To BOB,
HERE'S MY PATE[...] CURE FOR INSOMNIA,
CRAIG

Divided Loyalties

SUNY Series in American Labor History
Robert Asher and Amy Kesselman, Editors

Other books in this series include:

Divided Loyalties

*The Public and Private Life of
Labor Leader John Mitchell*

Craig Phelan

STATE UNIVERSITY OF NEW YORK PRESS

Published by
State University of New York Press, Albany

© 1994   State University of New York

For information, address State University of New York Press,
State University Plaza, Albany, N.Y., 12246

Production by Christine Lynch
Marketing by Fran Keneston

Library of Congress Cataloging-in-Publication Data

Phelan, Craig, 1958–
    Divided loyalties : the public and private life of labor leader
John Mitchell / Craig Phelan.
        p. cm.
    Includes bibliographical references and index.
    ISBN 0–7914–2088–4 (pb. : acid-free paper). — ISBN 0–7914–2087–6
(hc. : acid-free paper)
        1. Mitchell, John, 1870–1919. 2. Labor leaders — United States —
Biography. 3. United Mine Workers of America — Biography. 4. Trade
-unions — Coal miners — United States — History. 5. Anthracite coal
industry — United States — History. 6. Arbitration, Industrial —
United States — History. I. Title.
    HD8073.M5P48   1994
    331.88'12233'092—dc20
                                                                93–42744
                                                                    CIP

10 9 8 7 6 5 4 3 2 1

This book is dedicated to Monica,
who spent the last four years with
the uninvited ghost of John Mitchell and
waited with profound patience for his departure.

Thanks.

Contents

Preface

Organized labor greeted the dawn of the twentieth century poised for an unprecedented period of expansion. Labor leaders scrambled to exploit existing conditions to transform their tiny, besieged movement into a powerful force capable of securing economic justice for the majority of American toilers. After years of depression, prosperity had returned; muckraking journalists cultivated a degree of public sympathy for labor's right to organize; politicians in both major parties began to exhibit the reform spirit which came to be known as "Progressivism." These were exciting days for the struggling American Federation of Labor. Hopes ran high that labor could emerge from the shadows and take its place alongside industry and the state as masters of the nation's destiny.

For several years it looked as if this dream would become reality. Union membership skyrocketed from 447,000 in 1897 to 2,072,000 in 1904.[1] Nearly every region and economic sector witnessed an upsurge in unionism. How would employers respond to this changing industrial landscape? Would they simply intensify their age old war to eradicate the specter of unions? To the delight of working people, many employers, but by no means all, chose a new tack: the path of peace. Rather than resist what many regarded as the inevitable, leading employers signed national collective bargaining agreements with the conservative, responsible AFL unions. This trade agreement movement signalled what one scholar has dubbed the "honeymoon years of collective bargaining."[2] For many contemporaries this apparent surrender of employers heralded a new day in industrial relations, the dawn of union growth and class harmony, the coming of age of American labor.

More than any other trade union notable, even more than AFL President Samuel Gompers, John Mitchell personified the newly potent American labor movement based on the trade agreement. He embodied the youth, vigor, and dynamism of labor as it grew from its infancy to its adolescence. He was by far the best known and most celebrated trade unionist of his day. Not only did he preside over the largest and most powerful union of the period, the United Mine Workers of America, but he engineered the only victory of labor against a trustified industry before the 1930s. Indeed, his leadership of the anthracite mine workers in the strike of 1902 made him more famous and powerful than his predecessors could have dreamed. To the miners he was a demigod; to the working class as a whole, he was a hero, a champion of their rights; to progressive employers he was a straightforward, conservative man who had earned their respect; and to national politicians he was a power broker to be wooed and won over. He dealt with senators and robber barons as an equal, counted the president among his friends, and strode like a giant in the industrial world. With an army of miners ready to act on his command, he symbolized the movement's new status.

Yet Mitchell was only a shooting star in the economic sky. As quickly as he rose to the lofty heights of power and prestige, he descended once again into obscurity. After 1904 increasing numbers of employers broke their collective bargaining agreements and resumed their long standing war against trade unionism. An aggressive open shop movement effectively stymied further labor advances and killed the dream of class harmony. While the majority of workers and their leaders recognized that the "honeymoon" was over and that new strategies and tactics were necessary to combat the growing *anti-union* offensive, Mitchell refused to abandon his conviction that a permanent and peaceful solution to the perennial "labor question" had been found. After 1908, Mitchell's insistence that the trade agreement held the key to industrial justice and class harmony left him increasingly isolated in labor circles. As we shall see, his faith in trade agreements, while founded in the economic reality of the soft coal industry, ultimately served to strengthen the forces of reaction and cripple labor's efforts to take its place as a national power.

This book chronicles the rise and fall of a central figure in the pantheon of great American labor leaders. While his reign was brief, John Mitchell dominated one of the most significant and exciting periods of industrial relations, from the Spanish-American War to the outbreak of World War I. An investigation of his life provides insight into some of the salient developments of those years. Among the many themes we will investigate is the myth of the self-made man. In some ways his ascent reads like a proletarian version of an Horatio Alger success story. Deprived of all but the rudiments of a formal education, mired in the gripping poverty of an isolated Illinois coal town, his youth was an endless cycle of misery. His teenage and early adult years mirrored the experience of millions who labored under oppressive conditions to help build industrial America in the late nineteenth century. The mines in which he worked were death traps, the wages insufficient for existence, the conditions unspeakable. But while there were aspects of his personality which allowed him to rise above his station and assume command of the union, he understood that his authority ultimately rested on the brotherhood and solidarity of others of similar background and outlook. His rise did not represent individualistic success, but the collective might of coal diggers. In that important sense he was not the "self-made" man of the Alger myth.

A second theme is the transformation of union leadership in turn-of-the-century America. Early union leaders struggled and sacrificed to erect a powerful movement capable of securing economic justice. They endured hunger, slander, and even violence in their crusades to create viable institutions. In his early union days, Mitchell personified this noble warrior. Working without a salary, sleeping outdoors, forsaking a stable family life, he testified to the *idealism* and commitment necessary to become part of the great movement for uplifting the downtrodden. Once in power, however, Mitchell paved the way for future generations of union leaders who worked in plush offices at exorbitant salaries, and who viewed the labor movement as a profession rather than a cause. While he remained devoted to improving the lot of workers charged to his care, Mitchell grew quite fond of the comfortable life-style the union's success afforded. Indeed, he became so obsessed with personal gain he became involved in dozens of schemes to "mine the miners," several of which involved serious conflicts of interest.

A third theme is the impact of national collective bargaining on the relationship between labor leaders and the rank and file. Success of the trade agreement depended on the existence of a highly centralized and bureaucratic union. Mitchell could be quite ruthless in asserting his authority and subduing his rivals, and he laid the foundations of a union in which rank-and-file sentiment would exercise limited influence. Equally important, the trade agreement meant that he would spend an ever increasing amount of his time, both on the job and socially, with large scale coal operators who purchased the labor he sold and national political figures concerned with economic affairs. His removal from the social and physical setting of mine workers had a profound impact on his attitudes. The more he hobnobbed with the wealthy and powerful, the more he adopted their attitudes and culture. Perhaps to a greater degree than any other labor leader, Mitchell underwent what the German sociologist Robert Michels described as "embourgeoisement."[3] By the time he stepped down as UMWA president, his speech, his clothing, his associations, and, to a remarkable degree, his outlook more closely resembled those of employers than the rank and file.

A fourth theme, related to the third, is the tendency of labor officials to grow increasingly cautious and conservative over time. Mitchell's career beautifully illustrates this trend. Once ensconced in power, once in a position to begin working to create a more ethical basis of industrial relations, Mitchell underwent a slow process of change from the aggressive and militant voice of oppressed miners to the conservative head of an established institution. The change did not happen all at once, nor did he fully realize the change had occurred, but gradually and irrevocably he underwent a metamorphosis from labor leader to labor bureaucrat. The term "labor leader" connotes a champion of the working class, a spokesperson and interpreter of its desires, a warrior for its collective aspirations. John Mitchell, however, eventually became the epitome of the labor bureaucrat, a person for whom the demands of the union as an institution, ultimately, shaped his decisions. Even as he built the apparatus necessary to bargain with employers at the national level, he fell victim to the iron law of oligarchy: championship of the cause became secondary to the preservation of the institution. More and more of his actions as president were aimed at protecting the union from destruction. And throughout his presidency, he displayed an unwillingness to take chances for fear of damaging the union under his control. How and why this metamorphosis occurred is fundamental to an understanding of Mitchell and other labor officials.

A fifth theme is the development of alliances between labor leaders, reform politicians, and progressive employers. Since the power of coal unionism rested on the trade agreement, it was natural for Mitchell to join hands with other powerful men to promote this mechanism of labor peace. The institutional expression of this desire was the National Civic Federation, a voluntary association of wealthy capitalists, trade unionists, and representatives of the public. The NCF represented the promise of the early Progressive Era years, when increasing numbers of experts became convinced that there were no irreconcilable differences between capital and labor, that industrial relations could soon be permanently established on an ethical and mutually advantageous basis, that employers and responsible unions could work together to create industrial peace and economic prosperity. While his political allies and the NCF assisted Mitchell in his efforts to extend the trade agreement to hard coal, their assistance came with strings attached. As we shall see, Mitchell was quite willing to allow these elites to intervene in the affairs of the union and dictate policy on important union matters.

In addition to these and other themes, Mitchell's life offers a unique glimpse inside the personal life of a turn-of-the-century American. Although the telephone was already transforming long distance communications in the Progressive Era, Mitchell preferred to write letters. His correspondence to friends and family is voluminous and quite revealing. Unlike future labor leaders such as John L. Lewis, whose private lives are forever hidden from the most doggedly determined investigator, Mitchell's world is open to anyone willing to take the time to pore over his letters. The physical abuse he suffered as a child, his separation from his wife and family due to work, his close friendships with coal operators, his chronic alcoholism, his compulsive speculation on the stock market and his questionable investments, the physical and mental strains of his office that led to frequent illness and ultimately forced his retirement from the union presidency—all are revealed in his missives and make his life's story fascinating as well as important.

Chapter 1

The Emergence of a Labor Leader, 1870–1898

The bloody Civil War, which ravaged this nation and impacted so many millions, passed all but unnoticed on the barren prairie of central Will County, Illinois. When at last the war ended in 1865, the local historian described the area, located some sixty miles southwest of Chicago, as "nothing but a sea of tall grass, or in the winter a boundless field of snow, reaching out to meet the horizon, with scarcely a cabin intervening." The only inhabitants were "a few unthrifty farmers scattered throughout the neighborhood."[1] Just eight years later, however, this worthless tract was transformed into the bustling town of Braidwood. With a population surpassing 5,000, the town had a main street stretching for over half a mile. It had its own banks, daily newspapers, churches, schoolhouses, hotels, and stores. One amazed journalist suggested the change had been so rapid it must have come "by magic."[2]

The "magic" was bituminous coal. And its discovery came by accident in 1864, when a farmer, digging a well, discovered a significant vein of coal about eighty feet beneath the surface. While geologists explored and examined the vein, capitalists sank shafts to exploit the resource. Development was especially rapid because the vein was situated near the main line of the Chicago, Alton and St. Louis Railroad, and the product could be easily transported to nearby Chicago. By 1870, the area was abuzz with activity. Farmers sold their once worthless land at great profits, miners and their families rushed to find work, homes were built, and shopkeepers took up residence. The emerging town took its name from a Scottish immigrant, James Braidwood, who played a central role in the sinking and developing of the first mines. One of the earliest, and certainly the largest coal company to begin operations was the Chicago, Wilmington and Vermillion Coal Company, a group of financiers from Chicago and Boston. By 1868, the company had already invested over $475,000 in the area. Braidwood was a coal "boom" town and it quickly became the most important coal producer in northern Illinois.[3]

The vast majority of miners who flocked to Braidwood in the late 1860s were immigrants, and most of these were skilled coal diggers from Scotland, England, and Ireland. The growth of Braidwood coincided with tough times, for the mining industry in the British Isles was wracked by overproduction and unemployment. Alexander MacDonald, president of the Miners' National Association of Great Britain, encouraged emigration to relieve the miners' plight. "I would strongly encourage you not to think of continuing in the mines," he told a throng of Scottish diggers ready to set sail for America.[4] MacDonald's own brother moved to Gardner, Illinois, next door to Braidwood. Yet, once in America, the Scots found themselves enticed by coal operators with the promise of steady work and high wages; many took up their picks once again. When MacDonald himself visited Braidwood in 1867, he was greeted by 500 men, many of whom were familiar faces from the lodges of the Scottish unions. And when he returned two years later he found even more from his native land.[5]

The 1870 census revealed the ethnic diversity of Braidwood. Of the 630 heads of households listed, 449 had been born in England, Scotland, Wales, or Ireland. The Irish had a majority of 162, while the Scots were second with 143.[6] But there were other groups that lent the town a certain cosmopolitan air. Bohemians, Swedes, Germans, Italians, French, Belgians, Poles, and Russians, few with any mining or trade union experience, began to arrive in increasing numbers as the years passed. In 1874, a Chicago journalist found Braidwood "akin to Babel of old, as regards the confusion of tongues."[7] This clash of cultures would soon exacerbate the ethnic tension already existing between the Catholic Irish and Protestant Scots, but in the early years observers found the various groups working in "harmony and good feeling."[8]

Into this ethnic mix came Robert Mitchell. As with the majority of workers in nineteenth century America, almost nothing remains to chronicle his life. Born in Dublin to Protestant parents, he went to Scotland at an early age to work in the mines, living in a town named Killmornick. Sometime in the 1850s he embarked for America. At that time he was most likely in his late twenties. After working a short time in New York City, he moved near Buffalo and worked there as a farm laborer until the outbreak of the Civil War. It was probably in Buffalo that Robert Mitchell first married. His wife bore him three sons. Like so many immigrant miners, Robert enlisted in the Union army and served his full term.[9] At the end of his service, he moved to Braidwood with his family and returned to the craft of coal mining. Life in coal communities was often brutal and short, and Robert's experience was no exception. Soon after settling in town, his wife died. He married again, this time to Martha Halley, who gave birth to three children, two sons and a daughter. Then Martha died. Robert married a third time, this time to a widow who brought one child to the marriage, and the couple produced a son.[10]

Amid this bewildering assortment of marriages, births, and deaths, John Mitchell was born on February 4, 1870, the child of Robert Mitchell and his second wife, Martha Halley. Since his biological mother died when he was just two-and-a-half, he carried no memories of her into his adult years. He could not even recall her maiden name. Nor did he have the opportunity to develop lasting ties to his father. When John turned six, his father was crushed to death by a runaway team of horses. In later years, John remembered only that his father "looked like a Big Well Proportioned Man."[11] Young John was thus left in the care of his stepmother, Robert's third wife.

Scratching out an existence in the bleak coal towns was difficult enough with the family intact. The loss of the principal breadwinner, however, usually created a nightmarish struggle for survival, and Mitchell's early years were blighted by abject poverty. No laws existed to provide compensation for the widows and orphans of dead miners, although local union leaders were pressing for such measures at this time.[12] The poverty of the Mitchells may have been mitigated to some extent through charity, for Braidwood diggers prided themselves on their giving nature. A local journalist in 1875 commented on their "willing hands and generous hearts," which were "always ready to drive the wolf—want—from the door."[13] Whether or not the Mitchells received handouts is impossible to determine. Nor is it clear whether they received compensation benefits from the Illinois Miners' Benevolent and Protective Association. Robert Mitchell was undoubtedly a member of this union, founded in 1871, which had resolved to pay forty dollars to the survivors of members in good standing.[14] This union was financially weak by the time Robert Mitchell died in 1876, however, and it was probably incapable of paying benefits.

Mitchell's stepmother endured a cruel life of unremitting toil. While the eldest three children had left the nest by 1876, she was the sole support for John and the other four who remained. Only two legitimate means of earning money were open to widows in the coal camps—taking in boarders and doing laundry for the families of mine bosses and superintendents—and she engaged in both pursuits. Caring for boarders entailed cooking, cleaning, and doing laundry for single miners or married miners living without their families. In many coal communities, it was customary for each boarder to bring his own food for the woman to prepare, which made cooking much more time consuming than it would have been had she prepared the same meal for everyone.[15] Laundry and housecleaning in a coal town were even more onerous than cooking. Coal dust filled the air, covered the walls, and even entered the house. Every boarder required a daily bath to remove the accumulated grime, and their clothes had to be scrubbed often to remove coal and oil. Even fetching water was a heavy burden, involving numerous trips to often distant sources.[16]

Mitchell's stepmother supplemented her income by planting and tending a small garden. Those fruits and vegetables not eaten fresh were canned and stored. It is not known whether she, like many other women in coal camps, raised chickens and cows. But she undoubtedly spent many hours each day baking bread, pies, and cakes for her boarders and her family. She also saved money by making all necessary clothing, gathering chunks of coal that fell from the loading chute along the railroad tracks or at the slag heaps, and perhaps even sewing for other families. Her only comfort in this unending grind of work and poverty was religion. She strictly adhered to her Presbyterian faith and found solace by reading the Bible.[17]

Mitchell experienced an unhappy childhood. Rarely did he mention his youth in later years, but on those few occasions when he confided in his close friends and siblings, his bitterness and self-pity rose to the surface. "In those Days I used to consider my self (*sic*) the most unfortunate Being on Earth," he lamented.[18] He bemoaned the fact he had lost his natural parents, and he cursed his family's poverty. While all miners were poor, he was acutely aware of his deprivation relative to other children in the town. He resented the endless list of chores his stepmother assigned him. All miners' children were expected to contribute to the family economy at an early age, but Mitchell's chores were more numerous and exacting than most because survival of the fatherless family depended on them. He therefore had less time to play with friends, and he felt ashamed because his time was consumed by "girl's work" such as laundry, housecleaning, and babysitting his younger half-brothers.[19]

His chores also left less time for school. His stepmother could spare his labor only a few weeks each year, and as a result he fell behind the other students at the public school in Braidwood. "The humiliation and shame of lagging behind them caused me to lose interest in my studies," he later recalled.[20] After five years he stopped attending school altogether. Even for a miner's son, his formal education was slight. For the rest of his life, he was embarrassed by his ignorance and he came to prize education above all other accomplishments. Years later, when his brother became a father, Mitchell expressed the hope that the child would receive "a better education than either you or I had when we were lads together."[21]

The most lasting memory of his youth, however, was that of his stepmother. The only public comment he ever made about her was that she "failed utterly to understand my nature."[22] Even in his private letters, he almost never referred to her. Yet one handwritten letter to his sister revealed the depth of his emotion. The Mitchell children went their separate ways in the 1890s, and he tried to reestablish contact with his siblings once at the helm of the miners' union. When his sister replied to one of his missives, a flood of feeling was released. Her reply "recalled to my memory many long forgotten incidents of my Life. And Dear Sister for the first time in many years I sat down and cried." He had not "shed tears Since the unhappy Days of my youth when the occasion of my Sorrow was the sting of the cat-o-nine-tails (*sic*) on my poor little Nude Body in the hands of my Well Meaning But unthoughtful Step Mother." Certainly the physical punishment of children was not regarded with the same disapproval it is today, but the lingering psychological impact makes it difficult to downplay the significance of this abuse. "Many, many times I wondered if my Brothers or Sister had forgotten my existence," he continued. But he did not blame his sister for her failure to intervene. "I know you have had your own trials in this cruel world."[23]

The ultimate effect of this abuse is, of course, impossible to determine. Nor are psychological explanations essential to an analysis of his union leadership. But Mitchell's problems as an adult—his alcoholism, his powerful need to conform, his feelings of inferiority, his obsessive financial speculation, his discomfort with his own body, his inability to form intimate friendships, his compulsion to work himself to the point of exhaustion—were certainly not unrelated to his unhealthy relationship with his stepmother. As union president he carefully maintained his distance from her. Although he paid the rent on her home, he refused most of her invitations to visit.

Shut off from school and friends, overworked and abused, Mitchell believed he had been cheated out of a childhood. As an adult he regretted he had never experienced "freedom from care" in his youth, or a time "in which play and laughter and pranks had their place."[24] Circumstances for this unfortunate boy took another turn for the worse when he reached the age of ten and his stepmother remarried. She wed a skilled miner named Smith. Whether this new stepfather was also abusive cannot be determined from the record. But clearly Mitchell believed this man's presence made his home life intolerable, for soon after the marriage he ran away. Securing work as a water boy on a farm outside the town, he lived on the farm for the next two years, earned his own room and board, and visited home only at irregular intervals. At the age of twelve, he moved back to the home of his stepparents. The time had come to learn the craft of coal mining.[25]

Although Illinois state law required all mine workers to be at least thirteen, Mitchell at twelve was probably not the youngest boy in the employ of the Chicago, Wilmington, and Vermillion Coal Company. The first day must have been a harrowing experience. After rising early and walking to the mine entrance with his stepfather, they joined the others and rode down into the earth in the elevator or "cage." Braidwood mines were not as deep as many shaft mines, and the descent was probably no more than 100 feet.[26] But conditions in the mine were typical: cold, dark, and filled with strange and ominous noises.[27] Surface weather, either extreme heat in summer or cold in winter, did not affect the underground air, which stood at about sixty degrees. The only light came from lamps on the miners' hats, which allowed them to see only what was in front of them and left the rest in eerie shadow. Aside from the clinking of picks and shovels, and the squeaking of mule-drawn trains, he could hear the occasional crackling and rumbling of the roof.

The air he breathed on that first day was permeated with fine coal dust that obscured vision and within years could create the respiratory condition known as "black lung." The air in Braidwood mines was also filled with carbonic acid gas, which the miners called "black damp." If the gas became too thick, an explosion might occur. In smaller concentrations it simply made miners nauseous and numb. Braidwood mines were also noted for their lack of sufficient drainage, and it is probable that Mitchell found his feet submersed in cold water.[28] The dark, wet, and dust were not the only shocks to his senses. There were also large numbers of rats. In time he would come to regard the presence of these creatures as a sign of security, an indication the air was safe to breathe. Until then he had to adjust himself to the sight of rats scurrying around his feet and dinner pail. He also had to develop proper mine habits, such as learning how to relieve one's self without causing distress to one's work mates. Another future leader of the miners, John Brophy, remembered entering the mines at age twelve and receiving the following advice from his father: if a miner "had need for a bowel movement, he took care of that need over in the gob, and covered the waste with dirt and slack, to minimize the contamination of the air."[29]

Since the coal vein in northern Illinois was only three feet thick, Mitchell spent that first day continually bending and crouching without a single chance to stand erect and stretch. Over a period of years, this necessity to crouch would permanently affect the miner's posture. Mitchell claimed he would have been a taller, more graceful man had he not worked in the mines. "My Physique was Dwarfed and my Growth stunted" by mine labor, he cursed.[30] In his novel *King Coal*, Upton Sinclair wrote that miners, emerging from the pits at the end of the day, continued to walk with their head and shoulders hunched forward and looked like "a file of baboons."[31]

The unpleasantness of the mine, however, was probably not foremost in Mitchell's mind that first day. He likely was more aware of the possible dangers. All inhabitants of mining towns were attuned to what one scholar described as the "brooding expectancy of death."[32] As did all miners every work day, Mitchell must have wondered whether he would return that evening alive. Miners "constitute a class peculiarly exposed to hardships and perils," concluded the Illinois Bureau of Labor Statistics after surveying the state in 1882, the year in which Mitchell began to toil underground. "The air they breathe, the light they carry, the powder they use, the cage which sends them down, and lifts them out from the bowels of the earth, are all active and deadly agents against them."[33] Mitchell believed the constant fear of death made the job all but intolerable. Once he became president of the miners' union, he urged his brother to give up the "dangerous work" of mining and "seek employment in some other field."[34]

On February 16, 1883, young Mitchell witnessed the kind of ugly tragedy that could strike any miner at any time. While most mine fatalities involved one or two miners at a time, on that day between sixty-nine and seventy-four miners perished in the adjacent town of Braceville. The Diamond Mine Disaster occurred when surface water from the prairie broke through to the mine below, drowning the miners. More than a month passed before sufficient water could be pumped out to allow rescuers to remove the victims.[35] Although he was only thirteen, Mitchell took part in the recovery operation. A friend and fellow union official later recalled seeing blood on the prairie ice left by Mitchell's cut and shoeless feet.[36]

Constant danger and deplorable working conditions became Mitchell's reality in 1882, just as isolation from peers and physical abuse had been his reality as a child. But now he was acquiring the skills of a craft which would instill pride and independence. Late nineteenth century miners such as his stepfather, Smith, considered themselves an elite class of workers, set apart from general laborers in and around the mines by virtue of their ability to use a pick. They worked in relative isolation from other skilled miners, and they took a fierce pride not only in their ability to outproduce other miners, but also to cut coal with greater precision and geometric exactness. A fist fight or heated argument between two craftsmen over proper techniques was not uncommon. Skilled pick miners often worked with little or no supervision. Since they were paid by the ton and not the hour, they usually came and left as they pleased, missing entire days when personal emergencies arose. When supervisors visited the miners' "rooms," they often came to chat and rarely to reprimand.[37]

A miner's skills were handed down from generation to generation, father to son. Mitchell thus became his stepfather's apprentice in an underground workshop. Usually a youngster began his mining career as a trapper boy, the person responsible for opening and closing the wooden doors separating one section of a mine from another when mule-drawn trains passed through. While the trapper boy played a vital role in mine ventilation, his was a lonely job, often sitting in the pitch black by himself for several hours at a time. Mitchell claimed he avoided this entry-level position. "I never worked regularly as a trapper," he wrote, "although on some occasions when a trapper failed to report for work I took care of his door." Instead, he went straight to work as Smith's assistant, loading the coal cut by his stepfather, listening to his advice, and watching his technique.[38] Working for long hours in close quarters, sharing the dangers and the secrets of the trade, often created intense bonds of love and loyalty between fathers and sons. Such was the case with John Brophy and his father. Unfortunately, Smith and Mitchell never bonded in the same way. Mitchell recalled that his stepfather was a good miner, but a harsh taskmaster.[39]

At the age of fourteen, Mitchell ran away a second time, this time to Braceville. But he had not developed sufficient skill to obtain a job as a miner. After working as a mule driver for a short period, he returned home once again and rejoined Smith to complete his apprenticeship. He remained in Braidwood until he reached sixteen.[40] During this time, he became a master with pick and powder, and for the first time in his life, he took pride in himself and his accomplishments. Learning the craft of mining also helped him develop a social life. Since he was engaged in the same pursuit as his peers, he was no longer an outcast. He developed lasting boyhood friendships and became increasingly active in community life.

Physically, the community of Braidwood in the 1880s was an ugly wooden outpost on the bleak Illinois prairie. With the exception of the schoolhouse, the entire town was built of cheap wood.[41] One scholar described the town as "dark and dirty, gray and drab." Every house was small and unpainted, "with sagging front porches and decrepit steps." And because the town lacked sidewalks, "streets and paths were like swamps" when it rained.[42] Whether they were company owned or privately owned, Mitchell recalled that every house was "built of the cheapest material." One outhouse was built for every three or four homes.[43] Other than general stores, a few banks, and newspaper offices, the business district was comprised almost entirely of saloons. There were as many as eighty saloons in 1883, when the population was less than 10,000.[44] The town was also plagued by incredible numbers of dogs, hogs, sheep, and chickens roaming at will throughout the business district. One citizen estimated there were probably three dogs for each family, and since few dogs were kept tethered, a reporter protested that Braidwood was "literally overrun with canines."[45]

Not only was the town ugly, but like most rough-hewn mining towns, Braidwood was violent. Heavy drinking was the impetus for most brawls, while widespread gun ownership often turned brawls into deadly encounters. "The dirk and revolver have already too often made the name of Braidwood synonymous with crime and bloodshed," bemoaned one resident. Another declared the prohibition against concealed weapons was "a farce and a laughing stock."[46] A fearful outsider suggested that those who wanted "a foretaste of hell," an understanding of "what the world will become before it tumbles back into the arms of chaos," should certainly spend some time in Braidwood. A Chicagoan believed "every man in Braidwood owns a gun, a revolver, and a dog," and they "prowled" over the countryside, causing trouble and stealing food.[47]

Underneath the grime and violence, however, an exuberant culture thrived. The city was unequalled by towns of similar size, one reporter noted, in "institutions for improving the mind, morally, spiritually, socially, and intellectually." The public schools were "excellently conducted and well attended," six benevolent societies serviced the needy, a variety of fraternal, temperance, and miners' lodges provided profitable ways to spend one's leisure hours, and seven churches offered proof that Braidwood was "a moral town and God-fearing community." Town boosters also claimed "more reunions and sociables the year round than any other city in the state."[48]

More important than the institutional culture was the sense of community existing among the town's citizens. Due to the shared burdens of poverty, the danger of mining, and frequent strikes, the diverse ethnic elements of the town coexisted in relative harmony in the early years. The mayor of Braidwood, in his 1882 Fourth of July speech, asserted the town was "not so black" as outsiders imagined. Immigrant and native born, German and Scot, all "the thousands hereabouts could meet on social terms and enjoy themselves without outlawry and riot as well as any city on the continent."[49] The degree of cooperation among the various elements was revealed by the emergence of a particular Braidwood dialect. A Chicago correspondent believed outsiders would have difficulty comprehending the dialect, "which appeared to be a cross between Scotch, South of Ireland, and Yorkshire."[50]

Coexistence did not mean Braidwood represented a melting pot. Ethnic groups retained much of their traditional heritage, and the town was divided geographically along ethnic lines. The Bohemian neighborhood, for example, was located in "Lower Braidwood." Here residents spoke their native language and ran their own school.[51] Italians, Welsh, English, Scots, and Irish also had their own neighborhoods, clubs, games, traditions, religion, cuisine, holidays, and prejudices. While generally peaceful, ethnic rivalries and hatreds existed. One unsympathetic writer noted that the various "clans and nationalities" disagreed on everything except "drinking and fighting."[52] And at times ethnic hatred led to violence, as happened in 1883 when peaceful Italian picnickers were set upon by "some of the hoodlum Irish element."[53]

Braidwood also had a sizable African-American community. Imported as strikebreakers by the Chicago, Wilmington, and Vermillion Coal Company during a bitter strike in 1877, white miners at first were able to run them out of town by force. Weeks later some 600 African-Americans returned under the protection of the state militia. They remained, but they suffered discrimination at work and in the community. Only two of the twelve shafts employed them as of 1881, and while white miners encouraged them to join the local union, they were expected to live in their own segregated community, dubbed "Bucktown." Race relations were strained throughout the 1880s, and violence erupted periodically.[54]

Mitchell grew up in an enclave of Scots and Protestant Irish. All his adolescent friends were from the same neighborhood, and it is doubtful that he ever socialized with Italians, Germans, African-Americans, or others of dissimilar heritage. His closest friend during his teenage years was the child of a Scot, George McKay. "Many an up and down we had together," McKay recalled. Along with other chums, Mitchell and McKay spent their leisure time looking for fun, a chance to forget the long hours spent in the mines. A favorite activity was going down to the shop owned by "Old Man Miles." Here the boys purchased "taffy-on-a-stick" and sat "listening to the Old Man telling stories." The boys also challenged each other to foot races, and McKay remembered that Mitchell was the fastest among them.[55]

Not only was he beginning to take part in the social life of the town during his teenage years, but also he participated in the most important Braidwood institution, the local union. By the time he entered the mines in 1882, Braidwood miners had experienced an action-filled sixteen year labor history. In the late 1860s and 1870s, Braidwood miners exhibited remarkable solidarity and exercised a great deal of community control. Despite their ethnic differences, they created a local union strong enough to secure a wage agreement with the three operating coal firms in 1872. In the fall of 1873, the local union was one of the first in the nation to affiliate with the newly created Miners' National Association (MNA).[56] The fact that most of the early miners were British immigrants with trade union experience helps account for the strength of the local union. So, too, does the leadership skill of John James and Daniel McLaughlin. These two men, both Scottish immigrants, had learned their trade unionism directly from Alexander MacDonald. Indeed, the MNA, founded by Braidwood's McLaughlin and James, along with John Siney of the anthracite region, was "almost a complete replica" of MacDonald's British coal union.[57]

MacDonald's trade union philosophy was based not on direct action through the use of strikes, but on conciliation and arbitration of disputes, the establishment of friendly relations with employers, and the signing of annual wage agreements based on the sliding scale, in which wages would rise or fall according to the price of coal. John James, like his mentor, believed strikes were "ruinous" and should be sanctioned only when operators refused to bargain.[58] James and McLaughlin soon found, however, that the Chicago, Wilmington and Vermillion Coal Company, the largest in town, preferred battle to negotiation. In 1874, for instance, McLaughlin consented to strike only after the company closed the mines and refused to negotiate with the union. Although operators hired fifty Pinkerton detectives in an effort to provoke violence, union miners and their supporters remained peaceful and defeated the operators. Victory was a product of miner militancy, effective union leadership, and the active support of professionals and shopkeepers in the town who were dependent on the miners for their livelihood.[59]

The celebration of this victory was short-lived. McLaughlin was forced to call a second strike in 1877 after the company announced a wage cut of twenty-five cents per ton and demanded miners sign "yellow-dog" contracts, in which they promised never to join the union while employed by the company. This strike lasted nine months and ended in defeat when Illinois Governor Shelby Cullom ordered a large force of the state militia to Braidwood.

General Ducat of the militia arrested McLaughlin, who was at that time mayor as well as union head, for exceeding his municipal authority. The 1877 strike proved a catastrophe for the local union. McLaughlin and a dozen other leaders were blacklisted, and the union was effectively crippled for several years.[60]

Thus, when Mitchell received his union card, the local was too weak to resist the operators. Conditions in the mines were worse in 1882 than they had been when he was born, and they were steadily deteriorating. In that year, the six Braidwood coal firms employed 1,986 miners and extracted 649,000 tons of coal. Mitchell worked for the largest firm, the Chicago, Wilmington, and Vermillion, which employed 1,018 men at three main pits and accounted for nearly half the local output.[61] One symptom of union weakness was the decline in wages in the early 1880s. Braidwood miners accepted a five cent per ton reduction in pay in 1883, and a similar reduction in 1884. According to the Illinois Bureau of Labor Statistics, in 1884 the average mining family's expenses exceeded earnings by seven dollars.[62] A second symptom was irregular work. Mitchell and his comrades could expect to lose at least fifteen weeks of work during prosperous years and more during hard times. While all industrial workers in the late nineteenth century experienced unstable employment, the bureau stated that miners received the fewest weeks of steady work among all classes of Illinois laborers.[63] The absence of a strong union hurt Mitchell and the other miners in other ways. They had no means to protest the various techniques operators had devised to cheat miners when coal was weighed, and they had no means to force operators to ensure proper ventilation and safety precautions.

As grievances mounted in the mid-1880s, Mitchell and other Braidwood union men looked to their undisputed leader, Daniel McLaughlin, for solutions. And McLaughlin's creative efforts on their behalf would provide Mitchell with an object lesson in practical unionism he would never forget. McLaughlin's experience in the 1877 strike reinforced his belief that miners' demands "had to be expressed in other ways than by strikes and rioting."[64] In September 1885, along with John McBride of Ohio, he helped forge the National Federation of Miners and Mine Laborers (NFMML), which became, in the words of one scholar, "a movement more significant than any of the past."[65] McLaughlin had more in mind than simply founding the latest in a series of weak national miners' unions. His goal was to establish a system of collective bargaining that would make strikes and lockouts unnecessary. Labor-capital friction in coal, he believed, "stemmed from the existence of too many operators and too much production." Overproduction and cutthroat competition among coal firms forced the price of coal downward, and as profits disappeared, operators slashed wages, which provoked strikes. Strikes invariably caused hardship for the miners and ate up operator profits. To overcome these problems, miners and operators must meet together, establish uniform costs of production, and work toward limiting the output of coal. In a letter to the *National Labor Tribune*, he laid out his "plan of establishing a wage scale by a joint convention of miners and operators." The NFMML endorsed McLaughlin's plan, and the call went out to all coal operators to attend a joint convention.[66]

At least a dozen operators met with McLaughlin and other union officials on October 16 in Chicago. One of the most powerful operators attending was A. L. Sweet, superintendent of the Chicago, Wilmington, and Vermillion Company where Mitchell worked. A committee of three miners and three operators, including McLaughlin and Sweet, composed a letter urging all operators and miners to send representatives to Pittsburgh on December 15 to establish a joint conference. The letter referred to strikes and lockouts as "false agencies and brutal resorts for the adjustment of disputes and controversies" between employer and employee, which "generally involve waste of capital on the one hand and the impoverishment of labor on the other."[67]

For fifteen-year-old John Mitchell, the call for a joint conference was not a distant and inconsequential event. It was the most dramatic lesson in his early trade union education. At the conclusion of the Chicago meeting, the entire town of Braidwood erupted in celebration of "an improved feeling between employers and the employed." A parade marched through the town, two bands performed, and enthusiastic speeches were made by McLaughlin, Sweet, and local politicians. Mitchell and the whole town looked forward with anticipation to the Pittsburgh conference and the opening of a new era of labor peace and prosperity.[68]

They were not disappointed. While the Pittsburgh conference failed, at a second conference held in February at Columbus, Ohio, seventy-seven operators met with thirty-six miners and agreed on a wage scale to be effective from May 1, 1886, to April 30, 1887.[69] Hailed by one scholar as "a landmark in the history of collective bargaining,"[70] the agreement covered six states, including Illinois, where Braidwood miners were to receive a ten cent per ton advance. McLaughlin, now honored as "the father of the joint convention" in coal, returned to Braidwood in triumph.[71] Miners later celebrated his accomplishment with a mass rally, speeches, and, predictably, by drinking "oceans of beer."[72] Whether Mitchell was one of the guzzlers is impossible to determine, but he undoubtedly shared in the revelry, and he also absorbed valuable lessons. He learned that the basic thrust of MacDonaldism was not an abstract theory divorced from economic reality. Strike action was not always the best way to advance the interests of miners. Labor gains could be secured through peaceful means, through the shared interest of operator and miner in a rationalized industry, through the joint conference. These were lessons he would live by as union president.

As important as the interstate joint conference was, it by no means solved all the problems and frustrations of Braidwood miners. There were conditions which even the great McLaughlin could not control. One was the playing out of the Braidwood mines. While the mines were not yet exhausted, by the late 1880s companies found it increasingly difficult to locate profitable sites to sink new shafts.[73] The result of this decline was an intensification of the already unstable employment patterns in the area. A second condition was the increase in the number of immigrants from southern and eastern Europe. Beginning in the mid-1880s a flood of Italians, Bohemians, and Polish arrived in Braidwood. By 1889, these three groups outnumbered the "old stock" from the British Isles.[74] Competition for scarce jobs aggravated existing ethnic tensions and destroyed much of the community solidarity that had existed earlier. Violence and ethnic hatred flared. According to the biographer of Chicago politician and Braidwood native Anton Cermak, by the middle of the decade hostility between the various ethnic groups was "more or less continual; the boys, with willow switches and weapons, frequently carried it to the very gate of the school."[75] Lack of work and the decline of community explains Mitchell's decision to leave Braidwood in 1886.

At sixteen Mitchell was old enough and skilled enough to embark on his first great adventure. He said farewell to his family and friends to seek work in the faraway West. Such uprooting was the typical response of miners to hard times. For young miners it was almost a rite of passage, a chance to see the world before marriage and family. Miners lived a "gypsy life," wrote John Brophy. Geographic mobility rarely led "to any great improvement, but it was impossible to sit around and make no effort to do better."[76] As the mines declined in Braidwood, local miners dispersed in all directions in search of work, from New Mexico, Colorado, Oklahoma, and Texas in the West, to Indiana, Ohio, and Maryland in the East. And some immigrants retreated to their homelands.[77] While union leaders deplored the constant movement because it inhibited the development of stable unions and made the miners appear shiftless, the late nineteenth century miner was by necessity a "bird of passage," one who had to roam to find steady employment.[78]

With little money and all his possessions in one bag, young Mitchell rode the rails to Colorado. For the next two years he was a vagabond, working off and on in the coal mines of Colorado, Wyoming, and New Mexico. Little evidence remains to describe his experience, but later he recalled the deplorable conditions of work in the camps. Long hours, low wages, and unhealthy working conditions, similar to those in Braidwood, meant that his flight from misery had been unsuccessful. Dan McLaughlin's message of joint action had special meaning in Colorado, where intense overcrowding and lack of steady work helped lead "to the conviction that the only way out of this chaos and confusion lay in organization and concerted action."[79] It is probable that Mitchell also worked at the Sante Fe, New Mexico mine where another old Braidwood union leader, John James, had become superintendent.[80] In the desperate struggle for work, Mitchell's youth and lack of experience undoubtedly put him at a disadvantage, and his search for adventure was soon shattered by the hardship of the transient's life. Two years were enough. When he learned that new mines were opening in Spring Valley, Illinois, he trekked back to his home state. He arrived home penniless, but with a sharper appreciation of the common plight of miners nationwide. But by no means was he worldly—he still knew nothing of life outside mining camps.

Located on the Illinois River about forty-five miles west of Braidwood, Spring Valley did not develop as a coal town until the mid-1880s. Until that time the area was frontier prairie, although more wooded and with better farm land than Braidwood had offered in the 1860s.[81] When coal began to dominate the local economy, Braidwood miners were the first to take advantage of the new job opportunities. As Braidwood's population declined, from 4,641 in 1890 to 3,279 in 1900, Spring Valley's rose, reaching 6,214 in 1900. In addition, many of the immigrants in the continuing wave from southern and eastern Europe came directly to Spring Valley. By 1899 fifty-eight percent of residents hailed from southern and eastern Europe and there were few who had been born in the United States of native parentage. Perhaps hoping to avoid the racial strife of Braidwood, town officials followed the practice of racial exclusion and barred African-Americans from entering the city limits.[82]

Mitchell recalled that Spring Valley, at that time, was vital and dynamic, alive with activity and growth. "A thriving city had sprung up, as though over night, in what had been up to that time a peaceful farming district. The population had increased so rapidly that it was impossible to build schools (and other institutions) fast enough."[83] At first there was plenty of work. Mitchell found a job at the Spring Valley Coal Company, the largest employer in town. His first job was not as skilled miner, but as mine laborer responsible for "dead work" in and around the mines. For two years he sweated on some of the most back breaking chores in the mines, such as laying track for coal cars and timbering to support the roofs. He also remembered "pounding sand rock" for days on end.[84] It was difficult work, but he had a steady income; he was independent, and he had the camaraderie of fellow miners, some of whom he had known from Braidwood.

This tough but tolerable life did not last long. In early 1889, the interstate joint conference collapsed. Miners and operators had met on an annual basis since the founding of the movement in 1886, but many operators, including those in southern Illinois, never participated. Operators who agreed to pay union wages complained they could not compete against these nonunion operators. First, Indiana operators and then those from northern Illinois withdrew from the movement, and the 1889 joint conference adjourned without agreeing on a scale of wages. "The failure to agree will be regretted by all who believe in reason rather than force in the adjustment of the differences between operators and miners," predicted miners' leader John McBride. "It may be necessary to again plunge into industrial warfare to finally convince both operator and miner that any advantage to be gained by either party, from the dissolution of this movement, can only be temporary."[85]

Nowhere was the impact of the collapse of the joint conference more strongly felt than in Spring Valley. The Spring Valley Coal Company and other local operators immediately moved to destroy the local union and drive wages far below existing levels so they could capture markets dominated by cheap southern Illinois coal. In April 1889, without notice or provocation, the Spring Valley Coal Company locked out their 1,000 employees and closed the company store. In August, the company posted notice that mining would resume at a fifty percent wage reduction and that any miner seeking employment must sign a "yellow dog" contract. Other operators followed suit. Thus began the desperate eight-month struggle dubbed by Henry Demarest Lloyd, the famous reformer of the period, as the "strike of millionaires against miners."[86]

Mitchell and his comrades faced the full force of corporate power. Since most homes in the town were company owned, miners did not have the option to mortgage their homes to buy food as they had done during the Braidwood strike of 1877. Company housing also enabled operators to evict strikers. While some evictions occurred and many eviction notices served, operators understood that large numbers of evictions might incite violence and the destruction of company property. Operators tried to break the miners' will to resist by spreading rumors they were about to introduce African-American strikebreakers or permanently replace the majority of miners through the use of machinery.[87] Operators tried to sow dissension by urging men to listen to reason rather than the "shiftless minority"—the union leaders.[88]

Before long the lockout caused severe suffering. At the end of June, a Chicago correspondent asked "a bright, intelligent German housewife" how she and her family of seven children were faring after two months without income. She replied "with mute eloquence by bringing out an empty flour barrel and disclosing its hollow inwardness."[89] Hunger forced local union leaders to plead for arbitration time and time again. Each request was dismissed by operators. Yet the miners remained unified and defiant. When the Spring Valley Coal Company called off the lockout in August and encouraged the men to return at half their wages, they refused. And they paid the price for their resolve. By the end of August "death (hung) . . . over the town. From a cursory examination it (was) . . . a low estimate that seven of every ten families (were) . . . sick, seriously so," one reporter noted.[90]

Still the miners stood firm. And they were supported in their struggle by local businessmen and politicians. Local merchants signed a petition castigating the destitution brought on by the strike, and Henry Demarest Lloyd observed that while merchants often displayed class prejudice against working people, this prejudice was "tempered by the kindest personal feelings."[91] The national labor movement attempted to assist the strikers as well. Both the Knights of Labor and the American Federation of Labor declared boycotts of Spring Valley coal. The *Chicago Tribune* spearheaded relief efforts, such as benefit concerts, to raise money for the hungry men and women.[92]

Of all the support given, Mitchell was most impressed by the relief work of Henry Demarest Lloyd. When we were engaged in this "almost hopeless struggle," he remembered, when we had "battled on for many, weary, weary months, when starvation and eviction" stared us "in the face," Lloyd came to Spring Valley. He investigated conditions, he learned the story of our "hard, grinding lives," and he "took up the fight" through the daily papers. "He called public attention to the wrongs we had endured; he appealed to the patriotic and charitable citizens of the country." And as a result, provisions and money poured in, enough to keep death from their doors.[93] Mitchell would remember Lloyd's assistance years later and call on his aid during the anthracite strike of 1902.

Charity could not sustain the men, women, and children of Spring Valley forever. By mid-December hunger, combined with bitter cold, drove the miners back to work. Miners agreed to a twenty percent wage reduction and signed individual contracts promising to give up their union membership. According to Lloyd, signing these contracts meant miners bound "themselves, individually, not to take part in any combination to obtain better wages, and agree to leave the settlement of all grievances to the sole judgment and decisions of the company."[94] The company also blacklisted former union leaders and other miners who played a significant role in the distribution of food, clothing, and medicine to the starving and sick.[95]

Mitchell had not been a major player during the strike. He shared equally in the suffering, but he was able to return to work at the end of December. Less than a month later, on January 22, 1890, some two hundred and forty coal miner delegates from around the country met in Columbus, Ohio, and formed a new national union, the United Mine Workers of America (UMWA). The union was a merger of the two existing national organizations, the NFMML and the Knights of Labor's Trade Assembly 135. The UMWA represented a curious blend of different approaches to union advance. Some delegates envisioned a reform organization that would support cooperatives, while others pressed for a fighting organization that would strike for improved wages, hours, and working conditions. The result was an industrial union affiliated with the craft-dominated American Federation of Labor that accepted the existence of the wage system as "a natural and necessary part of our industrial system," but that also actively engaged in reform issues such as women's suffrage and the direct election of senators.[96]

For Mitchell the founding of the UMWA was not an event of great importance. Several national mine unions had come and gone in his lifetime, and this one did not appear very powerful. He had more pressing concerns in 1890, including the task of making a living after the lockout. Moreover, he had signed a "yellow dog" contract prohibiting him from joining the new organization. In the months following the lockout, Spring Valley miners found no respite from their misery. Operators had only partially resumed operations, creating the problem of half-time work for many men. Lloyd denounced this "policy of partial operation" as "but a turning more softly and slowly and secretly, so as not to awaken the public, of the old hunger-screw."[97] At the end of the lockout, operators had agreed to advance wages beginning November 1, 1890, but when that date came no advance was given. Only when miners resolved to strike again did the companies grant the increase, and operators took the occasion to raise charges for tool sharpening and coal used by the miners at home.[98]

By early 1891, Spring Valley erupted again. Without other means to redress their grievances, miners struck. The infant UMWA sent several organizers to the town, signed up 3,000 miners, and spent over $5,000 in a vain effort to win its first major battle. After ten grueling months, the union could no longer afford strike benefits and the men returned to work, defeated once again.[99] As did thousands of strikers, Mitchell vacated Spring Valley in the summer of 1891. Perhaps realizing the futility of this second clash against intransigent operators, unwilling to endure again the privation suffered in 1889, Mitchell traveled west once more.

He secured work at the Starkville Coal and Coke Company of Colorado, where his superintendent was none other than Dan McLaughlin. The "father of the joint conference" had been a state legislator until 1889, when the interstate movement collapsed and the lockout at Spring Valley began. Disgusted by developments, he gave up his seat in the legislature and joined the ranks of the operators.[100] Mitchell not only worked for McLaughlin but also spent many of his leisure hours with him discussing the coal trade, the need for effective national organization, and collective bargaining. Upon assuming the UMWA presidency, Mitchell told reporters his trade union outlook had been shaped "by the many lively discussions" he had with the old man in Colorado.[101] It is quite probable that while in Colorado Mitchell developed his understanding of and appreciation for the joint conference. It is also quite probable that he also began to consider a career in the trade union movement at this time.

In less than a year, Mitchell was back in Spring Valley. In the wake of the strike, so many had left and others blacklisted that Mitchell was able to find work once again. The hated "yellow dog" contracts were now gone, and

Mitchell joined the Spring Valley local of the UMWA. At twenty-two he was ready to settle down, to conclude his wanderings and establish a permanent home. Early in 1892, he met Katherine B. O'Rourke, and after a short courtship, they married. Kate, as she was called, was born in Catlin, Illinois, a small mining town five miles west of Danville on the Wabash River. Her father was Henry O'Rourke, a miner who was called "Old Man" even when young. Her mother had died when she was a child, and her only sibling was a brother, James. Soon after the mother's death the family moved to Belleville, where she attended public schools. In the mid-1880s the family moved to Spring Valley.[102] In many respects, Kate was similar to the man she married. She knew the trauma of losing a parent, she was accustomed to the daily privations of life in Spring Valley, she had survived the brutality of the lockout of 1889 and the strike of 1891, and she knew nothing of life outside mining camps.

There were several notable differences between John and Kate, however. Of least importance was the fact that she was two years older. More significantly, her father was one of the few miners in Spring Valley to own his own house. It was a double-family house. The O'Rourkes lived in one half and rented the other. This perhaps made Kate a more desirable mate, for marriage to her meant escape from the exorbitant rents and deplorable conditions of company owned housing. Another difference was religion. Kate was a practicing Catholic. Since escaping from his devout Presbyterian stepmother, Mitchell exhibited no religious convictions. Yet religion was an important dividing line between the various ethnic groups in mining camps, and the taking of a Catholic bride would have been an unusual if not a scandalous act. Mitchell did not convert to Catholicism, nor did he ask his wife to abandon her faith. Indeed, she continued to attend mass, and she raised their children in the faith.

The Mitchells were a handsome couple on their wedding day. Kate was slender yet strong, and the many years of hardship had not etched lines into her face, which was long and angular with remarkably high cheekbones. She had thin lips and a bulbous nose, but her large, round eyes dominated her visage and gave her an appearance of sincerity and warmth. Her dark hair, cut short just below her ears, made her look younger than her age. At five feet, seven inches, John was not much taller than his wife. His physique, common in the isolated mining camps, was muscular and lean. He was also blessed with a pleasant face. With olive skin and clear, expressive eyes, full lips, and well-proportioned features, all topped by dark, neatly combed hair, Mitchell looked intelligent, respectable, and likeable. His good looks would attract notice once he became a public figure.

After the wedding, Mitchell moved in with Kate and her father. Kate's brother James, himself a miner, had recently moved to Iowa and therefore did not live with the couple. Neither partner knew anything of the healthy functioning of a nuclear family. Mitchell's upbringing, in particular, gave him little insight on questions of love and affection. Nevertheless, in their first years together Kate and John were able to establish close emotional bonds that would last a lifetime. While in later years the couple would be separated most of the year by the pressing demands of his office, their marriage was one of love and commitment. Their marriage would prove fruitful as well. A little over a year after the wedding, Kate gave birth to Richard, the first of six children.[103]

Marriage and family were not the only signs indicating Mitchell's desire to establish permanent roots in Spring Valley. By the mid-1890s he had developed close friendships with fellow townsmen, and he began to take an active role in the institutional and cultural life of the town. And for the first time, he began to demonstrate leadership qualities that set him apart from ordinary men. While he did not begin reading law and philosophy at this time, as his first biographer claimed,[104] he did develop a voracious appetite for newspapers and conversation. He soon became recognized for his intelligence and insight, especially on matters relating to the coal trade and the local union. He was an active and well-liked member of the community, a joiner and a leader.

His mentor in these years was a Catholic priest, Father John Power, one of the most influential men among the miners. Unlike many priests and ministers who concerned themselves with spiritual matters only, Father Power was equally committed to improving the material conditions of his flock. He corresponded often with Henry Demarest Lloyd and was largely responsible for securing his aid during the 1889 lockout. In 1891 he testified in Springfield for the abolition of company stores, telling legislators "he found it hard to work to educate people in the paths of duty when soulless corporations were daily devising schemes to rob them of all they possess." His pro-union bias was sufficiently strong to prompt W. L. Scott, owner of the Spring Valley Coal Company, to pressure Bishop Spaulding of Peoria to remove Father Power from the town.[105] Power and Mitchell became close friends, and the priest helped Mitchell develop intellectually. Perhaps as a result of this relationship, Mitchell had a better understanding of the positive role priests could play in encouraging union growth, an understanding that would prove valuable during the anthracite strikes of 1900 and 1902.

Mitchell also joined an "athletic club" for coal miners. Drink and debate, rather than sports, were apparently the favorite activities of this club. The men would meet either in James Hicks's saloon, the union hall, or on a member's front porch and discuss mining issues. The long chats with Dan McLaughlin and Father Power served him well in these exchanges. One friend later wrote: "Many a time I look back to those Athletic Club days when we used to come together at times in debate. Even at that early date your judgment was considered superior to any of the older heads." Little wonder the miners selected Mitchell president of their club. Being recognized for his judgment and intelligence built his ego. And being noticed by the operators for his increasingly outspoken union views fueled a love of competition. He recalled these days fondly in later years, a time when "I was pounding sand rock in the mines . . . during the day, and fighting my good friend Dalzell at night." L. M. Dalzell was a foreman in the mines who later became general manager of the Spring Valley Coal Company. "I recall to mind the many times we sat devising methods by which we could compel an observance of the law regulating mines . . . and the attacks our mutual friend Heller used to make on us through his paper, the Spring Valley Press."[106]

In 1894, Mitchell's growing status in the community was demonstrated by his election as president of the Spring Valley Board of Education. He took his duties seriously and worked hard to alleviate problems caused by the rapid influx of immigrants. The schools at that time were "crowded beyond their capacity and teachers were worked to the utmost limit of endurance." He considered it his job not only to help build new schools but also to help cultivate a "spirit of unity, Americanism, and love of country" among the diverse ethnic mix of the town. He was successful enough to win reelection to the post the next year.[107]

Mitchell's rising popularity occurred during some of the blackest years for the UMWA in Illinois and nationwide. When Illinois miners met in convention in early 1892, there was little reason for optimism. The UMWA represented but a tiny fraction of the state's miners, and operators routinely ignored an 1891 law calling for weekly pay and outlawing company stores. The convention announced an organizing drive to drum up new members. The union circular asked miners "to consider their honor and manhood, their homes and the future of their families and not to allow themselves to be driven like dumb beasts or operated like so much machinery."[108] UMWA President John B. Rae announced in April 1892 that organizing Illinois, West Virginia, and Maryland was the "question of the hour." While the union spent $15,000 in Illinois in 1892 alone and successfully set up numerous locals, these locals "withered and died in early childhood." By 1894, only 500 Illinois miners were dues-paying members of the UMWA.[109]

Union leaders offered numerous explanations for their failures. Operator intransigence in the form of blacklisting of union members was a principal obstacle to growth. Ethnic tensions among the miners themselves stymied union appeals. Many immigrants from southern and eastern Europe displayed an "I-don't-care-if-I-am-a-serf" attitude, declared one Illinois leader. "One thing sure, we must organize the non-English speaking miners to make our organization effective."[110] By far the most deleterious effect on union growth, however, was the Panic of 1893 and resulting depression that left three million Americans idle by the end of the year. As industrial production plummeted, operators battled each other over the remaining coal markets. Operators slashed wages and curtailed production, leaving many of the nation's miners unemployed and hungry. Since the weak UMWA was powerless to save wage rates or jobs, miners saw no reason to join the organization.[111]

Events in the early-1890s radicalized many miners. The intense and often bloody labor wars of 1892—steelworkers at Homestead, metal miners in *Couer D'Alene*, railroad switchmen in Buffalo—demonstrated that the mining industry was not the only one in which employers, with their allies in government, ran roughshod over the rights of workers to organize and protect their interests. During the Depression of 1893, many miners turned to the Populist party and its premise that wealth belonged to those who produced it. And the miners could agree with the sentiments of Populist leader Mary Ellen Lease of Kansas that the time had come to "raise less corn and more hell." The miners supported Coxey's Army, the most famous of numerous "industrial armies" formed in 1894 that began to march toward Washington demanding relief. By the end of 1893, the UMWA journal merely reflected what was on the lips of many members when it warned miners that the "moneyed class would continue to rob them unless they organized economically and politically."[112]

The extent to which Spring Valley miners were radicalized in these years was demonstrated on Labor Day, 1893, when Lucy Parsons, widow of the Haymarket martyr, delivered an address denouncing capitalism and extolling anarchism to a large, cheering crowd. While there was a small anarchist club in town, comprised mainly of Italian immigrants, hundreds of miners and their families, both native born and immigrant, showed up to hear Parsons deliver "a terrible arraignment of the robber classes." On the stage behind her, according to one sympathetic observer, was "the blood red flag, symbolizing the brotherhood of man." After her two hour address, one miner asked for a vote of thanks, and "the motion was carried by a thunderous aye from the entire audience, accompanied by cheers which awoke the echoes along the quiet wooded vales of Spring Creek." Whether Mitchell attended the address is not known, but he undoubtedly would have agreed with the editor of the mine workers' journal that anarchism was not the solution to the diggers' desperation. "A little sound, persistent, and well directed trade unionism would, in our opinion, be more prolific of immediate results."[113]

UMWA leaders agreed. With an empty treasury and a membership of only 13,000, President John McBride and delegates to the April 1894 convention declared a nationwide strike of coal miners to restore wage cuts and stop layoffs. The union had supported numerous strikes in its infancy, but the strike of 1894 was its first national suspension. Coinciding with the Pullman strike and Coxey's army, the miners' strike was a desperate act representing the frustrations of hungry, angry, and increasingly militant diggers. The strike began on April 21 and 100,000 miners heeded the call to cease work. Before the strike was over, approximately 180,000 of the nation's 193,000 soft coal miners had joined the suspension.[114]

At Spring Valley the strike erupted in sporadic violence when operators attempted to import strikebreakers. Operators and an unsympathetic press played upon merchants' fears of working-class violence and radicalism to create near hysteria in the town. One local dry goods merchant told a Chicago reporter that anarchists armed with "dynamite bombs" were terrorizing the community. Another businessman from nearby LaSalle claimed that any "well-dressed stranger" entering Spring Valley was in "danger of his life." And a local deputy sheriff informed the press that "he did not consider the life of any newspaperman safe within the borders of Spring Valley."[115] The operators' accusation of anarchist violence was a ruse to discredit the strike and divide the miners, charged local union leader James O'Connor. The operators of Illinois were trying to split native born and "our non-English brethren — foreign anarchists, they are called. Most of them do not even understand the meaning of the term anarchy."[116]

There was more than enough violence during the strike, however, to lend credence to operator charges of anarchism. In their determination to make the walk out effective, Spring Valley miners organized themselves in military fashion and patrolled the mines in the area. Some 5,000 men, mostly from Spring Valley, marched to Centralia in mid-May when they heard mines were operating with strikebreakers. They were met en route by the county sheriff and his deputies, and seventy-five miners were put in jail. They were released after several hours, however, when their comrades surrounded the jail and chanted: "Shall we let our brothers stay in jail?" "No, burn it down."[117] A similar incident occurred at LaSalle the next day, and the marchers next headed toward Kewanee, where they forced the closing of several mines. When the miners reached Pana, they numbered 10,000, and a frightened Governor John Peter Altgeld called out the state militia.[118] Yet the militia at first only enraged the strikers and escalated the hostilities. To better elude the militia, miners hijacked trains to take them from one coal town to another. They also stopped trains entering the state carrying "scab coal" from West Virginia.[119]

Although Illinois miners effectively shut down coal production by early June, on June 12 the national union called off the strike and accepted an operator promise to stop further wage reductions. President McBride recognized that most operators were near bankruptcy and could not afford wage increases. He ordered the miners back to work. Miners in Spring Valley refused to heed McBride's order. On June 17, 12,000 of them adopted a resolution to "stand firm as bands of steel" in their "fight to the death" for a wage increase. They denounced the "cowardly surrender" made by McBride and demanded the resignation of all union officials who signed the back-to-work order.[120] By August 9, however, hunger and the use of African-American strikebreakers forced the resolute Spring Valley miners to surrender.[121]

Mitchell's role in the 1894 strike is a mystery. Whether he participated in the marches to neighboring towns or hijacked trains is unknown. But as president of the miners' athletic club and a recognized leader among the men, he undoubtedly played a significant role at the local level, if only by distributing strike aid. Whatever his role, when the mines reopened in August he was refused reemployment. Mitchell's first biographer asserts that he lost his job because the new superintendent was an Englishman who summarily discharged all Irish and that Mitchell's marriage to a Catholic of Irish heritage earned him the same fate. This assertion is probably not true. Local papers reported that Spring Valley operators rehired almost all strikers and made no mention of the discharge of Irish.[122] A more likely explanation is that Mitchell was fired for his activities during the strike.

At twenty-four, Mitchell found himself without the means to support his wife or infant son. His life had reached a crossroad, and he had to decide whether to uproot his family to seek work or find some way to remain in the town where he had laid down roots. During the strike he had made the acquaintance of William D. Ryan, and this chance meeting would determine the future course of his life. Born in Braidwood in 1861, Ryan had, like Mitchell, learned his trade unionism directly from Dan McLaughlin. In the early 1890s, Ryan served as the unpaid organizer and secretary-treasurer of the UMWA's northern Illinois subdistrict.[123] During the 1894 strike, he had been in charge of distributing strike relief. He also took it upon himself to entertain the strikers in an effort to distract them from their hunger. Exhibiting the racist insensitivity so rampant in that era, Ryan presented a skit entitled "The Mischievous Nigger" at the Braidwood Music Hall with white performers in black face that delighted "several hundred Irish citizens and their friends."[124] Although Ryan was nine years Mitchell's senior, the two men struck up a close friendship which endured for decades. Ryan saw in Mitchell the leadership qualities recognized by his athletic club associates, and he offered him the position of UMWA subdistrict organizer. Mitchell accepted.[125]

Why Mitchell chose to accept this post is a matter of conjecture. Monetary reward was certainly not the reason. Not only were organizers unpaid, but the subdistrict treasury had no money for traveling expenses. Organizers were dependent on the voluntary contributions of miners they spoke with in each camp.[126] Sleeping in the open air or in cheap flophouses was certainly not an attractive inducement. A plausible motivation was devotion to the cause of trade unionism. Perhaps he was fired with the same zeal to change the plight of miners that induced Mary Harris "Mother" Jones to become an official UMWA organizer around the time Mitchell did. An equally compelling motivation was the chance for advancement, a chance to escape the pits. Although the UMWA was in decline, Mitchell understood that if the union ever became powerful, there would be opportunities for those who helped it grow. And while he recognized "the attraction of mining," he believed "on the whole it is not a desirable vocation."[127] The slim hope that he could escape the horrors of coal mining surely must have been enticing to Mitchell.

Mitchell embarked on his new career during the darkest period for coal miners in the state and across the country. The lingering depression meant several years of subsistence wages and irregular work. Conditions were so deplorable in Spring Valley that three hundred miners in July 1895 publicly offered to accept "voluntary slavery" by foregoing all wages if the companies would provide their families with adequate food, fuel, and clothing.[128] For the year ending July 1, 1896, the average Illinois miner worked just 3.44 days per week and earned only $318, far below the amount necessary to sustain a family. Miners in northern Illinois earned an average of $299 for 1896.[129] One UMWA official mournfully reported at the end of 1894 that "charity, sweet though humiliating, has saved thousands of our miners from absolute starvation."[130] The UMWA limped through the mid-1890s. Too weak to battle operators after the defeat of 1894, the union now experienced precipitous membership loss, internal dissension, and discontinuity of leadership. President John McBride stepped down in 1895 and was succeeded by Phil Penna, who resigned after two unsuccessful years. By 1897 less than 10,000 coal miners belonged to the union. The union was simply too weak to resist periodic operator demands for further wage reductions.[131]

Desperate conditions heightened ethnic and racial tensions in the coal communities. In 1895, what was described as a "gang of blacks" in Spring Valley reportedly robbed and assaulted a white miner. Whites then petitioned the Spring Valley Coal Company to dismiss all of its African-American employees. When the company refused, white miners, "headed by an Italian band," marched on the African-American neighborhood chanting various racist epithets. One witness reported that forty were wounded as "shots were fired and bricks and missiles of every description were used by the combatants."[132]

Convincing men to join the union under such conditions was no easy task, but Mitchell set about his work with the single-minded resolution he would demonstrate in later years. Sometimes alone and sometimes with Ryan, he would travel from camp to camp, often on foot, pitching the union to the hungry miners. At each camp he would hold a public meeting and establish a temporary local. If miners could raise the money necessary to purchase a charter from national headquarters, a permanent local would be set up. Before leaving any camp, he made certain to ask who was the best man to talk to at the next stop. On one occasion he and Ryan arrived at a camp during a strike. He helped them collect food and make soup in a fifteen gallon pot. He and Ryan then ate with the men in a nearby orchard while they talked about the promise of the UMWA.[133]

Incredibly, Mitchell proved successful in his organizing work. At a time when miners across the country were abandoning the union, he helped achieve a minor victory for northern Illinois miners that convinced 7,000 to take out membership cards. The victory occurred in the summer of 1895 when Indiana miners were striking to resist a wage cut. Mitchell was then representing Spring Valley at a wage conference at Joliet between northern Illinois miners and operators. The two sides agreed to wait until the Indiana dispute was resolved. If the strike failed and Indiana miners were forced to accept the wage cut, northern Illinois operators would insist on a like cut in their mines. If, however, the Indiana strikers were victorious, then the existing wage scale would remain in effect for another year. Mitchell and other northern Illinois organizers busied themselves collecting strike aid for Indiana, and as a result the Indiana miners were able to hold out long enough to win their strike. Northern Illinois operators remained true to their word and did not insist on a reduction. The union's ability to protect wages in this instance led miners to join up.[134] While most of the new recruits left the union in the next two years, Mitchell had achieved his first union success.

This small victory at Joliet helped Mitchell win his first UMWA election. In early 1896, northern Illinois union miners chose Mitchell as the subdistrict's secretary-treasurer.[135] Ryan had vacated that post to run for office on the district executive board, and he no doubt sponsored Mitchell's bid to succeed him. The next year Ryan won the election for secretary-treasurer of Illinois (District 12), a post he held until 1908. Mitchell's new position still carried no salary, but at least his expenses were paid. His principal duties involved organizing, accounting for the subdistrict's finances, and lobbying at Springfield for positive mining laws. Traveling to the state capital by train, wearing a suit for perhaps the first time in his life, meeting with some of the state's most influential people—all this was new for the impoverished young man. Yet once again he proved himself capable. Along with other lobbyists, he helped secure an amendment to the state antitrust law, allowing operators and miners the legal right to fix a scale of wages. He also pressed successfully for a gross weight law. Illinois miners were paid according to the weight of coal dug, but until this law passed, they were not compensated for coal falling through the mine screen, the size of which varied from mine to mine. And he also helped strengthen existing prohibitions against child labor in the mines.[136] While the district union was too weak to force recalcitrant operators to comply with these laws, Mitchell did receive recognition for his successful lobbying efforts.

In 1897, Mitchell was elected to a seat on District 12's executive board. Ryan, now district secretary-treasurer, was probably instrumental in his candidacy. Mitchell had come a long way in three years, from unemployed digger to one of the top UMWA officials in the state. But it would be easy to overestimate his importance in early 1897. He was still a relatively minor player in one of the weakest districts of an impotent union. No one could predict that within two years he would emerge as the president of one of the nation's most powerful unions. In 1897 Mitchell rose like a phoenix out of the poverty-stricken prairie of Illinois.

The year began as inauspiciously as previous years for the miners and their union. The nearly bankrupt UMWA claimed less than 10,000 members, and in fact only a few thousand paid dues. Fewer than 200 delegates attended the January national convention, and more than half represented one district— Ohio. President Penna, who had already declared his resignation and would be replaced on April 1 by Michael Ratchford, recounted the pitiful details: demand for coal remained depressed; few operators had signed contracts with union miners in the past year, and those few had violated the contracts with impunity; the treasury was empty and the union could not afford to pay its organizers; and since the union did not exist in many areas, the calling of a second national strike was suicidal. Penna concluded there was little that could be done at the present time to reverse the union's fortunes.[137]

Ratchford did not view the situation with the same fatalism as Penna. He recognized the prospects for a successful strike were poor, but he also understood that failure to take risks might soon mean the death of the organization. Moreover, he was aware of growing militancy among exasperated miners. In late June, he invited national executive board members into secret session, and he convinced the board to issue the call for a national suspension to begin July 4. "Our suspension is not a choice," he thundered, "but it is the voice of an enslaved class urged to action by cruel and unbearable conditions, the protest of an overworked, underpaid people against longer continuing a semi-starved existence."[138] Although the only demand specified was a wage increase, the UMWA's real aim was the reestablishment of the interstate agreement.

If anything, Ratchford had understated the frustrations of the miners. Their response to the strike call shocked both union leaders and operators. Within days 150,000 diggers laid down their picks. The strike was almost completely effective in shutting off coal production in northern Illinois, Indiana, and Ohio. But in several important districts the strike was less than complete. Tens of thousands of miners continued to work in central Pennsylvania, West Virginia, and southern Illinois. W. D. Ryan led the strikers in northern Illinois with the battle cry of "shut the supply of coal off completely and victory will be ours." He then sold the furniture at District 12 headquarters in Springfield and returned to Braidwood to assume command in the field.[139]

While Ryan handled matters in the northern section of the state, Ratchford ordered Mitchell to southern Illinois. Stretching from Centralia to Cairo, southern Illinois was known as "Little Egypt" because of its shape. Settled mainly by Kentucky mountaineers, who carried with them the feuds and prejudices of their native state, it was a hotbed of "copperhead" activities during the Civil War. The first miners were farmers who dug coal in the winter and raised corn in the summer. And they resisted unionization as an infringement on their independence. Although the area was not yet the important coal producer it would be in later years, southern Illinois miners were digging enough black gold to upset the union's plan to choke off the nation's coal supply. To assist Mitchell in this important task, Ratchford assigned John H. Walker, a Scotsman who lived in Braceville near Braidwood, and a future ally of Mitchell's at the national level. Since there were no funds for train fare, Mitchell and Walker walked from camp to camp, sleeping under the stars and eating whatever the miners would give them. Their appeals on behalf of the union induced thousands of men to refrain from work. Although he never achieved a shutdown of the southern Illinois field, he was successful enough to attract the notice of Ratchford and other UMWA leaders.[140]

As had happened during the 1894 strike, hunger stalked the coal towns within weeks of the stoppage. "Swarms of ragged children are beginning to forage around the mining communities for food to keep them and their parents from starving," observed a Chicago journalist in mid-August.[141] If the strike were to succeed, the moral and financial support of the public was essential. And public support, Ratchford and other leaders understood, would not be forthcoming unless strikers remained peaceful. Hoping to avoid a repeat of the violence that occurred in the 1894 strike, UMWA officials continually urged the miners to refrain from property destruction and physical confrontations. The message took hold. In Illinois, for example, the Bureau of Labor Statistics reported at the end of the strike that it had been "conducted in an admirable manner and singularly free from violent demonstrations."[142] A major reason for the lack of violence and, indeed, for the success of the strike, was a general agreement among leading operators not to reopen their mines with strikebreakers. Many forward-looking operators had been looking for a way to reestablish the interstate joint conference ever since its collapse in 1889. Many even understood that a strong national miners' union, by standardizing wage rates, could help stabilize the industry. Thus, more than a few operators privately prayed for a UMWA victory in 1897.[143]

The peaceful strikers received support from numerous quarters. The governors of Illinois, Indiana, Ohio, and West Virginia expressed their sympathy for the legitimate demands of the downtrodden miners. Illinois Governor John Tanner, for instance, welcomed a delegation of strikers to the state house and refused to order the state militia despite the pleas of panicky sheriffs. Heart wrenching coverage in the nation's press produced gifts of food and other forms of material aid from thousands of citizens. The American Federation of Labor lent organizers. Eugene Debs of the defunct American Railway Union and James R. Sovereign of the Knights of Labor, two of the nation's best known labor leaders, offered their services.[144]

The AFL sponsored three mass rallies to raise money to aid the strikers, at Pittsburgh, Wheeling, and St. Louis. The rallies attracted labor supporters of every stripe—socialists and anarchists, Populists and Knights, middle-class reformers and hard-bitten radicals. Mitchell took time out from his organizing work to attend the St. Louis convention. William D. Ryan and he traveled by train from Springfield in August. For the next few days, he listened while speakers focused on West Virginia, the biggest obstacle to labor victory. The state was quickly becoming a leader in coal production, and operators there were viciously antiunion. The isolation of the camps in mountainous regions, company owned roads, private police forces, and judges who made liberal use of their power to issue injunctions against union representatives—all made organizing exceptionally difficult. Mother Jones and other UMWA organizers who traveled there in 1897 were promptly thrown in jail. Mitchell sat while Eugene Debs and others blasted the combined power of state and capital as represented by the injunction. In the not too distant future, Mitchell would gain personal knowledge of the force of injunctions in West Virginia.[145]

The 1897 strike was one of labor's great struggles, and Mitchell believed he was part of history in the making. His central role as the organizer in southern Illinois, attendance at his first mass rally outside Illinois, and the national focus given the strike made the summer of 1897 memorable and fired him with enthusiasm for the cause of unionism. Years later he recalled "the long struggle . . . that marks the turning point in our craft's contest for higher wages." He remembered "the determined faces of that great army of toilers who, on July 4th, threw down their picks . . . with a resolution that would have done credit to the warriors of old." And he took pride in being one of "that small band of toilers who marched from place to place, foot-sore, weary and ill, pleading and urging others to join them in their struggle for justice." Unlike soldiers who fought for the defense of the country, the strikers did not go forth with flags waving, drums beating, and the public applauding. Nevertheless, "with undaunting courage they pressed on, overcoming what seemed to be insurmountable obstacles."[146]

Miners held firm until September, when both sides were ready to settle. Midwestern operators feared losing their markets to West Virginia competitors who had succeeded in keeping their mines open. Ratchford and other UMWA leaders also realized that if major operators lost their markets, they could not afford wage increases. Moreover, Ratchford received reports that hunger was driving some miners back to work. By the time a special union convention was held in Columbus, operators had offered a compromise—a wage advance less than the miners demanded and a promise to reestablish the interstate joint conference in January 1898. Many delegates opposed the offer, believing the strike should continue until all demands were met, but Ratchford ultimately convinced a majority to accept the terms as the best possible under the circumstances. The offer was accepted and the strike was called off. Although it ended in compromise, the 1897 strike marked the first national victory for the UMWA and signaled its emergence as a powerful force in the industry.[147]

The contrast between the failure of 1894 and the success of 1897 contained valuable lessons for Mitchell and other aspiring union leaders. Both strikes were acts of desperation, conducted during a depression when the union was weak and demand for coal low. Both strikes had unleashed a torrent of militancy among the nation's diggers and were successful in the early weeks. In 1894, however, the union had been unable to prevent militancy from turning to violence. Violence had turned public sympathy against the miners, and state governments had intervened to protect life and property. In 1897 Ratchford and his associates succeeded in harnessing militancy. They made certain the work stoppage was quiet and lawful. A peaceful strike won over journalists whose sympathetic coverage ensured public support. A peaceful strike also guaranteed at least the neutrality of state governments. Governors could not justify ordering state militias to intervene when property and life were not threatened. In 1897 Mitchell learned that public support, the neutrality of the state, and the orderly conduct of a strike were the intimately connected elements which made success possible.

Mitchell had little time to reflect on these lessons, however. While miners joyfully returned to work in Ohio, Indiana, and western Pennsylvania under the terms of the Columbus settlement, a majority of miners in his home state balked. Illinois diggers believed their national and district officers had sold them out by not insisting on the full wage increase. Emboldened by dramatic growth in district membership, Illinois miners refused to return to work unless operators agreed to their original wage demands.[148] Mitchell had an important decision to make. Would he side with the majority in his district, continue the struggle, and exact higher wages from weakened operators? Or would he side with Ratchford and the national officers and try to force the miners in Illinois to accept the compromise they so detested?

Mitchell's decision affords us the first real glimpse at his trade union predilections. As soon as the Illinois miners rejected the Columbus settlement, Mitchell took to the road, moving from colliery to colliery, in an effort to convince the men that their continuation of the strike was foolhardy, that the best course of action was to accept the contract and return to work. Certainly there was an element of ambition in his decision to uphold the Columbus settlement. If he could get the Illinois miners back on the job, he would endear himself to President Ratchford and perhaps through his patronage advance up the union hierarchy at a time when the union was expanding. For a married man who now had two children, no steady income, and no desire to return to the pits, personal advance was an important concern. There was also an element of principle in his decision. Having learned his trade unionism from Dan McLaughlin, Mitchell believed that a strong national organization and the reestablishment of the joint conference was far more important than wage advances at the district level. Without a strong national union and an interstate agreement with operators, any district gains would soon be reversed. Coal was a national industry, McLaughlin had told him, and any successful movement of miners had to be national in scope. The time for incessant wars at the local level had passed. Mitchell thus stood ready to cripple militancy in Illinois for the sake of national advance.

Mitchell not only foreshadowed the trade union philosophy he would pursue in later years, he also ably demonstrated his skills as conciliator. In his face-to-face discussions with miners, he came across as sincere, understanding, rational, and patient. As we shall see, he did not regard the average miner as intelligent and had little respect for his opinions, but by nature he was one who would listen to his opponent and coolly discuss the issues point by point. While Mitchell convinced few miners to return to work, he earned their respect and confidence as a straightforward and honest official. Thus, when Illinois miners forced the suspension of district President James Carson on charges of "selling out," they did not heap abuse on Mitchell.[149] Mitchell also proved adept at press relations. During his tour of the state, he met an influential pro-union reporter for a Springfield paper, Edward R. Smith. The two men became fast friends, and Mitchell convinced Smith to use his column in support of the Columbus settlement.[150]

Mitchell's machinations did not end the strike in Illinois. At the end of October, the majority still held firm. In early November, however, operators broke the miners' resolve with the threat to import large numbers of Chinese strikebreakers from Wyoming. Preparations for transportation, housing, and police protection were soon underway. Within days, numerous local unions accepted the Columbus settlement and ordered their men back to work.[151] The Chinese threat and the defection of these locals forced Illinois miners to seek peace. On November 22 at Joliet, operators met with Mitchell, Ryan, and other union representatives. After two days, a compromise settlement was reached that gave Illinois miners a slightly higher advance than called for in the Columbus settlement.[152] The strike was effectively over in Illinois, and Mitchell and Ryan were given most of the credit. Ryan was rewarded with a seat on the national executive board, and Mitchell had once again caught the eye of President Ratchford.

The January 1898 UMWA national convention at Columbus was a jubilant celebration of the first great national victory in coal. Mitchell was there. It was his first national convention and, at age twenty-seven, only the fourth time he had been outside Illinois. Along with the hundreds of other delegates, he sat in the convention hall and peered through the cloud of tobacco smoke while he listened to Ratchford triumphantly proclaim that the union had finally come of age. Membership gains of more than 300 percent, the emergence of powerful district organizations in the Midwestern states, rapidly increasing interest in the "outlying fields" such as Alabama and Wyoming— all this and more had been accomplished in the past few months. "Our trade shines brilliantly with the victories and achievements of 1897," Ratchford boasted.[153] When the cheering and clapping died down, delegates got down to work. They had to prepare for the upcoming interstate conference and elect their new officers.

Elections for two of the top three posts were carried out without rancor. For their able strike leadership, delegates reelected President Ratchford with minimal opposition and Secretary-Treasurer W. C. Pearce with no opposition. The vice presidency was a different matter. The incumbent, John Kane, had died several months earlier and the office stood vacant. Moreover, there were rumors that Ratchford would soon step down to assume a political post. The contest for the vice presidency was thus a free-for-all with important implications for the future leadership of the union. Eleven nominees jockeyed for position, making promises and lining up support from as many delegates as possible. Illinois alone put forth three nominees—Mitchell, Ryan, and district President John "Dad" Hunter. Of the three Mitchell was by far the least powerful. He was an inexperienced unionist virtually unknown outside his own district, while Ryan and Hunter were popular men who sat on the union's highest council, the national executive board. Yet soon after the contest began, both Ryan and Hunter bowed out and threw their support to Mitchell.[154] Exactly why they did cannot be determined from the record. But since Ryan in years to come turned down repeated offers to run for national office, he most likely had no personal ambitions to become vice president in 1898. And it is possible that Hunter declined to run because he believed his present post was more powerful than the number two slot in the national organization. Whatever the reasons, the departure of Hunter and Ryan made Mitchell an unlikely but strong candidate.

Mitchell's victory was by no means assured. Because delegates usually voted along district lines, factional fights for office were a matter of district voting strength. And while Illinois had become one of the strongest districts in the union, its 110 votes could not match the 150 votes of Ohio. Fortunately for Mitchell, there was an unspoken rule in the union that the two top posts could not go to the same district. And since Ratchford was an Ohioan, no Ohio candidate was seriously considered for the vice presidency. At the time of the election, Mitchell's only serious rival was Patrick Dolan of District 5, western Pennsylvania. A boisterous and jovial man, Dolan seemed to have the advantage in terms of experience and influence. He was a district president, albeit of a poorly organized district, he was a member of the national executive board, and he was popular among the rank and file. Most importantly, Ratchford, although he thought highly of Mitchell, had earlier promised to support Dolan's candidacy.[155]

The contest pitted Dolan's popularity against the political skills of Mitchell's mentor, William D. Ryan. And Ryan's maneuvering ultimately prevailed. Ryan apparently made a deal with the Ohio delegation, promising Illinois' support of an Ohio candidate for the union presidency once Ratchford stepped down if Ohio delegates voted for Mitchell. Although it cannot be verified, the Ohioan he promised to support was probably Tom L. Lewis.[156] The combination of votes from the two most powerful districts put Mitchell over the top. On the first ballot Mitchell outpolled Dolan 215 to 195. Two minor candidates picked up twenty-one votes, however, leaving Mitchell one vote short of a majority. The fourth place candidate was then asked to withdraw and a second ballot held. This time Mitchell defeated Dolan 228 to 196. Mitchell was probably more stunned than anyone in the hall when he was announced the new UMWA vice president and called upon to make a speech. Embarrassed, Mitchell rose, thanked the delegates for the honor bestowed, pledged to do his utmost for the organization, and expressed his hope that at the next annual convention no one would have cause to regret his election.[157]

Immediately upon the adjournment of the convention, Mitchell and other select delegates boarded a train for Chicago, where they met with operators in joint conference beginning January 17. This was the first national joint conference held in more than a decade, and it signalled a new era in soft coal industrial relations that would last, with occasional lapses, for nearly three decades. Since union attempts to organize West Virginia and other outlying districts had failed, the joint conference involved only the Central Competitive Field— western Pennsylvania, Ohio, Indiana, and Illinois. The basis of unity between capital and labor in soft coal was the mutual desire to maintain labor peace over an extended period. With the depression lifting, both sides hoped to benefit from the resurgence in coal demand. Labor peace meant higher profits for operators and higher wages for miners.[158]

The primary consideration at the Chicago conference was wage rates. Wages represented two-thirds of mining costs, and wage slashing bred ruinous competition and labor unrest. While operators naturally hoped to keep wages as low as possible, progressive operators understood that wage levels were less important than the health of the industry. If all operators in the Central Competitive Field (CCF) had uniform labor costs at levels the union could tolerate, the primary basis of competition and labor strife would be eliminated. Operators therefore agreed to the union's demand for an advance in wages of ten cents per ton.[159]

Although the bargaining sessions were often heated, operators ultimately agreed to other union demands at the joint conference. Many operators appreciated the need for a powerful trade union in coal. Only a strong UMWA could successfully organize the outlying coal fields, especially West Virginia, which threatened their markets with cheap nonunion coal. To give the union the strength necessary to organize these districts, operators accepted the union's demand for the checkoff of dues, which guaranteed a constant flow of money into the union treasury. And to the surprise of many miners, operators granted miners the eight hour day. This traditional union goal, which had been staunchly resisted for years, was now accepted by operators as a way to limit production. While miners praised their union for achieving this goal, progressive operators were happy to use this mechanism to relieve the chronic overproduction that plagued the industry.

Upon Mitchell's election as vice president, the editor of the union's journal described him as a "promising young man," but observed that his "experience in the broad field of national mining affairs is more limited than that of most of his colleagues."[160] His inexperience proved a handicap at the joint conference, where he assumed the role of a bit player in the discussions. He could do little more than listen and learn while Ratchford and other more knowledgeable union men engaged in verbal battle against the employers. It was his first national experience with the arguments and bargaining strategies of operators. He used the conference as a learning experience, and the next time the two sides came together, Mitchell would not hesitate to take charge of negotiations.

Leading economists such as W. J. Ashley, the internationally known editor of the *Quarterly Journal of Economics*, praised the joint conference system in soft coal as a major step toward the solution of the "labor problem." It was an orderly, nonviolent, nongovernmental approach to industrial relations that promoted class harmony and cooperation. Numerous journalists, academics, and political leaders agreed and called for the adoption of this system by other industries.[161] So, too, did young John Mitchell. He believed the coal accord should be "regarded as an epoch in the industrial movement of our country." During those eleven days in Chicago, representatives of capital and labor, "those two forces formerly so antagonistic," met and "agreed to apply reason and intelligence, instead of force and coercion, in the adjustment of wage differences." Unlike the middle-class economists and social commentators, however, Mitchell was acutely aware of the militancy and collective power which had forced operators to the bargaining table. "The knowledge that behind the miners' just demands were one hundred and fifty thousand workers ready to throw down their picks and again renew, with all the vigor of their natures, the struggle of '97 . . . finally impelled the operators to give way."[162]

Elevation to the vice presidency altered Mitchell's life in numerous ways. For the first time in his union career, he received a salary. $900 per year did not make him a wealthy man, but his annual income was more than twice that of the average coal miner. Kate had given birth to a third child, Robert, during the 1897 strike, and Mitchell could feel secure in his ability to shield his boys from the hunger and poverty he had known as a child.[163] And as we shall see, Mitchell quickly acquired tastes far beyond the means of his former work mates, and he proved adept at real estate and stock market investments that multiplied his wealth. His new job also meant he would never have to return to the pits. Although his organizing efforts were difficult and at times exasperating, he was now forever free of the backbreaking toil in underground caverns that sapped men's spirits and destroyed their health. The principal drawback of his new post was separation from home and family. The vice presidency involved not only office duties at Indianapolis, but a great deal of organizing work in the weakly organized and outlying districts. There would be few opportunities to rush home to Spring Valley for even a weekend. And the uncertainties of holding union office made him reluctant to sever long established ties to that community and relocate his home and family in Indianapolis.

One of the most dramatic changes in his life was the fanfare and admiration he received from the people of the mining towns. Whenever he traveled in organized areas, miners, their wives, and even their children came out to see him, to shake his hand, to listen to his speeches. In the wake of the victory of 1897, Mitchell became something of an instant hero. Returning home to Spring Valley after the joint conference, he found his townsmen had planned a parade in his honor. Community leaders sang his praises in the town square.[164] Just four years earlier he had been an unknown, unemployed miner, an impoverished face in the crowd. Now he stood before them as a leader, the personification of their hopes for a better life. Throughout his union career, Mitchell remained ambivalent about the adulation he received. It flattered him and boosted his ego, but it also carried an enormous obligation to remain vigilant and secure tangible victories. In later years, the strain of this obligation would exacerbate physical and emotional problems.

Mitchell's first assignment as vice president proved the most difficult. Ratchford placed him in charge of an organizing team designed to accomplish what the strike of 1897 could not: bring West Virginia into the union fold. West Virginia coal seriously jeopardized the interstate movement. Not only was the coal of high quality grade, but nonunion labor made it cheaper than coal from the CCF. As long as the state remained unorganized, West Virginia operators could undersell their CCF competitors and steal their markets. At the joint conference, operators had warned that the continuation of the interstate movement hinged on the UMWA's ability to organize West Virginia. "We are willing to cooperate with you," Ratchford told union operators, "we do not want West Virginia coal to put you out of the market."[165] The enormous importance of this task revealed Ratchford's confidence in his young subordinate.

Accompanied by John Walker, who had assisted him in southern Illinois, Mitchell traveled to West Virginia in March 1898. Even though he had heard horror stories about West Virginia at the St. Louis rally in August 1897, he was shocked by the conditions he found. He had spent his entire life in poor coal towns, but he claimed he had never witnessed such suffering. Miners' homes were not fit for animals, and yet operators charged exorbitant rents. Miners worked twelve hour days in unsafe conditions for wages that could not cover expenses at the company stores.[166] West Virginia operators opposed the union with savage determination. To keep organizers out, operators relied on injunctions and violence. Miners brave enough to sign up faced dismissal and blacklisting. Mitchell knew he had his work cut out for him.

The extant letters from Mitchell's West Virginia experience reveal a great deal about the man and the early UMWA. Unlike today's well fed and generally well educated union officials, Mitchell traveled on a very tight budget. He walked from camp to camp. This reflected not only the isolation of the camps in mountainous terrain, but also the financial constraints on a growing but still small union. Only when he had to travel a good distance rapidly did he ride trains, and even then he made certain to travel second class. Although he was afforded the luxury of sleeping at hotels rather than outdoors, he went to great lengths to secure the most inexpensive lodging available. One of his first stops was Fairmont. He stayed at "The Tavern," which had as a motto, "you can't beat it unless you cheat." Even then Mitchell apologized to Ratchford because the room was $1.50 per day. "It's the best rate I can git (sic)," Mitchell explained.[167] Another indication of the budgetary restraints was Mitchell's lack of stationery. Every one of his reports was written on paper with hotel letterheads.

The grammar and spelling of these reports reflects Mitchell's lack of education. As union president his prose would improve dramatically through sheer effort and the guidance of his secretary, but as vice president his letters were chock full of misspellings, improper punctuation, subject-verb disagreements, and every other mistake imaginable. Even capitalization was a problem. His use of colloquialisms shows that his language was still that of the average miner. To cite but one example, when speaking of an earlier organizer who may have been in the employ of the operators, he wrote "there was one of them Who Done you Dirt."[168] Yet one can also see in these letters a man struggling to improve himself, to set himself apart from the rank and file, to demonstrate his worthiness to Ratchford. When he believed a word was misspelled, he scratched it out and rewrote it two, three, or sometimes even four times until he thought it was spelled correctly. More importantly, these letters offer us the first glimpse of Mitchell's attitudes toward his fellow miners. Having risen above his station, he began to view them with a combination of paternalistic affection and utter contempt. Expressions of sincere sympathy for their plight were liberally mixed with harsh invectives such as "these Dam cattle."[169] This superior and ambivalent attitude toward the rank and file would grow over the years.

Following Ratchford's instructions, Mitchell first approached operators rather than miners. He called on the various companies, hoping to convince operators to participate voluntarily in a union-sponsored, district-wide joint conference. The threat of strike action was implied in his invitation, but he also hoped to demonstrate that the UMWA was led by conservative men with reasonable demands. His first efforts to "make a favorable impression on the companys (*sic*)" gave him "some hopes" that a joint conference could be arranged. After speaking to two leading operators in the northern section of the state, however, he learned their real attitudes. "Sorry to report that the companys (*sic*) refuse to have any thing to do with us," he wrote.[170]

Turning his attention to the miners, he tried to arrange mass meetings to ignite a fire of union sentiment. While he found the miners "allright" in terms of support for the union, he learned that fear of dismissal and blacklists kept them from attending. Often the men would promise to attend, then fail to show up. For one large meeting, he printed handbills and delivered them to each miner's house in the area, but the response was "the same old Story." No more than twenty-five miners attended "and about four Straw Bosses . . . sent there to watch us." At another meeting, the "Pit Bosses" interrupted Mitchell and told the miners "they would be discharged if they stayed to hear me." He soon admitted he was at a loss as to his next move. "I have tried every plan that I know of to git (*sic*) the men to attend a meeting," he despaired. His only suggestion was that Ratchford send Chris Evans, a longtime coal union activist who had organized in West Virginia during the 1897 strike. The miners respected Evans and might attend a meeting if he were present, Mitchell wrote, "although I am afraid they would not come if Christ him self would speak here."[171]

There were other frustrations. Bad weather hampered travel, companies discharged all miners he succeeded in signing up, and he faced increasing threats from operators to keep off company property. The low point of the drive occurred when he was delivering circulars at mines owned by the Watson Company. When ordered to leave, Mitchell refused. Company bosses, assisted by the deputy sheriff, then "took hold of us and Pushed us off." He was infuriated not by the use of force by the operators, but by the fact that "some miners stood and laughed at us when they were doing it."[172]

After the humiliation at the Watson mines, Mitchell was ready to concede defeat. He called several more meetings but informed Ratchford that unless he met with greater success he was ready to abandon the field. Failure was a blow to his ego. His last report from West Virginia revealed an intense competitive drive, a need to accomplish what others could not, a desire to surpass even the organizing abilities of Eugene Debs, Mother Jones, and Samuel Gompers, who had tried to organize the state in 1897. "I would have been the happiest person on Earth if I had succeeded in organizing these men after all the great Labor leaders who were here last year failed," he lamented. Yet he was careful not to give Ratchford the impression that his failure in this important mission stemmed from a lack of effort on his part. He assured his superior: "I have done my best and that is all any Person can do."[173]

Unable to make headway either with operators or miners, Ratchford withdrew Mitchell from West Virginia. Organizing efforts in the state ceased for the time being, and the UMWA tried a different approach—the boycott. The union issued a circular in mid-May asking trade unionists and their supporters to refrain from purchasing nonunion West Virginia coal. The boycott was a traditional method of combating obdurate employers, one founded on working-class solidarity, but in this instance it had little effect. According to one scholar, the boycott may actually have increased sales of West Virginia coal because operators in that state could now claim the union was conspiring with CCF operators to destroy the industry in their state.[174]

Failure in West Virginia did not lessen Ratchford's confidence in his vice president. Indeed, soon after he recalled Mitchell from that field he reassigned him to another problem area, Illinois. The signing of the interstate agreement had been only the first step toward establishing harmonious relations between miners and operators. The joint conference did not work out specific pay scales for all miners. It simply fixed the scale at certain "basing points" in each of the four districts. The next step was to work out pay scales at the district level based on these "basing points." The process was complicated, involving a myriad of details concerning local conditions. Illinois operators and district officials signed a contract in early 1898, but neither side was happy with the terms. By the time Mitchell reached Illinois in late April, operators and miners in the state had failed in their attempts to readjust the scale. Several local strikes had erupted and operator resistance was hardening. A district-wide dispute at this critical juncture posed a serious threat to the continuation of the interstate movement.

After establishing headquarters in Springfield, located within easy reach of the areas on strike, Mitchell spoke with district leaders and operators. He concluded that miners in many subdistricts were making unreasonable demands. Operators in these areas could not afford to pay the wages demanded and remain in business. It is interesting to note that Mitchell never claimed the wage demands were out of line with the joint agreement. He claimed only that they were out of line with the companies' ability to pay. The "Mad Demands" of local strikers threatened labor peace in the entire state. District officers of the union were afraid to oppose these militants, and operators were considering a "united Stand against the Organization unless they are treat (*sic*) with more consideration." The Illinois situation provided Mitchell a golden opportunity to demonstrate his skills as a peacemaker. He arranged a joint conference of the district executive board and operators on May 10 and was able to resolve some of the problems.[175]

For Mitchell and Ratchford the crucial problem in Illinois was not local wage rates. The critical issue was union discipline. Unless the UMWA proved itself able to curb the militancy of its members and prevent local strikes, then united action was impossible and operators would have no reason to bargain with the national organization. After decades of localized warfare, miners had to accept the authority of the national union and resolve their grievances through proper union channels. Mitchell volunteered to become the enforcer of union discipline in Illinois. "The miners of this State need Someone to visit all there (*sic*) meetings to tell them What Dam fools they are making of themselves," he wrote, "and if you think it Best I Would Be Pleased to Do it." Ratchford told him to proceed. Over the next two weeks he traveled from camp to camp, scolding the miners that "they Must Stop coming out on strike With out (*sic*) first trying to adjust Differences through the Organization." His lectures were partially successful in encouraging rank-and-file moderation. Several local strikes were called off, and by the end of the month Mitchell could boast that due to his "good Work in Educating the Miners," Illinois diggers "Will use more good Sence (*sic*) and Reason in the future than they have in the Past."[176]

Mitchell's difficulties in Illinois were far from over, however. In the southern part of the state, several operators had refused to negotiate with the union at all. The resulting local strikes threatened to explode into open war when operators resorted to the importation of African-American strikebreakers. At the end of May, Mitchell learned that the St. Louis and Muddy River Company mines at Carterville had shipped in over four hundred African-Americans and erected a guarded compound for them.[177] As a child during the 1877 Braidwood strike, he had witnessed the kind of violence that could result from such action, and he therefore rushed to the scene. When he arrived in Carterville, he found some 2,000 white miners assembled and prepared to march to the mine where the scabs were working. Their intent was "to Burn the Shaft down." He courageously confronted the men and ordered them to desist. Although he was successful in preventing violence, he was unable to convince the strikebreakers to join the walk out.[178]

Fearing whites would soon return to work themselves, Mitchell asked Ratchford for strike relief and funds to remove miners from the area and reestablish them at union mines. Ratchford sent a check for $200, but he specifically instructed Mitchell not to use the money for strike relief or transportation. Such funds must come from the district treasury, Ratchford explained, and he did not want his vice president to set "a bad precedent." The

$200 was to "pay the fare of the negro scabs back to their homes." Mitchell's response to these instructions demonstrates that while he was anxious to cultivate his superior's trust and admiration, he was unwilling to serve as Ratchford's lackey in the field. He disagreed with the president on this issue, and he was not afraid to let him know. The district treasury was empty and money was needed in Carterville. "And if I am not Permited (sic) to use my own Judgement (sic) as to the Best Way to use it," he wrote, "the check Will Be Returned to you." A surprised and somewhat annoyed Ratchford responded with a three-paged missive on union finances. Claiming Mitchell reached his conclusions "hastily," he explained that strikers in every district demanded money. He could not give in to one group and refuse another. And he hoped Mitchell would not take offense because this was not "a personal matter." Mitchell did take the matter personally. He returned the check and included an angry note. He had spent some of his own money to assist the miners, and he had made promises to help others, but without funds he was placed "in a Very embarassing (sic) Position."[179]

Unable to settle the Carterville strike, Mitchell soon found himself embroiled in an even more explosive situation in Pana and Virden, Illinois. Operators in these two towns claimed the contract they had signed with district officials earlier in the year priced them out of the Chicago market. They sought relief from the state board of arbitration, but when the board rejected their contentions they repudiated the board's decision. On August 8 operators turned to the UMWA national executive board, asking the union's national officers to arbitrate and agreeing to be bound by their decision. But when Ratchford and the executive board also rejected their demands, operators locked out the miners.[180] The lockout did not simply represent another local conflict. Led by the largest coal producer in the state, the Chicago-Virden Coal Company, the Pana and Virden operators were some of the most powerful in Illinois. If they successfully resisted union wages, other firms might be emboldened. It was thus up to Mitchell to bring Pana and Virden into line.

After failing to reopen their mines with white scabs, operators sent agents to Alabama to round up African-American miners. These agents promised good wages and steady work but made no mention of labor trouble. On August 24, one hundred and fifty African-Americans arrived by train in Pana. District President "Dad" Hunter and local UMWA leaders were there to greet them. Hunter did a remarkable job explaining the situation to these men. By the time Mitchell arrived on the morning of the 25th, two-thirds had joined the strike. Hunter then left Mitchell in charge and traveled to Birmingham himself to try to prevent further importation of scabs.[181]

With Pana relatively quiet, Mitchell left for several days to attend to other duties and briefly visit his wife and children in Spring Valley. He arrived back in Pana on the evening of September 1 and, to his dismay, he found local miners in the midst of a mass meeting and "Preparing to March to the mine and take the (remaining) Negroes out." Since the scabs were quartered in an armed compound, Mitchell understood that their removal could easily lead to bloodshed, the calling of the state militia, and the certain defeat of the miners. He counseled patience and assured the miners he had a better plan. Since the mine was being operated without a fire boss as required by law, he was going to apply for a court injunction to shut it down legally and peacefully. He asked only that miners adjourn their meeting until 2 P.M. the next day. The miners approved his plan.[182]

At noon the next day Mitchell was in the Hotel de Pana conferring with David Ross, Illinois Commissioner of Labor, when he heard commotion outside in the street. Approximately thirty miners had grabbed David and Levi Overholt, president and superintendent of the mining company, "and started them towards the mine." Mitchell then witnessed the sheriff approach the mob "when some one (*sic*) Put a gun up to his head and told him to Run Which he Did." In a matter of minutes the crowd had grown to "about 1000." The men marched with the operators in front "so that the sherif (*sic*) would not order his Deputies to Fire on the mob." Halfway to the mine the men stopped and sent a committee to demand the sheriff to bring out the strikebreakers. "I was trying all the time to get the mob to Reason With me But they Were all angery (*sic*) and Excited and Would not listen to any thing." When the committee returned and reported that the sheriff refused to round up the strikebreakers, the crowd quieted down. Mitchell then seized this opportunity to restore order. "I made a Speach (*sic*) advising them to Release the prisoners and observe the law." After other local union officials made similar speeches, the miners released their hostages "and there was no harm Done."[183] The strike was not settled until the following spring, but Mitchell had helped defuse a dangerous crisis.

Far more than any other action, Mitchell's peacekeeping efforts in Pana made him a popular and respected union leader among the rank and file. His subsequent indictment by a county grand jury on charges of participating in the Pana riot may actually have increased his popularity.[184] Despite his West Virginia failure and his inability to settle the strikes at Carterville and Pana, miners began to develop the high regard for his courage, sincerity, and enthusiasm that would increase over the years. Equally important, Ratchford became convinced that Mitchell possessed the requisite qualities of dedication and levelheadedness to assume command of the UMWA's destiny.

Each of the first three UMWA presidents had used their office as a stepping stone to more lucrative careers. John B. Rae became a well-paid hospital administrator; John McBride, after serving one term as AFL president, eventually became commissioner of labor statistics in Ohio; Phil Penna sold his negotiating talents to the mine operators of Indiana.[185] Now it was Ratchford's turn. In September 1898, he accepted President William McKinley's invitation to become a member of the newly created United States Industrial Commission. His new duties were to begin October 20, when the first session of the commission was slated to open.[186] None of the previous presidents had played a significant role in union affairs after their departure, and Ratchford planned to make a clean break as well. Yet he was deeply concerned about the future success of the organization that had grown so dramatically under his charge in the past seventeen months. And he therefore took pains to make sure the most gifted man succeeded him.

Exactly why Ratchford believed Mitchell was the best candidate is impossible to determine with any degree of accuracy. There were certainly more experienced and knowledgeable men, most notably Ohio District Secretary-Treasurer Tom L. Lewis, who was regarded as perhaps the best debater and the best informed on coal mining issues. Nor did Mitchell possess the rhetorical skills, the commanding presence, or the sheer popularity of western Pennsylvania District President Patrick Dolan, whose abilities earned him the absolute attention of miners at conventions.[187] But Mitchell had demonstrated other leadership qualities even more valuable to the UMWA after the establishment of the interstate movement. In 1898, the union had embarked on a new course. After years of class warfare and confrontation, the goal was now to uphold peaceful contractual relations. This new course required new skills—soundness of judgment, deliberate and calculated rationality, willingness to compromise, an ability to persuade the rank and file to live up to existing contracts rather than inspire them to fight. And while Mitchell had not always succeeded in his efforts as vice president, he seemed to understand the new rules of the game at least as well as anyone else. By convincing Illinois miners to back down from their "mad demands," by obtaining small concessions from Illinois operators, and by cajoling miners in Carterville and Pana to refrain from breaking the law, Mitchell assured Ratchford he possessed the necessary talent for continued union victories.[188]

Ratchford's choice of Mitchell by no means guaranteed victory for the young man. There was no traditional pathway from the UMWA vice presidency to the presidency, and former union chiefs gained office only after bitter and even ruthless infighting. Ratchford understood that by stepping down before the end of his term a power struggle would ensue. But Ratchford, a wily veteran of intra-union battles, devised a means by which Mitchell's chances would be greatly improved. Rather than resign, he chose to remain official head of the union until the expiration of his term on April 1, 1899. And he installed Mitchell as "acting president," a position not provided for in the union's constitution. This subversion of union law would greatly assist Mitchell in the January 1899 elections. As head of the administration, Mitchell could take credit for all UMWA advances in 1898, and he had control of the internal mechanisms of power, such as the union's journal and the staff of organizers, to help defeat his enemies. Ratchford's maneuver had another advantage. Since he officially remained president, he—and not the inexperienced Mitchell—would preside over the national convention and lead the miners' bargaining team in the next joint conference.[189]

By October 20, then, the twenty-eight year old Mitchell took charge of the day-to-day affairs of the UMWA. His rise had been a matter of luck, ambition, and talent. Equally important, his advance demonstrated the viability of what one scholar called the "informal protege system" as a path to power.[190] Just as Terrence Powderly had attached himself to Uriah Stephens in the Knights of Labor, and just as Samuel Gompers won the support of Adolph Strasser in the Cigar Makers' Union, so, too, did Mitchell first win the patronage of William Ryan in Illinois then Michael Ratchford at the national level. Much of Mitchell's early success stemmed from his recognition that pleasing his superiors was even more important than cultivating the support of the rank and file. And once in office, Mitchell remained strongly inclined to prove his worthiness to those more powerful than himself. Indeed, his desire to gain the approval of important men such as Senator Mark Hanna and President Theodore Roosevelt became somewhat of an obsession, affecting his dress, language, attitudes, and actions.

Acting President Mitchell received valuable on-the-job experience in the handling of a growing bureaucracy. He now spent most of his time at union headquarters located in the Stevenson Building in Indianapolis. And for the first time he grappled with questions involving union finances, the assignment of organizers, public relations, the national executive board, and district-national relations. While his salary was not increased, his duties multiplied tenfold.[191] His first major challenge was the unsettled business in southern Illinois. In the weeks that passed since he left the Pana-Virden field in early September, tension was mounting as operators once again looked to Alabama for scab labor. If Mitchell could resolve the situation peacefully, his chances of election in January 1899 would be greatly improved. If he failed, not only might he lose the election, the entire interstate movement might crumble.

The Chicago-Virden Company on September 28 attempted to unload a train of strikebreakers, but well-armed Virden miners were waiting and the engineer refused to stop. After this incident, Mitchell left Indianapolis and headed to Virden, where his presence helped keep the peace. On October 10, he reported that a second "train load of Negroes are Expected in Virden any time," but he was confident "there are Enough Miners Waiting for them" to prevent the engineer from stopping. On October 11, Mitchell was in Springfield seeking a legislative solution to the problem. He addressed a rally at the state house and demanded legal action to stop firms from importing replacement workers into the state.[192] The next day the second train of strikebreakers arrived in Virden. This time armed guards were on board. When the train stopped at the mine, heavy gunfire erupted between miners and guards. Eleven died, six miners and five guards, and thirty-five were wounded in the infamous "Virden Massacre." Mitchell rushed to Virden from Springfield and went immediately to the hotel that had been turned into a temporary morgue. The scene at the hotel left a lasting impression: "There were six dead union miners laid out on the floor. All of them had left their homes in other mining towns to come to Virden to assist the miners of Virden to protect their homes from the imported 'criminals' and 'ex-convicts' from Alabama."[193]

The massacre led to a quick resolution of the strike. Governor Tanner, who had supported the miners during the 1897 strike, dispatched the state militia to protect the miners and prevent further efforts to import out-of-state labor. By November, the Chicago-Virden Company admitted defeat and agreed to abide by the union contract. Trouble at nearby Pana continued until the spring of 1899, but there, too, operators eventually were brought to heel.[194] The bloodshed and subsequent victory at Virden contributed to Mitchell's growing reputation among miners. His arrival in Virden immediately follow-ing the massacre to provide for burial of the dead demonstrated his concern for the rank and file, and his ability to force powerful and hostile operators to adhere to the joint interstate agreement proved his leadership skills.

The southern Illinois crisis also revealed much about Mitchell's racial attitudes. While he never used racial epithets, he certainly shared the prevail-ing attitudes of the northern white miners, whose racist leanings were exacer-bated by the frequent use of African-American strikebreakers. His first experi-ence with African-Americans came in Braidwood when he was just seven. They were imported to take the place of striking white men, run out of town by force, and returned under the protection of the state militia. They lived in a segregated neighborhood and were frequently under attack from whites. A similar situation developed in Spring Valley during his early adult years, and he watched the pattern repeated in southern Illinois. Like other Illinois miners, he used the terms "scab," "strikebreaker," and "Negro" interchangeably.[195] Since his only real knowledge of African-Americans was their apparent will-ingness to commit the "sin" of strikebreaking, he came to regard them as less moral than whites and less desirable union members. After white miners in Pana initiated a full-scale race riot in the spring of 1899 that left seven dead, Mitchell justified their action. "Colored persons" had come to Pana, had "taken the places of white miners," and had "driven them from the homes and towns they developed, where they have been living all their lives."[196] As union president, Mitchell would uphold the UMWA's nondiscriminatory member-ship policy, but he made little effort to establish full racial equality within the union and never criticized the exclusionary practices of other unions.

Once back at union headquarters, Mitchell turned his attention to the upcoming union election. He approached the campaign full of confidence because he knew that numerous factors made victory probable. First, he represented the administration that had won the great strike of 1897 and followed up this victory with a long list of accomplishments in 1898—the eight-hour day, membership gains, wage increases, the creation of new district organizations in Arkansas and Indian Territory (District 21) and Kansas and Missouri (District 14). He was riding the wave of prosperity and union growth. Second, he controlled national organizers and the union journal. Organizers were dispatched to well organized districts to campaign for Mitchell and disparage his opponents. Under the pretext of maintaining harmony within the union, Mitchell and Ratchford prevented rival candidates from using the journal as a platform. Journal editor Thomas W. Davis, a strong Mitchell supporter, announced during the campaign that "all references to the merits or demerits, if any there be, of candidates for office, at our coming annual convention at Pittsburgh, will be excluded from the columns of the Journal."[197] In practice, this policy allowed Mitchell's achievements to be covered in detail while opponents were silenced.

Mitchell sought to increase his chances by taking actions calculated to win over the miners. In late September, he issued appeals to local unions to provide financial assistance to aid miners presently on strike. The appeal would probably not increase aid, he told Ratchford, but it might win votes among strikers by showing the national's concern for their well being. He targeted the increasing foreign element in the union by vigorously defending the UMWA's policy of accepting all miners regardless of race or nationality in the journal. Yet throughout the campaign Mitchell upheld the unwritten code of UMWA politics that one should not actively seek office. In response to a miner who publicly announced he supported the acting president, Mitchell proclaimed in the journal that he "never solicited the assistance of you nor anyone else employed by our organization."[198] With Ratchford's assistance, Mitchell quickly mastered the electioneering skills necessary for survival in the rough and tumble world of UMWA politics.

Despite his advantages, there were still pitfalls and question marks regarding his candidacy. His youth and inexperience caused concern, and his West Virginia failure did not help his chances. His few months as acting president did not give him sufficient time to build bases of support outside Illinois, nor had he been in Indianapolis long enough to establish close personal ties to other executive board members. He was not yet regarded as "one of the boys." Geography was also a major problem. Ohio remained the largest district and Ohio demanded the presidency. Finally, Mitchell's opponents were two of the most influential men in the union—Tom L. Lewis and Patrick Dolan. Lewis and the power brokers in Ohio recalled Ryan's promise at the 1898 convention to throw Illinois support behind an Ohio candidate for the presidency. Dolan controlled the Pittsburgh district, where the convention would be held, and held a personal grudge against Mitchell for "stealing" the vice presidency from him in 1898.

But Mitchell had the trump card—Ratchford. When delegates gathered at the "Old City Hall" in Pittsburgh on January 9, 1899, President Ratchford presided. He all but guaranteed Mitchell's victory through his power to control debate and make committee appointments. The most important committee affecting union elections was the credentials committee, and Ratchford made certain it was packed with administration supporters. This committee examined the credentials of each delegate and decided, on the basis of how many members each delegate represented, the number of votes each delegate possessed. Thus, even though Ohio was considered the strongest district, few were surprised when this committee reported that Illinois delegates controlled 261 votes and Ohio just 154.[199] Recognizing this meant his certain defeat, Tom L. Lewis bowed out of the presidential race on the second day of the convention. Before doing so, however, he charged that union funds had been used to promote the candidacy of "certain aspirants" for office. Mitchell thereupon rose to defend himself against the charge.[200]

Patrick Dolan, commanding a mere 81 votes in the western Pennsylvania district, refused to give up without a fight. He charged that Ratchford and Mitchell forces were guilty of foul play in assigning delegate voting strength. He accused Ryan of increasing Illinois voting strength in 1898 by setting up "paper locals" and national Secretary-Treasurer W. C. Pearce of illegally bolstering the voting strength of Mitchell's supporters at the present convention. On the third day of the convention, Dolan supporters demanded the convention be delayed so that official membership and payment records could be obtained from union headquarters in Indianapolis to make certain the credentials committee had been honest. When a majority of delegates voted down this recommendation, Dolan, too, saw the handwriting on the wall and withdrew from the race.[201]

With the removal of the opposition, the election itself was a mere formality. On the eve of the election, an excited Mitchell wrote his brother-in-law that he would become president "by acclamation." The only other candidate was a crank from the anthracite field named Clatworthy, who did not even have the support from his own local. Mitchell was already thinking of the power, fame, and fortune the office might hold. He wrote of his hope that "the salary will be increased to fifteen hundred dollars ($1500) a year." The next day Mitchell received 571 of the 613 votes cast.[202]

In numerous ways Mitchell's youth was similar to that of hundreds of thousands of nineteenth century coal diggers. He had intimate knowledge of the daily grind of poverty and hunger, the horrendous working conditions and the daily fear of death in the mines, the uncertainty of employment that forced miners to adopt a "gypsy's life" of constant travel, and the brutality of strikes and lockouts that cast the pall of outright starvation in the coal communities. The solidarity which bound those who shared these horrors was etched upon his soul. He was one with other miners. Yet in some ways his experience had been more unfortunate than most. The loss of his parents at an early age, the physical abuse he suffered at the hands of his stepmother, the paucity of his education and the subsequent alienation from his peers—all made him a pitiable character even by the heart wrenching standards of coal towns.

Perhaps it was his privation that had ignited the spark of ambition. From the gripping poverty of his fatherless home in Braidwood, Mitchell had ascended with remarkable speed to the lofty height of the UMWA presidency. At the age of twenty-eight Mitchell stood at the helm of a stable and prosperous union. Largely through his natural intelligence, his gift for conciliation, and his talent for inspiring confidence in his superiors, he had become more powerful than he ever could have dreamed as a lonely child. A practicing miner just five years earlier, in many ways he was little different than the rank and file he had been chosen to lead. Yet he also exhibited strong tendencies that would soon leave him divorced from rank-and-file sentiment. His ambition, his self-confidence, his compulsion to win the approval of elites—all had helped separate him from his fellow miners. As we shall see, his newly won power and fame would soon widen the gulf between Mitchell and the membership.

Chapter 2

The Boy President, 1899

In one sense election to the union presidency was a crowning achievement for the young and ambitious Mitchell. He had struggled and sacrificed for many years to help create a powerful union. He had known privation and had given up any semblance of a stable family life to be part of a great movement for uplifting the downtrodden. For his idealism and commitment to the cause he had been amply rewarded. Not only was the UMWA, as a result of the joint agreement, established on a sound and lasting basis, but Mitchell himself now controlled the destiny of this great movement. The cause was in his hands. The promise of a better life, a more just life, for the nation's miners was his to safeguard and make real.

His first task as union president, therefore, was to erect a bureaucratic apparatus capable of transforming the ideals of the movement into reality. One by-product of national collective bargaining was the necessity to centralize decision making at the national level, to shift authority from the local and district levels to the national board and president. Before 1897, when miners and operators of a single state met to devise wage agreements, national officers were conspicuously weak, performing mostly administrative functions. Interstate bargaining, however, forced a high degree of coordination and collaboration between districts. Conflicting goals had to be balanced, and the demands of individual districts had to be subsumed under the interest of the national organization. Negotiating and enforcing national contracts required strong centralized control over constituent bodies. Only the president and the national board could be counted on to see the larger picture, to transcend local interests. Once attaining power, therefore, Mitchell naturally strove to subdue the power of locals and districts and centralize authority. When he met with entrenched resistance to centralization, he could be quite ruthless in asserting his authority. By both fair means and foul, Mitchell created a strong central union, able to draw up and enforce national contracts.

While the process of centralization was essential to the permanence of the union, the process also worked to undermine union democracy. At the local and district levels, the rank and file exerted considerable control; at the national level, as we have seen, incumbents were able to use organizers, union funds, and the union journal to all but assure their own reelection and the passage of almost any resolution they desired. Moreover, when the convention was not in session, the president enjoyed a monopoly of power and remained all but immune to rank-and-file pressure. Thus, even while Mitchell continued to portray the union as the purest expression of democracy in action, he was aggressively working to create a union in which rank-and-file sentiment would exercise limited influence.

John Mitchell was by no means an imposing physical specimen. While he was never one to hesitate when trumpeting his own accomplishments and virtues, he was uncomfortable with his looks. In a letter to his sister Maggie, he gave an unusually honest description of himself. Maggie and John had not seen each other for many years, and when Maggie wrote of her wish to be reunited with her brother, she remembered a beautiful child and expected a handsome man. Mitchell tried to disabuse her of that expectation:

> I am not the Big Broad shouldered good looking Fellow you Evidently think me—though I might have been had I not been compelled to go in to the mines When so young and work so hard that my Physique was Dwarfed and my Growth stunted. . . . I wish I was a Well Built—I am about 5–7 and weigh 165 Pounds. My shoulders are only square when I have my Tailor made coat on—and as for my looks Dear Sister I fear the photographer must be called upon to explain how he makes me look so well.[1]

At the beginning of his presidency then, Mitchell was stalwart of build but not yet paunchy as he would be in later years. He had the squat body so common among miners, and his discomfort with his frame is obvious from his remarks. Yet the handsomeness that Maggie remembered had not vanished with the years. He had an impressive face. His guise was both highly intelligent and sensitive. His swarthy skin and dark hair set off oversized facial features: brown expressive eyes and square jaw. Several contemporaries and historians have commented that Mitchell, in his prime, had the appearance of a priest.[2] These commentators focused on his apparel in making their judgment—the long, western miners' coat and straight collar. Less well known is that Mitchell's contemporaries also likened him to a priest, not for his clothing, but for his visage. Thomas I. Kidd, secretary of the woodworkers' union, was perhaps the first to make the comparison. In 1900, after Mitchell had sent him a photograph of himself taken upon his initiation into the Elks, Kidd noted "if you only had a high front vest and were without the emblem of the Elks, 999 people out of every thousand would take you for a priest."[3]

If his face was priest-like, his clothing preference was anything but clerical. The long coat and high collar noted by historians was the style of Illinois miners and was useful when attending miners' conventions or touring unorganized territory, but when dealing with coal operators, politicians, and other men of wealth and position, Mitchell soon displayed a taste for sartorial fineries. When a writer in the *New York Journal* described his coat as shabby, he took offense. The coat in question was a "brand new Prince Albert coat" and not in the least shabby, he complained.[4] And by early 1900, he sported an expensive gold ring, decorated with six small diamonds.[5] Mitchell's taste for expensive clothing and jewelry grew with time.

The new union president was in many ways a remarkable man. Most obviously, he was remarkable for the speed in which he gained power. He had been elected president just one year after attending his first national convention. This meteoric rise bucked a national trend toward slower ascents through union hierarchies in the United States in the Progressive Era.[6] Also notable was his youth. A few weeks shy of his twenty-ninth birthday, he was the youngest president of a major national union in the Progressive Era.[7] Mitchell was well aware that his youth and inexperience were perceived by many as serious liabilities. Soon after taking office, he informed a friend in Spring Valley that "at the close of the Pittsburg convention many of those who antagonized my election vigorously there made the prediction that the agreement reached in Pittsburg would never go into effect; in other words it was contended that with my youth and inexperience I would not be able to shoulder the responsibility placed on me by that convention."[8]

In addition to the "crime" of youth, he was also profoundly cognizant of the responsibilities of his charge. In a speech given at Spring Valley in early February, he assured his fellow miners he was "painfully conscious of my own imperfections" and "fully aware of the stupendous difficulties which must be met and overcome in harmonizing all the conflicting interests connected with the coal industry." The UMWA "has grown to such vast proportions, has spread over so great an expanse of territory within the last year, that I sometimes tremble with fear, lest by some error or mistake on my part, its progress should be retarded, or the victories won, at the cost of so much suffering and privation by the toilers, taken from them."[9]

In part because of the onerous responsibilities of office, Mitchell was ambivalent about his new position. On the one hand, he was intensely proud of his election. "There is a wonderful change in my life in the last few years," he wrote to a friend, "from practical obscurity to the presidency of the strongest labor organization, numerically, in the world, is indeed a long stride." And undoubtedly he was quite relieved to have escaped the fate of the vast majority of miners—a life of drudgery and danger in the pits. On the other hand, the constant travel, public scrutiny, and above all, the often unrealistic expectations of the rank and file, gave him reason for pause. "I cannot say ... that I feel any personal gratification in my elevation to this position; there are certainly many features connected with the leadership of our organization that are very undesirable, but I presume this is not more true in my own case than it was with my predecessors. It seems to be the lot of those engaged in the labor movement to be idolized by some and stigmatized by others; glorified and crucified."[10] Nor did his dislike of the job lessen as the months passed. On numerous occasions during his first year in office, Mitchell contemplated retirement. In September, he wrote one of his organizers that if he could find someone "in whose hands the interests of the organization would be safe, I should be happy, indeed, to be relieved of the responsibilities of office."[11] Were he to step down, he felt certain that he could find a higher paying and less taxing job. "My personal interests would be best served by my retirement, as I can secure employment which would not only be congenial, but would pay a much higher salary than is paid me by the miners."[12]

His ambivalence about the presidency did not stem from a lack of confidence to perform the job well. While he might tell audiences that he "trembled with fear" under the weight of his responsibilities, close friends learned that he took the new job in stride and planned to approach union work much as he had in years past. His new circumstances, he explained, would not "influence my actions in the least." He would proceed along the lines "I always did when you knew me at my home." If this course won the approbation of the rank and file "I shall feel entirely satisfied; on the other hand should they disapprove of it, it will make no personal difference to me. I shall neither court favor nor invite enmity, but I shall be guided entirely by what my own judgment and conscience tell me is right."[13]

His mixed emotions were intimately tied to his desire to set himself up in business and amass a personal fortune. Within three weeks of taking office on April 1, 1899, he began to reveal the avaricious side of his personality, labeled by one historian the "acquisitive spirit."[14] Throughout his presidency, he actively sought investments, partnerships, and endorsements, some of which represented serious conflicts of interest, and all of which attested to his craving for wealth. On April 20, he wrote a friend in Spring Valley, William Hawthorne, a lawyer specializing in real estate and investment law, stating that he understood a hardware business in Spring Valley was for sale. After carefully thinking the matter over, he suggested that a "stock company of three or four persons" could be formed, with each person investing $1000 or $1500, to take over the business. "I am anxious to engage in some kind of business myself," he continued, and "I would not mind taking at least a thousand dollars worth of stock in the company." Because such a venture might cause rank-and-file concern that he was not devoting all his energies to his office, and would certainly lead miners to wonder how a union leader who made $900 a year as vice president and acting president might have $1000 to invest, he qualified his suggestion. "Of course I would want to be regarded as a silent partner, at least during the time I am holding the position that I do at present." Unfortunately for Mitchell, Hawthorne responded that while the hardware store was for sale, it was not a good investment. However,

Hawthorne did have an investment proposition for Mitchell "that will bring fair returns." Hawthorne was buying property in Spring Valley and wanted him to invest $1000 to help purchase two lots near the town's post office on which Hawthorne hoped to build offices. Mitchell did invest his money, but he obviously did not find that golden opportunity that would allow him to leave his post.[15]

In September 1899, Mitchell was exploring another business venture that would allow him to retire from union activity. He wrote his good friend Billy Ryan that a St. Louis tobacco manufacturing firm that would be ready for production by January 1900 "made me a very flattering offer to work for them." He was less interested in this job offer, however, than in organizing his own tobacco manufacturing business. He had made inquiries and concluded the business was potentially profitable. "I feel confident that if we could organize a company of three or four, with a capital stock of five or six thousand dollars we could clear up a handsome little stake each year."[16] As with the hardware store, nothing came of this idea. While he continued to entertain hopes of finding alternative employment, he soon came to realize that his dreams of wealth could best be realized by exploiting opportunities that came to him as head of the union. In short, despite the unpleasant and burdensome nature of his position, the union presidency offered financial rewards far beyond its salary. By the spring of 1900, he was able to write "I am, of course, well aware of the many inducements which are continually held out to men prominent in the trades union movement, the acceptance of which would stultify and debauch a man to such an extent that he would despise himself and make his life a living hell on earth."[17]

Of all his complaints about union work, the one aspect of his post he liked least was the demand it made on his time. As he explained to his brother Robert, "my time and attention are so completely taken up with the duties of my office that I have very little time to devote to the pleasures of life."[18] Rarely did he have the chance to visit his wife and children in Spring Valley except for holidays. He was an absentee father and husband, able to express his love and show his affection only over the telephone and through letters and telegrams dictated to his secretary. In January 1900, Mitchell had four children—Richard (seven years old), James (five), Robert (three), and Marie (one).[19] The youngest two children probably knew little of their father. He was never there to cope with the daily problems or celebrate the little joys in their lives. On one occasion he completely forgot Marie's birthday, failing even to send a gift.[20]

A reading of the extant letters between Mitchell and his wife reveals a loving relationship based on affection and humor. He wrote with pride about his accomplishments and detailed his minor physical ailments. He would then jest about family members, referring to a sister-in-law they both liked as "my next wife." Nothing in their correspondence indicates that Mitchell's absence from home was anything other than a profound source of regret.[21] As we shall see, upon his retirement from the presidency, one of his primary considerations would be to secure employment involving less travel.

Although isolated from his wife and children, he sought to reestablish ties with his brothers and sister in early 1899. He wrote a series of letters trying to locate them and discover what had become of them. The picture that emerges is that of a man who desperately hoped to create a closeness to his siblings that he had been denied as a child. Through the dogged determination of his secretary, Mitchell found his brother Robert working on the railroads in Cascade Tunnel, Washington, his brother Ed employed as a salesman in Maplewood, Ohio, his brother David working as a coal miner in Renton, Washington, and his sister Maggie living on a farm in Fresno, California. His letters indicate he had not seen his siblings for many years and that he knew nothing of their lives. He had not seen Maggie for twenty-three years, and he obviously did not know the names of his brothers' wives, referring to each one only as "Mrs. Mitchell."[22]

As early as February, Mitchell made plans to visit Maggie in Fresno. She was much older than Mitchell, and he had not seen her nor heard from her since he was six years old. The urge to reestablish ties was strong. Even though the UMWA did not provide vacations for its officers, he was determined to "absent myself from the office for two or three weeks" to visit her. In late June, he wrote an operator friend and obtained a free railroad pass to make the journey. This was the first of many times he would take advantage of his connections among coal and railroad officials to travel free. And he was certainly aware of the risk involved in taking an extended trip without union approval. Before he left, he received a warning from his friend Ed Smith, a reporter for a Springfield paper, not to let anyone find out about his travel plans. "Say John this is none of my business but if you go out to California for God's sake don't let it be known as the—- things in Ohio, Pa, and some of the Ills boys (*sic*) will say he is a nice fellow to go off on a trip during so much trouble. Where did he get the money etc."[23] The fact that Mitchell went on the journey despite the potential consequences demonstrates his profound desire to capture a semblance of familial togetherness.

Mitchell stayed in Fresno for eleven days. His secretary forwarded to him summaries of all union correspondence and, recognizing the trip was a secret, told no one where he was. For Mitchell the trip "was the happiest event of my life." His sister, Maggie, and her two daughters, Mae and Agnes, both married adults, "left nothing undone to make my visit with them a continual source of pleasure." He described Maggie as "a well-preserved, pleasant looking lady" and his nieces as "talented, highly educated girls." He was also taken with Fresno, "a very beautiful city," and wrote that he was "so favorably impressed . . . I became imbued with the idea that upon severing my connection with the labor movement I would probably make that my future home." After his return to Indianapolis, however, he realized that Fresno, despite its charms, would not be a suitable place "for me to engage in business which would prove profitable." Yet while there he enjoyed himself immensely. With his new found relations he could relax and let down his guard. He went on walks with his nieces, went swimming, and played various games. In Fresno he found the extended family for which he longed. And the nieces were enchanted with their uncle. For years thereafter, both Mae and Agnes wrote him letters, begging him to give up union life and move to California.[24] But for Mitchell Fresno would remain just a happy memory and a constant reminder that as long as he was UMWA president, he would never enjoy a close family life.

As a slave to union affairs, Mitchell often lapsed into melancholy moods. "I desire to say (although it may surprise you) that I do not enjoy myself very well," he wrote an old Spring Valley chum, "as I have reformed and have settled down to be an old business man whose entire time is devoted to the affairs of our organization." It is quite possible, although perhaps impossible to prove, that his use of the term "reformed" referred to the consumption of alcohol. Other such references in his correspondence also point to the possibility that he had been a heavy drinker before assuming office and had taken a pledge of sobriety or at least moderation in 1899. When another Spring Valley friend invited him for a visit, he told Mitchell "you will have to behave yourself" and that he had heard Mitchell had "reformed and was living a different life." If he was in fact a problem drinker before 1899 and had pledged to quit, this would help explain why he never seemed to have spending money. Time and again, he had to ask his wife to forward personal checks to cover expenses he incurred while visiting friends. And several times he complained to his wife about being "dead broke." It is possible that Kate controlled the family finances and that she was careful to limit the amount of her husband's pocket money in a joint effort to discourage his drinking. Another possible indication that he had alcohol problems was his apparent physical breakdown in March 1900. As early as January he complained, first to his wife and then to his niece, of "extreme nervousness," a euphemism he would again use in 1907 when his alcoholism became acute. He explained to another relative that "the long physical and mental strain which I labored under during the convention, has left me so nervous that I am unable to write legibly with a pen." By early March his "nervousness" left him under a physician's care in a Chicago hotel, unable to attend to union business, for over a week. He informed his wife of his illness only when he had sufficiently recovered to resume his duties, and he never asked her to attend to him.[25] It is significant that he did not return to Spring Valley to recover or that he never asked his wife to travel to Chicago to visit him, as if he were embarrassed by or guilty about his condition.

Whether or not Mitchell had a drinking problem at the start of his union presidency is impossible to determine with any degree of accuracy, but the closest approximation to "proof" was provided by Mitchell himself in August 1900. A large parade and rally was held in Indianapolis for William Jennings Bryan, Democratic candidate for president. Mitchell had been invited to view the parade from the cold storage room of the Indianapolis Brewing Company. He declined this invitation when offered a seat on the official viewing platform. "Of course," he wrote his friend, "I know you won't believe I left the brewery on that account." Such joking about alcohol takes on new meaning, however, when contrasted with the invitation, in the same letter, that when this friend came to Indianapolis Mitchell would take him out for a "Ginger Ale."[26]

Perhaps to compensate for his lack of family life in Indianapolis, Mitchell joined several fraternal societies. By January 1900, he became a member of both the Red Men and the Elks. His initiation into the Elks involved an "exalted ringmaster" who drove around the lodge a goat on which the initiate rode. Mitchell was apparently not put off by this bizarre experience, for just five days later he wrote his wife that the Elks were "an excellent organization, and I am more than satisfied with it."[27] His desire to join these essentially middle-class social clubs was by no means unusual among labor leaders. One historian asserted that the fraternal connections of some turn-of-the-century union officials "would put Sinclair Lewis's Babbitt to shame."[28] Like his fondness for expensive clothes and jewelry and his desire to enter business, his determination to participate in such clubs testified to his thoroughly middle-class aspirations and his rising status in the community.

Even while he sought middle-class respectability, Mitchell believed himself inferior to those born and raised to wealth and quality. He was a powerful man as head of the union, who could already display the symbols of that power in the form of property and community status, but he still considered himself the ignorant hayseed in the presence of successful operators and politicians. The envy and admiration he felt when he met Ohio Senator Mark Hanna and other politicians during an early 1899 AFL Executive Council meeting was noted in a missive to his brother Robert. "Have just returned from Washington, D. C. where I had the pleasure of meeting and conversing with that renowned statesman, Mark Hanna, as well as many senators and congressmen of National fame." How impressed he was! How intermingled were the feelings of pride and inferiority—pride that he, a coal miner, had risen to such lofty heights, and shame due to his own ignorance of high culture and national affairs. Of great significance was the response of his brother, a coal miner in Washington state. "You know your busness (*sic*) but if it was me I could not speak or write of Mark Hanna as a Honerable (*sic*) man because in the sight of most Western labors (*sic*) he appears quite Rotten."[29] This exchange between brothers revealed a growing disparity between a class conscious miner and a young mine worker official already succumbing to the blandishments of the wealthy and powerful. Mitchell did not respond to his brother's criticism of Hanna. He was dazzled by the men he met. He wanted the Hanna's of this world to treat him as an equal, yet he felt backward and ignorant. His painful awareness of his own lack of education was apparent in letters to brothers and friends, encouraging them to make certain their children received the best education. For instance, when the son of UMWA Vice President Tom Davis graduated from high school, Mitchell wrote to congratulate him on the "education that you have been so fortunate to receive."[30]

Bedeviled by onerous office duties, isolated from his family and closest friends, longing for bourgeois respectability yet hamstrung by his own lack of education, and possibly grappling with alcoholism, Mitchell was by no means satisfied by his election to the presidency. Assistance was near at hand, however. His new position entitled him to a full time secretary, and he was truly blessed with the one assigned to him, Elizabeth Catherine Morris. Morris and Mitchell established a working partnership that lasted until his death in 1919. They formed a relationship that transcended employer and employee. Morris's origins are obscure, but she was undeniably well educated. She had taught school and had served as personal secretary to May Wright Sewall, founder of the International Council of Women and headmistress at the Girl's Classical School in Chicago. Although she claimed in 1900 to be "so ignorant of mining and mining terms that I scarcely know how to express myself," she learned from Mitchell about the cause of labor and became a staunch behind-the-scenes supporter of the movement. Mitchell gave her not only employment but also a calling.[31]

Yet it was Mitchell who benefited most from the relationship. First, Morris proved to be a gifted office manager. She handled all the day-to-day correspondence that cluttered his desk; she kept his appointments and made out his schedules; she corresponded with organizers to keep him informed of the machinations of his internal enemies. She thus freed him from many of the mundane but necessary tasks performed at national headquarters. Second, Morris became a friend, a confidante, a companion for Mitchell. The many hours they spent together each day in the office, on organizing trips, and on speaking tours, helped their relationship blossom. Although she always referred to her boss as "Mr. Mitchell" and Mitchell always addressed her as "Miss Morris," there was a deep affection in their bond. He spent far more time with Morris than with his wife, and in some ways she provided him with the support and day-to-day nurturing that was absent in his home life. Moreover, Morris usually accompanied him on business-related social functions as well. For example, during the 1902 anthracite strike, Ralph Easley of the National Civic Federation invited Mitchell to come to dinner and attend a Broadway play with himself and George Perkins of the House of Morgan. The evening was to combine business and pleasure, and Easley took it for granted that Morris would come along.[32] Undoubtedly Morris eased Mitchell's loneliness. Third, and perhaps most importantly from Mitchell's perspective, Morris provided him with an informal "finishing school." By rewriting his dictated letters and speeches, she helped him present a more polished front. She eradicated the countless grammatical errors and country expressions that permeated his correspondence and speeches prior to 1899. She also helped him pronounce the big words he enjoyed using. And quite likely she helped him with table manners, coordinating his clothes, selecting gifts for operators and politicians, and all the other little things that would make him more respectable and sophisticated in the eyes of those he truly admired—the wealthy and powerful. Because of Morris, Mitchell felt less of a nabob.

The establishment of the interstate agreement in 1898 made the UMWA a permanent force in the soft coal fields. It was without a doubt the single most important reason for the success of Mitchell's presidency. But the joint agreement implied obligations as well as permanence. One principal obligation of the union was to expand its control beyond the boundaries of the Central Competitive Field and organize all miners. If the UMWA failed in its efforts to organize all coal fields, to force all coal operators to pay union wages, CCF operators paying high union wages would be unable to compete for markets against nonunion operators paying low wages. Such a situation would eventually force CCF operators to demand extensive wage cuts from the union. Mitchell recognized the threat of nonunion fields all too well.

In the union's need to expand, the interstate agreement itself proved invaluable as a selling point to both operators and miners. Mitchell and his corps of organizers could hold out the promise of high wages and the eight hour day to entice nonunion miners to join the fold. Operators were told about the relative labor peace that meant steady production and the end of cutthroat competition among coal firms. With such a package to offer, it is hardly surprising that membership skyrocketed and the number of signed contracts with operators mushroomed after 1897. By January 1900, union membership stood at 93,000, a figure that did not include the thousands exonerated from paying dues because of strikes and lockouts. Hundreds of new locals had been formed, lapsed districts were revived in Iowa, Alabama, central Pennsylvania, and Kentucky, new districts were created in Maryland, Kansas, Missouri, Michigan, Arkansas-Indian Territory, and the anthracite region of northeast Pennsylvania.[33]

Mitchell's incredible success in organizing the unorganized in 1898 and 1899 was not a simple matter or salesmanship, however. As acting president and then in his first year as president, he was often forced to flex union muscle. He engineered large scale and militant organizing drives that forced recalcitrant operators to submit to the growing power of the union. That this boy president proved such an able field general surprised many, including some of his own supporters. Any appreciation of Mitchell as a strike leader and organizer, and hence his popularity among the rank and file, must include an examination of his two great campaigns of this period. The first came in Arkansas-Indian Territory and the second in central Pennsylvania.

The officers and members of the newly created District 21, comprising the mines of Arkansas and the Indian Territory (Oklahoma), met in convention in early 1899 and, following standard practice, adopted a list of demands. The most significant demands were a no discrimination clause against union membership and the check off of union dues. Before adjourning, the miners issued a call to operators of the area to meet with district UMWA representatives in joint convention on March 1, 1899. When the operators failed to show, some 6,000 miners across the district struck.[34]

Operators quickly adopted aggressive tactics to break the strike. At mines owned by the two major railroads in the territory, the Missouri-Pacific and the Kansas & Texas, UMWA miners were dismissed and driven from their company homes, and operators throughout the area imported strikebreakers. In addition, because Indian Territory was administered by the federal government through the Department of the Interior, operators were able to exploit a federal law requiring miners on Choctaw land to pay a resident fee. The fee was customarily deducted from the miners' pay, but once miners went on strike the fee was no longer collected. Miners thus became trespassers on federal land, and government officials cooperated with coal operators to have them expelled from the territory.[35]

Mitchell responded immediately to what he called the most important strike ever to occur west of the Mississippi. First, he appealed to all UMWA members to contribute to the struggle, informing them their union brothers in Indian Territory "were compelled to suspend work" because their righteous demands "have been received with scorn and indignantly refused by these unfair and unscrupulous corporations." Second, he allocated union funds to provide food and clothing and set up tent colonies. Third, as had been done in southern Illinois, he urged strikers to meet strikebreakers at train depots, appealing to their sense of fair play and asking them to return.[36] Fourth, he gave the strike wide publicity to secure the support of the public. His press releases contained a militant class-conscious rhetoric he would abandon in later years. Toward the end of 1899, he pointed to Jay Gould and his wife Helen, who held interest in the railroads, as being personally responsible for the suffering and privation visiting the tent colonies. "Helen Gould has posed as a woman of Christianity for many years," he told an Indianapolis paper. "If the people of New York City could see the Gould employees in Indian Territory and elsewhere in the Southwest, they would ostracize her from society."[37]

Fifth, he aggressively addressed the question of federal law by writing directly to the Secretary of the Interior, Edward A. Hitchcock, and demanding that federal authorities refrain from interfering in the strike. When federal authorities began notifying strikers they would have to vacate Indian Territory, he tried to enlist the support of the entire labor movement by urging all unionists to write Secretary Hitchcock and condemn the "un-American" behavior of the coal companies and federal authorities.[38]

Railroad executives responded to Mitchell's actions by stepping up their attack. They continued to import scabs, many whom were African-Americans from Alabama and southern Illinois. When strikers learned that several car loads of strikebreakers were on the way, they threatened they would not permit the scabs to disembark. With violence imminent, the companies applied and secured a federal injunction restraining the strikers from "in any way interfering with the operation of the mines or the importation of non-union labor." What followed was an unusual and confusing contest between the federal courts and the state government of Arkansas. The Arkansas Circuit Court countered the federal injunction by issuing an injunction of its own restraining railroad companies from importing strikebreakers. Mitchell reported with glee that the governor of Arkansas backed up the state circuit court by ordering the sheriff "not to permit the niggers to land in Arkansas." The federal court then intervened and enjoined the sheriff from carrying out the governor's instructions. In the meantime, the railroad companies appeared before the state circuit court in an effort to dissolve the injunction restraining them. When the hearings before the state circuit court began, Mitchell traveled to Arkansas to testify on behalf of the strikers.[39]

Throughout his testimony at the circuit court hearings, Mitchell demonstrated his growing ability to influence his listeners through appeals to their reason and sense of fair play. This type of argument, rather than the emotional and class-conscious attacks on employers such as the one against Helen Gould, would come to dominate his speech making. He chronicled the history of the UMWA and its efforts to bring collective bargaining and labor peace to the coal fields. He cited the efforts of the UMWA to bring operators in District 21 to the bargaining table, only to be ignored. He then addressed the heart of the matter, providing, in his words, "expert testimony on the evil effects of the importation of colored labor to take the place of striking miners." He described the violence at Pana and Virden to portray the consequences of importing African-American strikebreakers. Introducing these scabs, he concluded, was certain to result in the spilling of blood. In the end, the circuit judge ruled that the injunction against the importation of scabs would be upheld.[40]

Despite this favorable legal decision, the UMWA was no closer to victory in the strike. The railroad companies had the determination and economic resources to conduct a long-term battle. In addition to their mines in District 21, the Missouri-Pacific and Kansas & Texas both owned mines in Kansas which were still in operation. In May, Mitchell escalated the strike by calling out miners in the neighboring District 14 (Kansas) who worked for the Missouri-Pacific or Kansas & Texas, thereby attempting to close all the mines owned by these railroads.[41] This move on Mitchell's part demonstrated a willingness to engage in large-scale economic warfare. His prompt support of this strike, his aggressive action, and his militant rhetoric all contrast with the hesitation and restraint he would show in later years.

Even this maneuver did not cripple the railroads. Both corporations were able to purchase enough coal to run their trains and supply their customers from operators elsewhere in Kansas and in southern Illinois. This was an expensive arrangement, to be sure, but both corporations seemed determined to stand firm against the union whatever the cost. As the strike dragged on, miners petitioned Mitchell to widen the strike and call out all miners in District 14 and southern Illinois working for operators who supplied coal to the two railroads. On this issue he balked. The miners he had already called out in District 14 were not working under union contracts, and thus he could not be accused of violating the sanctity of agreements. A walk out by the remainder of District 14 miners and those in southern Illinois would have necessitated breaking signed contracts, something Mitchell was not prepared to do, even when those contracts supplied railroads against whom the UMWA was striking. As an alternative strategy, he secured promises from a number of southern Illinois operators not to supply coal to the struck railroads.[42]

His refusal to widen the strike provided an excellent example of his priorities. Although his commitment to victory could not be questioned, he was unwilling to take the steps necessary to cripple the railroads economically by choking off their coal supply. He was unwilling to violate existing contracts in Kansas and Illinois in order to secure victory in Indian Territory. Such a move, he believed, would provide at best a pyrrhic victory; it might win this strike but it would irreparably damage the union's reputation as an organization that abided by its agreements. Rather than relying on a sympathy strike, an expression of labor solidarity, Mitchell aided the strikers by relying on his positive relationships with operators. To his credit, however, he tried hard to make certain the Illinois operators lived up to their promise. He did not rely solely on their good word. He placed UMWA members at several bridges crossing the Mississippi to determine whether Illinois operators were sending coal south to the strike area.[43]

The decision not to break contracts gave proof to union operators that Mitchell knew the rules of the game. He needed to organize the outlying districts to prevent their takeover of markets, but his principal obligation was to respect agreements made with union operators and keep their mines in continuous production. By keeping his word he may have undermined the sense of solidarity existing among coal diggers, but he earned something he believed far more valuable to a union president with a collective bargaining agreement: the admiration of union operators. Charles Devlin was one such union operator. Devlin was the president of a large coal company in District 14, the Mt. Carmel Coal Company of Topeka, Kansas. So impressed was Devlin by Mitchell's conduct of the strike he offered to assist Mitchell during the dispute in any way he could be of service. Without being asked, Devlin posted a $3,000 bond to secure the release of Mitchell's chief organizer in the strike field, who had been arrested for violating an injunction. Overjoyed by this symbol of respect and appreciation from an operator, Mitchell, in his letter of thanks, informed Devlin that he would not "fail to reciprocate your kindness should the opportunity present itself."[44] This display of mutual back scratching not only demonstrated the businessman's way of conducting business between Mitchell and union operators, but also helps explain why he was always so careful to cultivate the friendship and respect of union operators.

Due to his unwillingness to expand the strike and the railroad companies' determination, the strike dragged on and on. By the end of 1899, after more than nine months of struggle, only twenty-five small operators in District 21 had signed union contracts. More than 2,500 miners continued the strike in 1900 against the larger firms, including the major railroads.[45] The railroads resisted unionization until 1903. The strike was not therefore an immediate and unqualified success, but Mitchell could point with pride at his union's ability to withstand the full economic and legal force of corporate America and emerge stronger than ever, with its reputation for abiding by agreements intact.

The southwest was certainly not the only area of the country where the union was weak in 1899. Of the nearly 50,000 miners the bituminous fields of central Pennsylvania (District 2), only 633 were dues-paying members of the union.[46] Miners in the district suffered the same hardships and degradations common to all unorganized coal diggers. In addition to low wages, miners complained of dockage excesses in the weighing of coal, exorbitant rents for company housing, and the presence of "pluck me" stores in many localities.[47] To ameliorate these conditions and to prove to CCF operators that the UMWA was able to bring nonunion operators to the conference table, Mitchell flooded the field with organizers and arranged for a District 2 conference to be held in March 1899 at Tyrone.

The Tyrone conference did not, as was the usual practice, put forth a list of demands and invite operators to meet in a joint convention. Too few of the miners were organized for this strategy. Instead, the conference encouraged miners to join the union and secure redress of grievances on a mine by mine basis. If negotiations did not achieve the desired goal, locals were to strike with the understanding they would have the full backing of the national union.

Also at the Tyrone conference, delegates elected a new slate of district officers. The new president was a Scottish immigrant who was soon to rise even higher in the union hierarchy, William B. Wilson.[48]

When the conference adjourned, delegates were sent throughout the district, promoting the union, enrolling new members, and giving instructions on how to proceed. John Brophy, at this time a sixteen-year-old miner but later district president and a moving force in the early CIO, referred to this as the "period of great awakening" for the miners of District 2.[49] Miners responded aggressively to the appeal and support of the national by joining the union in large numbers and pressing for their liberation from industrial serfdom. The success of several small strikes emboldened other locals to walk out as well, until a sort of chain reaction sparked work stoppages across the district.

The two largest operators in the district, W. L. Robinson of the Buffalo, Rochester, and Pittsburg Coal and Iron Company and Harry Berwind of the Berwind, White Company, employed well over 15,000 miners between them. Lasting success in District 2 necessitated winning recognition from both these men. According to one UMWA organizer on the scene, both men were receptive to unionization, willing to grant recognition and the check off of union dues, but both believed William B. Wilson was too radical to deal with in a businesslike fashion. Employers shunned him for his refusal "to recognize business facts," the organizer wrote, noting also that Wilson's very radicalism had made him popular among the miners "as you know that is usually the case." Apparently, these two operators would deal with the union only if Wilson were removed as district president.[50] Mitchell refused to move against Wilson, however, and when negotiations failed, he called out the miners against both operators. Through liberal use of the discharge and labor spies, Berwind successfully withstood the strike, but Robinson eventually came to terms with the UMWA.[51]

Mitchell was ecstatic about the success of the strike against the Buffalo, Rochester, and Pittsburg Company, calling it the decisive victory that "insures continued growth of our organization in that field." In typical Mitchell fashion, he privately credited himself for securing victory. Rather than applauding the miners themselves for their unity and determination, he honestly believed "their victory is entirely due to efforts made by me. I have kept men there, paid their salaries from the national treasury, and have practically paid the salaries of the District officers." He believed that for his victory he would be handsomely rewarded at the next national convention. All the newly organized men would support him at the convention, he wrote, "unless these men display the basest ingratitude."[52]

By the end of 1899, more than 20,000 miners in District 2 had secured wage advances, and more than 8,000 had enrolled in the union. Indeed, the union had become so popular in District 2 that Mitchell's primary concern was no longer organizing the unorganized, but making certain the organized men did not grow too enthusiastic, too strident in their demands. At a district convention held at the end of the year he made certain a trusted national board member was present so he could "prevent radical measures being adopted, if possible."[53]

His egotistical assumption of credit for victory, his cold calculation of the ramification of that victory, and his determination to suppress radicalism were all part of the same transformation he brought to the UMWA at the end of the century. In order to fulfill his personal ambitions, the union had to succeed. And union success was predicated on the survival and growth of the CCF and all that interstate collective bargaining implied: the organization of nonunion fields, the centralization of authority within the union, and the pacification of the rank and file. Mitchell had proven to CCF operators in 1899 that the UMWA could bring nonunion operators into line. Yet he also needed to show these operators that he alone spoke for the miners, that he could force local leaders to abide by his decisions, and that the miners themselves, once organized, would follow his orders and live up to signed contracts.

By no means did Mitchell feel secure upon his election. Although as incumbent he had the upper hand in national union elections, the internal union enemies created by the 1899 election were still powerful in their own districts and therefore posed continuous threats to his regime. He understood that his principal opponents, Tom L. Lewis and Patrick Dolan, had to be silenced. He therefore set after them with a vengeance, using all weapons at his disposal, including subterfuge and illegal means. In the process, he built the basis of a political machine.

His ruthless pursuit of Dolan, Lewis, and other internal foes exposed a number of points about his personality and the nature of union leadership in the Progressive Era years. First, he demonstrated his own aggressiveness, his love of confrontation and intrigue. He had a love of the hunt and a taste for blood. Second, he brought to light his sophisticated understanding of power. Despite his early mistakes and clumsiness, he proved to be a master of political manipulation. Third, his questionable tactics revealed how power was really exercised within the union and how corruption already began to seep into union affairs. He thus set the stage for a John L. Lewis in the 1920s. Fourth, his machinations were an object lesson on how the role of national officers expanded with the establishment of interstate collective bargaining. The struggles between Mitchell and the district leaders were not only personal power struggles, but also part of the process by which the national absorbed more and more authority formerly held by the district organizations. Fifth and finally, because he was not able to unseat the obstinate district officials, the power struggles reveal that union leadership at the turn of the century was still in part a matter of oratory and personal relationships as it had been in the Reconstruction Era. Despite his control of the union press, union funds, and his knowledge of how to control an election, he proved unable to drive from office popular district officials. In the end, he made them more or less loyal to his administration, but he was never able to completely crush their independent authority as John L. Lewis would in the 1920s. Indeed, one opponent, Tom L. Lewis, was able to outmaneuver Mitchell and capture the national vice presidency, where he hoped to obstruct Mitchell and succeed him in office.

Because Mitchell's rise to power coincided with the establishment of interstate collective bargaining in soft coal, one of the primary concerns of his tenure was the centralization of power. The interstate joint conference necessitated a strong central leadership able to negotiate a national contract and enforce its terms. While the process of centralization was in many ways a natural result of the joint conference, there were those in the union who opposed this trend. Before 1897 the focus of power in the union had been the district, and a few district leaders proved unwilling to abdicate their authority voluntarily. Over the years, these officials had created their own fiefdoms, their own political machines and mechanisms of power. When Mitchell moved to impose national authority, these district leaders were thus able to entrench and resist quite effectively for some time.

In his campaign of centralization, Mitchell employed questionable strategies and tactics. Rather than engage these leaders in the open forum of the convention to decide through democratic means who would control the use of organizers and strike funds, and what the proper relationship between district and national should now be, he engineered covert operations and rear guard actions involving subterfuge, duplicity, and intrigue. He misused national funds, used national organizers as personal spies and campaigners for himself and district favorites, and he showed a propensity for ignoring constitutional restraints. His machinations helped pave the way for the corruption and dictatorial control that infested the union for much of the century.

Moreover, in his secret wars to undermine district autonomy, the young and inexperienced Mitchell made numerous mistakes. He placed his trust in incompetent insurgents whose bungling jeopardized his reputation. He built up opposition blocs but proved unable to control them. He often found himself lost in the quagmire of a district's struggles involving personal jealousies and animosities. He exposed himself to potentially damaging accusations. And his inexperience even permitted the rise of one of the most powerful district opponents, Tom L. Lewis, into the national vice presidency, where his obstructionism continued unabated.

Despite Mitchell's clumsiness, by 1900 the process of centralization had stripped districts of the former power. District autonomy had become a dead letter. By no means were all district leaders transformed into Mitchell boosters, but they found that continued obstruction was a futile and damaging policy. District leaders had become dependent on the national for strike funds and organizers, and they found that Mitchell had become so popular among the rank and file that public attacks on the new president threatened their own hold over the miners in their districts.

After Mitchell's election to the presidency, the most pressing internal political problem was that of Tom L. Lewis and District 6. The Ohio district was the largest in the union and Tom L. Lewis controlled its affairs with an iron hand. Technically, Lewis was not the head of the Ohio miners. He served as District 6 secretary-treasurer. The president was William Haskins, but Haskins was known to be only a cog in the Lewis machine. Lewis was an outspoken opponent of Mitchell with unfulfilled ambitions to dominate the union. As long as the affairs of District 6 were left in Lewis's hands, therefore, not only would Mitchell's presidency be insecure, but Ohio could prove to be an obstacle to the centralization of authority necessary to maintain the national contract. Mitchell's efforts to crush the Lewis gang is instructive since it represents his first attempt at asserting national authority against entrenched district opposition and developing his own loyal district regime.

As early as March 1899, Mitchell became aware of a nascent opposition group within Ohio that hoped to defeat the Lewis machine. The opposition bloc believed Lewis was losing prestige as a result of his lengthy tenure as secretary-treasurer. Miners in the district were more than ever inclined to turn out the incumbent and elect a clean slate. But these men still recognized that to defeat Lewis or his faction it would be necessary to enlist the full support of the national office. As one Lewis opponent put it, "I realize that with the support of the National office the battle is half won." By July Thomas Cairns was openly campaigning for secretary-treasurer of District 6 and asking for Mitchell's support. "If you see your way clear to assist me at any time," he wrote Mitchell, "I shall always consider myself greatly indebted to you."[54]

Mitchell hesitated. He needed more time to assess the situation, to measure Lewis's strength and that of the opposition bloc. He wanted to avoid a public feud with Lewis because such a feud had no chance of positive results for his administration. For observations and advice on the Ohio situation, Mitchell relied heavily on Ralph Mason. Mason had been a staunch supporter of Ratchford, had promoted Mitchell for president, was a member of the district board, and, as agent of the UMWA *Journal* in Ohio, he was in a unique position to quietly canvass the sentiments of the rank and file throughout the state. Even though Mason agreed that Lewis's fortunes were declining, Mitchell continued to wait and watch.[55] Indeed, he waited until August, when a change in his own national administration provided an opportunity to act.

In August 1899, national Vice President Tom Davis resigned his post to become Commissioner of the Michigan Coal Operators' Association. Since the UMWA constitution specifically denied him the power to appoint a replacement, Mitchell was forced to leave the office vacant until a new vice president could be elected at the January 1900 convention. Within weeks he learned from Mason that Lewis would make a bid for the national vice presidency.[56] Although he was certain Lewis would attempt to secure the election of one of his henchmen as district secretary-treasurer, the withdrawal of Lewis opened the door for a strong push by the opposition in the district elections scheduled for January 1900. Only now did Mitchell intervene in the affairs of District 6. He would soon find that coordinating an insurgent movement at the district level was fraught with hidden complications.

His first step was to meet with the opposition bloc and discuss strategy. He made arrangements to give his annual Labor Day speech at Nelsonville, Ohio, in the heart of the Hocking Valley, the home of the principal leaders of the opposition. Here he met, for the first time, Thomas Cairns, George Schachert, and John Lanning, ambitious men eager to obtain Mitchell's backing and advance their careers. Mitchell suggested, and the others agreed, that Cairns should make the bid for the post vacated by Lewis. To form a geographically balanced ticket, therefore, any candidate for president must come from outside the Hocking Valley. He told the men to locate a suitable candidate willing to run against the incumbent President William Haskins.[57]

Although Mitchell considered the meeting a success, he soon encountered a series of difficulties that made victory all but impossible. First, there was significant delay in starting the campaign after Ralph Mason decided he wanted to make a bid for secretary-treasurer in the place of Cairns. Second, none of the insurgents could think of a single Ohio miner who could make a strong race for president or vice president. Third, the campaign techniques of at least one insurgent were so aggressive that they created a groundswell of opposition to Mitchell in Ohio. Mitchell himself contributed to each of these difficulties by refusing to take complete control of the opposition forces and dictate the terms of his support. In the process, he learned invaluable lessons that would help him in future union battles.

This problem of jealousy and ambition for office among insurgents was a natural by-product of opposition bloc formation. The only way to mitigate it was through strong and consistent leadership on the part of Mitchell. And this he failed to provide. Just weeks after the Labor Day meeting, when Ralph Mason decided he wanted to make a bid for district secretary-treasurer in the place of Cairns, Mitchell paused. He wrote Mason that Cairns was already "an aspirant for the place, and was given some encouragement by me." Yet Mitchell allowed Mason to have his way, telling him "you can depend upon me giving all possible support in the campaign." Mitchell wanted to make certain, however, that Cairns approved of the change in plans as his assistance would be required during the campaign. To ease Cairns's disappointment,

Mitchell suggested that Mason promise Cairns that "a place will be provided for him" after the election.[58] Cairns, however, must not have been placated by this promise, for he seems to have taken little part in the insurgent movement from that point on. If Mitchell wanted to succeed in Ohio, he needed to be more forceful and consistent in his handling of his supporters.

The second problem, that of finding suitable candidates for district president and vice president, proved even more troublesome. Once again, Mitchell failed to take charge. The Hocking Valley men came up with no suggestions. If Mitchell hoped to defeat the Lewis machine, he therefore needed to cultivate his own opposition slate. He certainly recognized the problem, for as early as October he admitted "there is no use going into the state convention haphazard or without any well-defined understanding." His policy, however, was simply to wait and hope that Mason and the others would find someone on their own. "I wish our boys would get together," he wrote dejectedly, "and determine who would be the candidates for the various places." Despite his pressing the Hocking Valley men to redouble their efforts to find "good strong men to run for President and Vice-president," he despaired as early as October 11, writing "I hardly know how we should proceed to find a man." On only one point was Mitchell insistent. Any candidate for president must come from outside the Hocking Valley. If any presidential candidates emerged from the Hocking Valley, Mason was instructed to "set a movement on foot to sidetrack them." Mitchell would have preferred a presidential candidate from Guernsey county, the home of Tom L. Lewis.[59] Mason never found running mates, and his chances of success were thus seriously jeopardized. Mitchell should have realized that, once the insurgents themselves proved unable to field a full slate, it was his responsibility to put a man forward with the full backing of the national office. His failure to do so was a sign of inexperience as a national leader and a demonstration that he lacked control over the insurgent movement.

Mitchell was able to give Mason some sage advice on the proper conduct of a campaign, imparting knowledge he had acquired in recent years. UMWA elections, as we have seen, were tricky affairs. One had to know how to campaign without the appearance of campaigning. Take care so as "not to appear to be making a canvass for the place." If you are too obvious in your pursuit of office, you will array against you "that element among the miners who are opposed to men seeking office, and who would antagonize you if they thought you were devoting your time to campaign at the expense of the miners." Equally important, Mitchell assisted Mason in more obvious ways. He had directed the editor of the UMWA *Journal*, W. H. Scott, to provide Mason positive press coverage. Control of the union journal had been instrumental in Mitchell's victory in January 1899 and he no doubt believed it could do the same for Mason at the district level. Moreover, Mitchell had ordered the national secretary-treasurer, W. C. Pearce, to support Mason's campaign financially.[60] If the use of the national journal to support a Mitchell favorite in a district campaign was of dubious morality, the use of national funds was certainly illegal. Mitchell offered no justification for these practices. This was the nature of UMWA electioneering.

The third problem involved lack of judgment on the part of certain insurgents. The most obvious incompetent was George Schachert, who had Mitchell's tacit support in his bid for the district executive board. Schachert's shortcoming was a lack of subtlety. Mitchell learned to his chagrin that Schachert was not only openly campaigning for office, but brazenly suggesting that he had Mitchell's support. This was the type of campaigning Mitchell had warned Mason not to pursue. It was counterproductive and could also tarnish Mitchell's reputation among the rank and file. He did not confront Schachert directly, and he seems to have feared too close an association with this untrustworthy ally. Instead, he instructed Mason to set Schachert straight. Schachert must learn to be discreet. He must gauge the prevailing sentiment among the miners and local leaders he visits, Mitchell wrote, "and if he can casually say something that will have effect, why O. K.; but he should not openly advocate the election of anybody, or the defeat of anyone else."[61]

Lack of discretion in his own campaign was not Schachert's only crime, however. Without Mitchell's approval, Schachert also openly promoted national executive board member Fred Dilcher for the post of national vice president. In Mitchell's eyes, this was an unpardonable crime of meddling in national affairs. Schachert's promotion of both Dilcher and Mitchell made it appear that Dilcher was Mitchell's running mate. This was not the case at all. "Between our two selves," he told Mason, "Dilcher will not be the choice of myself or others for Vice-president." He indignantly concluded that he did not intend "to be embarrassed by having official colleagues forced on me" by thoughtless supporters such as Schachert.[62]

Schachert had proven a man not to be trusted with any degree of confidence, and when he asked Mitchell's permission to campaign in another part of the state, Mitchell refused to allow him. The now disgruntled Schachert moaned that he had spent some of his own money promoting Mitchell's presidency the year before and had never been compensated. Mitchell replied that while he appreciated Schachert's efforts on his behalf, he had never spent any union funds advancing his own interests and was not about to start now.[63] Mitchell had blatantly lied. He had spent considerable sums from the union treasury on organizers to campaign for himself and for his favorites in district elections. At the time he wrote this letter, he had numerous organizers in the Pittsburgh District supporting a candidate for district secretary-treasurer and counterattacking anti-administration sentiment. He also had organizers on the national payroll assisting Mason's campaign in District 6. Mitchell had lied to protect himself. He wrote Mason that his message to Schachert "was not intended to apply to you." Mason could still count on Mitchell's financial support. The letter to Schachert was written "so that if he made anything public the letter would be on file, and would be a vindication."[64] This kind of duplicity and intrigue represented the very essence of Mitchell's attempts to undermine his union opponents.

As the district election approached the insurgents were still without a presidential candidate. Mitchell therefore took it upon himself to determine whether he could win over Lewis's man, District President William Haskins. He had kept close watch on Haskins since September, and just days before the mid-November meeting of national executive board and district presidents in Indianapolis, Mitchell decided it was time to have a "private conversation" with Haskins. Mitchell wanted to determine whether Haskins "would go into a deal to throw his influence to you, providing we will put no candidate in the field against him." Mitchell held out little hope for the success of this meeting, however, believing that Haskins was loyal to Lewis and would not abandon him.[65]

Much to Mitchell's surprise, Haskins proved ready to strike a deal. He reported that at the secret meeting Haskins "indicated a desire to work with the National even to the extent of separation from Lewis."[66] He did not explain why Haskins was prepared to break with the powerful Lewis and had become so anxious to secure the support of the national office. It is possible that Haskins feared that Tom L. Lewis's future in the union was about to self-destruct. District 6 was currently investigating charges made by the Ohio Valley Trades and Labor Assembly that Lewis had assisted a street railroad company defeat street-car strikes at Bridgeport, Ohio, and Wheeling, West Virginia earlier in the year. It is also probable that Haskins realized the futility of continuing to resist an increasingly popular and powerful national president. By early December, it was widely known that Mitchell would once again win the national presidency. Perhaps Haskins thought it best to accept Mitchell's peace terms before he was branded an enemy of the administration.

Whatever the specific reason, Haskins's apparent readiness to become a Mitchell supporter was a significant victory for the young national president. Perhaps to prove his new found loyalty, Haskins and several members of his district board traveled to the Hocking Valley late in December to campaign for themselves and for Mitchell's administration. Mason reported that Haskins and the others "spoke very highly of National President Mitchell and of the kind treatment extended to the Ohio officers by him and of the friendly relations between the national officials and the Ohio officers." Although Mitchell claimed to be "rather surprised to learn of the compliments," he figured that the Ohio officials "are all bidding for the support of the administration, which they now realize is popular with the miners of the country."[67] More likely was the recognition that strike funds, organizers, and other essentials were controlled by the national and might be withheld from District 6 unless district officials demonstrated their support for Mitchell.

The District 6 elections of January were anticlimactic. Just weeks prior to the district convention, Mason withdrew from the race for secretary-treasurer in favor of a candidate more favorable to Haskins. And with Mitchell's backing, Haskins and his slate were reelected by wide margins. Thus, despite Mitchell's inability to develop an opposition slate and his inability to successfully control and coordinate the insurgents, he had accomplished his mission in District 6. He now had a district organization solidly under his control that would no longer pose a serious impediment to his plans for the centralization of authority. All of his scheming and misuse of funds had not secured the desired end. Rather, District 6 had been brought into line because district officials understood that power in the union was shifting inexorably toward the national office.

Simultaneous with his efforts to subdue a potentially hostile District 6, Mitchell also had to grapple with an even more serious challenge in western Pennsylvania (District 5). Centralization of control often necessitated confronting dangerous district opponents, and in this instance it entailed combatting the militant and popular Patrick Dolan. Dolan's personal animosity toward Mitchell for having "stolen" the vice presidency in 1898 no doubt multiplied when Mitchell was able to steal the presidency. Yet Mitchell had no immediate plans to undermine Dolan's district presidency, and may even have been inclined to offer the olive branch to his powerful foe. Just days after the interstate joint conference, however, Mitchell received disquieting information concerning Dolan from a trusted source within the District 5 administration. He learned that Dolan not only continued to denounce Mitchell in public speeches, but that Dolan actually had declared that "rather than see you successful he would do all in his power to destroy the organization in the Pittsburg District." This same source also told Mitchell he had "proof that the operators are contributing money to insure the election of Dolan" in the upcoming District 5 elections."[68] Upon receiving this information, Mitchell determined that Dolan had to be subdued.

The source of this information was William Warner, secretary-treasurer of District 5, a man who had aided Mitchell in his recent election and a man Mitchell trusted implicitly. Warner, however, was not moved to write solely out of altruistic concern with the success of Mitchell's presidency. He had personal reasons to encourage Mitchell to move against Dolan. For his support of Mitchell, he had earned the wrath of the district president and, as early as November 1898, he was convinced that Dolan's "intention is to banish me from official existence."[69] Warner requested that Mitchell send national organizers to help him in his own reelection bid at the district convention scheduled for February 1899. To maintain his district office, Warner needed Mitchell's help, and he therefore may very well have overstated Dolan's challenge to Mitchell.

In his desire to promote an important supporter and crush a powerful rival, Mitchell followed a duplicitous strategy. While swearing to Dolan that he had no desire to meddle in the affairs of a district organization, he simultaneously ordered national board members G. W. Purcell and Fred Dilcher to District 5 to campaign surreptitiously for Warner. He compounded his subterfuge by offering Warner direct advice on effective campaigning. He encouraged Warner to utilize his ties with the United Labor League by having members of this group speak in favor of his candidacy. He also suggested how Warner might secure the removal of the Pittsburgh Press's labor reporter, Al Hamilton, a known friend and supporter of Dolan. Finally, he demonstrated his readiness to abandon constitutional restraints by instructing Warner to employ "suitable men" to assist his campaign "and have their bills sent to me." His use of national funds to hire local campaign workers on behalf of his supporters in district elections was an obvious breach of union law.[70]

Of all the strategies employed by Mitchell to assist Warner's reelection bid, the most important, in retrospect, was his use of national organizers to promote Warner's candidacy. Although the practice was nearly as old as trade unionism itself, the use of national organizers as campaigners in union elections was of dubious constitutionality. In the UMWA, the question of who ultimately controlled organizers had never been conclusively decided. Once assigned to a particular district, were the organizers under the authority of the district president or the national president? The question was of grave importance in a time of growing centralization of authority. District presidents such as Dolan, who bemoaned the steady flow of power from district to national office as a result of the interstate joint agreement, were determined to stymie all further encroachments on what they considered to be their traditional rights. The resulting struggles between national and district officials were like those of the fifteenth century in rising European nation-states between an increasingly powerful monarch and a nobility desperate to defend its ancient privileges.

Dolan, of course, was not fully aware of every aspect of Mitchell's machinations, but he soon learned of the activities of Dilcher and Purcell and was quick to take umbrage. Dolan's protest took the form of a constitutional challenge: once organizers were sent to a district, he argued, they came under the authority of the district president. Therefore, Dilcher and Purcell must receive their orders from Dolan and report directly to him. "Take my advice at the beginning of your administration," Dolan warned, "send your organizers to work where the miners of the country will be benefitted by their efforts, not into the Pittsburg District." And then, as if to emphasize that he understood

Mitchell's challenge to the long held prerogatives of district presidents, Dolan concluded tersely: "I want to be very plain in this matter, and I repeat again, that no man, whether he is a National Board member or national organizer or any other man will be tolerated in this District, as long as I am president, without my consent, and they come under my jurisdiction."[71]

Mitchell wrote a scathing response to his adversary. He claimed Purcell and Dilcher were in District 5 not to campaign, but to make certain that scale rates for mining were enforced.[72] Not content with this line of argument, he was also more than happy to take up the constitutional challenge. "I believe, if you will consult that section of the Constitution defining the duties of the National President," Mitchell lectured, "you will discover that he is authorized and empowered to exercise general supervision over the workings of the organization everywhere." Maintaining that while it was not "my intention to usurp any of the powers or prerogatives which properly belong to you," he threatened Dolan that if he persisted in denying board members, "my direct representatives," the right to hold meetings in District 5, "I shall be compelled to resort to lawful and constitutional measures to prevent you from usurping (my) authority." In the missive's conclusion, he so much as told Dolan he did not want to hear any more of the district president's views on the constitutionality of his actions: "The absurdity of your position becomes so apparent that it should not warrant any serious consideration."[73]

Once the battle had been joined between Mitchell and Dolan, Mitchell was surcharged with enthusiasm. He believed his letter, because it carried with it the authority of the national office and contained the threat of action against Dolan at the next convention, had settled the matter of organizers. He reported to Warner with glee that his barbed letter must have "caused Dolan much agony and indignation" and he hoped Dolan had been "driven to the wall." He warned Warner to be careful in his campaign addresses and public statements, however, noting "that as long as Dolan and his friends refrain from attacking you in meetings, you cannot afford to invite attack from them." Although the temptation might be great to assail Dolan and his cronies, "we must be careful what we say and write to them, so that they can have no justification on which to attack us in the next National Convention." As the District 5 elections drew near, Mitchell expressed his hope that his efforts on Warner's behalf had been enough to secure his reelection, and he even apologized for being too busy to travel to Pittsburgh to campaign in person.[74]

Yet perhaps Mitchell had underestimated Dolan's challenge and his grip on District 5. Dolan did not back down on the issue of control over national organizers, and his correspondence on this issue grew even more caustic. "Unless a man is very dull in comprehension he can readily see what your object is," Dolan fumed. "You have men going from one mining camp to the other at the present time, paid by the National organization, lectioneering (sic) contrary to the wishes of the Executive Board and President of this District."[75] This issue, obviously, would not disappear with a mere show of resolve on the part of Mitchell. More importantly, in the district election on February 14, not only did Dolan win reelection, but Warner was defeated and Dolan's man, William Dodds, won the office of secretary-treasurer.[76] Mitchell's advice, his organizers, and his funding of Warner proved inadequate to offset the personal appeal and local control of Dolan's district machine. The defeat of Warner proved that the power shift from the district to the national was by no means an accomplished fact.

Warner's defeat forced Mitchell to try a different strategy. Rather than confronting Dolan, he sought to pacify him through conciliation. Mitchell sent out a peace feeler to Dolan on February 21, suggesting that "past differences, if any existed, will be forgotten." He then asked Dolan to name men he wanted as organizers to serve in District 5 and promised to send these men commissions. He still refused to yield on the substantive issue in the dispute, however, that of control over the organizers once assigned. Perhaps sensing that Mitchell was bargaining for peace from a position of weakness, Dolan rejected the overture. Dolan refused to provide the list of names and reiterated his position that all organizers must be under the direction of the district office. Dolan's obstinacy angered Mitchell, who soon abandoned conciliation and returned to his earlier policy of threats and intimidation. Numerous letters, each increasingly strident, were exchanged between Mitchell, Dolan, and William Dodds. In a four-page letter written in April, Mitchell cited specific constitutional provisions supporting his position: Section 3, Article 1, stating that the national organization had jurisdiction over all local unions; and Section 2, Article 2, granting the president power to supervise the workings of the organization as his judgment dictated. Dodds responded by pointing to the "established precedent" of district control over organizers.[77]

Mitchell's apparent legalistic focus belied his true motivation: the centralization of authority. Indeed, he was certainly no stickler for constitutional restraints. If the union's framework worked to his advantage, he might insist on upholding it. But if it stood in the way of his objective, he would often overlook it. He never regarded the constitution as sacrosanct. "To a certain extent," he later wrote, "the formal written constitution of a trade union is rather a statement of principles and a formulation of present policy of the union than a hard and fast determination of its future laws."[78] Power, not law, motivated Mitchell. The right to control organizers was just one stage in the process of asserting national control over the districts. As he informed one organizer he had assigned to the Pittsburgh District, he was determined to "demonstrate to the interests of all concerned that my authority does not stop at simply advising with the District officers."[79] Were he to concede control of organizers to Dolan, it would establish a dangerous precedent for other district leaders.

His growing obsession with Dolan's challenge to his authority led him in early April to appoint as organizer for District 5 Edward Soppitt, a trusted friend. Mitchell forwarded to Soppitt all correspondence between himself, Dodds, and Dolan, and instructed Soppitt to note what district officials were saying about him at union meetings.[80] By May, Soppitt and other friends of the administration had terrible news to report. Dolan was not only making his usual personal attacks on Mitchell at district headquarters, but also he was now assailing the president publicly with new ammunition. Dolan had in his possession all the letters Mitchell and Warner had exchanged before the district convention, letters that detailed all of Mitchell's scheming to undermine Dolan and reelect Warner, even Mitchell's offer to use national funds to support Warner's candidacy. Exactly how Dolan came into possession of these letters is unclear. Warner, now working as an organizer in Central Pennsylvania (District 2), claimed he had taken every precaution to prevent such an embarrassment. He swore he kept the letters locked in his desk while in the office and always took the letters with him when away from his desk. Later he suggested that one of Dolan's men had stolen them from his pocket.[81] Once Dolan had the letters, he made effective use of them to discredit Mitchell. He began showing the letters around to local unions throughout the district. The feud between Mitchell and Dolan had escalated far beyond a debate over organizers.

Mitchell, of course, was dumbfounded. Obviously, his trust in Warner had been misplaced. Not only did the letters offer Dolan the chance to damage Mitchell's reputation among the rank and file, but the letters also made Mitchell appear incompetent and amateurish to his leading supporters. He was uncertain how to counterattack. In vain he tried to convince his supporters that he had never trusted Warner and that the letters contained nothing that could seriously damage the administration. "Of course you are aware that I was suspicious of him," he wrote one organizer. He even hesitated to sack Warner because he had helped secure Mitchell's election. "Were it not for the fact that he tried to do us some favor at Pittsburg during the annual convention, I would dismiss him from the service."[82] But as the crisis deepened and as the number of unionists who had seen the letters multiplied, Mitchell was forced to recognize the gravity of the situation. In a gut wrenching letter to Warner, Mitchell impressed upon his one-time confidante the nature of his crime. "It is the one thing in connection with my official life in the mining movement that has ever occurred to which I would not invite the closest investigation," he wailed. "Dolan is now parading them (the letters) before everyone who comes into his office, and is frequently visiting the Central (Pennsylvania) District, showing them to everyone there and in fact doing all in his power to destroy my standing among the miners of the country." In response, Warner could only offer apologies and his opinion that, despite the crisis, the vast majority of miners in District 5 and District 2 would still vote for Mitchell in the next election.[83]

Mitchell tried to make light of the matter as best he could. When he learned that Dolan told a local union meeting that Mitchell had launched a conspiracy to topple him and threatened to expose Mitchell to the world, Mitchell nervously joked that "Pat ought to join some burlesque company; his tragic poses would prove quite amusing to the public." At all times, however, Mitchell understood the situation with a clarity that underscored his grasp of the nature of power. Dolan was a district leader who sensed that power was shifting inexorably toward the national. Like an untamed animal, Dolan might prove even more dangerous when wounded. "As Pat sees his influence dwindling he is liable to do anything that would discredit other men," he told one organizer, "and I would advise you to keep close watch on him."[84]

The controversy over the letters, however, would not die. Mitchell received a number of piercing queries from local officials demanding an explanation.[85] Having been caught red handed by a union opponent using questionable if not illegal tactics, and watching the opponent make significant capital out of the affair, he now faced the dilemma well known to all politicians and union leaders faced with charges of wrongdoing they cannot deny. He could come clean, confess his crime and the circumstances making the crime necessary, and hope for a pardon by the rank and file. Or he could get even dirtier by fashioning some type of cover-up. Like so many leaders before and since, Mitchell chose the latter course.

The cover-up was detailed in a letter to Warner late in October with the national elections looming on the horizon. Mitchell instructed Warner to come to national headquarters in Indianapolis so that both of them could "fix up letters from you to me which will justify answers such as I sent so I will be in a position to defend myself." His response, therefore, was to use forgery to obscure the truth and maintain his reputation. Even the instructions he gave Warner on how to travel to Indianapolis were devious. Warner, who was now organizing in Maryland, was to announce to his colleagues that he had business in Pittsburgh, then take a train directly to Indianapolis. Mitchell's own justification for arranging the cover-up revealed misguided morality; it was proper to fight the evil of Dolan by resorting to unethical behavior. "If everyone knew Dolan as you do and I do there is no reasonable miner who could take exception to those letters," he argued, "but the fact that the mine workers generally do not know whether Dolan is a good man or bad man makes it necessary that I be placed in a position that will not compromise me in the eyes of the miners or in our convention."[86]

If Mitchell had erred by trusting Warner in the first instance, he erred again by trusting Warner to assist him in the cover-up. Warner proceeded to demonstrate his incompetence by bungling his simple assignment. Perhaps at Mitchell's request, Warner took the forged correspondence between himself and Mitchell to a publisher, the *Lonaconing Review*, and had them printed in pamphlet form. In a show of unbridled idiocy, however, Warner had included in this cachet of letters the one in which Mitchell told him to come to Indianapolis to prepare the cover-up! One might readily imagine Mitchell's horror upon receiving a copy of this pamphlet. "To say that I am thunderstruck . . . would be, to say the least, stating it mildly," he told Warner. "It appears to me that it is bad enough to have my enemies antagonize me, but it certainly causes me much more sorrow and pain to have my confidence betrayed by my friends." Mitchell ordered that all pamphlets and original letters be destroyed. And he concluded by exiling Warner from his confidence. Due to the "irreparable injury" Warner had inflicted, Mitchell would no longer correspond with Warner on any topic "except matters strictly pertaining to the organization and its business."[87]

Fortunately for Mitchell, none of the pamphlets fell into the hands of Dolan. Yet Dolan was still making use of the letters he did possess to damage Mitchell's reputation in Pennsylvania. Thus, Mitchell recognized Dolan as a continuing threat to his reelection plans. Although he was confident he could retake the presidency without a single vote in District 5, he took the precaution of sending numerous organizers into the district as early as October to campaign for him. In November, he wrote of his decision to "place large numbers of organizers in the Pittsburg District, to stir things up there in preparation for the Indianapolis convention" of January 1900. He planned to make a few speeches himself in the district, noting that "the one that will give me the greatest pleasure will be the one which is being arranged at Bellevernon," where Dolan had first read the letters between Mitchell and Warner. Soon his chief organizer in the district could write that the question of the letters was no longer a vital concern among the rank and file.[88]

Despite his own blunders and those of Warner, the fact that Mitchell could send in his organizers and use them as he pleased over the protests of district officials proves that he had in fact won the battle over who would control organizers. The constitutional question had never been resolved, but because Dolan had no adequate means of redress, Mitchell had secured victory in actual practice. By late November, even the usually bellicose Dolan had recognized his own defeat on this issue. By that time it was obvious to all who followed the union's affairs that Mitchell would be reelected. Due to his own propaganda efforts and the union gains made in 1899, Mitchell's popularity was soaring. Dolan realized that continued opposition could prove suicidal. Were he to remain Mitchell's enemy, he could easily find himself cut off from union funds to support local strikes. He might also be denied the use of organizers to enroll nonunion miners. District officials, even those such as Dolan who fought to maintain district autonomy, found out sooner or later that the centralization of authority was an inevitable result of the interstate agreement. Mitchell's chief organizer in District 5 reported in late November that

Dolan had become "as nice as Pie." "He sees it will suit him better to be friendly to us than to continue trying to down us. He has tried that and failed." Dolan officially waved the white flag of surrender in early December when he petitioned Mitchell to have four national organizers remain in District 5 to help him sign up nonunion miners. This request did not contain the usual qualification that these organizers were to be under his control.[89]

The Mitchell-Dolan affair of 1899 was a significant episode in the diminution of district authority and the creation of a more powerful, centralized union. Mitchell's assumption of the right to control organizers was the most important step toward the creation of his own personal political machine. Organizers functioned as his eyes and ears at the local level, were responsible to him alone, and held their appointments only as long as they contributed to his power and prestige. In addition to enlisting nonunion workers, organizers served as Mitchell's informants on local opposition, helped him settle local disputes in violation of contracts, popularized his policies, and praised his accomplishments. Mitchell was by no means the only labor leader to use organizers as the basis of a political machine. Gompers had more than seven hundred organizers at his command by 1900, and by 1902, according to one historian, the leadership of the Carpenters had "swarms of professional organizers and hence a political machine."[90]

The affair was significant as well for what it revealed about Mitchell's personality and leadership style. He obviously relished the infighting that was commonplace among UMWA officials, and he had an inherent knack for political maneuvering. He had no qualms about concocting amoral and secretive schemes, nor did he shy away from illegal and devious methods to establish his personal rule. The comic episode involving Warner proved that his skills at chicanery were not yet perfected, for he was still too trusting of those who supported him, and he therefore had left himself exposed to potentially career-ending charges. In the future, Mitchell would be more careful and circumspect but just as ruthless in stamping out internal dissent.

Having experienced some success in organizing outlying fields, and having brought to heel the most recalcitrant district administrations, Mitchell could look forward to consolidating his control of the national administration through a well orchestrated campaign to secure his own reelection in January 1900. And by demonstrating to operators he was in full command of the union, he would be in a better position to win a wage increase at the upcoming interstate joint convention.

Since the time of his election in 1899, Mitchell had informed his close friends and associates he might not be a candidate in the 1900 election. As we have seen, Mitchell detested many aspects of his new job and believed he could earn more money and be happier with a career in business. His attempts to enter the hardware business and the tobacco manufacturing business were obvious efforts to find alternative employment. When the tobacco partnership failed to materialize, however, he resigned to run for the presidency once again. He would continue to entertain hopes of leaving the presidency, and he certainly exploited numerous money-making ventures that came his way, but he no longer actively pursued full-time business careers. While he never developed a love of the office, he did come to recognize that his own personal fortunes were inextricably tied to the union presidency.

Ironically, he continued to use the threat of retirement as a campaign strategy. He found this threat an effective means of maintaining the active support of the most ambitious men in the union. First, the threat of retirement was an attempt to convince his boosters he was not overly ambitious for office. Office-seekers who campaigned too aggressively violated an unspoken code among miners and jeopardized their chances. Second, boosters who believed he might actually step down in the near future wanted to demonstrate their loyalty to him and their effectiveness in securing support for him. In this way, they could hope to succeed him as he had succeeded Ratchford. Third, the threat proved a unobtrusive way of canvassing his friends to determine rank-and-file support for his candidacy. If supporters informed Mitchell that he was obliged to run for reelection because miners in their district were solidly behind him, then Mitchell knew he did not have to campaign hard in those districts.

His threats of retirement revealed his cunning calculations and his expertise in the use of propaganda even among his closest confidantes. He dangled the prospect of high union office in front of their noses like a piece of red meat. On several occasions he insisted he would step down immediately were it not for the possibility that Dolan or Lewis might capture control of the union. Either man might "forage our treasury" and possibly destroy the union altogether. "If I were satisfied that a candidate could be brought forward who would antagonize the Dolan-Lewis combination, and in whose hands the interests of the organization would be safe," he wrote, "I should be happy, indeed, to be relieved of the responsibilities of office." By giving the same message to several underlings, Mitchell was certain each would do his very best to prove he was the candidate for whom he was looking.[91]

Once he had committed himself to run again, he was careful to explain that his desire for office was not a matter of personal ambition. He argued that while he personally hoped to step down, his close associates in the union would not hear of it. "It appeared to be the consensus of opinion of all my friends and official colleagues that it would be almost criminal to leave the movement at this time."[92] In this way, he could claim he was simply accepting the urgent pleas of his associates to save the union from destruction. He did not covet the office; he had been drafted.

At no time did he fear he would lose his bid for reelection. As early as

July he expressed confidence that "if I want the place I can have it without opposition."[93] And what was there to fear? The price of coal was up and miners could therefore expect a wage increase at the upcoming interstate conference. He had success as an organizer and strike leader, and he had subdued his most vocal critics. He had even more direct control of the union's journal than he had in the election of January 1899. Before August 1899, the editorship of the UMWA's *Journal* had been the responsibility of the vice president. When Tom W. Davis retired in August 1899, however, Mitchell did not replace him and instead, created the position of journal editor. The new editor, W. H. Scott, was a man whose career was dependent on his ability to follow Mitchell's orders and serve his interests well. Scott did not disappoint his boss. The UMWA *Journal* became an even more pliant tool of the administration. Finally, Mitchell made effective use of national organizers to campaign in areas where his support was weakest. Even though nominations for national office were to be seen only by the secretary-treasurer, Mitchell subverted the constitution and kept close track of the nominations as they came in to headquarters. He made careful note of those locals nominating anyone other than himself for president and sent organizers there to speak for him. "I shall look over the list," he told his chief organizer in District 5, " and let you know the number of the Local, and name of the town in the Pittsburg District that has nominated any other person than myself."[94] Thus, Mitchell not only used his organizers to campaign, but he knew exactly where to send them.

One source of potentially serious trouble in the upcoming election was his inability to select a vice presidential running mate. When Tom W. Davis resigned in August 1899, Tom L. Lewis quickly announced his candidacy. The fact that Lewis refused to make a bid for the presidency showed Mitchell's increasing power and prestige. Were Lewis to capture the vice presidency, however, Mitchell would be faced with a kicker within his own administration, a powerful foe bent on causing Mitchell's downfall and replacing him. Moreover, were Lewis to secure the vice presidency, it would be a clear sign to operators that Mitchell was not in full command of the UMWA as he professed. Lewis had to be defeated at all costs.

Soon after Lewis announced his candidacy, Mitchell heard the news that Lewis had compromised his union principles during street car strikes at Wheeling, West Virginia and Bridgeport, Ohio. To his delight, he learned that the Ohio Valley Trades and Labor Assembly charged Lewis with assisting the street railroad company involved in the strike. M. F. Tighe, president of the OVTLA, sent Mitchell copies of a circular exposing Lewis's "crimes." "If these charges are true, and they are certainly reasonable men who make them," he gleefully told his chief supporter in Ohio, Ralph Mason, "it means Lewis's everlasting defeat in Ohio." Mitchell then secured "a dozen or two" of the OVTLA circulars denouncing Lewis, and he quickly distributed them to powerful members of the union with curt notes that spread the news: "I presume you have not heard of the downfall of the leader of the opposition, the gentle gentleman that was always against the administration." When his supply of circulars ran out, he asked a subordinate to secure as many of them as possible and "place them in the right parties' hands." For a while it seemed as if the propaganda campaign against Lewis was having the proper effect. In October, he learned from Mason that the miners of Ohio were denouncing Lewis in the most bitter terms. "John, I think we have the Clique by the Heels, and we will turn the tables upon them."[95]

The speed with which Mitchell tried to eliminate his opponent was remarkable. He had the killer's instinct to attack when his opponent was in trouble. Whether or not Lewis was actually guilty of sabotaging a strike was a secondary consideration. Mitchell never investigated the allegations. If the issue could be used to remove an obstructionist, the truth of the issues were of little consequence. Certainly Mitchell can be criticized for his "questionable tactics" and his "underhanded efforts,"[96] but it is equally certain that Lewis would have done the same had the roles been reversed. Internal union politics was an amoral game, not to be played by the faint of heart.

Unfortunately for Mitchell, the furor soon died down. The Ohio executive board, dominated by Lewis, issued its own circular vindicating Lewis's actions during the strike. While Mitchell believed the Ohio circular a farce that would convince only the "extremely gullible," it raised enough doubt about Lewis's guilt for the episode to fade away without noticeable damage to Lewis's reputation in Ohio or elsewhere. A frustrated Mitchell could only make the empty promise to Tighe that when the proper time came, "I shall see that he (Lewis) is held to a strict accountability for his disloyalty to the trade union movement."[97]

Having allowed his prey to escape unharmed, the only way remaining for Mitchell to block Lewis's bid was to find an acceptable candidate of his own and provide him the full backing of the administration. Yet Mitchell never named his running mate, and as a result, Lewis became vice president. This was Mitchell's greatest failure in 1899 and the reasons for it revealed a great deal about union politics.

Mitchell's failure to name a running mate was not due to lack of qualified underlings. There were several ambitious and respected men ready to become second-in-command at union headquarters. One was William B. Wilson, president of District 2 in central Pennsylvania. Although Mitchell did not know Wilson well, Wilson was the person Mitchell wanted. This was in part because of Wilson's effectiveness in organizing that district and his ability to control the radical element there. Mitchell learned, however, that a movement for Wilson would be strongly opposed in the southern districts and would therefore cause division within the Mitchell forces. William Fairley, executive board member from Alabama, despised Wilson because of an alleged injustice that had occurred several years before, and had promised to fight Wilson's nomination to the end. Because of the intensity of this animosity, Mitchell decided that "unless the movement has been started I think it would be well to drop him."[98]

With his first choice out of the running, Mitchell was uncertain how to proceed. Several of his proven supporters petitioned him to give them the nod. Among the leading contenders for office were: William Fairley, John P. Reese of Iowa who had served as chief organizer in the Indian Territory strike, W. D. Van Horn, District 11 (Indiana) president, Fred Dilcher, national organizer, and W. H. Scott, editor of the UMWA's *Journal*. All these men were members of the national executive board. While Mitchell liked all these men and considered their petitions carefully, he did not believe any were appropriate. The primary consideration for Mitchell was not the candidate's ability, popularity, or loyalty to the administration. For Mitchell the key issue was geography. Mitchell was very concerned about having a geographically balanced ticket. He considered himself a "western man," and the secretary-treasurer W. C. Pearce was from Ohio. Thus, Mitchell believed the best candidate would be one from a well organized part of the East, meaning Pennsylvania. This is the principal reason he wanted William B. Wilson. None of the other candidates were Pennsylvanians and he believed this would hurt their chances in the upcoming election.[99]

Geography had always been an important factor in UMWA elections, and Mitchell was right to emphasize it. When an acceptable candidate from Pennsylvania failed to materialize, however, he should have thrown his support to one of the other men as quickly as possible. And he should have explained his reasons to the other contenders in a manner designed to maintain their loyalty. Instead, he abdicated responsibility and made no choice at all. His failure to do so revealed he was not so much the absolute commander of the union, but the fledgling political boss trying to satisfy all his supporters. His failure to name a running mate also made Tom L. Lewis's bid for office all but inevitable. All through October and the first half of November Mitchell grappled with the problem of how to select a running mate without antagonizing the other candidates, a problem that was the source of "considerable worry."[100] He tried gently to discourage the candidacies of Reese and Fairley, apparently without success. In mid-November, when local boosters began to query Mitchell on who they should nominate for vice president, Mitchell grew despondent. He wrote one local official from Illinois that having "so many candidates among our Board members makes it embarrassing to me, and I could not, with justice to myself or them either, express a preference for one over the others."[101]

Having failed to take charge of the issue, he then determined that the various contenders should resolve the issue themselves. He held out hope that at the November 15 national executive board meeting "the boys" would take it upon themselves to "fix the matter up." This hope proved unfounded, however. At this meeting several board members proved willing to give up their candidacies but John P. Reese and W. D. Van Horn were more determined than ever to stay in the race. The meeting ended on a most unpleasant note with board members hurling insults at each other. The all-consuming thirst for office by ambitious men not only jeopardized the vice presidential race, but it also disrupted the harmony among Mitchell's supporters. Still Mitchell refused to intervene. At the conclusion of the board meeting, he wrote that while he regretted the "unsatisfactory feeling" among his loyal lieutenants, as far as he was concerned the vice presidential race would be an open contest. No candidate would receive his support. Only in this way, he believed, could he maintain the friendship of all office seekers.[102]

The failure of the board to agree on a single candidate, Mitchell knew all too well, set the stage for Tom L. Lewis's victory. "It was obvious to me," he informed Reese after the election, "that with yourself and Van Horn in the race Brother Lewis was sure to win." This was not because Lewis had more support, "but because the men who were in a position to influence the votes of the delegates had their hands tied because of their friendship for both yourself and Van Horn."[103] Between Reese and Van Horn, Mitchell preferred Van Horn. Van Horn was more experienced and he hailed from a state that was part of the CCF. While Mitchell officially maintained his position of neutrality throughout the campaign, he let several influential people know in confidence that Van Horn was preferable.[104] In this way he hoped perhaps that the news would leak out that Mitchell supporters should vote for Van Horn. If this was in fact his strategy, it did not work.

At the 1900 convention, the inevitable occurred. Reese and Van Horn divided the pro-administration vote and left Tom L. Lewis a winner. On the first ballot, Lewis received 370 votes, Reese 323 and Van Horn 212. Had Mitchell been able to force either Reese or Van Horn to bow out of the contest, Lewis probably would have been defeated. It was not until a third ballot was taken that Lewis received a majority of the votes cast.[105] Lewis's election as vice president was Mitchell's first serious defeat. He had blundered in his moves against opposition in Districts 5 and 6, yet he had still come out on top in both cases. Through his unwillingness to select a running mate, he had erred in his handling of Lewis's bid for national office. This time he lost. As a national officer, Lewis could now claim for himself a share of all praise bestowed upon Mitchell's administration. Lewis was now in a position where he could build a national rather than merely a district following. And worst of all from Mitchell's standpoint, Lewis now had an opportunity to work against Mitchell from inside union headquarters. He was aware of the problem Lewis's vice presidency presented, but he remained confident in his ability to avoid the worst possible scenario. "You can rest assured," he wrote the former vice president, "that the Presidency of the organization will not pass into the hands of Lewis if I can prevent it."[106]

When the UMWA convention opened on January 15, 1900 at Masonic Hall in Indianapolis, Mitchell and the delegates were in a celebratory mood. It was a time to pat themselves on the back for the accomplishments of the past year and to prepare for an interstate joint convention in which they could rightly expect a significant advance in wages. The fact that Gompers himself delivered the opening address was testimony to the growing national importance of the UMWA. There was much to celebrate. Official membership had risen to 93,000, an increase of 38,000 in one year; nearly 500 locals had been either organized or reorganized; more than $70,000 had been expended for organizing purposes in the past year and the treasury still held almost $40,000.[107]

Although he had been president of the organization for nearly a year and a half, this was Mitchell's first time to chair the convention. Not yet thirty years old, and with a self-confessed tendency to speak far too quickly,[108] the boy president showed no visible signs of nerves and performed the task like an old hand. He demonstrated a remarkable grasp of parliamentary procedure, handling motions, points of order, and all the technical jargon in expert fashion. He was also careful not to dominate the discussion on all issues, opting to give the delegates opportunity to speak freely, thus avoiding the appearance of dictatorial control. His own speeches, as usual, were filled with large words and rambling sentences. They lacked precision, yet his meaning was generally clear. Unlike so many effective stump speakers of the day, his speeches did not contain many classical or biblical allusions. His was not adept at emotional "speechifying"; his gift was sincerity and humility. Always ready to "bow to the wishes of the delegates," or "accept the dictates of the majority," forever "pleased to remain your humble servant," he sometimes sounded like Charles Dickens's Uriah Heep. And like Heep, whose protestations of humility masked his grossly ambitious nature, Mitchell's ingratiating humility masked a determination to have his own way.

A beautiful expression of Mitchell's false diffidence was the convention debate over officers' salaries. By voice vote, the convention approved a salary scale of $1,500 for president, $1,200 for vice president, and $1,300 for both the secretary-treasurer and union journal editor. Later, when an unnamed delegate rose to question the significant increases before there was an advance in the mining rate, Mitchell quickly asserted himself. Claiming to be in an "embarrassing position," he let it be known that his interests were secondary to the interests of the miners. Because the vote to advance his salary had not been unanimous, he began, "the thought occurred to me that perhaps the best interests of the organization were not being served." He appreciated every honor the union bestowed on him, and he assured the delegates "that if advancing my salary would injure the organization, if one man was to go away from here dissatisfied about the matter, then I say you should put the salary at last year's figure, or even make them smaller." He concluded by declaring that he loved the UMWA too much to allow a salary increase to injure it.[109]

Of course this was sheer nonsense. Mitchell's fondness for "mezuma," as he often referred to money, easily outweighed his "love" of the UMWA. As we shall see, after the 1900 anthracite strike, Mitchell himself initiated a move to have anthracite workers "surprise" him and his family with the gift of a new home. The point here is that his public posture was that of an altruistic, self sacrificing servant of the miners. It was a posture that proved very effective in earning and maintaining the admiration of the rank and file. The convention, of course, voted to uphold the wage increase, and Mitchell wrote with joy and satisfaction to his niece that "it is of course needless to say that the increase in salary was not declined."[110]

Mitchell's posture contrasted sharply with that of the new vice president. Tom L. Lewis made no secret of his desire for the increase. He believed he deserved it. And in a rather clever way, he claimed the raise would help the union at the interstate conference. Any failure to raise the salaries of officers, Lewis suggested, would give operators a chance to argue we did not do so because we did not expect to get an advance in mining rates. Whereas Mitchell appealed to the delegates' sense of fair play, Lewis called upon their militancy. "I am one of those people who if I think my services are worth a certain sum are going to ask for it," he barked, "and if I don't get it I am going on a strike."[111] Lewis was no more radical or aggressive than Mitchell in his approach to union matters, but his public posture was certainly that of a street fighter and strike leader.

Elizabeth Morris, Mitchell's secretary, once noted in a panegyric essay that Mitchell always knew what he wanted a convention to do and always carefully planned his approach.[112] This was the case in 1900. He encouraged the delegates to celebrate a year that "has been resplendent with notable victories and grand achievements."[113] But Mitchell himself had not come to make merry. He was planning to push through constitutional changes that would greatly add to presidential power. He had hand picked members of the committee on the constitution and had named his friend Billy Ryan as chair. Usually not as significant as the resolutions or credentials committees, this year the constitution committee had an extremely important role to play in shaping the type of union Mitchell envisioned.

On the morning of January 30, the committee introduced eighteen amendments to the constitution, of which all but one passed. By far the most important amendments involved expanding the powers of the president.

Mitchell had prepared the way for these amendments in his opening address. He had told the delegates that his experience as president had convinced him "that the constitution is entirely too indefinite and incomplete to serve the purpose for which it was intended."[114] Presidential powers were expanded in a number of ways. First, the president would be given the right, with the consent of the executive board, to fill all vacancies occurring in the national office. This was a matter of closing the stable door after the horse ran off. Had he possessed this power in August when Tom Davis resigned, Mitchell could have replaced him with one of his own boosters, making it all but impossible for Lewis to defeat an incumbent. Second, the president was given the right, again with the consent of the executive board, to "suspend or remove any national officer for insubordination, for just and sufficient cause." This was an obvious threat to Lewis not to subvert his presidency. Third, the president was empowered to appoint as many organizers and other workers as he believed were required. The number of organizers had risen dramatically in 1899, and he did not want limitations placed on his right to increase staff. Fourth, the president was empowered to attend in person, or send national organizers, to visit locals, district conventions, and "any other places in the districts . . . when convinced that such services are required." In short, he had resolved the issue in dispute between himself and Dolan. He now had explicit constitutional authority to send his organizers anywhere he wanted. Fifth, the president had the right to appoint one or more officers to examine the financial accounts of local unions. This was designed to make certain that all dues and assessments owed the national were paid. If properly enforced, this amendment would greatly add to the national treasury. Sixth, the president shall "decide all questions of dispute on constitutional grounds." After a close voice vote on the floor, Mitchell declared that all the proposed amendments had been adopted.[115] In one mighty chop, Mitchell had struck at the very roots of local and district sovereignty and had centralized authority in a way unthinkable a few years earlier.

His agenda was not yet complete. The constitution committee also moved to create a central defense fund. In 1898, miners had defeated the creation of a national strike fund through referendum vote. This time he avoided the pitfalls of such direct democracy by asking the convention to place authority in the hands of the president and executive board to levy assessments in support of those on strike. "Never in the history of our movement," Mitchell told the delegates, "has the necessity of establishing a defense fund been more obvious than during the past year."[116] The amendment made each member's standing in the organization contingent upon prompt payment of the assessments. After a great deal of squabbling, this amendment also narrowly passed by voice vote.[117] The creation of the defense fund was a major step toward centralized control. Only strikes approved by the president and the national board received strike funds, thus giving Mitchell incredible power to discourage wildcat strikes through the withholding of money.

Having obtained what he wanted from the convention—unanimous reelection, a pay raise, and a revised constitution—he began preparing for the interstate conference. Before he adjourned the delegates, however, Mitchell warned his followers to abide by their agreements and not to expect too much from the upcoming scale negotiations. If the members hoped to perpetuate the new found power of the UMWA, "we must conduct our affairs as prudent business men, and on business lines." While we will insist on every penny market conditions entitle us, "in the same spirit, we should accord to the operators that portion of the profits accruing from increased business that they are properly entitled to." He aimed to serve the immediate interests of the miners and also to "command the respect and confidence of the public at large."[118] In short, the UMWA must be reasonable, peaceful, and acceptable to middle-class society if it hoped to prosper as a working-class institution.

The interstate joint conference was a ritualized dance between two hostile powers. Shifting from joint discussions to scale committees to sub-scale committees, the two sides followed prescribed formulas as they sized each other up, using taunts and jokes and statistics to measure the other side's war readiness and to determine the minimum price of peace. It was the most important human element in the bituminous coal industry. Its outcome determined whether or not there would be a strike, a wage increase, or a decrease. Only expert negotiators able to withstand marathon bargaining sessions could succeed. This was Mitchell's third interstate conference, yet he was a veritable rookie. He had essentially been mute in 1898, and Ratchford was still in charge in 1899. Now it was Mitchell's turn to prove his meddle as the miners' leader in the "new era" of collective bargaining.

Not surprisingly, Mitchell demonstrated amazing skill as a negotiator. It was at the joint conferences that his brilliance shined. He was in his element, among powerful men he respected and from whom he desperately wanted to earn respect. He came armed with an impressive arsenal of facts and arguments. Without a second's hesitation he could bring forth statistics on the tonnage of coal produced in each district, the price that coal brought on the market, the wages presently paid each category of mine worker, differentials between pick and machine mining, and the costs of living for miners down to the price of beer. While he acted meek and humble before delegates to the UMWA convention because that served his purpose, at the joint conference he was the aggressive and confident salesman with exclusive rights to a necessary product, mine labor.

His confidence was especially strong in 1900, for his statistics told him that "there has never been a time . . . when the prices of coal have been as high . . . and there has never been a time when the cost of living to the Miners has been as high." The only question in his mind was how great the advance would be. When operators offered what he considered to be the paltry sum of nine cents a ton, he retorted: "I am reluctant to believe that the Operators have presented the scale they have seriously. I imagine that they are trying to have some fun with the Miners; that they are only joking."[119] He knew, however, that the dance had only begun.

At various times he would plead for fairness. "The Miners do not expect you to run your mines except at a profit," he told them, "but they do expect you to pay them a fair share of the profits accruing from any increased business." At other times, he threatened a walk out, claiming he had 150,000 men ready at his command to "paralyze the wheels of industry" unless the operators came across with a more reasonable offer.[120] In the end, he heard what he wanted to hear, a compromise he could accept. The operators offered an advance of fourteen cents a ton for picked, screened coal, nine cents a ton for run of mine coal, and twenty cents a day for day laborers. Although there were many aspects of the agreement to which he objected, he believed he had received the best offer possible without resorting to strike action.

He realized that his job was not finished with the signing of the accord with the operators. Indeed, in many ways his duties had just begun. First, he had to convince the miners that the advance was the best possible. To those miners who came expecting more than they received, Mitchell proved a capable pitch man, describing the contract in such glowing terms that one would hardly recognize it as the product of a compromise with which he was not completely satisfied. "There has never been a time in the history of mining, even within the recollection of the oldest one among you," he told miners assembled at the joint session, "when an advance so great as this, and applied to so great a number of men, was secured." Second, he had to make certain, for the life of the contract, that operators abided by the terms of the contract. Addressing the operators, he noted that some of them had refused to comply with contracts signed with the UMWA, and that others had discriminated against miners because they were union men. "Operators must not throw stumbling blocks in the way of the Miners," he warned. "I will serve notice to the Operators now that when they go home unless they keep the agreement inviolate we will call the men out." Third, and most important, he had to control his own members and guarantee they would maintain absolute compliance with the terms of the agreement. Now he spoke to the miners. He had received numerous complaints in the past year that mine workers had violated the last contract, had struck in violation of the agreement, had refused to obey the laws of the UMWA. "Miners must not strike contrary to the laws of the organization," he insisted. "I will serve notice on the Miners that unless they keep the laws of the organization we will suspend them from the organization."[121] Mitchell the negotiator had turned Mitchell the policeman, standing between labor and capital to maintain labor peace through coercion.

For Mitchell, the interstate conference was the salvation of an industry in despair, beset with too much competition and declining prices. It represented the fruition of the dreams of Dan McLaughlin and John James, those noble pioneers of coal unionism who had impacted his youth and shaped his ideals. Only by bargaining in good faith, and sharing whatever profits existed, did the industry have a chance to emerge "out of the slough of despair in which it has wallowed for so many years." While this particular contract did not solve the problem of the differential between pick and machine mining, he was aware "all the evils and wrongs that have accumulated during the past thirty years" could not be rectified overnight. It would take time, but "if we continue to progress at the same rate we have during the past three or four years, the time is not remote when our people will take that place in the industrial movement to which they are so rightly entitled."[122] For Mitchell the interstate movement was no stopgap measure to prevent the worst abuses of capitalist exploitation. It was the harbinger of a free enterprise utopia on the not too distant horizon in which workers and owners shared profits equitably. As long as coal production expanded and prices continued to rise, many miners were willing to accept his solution to the labor problem.

Soon after the interstate conference Mitchell felt compelled to squelch the voices of opposition in his hometown of Spring Valley. By the fall of 1899, there was a movement underfoot by the radical element in Spring Valley to undermine Mitchell's reputation. He perceived the danger at once. Failure to receive the nomination from his hometown would discredit his candidacy. "I should rather lose a hundred votes in any other state that one from my home town," he wrote a friend in Spring Valley.[123] That the miners of Spring Valley should oppose the local hero was hardly remarkable. Spring Valley was still known as the "banner anarchist city of the United States,"[124] with a large number of radicals of all persuasions. It was still densely populated by recent immigrants from Italy who had not been raised in the tradition of John James and Dan McLaughlin. Moreover, these miners knew Mitchell better than any other element among the rank and file. They not only were aware of his relative wealth, but they knew that he counted no miners among his closest friends, that he was no longer one of them. When Mitchell went to Spring Valley in February 1899 to attend a celebration of his recent election, the speeches praising Mitchell were not made by miners but by the "leading lights" of the town, as Mitchell described them: Father John Power, the attorney William Hawthorne, and the operator Ed Dalzell.[125] These were his friends and companions. These were the men he respected.

When the Spring Valley opposition surfaced, he treated it as an irritant rather than a fundamental challenge to his outlook and life-style. He could not afford to spend much time there himself, he told a friend, so he had to "depend upon my friends to line the boys up for me." He instructed his friend to get him as much publicity in the local papers as possible. He wanted to see articles printed that listed his achievements and highlighted his growing national reputation.[126] The fact that he believed such an approach would undercut a class conscious protest revealed his increasing alienation from rank-and-file sentiment. The opposition did not subside.

When Mitchell went home for Christmas that year, he heard disheartening news. At a recent meeting of Spring Valley Local 43, which Mitchell did not attend, several speakers attacked the administration. One speaker arose and, "with due solemnity, roasted the whole gang, from Mitchell down, declaring that we were a set of robbers, who were waxing fat at the expense of the poor down-trodden coal diggers." In a letter to his old mentor and friend Billy Ryan, Mitchell mocked his opponents, suggesting their demands were absurd. Local coal diggers wanted one dollar per ton as a minimum price for mining, and a sliding scale "which must always slide upward," and a resolution that the UMWA "abandon the plutocratic Democratic and Republican parties, and embrace simon pure socialism." If the operators refused to grant these terms, Mitchell continued, "the miners of Spring Valley will refuse to work, and let the industries of the country shut down through lack of fuel." As soon as he had time, he would attend a meeting of local miners for the purpose of "taking them to task and insisting on either a withdrawal of the charges, or that they make them specific." Ryan was not at all surprised by the Spring Valley opposition, "considering the kind of men that have drifted in there."[127] Mitchell's contempt for the radical miners of Spring Valley foreshadowed his attitude toward the socialists who began to play so great a role in union affairs after 1901.

Although the Spring Valley radicals did not succeed in disrupting Mitchell's convention plans, he found them a continuing source of vexation. The new interstate agreement had given the local miners their highest mining rate ever, and still these miners had the temerity to complain about his administration. "I presume that Christ himself, if he were in attendance at this convention and had the responsibility of directing its progress, could not have satisfied some of the men whom Spring Valley is unfortunate enough to have in it as residents," he wrote a friend.[128] The wit and sarcasm of this comment was typical of the humor he displayed to his friends and generally hid from the public at large. It was this honest expression of his feelings, contrasted with the false expressions of humility he presented to the public, that made him such a welcome guest or drinking companion.

By mid-March Mitchell returned home to deal with this local opposition. As the local hero, his return home was always a cause for celebration, and it would take a brave man to square off against him in public. Nevertheless, he recalled the union meeting as "one of the hottest I ever attended." He set the scene for his friend Billy Ryan: "The Anarchists and Scotch tramps were there in full force, and what they tried to do with me was a plenty." Like a friend bragging about a barroom brawl, he probably exaggerated the size and strength of his opponent before describing how he began his counter assault. "I handed them up a few, particularly to the gang that stands on the corner from morning until night telling everyone how Mitchell, Ryan, and Company are growing fat at the expense of the poor down-trodden working men." Mitchell landed a few jabs against Ned Flood, apparently one of the leaders of the anarchists, calling him a character assassin who attacked without warning. Then Mitchell detailed the knockout blow. Flood approached the platform, flailing his arms and hurling insults, and suggesting that the money spent on officers' salaries might as well be thrown in the river. Mitchell waited for order to be restored, then asked Flood whether he knew how much miners received in return for this expense. Flood could not answer. "When I told him the advance was not less than eight or nine million dollars he appeared so astonished that his sight was almost restored to his blind eye."[129]

Local opposition certainly did not melt away. Anarchists and socialists who lived in Spring Valley continued to belittle his accomplishments and advocate more fundamental solutions to the plight of working people. Yet this scene in Spring Valley revealed Mitchell's attitudes toward radicalism of any sort. He perceived radicals as complainers and hecklers who stood on the sidelines while men such as himself performed the real work of advancing the interests of the miners. The story of Ned Flood symbolized his desire to open the eyes of all radicals by securing significant wages advances through the interstate movement.

In April 1900, Mitchell's administration underwent drastic change. Not only did Lewis begin his duties as vice president but there was also a change in the post of secretary-treasurer. A potentially embarrassing scandal forced Mitchell to demand the resignation of the current secretary, W. C. Pearce. On April 4, Mollie Meredith, who worked in Pearce's office, informed the editor of the union journal that Pearce was defrauding the union of its funds by raising the figures on receipts for money spent on postage stamps. On April 18, the journal editor relayed the story to Mitchell, who said he was "dumbfounded and incredulous when given this information." Mitchell first went to the postmaster to verify the story and next to the bank, where he told bank officers not to honor any check from Pearce for more than the "usual amount." On the next occasion Pearce purchased stamps, Mitchell obtained the official post office record, which showed Pearce had spent $20. Mitchell then looked at Pearce's receipt and cash book. According to Mitchell, "The receipt showed that the figures (twenty dollars) had been erased and thirty dollars inserted; and an entry of thirty dollars made in the cash book." An investigation revealed Pearce had used this same scheme to embezzle $160 over the past year. On April 30, Mitchell confronted Pearce, and, although Pearce admitted guilt and soon reimbursed the union, Mitchell demanded his immediate resignation. Had Pearce been a staunch ally of Mitchell, perhaps this indiscretion could have been rectified. But since Pearce was never Mitchell's confidante and since Lewis was ready to expose any possible cover-up on Mitchell's part, Mitchell had no choice but to force Pearce from office. This scandal was never brought to the attention of the rank and file. It was handled exclusively by the national executive board.[130]

As a result of the new constitutional provisions he had pushed through the recent convention, Mitchell could appoint a replacement. He did not have to wait until the next convention before a successor was elected. Mitchell's first choice for the vacancy was Billy Ryan, his old mentor, his close friend, and presently secretary-treasurer of the Illinois district. Perhaps Mitchell wanted to repay the debt he owed Ryan for advancing his career; perhaps he sensed that Lewis would be no match for the combination of Mitchell and Ryan. Ryan, however, did not want the job. He had just one year earlier purchased a house in Springfield, had settled his family there, and did not wish either to relocate his family in Indianapolis or live without his family for most of the year as Mitchell did.[131]

Casting his eye among the other potential candidates, geography once again became the primary issue. Pennsylvania's two large districts were still unrepresented in the administration, and while he could find no acceptable man in Dolan's Pittsburgh district, central Pennsylvania's district president had a great deal to offer. William B. Wilson, it will be remembered, had been Mitchell's personal choice for vice president. The two were by no means friends, but Wilson had proven his worth during the 1899 organizing drive in his district, and he had favorably impressed Mitchell at the recent national convention. Even so, Wilson recalled being "very much surprised" when Mitchell offered him the position because "I had but a slight acquaintance with Mr. Mitchell before that time."[132] At its May 1900 session, the executive board commended Mitchell for "demanding the resignation" of Pearce and ratified Wilson's appointment.[133]

Born in 1862 in Blantyre, Scotland, Wilson emigrated to Arnot, Pennsylvania in 1870; he began work in the mines at the age of nine.[134] He had been a member of the UMWA's executive board from 1891 to 1894, had been elected to the presidency of District 2 in 1899 and again in early 1900, and he would serve as UMWA secretary-treasurer until Mitchell's retirement in 1908. Mitchell and Wilson could hardly have been more different in terms of temperament. Wilson was an intensely religious man, maintaining the strong Scotch-Presbyterian outlook of his youth. He did not possess Mitchell's hearty humor and took himself quite seriously. He shunned alcohol and gambling, two things Mitchell enjoyed far too much, and which formed the basis of camaraderie among union officials. Wilson was never "one of the boys." He was a loner who took delight in reading and writing sentimental poetry.[135]

In terms of their approach to unionism, however, Mitchell and Wilson were eminently compatible. Both had a rare talent for negotiation, both shunned the use of the strike except as a last resort, and both had a deep commitment to collective bargaining. Wilson's presence in the national office would serve to reinforce Mitchell's conservatism. Mitchell quickly came to regard Wilson as his closest advisor, a man who could be trusted to handle any union issue. As Mitchell himself put it, Wilson became his "wise and sagacious counselor."[136] The relationship between the two men was based on trust, mutual respect, and commitment to a common cause. Wilson and Mitchell also became friends. Although a man of many acquaintances, Mitchell had few close friends. Wilson, however, became one of a small handful of men who enjoyed his complete confidence.

The period between the summer of 1898, when he became union president, and the spring of 1900, when Wilson became his secretary-treasurer, was a time of triumph for Mitchell and the union. After less than two years as head of the union, he had laid the groundwork for a highly centralized political machine. He had laid to rest any lingering doubts that he was too young and inexperienced to handle the affairs of the UMWA. The basis of his success was, of course, the general economic expansion after 1898 that precipitated union growth nationwide. At no other time of peace did unions experience such remarkable membership growth. Production soared, profits multiplied, and labor markets tightened. Many employers responded to the new situation by signing contracts with unions.

Because so much of the industrial expansion around the turn of the century was dependent upon coal, output and profits in that industry were remarkable. Peace and stability were essential for continued production. Since labor peace meant profits, many operators in soft coal willingly accepted what coal miner leaders had wanted all along—collective bargaining. The establishment of the CCF in 1898 formed the core of Mitchell's power. To maintain that power, he was obligated to bring all miners into the union fold and coerce them to keep the peace. He needed to organize the outlying fields, and his success in central Pennsylvania and Indian Territory proved he had the power to do just that. He needed to centralize power so that the union could negotiate national contracts and maintain them. Mitchell's success in subduing the recalcitrant districts, in creating a national strike fund, and in expanding the constitutional powers of the president demonstrated that he was well on the way to building a powerful national machine. His inability to keep Tom L. Lewis out of the national administration, however, showed that this machine was not yet complete. Above all, Mitchell was obligated to force miners and operators to comply with contracts once signed. And as long as mining prices, output, and tonnage rates continued to rise, most miners and operators were willing to accept his leadership.

Mitchell himself was changed by his first years in office. His rising income and his newly established social relationships with operators and other men of means allowed him to cultivate expensive tastes for clothes and jewelry, to join middle-class fraternal societies, to ponder real estate and other investments, and to begin dreaming of a life on "easy street." The pressing concerns of office work, constant travel, and the separation from his wife and family had created a state of "extreme nervousness" if not alcoholism. Most importantly, his new social circle and wealth, as well as his new role as enforcer of the contracts, created a growing gulf between himself and his fellow unionists, a separation from the day-to-day concerns and problems facing the rank and file that would only become more glaring with time. The boy president still looked the same. He was still lean and angular, still youthful and vigorous, but he had already shed much of his coal digger culture. His speech, his manners, his clothes, his associations, and even his attitudes all gave evidence that John Mitchell was adopting the culture and attitudes of the employing class.

Chapter 3

The Anthracite Strike of 1900

The anthracite strike of 1900 was a remarkable turning point in Mitchell's career. Never was he more militant than during the organizing drive and strike call. At the start of the campaign, all signs pointed to union failure: the union had almost no organization in the hard coal fields; the labor force seemed hopelessly divided by region, skill, ethnicity, and other factors; Mitchell and other union leaders were densely ignorant of the anthracite industry, which bore little resemblance to soft coal; and above all, hard coal operators were powerful men, ruthless and sophisticated in their opposition to unions, who did not need to rely on union strength to ensure labor peace and the stability of trade. Despite the enormous odds, Mitchell spearheaded an aggressive drive to organize as many mine workers as possible, expending a great deal of money and resources. The drive met with only limited success. Then, over the cries of local officials that a strike would surely fail, Mitchell called the men out, initiating a labor-capital confrontation even greater than the soft coal strike of 1897.

The resolution of the strike, however, foreshadowed Mitchell's conservative future. Bowing to political pressure, he accepted a limited settlement made in the interest of securing the reelection of the Republican administration of President William McKinley. The Republicans' desire for labor peace during the election year, not a lack of solidarity on the part of the strikers, led Mitchell to call a halt to the walk out just five weeks after it began. And even though the settlement addressed none of the mine workers' leading demands, even though strikers were prepared to remain out until a more complete victory was achieved, Mitchell demonstrated his mastery of the situation by convincing workers to accept the settlement and return to work.

The 1900 anthracite strike also represented Mitchell's first major test as field general. The press and public scrutinized his actions for the first time. And to their delight, he proved a "responsible" union leader, a man who could be trusted to keep the peace, a man who was bold enough to take on monopoly capital but "rational" enough to end the hostilities when reasonable offers were made. When the strike was over, the press made him a hero. He won the praise of liberal and conservative alike. Here was a labor leader the American people could trust.

For Mitchell, 1900 was a proving ground in all aspects of strike management. He learned how to control his forces, how to unite the disparate elements under his command, and how to prevent their actions from bringing down on the union the wrath of adverse public opinion. Equally important, he learned the complicated tactics of behind the scenes maneuvers, the give and take that goes on in corporate boardrooms, the political realities of industrial relations. Mitchell proved a quick study, for he was able to translate his limited victory into significant union growth and secure for himself the friendship of some of the most important politicians in Washington.

John Mitchell's recent victories convinced him of the need to continue organizing until all mine workers were UMWA members and were protected by trade agreements. By his own reckoning, there were still well over 300,000 diggers outside the union fold.[1] Of these, nearly 150,000 were mine workers concentrated in the anthracite fields of northeast Pennsylvania. A single organizing drive could more than double the size of the union. It was thus natural that he should turn his attention to hard coal. Mitchell was the first UMWA president to devote any significant attention to the anthracite fields. The union was too weak and divided in its early years to consider organizing hard coal, there seemed to be little interest among anthracite workers in the UMWA, and soft coal miners had little appreciation of the special problems and conditions of the anthracite industry. Mitchell shared this ignorance but was determined to overcome any obstacles.

On the surface, the obstacles did not seem insurmountable. Mitchell could "sell" the union to both workers and owners by pointing to the already successful operation of the interstate agreement in maintaining production and profits while raising living standards for bituminous miners. He carried the weight of public support in his efforts to ameliorate living and working conditions while respecting the rights of property. And he was also buoyed by the geographical concentration of the anthracite industry. While bituminous coal deposits could be found across the continent, anthracite coal was deposited almost exclusively within five counties of northeast Pennsylvania. This meant, or seemed to mean, that organizers would have less difficulty traversing the field, keeping the rank and file informed of developments, and ensuring compliance to any directives.

Mitchell would soon come face to face with the hard realities that made the anthracite industry all but impervious to unionization. By far the most significant impediment was the near monopolization of the industry. The geographical concentration that made travel less strenuous for union organizers also encouraged powerful railroad corporations, which had penetrated the area and bought up significant slices of the anthracite pie. Beginning in the 1870s, railroad companies began to absorb or force out of business the smaller independent operators. In the 1890s, the J. P. Morgan interests accelerated the drive toward monopolization by reorganizing the railroads and establishing interlocking directorates. By the turn of the century, when all the lawyers' ink had dried, six railroads controlled more than 96 percent of all anthracite coal lands. Coal prices, production levels, wages, and working conditions in hard coal were all determined in a few corporate offices located in New York and Philadelphia.[2]

Thus, the anthracite industry bore little resemblance to the bituminous industry, in which there were hundreds of operators, most of them far weaker than the union. In soft coal, operators needed the power of the union to impose some type of discipline over their workers; in hard coal, order and discipline of the workers was complete. It had been established from above. It is not surprising, therefore, that the owners of hard coal were among the most ferocious and calculating opponents of unionization. They did not need the trade agreement. They were not susceptible to Mitchell's rational arguments about its positive impact. Monopoly control made the magnitude of Mitchell's task historic. If Mitchell hoped to organize anthracite workers, he had to accomplish something never before achieved in American labor history. He had to succeed where the Homestead strikers had failed in 1892, where Eugene Debs and the Pullman strikers had failed in 1894. Success in anthracite meant cracking the nut of concentrated capital.

The degree to which the railroad corporations cooperated with each other to dominate their work force could be seen in their encouragement of immigrant labor to the area. Importing thousands of immigrants, mainly from southern and eastern Europe, not only provided an abundance of cheap labor, but also helped to divide the mine workers along ethnic lines. When the new immigrants arrived, many of the older English-speaking mine workers left the area, so that by 1900 well over one-third of all anthracite workers were eastern and southern Europeans.[3] The resulting antagonism between ethnic groups so different in their language, customs, and religion was significant in helping to stymie collective action.

Ethnic differences were aggravated by another aspect of corporate control over the work force. Unlike bituminous mining, in which most underground toilers were skilled miners, anthracite exhibited a more complex occupational structure. Skilled miners worked as contractors and paid the wages of the unskilled "helpers" who assisted them. The division between skilled and unskilled largely fell along ethnic lines, with English-speaking men assuming the skilled positions and recent immigrants serving as helpers. Grievances experienced by the helpers were often directed against those who paid their wages, the skilled miners. In addition to the issue of wages, helpers complained that skilled miners deliberately blocked their entry into skilled positions.[4]

Despite the monopoly control by the railroad corporations and their resistance to unionization, Mitchell decided to forge ahead with an organizational drive in early 1899. An investigation into the current state of affairs of the

UMWA in anthracite could not have impressed him. The halfhearted efforts of the union up to that point had created but ninety locals, very few of which were in good shape, and only one district organization to cover all of anthracite, District 1.[5]

The drive got off to an inauspicious start. He began a correspondence with John Fahy, the most prominent UMWA official in anthracite. Fahy had been a member of the UMWA's national executive board in the mid-1890s, and was president of the anthracite district since 1896. Yet Fahy was something of a maverick. He rarely toured his district, preferring instead to spend his time lobbying for beneficial mining legislation at the state capital. His answer to Mitchell's request to supply the names of men who might serve as organizers was a cryptic and ponderous account of his activities in Harrisburg.[6] If this was the leader of the union in anthracite, Mitchell must have thought, things could not be worse. However, he believed that sending members of his own organizing corps would be a mistake. Anthracite workers "would resent a movement of this kind," he told one national organizer. "Bituminous miners are not sufficiently familiar with conditions surrounding the anthracite mines to enable them to discuss intelligently questions affecting anthracite miners."[7] Mitchell was already learning the basic facts of hard coal.

In the summer of 1899, more bad news from anthracite reached his desk. The news again concerned Fahy, who was engaged in an apparent rebellion against the district and national. In May, Fahy had been defeated for the presidency of District 1, but he refused to acknowledge the new officers and failed to relinquish control of his authority. He had established his own headquarters in Shamokin, far to the south of District 1 headquarters in Scranton. Thus, there was a great deal of confusion among members as to who was actually district president. Most troublesome was Fahy's order to locals in the southern anthracite counties to pay their district and national assessments directly to his Shamokin office. Distressed local leaders asked Mitchell what to do.[8] Fahy excused his mutiny by declaring he was withholding the funds in an effort to coerce Mitchell to send organizers into anthracite, especially the southern field.[9] This was a strange response considering Mitchell's previous attempt to get Fahy's advice on the selection of organizers, and considering Fahy's own neglect of the district.

Fahy's rebellion had to be crushed before the organizing campaign could commence in earnest. By commandeering the per capita tax, Fahy posed a direct challenge to Mitchell's authority and revealed the chaotic state of union affairs in the region. In early August, Mitchell decided to hold a convention of all organized miners in the district, and he indicated his intention to attend in person this meeting slated for August 24 in the city of Wilkes-Barre, in the northern field.[10] The threefold purpose of the meeting was to discredit Fahy, devise a strategy for the organizing drive, and demonstrate the national's sincere intent to succeed in hard coal. Of the three purposes, the one which excited Mitchell most was the ruination of Fahy. Once again demonstrating his love of battling internal opponents, Mitchell likened the coming confrontation to a boxing match. "I presume it will be necessary for me to take a fall out of Fahy," he wrote ex-Vice President Tom W. Davis, "but that matter causes me no loss of sleep as I anticipate being able to put him on his back in the first round."[11]

The Wilkes-Barre convention was successful in all respects. Mitchell's mere presence convinced many that the national, for the first time, was now interested in hard coal. Delegates resolved a long standing bone of contention by agreeing to reorganize the field into three separate districts. Henceforth the southern counties became District 9, the middle counties District 7, and the northern counties District 1. Also, a general scheme for the organizing drive was adopted. In his description of the convention, however, Mitchell focused on his solution to the problem of Fahy. With a great deal of pride Mitchell explained how he had "added materially to my reputation as a fighter." According to Mitchell, Fahy became so vexed at one point he rose from his seat and walked down the aisle toward Mitchell, convincing many delegates he was about to become violent. To Mitchell's amusement, however, "he offered his hand and practically begged for mercy." The defeated Fahy agreed to relinquish all taxes and recognize the authority of elected officers. "I can say without egotism that I gave him the worst turning down that he ever received in his life."[12]

Mitchell would hear no more of John Fahy. Or so he imagined. In October, when the first convention of District 9 was held, the supposedly deceased Fahy was resurrected and elected district president and national organizer. Mitchell flew into a rage. Delegates had certainly demonstrated a great deal of "nerve." "It was bad enough to elect John Fahy President," he fumed, "without also electing him National organizer at our expense." Mitchell even contemplated refusing to pay Fahy's salary as an organizer.[13] Obviously, he had underestimated Fahy's popularity in the southern anthracite field. It was now Mitchell's turn to beg for mercy. In November, he wrote Fahy a polite letter in which he explained his desire to cooperate fully with the district leader in organizing the mine workers. He then asked Fahy's suggestions on hiring organizers.[14] In a matter of weeks, once he came to realize that Fahy did not pose a threat to his authority, and once Fahy accepted Mitchell's sincere interest in organizing anthracite workers, the two formed a working relationship.

The August convention in Wilkes-Barre marked Mitchell's first visit to the anthracite region. He saw for himself the desperate conditions of industrial servitude, and he heard for the first time from the lips of mine workers the failure of past campaigns and their present grievances. Perhaps for the first time he became fully cognizant of the plight of these families. The hardships

anthracite families endured were even more stultifying than those in bituminous towns. Mean annual earnings of about $375 were not enough to sustain a
family, forcing women and children to seek employment. The number of
working days averaged only 190 a year.[15] In comparison to bituminous communities, the accident rates and death tolls were significantly higher, the system of company housing and company stores more rampant, and child labor
more common. Coal companies often controlled local politics and enforced
law and order through the infamous Coal and Iron Police.

Mitchell returned to Indianapolis with an even stronger conviction to
organize hard coal.[16] He flooded the field with organizers, he later explained,
"in order to rouse from their lethargy the thoroughly subdued workers . . . to
revive their hopes and rekindle in their hearts the spirit of resistance."[17] And
he confided to ex-Vice President Davis as early as September 1899 he was
"seriously contemplating a general movement in the Anthracite region." He
wanted the strike to begin in October, when demand for hard coal would reach
a peak. Fahy dissuaded him for the moment by suggesting that any strike must
wait until the membership had grown and depleted treasuries rebuilt.[18] It was
clear, however, that Mitchell was determined to organize the area and that he
understood a strike involving the entire region would probably be necessary to
achieve results.

If he had developed a true personal sympathy for hard coal miners, he certainly did not yet understand them. His reference to "thoroughly subdued
workers" was far from an accurate description. Indeed, in 1899 hard coal miners, like soft coal miners in 1897, were impatient for a showdown against their
employers. Numerous local strikes underscored a rising tide of rank-and-file
militancy. In March and April 1899, strikes involving more than 10,000 workers occurred at the District 1 towns of Nanticoke, Duryea, and Pittston. Local
strikes were often against the wishes of district officials and organizers who
hoped to preserve the union's strength. Mitchell himself was critical of the
Nanticoke strikers, stating he "would have preferred that the miners endured
for some time longer before engaging in a strike." The success of the eight-
month Nanticoke strike in securing a wage increase and other concessions,
however, certainly heightened enthusiasm for the UMWA throughout the
region.[19] The success of the Nanticoke strike also emboldened the leaders of
District 1. After a special convention held in late December 1899, district leaders invited operators to attend a joint conference on January 9, 1900. Mitchell
thought the idea premature. One local strike victory in one anthracite district
would not force union recognition from the railroad corporations. "I fear very
much that they (the operators) will either decline or ignore any invitation until
the entire Anthracite region is prepared to move together." As he predicted, the
operators ignored the invitation. District 1 leaders then petitioned Mitchell and
the executive board to inaugurate a strike throughout the anthracite field.[20]

At the national convention in January 1900, Mitchell presented a roseate view of the previous year's organizing drive. Union growth in the region had been "almost phenomenal." And while the drive had been expensive and laborious, the supposedly unorganizable anthracite workers were starting to "realize the disadvantage and folly of isolation" and would soon join bituminous miners in the "onward march toward the realization of their hopes and the consummation of their aspirations."[21] His assessment obscured reality. Membership in anthracite, which had been negligble one year before, now approached 9,000. This was significant, but hardly remarkable considering the expense and energy of the effort. Moreover, not all districts grew at the same rate. District 1 membership stood at more than 7,000, while District 7 had only 341 members. The high figure for the northern field suggested to many that UMWA organizers were less important than the recent Nanticoke victory. And while 9,000 members represented growth, it was far less than necessary to win concessions.[22] Delegates then pledged to anthracite workers the moral support of the organization "should the operators persevere in their defiant and haughty attitude and refuse to meet their employees in joint conference." A section in the original resolution calling for the financial support of the organization had been deleted, however, suggesting that a majority of the delegates were not prepared to shoulder a strike when so few were organized outside District 1.[23] Mitchell may have been preparing for a strike in anthracite, but others in the union were far more cautious.

At the February 1900 session of the national executive board, Mitchell addressed the petition of District 1 for a region-wide strike. The presidents of the other two anthracite districts were summoned to this meeting to express their views on the matter. Most intriguing about this meeting was the fact that Mitchell was more enthusiastic about the possibility of a strike than either of these district presidents. Benjamin James, a national board member who spoke for District 7, opined that less than 10 percent of the collieries in his district would walk out. Too few of the mine workers in his district were union members for a strike to succeed. "The time is coming when we shall have to inaugurate a strike," James concluded, "but the time is not now; we should have more in the organization." District 9 president Fahy was even less inclined toward strike action. With so few men in the union, he said, a strike "would be futile, and jeopardize the organization we have." After listening to these comments, Mitchell understood that a strike at the present time was impossible. While the union constitution gave him considerable power, he realized "it would be the height of folly for this Board to act favorably on the application" of District 1 with the other two districts opposed.[24]

Mitchell then tried to impress upon James and Fahy that, despite the weak organization of their districts, a region-wide strike was going to take place in the near future. He favored a joint conference involving officers and delegates from all three districts, at which the men would draw up a list of demands and invite the operators to meet with them. "If they fail," he said in no uncertain terms, "a strike (will) be inaugurated at the proper time." As to the dearth of members in Districts 7 and 9, he countered with the argument that "strike sentiment often carries unorganized men with it." He concluded his remarks with the prediction that "if we get everybody working together, I believe it possible to inaugurate a strike that will sweep the district."[25] His prediction would prove uncannily accurate.

Also at the board meeting, he proposed a method to boost organizing throughout the region. If organizers could not reach every pit, every community, then the union should try circulars. "I am a firm believer in circulars," he told the board. "A circular from the National reaches more men than all the organizers we can employ." He suggested circulars be sent each month. This was added proof he was much more aggressive than leaders in Districts 7 and 9 in his determination to make a move in anthracite.

Operators in District 1 did not sit idly by while their mines were organized. According to T. D. Nicholls, district president, some of the collieries had announced wage reductions in a deliberate effort to spark local strikes. "I believe that the companies are trying to involve us in small strikes, and break our strength before we get ready to move together," he complained to Mitchell. Operator policy was effective. Numerous local, uncoordinated walk outs, many without the approval of the district officers, rocked the district in the spring of 1900. The result was discord and frustration. When the district counseled against strikes and refused to support them, the rank and file began to question the union's worth. The only solution to the problem, Nicholls wrote, was for Mitchell to call a convention of all three districts "to consider the advisability of a general move, asking the operators of the entire region to meet with us in a Joint Convention giving them to understand that in the event of their refusal that a strike will be inaugurated."[26]

Again District 1 was pushing for positive action, and again the other anthracite districts were hesitant. Fahy of District 9 counseled caution. He believed it wrongheaded to call a tri-district convention at the present time. With only a handful of the men organized, few delegates would attend the convention, which "would become but a laughing stock." Were this to occur, mine workers in and out of the union would become discouraged, while operators would be encouraged to blacklist union members. In a particularly revealing paragraph, Fahy then offered his opinion on why so few anthracite mine workers joined and remained in the union. He believed it a matter of "childishness." "It seems strange that in such matters coal workers talk and act so much like children, but they still do," he confided, "and it seems to me that if it were not for this, what I might call childishness among them, that today our organization would have twice as many members."[27] Fahy did not stop to consider why mine workers would suffer the threat of blacklisting and eviction from their homes to join a union that refused to move against their employers.

Mitchell held his own unflattering perceptions of the rank and file in hard coal, although he was more apt to refer to them as "cattle" rather than "children."[28] Nevertheless he considered Fahy's position absurd. The organizing drive had achieved its success, perhaps not in terms of membership growth outside District 1, but in terms of creating a martial spirit among the men. Local strikes were expressions of that spirit. Militancy, however, was a fleeting emotion. It would soon dissipate unless tangible rewards were secured. Militancy must be used to force concessions from the railroad companies; it could be used as a threat, but if the threat failed, the union must be prepared to strike. Although Mitchell did not respond to Fahy directly, less than two weeks later he sent two national board members to anthracite to coordinate activities. Obviously he had made up his mind that the time to act had come. "From this time on," he wrote, "we intend to center as much of our force in the Anthracite region as we can spare from other Districts, preparing for our fall movement." The force of Mitchell's conviction was demonstrated by his plan to get Tom L. Lewis out of the way so that he would not obstruct the major undertaking in hard coal. Lewis was ordered to assist Pat Dolan in troubles bedeviling him in the Pittsburgh district. "God bless them," Mitchell remarked with more than a little sarcasm at the thought of his two rivals joining hands.[29]

More than mine worker militancy motivated Mitchell to initiate a move in hard coal in the first half of 1900. The political situation also favored action. 1900 was a presidential election year. Ohio Senator Mark Hanna, chairman of the National Committee of the Republican party and the leading force behind the reelection bid of President William McKinley, had strong ties to the UMWA and kept close tabs on their activities. In 1900 Hanna was concerned with more than the voting power of the nation's largest union. The effectiveness of the Republican party's theme of the "full dinner pail" hinged on continued economic prosperity. Uninterrupted production, high profits, and high wages would keep McKinley in the White House. Thus to ensure prosperity, massive outbreaks of labor unrest had to avoided. By March 1900, Mitchell had received word from the National Committee of the Republican party that a major strike might jeopardize McKinley's chances. "From information reaching us some time ago," he confided to his friend Ryan, "we learned that the Republican administration were (*sic*) very desirous of having all labor disputes settled before the campaign opens, and particularly in the mining regions."[30]

To his great credit, Mitchell had the savvy to recognize the opportunity before him. If anthracite workers were prepared to strike in unison, if 150,000 miners were ready to to walk out and create a fuel shortage, then Hanna and the Republicans would be forced to intervene and apply political pressure on the railroad corporations to grant concessions. The Republicans' need to curtail strikes played into Mitchell's hands. Reflecting on events in hard coal two years later, Mitchell was frank about the political opportunism he displayed in 1900. "We cared nothing for one party or another," he said matter of factly. "It made no difference to us who won or lost." If the Republicans required labor peace, the UMWA should take advantage. "If the political organizations of this country are in trouble, and the coal miners can benefit by their trouble, I am willing to see the coal miners benefit, even if the political organizations suffer."[31] At just thirty years old, he was learning the art of economic and political warfare at the highest level. The events in anthracite in 1900 would prove just how adept a general he was.

On July 17, he issued a circular call for a convention of Districts 1, 7, and 9 to meet August 13 in Hazleton, Pennsylvania. The stated purposes of the convention was to draw up a list of demands and to arrange a joint convention of both mine workers and operators. To inspire interest in the convention, the circular noted that organized bituminous miners had won increases from 25 to 50 percent over the last two years. In addition to wages, the convention would also address the need to abolish the "infamous system of dockage" and the long ton.[32] While Fahy and others believed few would attend this convention and that nothing positive would result, Mitchell was convinced that the August 13 meeting would not only be "the most important convention ever held" in anthracite, but that it also would lead eventually to a strike call. "Unless things turn out different from my anticipations," he told his lawyer friend in Spring Valley, "within the next month there will be a movement made in mining affairs which will startle the country."[33]

As announced, at the conclusion of the tri-district convention, delegates issued a circular inviting operators to meet UMWA officials on August 27 in Hazleton to consider grievances.[34] The operators, as expected, refused to respond. Delegates then reconvened on August 29, drafted a list of demands, and petitioned the national executive board to initiate a strike on Monday, September 10. Mitchell and the board did not respond to the petition until September 8, when the petition to strike was denied. On that same day, however, Mitchell, Lewis, and Wilson wrote an open letter to the mine workers stating that if they could "restrain themselves" and "hold themselves in readiness," the board would call a strike for September 17.[35]

Mitchell had postponed the strike one week because he was then engaged in secret negotiations. Having demonstrated the resolve of the mine workers to walk off the job, he was hoping that Hanna's influence would bring the operators to heel before inaugurating a strike of such magnitude and expense. Instead, he received his first taste of the intransigence of the railroad presidents. Hanna did in fact apply pressure on the railroad men, but he failed to arrange an interview between Mitchell and the railroad chiefs. Probably on Hanna's suggestion, Mitchell traveled to New York anyway. His education began after he arrived. Despite Hanna's assistance, Mitchell was not permitted entry to the corporate offices of the railroad chiefs. Mitchell later recalled what transpired next:

> Finally I was told there was a man at the Astor House (Hotel) who was connected with the railways who would see me. They did not even give me his name, simply gave me the number of the room where I could see him. I went to the room designated and met the man. I told him I had been sent there to meet a representative of the Erie Railroad. He asked me who I was. I told him, and he said he expected to see an old man. I told him all about the troubles here, told him the men were not receiving proper wages and that they were not working under proper conditions, and that they were threatening to strike if they did not receive them. He laughed and said we could not call a strike; that our organization was not strong enough, and that the Anthracite miners were satisfied with their conditions. This man turned out to be the Vice-President of the Erie Railroad. He refused to help me to get an interview with his superiors.[36]

Mitchell returned to Indianapolis dejected but wiser. He now had a clearer notion of how determined anthracite operators were to maintain complete control over their work force. But if the remarks of Erie's vice president were any indication, Mitchell now also understood that the operators were unprepared for a strike. On September 12, Mitchell and Secretary-Treasurer Wilson sent identical telegrams to the presidents of the major anthracite railroads requesting that the "whole question of wages and conditions in the Anthracite coal fields be submitted to arbitration." Operators were requested to respond by the end of the day.[37] When the operators failed to respond, the call was issued by the national executive board for the strike to begin on Monday, September 17.

Mitchell's public relations campaign to elicit public sympathy began even before the strike started. On September 13, he and Wilson issued a circular to the public explaining why the strike was necessary. "We have done all that honorable men can do to avoid this conflict," Mitchell told his audience. "The great Jehovah knows and understands the rectitude of our purpose." By placing the blame squarely on the shoulders of the operators, he was then able to appeal to the American people to assist the mine workers and sustain them in the "hour of trial."[38] The strike of 1900 was about to begin.

"Congratulations, old man," Fahy gushed in a letter to Mitchell on the second day of the strike, "she's a beaut (*sic*), and all it needs is to continue for a short while as it has been and then as sure as the stars shine above tonight I feel we're a winner, and then O Lord! won't we shout and jubilate."[39] Fahy, who had consistently opposed the strike and had predicted its early doom, was not alone in his amazement at the response to the strike call. Operators were also stunned. While exact figures will never be known, Mitchell estimated that on the first day between 100,000 and 112,000 of the 142,500 mine workers refrained from work. He later revised that estimate and suggested between 80,000 and 100,000 miners struck on the first day.[40] Within two weeks the anthracite fields had virtually shut down.

Mitchell left Chris Evans, longtime coal union leader, in charge of UMWA affairs in Indianapolis, and established strike headquarters at the Valley Hotel in Hazleton. He brought several members of the office staff with him, including his personal secretary, Elizabeth Morris. The Valley Hotel was not known for luxury. Mitchell once jested to a reporter that the proprietor was "up in arms" because the reporter had dubbed the hotel a "second class hostelry" and had criticized the bill of fare. Morris complained that even with the unseasonably cold weather Pennsylvania was then experiencing, the proprietor refused to light a fire. "The hotel is as cold as a barn," she told the editor of the union journal, "and I work all day with my coat on."[41]

Mitchell had little time to complain about his accommodations, for his time was consumed by the onerous demands of managing a strike of such magnitude. And it was his unparalleled success as a strike leader in 1900 that transformed him into a truly national figure. The anthracite strike of 1900 made Mitchell second only to Gompers as the best known labor leader in America. The young man proved superlative in all aspects of strike leadership: negotiations, handling the press, avoiding violence, winning public support, forging community ties, and maintaining morale among the strikers. At all times, Mitchell appeared in complete control of the forces he had unleashed, while his quiet resolve and readiness to negotiate won him respect and admiration from friends and foes alike.

Throughout the course of the strike, coal operators charged Mitchell with having stirred up a contented labor force, with exploiting the mine workers to quench his own thirst for power, with being a dictator in the strike field. To this last charge Mitchell pleaded guilty. As in all his union work, he believed that in this strike there were very few associates upon whom he could rely. While he considered his official colleagues to be "earnest and honest," some lacked experience and others were devoid of "cool deliberate judgment." Thus, against his own wishes, "I have been forced into the position of being almost a dictator, or autocrat, in this field."[42] He found that the anthracite men knew nothing about unionism, and the bituminous men he brought with him failed to assume responsibility. "The whole thing is forced on to my shoulders," he lamented.[43]

Adding to his oppressive burden was his belief that the mine workers in hard coal were a particularly volatile lot prone to irrational behavior. Never one to praise the virtues of the proletariat, Mitchell described the largely ethnic work force in hard coal as even less sufferable than soft coal miners. Confiding in his friend Billy Ryan, he wrote: "Of course, these miners are not like the men we know in the West; they remind me very much of a drove of cattle, ready to stampede when the least expected. In our meetings they are so impressionable that they are swayed from one side to the other in accordance with the force or eloquence of the speaker."[44] These were strange words indeed from a man soon to be all but deified by these "cattle." His harsh assessment of the anthracite mine workers stemmed in part from his anti-foreign views, which were quite ugly. When violence erupted at Shenandoah, he privately blamed the Hungarians, telling his secretary that Hungarians were "hard to control, and in the habit . . . of throwing rocks every time a flag is raised, or a holiday comes along."[45]

Needless to say, Mitchell never uttered such ethnic slurs in public. Indeed, throughout the organizing drive and strike, he proved remarkably sensitive to ethnic concerns. The UMWA under Mitchell was one of the few unions of the time that actively sought to enlist immigrants from southern and eastern Europe.[46] He overcame the language barrier by hiring organizers conversant in the various tongues. He demonstrated his concern for the welfare of the various nationalities by visiting many of their enclaves in person. And he showed respect for their institutions by establishing close ties to their religious leaders, especially Bishop Michael Hoban of Scranton.[47] These actions made him immensely popular among the immigrants and helped ensure their participation in the strike, but his personal prejudices meant that the large number of immigrants would remain a constant source of worry.

In addition to subordinates he did not trust with responsibility and a rank and file unschooled in responsible unionism, Mitchell felt other types of pressure during the strike. Newspapers that were owned or controlled by the operators made him a target of numerous personal attacks, hoping to destroy the confidence of the men in their leader. The relentless vilification of one's character might be easily handled by some men, "but you, knowing that I am naturally sensitive, can realize that false allegations, coming from sources that have the outward appearance of responsibility, do not rest lightly upon me."[48] Operators also hired detectives who hounded him day and night. "I cannot even steal out of my room without being shadowed by detectives, who seem to have a peculiar desire to know what I am doing," he moaned.[49]

In the face of such pressure, and of the grueling schedule of strike meetings and negotiations and press conferences, it was not surprising that Mitchell looked forward to the conclusion of the strike. After just one week, he declared he needed a vacation. Just two weeks after the start of the strike, the problem of "extreme nervousness," which had left him in the care of a physician in March 1900, began to resurface. "It is needless to say that I shall be happy indeed, when the strike is over. The nervous strain under which I am laboring is fearful, and if continued will unquestionably undermine one's health."[50]

If the strike was a monumental personal burden for Mitchell, his spirits were buoyed by the admiration strikers and their families heaped upon him. While he had no love of the rank and file, he was moved by the affection they showed in return. Within a few weeks, he was already becoming the object of hero worship to the working people of the anthracite region. Exactly why this happened is a matter of conjecture. Some observers pointed to his success in bituminous coal, which held out the promise that he would bring that success with him. Others focused on his appearance and personality. To English-speaking miners, he was regarded as a brother, one of their own kind, and, to the foreign-born, his somber and thoughtful visage, combined with his long western miner's coat and high collar, reminded them of one of their own priests. Still other observers pointed to his message of unity, his public declarations that miners must forego ethnic antagonisms and join hands in the struggle. He was often credited with having uttered, "The coal you dig isn't Slavish or Polish or Irish coal, it's coal."[51]

While these factors were certainly noteworthy, they tend to mystify Mitchell's popularity. These factors suggest there was something peculiar in the makeup of working people in the anthracite region that made them especially prone to hero worship, or that there was something especially remarkable about Mitchell which made the rank and file tremble in awe. Nothing could be further from the truth. The admiration for Mitchell was neither mysterious nor unique. On the contrary, the strikers quite naturally looked to him, as strike leader and union president, as the champion of their demands and hopes for a better life. He had not created strike sentiment. He simply gave organization and direction to their protest through the strike and the union. Other strike leaders received the same adulation. John Siney, Dan McLaughlin, Chris Evans, William B. Wilson, and Mother Jones all had received hero treatment for their leadership of coal strikes.

Whatever the reason for his popularity, Mitchell himself was moved by the reception he received. He was constantly on the go, visiting at least two meetings a day while in the strike area, and everywhere he went the response was the same. "There has been a constant ovation ever since I set foot in the region," he exclaimed. "All the large meetings and parades I have attended have been the greatest turnouts in the history of the towns where they have taken place."[52] By the end of the strike, he was aware that the strikers and their families had come to regard him as a "Moses whose (*sic*) has come to deliver them from their oppressors."[53] The hoopla and celebration attending the many picnics and parades honoring Mitchell was a source not only of pride but also of amusement for the boy president. One humorous incident involved Elizabeth Morris, who usually sat next to Mitchell in the open carriage during parades. "An over enthusiastic admirer" ran toward the carriage and, amidst thousands of spectators, shouted at the top of his voice, "Hurrah for Mitchell and Mother Jones!," mistaking Morris for the angel of the miners. This embarrassed Morris, making her feel "like thirty cents." The "villain" persisted, racing down the street to meet the carriage on every corner, greeting them with the same cry. When the parade ended at the baseball park where Mitchell was to speak, the first man to greet them was the "same mysterious fellow," who pushed forward in the hope of shaking the hand of Mother Jones. Mitchell at last informed the admirer that he was mistaken, and the man turned away, obviously disappointed, muttering "Well, I did the best I could."[54]

Mitchell understood, however, that the applause he heard today would turn to jeers tomorrow if the strike went badly. His awareness of the fleeting nature of a labor leader's celebrity helped to temper his ego. "The labor movement is not like any other movement in this world," he told his brother. "For a time labor leaders are hailed as heroes, received with cheers and applause and their path is, figuratively speaking, strewn with roses." A lost strike would soon strip leaders of their hero status. If workers believed their interests had been betrayed, labor leaders would find that "instead of being idolized they are stigmatized; instead of being glorified they are crucified."[55]

The accolades and enthusiasm of the mine workers and their families helped sustain Mitchell's spirits during the strike. So, too, did the sincere sympathy he felt for the breaker boys. Mitchell was not a man easily given to sentimentality. Having experienced deprivation as a youth and having witnessed so much suffering in his organizing work, he had become somewhat inured to poverty. Yet when he observed the breaker boys he was moved to pity. The towering breaker was the most important building at a hard coal mine. After coal had been brought from below by mine car, it was tipped to dump the coal at the top of the breaker where it passed through revolving cylinders that crushed and separated the coal into various sizes. Then the coal was forced downwards through a series of chutes, where breaker boys picked out slate and other refuse. Boys as young as eight worked ten hours a day, six days a week in an atmosphere of dense coal dust and deafening noise. The foreman's club or leather switch enforced work discipline.[56] These boys, who had been denied their childhood for the sake of corporate profit, represented one of the most glaring expressions of capitalist exploitation. And perhaps because they reminded him of his own misery as a youth, Mitchell was quite touched by their plight. In a letter to ex-Vice President Davis, he wrote:

> I have never seen anything which appealed so much to my sympathies as the little breaker boys in the Anthracite region; at eight or ten years of age they

seem as serious and thoughtful as men; and in our meetings they listen as attentively as though they understood the industrial question. In their parades they carry banners saying "Give our fathers justice and we can go to school"; and as they pass my carriage they continually yell, at the top of their voices, "What's the matter with Mitchell? He's all right. Who's all right? Mitchell!"[57]

Mitchell's actions as strike leader must therefore be measured against this backdrop of pressure, applause, and emotion.

Mitchell likened the strike to a military engagement, with one major exception: public opinion. The outcome of a strike, unlike the outcome of a battle, depended on more than strength and skillful maneuvers. A strike's resolution also hinged upon the ability of each side to cultivate public sympathy. Public opinion was a powerful voice in determining victory or defeat. If a union could plead its case effectively in the public forum and conduct the strike lawfully and peacefully, then that union stood a sound chance of forcing the employer to the bargaining table. He thoroughly understood the important role of the public, and he therefore utilized the press to an extent never before seen in American labor history.

He had the advantage of a generally friendly press from the outset of the strike. His willingness to arbitrate and the shocking poverty of the hard coal towns gained him the sympathy of most papers, even some of the most conservative ones across the nation.[58] Mitchell must be credited, however, with his relatively sophisticated understanding of how to maintain the press's friendliness. Within a remarkably short time, he educated himself on the proper handling of reporters. He recognized which wire services were inaccurate and tried to avoid them. He learned to issue his press releases early enough for the wire services to distribute copies to affiliated newspapers before deadlines. He kept his press releases short so they were less likely to be butchered and distorted when presented in the papers. He seldom refused an interview, even when he had nothing new to report. And he frequently called the press's attention to letters offering moral and financial support.[59]

Not all press coverage was friendly. The railroad corporations were also adept at manipulating the press, and they worked hard to assassinate Mitchell's character and make that the focus of attention. To counter these efforts, Mitchell tried to obtain testimonials for publication from elites who knew him intimately. His success in this regard was limited. For instance, Charles J. Devlin, a major soft coal operator, had written a letter on Mitchell's behalf to a hard coal operator in late August in an effort to arrange a conference between the two men. The letter was highly laudatory, praising Mitchell as "a very conservative man in every way, strictly honest." Mitchell received a copy of this letter, and he wanted to offer it to the press for publication. Devlin refused, citing "business reasons."[60] Another instance involved Father John F. Power of the Immaculate Conception church in Spring Valley. Power, it will be remembered, had been a guiding influence in Mitchell's youth. Thus, when unfriendly papers referred to Mitchell's "shady" public activities in Spring Valley, Mitchell asked Power to write a letter for publication giving his impressions of Mitchell as a private and public man. Power evidently misunderstood the instructions, for while his letter expressed indignation at the "lying attacks" made on Mitchell's good name, it made almost no reference to Mitchell's early career and was therefore unsuitable.[61]

Keeping the strike peaceful was the key to maintaining the support of the press and public. And to Mitchell's amazement, the "cattle" did not "stampede" in large numbers very often. At the 1901 UMWA convention, he claimed there had been an absolute absence of lawlessness during the strike.[62] That observation was absurd; disturbances occurred on an almost daily basis. Yet, there was little blood spilled, and Mitchell successfully convinced reporters that the infamous coal and iron police had incited much of the violence which did take place. The press therefore focused on the peaceful nature of the strike and Mitchell's claim that the strike was singularly free of violence went unchallenged.[63]

The need to refrain from violence even took precedence over the need to keep the men from returning to work. Traditionally, miners organized marches of strikers, called "raids," to travel from mine to mine to ensure complete compliance with the strike order. Mother Jones, who was seventy years old in 1900 and probably the union's most militant organizer, was placed in charge of these raids. Raids were of questionable legality, and Mitchell never publicly sanctioned them. When informed by police that force would be used to prohibit raids, Mitchell, fearing outbreaks of violence, immediately halted the practice.[64]

The one major outbreak of violence that did occur came early in the strike at Shenandoah. The large immigrant community at Shenandoah responded quickly to the strike call, but many of the English-speaking residents continued to work under police protection. On September 21, several hundred strikers went to the collieries and drove the scabs out. When the sheriff and his deputies tried to escort the scabs to safety, the immigrant strikers shelled them with rocks and beer bottles. The besieged police opened fire, killing one and seriously wounding seven others.[65] Mitchell immediately condemned the killing and absolved the strikers of any blame. In his press statement, he said the shooting was "entirely uncalled for, inasmuch as the strikers had not injured a single member of the sheriff's posse." The incident was a clear illustration of "the ruthless disregard the sheriff and his deputies have for the lives of persons."[66] Governor George Stone disagreed. He ordered 2,200 troops of the state militia under the command of General William Gobin to restore order in the community. Mitchell, of course, publicly protested this action. He believed the strikers were "fully impressed with the necessity of observing the law and conducting themselves in a peaceful manner at all times," and he criticized the governor for acting "inconsiderately and without a thorough investigation."[67] Privately, Mitchell complained that the strikers needed to remain "steady and patient" to gain victory.[68]

In addition to refraining from violence, another key to maintaining the support of the press and public was to express a continued willingness to arbitrate. By standing ever ready to arbitrate the dispute, he was quite successful in presenting himself as eminently fair and depicting the railroad presidents as underhanded and greedy. "I, speaking for the 130,000 mine workers this day on strike, recognize these railroads as our real enemies," he declared at a press conference four days after the start of the strike, "and name their Presidents as the men responsible for refusal to arbitrate or even confer upon the differences which have grown up. . . . " Even though the railroad chiefs had refused to acknowledge every "cordial invitation" to discuss the issues of the strike, he was still prepared to confer at any time. "It ought to go without saying, at this late date, that I am a staunch advocate of the principle of arbitration," he continued. He argued that the ideal solution would be one along the lines of the trade agreement established in soft coal. The interstate conference was the best method to avoid strikes and turmoil and to ensure a proper distribution of the profits of industry. Yet, he did not insist on a trade agreement. Nor did he insist on any form of union recognition. If the railroad presidents "meet committees of their own employees and come to a peaceful agreement," he pledged not to make union recognition an issue.[69] He thus appeared reasonable, and the operators, who continued to refuse arbitration, appeared intransigent.[70]

In truth, Mitchell had little desire to arbitrate the issue. As a public relations ploy, arbitration was useful, but the outcome of arbitration was too risky. He was banking on the operators' unwillingness to accept his offer. One independent operator, however, tried to call Mitchell's bluff. Since 1884, employees at G. B. Markle and Company, an independent firm in District 7, had been forced to sign a "no strike" contract as a condition of employment. The contract stipulated that employees would not join a union and that all labor disputes would be submitted to an umpire for binding arbitration. On September 19, when Markle's 2,400 employees held a meeting at the Jeddo school house to consider joining the strike, John Markle, manager of the firm, attended the meeting and reminded the men of the arbitration clause. At Markle's request, Father Edward Phillips of St. Gabriel's church in Hazleton also addressed the meeting and counseled the men to honor their contracts and vote against the strike. Phillips also announced that Archbishop Patrick Ryan of Philadelphia was willing to serve as arbitrator. This was one firm, then, that seemed to offer what Mitchell demanded. Markle was willing to meet with representatives of his workers and submit the issues in dispute to an impartial hearing. If mine workers rejected arbitration, the operators would win an important propaganda victory.

Mitchell also attended the September 19 meeting. His speech was not an emotional plea designed to stir the men, but rather a reasoned argument to show why arbitration in this instance should not be accepted. He had to tread lightly, for the public could not be expected to recognize immediately the difference between this arbitration plan and the one supported by Mitchell. Moreover, while it was relatively easy to question the morality of the Morgan and Vanderbilt interests, in the Markle situation he was dealing with a firm that claimed a close personal relationship with its employees. His argument was twofold. First, employees must not be bound by ironclad contracts they had been forced to sign as a condition of employment. Such "yellow dog" agreements were violations of the freedom of contract and need not be respected. Second, Mitchell contended that arbitration, to be effective, must cover the entire region. It simply would not work on a firm by firm basis. Even if arbitration in the Markle case was impartial, even if a board of arbitration granted Markle's employees all they desired, "that award could be lived up to by Markle only so long as the strike continued elsewhere." Wages and other concessions won by Markle's employees would not endure long unless the same wages prevailed throughout the region. To be effective, arbitration must include the railroad corporations who controlled production and conditions of labor.[71]

It is a rare occurrence when the force of one's argument in a debate creates a change of attitude in one's opponent. Yet Mitchell's pitch led Father Phillips to rethink his position. "The logic of his position impressed me so forcibly and so favorably on reflection," Phillips later recalled, "I acknowledged the superiority of Mr. Mitchell's judgment and tactics . . . and professed absolute confidence in the general and his plans." The very next day, at the suggestion of Phillips, Mitchell and the priest traveled to Philadelphia to confer with Archbishop Ryan. After this meeting, Phillips issued a press statement informing Markle's workers he now advised "the adoption of Mr. Mitchell's plans." Markle's employees then joined the strike.[72]

The Markle affair represented an important propaganda victory for Mitchell. By defining the type of arbitration that was acceptable, he was able to maintain the support of the press and public. By persuading Phillips to accept his position, he had won for himself and the union the friendship of a powerful priest.[73] And he had demonstrated to all anthracite workers that he was a wise general able to keep the strike intact. His victory in the affair was so complete that even John Markle himself was forced to admit that "The Laborers . . . believed he could accomplish anything."[74]

The tie up was all but complete. The vast majority of workers held firm and coal production was negligible. Violence had been avoided to a remarkable extent and the union was winning the propaganda war. The railroad presidents, however, maintained their obstinate stance, declaring they would never deal with Mitchell and the UMWA. It looked to outside observers as though this strike might be of long duration since each side showed equal resolution. But Mitchell was confident of victory from an early date. After just one week of the strike, Mitchell privately declared "we are sure to win."[75]

His confidence stemmed from the political situation surrounding the presidential election of 1900. As stated earlier, his awareness that the Republican party desired labor peace had been a major factor in his decision to call the strike. Once the strike started, he knew that Hanna and the Republicans would soon apply fierce pressure on the railroad presidents to grant concessions before the strike grew violent and made a mockery of their "full dinner pail" campaign.

His strategy worked to perfection. Throughout the strike, press reports and editorials charged the walk out was politically motivated. One New York paper asserted it was "an established fact" that the strike was started and supported by "conspirators" who wished to secure the election of William Jennings Bryan, the Democratic candidate.[76] Another press report stated Mitchell had planned the strike in Indianapolis with the Democratic mayor of that city and members of the Democratic National Committee. On several occasions, Mitchell made strong public denials of these reports. He responded to the second story in dramatic fashion, declaring that "any man who would inaugurate a strike in the interest of any political organization would be deserving of the severest punishment which could be meted out to him."[77]

Indeed, Mitchell's motives were not overtly political. He did not inaugurate the strike in the interests of the Democratic party, nor did he hope to injure the Republican campaign. He simply hoped to exploit the political situation; he simply hoped to pressure Hanna and the Republicans into the role of peacemakers. And his calculations proved accurate. From the very beginning of the strike, Hanna goaded the coal barons to grant concessions and end the strike. Any prolonged strike, he warned, would result in a Democratic victory that would spell disaster for the propertied interests of the nation.

Hanna and Mitchell were not friends at this time. They had met on several occasions and each was impressed by the other, but there was little direct contact between them throughout the negotiations. While Mitchell and Hanna spoke on the telephone several times during the strike,[78] the major path of communication between the union president and the Ohio senator went through Daniel J. Keefe, president of the International Longshoreman's Association (ILA). Keefe and Hanna were close associates. Keefe's union had a trade agreement with Hanna's shipping interests in the Great Lakes and both men were members of the Chicago Civic Federation. From Keefe, Mitchell learned he had Hanna's respect and trust. Hanna felt confident and satisfied, according to Keefe, "that there was one man connected with the Miners who could not be juggled with in any manner and that man was John Mitchell."[79]

One week after the start of the strike, Mitchell provided Hanna, through Keefe, with an outline of the terms he would accept for a settlement. First, he desired a conference between the operators and himself. If this proved untenable, he would accept a conference between the operators and their own workers, but only if these meetings were held in the same city on the same day so that he could direct matters behind the scenes. Second, he listed "the grievances which would have to be remedied": abolition of the company store, reduction in the price of powder, "and an advance on day labor of at least 10 percent."[80] On September 26, Hanna met the railroad presidents in the offices of J. P. Morgan.[81] One of the operators present, George Baer, president of the Reading Railroad, recalled that Hanna presented Mitchell's offer with dire warnings about the future of the nation were it to be rejected. Hanna "insisted that if the strike was not settled it would extend to Ohio, Indiana, and Illinois, and the election of Mr. McKinley and Mr. Roosevelt would be endangered." At the conclusion of the meeting, the operators agreed to advance wages 10 percent.[82]

Mitchell was ambivalent about the results of this meeting. He was pleased that the power of the Republican National Committee had been brought to bear against the railroad presidents and had secured the 10 percent advance. And personally he favored acceptance of the offer, knowing it would "result in a big organization." He despaired, however, that the offer failed to mention how long the advance would remain in effect and that it did not "correct many of the abuses under which the mine workers labor." The offer thus placed him in a difficult position. Mine workers themselves might reject it. He feared that if he brought this settlement to a vote in convention, "a large majority of the miners will favor continuing the strike." This scenario filled Mitchell with dark thoughts. If mine workers rejected the wage advance and held out for a better settlement, Mitchell believed, the "pangs of hunger" already being felt by some strikers would force them to yield. He needed to convince mine workers to accept the proposal. "If they are not guided by my advice I fear that they will be whipped so badly that they will never, at least for years, get together again."[83]

By October 2, three of the leading operators had posted notices of a 10 percent advance and encouraged its employees to resume work.[84] At a mass meeting in Wilkes-Barre, where 25,000 people were expected, Mitchell told the mine workers not to return to work. He was going to call a convention where workers would decide, in democratic fashion, whether or not to accept the wage advance. Even though he instructed his listeners not to allow any single person, not even himself, to decide their destinies, he concluded his speech with a ringing endorsement for acceptance of the wage advance: "Now, my fellow workingmen . . . you cannot reasonably expect to remove and eradicate all the evils, all the injustices that have been heaped upon you for forty long years of no organization, but I do believe that a victory has been gained."[85]

At the same time he began to sell the acceptance of the wage advance to the mine workers, he also applied pressure on Hanna to see if he could obtain a better settlement. He informed Keefe that his organizers had been sent to "feel the pulse of the people," and that mine workers were overwhelmingly opposed to any settlement that did not establish an advance for a fixed period or abolish the company stores. Mitchell would remain true to his word. When all operators posted notices of the wage advance, he would call a convention and try to convince them to accept the terms. However, he could make no promises regarding the outcome of the convention. "Notwithstanding my position with the men," he wrote, "I am almost convinced that they would refuse to accept my advice in a convention." In a veiled political threat to Hanna to continue his pressure on the coal barons, he stated the union would soon have to make public appeals for the financial support of the strikers. Were the public appeal to go out, Mitchell wrote, "politicians of the opposing party would use the cries of distress going up from honest men, women and children who are battling for what they believe to be their rights, to dissipate the prosperity arguments which are made by those favoring the administration."[86]

On October 8, Mitchell sent out an official call for a tri-district convention to be held October 12 at Scranton, where delegates would vote on the operators' offer. In the days before the convention, however, he continued to apply political pressure on Hanna. "The miners believe the operators are handing them a gold brick," he told Keefe. He hinted that if Hanna could do nothing about the price of powder, dockage, and company stores, the senator should at least get operators to give him a wage advance for a specified period of time. "If some delegate in the convention asks me how long this rate of wages is going to prevail I, of course, shall be unable to answer him."[87]

More than eight hundred delegates attended the Scranton convention. In his opening address, Mitchell pointed to the achievements of the strike thus far. In addition to the wage advance, there had been tremendous growth in the power of the union in hard coal, and through the union greater unity in the region. While the union would not be recognized as a result of the strike, the day when recognition would be granted was not too distant. The strength of the union could be seen in the fact that "there can be no resumption of work in the anthracite field until the United Mine Workers of America gives its consent." As Mitchell had predicted, a majority of the delegates disapproved of the operators' offer as it stood. While some wanted to continue the strike until the union was officially recognized, the majority accepted Mitchell's advice and voted for a more moderate position. The delegates resolved not to return to work until all operators agreed to abolish the sliding scale, maintain the wage increase until April 1, 1901, and agree to meet with committees of their employees to settle all outstanding grievances.[88]

Most of the operators soon posted notices agreeing to these demands. Mitchell and union officials then met on October 24 in Hazleton to decide whether to conclude the strike or wait until all operators posted notices. Mitchell was in haste to close affairs for numerous reasons: the expense of the strike; editorial opinion turning against a union that appeared reluctant to call off hostilities; and employees of companies that had already posted notices were becoming anxious. "The Lithuanian people are becoming restless," he declared. Concerning those operators who had not yet posted notices, he was certain they would fall into line. "So many men have left the region since the strike began," he reasoned, "they will have scarcely enough (employees) to run the mines as it is."[89] The following day, therefore, union officials issued the order to all hard coal mine workers to resume work on October 29.[90] The strike of 1900 had ended.

The strike left Mitchell exhausted. He was "almost completely worn out," according to his secretary, and he went home to Spring Valley for a short period of recuperation. Among other ailments, he suffered from a chest cold severe enough to make him believe for a while that he had contracted consumption. Within a few days, however, he was back at union headquarters in Indianapolis. He had hoped to take part of his vacation at this time, perhaps even visiting California, but he found that the success of the strike and the addition of so many new members left him busier than ever.[91] Moreover, he had to prepare for the AFL convention in December and the UMWA convention in January.

The strike of 1900 was of immense historical significance for the anthracite mine workers. For the first time since the Long Strike of 1875 and the mass importation of southern and eastern European labor, the workers demonstrated an ability to overcome regional, ethnic, and skill differences and present an organized front to their employers. Their new found unity, determination, and discipline represented the real victory for mine workers. Their proven ability to act together without violence sent a message to the railroad presidents and union officials who had heretofore considered them incapable of sustained and coordinated strike action. Through their own efforts they had created a greater sense of confidence in their own ability to challenge the complete control of the railroad corporations.

To what extent Mitchell deserves credit for cultivating this unity and determination is conjectural. It is safe to say that Mitchell in many ways helped foster latent solidarity. First, his conviction that anthracite workers could in fact be organized and would strike in unison ran counter to many district officials. Thus, his expressed confidence in the workers themselves helped them develop their own confidence. Second, his special attention to the organization of immigrants helped make them feel an equal part of the struggle. Despite his own anti-foreign prejudices, the effort he made to win the support of the Catholic clergy, and his use of immigrants as organizers, made the immigrants believe he was sincerely concerned about their welfare. Third, his deep concern with the plight of the breaker boys, which became something of a personal crusade, gave mine workers an emotional focal point that helped them bridge all the differences between them. And finally, the hero status accorded to Mitchell himself at the outset of the strike both reflected and inspired camaraderie. At the parades and rallies honoring Mitchell, skilled miners and unskilled helpers, Poles and Irishmen, boys and old men, all stood side by side to hear Mitchell's message of strength through solidarity.

If anthracite workers could rightly declare victory, the railroad presidents could remain smug in defeat. The 10 percent advance had been surrendered, but operators had not been forced to consider any of the grievances regarding methods of payment, working conditions, and company stores. Operators had faced the greatest show of militancy ever to occur in the region and had emerged as they had entered—in complete control over all aspects and conditions of mine work. Despite the intense political pressure exerted on them, the railroad presidents had kept John Mitchell and the UMWA out of their affairs. They had succeeded in their adamant refusal to negotiate with Mitchell or in any way recognize the union. The coal barons rightly regarded Mitchell and the trade agreement as a direct challenge to the entire system of social control they had established in anthracite, and if a 10 percent advance was the price they had to pay to maintain control, they were willing to pay it.

Despite his failure to achieve union recognition, Mitchell could also claim victory for the union. At January 1901 UMWA convention, he boasted that the strike had been "the most remarkable contest between labor and capital in the industrial history of our nation." Remarkable because of the number of strikers, because of the lack of violence, "and last, but not least, because it was the only great contest in which the workers came out entirely and absolutely victorious." The union was now an established force among anthracite mine workers. From the 7,000 District 1 members at the end of 1899, more than 53,000 were members at the conclusion. District 1 became the second largest district in the entire union behind Illinois. District 9 had become the fourth largest. Moreover, Mitchell remained sanguine that the union could achieve true recognition from anthracite operators in the near future without having to resort to another strike. "I feel confident," he told delegates, "that the time is not remote when, if the present policy in regard to that field is continued, harmonious relations will be established between operators and miners."[92]

All three participants—the union, the railroad presidents, and the workers themselves—were thus able to claim victory after the strike. The failure of the strike settlement to address fundamental grievances, and the adamant refusal of the operators to deal with the union, however, made it quite clear that the strike had resolved very little. The peace in anthracite proved fragile.

The most obvious victor in the anthracite strike of 1900 was John Mitchell himself. Within the UMWA, Mitchell now reigned supreme. His successful conduct of the strike crushed the remnants of power wielded by his two leading internal opponents, Tom L. Lewis and Patrick Dolan. Before the strike Mitchell had expressed his desire to run for reelection but was concerned about the "Lewis-Dolan combination."[93] By mid-November, Mitchell, still engaging in the illegal practice of looking at nominations for office, could predict with confidence he would be virtually unchallenged for reelection. Lewis was making a halfhearted bid for the presidency and had received just 3 percent of the nominations. Mitchell concluded Lewis was no longer "a dangerous opponent; although I understand he is corresponding with everybody he knows in America, trying to keep his fences together for Vice-President." Ryan agreed. There might be a handful of "kickers" at the next UMWA convention, Ryan informed Mitchell with his usual wit, "but they will be so lonesome that they will certainly be ashamed of themselves."[94]

Not only had Mitchell silenced his internal union opponents, he won for himself the admiration and friendship of Mark Hanna. Indeed, the strike was more than a conflict between workers and employers; it also had been something of a personal test for Mitchell, a test prepared and administered by the powerful Ohio Senator. Mitchell had started the strike as a political opportunist, exploiting the political situation to the union's advantage, but during negotiations, he demonstrated his appreciation of the broader political ramifications. He quickly came to recognize that Hanna's efforts on the union's behalf carried with it an obligation to toe the Republican line. By October 4, weeks before the strike had concluded, Mitchell revealed his awareness of the price tag on Hanna's intervention. In a letter to Daniel Keefe, he wrote that "For the Senator, regardless of what others may say, I have the highest esteem. He has done all he could . . . and you can assure him, for me, that *I shall be ever vigilant in keeping out of the movement anything that would militate against the success of the interests he represents in this campaign.*"[95] He implicitly understood that he had to keep the strike peaceful and, more importantly, he had to end the strike after Hanna's political pressure had secured a compromise offer from the operators, even if that offer was not acceptable to the majority of the mine workers. Mitchell's ability to control the strikers, to get them to return to work before their grievances had been addressed, to prevent headline-making bloodshed, all helped ensure the labor peace necessary for a Republican presidential victory in the fall. Here was a labor leader that Mark Hanna could trust. Here was a labor leader who acted "responsibly."

Mitchell passed Hanna's test of trustworthiness with flying colors, and the two men quickly established a mutually beneficial relationship. The use of Daniel Keefe as a communication link slowly disappeared as the bond between Mitchell and Hanna became intimate. Mitchell affectionately referred to Hanna as "the Captain," and he frequently corresponded with him and even visited him at his Cleveland home. In the first weeks following the 1900 strike, Mitchell was already making use of his new friend to assist the union. Lingering strikes in the southwest bituminous fields prompted him to travel to Cleveland where he "called upon the Captain in reference to our South-west trouble. He promised me to go to New York and do all he could to bring that matter to a close." True to his word, Hanna not only met with the operators but solved the difficulty to the satisfaction of Mitchell before the year was out.[96] Mitchell also saw in Hanna a veritable mother lode of opportunity to obtain government patronage posts for his friends. When Daniel Keefe informed Mitchell he sought the post of U. S. Commissioner of Labor, Mitchell advised Keefe to get an endorsement from Hanna: "If we cannot land the place we want put in a bid for the chief of the Bureau (of Immigration) at New York City, which pays almost as much and which has considerable patronage to be disposed of. One thing is sure, we must have a good berth."[97] While Hanna's influence could not land this particular office, the Senator's power over government appointments made Mitchell and Keefe drool with anticipation. Lest their excitement make them look foolish, Mitchell cautioned Keefe that it was "good policy to preserve our dignity, and not appear to be tumbling over ourselves in getting the good things."[98] Within a few months, however, Mitchell and Hanna were having frank discussions about patronage jobs. "While in Washington I called upon the Captain," he explained to Keefe, "in fact he sent me an invitation—and had a heart to heart talk with him concerning some of the good things. He told me that he had the District Superintendency of a free postal delivery in view for you; that he told the Postmaster General that you must have it."[99]

The 1900 strike not only earned for Mitchell a powerful political ally, it also transformed the "boy president" into a truly popular national figure. Editorials across the nation praised his conservative generalship, his willingness to compromise, his rational style. Offers asking for commercial endorsements crossed his desk, organizations of all descriptions asked him to give lectures and attach his name to their cause, and one of the leading national magazines, the *Independent*, paid him to publish his account of the strike.[100] Within the labor movement, Mitchell was being touted as the next AFL president. Statements appeared in the Chicago papers that he would be a candidate to replace Gompers at the December 1900 AFL convention. The reports hinted that Senator Hanna was backing his candidacy.[101] Mitchell also was invited to attend the first conference of the National Civic Federation, an organization designed to bring together the most powerful people in the nation. Mitchell, with more than 150,000 miners now under his command, had entered the power elite.

The strike also was a victory for Mitchell in the sense that the limited nature of the settlement did not detract from the prestige accorded him by the hard coal mine workers. He remained their savior, their Moses, and they showered him with gifts and other signs of affection at the conclusion of the strike. Union members in hard coal voted October 29 "Mitchell Day," a holiday in his honor. At the conclusion of the strike he began what he called a "jollification" tour,[102] stopping at numerous towns throughout the region to receive the gifts and accolades of the people. The highlight of the trip was a celebration at Scranton, where thousands of breaker boys paraded through the streets in his honor and presented him with a gold medallion. Mitchell thanked them and, in a show of paternal affection, he explained what the breaker boys meant to him: "They have the bodies and faces of boys but they came to meetings where I spoke and stood as still as the men and listened to every word. I was shocked and amazed . . . as I saw those eager eyes peering at me from eager little faces; the fight had a new meaning for me; I felt that I was fighting for the boys, fighting a battle for innocent childhood."[103] He felt a sincere bond with the breaker boys. When the Illinois district was planning a brief biographical sketch of Mitchell, he wrote that in northeast Pennsylvania he had become known to everyone as "the Breaker Boys' Friend." He was "particularly proud of this title" and wanted it used in the sketch.[104]

At the end of the strike, Mitchell insisted "I am still the same man I was when I came here." The only possible change was that he had "learned to love my people more, and I have been filled with a new inspiration to do something for them if I can."[105] Yet, in terms of the political alliance forged with Hanna and the Republican party, the spectacular growth of the union, his increased control over internal union affairs, and his tremendous popularity among the rank and file, both Mitchell and the UMWA had changed remarkably in the wake of the strike. In some ways, however, Mitchell did remain the same man. When describing the jollification tour to friends and family, he displayed a singular concern for the price of the gifts he received. He provided one of his nieces in California with an inventory of his loot. At the top of the list was a "magnificent" silver loving cup presented by the Elks of Scranton and valued by Mitchell at $325. He also received, among other things, a gold headed cane, a "silver mounted" umbrella, a gold medal, two candelabra, and a gold mounted clock bearing the figure of a woman with a scroll that read "Veni, Vidi, Vici."[106] He gleefully wrote a friend that the aggregate cost of the booty "could not be less than one thousand dollars!"[107]

In terms of avarice, then, Mitchell was the same man. And his preoccupation with wealth quickly transformed his gratitude into greed. Starting in December 1900, he sought to exploit his status in the three anthracite districts by scheming to have the rank and file buy him a home.[108] He pressured the three district presidents and other trusted administration supporters do his dirty work for him. At the annual district conventions, Mitchell's men were to secure passage of special assessments to buy him a house in gratitude for his efforts during the strike. The rank and file certainly were not aware that the house was in fact Mitchell's idea. "Now when you get word that the Boys in 9 *have started* the Ball rolling be *Surprised*," executive board member Fred Dilcher wrote Mitchell on the eve of the District 9 convention. The district convention dutifully passed the assessment, and again Dilcher warned Mitchell to "be Very Much Surprised when you learn of it."[109] George Harris, a national organizer, reported that progress toward the collection of assessments was also being made in District 7. "You are certainly worthy," Harris told Mitchell.[110] In January 1901, Mitchell was already making plans to move his family from Spring Valley to a brand new home in Indianapolis.[111]

A full year passed without much progress, however, and Mitchell was growing impatient. Despite the assurances of Dilcher, he fretted that collecting assessments by itself would never raise sufficient capital. "I would suggest that in addition to having the miners contribute a small amount," he wrote Dilcher, "that committees be selected from each Local Union to wait upon the business men, and give them an opportunity to contribute." Recognizing that soliciting operators and merchants might not be regarded as "the proper thing," he advised Dilcher that the suggestion should be "dropped altogether" if he ran into resistance. But he wanted Dilcher to try this method because housing was so expensive where he wanted to live. Mitchell apparently was having second thoughts about moving his family to Indianapolis. "You know you cannot purchase any kind of a home either in Indianapolis or Chicago (and I think I should prefer it in Chicago) for less than five or six thousand dollars."[112]

At the end of 1901, Mitchell began to rethink the whole house scheme. He read an Associated Press dispatch declaring that at a convention in Pottsville the hard coal miners had decided to present him with a home. He wanted organizer Harris to tell him "candidly" if there had been significant opposition. "Under no circumstance," he informed Harris, "would I accept a gift, no difference how valuable or desirable, unless it came to me from willing donors." He then told Harris if there had been opposition, he would "prefer that the whole matter be dropped."[113] Evidently, there had been opposition at Pottsville. Mother Jones attended that convention and recalled what transpired in her autobiography. She wrote that when the petition for Mitchell's house was being passed around, she spoke against it: "If John Mitchell can't buy a house to suit him for his wife and for his family out of his salary, then I would suggest that he get a job that will give him a salary to buy a $10,000 house." From that time on, Jones remarked, "Mitchell was not friendly to me."[114] Mitchell never received the gift of a home. Nevertheless, the drive for a free house demonstrated not only Mitchell's love of money and his opportunism, but also his willingness to "mine the miners" for personal profit.

If the strike of 1900 did not provide Mitchell with a free house, there were other ways that he could "cash in" on his new found fame. While resting in Spring Valley just days after the strike, he wrote his attorney friend Hawthorne that "I contemplate making some investments in the near future."[115] This proved to be a gross understatement. Mitchell embarked on a staggering variety of money-making schemes, all of which sought to increase his earnings from the pockets of the miners, but none of which landed him on the "Easy Street" of which he so often dreamed. One scheme involved an effort to sell an enlarged, framed photograph of himself to the miners. Quite naturally, he hoped to find a firm in the anthracite region where he was most popular. When A. P. O'Donnell of O'Donnell's Undertaking and Livery Stables in Scranton offered to handle the picture sales, Mitchell's primary concern was "what commission it would be fair for me to expect." The two apparently never agreed on the proper commission, and the project fell through.[116] A second scheme that Mitchell pursued with greater vigor involved starting up a "John Mitchell" cigar company. The idea was to sell cigars bearing Mitchell's name and likeness on the box. Mitchell and Keefe discussed the opportunity at length with John C. Dernell of New York City at the December 1900 AFL convention. For unknown reasons, however, the project took a long time to get off the ground. It was not until January 1902 that Mitchell invested $750 of his own money to start the venture, and by that time he was less certain it would prove profitable. "Don't fail to send a box of the weeds," he told Dernell, "so that we can have a smoke, at least, for our money."[117] The most attractive financial windfall from the 1900 strike was a job offer from the American Relief Association, an insurance firm headquartered in Philadelphia. The company believed Mitchell's popularity would make him an invaluable partner to secure new business. Eventually the company offered him a vice presidency, a salary of $4,000 per year, plus $1,000 worth of stock each year.[118]

The money making efforts and his consideration of the insurance job offer revealed that even after the 1900 strike Mitchell still had not resolved his ambivalence toward the UMWA presidency. On January 23, 1901, the very day he was unanimously reelected UMWA president, Mitchell expressed his conflicting emotions to one of his nieces. "I don't know, really, whether to feel elated or depressed about it (his reelection)," he began. "While I do not underestimate the high honor of my position, I look with apprehension upon the exacting duties I shall be compelled to perform during the next year." On the one hand, he believed he would be much happier were he to abandon his responsibilities, to "settle down and look after my own affairs." On the other hand, he considered the trust placed in him by the rank and file a duty "which I am morally compelled to perform."[119]

The conflicting emotions Mitchell felt regarding the UMWA presidency lingered long after the 1900 strike. The position involved too much work and paid too little money. "Personally I am sick and tired of doing three men's work for one man's pay," he complained, "and while the miners would probably pay me more salary if I were to indicate that I wanted it, yet they will never give me as much as I can get in other lines of work." He wanted an arrangement that would put him "on the shady side of Easy Street."[120] In addition to the money, he often found union work itself discouraging, and complained that the "constant bickering makes the work unpleasant and unsatisfactory."[121] His success as president, however, did give Mitchell a sense of satisfaction and pride of accomplishment. For the first time since assuming the presidency, he began to reveal strong emotional ties to the UMWA. As he explained to a friend, "my whole heart is in the organization which I have seen grow from few in numbers to its present magnificent status; and a separation from it would be like severing my connection with what seems to me to be a part of myself."[122] Despite all the national acclaim, all the affection of his membership, all the power he wielded, the great victory he had achieved in 1900 had not resolved Mitchell's inner crisis. A full year of contemplation passed before he finally turned down the offer of the insurance job.[123]

Anthracite mine workers had many terms of affection for Mitchell. One of the most apt was "young old man." Still only thirty years of age, Mitchell had accomplished more than he ever could have dreamed. He had risen to the pinnacle of the labor movement, undisputed head of the largest and most powerful union in the nation. He consorted on a daily basis with national politicians, the national media, and other members of the elite. His counted among his closest personal friends leading soft coal operators such as Harry Taylor and Joseph Cavanaugh, both with headquarters in Chicago and whom he referred to as "the heavenly twins."[124] He went on jaunts with them to Lake Michigan and was a member of their Lake View Bowling Club.[125] He was welcome in the home of Mark Hanna, and he had matched wits with J. P. Morgan across the conference table. The "young old man" had certainly come a long way in the past few years.

Yet, in other ways, his career was just beginning. The 1900 strike catapulted Mitchell into the national limelight, and in the years that followed, he would be recognized not only as the president of the miners, but also as a spokesperson for the entire labor movement. The year 1901 witnessed Mitchell's entrance onto the stage of national affairs. Through his participation in the National Civic Federation, he would share the spotlight with powerful employers and politicians, voicing his views on the important issues of the day. He would find, however, that as his contact with elites increased, so did his alienation from the source of his strength, his own the rank and file.

Chapter 4

Mitchell Enters the National Scene, 1901

The years between 1898 and 1904 witnessed unprecedented economic expansion and union growth. The success of the UMWA under Mitchell was only the most spectacular illustration of a national trend that saw union membership more than quadruple, from 447,000 in 1897 to 2,072,700 in 1904.[1] Trade unions flourished in almost every region and economic sector. Employers, naturally, responded to the changing industrial landscape. Many, but by no means all, chose the path of peace and signed contracts with "responsible" unions. The public, too, began to demonstrate cautious sympathy with labor's right to organize. Compared to the vicious industrial strife of the 1890s, there seemed a real desire on the part of many Americans to devise peaceful solutions to the so-called labor problem. The National Civic Federation (NCF) was the institutional embodiment of the new approach to industrial relations. Its stated objective was to bring together leading figures from capital, labor, and the public in an effort to rid the nation of the industrial anarchy that had characterized the 1890s and establish lasting industrial quiescence. Declaring that antiunion employers were as great a threat to industrial peace as socialists, NCF leaders actively encouraged moderate unionism and the trade agreement as the cornerstones of stability.

Like other trade union officials, Mitchell approached the new organization with a pragmatic eye. His primary consideration at first was whether the NCF could assist him in negotiations with anthracite operators. During the 1900 hard coal strike, he had seen that his organizational and leadership talents were not enough to bring powerful antiunion operators to heel. The role of the press and especially Mark Hanna's involvement proved that wider political and social forces had to be mobilized for union success in anthracite. He thus perceived the NCF, with its stated commitment to collective bargaining and its condemnation of antiunion employers, as a potential ally in his struggle to extend the trade agreement to hard coal.

Over time, however, the NCF came to mean a great deal more to Mitchell than a body of useful negotiators and propagandists. The more familiar he became with the organization, the more he came to appreciate its strategies and goals. He would eventually become the NCF's most active and dedicated labor member. While Samuel Gompers and other trade union officials maintained a utilitarian stance, using the NCF's assistance to help them resolve various crises and encourage public support for labor, Mitchell developed an intense ideological commitment to the overall purposes of the organization. He came to perceive the NCF, and particularly its promotion of the trade agreement, as the ultimate solution to capital-labor relations. The method that had brought stability and peace to soft coal, he prophesied, could bring stability and peace to all industries. The method that allowed soft coal miners to share in the profits of industry, he urged, should be promoted across the land. For him, the NCF embodied the proper direction of labor relations and he gave it his enthusiastic support.

The NCF was the brainchild of Ralph Easley, a Chicago newspaper reporter. After a successful September 1899 conference on trusts arranged by the Chicago Civic Federation, Easley set about establishing a national organization. To assist him, he created an advisory council of five hundred leading representatives of capital, labor, and the public. All these men were "conservative, practical men of affairs," according to Easley, and no "cranks, hobbyists or revolutionists have been knowingly included."[2] Mitchell was one of thirty-four labor representatives Easley selected to serve. Uncertain how to respond to this invitation, he sought the advice of Samuel Gompers, asking the AFL president if he thought participation on the committee would be advantageous to the labor movement. Gompers's reply was noncommittal. "I do not know where the actual advantage would come," he wrote, "but it seems to me that it might not be amiss for some of our active, earnest union men to accept membership . . . in order to be advised of what is going on."[3] Both Mitchell and Gompers joined the new organization, and Gompers was elected to the NCF's executive committee.

In its earliest days, the NCF did not confine itself to examining industrial relations. Its program was far more ambitious. Easley hoped to discuss all matters of national importance, international as well as domestic issues. In the winter of 1900–1901, for instance, Easley planned three separate conferences on municipal ownership, taxation, and industrial conciliation.[4] Very soon, however, the focus narrowed almost exclusively to relations between capital and labor. NCF leaders believed that if all the resources of the organization could be brought to bear on that one mighty issue, perhaps a lasting solution to the "labor question" could be found.

Mitchell was invited to speak at the NCF's first conference, on industrial conciliation, which was held on December 17 and 18, 1900 in Chicago. The gathering of so many illustrious power brokers attracted widespread media attention. There was a general sense that this was the origin of a major new force on the national scene. Although the conference was intended to debate the relative merits of voluntary conciliation and compulsory arbitration, most of the speakers, whether employers or union officials, represented industries where the trade agreement was in effect. Therefore, most speeches were emphatic pleas in favor of extending the principle of the trade agreement to all industrial sectors. No speaker was more emphatic in support of the trade agreement than John Mitchell.

Having just recently concluded the 1900 anthracite strike, Mitchell demanded the attention of the large crowd when he took the stage to deliver his speech. "I am of the opinion," he said, "that the best and most practical plan that could be adopted to avert strikes and lockouts would be for the employers of labor and the representatives of labor organizations to meet in joint conference, as is done by the soft coal miners and operators of this country, and mutually agree upon contracts governing the scales of wages and conditions of employment." Before the interstate movement, the soft coal industry was anarchic. Miners would meet in convention at the end of each scale year and formulate demands. If operators refused the demands, a strike ensued. At other times operators made demands for wage reductions. If miners refused, a lockout began. "But during the past few years, and as a result of severe punishment inflicted upon both operators and miners, we have realized that the better plan is to adjust our differences and formulate our wage scales is by meeting together, like prudent business men, and staying together until we reach an agreement."

The trade agreement not only ensured peace for the coming year, it helped foster lasting peace by creating mutual respect between employee and employer. Mitchell recalled that as a youth, when just becoming active in the labor movement, "I looked upon the man who owned a coal mine as my natural enemy, simply because he owned a coal mine." Those days had passed, he continued, "and the men I regarded then as my natural enemies. . . . I have grown to respect . . . and I believe that the mine owners have grown to know and respect the opinions of the miners." If all employers and unions met and reasoned with each other, he concluded, "the public would have less cause to fear industrial eruptions and disturbances."[5]

During this conference, the NCF established a committee on conciliation and arbitration. Twelve members were appointed, half were employers and half were labor men, including Mitchell and Samuel Gompers. The committee's first act was to issue an appeal calling for the adoption of annual or semiannual joint agreements. When the conference concluded, the *Chicago Tribune* declared it "perhaps the most important discussion ever held in this country of the broad and urgent subject of how to promote industrial peace."[6]

Since Mitchell never mentioned this conference in any of his private correspondence, it is unlikely that he regarded the founding of the NCF as a particularly significant development. Despite the attention given the conference, there seemed to be no direct connection between the NCF and the UMWA. His head must have turned, however, when he read in the newspaper that

Mark Hanna, who at this time was not a member of the organization, gave the NCF a ringing endorsement. Its founding provided the means "for the total abolition of strikes in the United States," the Senator declared.[7] Always eager to prove his loyalty to the Captain, Mitchell wrote Hanna that he, too, supported the aims of the NCF. "Personally I believe you know," he chirped, "that I am in favor of peace and the establishment of harmonious business relations with the employers of labor, to the end that strikes and lockouts may become unnecessary."[8] The awareness that the "savior" of the 1900 hard coal strike was interested if not involved, undoubtedly sparked Mitchell's commitment.

As usual, Mitchell first demonstrated his interest by hoping to feather his own nest. At a January 1901 meeting in Chicago, the conciliation committee of which he was a member, was expanded to forty members. Along with Herman Justi, commissioner of the Illinois Coal Operators' Association, and E. D. Kenna, vice president of the Acheson, Topeka, and Sante Fe Railroad, Mitchell had been appointed a member of a subcommittee to determine the best method to set up trade agreements in industries presently without them. In a letter to Justi, Mitchell suggested the first step would be the hiring of two full time commissioners. Because these men would be fully independent of any employer or labor organization, and therefore perceived as impartial, they would be in a position to organize joint conferences and act as arbitrators in the event the joint conferences became deadlocked.[9] Justi apparently discussed the matter with Easley, and Easley then informed Mitchell he liked the idea. Two commissionerships would be created with salaries of $5,000 per year. Moreover, Easley was seriously considering Mitchell and Justi for the two positions. Mitchell could hardly believe his good fortune. "Now I think that would suit me all right," he bubbled to Keefe, and "when the time comes I would like to have matters fixed up all O.K."[10] In the end, Mitchell was never offered the job.

If the NCF failed to put him on "Easy Street," it did prove immensely valuable in his ongoing negotiations with the anthracite coal operators in the spring of 1901. The anthracite situation provided the NCF's committee on conciliation, which until this time had no clear focus, its first opportunity to perform important mediation work. Mitchell was very impressed. Indeed, the services provided by the NCF during these negotiations transformed him from a lukewarm participant in the organization to a thoroughgoing booster. He found the NCF much more than a social club, holding dinner parties and lining up speakers to discuss the labor question. The NCF, as far as he was concerned, demonstrated its ability to intervene in labor disputes and put its ideals into action. As had Senator Hanna the year before, the NCF had become his partner in his effort to bring hard coal operators to terms.

The settlement after the 1900 strike was no more than a temporary cease-fire. Before the ink had dried, both sides were maneuvering for better position in the next round of hostilities. Determined to destroy the union, operators blacklisted union activists and placed contingents of coal and iron police at mine entrances. Stockades were constructed to afford troops protection in the event of violence. Mitchell was also busy, flooding the field with organizers to enlist the more than 90,000 hard coal men who remained outside the union fold. As they traveled from camp to camp, organizers trumpeted the same message—operators would never improve conditions unless all mine workers belonged to the union.[11]

Mitchell's goal had not changed. He hoped to establish the joint conference in anthracite and negotiate a trade agreement. With the wage advance set to expire on April 1, 1901, he had little time to spare after the January UMWA convention to induce operators to bargain with the union. He arranged for a special anthracite mine workers' convention to be held on March 12 in Hazleton. On February 15, he wired the presidents of the coal carrying railroads, inviting them to attend a joint conference of operators and mine workers to be held immediately following the Hazleton convention. By the very next day he unhappily reported that two of the railroad chiefs had already declined and he expected "that this attitude will be assumed by all of the companies." Undaunted, he issued the call for the Hazleton meeting of the mine workers.[12]

In the weeks prior to the Hazleton convention, Mitchell held out little hope that a satisfactory settlement with the railroad chiefs could be reached before the April 1 deadline. Not only had the operators refused to attend the joint conference, but they also had begun posting notices that the advance in wages received in October would be continued for another year.[13] In a letter to his soft coal operator friend, Harry Taylor, Mitchell vented his anger at the intransigence of the railroad presidents, hinting that a second strike might be necessary to subdue them. "It seems to me that those laddie bucks in New York will have to be given another round," he wrote, "before they realize the necessity of taking cognizance of our existence."[14]

The refusal of these "laddie bucks" to negotiate represented only one half of Mitchell's hard coal dilemma in the spring of 1901. The other half was the apparent breakdown of unity among the rank and file. Most of the men were new to unionism, and they lacked the discipline and respect for proper procedure Mitchell had come to expect from soft coal miners. When the six hundred delegates to the Hazleton convention met on March 12, Mitchell was amazed by the amount of infighting and unruly behavior. "They are about a wild a set of men you ever saw in your life," he complained to an old friend. "The whole bunch wants to talk at the same time, and some of them have very decided opinions as to the proper method of running a labor organization." Recriminations abounded, and he feared the organization had disintegrated greatly since the strike.[15]

When operators failed to appear on March 15 for the scheduled joint conference, the convention voted unanimously to send telegrams demanding their appearance in Hazleton. When these telegrams were also ignored, the convention resolved that Mitchell, the national executive board, and the officers of the three anthracite districts be authorized to arrange a joint conference by April 1. If a joint conference could not be arranged, these men were further authorized to initiate strike action.[16] Mitchell now found himself between a rock and a hard place. Operators refused to budge, and an unruly rank and file was clamoring for a strike. "We are up against a pretty hard proposition here," he confided to his friend Billy Ryan, "and I should not be surprised if we engaged in another strike."[17]

At all costs, Mitchell hoped to avert what would be a second strike in two years. Mine workers were divided, operators were beefing up the number of coal and iron police, and public opinion could not be expected to rally behind the diggers just months after a strike victory. Moreover, Mitchell had information that operators were stockpiling coal and in fact desired a strike.[18] Since there were less than two weeks until the April 1 deadline, Mitchell had to work quickly. He desperately sought assistance to help him arrange a meeting with the railroad chiefs and effect some type of settlement. Mitchell first turned to Ralph Easley and the National Civic Federation. This organization's committee on conciliation had not, as yet, engaged in any high level negotiations, but Easley claimed powerful friends and offered to assist. Easley agreed with Mitchell that another anthracite strike would be disastrous for the union. He promised that if a strike could be averted, by April 1902, the NCF's committee could pressure the railroads to "enter into official agreement" with the union.[19]

Given this opportunity to prove the value of the NCF, Easley was determined to succeed. He exploded onto the scene, contacting everyone in New York who might bring pressure to bear against the operators. Among others, he spoke to Albert Shaw, influential columnist for the *Review of Reviews*, Episcopalian Bishop Henry Potter, and Seth Low, prominent politician and future mayor of New York. Easley's pressure was successful in arranging two private conferences between Mitchell and George W. Perkins, the partner of J. P. Morgan. Both conferences took place in New York, one in Shaw's home and the other at Perkins's office.[20] Although these two meetings bore no fruit, Easley was not finished. He secured for himself a personal talk with E. B. Thomas of the Erie Railroad. Thomas's message, however, was not one to lift Mitchell's spirits. While Thomas believed J. P. Morgan was willing to talk with Mitchell, he was even more confident that Morgan would never interfere in the management of the railroads.[21]

Easley's initial efforts had not resolved the impasse, and the April 1 deadline was drawing ever closer. After the unsuccessful meeting between Easley and Thomas, Mitchell commented that affairs in hard coal had "assumed a very aggravated form. The companies appear determined to ignore our repeated requests for a conference," he noted, "and the sentiment among the miners is growing decidedly in favor of a suspension of work."[22] Unwilling to wait any longer, Mitchell decided to call upon his political ally, Senator Hanna. By turning to Hanna, however, he was by no means turning away from the NCF. He was simply enlisting all outside pressure he had at his disposal to avoid a strike. Indeed, the NCF continued to be very active in the negotiations, and he was quite impressed by the efforts of Easley and other NCF negotiators on his behalf during the crisis. Mitchell had nothing but praise for indefatigable efforts of Easley. To his friend Keefe, Mitchell declared that Easley "is proving of valuable assistance to us. He is one of the best men I have met yet."[23]

Mitchell's letter to "My dear Senator Hanna" on March 20 was a desperate plea for help. He recounted his efforts to arrange a conference, described the mounting strike sentiment among the men, and appealed to Hanna to use his "good offices" to intervene. If only Hanna could arrange a conference between Mitchell, the three district presidents, and the railroad presidents, Mitchell was certain the crisis could be resolved. He expressed his confidence that at such a meeting "we could reach an understanding which would be satisfactory to all concerned and would not necessarily mean any loss of dignity on the part of the railroad Presidents." Nor did he forget to remind Hanna of the possible political implications of a strike at this time. When the 1900 strike was settled, Mitchell wrote, opponents of the Republican party predicted that once the election was over the railroads would destroy the union in anthracite. If operators continued to refuse a conference and the union was forced to strike, Mitchell feared "that those who made predictions then will claim that the present action of the coal companies is a verification of their prophecies during the campaign."[24]

Hanna, of course, was more than willing to do what he could to prevent another outbreak of labor unrest with potentially adverse political ramifications. He immediately responded to Mitchell's plea with a promise to go to New York that weekend, talk to as many of the railroad presidents as he could, then confer with Mitchell at the Waldorf Astoria. "I will be only too happy to do anything I can for the mutual interest of the operators and men," he assured Mitchell.[25] Now that the "Captain" was on the job, Mitchell expressed his first hint of optimism. While in his New York hotel room that weekend waiting for Hanna to arrive, he noted that although the situation was complicated, "a ray of hope appears to-day in the person of my dear friend, the Senator."[26]

Between the day he asked Hanna to come to the rescue and the day Hanna actually met with the railroad presidents, no doubt an exasperating few days, Mitchell reached a personal decision. Under no circumstances would he conduct an anthracite strike in 1901. The entire situation became clearly focused in his mind. "To begin with, if a strike is engaged in it will be to a finish," he wrote, referring to recalcitrance of the operators and their apparent readiness for confrontation. Second, "there are disintegrating influences at work among the miners" which might cause a break in the ranks. Mine workers were being deceived by men in the employ of operators to believe union officials had been dishonest during the last strike. And finally, he had "conclusive proof" that certain union officials "in our midst" were acting as spies for the operators. All these factors spelled doom for strike action. Mitchell was also confident he could sidetrack the widespread strike sentiment among the rank and file. In a particularly revealing statement about the growing centralized control over union decision making, he wrote: "It is generally assumed, and believed by everybody, that I can determine the miners' course, and while I of course deny this publicly, I have no hesitancy in saying to you that a majority of the Committee to whom the question of strike or no strike was referred, will vote as I wish." Of course, he concluded, the threat of a strike would still be used to obtain concessions if at all possible.[27]

Reaching this decision, however, did not lessen the intense nervous strain of negotiations. While in his room at the Ashland Hotel in New York, waiting for his meeting with Hanna and busily conferring with all interested parties, he felt ill and fatigued. He claimed that for two days he had grave difficulty walking. His joints were stiff and sore, and he had "coughed hard" for the past two weeks. He desired a rest. Other factors combined to make him truly miserable. His sister, Maggie, was bedridden and he wanted to visit her in California. Equally unnerving, at this time a labor paper in Scranton, the *Scrantonian*, accused Mitchell of, among other things, being intoxicated at union meetings and having an extramarital affair with Elizabeth Morris, his secretary. Once the negotiations were over, he intended to sue the editor of the paper for libel "and send him to the penetentiary (*sic*), where he properly belongs." He intended to do something else at the conclusion of negotiations. He wanted to retire. "If I can get this closed up with credit to our organization," he wrote Secretary-Treasurer Wilson, "I believe, Billy, that I shall sever my connection, officially, with our union."[28] Mitchell had reached a spiritual low.

Hanna arrived in New York on March 25 with his son, D. H., who managed his father's commercial interests and was a member of the NCF executive committee. Easley joined them. Mitchell recognized the close link being established between his two allies. "The Captain has taken hold like a good fellow," he wrote, "and by to-morrow I expect to know what our fate will be."[29] The "Captain" did take hold, and the next day he and Mitchell went together to see E. B. Thomas of the Erie Railroad. Even with the senator at his side, he found it was no easy task to talk to the coal barons. "You cannot imagine how much red tape there is in New York," he wrote in amazement. "First we had to see the ministers who preached to these fellows; then saw the college lectures (*sic*) and editors of magazines . . . before we could work our way into the presence of the magnates." At last the long awaited meeting took place. According to Mitchell, Thomas was authorized to speak for "a large number" of the railroad presidents. In no way would Thomas grant union recognition to the UMWA, but as far as his own company was concerned, he was willing to receive committees of men to adjust grievances. Mitchell considered this a significant concession, for until that time the railroads had met only with individual employees. After the conference, Hanna dashed off to ascertain whether the other railroad presidents would concede this point. "If we are able to obtain even this concession all along the line," Mitchell concluded, "I shall feel that a great victory has been achieved."[30]

Hanna was also in close contact with J. P. Morgan, and as Mitchell knew, "what Morgan says goes with the railroads." According to Hanna's reports, Morgan believed that if a settlement was worked out this year, full recognition would be accorded the union in April 1902. This proposal was contingent, however, on the demonstrated ability of the union to prevent unauthorized strikes over the next twelve months. There had been so many local strikes since the settlement in October that operators did not believe the union could impose discipline. The greatest obstacle to a joint conference, as Mitchell understood it, was "the lack of confidence in our ability to control our own men." Mitchell was both delighted and perplexed by Morgan's proposal. He wanted to earn the respect of the operators, but he knew that local strikes were symptomatic of an industry without a trade agreement. Only after an agreement was signed could the union "act as a restraining influence against local strikes."[31]

Just a few days prior to the April 1 deadline, Hanna informed Mitchell that several other railroad presidents agreed to the concession to meet with committees of their employees and consider a joint conference with the UMWA the following year. And with praise that must have made Mitchell tingle with pride, Hanna wrote, "I congratulate you on your conservative management and assure you that you have strengthened your cause and influence with the interests here."[32] The operators' agreement to meet with employee committees was Mitchell's "victory," and with it he gathered together the national executive board and officers of the anthracite districts on March 29. The question of whether this concession was enough to block the will of the mine workers to strike was yet to be decided. According to Mitchell's secretary, who was present at this meeting: "Mr. Mitchell told me that many of the District Board members had come instructed to vote for complete recognition or a strike."[33] What Mitchell had to offer was a far cry from complete recognition. He had only the vague promise of recognition a year hence if the union could prevent local strikes. But just as he had predicted, the union men violated their instructions and acceded to his wishes.

In an effort to sell this settlement to a rank and file determined to strike, Mitchell's statement to the anthracite mine workers, issued on March 29, portrayed the entire affair as a stunning union victory. The agreement to meet with employee committees was dubbed "partial recognition," which represented a "step in the right direction, and presages more harmonious and equitable relations between employers and employees than have prevailed in the anthracite region heretofore." And if mine workers demonstrated their willingness to forego local strikes in the next year, "full and complete recognition would unquestionably be accorded at a future date."[34]

Although Mitchell stated the negotiations were "one of the most trying experiences of my life,"[35] the results hardly could have pleased him more. The movement for a potentially disastrous strike had been derailed. A small measure of success could be claimed for the union, and greater successes had been promised for the future. He also had cemented his friendship with the "Captain." The developing relationship between Hanna and Mitchell was based on the solid edifice of trust and mutual admiration. Mitchell had once again proven his ability to impose on the rank and file compromises reached through behind the scenes negotiations, and Hanna had once again rescued Mitchell from a difficult position through the exercise of his political clout on Wall Street. Moreover, Mitchell had found in the NCF a new and powerful partner to assist him in extending the trade agreement to hard coal. Easley's tireless efforts on Mitchell's behalf were greatly appreciated. When the crisis had passed, Mitchell expressed his gratitude to Easley, whom he said "contributed very much to our success in obtaining the concessions which resulted in a continuance of work in the anthracite coal fields."[36]

By the spring of 1901, therefore, Mitchell had come to the conclusion that the economic power of the union alone was insufficient to achieve union goals. Political alliances needed to be established and maintained. He had witnessed on two occasions how political pressure, in combination with strike action or the threat of a strike, had achieved tangible results in the anthracite region. He considered the alliances with Hanna and the NCF invaluable to union growth and stability, and he was learning to depend on their intervention. At this time, however, he seemed oblivious to the possible pitfalls such political alliances represented. Dependence on elites such as Hanna and Easley often necessitated violating the collective will of the rank and file, the ultimate basis of his authority as union chief. Having snuffed out the widespread strike sentiment in March and having committed the union to a full year of labor peace, he had earned the praise of Hanna and Easley but he jeopardized squelching the very militancy that made the union powerful. In the spring of 1901, however, losing touch with rank-and-file sentiment was the last thing on Mitchell's mind.

While the specific aims of the NCF were somewhat ambiguous at its founding, the role it played in anthracite negotiations helped it to establish a clearer focus. And Mitchell helped define the NCF's program. In January 1901, he had been appointed to an NCF subcommittee to determine specifically how the organization might advance the cause of labor peace. In May, this subcommittee made its recommendations at a public meeting of the committee on conciliation. Easley considered this public meeting so important he later referred to it as the true beginnings of the NCF.[37] The meeting took place in New York at the Cooper Institute, and Easley made certain the press gave the event wide coverage. "Don't let anything but death keep you from coming down here at that time," he told Mitchell.[38]

Mitchell's subcommittee presented its ideas to Easley and the other NCF leaders in private. Then Easley, in front of a large audience, explained the newly defined aims and strategies of the organization. The NCF would concentrate exclusively on relations between capital and labor. It would be the first private organization of any consequence to deal scientifically with industrial relations. It would employ a two-pronged approach. First, the NCF would play an educational and propagandistic role in helping to extend the trade agreement to all industries. Interested employers could use the NCF to obtain information on existing agreements and advice on how to set one up. Second, the NCF would provide private mediation and conciliation services. It would directly intervene in ongoing industrial disputes in an attempt to resolve them as quickly as possible. By so doing the NCF hoped to convince both workers and employers that strikes were avoidable, and that the best method of avoiding them was the trade agreement.[39]

Just as Easley had hoped, the June conference attracted widespread public acclaim. To the press and public at the turn of the century, the idea of scientifically approaching capital-labor relations and the promise of ending labor strife through trade agreements was something quite new and remarkable. Mitchell was taken aback by the public reaction. Although less than enthusiastic when the conference began, he became excited after reading the favorable comments in the newspapers. With its new approach, he now gushed, the NCF was certain to have "a far reaching effect."[40]

Less than three weeks after the May 7 meeting, the NCF's conciliation committee faced the first major challenge to its professed ability to resolve strikes and uphold trade agreements. On May 20, 45,000 members of the Machinists' union initiated a nationwide strike when union leaders and employers failed to agree on terms for a renewal of their one-year old "Murray Hill" trade agreement. The Murray Hill agreement, like the one in soft coal, had been hailed by the NCF as a model for other industries. Members of both parties to the agreement, union officials and employers, were represented on the NCF's conciliation committee. Unless a settlement was reached quickly, Easley explained to Mitchell, the NCF would look ridiculous before the public.[41]

Mitchell, however, went on vacation soon after the start of the strike. Still suffering from the strain of the anthracite negotiations, he consulted physicians who told him his condition was "nervous exhaustion," and that immediate rest was required. Declaring there was no place on earth where he could be more contented, Mitchell headed to Fresno to visit his sister and nieces. He remained for several weeks, enjoying himself thoroughly, taking part in pillow fights and other shenanigans, and he did not return to Indianapolis until early June.[42] Upon his return, Easley was in an agitated state over the metal trades dispute. On June 11, he attended a meeting of the employers' group, the National Metal Trades Association, and found it firmly "in the hands of the radicals," by which he meant those determined to crush the union and terminate the agreement. He needed Mitchell's help to get the conciliation committee together and take charge of the situation. Mitchell assured Easley that their committee "would render great assistance in bringing the warring elements together," but both the union and the employers resisted all attempts at NCF mediation and the strike dragged on.[43]

The metal trades strike embarrassed the NCF. The heralded Murray Hill agreement was lost forever and the prestige of the infant NCF had suffered a setback. Its first effort to deal scientifically with labor disputes and prove the viability of trade agreements collapsed in the face of union militancy and employer intransigence. Obviously, there were a great number of employers who did not share Mitchell's and Easley's vision of a harmonious world based on a commonality of interests. In response to the metal trades defeat, the two men embarked on a mission to induce other men of high standing to join the NCF, endeavoring to make the movement so prestigious that its counsel could not be ignored in future disputes. Hanna also assisted in this effort. According to Easley, the Senator sent telegrams "at the right time to the right people," which was of tremendous help in signing up "the strong men of the country." Easley then suggested Mitchell contact Marshall Field, the commercial magnate of Chicago. Field had taken "quite a fancy" to Mitchell at a lunch they had together in Chicago at the NCF's January 1900 conference, and Easley believed a line from Mitchell would be worth more than an invitation from anyone else on the committee. Mitchell dutifully wrote Field but Field politely declinee, citing a lack of time. Undaunted, Mitchell suggested to Easley that they "should look around for other men whose reputation is so firmly established that their connection with our organization will give it strength and prestige."[44]

Despite the metal trades fiasco, in the summer of 1901 Mitchell assumed a leadership role in the NCF's affairs. Although this added to his already oppressive workload, he knew his NCF activities would eventually pay dividends to the union. By serving as Easley's most energetic labor representative, he knew he could expect Easley's assistance in future anthracite negotiations.

By encouraging powerful employers to join the NCF, he was adding to the strength of a proven UMWA ally. By taking an active role in this national movement, he retained Hanna's attention and affection. Thus, there were numerous pragmatic reasons why Mitchell would assume such a leading part in the NCF. But it would soon become increasingly obvious that there were other motivating factors at work. The praise he received from "the strong men of the country" and the national exposure given his activities fed his ego and his craving for acceptance by elites. What other association provided him an opportunity to dazzle Marshall Field at an informal lunch? The more prestige the NCF gained, the more prestigious Mitchell became. Moreover, the zealous approach Mitchell took to his NCF work also indicated that he was developing an ideological commitment to the organization. When he joined the NCF, his knowledge of capital-labor relations was confined to the mining industry. As he learned more about other industries, he increasingly became convinced that the trade agreement could be successful in all sectors of the economy. By the summer of 1901 it was apparent that he was not simply mouthing the NCF's "line" to fulfill obligations owed to Easley, but that he had come to believe the NCF's approach was the proper one.

The emerging affinity of outlook between Mitchell, Easley, and Hanna had significant implications for the future of the American labor movement. This was demonstrated quite clearly during the steel strike of 1901. During this strike, which threatened to become a full scale war between organized labor and monopoly capital, Mitchell was faced with a clear decision. Would he side with the forces in his own union, demanding solidarity with steel strikers in a momentous confrontation? Or would he once again demonstrate his conservative leadership to employers and politicians by upholding the sanctity of contracts above all else? The steel strike of 1901 revealed that the alliances Mitchell had created could only be maintained through the sacrifice of labor solidarity.

The formation of the mammoth U.S. Steel Corporation in early 1901 captured the attention of the entire labor movement.[45] The nation's first billion dollar corporation, U.S. Steel employed nearly 148,000 of the 160,000 workers in the steel industry. If this example of monopoly control represented the wave of the future, the labor policy of the trust became a matter of intense interest.

The Amalgamated Association of Iron, Steel and Tin Workers had the most pressing concern. Defeat during the Homestead strike in 1892 had led to a steady decline in membership for the Amalgamated, and by 1901 the union represented less than 10,000 members. It was clear to T. J. Shaffer, president of the Amalgamated, that drastic action was necessary to prevent steel unionism from disappearing altogether. Shaffer hoped that the establishment of the giant trust would provide him with an opportunity to resuscitate his union.

Members of the steel trust's executive committee were viciously hostile toward unions. They were also concerned, however, with establishing financial stability and positive public relations. Ultimately, these conflicting concerns led to the adoption of a seemingly moderate position on union representation. U.S. Steel declared it would seek labor peace. While the Amalgamated would not be allowed to organize nonunion mills, it would be allowed to retain its presence in union mills. Shaffer knew that this peace proposal was more apparent than real. Multi-plant corporations in the steel industry had long employed the practice of closing organized mills and transferring work to nonunion mills. If U.S. Steel adopted this policy, it would be only a question of time before the Amalgamated lost all of its dwindling membership.

During contract negotiations in the spring of 1901, Shaffer demanded union recognition for all the mills of the American Sheet Steel and American Steel Hoop companies, two subsidiaries of U.S. Steel. When these companies refused to recognize the union for mills without existing union contracts, Shaffer declared a strike against each company. By July 10, some 36,000 steel workers, most of them until now unorganized, joined the walk out. Shaffer then began threatening to close down all of U.S. Steel. In widely publicized statements, he claimed to be waging a war against J. P. Morgan, dictator of steel, railroads, and mining. He also hinted that other unions were prepared to assist him in this war, particularly the railroad brotherhoods and the UMWA. These unions, Shaffer said, would strike in sympathy because they realized that if Morgan killed unionism in steel, he would soon destroy unionism in other industries under his control.

Shaffer's mention of a possible sympathy strike by the miners was reinforced when District 5 President Patrick Dolan was quoted in the newspapers threatening to call out the miners in his district in support of the steel workers. Alarmed, both Hanna and Easley sprang into action. Even the vaguest possibility that miners might join the strike and thus create a titanic struggle between labor and the House of Morgan sent chills down their spines. Hanna wrote Mitchell on July 16 concerning Dolan's statement and urged him to "stop that kind of talk." The mere mention of sympathetic action "hurts what you and I are trying to accomplish in the interest of organized labor." Hanna also wished Mitchell would try to curb Shaffer's recklessness, to induce him to be "more conservative in the management of the present tumble." "Can't *we* do something?," he asked pointedly.[46]

Mitchell was quick to allay Hanna's fears. Not only was Dolan's statement "entirely unauthorized," but Hanna also could rest assured there was "no prospect of the miners becoming involved in the present difficulty." As to straightening out Shaffer, Mitchell would be "very glad indeed" to be of assistance in resolving the strike. Hanna found Mitchell's comments "very satisfactory" and was relieved he could count on Mitchell's conservative approach. As far as the miners were concerned, Hanna knew "nothing would come up to plague us."[47]

On July 27 and 29, two conferences were held between the officers of the Amalgamated and those of U.S. Steel. J. P. Morgan offered a compromise to end the strike. He promised to pay union wages but would not extend recognition to mills presently nonunion. Claiming he was personally sympathetic to the cause of labor, Morgan predicted that within two years all the mills of U.S. Steel would be operating under union contracts. Just as Mitchell four months earlier had accepted the promise of future recognition in anthracite, Shaffer now attached his signature to Morgan's proposal. When he brought this proposal to the Amalgamated's executive board, however, the board refused to ratify it. The board made a counter offer but Morgan claimed the agreement signed by Shaffer was binding on the union. Caught between his own executive board and an inflexible J. P. Morgan, Shaffer sided with his union. He issued a general strike call against U.S. Steel on August 10. While the answer to this call was far less than Shaffer hoped, 62,000 steel workers were now on the picket line.[48]

Urged on by Hanna, Easley in late July assembled the members of the NCF's conciliation committee. Besides Mitchell and Easley, this group included Samuel Gompers, economist J. W. Jenks of Columbia University, Henry White, secretary of the United Garment Workers, and Frank P. Sargent, grand master of the Brotherhood of Locomotive Firemen. Hanna himself took an active role in the committee, although he did not want his involvement to be made public. After the two conferences between Shaffer and Morgan, the conciliation committee, according to Easley, struggled "night and day to bring about a renewal of negotiations."[49] Unable to bring the warring factions together, the NCF's committee focused its efforts on preventing any type of sympathetic action that might widen the conflict.

The fear of sympathetic action was not without foundation. In a number of unions, there existed considerable rank-and-file pressure to join hands with the Amalgamated and make this strike a true showdown between capital and labor. This sentiment was strongest in Mitchell's own union. When the UMWA executive board met on August 10 to consider the steel strike, the depth of this sentiment became apparent. Two strong resolutions were adopted. One asked Gompers to convene a council of all presidents and secretaries of the AFL's constituent unions "to devise a plan for assisting the Amalgamated Association in its struggle." The second "heartily" endorsed the steel strike and pledged the strikers "the support of the United Mine Workers in every possible manner."[50] According to Tom L. Lewis, the union's vice president, both resolutions were passed over Mitchell's protest.[51]

The UMWA national executive board did not call directly for a sympathy strike, but Mitchell was beginning to feel pressure from his own union to assist the strikers in a meaningful way. The need to resolve the conflict as speedily as possible was growing, and Mitchell redoubled his efforts. On August 14, he met with the NCF's conciliation committee in Cleveland, and the following day the group met in Buffalo. On August 23, Mitchell, Easley, Jenks, and White traveled to Pittsburgh where they had a long talk with Shaffer and other Amalgamated officers. By this time, U.S. Steel had introduced strikebreakers, and Shaffer had begun to question his chances of victory. Mitchell was therefore able to convince Shaffer to consider his plan for peace. According to Mitchell's plan, the union would accept the proposition made by J. P. Morgan on July 29, calling for union wages but not union recognition, and all strikers would be reinstated without discrimination. Mitchell himself volunteered to approach U.S. Steel executives if the Amalgamated accepted this plan. Shaffer agreed to submit Mitchell's plan to his union's executive board. By means of a circular letter, Shaffer asked his executive board to consider Mitchell's proposal.[52]

Shaffer also stated in this circular letter that if Mitchell's mediation efforts failed, Mitchell had agreed to call out the miners in a sympathy strike and try to induce the railroad men to strike as well. Whether or not Mitchell had actually made this promise or whether it was simply a ploy by Shaffer to obtain his board's compliance would become a matter of great debate. Mitchell, however, did not publicly deny Shaffer's claim at this time. Believing the mine workers would join them in case of failure, the Amalgamated's board voted to accept Mitchell's peace plan. On August 29, Shaffer notified Mitchell of the board's decision.[53] Mitchell was overjoyed. He immediately wrote Hanna claiming he had engineered "a clear back down on the part of the Amalgamated."[54] He then wrote Easley and asked him to help set up a conference with U.S. Steel executives. In his letter to Easley, he lent credence to Shaffer's claim that he had in fact promised some type of assistance. "If the terms outlined in this proposition are not accepted," he warned, "the steel strike will have the unqualified support of the American labor movement; and President Gompers will unquestionably call the Executive Council together for the purpose of devising methods to help them."[55]

Mitchell's negotiating mission was, in his own words, "a complete failure." He assembled several members of the conciliation committee, including Gompers and Easley, and met with Morgan's representative, Charles Schwab, on September 4 at U.S. Steel headquarters. Although Mitchell found Schwab to be "open and frank," Schwab dismissed Mitchell's proposal out of hand. Schwab provided statistical evidence that the Amalgamated was "at his mercy." Impressed by Schwab's evidence, Mitchell concluded there was "no hope left for the steel workers."[56] Schwab then proposed terms for a settlement. Union contracts would be signed for all mills which had been organized the previous year except nine, which would now become nonunion. If these terms were not accepted within twenty-four hours, Schwab said, negotiations would be discontinued. Mitchell contacted Shaffer and advised him to accept the terms and call off the strike, but Shaffer refused to act without the approval of his executive board and asked that the deadline be extended another day. Mitchell received the extension, but this, too, passed without official notification from Shaffer.[57] The strike lingered on until September 14, when the union was forced to surrender on terms even worse than those outlined by Schwab on September 4. The disastrous steel strike was one of labor's greatest setbacks in the early twentieth century.

In the wake of the disaster, the labor movement was consumed by vitriolic debate over who was responsible. Shaffer publicly attacked Mitchell and Gompers for sabotaging the strike. He accused Gompers of refusing to offer the financial assistance of the AFL, and he denounced Mitchell for failing to live up to his promise to call a sympathy strike after U.S. Steel had rejected Mitchell's peace proposal on September 4.[58] Meeting at the Ashland House Hotel in New York, Gompers and Mitchell composed a letter to Shaffer on September 25 demanding an investigation of all the charges. "Pillory us if we deserve it," they declared, but public charges could not be allowed to "stand unanswered and unchallenged." They stated their willingness to go before a committee of three union officials selected by Shaffer from a list they provided. If found guilty, both promised to resign their present posts in the labor movement.[59] Shaffer rejected this offer.

Mitchell next appealed to the other members of the NCF's conciliation committee who were with him in Pittsburgh when he supposedly promised a sympathy strike. He requested Easley, Jenks, and White to refute the charge made by Shaffer against him. Both J. M. Jenks and Henry White responded with ringing affirmations of Mitchell's position. Mitchell had never made such a promise, nor was there ever an implicit understanding that the miners would be called out.[60] Easley, however, claimed to be "surprised" by Mitchell's request. He recalled seeing the circular of August 23 in which Shaffer noted Mitchell's promise of a sympathy strike. He vaguely remembered asking Shaffer at that time whether Mitchell had in fact made the promise. Although he did not recall the "exact phraseology," the "effect produced on my mind" at the time was that Shaffer was simply trying to gain his board's approval. But Easley's feeling on this matter was "completely reversed" when he received Mitchell's letter of August 31 stating the strike would have the unqualified support of the labor movement. From Mitchell's later comments and actions, however, Easley realized that he had "put too serious an interpretation on that letter."[61]

Mitchell was distressed by Easley's lack of faith. The suggestion that Easley, of all people, would question his commitment to the sanctity of contracts wounded his pride. Shaffer used the suggestion of a sympathy strike "simply as a ruse," Mitchell insisted. "Personally, I did myself the credit to believe that I had demonstrated often enough my regard for the inviolability of contracts to satisfy anyone who knows anything of me or of my course in the labor movement and place me beyond the suspicion of having ever suggested the possibility of violating contracts between my organization and the coal operators."[62] That Easley, his powerful ally, should have cause to doubt his conservatism, even for a moment, was a powerful blow. Mitchell vented his anger in an explosive attack on Shaffer. It was Shaffer's "criminal incapacity" that had undermined the strike, and the Amalgamated leader had tried to pin the blame on others through "false and cowardly attacks" on himself and Gompers.[63]

Private hatred between Mitchell and Shaffer endured far longer than the public debate over responsibility for the defeat of the strike. Although conclusive proof will never be found, it was most improbable that Mitchell ever promised Shaffer a sympathy strike. Such action represented a direct violation of the reputation Mitchell was trying to create for himself as the conservative trade union leader who could be trusted by employers. A union leader as intent as Mitchell was on maintaining alliances with Hanna and Easley would not consider lightly the sympathy strike. Indeed, Mitchell's "crime" during the strike was that he never seriously considered extending any assistance to the strikers. In his zealous eagerness to prove to Hanna and Easley that he was reliable, he used the offices of the NCF to secure a settlement as quickly as possible regardless of the consequences for steel unionism. Although the UMWA national executive board instructed him to assist the strikers and secure AFL support, Mitchell did neither. He should be condemned for failing to appreciate the importance of this struggle and for failing to support it wholeheartedly. In part because of Mitchell, steel unionism would not become a reality until the 1930s.

Mitchell's true intentions during the steel strike can be discerned from several candid comments made by him and his associates during and after the dispute. Mitchell concentrated far more on his own union and especially the anthracite field than the struggle of steel workers. Several years later, he admitted that at the time of the steel strike he was attempting to secure a conference with anthracite operators, and since the House of Morgan controlled both steel and anthracite, "a good impression made in one arena (would) transfer to the other arena."[64] After the August 23 Pittsburgh conference with Shaffer, Easley fed Mitchell's hopes that his ability to settle the steel strike would help his union in hard coal. "Carry out the policy you spoke of or see if you can," Easley wrote, "and we will get you in such a position . . . that you can get anything you want for your organization."[65]

If the strike was a disaster for the Amalgamated and the labor movement as a whole, it had done much to enhance Mitchell's prestige as a conservative labor leader. Notwithstanding Easley's momentary doubt as to his disdain for sympathy strikes, Mitchell had good reason to believe the strike had put him in good stead among the capitalists of the East. After his September 4 meeting with Schwab, he was almost giddy from the praise he received from J. P. Morgan's right hand man. Schwab had told him in confidence that "any time I wished to discuss labor matters with him he would receive me and give careful consideration to all I said." Mitchell was convinced that Schwab was now in his corner and that the "steel corporation can be used to help us should we need it."[66] Because of Mitchell's conservative approach to the strike, according to fellow conciliation committee member Frank Sargent, "the representatives of capital look upon you as a strong man, wise in your decisions and absolutely fair in your relations between capital and labor."[67] Indeed, during the steel strike Mitchell had demonstrated unstinting loyalty to Easley and Hanna, and he had upheld the sanctity of the contract against the wishes of many within his own union. He had undermined labor solidarity and, in the process, he became the golden boy of the NCF. As the NCF's friendly historian has written, "here was a labor leader upon whom the Federation could count."[68]

In the anthracite region, Mitchell immediately set about translating the goodwill he had earned from Hanna, the NCF, and the Morgan interests into union gains. In return for Morgan's vague promise of a trade agreement in April 1902, Mitchell had committed himself to a full year of labor peace in the region. For Mitchell this seemed a reasonable bargain. He trusted his allies, Hanna and Easley, to make certain railroad presidents kept their word. He would find, however, that the alliance he had forged was not as powerful as he believed. No force, it seemed, was strong enough to bring the hard coal operators to the bargaining table.

In the summer of 1901, Mitchell also found that keeping his promise to prevent local strikes was virtually impossible. He kept numerous organizers in the field to teach the men that local strikes were injurious to their long term interests. While in Fresno on vacation in late May, however, he learned from his organizers that the message was having little effect. Mine workers who regarded strike action as their only means of redress continued to walk out. One organizer noted the "great restlessness in that field, and considerable trouble in making the men understand the principles of the organization." Another organizer regretted "the tendency of the mine workers to strike on the slightest pretext."[69] Despite the efforts of his organizers, the situation did not improve.

What was the reason for this plethora of unauthorized strikes? Did the mine workers not understand that one year of sufferance would lead to union recognition and the redress of their grievances? Mine workers understood the message of the union, they simply did not believe it. Writing Mitchell in August, district presidents claimed the reason so many unauthorized strikes occurred was that, unlike Mitchell, mine workers did not believe a joint conference would be held in 1902. Operators violated so many posted notices and verbal agreements with employee committees that "a large number of people . . . doubt the sincerity of the employers in holding out the hope of a joint conference." District presidents therefore invited Mitchell to attend a tri-district convention on August 27 at Hazleton to convince workers that a trade agreement would in fact be worked out. "If it can be definitely understood that a joint conference will take place," they concluded, "it will do much toward relieving the present tension."[70]

In the midst of steel strike negotiations, Mitchell returned to the scene of his great triumph and took up his room at the same Valley Hotel. When the Hazleton convention opened, Mitchell quickly became alarmed. The numerous complaints that operators were violating the April settlement had created a militant mood. It did not take long before he realized he needed the assistance of Hanna. Because the "men are chafing under alleged violations of agreement on the part of the companies," he warned the "Captain," "radical action was contemplated." It was only through his own influence that "the conservatives finally got control." Upon his request, a resolutions committee was formed and resolutions drafted. He then asked Hanna to help him arrange a conference "with the proper people in New York" to discuss the resolutions.[71]

Hanna's response was less than encouraging. He considered it unfortunate that the anthracite problem should spring up again at the same time "Mr. Morgan and his associates are so disgusted with the Shaffer business." Hanna suggested Mitchell contact E. B. Thomas of the Erie Railroad. Thomas was the most "practical" of the operators and Mitchell had already established a working relationship with him.[72] Mitchell agreed. He was certain that a consultation with Thomas would do much to rectify the trouble. Perhaps Thomas was not even aware that his mine superintendents and foremen were "going out of their way to antagonize our union."[73]

Mitchell had no success securing an appointment with Thomas. Indeed, the Erie president failed to respond to his letters at all. Thus, he called upon the assistance of Easley. Yet even this ally found difficulty arranging an interview for Mitchell. Easley tried to convince Thomas that Mitchell was a reasonable man. "I went all over the part you had taken in the steel strike and the splendid impression you had made on Mr. Schwab and the steel people by your breadth and fairness," Easley explained. Still Thomas was unmoved. Thomas was angered by a letter Mitchell had written him supposedly demanding an interview and threatening a strike.[74] Mitchell now recognized his dilemma. How could he keep control of a restive rank and file while operators remained obstinate? "If Mr. Thomas knew the efforts which I have made to keep down hostile action on the part of others he would not have refused to even reply to my letters." The letter he had sent to Thomas, he explained, contained no strike threat. He had merely stated the fact that mine workers were ready to walk out with or without union support unless their grievances were addressed. If the railroad presidents "are so sensitive that they cannot receive a committee with their mines in operation, they may have an opportunity of receiving them with their mines idle."[75]

Such militant language from his trusted friend convinced Easley of the seriousness of the situation. Easley asked Hanna to intervene and he conferred with Thomas, but nothing concrete developed. At a loss as to what the next step could be, Easley then suggested all action be deferred until after the annual conference of the NCF scheduled for December. Mitchell reluctantly agreed. He could only hope that the NCF conference, at which powerful employers would dine and converse with labor leaders, might have a "far reaching" moral effect on the railroad presidents.[76]

Despite the NCF's failure to settle the two major disturbances of the past year, the steel strike and the machinists strike, Easley had grand hopes for the December 1901 NCF Conference on Industrial Mediation and Conciliation. "I feel sure we can make this the biggest industrial conference ever held in this country," Easley declared. No one but "top-liners" from capital and labor would be invited. He hoped to induce Schwab and Morgan to attend, and "a big Railroad President, and a big manufacturer, so that, when the largest leaders of labor come here, they will meet the largest leaders of capital."[77] Easley's optimism stemmed from his knowledge that Mark Hanna had now committed himself publicly to the NCF and was going to play a central role in its affairs. Although Hanna had always expressed an interest in the organization, he did not officially associate himself with it until the fall of 1901.[78] Hanna had the contacts and influence among politicians, industrialists, and labor leaders to make the NCF a viable organ for industrial peace. As far as Mitchell was concerned, Hanna's affiliation with the NCF meant a merger and a strengthening of his two allies and was therefore a cause for hope and celebration.

The conference exceeded Easley's expectations. A dazzling list of elites paraded to the podium, each reciting the happy refrain that the NCF's educational and mediational work would soon eliminate all industrial strife. "Tribunal of Peace" read the headline in the *Chicago Tribune*, while the *Catholic World* called it "The Marriage of Capital and Labor."[79] Mitchell played a starring role in the drama. He provided the crowd with another one of his increasingly famous pleas for the adoption of the trade agreement as the basis of lasting industrial harmony. The relationship between capital and labor was "not a complex problem." It was simply a matter of "reason and common horse sense" on the part of employers and workers. He claimed he had never, in all his experience, seen a strike that could not have been averted through a joint conference. The NCF understood the importance of the trade agreement, and if everyone involved gave it enough time and energy, it would significantly reduce industrial strife. "If through the medium of this movement we can bring the representatives of each of these apparently antagonistic forces together, if we can sit down, look into each other's eyes, tell each other the exact truth, then the happy days of industrial peace and prosperity for all shall have arrived."[80]

Rarely did Mark Hanna make public speeches, but he made an exception at this conference. Since Hanna would dictate the NCF's affairs for the next two years, it is therefore essential to understand fully his attitudes toward the labor problem. For Hanna the labor question was essentially a political question, and he endorsed the trade agreement for political reasons. Industrial warfare raised the specter of working-class radicalism, a process which could only be diverted by cultivating responsible, conservative unionism. In his NCF address at the December conference, he summed up this view with precision. Both trusts and trade unions developed naturally, he said, since both "are but forward steps in the great industrial evolution that is taking place." The proper policy toward unions should not be one of destruction, but should be an attempt to steer them in an evolutionary rather than a revolutionary course. Pitched battles such as those that had occurred at Homestead and at Pullman were inherently dangerous. They jeopardized continued economic growth, and worse, they fostered political extremism among workers. If, on the other hand, unions were granted recognition and accepted as legitimate social institutions, the political threat arising from class conflict would be defused. He announced that his "plan is to have organized labor Americanized in the best sense, and thoroughly educated to an understanding of its responsibilities, and in this way to make it the ally of the capitalist, rather than a foe with which to grapple."[81] Thus, Hanna's political motivation for supporting trade agreements was not identical to Mitchell's motivation, which was rooted in the economic reality of the soft coal industry where the trade agreement had increased union growth and living standards.

After the speeches, the conference participants and guests wined and dined and talked. Mitchell gabbed with corporate executives, bishops, politicians, a university president, and even ex-President Grover Cleveland. How could Mitchell not be impressed? He supped on extravagant food and drank expensive wine. He was socializing with the most powerful men in the nation. He craved their respect and they apparently respected him. All of these were things beyond the wildest dreams of a fatherless child of the pits. Yes, he told these men what they wanted to hear, but to say that he was insincere would be to miss the point. For Mitchell was expressing ideas he was honestly coming to believe as he formulated, for the first time, his position on the proper role of the labor movement in American life. And he was encouraged to believe these ideas by the acceptance they found among his fellow NCF members. How could hundreds of the most powerful people in the nation—union leaders among them—be wrong?

The organizational structure of the NCF was also revamped at this conference. The old conciliation committee became the Industrial Department with a membership of three hundred. Mark Hanna was selected chair of the new department. The goal was still the promotion of trade agreements and the mediation of strikes, but new means to achieve these twin goals were devised. To help disseminate information, a journal was to be founded. To deal with smaller strikes and lockouts, permanent boards of conciliation were to be set up in all major cities.[82] Many believed the NCF was no longer just talking about peace, it had recruited the people and set up the institutions to make industrial peace a reality.

Mitchell was one of those believers. He carefully read the press comments he received through the UMWA "clipping bureau," and he was amazed to find that even his high expectations of the conference had "proven too conservative." The conference was "the biggest thing of its kind in the history of our country," he told Easley, "and its beneficent effect is sure to be felt everywhere." The only thing lacking was an actual example of the NCF's ability to avert a strike and introduce a trade agreement in a major industry that appeared impervious to unionization. Mitchell implied the anthracite industry would be a good choice. Reminding Easley of the turbulence among hard coal's rank and file, he wrote that "I have no doubt that the time is not remote" when the services of the Industrial Department "may be called upon."[83]

By 1901, Mitchell was no longer simply the president of the miners. Whether he liked the idea or not, his fame had made him a spokesperson for the entire labor movement. Therefore, his attitudes on numerous issues took on new meaning. How should the labor movement respond to the growing numbers of immigrants and African-Americans in the nonfarm work force? Should the craft union structure of the AFL be discarded in favor of industrial unionism to accommodate the rising tide of unskilled workers in mass production industries? Should the AFL become more active in the political arena to combat its powerful foes? American workers eagerly awaited answers to these and other fundamental labor issues from the new star in the movement's galaxy, the militant hero of the hard coal strike of 1900, John Mitchell.

For those working-class Americans who envisioned a bold transformation of the labor movement, Mitchell's views were disappointing. For those who regarded the AFL as the conservative bastion of native-born, white, male, skilled workers and were pressing for a more inclusive movement,

Mitchell proved an obstacle rather than an ally. And for industrial union advocates and those demanding the formation of a third political party to advance labor's cause, Mitchell represented the status quo. Although he was the head of an industrial union with a positive record on the organization of immigrants and African-Americans, and although he was second vice president of the AFL, Mitchell failed to champion the cause of progressive reform within the national labor movement. To the great dismay of radicals and reformers, his conservative views on the salient labor questions of the day buttressed the cautious and increasingly outmoded policies of Gompers and the AFL Executive Council.

Indeed, in many ways, Mitchell personified the conservative trade union leader of the Progressive Era. Radical opponents found him on the wrong side of every issue. His acceptance of industrial capitalism and pursuit of capital-labor harmony was a denial of the class struggle. His participation in the NCF, an organization controlled by monopoly capitalists, served only to "chloroform" the class consciousness of working people. His outspoken condemnation of sympathy strikes and belief in the sanctity of contracts undermined labor solidarity. His sabotage of the steel strike killed an opportunity to begin the organization of mass production industries. Moreover, radicals found him wanting on the questions of race, ethnicity, industrial unionism, and political action.

Mitchell's stance toward African-Americans and immigrants reflected the racist and anti-foreign attitudes he had learned as a youth. Despite the positive role immigrants had played in the 1900 hard coal strike, despite the many accolades they had given him, Mitchell went on public record to say that immigrants did not make good unionists. Speaking before the U.S. Industrial Commission, he claimed that "people from the non-English speaking countries of Europe" were responsible for lowering the standard of living in mining districts. While immigrants from the British Isles had solid trade union backgrounds, he knew of "no trade unions in Hungary and Italy, and those people have been undesirable as far as our organization is concerned." Therefore, Mitchell believed "a law should be enacted prohibiting immigration of foreigners to this country."[84]

Similarly, despite the fact that African-American miners were loyal to the union and held numerous positions of authority at the district and local level, he condemned them before the commission with the same contempt he held for immigrants. When asked if African-Americans were "a desirable class of miners," he answered: "No; their standard of morality is not as high as that of white people; they are not as desirable citizens." While mentioning that the UMWA "does not make distinctions between classes," he found blacks lazy and a danger to the union because they were willing to accept a lower scale of wages. "My opinion is usually that colored persons in the mine are not satisfied to work to a large extent at all; but when they do work they will accept less than white men."[85]

In comparison to other unions at this time, the UMWA had an outstanding record on organizing immigrants and African-Americans. The UMWA was one of the few unions to actively recruit immigrant and African-American workers and enroll them on an equal status with native born, white members. Moreover, before union conventions and other labor gatherings, Mitchell never disparaged African-Americans or immigrants. Except for occasional public remarks, his views were largely personal ones. As far as can be discerned from his personal papers, although he certainly never encouraged the promotion of African-Americans or immigrants to powerful posts in his administration, he never denied union membership or advancement on the basis of race or ethnicity. As Mitchell's personal views indicate, however, union policy on race and ethnicity sprang from the nature of the industry, not the "progressive" outlook of its president.

Outside the UMWA, the great majority of unions in the Progressive Era discriminated against immigrants and African-Americans. Sometimes unions did so explicitly through constitutional restrictions, and other times the restrictions were implicit. Since most unions organized skilled workers only and regulated the apprenticeship programs necessary to obtain those skills, few except white, native born males could gain entry. The craft union policy of the American Federation of Labor, therefore, posed a serious impediment to a more inclusionary labor movement and industrial unionism became the battle cry for those who wanted to organize all workers regardless of skill, race, ethnicity, or gender. Since the UMWA had been, since its founding, the most powerful advocate of industrial unionism, Mitchell's views on this subject were of great significance for the future direction of the labor movement.

The UMWA constitution claimed the right of the union to represent all workers in an around the mine. This industrial union stance reflected the nature of the industry. At every mine there were numerous employees who, while not miners, were vital to the mining process. Blacksmiths, engineers, carpenters, and others provided essential skills. If each skilled group belonged to a separate union, a strike by a small number could shut down the entire mine. Thus, pragmatic considerations forced Mitchell and other UMWA leaders to adopt industrial unionism. And in his attempt to make industrial unionism a reality, Mitchell never sought to join forces with those who saw it as an ideological issue.

At the 1901 UMWA convention, Mitchell pushed for passage of a resolution demanding an industrial charter to organize all workers in and around the mines. Delegates dutifully responded.[86] He then led the fight at the 1901 AFL convention to obtain an industrial charter. The thrust of his argument at the AFL convention was that the UMWA could only live up to its contracts with operators if it controlled the "outside" workers' right to strike. Gompers agreed, and the result was the adoption of the Scranton Declaration, granting an industrial union charter to the UMWA.[87] Mitchell's intent was hardly the radicalization of the AFL by promoting industrial unionism. As we shall see, in later years when socialists introduced resolutions in favor of industrial unionism, he stood by Gompers and the craft union heads of the AFL and helped defeat these efforts.

Other than his desire to secure an industrial union charter, he showed very little interest in the affairs of the AFL during his early years in office. Although he was second vice president of the Federation, and as chief of the largest union he was in a position to exert real power over its policies, he did not view the AFL as a vehicle to promote his interests. He correctly regarded the AFL as a weak organization. True power rested in the affiliated unions. Mitchell was, of course, flattered when urged by friends to replace Gompers as president, and he was quite certain he could have the post if he wanted it, but he never expressed a desire to fill Gompers's shoes. He considered the AFL presidency less powerful and less demanding than his present position. "Possibly when I grow old and frail and want a job where you have nothing to do but draw your salary and look wise," he wrote just before the 1901 AFL convention, "I will be willing to accept the prestigious honor of presiding over the destinies of the American Federation of Labor."[88] The same recognition of his own power in the AFL and lack of interest in its activities was illustrated again in 1901 when his friend Billy Ryan wanted him to help out a mutual acquaintance by getting him a job as AFL organizer. Mitchell replied that Gompers would agree or he would make trouble. "I have asked very few favors at the hands of the A. F. of L.," he wrote.[89]

By 1901, Gompers and Mitchell had begun to develop a close working relationship. Letters that passed between them, other than routine administrative business, were marked "Dear Sam" and "Dear John." That a certain intimacy developed was not surprising. Despite coming from radically different backgrounds, both shared a fondness for alcohol and intrigue, and to a great extent, both shared similar outlooks on most social and economic issues. Thus, to the extent Mitchell did involve himself in AFL activities, his stance was largely in accord with the attitude and policies of Gompers. Mitchell was perhaps less doctrinaire than Gompers on the positive role of state intervention in economic affairs, calling for a compulsory eight-hour-day law for instance, but he was in basic agreement with the AFL president that trade union economic power was the best method to advance their interests. Mitchell therefore upheld the voluntarism of the AFL. Coal would be stabilized through collective bargaining between consenting private interests. Government interference could only undermine the relationship between operators and the union. Nationalization schemes were rejected out of hand.

Similarly, Mitchell had little objection to the AFL's nonpartisan policy. His political vision, at this time, amounted to little more than the often repeated call for the labor movement to reward its friends and punish its enemies. Believing there was no clear cut distinction for working people between the Republican and Democratic parties, Mitchell accepted the current practice of submitting the AFL's political program to both national conventions and informing union members of candidates' attitudes toward labor's agenda. While he urged a revitalization of the AFL's political commitment in 1903, asking that the AFL become a "central clearinghouse" of political information, he never questioned the nonpartisan policy itself.[90] He counseled against the formation of an independent labor or socialist party. A special interest, such as organized labor, could gain more concessions by lobbying the two dominant parties. "A strong, well-organized group of men determined upon a given line of policy," he wrote, "can usually secure all or a portion of their demands from one or the other of their parties by maintaining neutrality between them."[91]

A variety of criteria can be used to judge the legacy of any historical figure. Words, actions, intentions, and accomplishments are all valid bases of assessment. Especially useful in analyzing Mitchell's legacy is the issue of missed opportunities and actions never taken. His role in the AFL begs the question of what might have been. He could have thrown the weight of the AFL's largest affiliate behind the push to restructure the labor movement along industrial lines. He could have used his prestige and power to break down racial and ethnic barriers in other affiliates. He could have led a progressive crusade to create a more inclusive, and hence more potent, labor movement. Yet he never considered joining, let alone leading, such a crusade. To the radicals his views were thoroughly bourgeois and conservative, symptomatic of a labor movement that cowered before the capitalists.

Mitchell, however, scoffed at such assessments. The AFL was making steady advance along its present course. Other affiliates were experiencing membership growth and securing wage advances similar to his own UMWA. Many employers were slowly accepting union existence for the first time in the nation's history, and the NCF served to goad the dwindling number of employers who insisted on fighting unions tooth and nail to see the error of their ways. Unions could continue to prosper as long as they convinced capitalists they were "responsible," meaning as long as they lived up to their contracts and refrained from political radicalism. In his eyes, there was no need for a crusade to alter the course of the labor movement. The day was not distant when most workers would enjoy the peace and prosperity afforded by the trade agreement. As for immigrants and African-Americans in mass production industries, his personal prejudices denied them a role in his vision of the movement's future.

While he often mused about the national labor movement, Mitchell always remained focused on the affairs of his own union. And by the end of 1901, he not only faced problems in anthracite, but there was also an imminent threat to the joint conference system in the bituminous industry: West Virginia. The problem posed by West Virginia had not been addressed since his efforts to organize that district as vice president in 1898. Indeed, the problem was growing. By 1901, West Virginia was one of the largest coal producing states in the nation. Cheap nonunion coal stole markets from union operators, and union miners felt the pinch when their hours were reduced. Unless he organized West Virginia, he would be met with the demands of union operators to accept a sizeable wage reduction. He realized the "prospect of any improvement on our interstate scale, or even its renewal, is very much endangered by the situation in West Virginia."[92] As he approached this crisis, he recalled the difficulties he had encountered several years before—the injunctions preventing organizers from reaching the miners, the isolation of the mining camps, and the apparent willingness of the miners to work for low wages. West Virginia did not bring back pleasant memories.

At a national executive board meeting in August 1901, he outlined the plan of organization. It had a familiar ring. A corps of organizers would be sent in. Through private discussions, mass meetings, and circulars, organizers would create dissatisfaction with existing conditions and enroll new members. A convention of miners would then be held, after which operators would be invited to a joint conference. If operators failed to attend, miners would establish a wage scale "and set a date for its enforcement by strike if necessary."[93] The only difference between this and other drives was the larger number of organizers involved. Mitchell was prepared to spend as much money as it required to take West Virginia once and for all.

Because so much of his time was consumed by anthracite affairs, Mitchell reluctantly agreed to place Vice President Tom L. Lewis in charge of the organizing campaign. Mitchell's inability to trust Lewis, and Lewis's apparent determination to sabotage Mitchell's administration almost proved the undoing of the campaign from its very inception. The hostility between the two men was so intense that when Mitchell formulated specific instructions for the drive, he sent them to Secretary-Treasurer Wilson and not to Lewis directly. Nor did he bother to inform Lewis directly that he was in fact to head up the organizing drive![95] Not until September 21 did Mitchell communicate with Lewis. He ordered Lewis to go to West Virginia, familiarize himself with the various sections of the state, hold a meeting of organizers on October 1 in Parkersburg, then establish a campaign headquarters where he would remain and supervise the drive.[94]

Lewis dutifully went to West Virginia and held the meeting of organizers, but then left to attend to prior engagements in Ohio. He simply refused to take responsibility for directing the organizers.[96] Frustrated and angry, Mitchell remained the consummate tactician. Rather than challenge Lewis's insubordination directly, he chose to interpret Lewis's failure to follow orders as a simple misunderstanding. In the future he would try to "make my instructions sufficiently plain that they cannot be misunderstood." And in clear and precise language, Mitchell stripped Lewis of authority. One national organizer in each of the five principal fields would now be responsible for organizing work, and these organizers would report directly to Mitchell. This increased his already burdensome workload, but it reduced Lewis's role considerably. Lewis would now serve only as a speaker, using his prestige as national officer to convince West Virginia miners of the need to join a union. Mitchell planned the first convention of the drive for October 31 in Huntington, and he wanted Lewis to drum up as much support as possible.[97]

Lewis proved unwilling to fulfill even this light duty. He again went to West Virginia, but he remained just three days before returning home to Ohio. With the nerve for which he was known, he claimed "the instructions given me did not convey your idea of what I should do in West Virginia." Besides, wrote Lewis, "I was called home on urgent matters." Mitchell sarcastically inquired whether Lewis had settled his affairs satisfactorily and whether he now saw fit to devote attention to union matters. Lewis then mysterious fell ill with "the Grip" and did not return to West Virginia until October 21.[98]

Lewis, of course, was far less interested in promoting unionism in West Virginia than he was in promoting his own candidacy for the UMWA presidency. Mitchell knew full well that Lewis planned to run against him in the next union election. He had information that Lewis was making campaign speeches in Ohio, and that Patrick Dolan of District 5 and former UMWA and AFL President John McBride were actively promoting him.[99] While Mitchell did not fear losing the contest, he did resent Lewis's brazen obstructionism that risked an important organizing drive and added to his own tasks. Although his administration might appear harmonious, he informed his brother-in-law, "under the surface there is a bitter fight being waged against me by the Lewis, McBride, Dolan element." He would undoubtedly defeat these foes as he had in years past, but "the fact that Lewis is Vice-President compels me to do more work than I should, and more really than I am physically able to stand." He could not afford to give Lewis his "confidence, or entrust him with any important duty, as he has taken advantage of every opportunity which presents itself to do me injury."[100] Unable to dislodge Lewis from his present post, unable to retire for fear that Lewis would gain the presidency and ruin the organization, Mitchell saw no choice but to carry on stoically with his enemy as vice president.

After receiving mixed signals from organizers in the field, Mitchell could not be certain how successful the miners' conference at Huntington would be. Mitchell, Wilson, and even Lewis attended, demonstrating the importance of West Virginia for the future of soft coal. Yet only 120 delegates showed, far fewer than was hoped. Nevertheless, Mitchell decided to follow the plan of organization outlined in August. The convention drafted a circular calling for a joint conference with the operators to be held November 27.[101] At the close of the convention, he returned to Indianapolis where he devoted as much of his time as possible writing letters and making phone calls to operators in organized districts in the hope they would exert pressure on West Virginia operators to attend the joint conference. He also encouraged organizers to redouble their efforts so the upcoming joint conference would be a success.[102]

Initially, Mitchell received some positive feedback from both operators and organizers. The antics of Tom L. Lewis, however, continued to plague the entire campaign. At the conclusion of the Huntington convention, Lewis was to embark on an extended speaking tour in a final effort to rally the miners. As soon as the convention adjourned, naturally, he left for Ohio under the pretext of pressing district business. Lewis agreed to begin the tour on November 11, so Mitchell went ahead and lined up several meetings at which Lewis was to be the featured speaker. Lewis never attended those meetings. He remained in Ohio where he claimed matters were still unsettled. On November 14, Lewis informed Mitchell that his services would be required in Ohio for the next few weeks! Lewis's irresponsibility left Mitchell more dumbfounded than angry. He found it hard to believe the vice president would disregard instructions and injure the entire movement in West Virginia "at a time when so much depended upon the sentiment which we might be able to create" before the joint conference.[103]

Tom L. Lewis was not the only one who undermined the organizing drive. West Virginia operators played an even more conspicuous role in upsetting Mitchell's plans. In the weeks prior to the proposed joint conference, union sympathizers were discharged in large numbers and private mine guards hired, making their attitudes toward the unionization of their mines quite obvious.[104] And when operators failed to attend the joint conference on November 27, the union was unprepared to carry out its threatened strike. Only 5,000 of the state's miners belonged to the union, and continued organization would be necessary before a strike was initiated.[105]

The failure to organize West Virginia before the end of the year had disastrous consequences for all union soft coal miners. At the interstate joint conference in February 1902, operators voiced their anger over the union's inability to crush this threat to their markets. One powerful operator from the Pittsburgh district, F. L. Robbins, charged that every year on the eve of the interstate conference a few union men were sent to West Virginia to organize that state "and you call that organization! I call it a simple blind attempt to make a show to present to the operators of this interstate conference and nothing else."[106] Operators therefore refused to grant a wage advance.

In the weeks that followed, Mitchell fully came to appreciate how the West Virginia failure jeopardized soft coal trade agreements. During the lengthy process of negotiating district settlements, the rank and file grew restive, many demanding strike action rather than accept the same scale. Mitchell needed all his powers of persuasion to hold the miners of Illinois on the job.[107] "Every settlement we have made," he confided to a friend, "has been against the wishes of a majority of our delegates. We have literally been compelled to shove our agreements down the throats of our delegates." It was difficult enough to battle operators at the conference table, "but it is even worse to be forced to fight our own people, who seem to think they are strong enough to force any condition they desire."[108] He understood that if West Virginia remained unorganized, the trade agreement in soft coal might soon collapse.

When Mitchell burst onto the national scene after the 1900 anthracite strike, his words and actions set the standard for conservative trade union leadership. His enthusiastic participation in the NCF, his public condemnation of strikes, his political nonpartisanship, and his refusal to support the steel strike earned for him the respect and admiration of corporate capitalists and conservative politicians. He considered these men partners in his efforts to extend the trade agreement to the hard coal fields as the basis of labor peace. These men had promised him their influence would soon bring the hard coal barons to terms. And Mitchell believed them. He placed even more faith in their promises than he did in the power of a rank and file who idolized him.

Yet not all was rosy for the conservative labor leader as he faced his prospects in 1902. In the organized bituminous fields the inability to take West Virginia and the consequent failure to advance the mining scale had created widespread dissatisfaction among the rank and file for the first time in several years. Unless he acted decisively and aggressively, the trade agreement bequeathed to him in 1898 would be shattered. In the anthracite fields Mitchell faced an even more explosive situation. The militancy of the hard coal diggers had been mounting steadily since the 1900 strike, erupting in numerous local strikes that Mitchell had vowed to prevent. Unless Hanna and Easley could make good on their promises to bring about a joint conference in anthracite, he would have no choice but to unleash that militancy for a second time in what might well be a fight to the finish.

Chapter 5

The Great Strike of 1902

Mitchell was already a well-known labor leader in early 1902. The hard coal strike of 1900 had given him a measure of fame and approval uncommon in an era when organized labor was depicted as a radical movement operating on the pale of social respectability. It was the hard coal strike of 1902, however, that ensured his place in the pantheon of great labor leaders. His Herculean efforts on behalf of the 150,000 anthracite mine workers in a righteous but socially responsible war against the coal barons was the focus of national media attention for more than five months. His ability to control the strike field, and at the same time maneuver successfully on the complex terrain of national politics, earned for him the devotion of working people and the admiration of the press and political establishment. By the time the strike ended, Mitchell had become a national hero, a larger than life symbol of the collective aspirations of the dispossessed.

In his annual address to the national convention in 1902, Mitchell spoke on developments in the anthracite region over the past year. And in his mind the positive far outweighed the negative. It was true that the railroad presidents had "for reasons best known to themselves" refused to meet in joint conference with union officials in the spring of 1901. Despite this failure, mine workers had stood by their union. Indeed, membership figures for the three anthracite districts showed an increase. An equally pleasing development had been his meeting with the president of the Erie Railroad, E. B. Thomas, "to whom all other companies had delegated authority to act for them." Thomas had promised that "if matters ran along satisfactorily during the year" the railroads would give "fair consideration" to entering into a trade agreement. Mitchell never mentioned his inability to secure a second meeting with Thomas in the fall of 1901, nor did he comment directly on the local strikes that plagued the industry and seemed beyond his control. He did, however, indirectly concede that matters in the anthracite region were reaching a boiling point and that he was prepared to lead them in strike action if negotiations failed. The "paramount" issues in anthracite were the eight hour day, a minimum wage scale and union recognition, he concluded, and "I believe that I voice the sentiments of all anthracite mine workers when I say that they are ready and willing to take any step this convention may determine upon to attain these ends."[1]

Mitchell guided the convention to adopt the steps he believed necessary. He secured passage of a resolution granting him control of negotiations. A second resolution pledged the financial assistance of the union to a hard coal strike if one were "forced upon" the union. In a beautiful display of solidarity, soft coal and hard coal workers joined together and adopted a third resolution stating that in the event of a strike, if it was found that soft coal was being used to maintain hard coal markets, the national executive board was empowered to order "a national suspension of work."[2] Mitchell, of course, had no intention of ordering a nationwide walk out in both bituminous and anthracite no matter how desperate the situation became. Such a move entailed the violation of existing contracts with soft coal operators, something Mitchell would never seriously contemplate. Yet the fact Mitchell controlled the resolutions committee, and that the resolution had been introduced by one of his trusted supporters in anthracite, Thomas Duffy of District 7, and supported on the floor by one of his ablest lieutenants in bituminous, John P. Reese of Iowa, left little doubt that Mitchell approved the resolution and recognized its strategic value as a threat to hard coal operators.

Anthracite was a tinderbox ready to explode in February 1902. Local unauthorized strikes still occurred with regularity, and Mitchell had received no word from Hanna or Easley to indicate that the railroad presidents had become more receptive to union overtures. It was therefore with a sense of emergency that he set about negotiations which would defuse the situation before the April 1 deadline. He and the three district presidents wrote E. B. Thomas on April 13. Reminding Thomas of his pledge to arrange a joint conference, Mitchell notified him that the time had come to make good on this pledge. Recognition of the union need not be something to fear, Mitchell assured him. Where the joint conference was now in operation, the UMWA met with the "unqualified approval" of the operators involved. Let us now apply our union's "business principles" to anthracite.[3] Mitchell then sent invitations to all the railroad presidents for a joint conference of operators and miners to be held March 12 at Scranton.[4]

Thomas's response showed the direction negotiations would take. The Erie president was the "reasonable" one, the one who, according to Mitchell, had spoken for all of the railroad presidents when he promised a joint conference in 1902. Now Thomas adamantly denied ever having represented other railroads. "If you will recall what passed at that interview between you and me last year, you cannot fail to recollect . . . my distinct, positive and unequivocal statement to the effect that I represented no interests whatever other than those controlled by the Erie Company." The fact that other railroads took similar action was a matter of coincidence. As to the hope of a joint conference, he reminded Mitchell that the promise was contingent upon the union's ability to control the mine workers. This the union had failed to do. He declared that "at no time during the last twenty years has a greater spirit of unrest and agitation prevailed upon the anthracite miners than has existed during the past year." Thomas declined the invitation to Scranton. So, too, did all the other railroad presidents. While Mitchell probably expected rejections, the operators' apparent denial of the impending crisis in the industry must have taken him by surprise. In a typical response, W. H. Truesdale of the Delaware, Lackawanna, and Western Railroad suggested his mine workers were "all well satisfied with their present rates of wages, their hours of work, and the general conditions under which they perform their work for us."[5]

Mitchell also worked behind the scenes through the new NCF Industrial Department to gain a hearing with the coal barons. When the executive committee of the department convened in February at New York, Hanna and other committee members tried without success to arrange a meeting with the railroad presidents. Hanna was able, however, to arrange an interview between Mitchell and J. P. Morgan in February. Mitchell recalled vividly the assurance Morgan gave him: "If the railroad presidents were wrong he would not sustain them; if the miners were wrong he would not help them." Even though Morgan vowed to "do what was right in the matter," the mighty financier refused to intervene at this juncture. Mitchell was unable to comprehend why Morgan would not involve himself before negotiations broke down. Easley offered the implausible excuse that Morgan had "a lot of unruly (railroad) presidents on his hands who are willing to resign any minute if he undertakes to coerce them."[6]

With coal barons refusing to recognize the coming crisis, with his NCF allies apparently unable to bring about a conference, and with Morgan simply refusing to intervene, the situation in anthracite became increasing worrisome. A tri-district convention had been scheduled for March 18 in Shamokin, and as the convention date approached, operators began posting notices that the current wage rates would be continued for another year.[7] Mitchell understood that mine workers were in no mood to accept a continuance of the present wage scales. Before leaving for Shamokin, he contacted Easley and asked him to attend the convention. "Matters there are assuming dangerous proportions," he wailed, "and I fear that unless the railway Presidents will give our organization some recognition and some concessions, trouble will ensue." Moreover, he was not about to try to force the mine workers to accept the situation without protest. He explained that while he did not relish a strike, "I will not advise the anthracite miners to lay down unless the railway Presidents show some disposition to meet them half way."[8]

Easley did not attend the Shamokin convention, preferring to stay in New York and keep pressure on the operators. Mitchell was thus left to face the restive mine workers on his own. While he made no attempt to silence those who demanded strike action on April 1, he did recommend the NCF be given one more chance to mediate the dispute. His description of that organization revealed his immense respect for both Hanna and Easley. "In view of the fact that a great and powerful organization has been formed whose object and purpose is to try to avert strikes by brining employer and employee into conference," he counseled, "I believe that a strike in the anthracite field should not be engaged in until that tribunal has been appealed to." If the NCF failed, then the strike call would be issued. The delegates approved Mitchell's plan.[9]

Even before his advice was adopted, he had been in constant contact with both Hanna and Easley urging them to arrange a conference with the operators.[10] This time, with the real threat of a strike staring them in the face, operators agreed to have a meeting with Mitchell and the three district presidents under the auspices of the NCF. At long last, Mitchell had secured his meeting with the railroad presidents. At long last, he had his opportunity to realize the vision of capital-labor harmony he had expressed at the December 1901 national conference of the NCF: if employers and employees sat down, looked into each other's eyes, and told the truth, strikes would be made unnecessary. The anthracite operators must not have heard this speech, for although the meeting was held, it served only to postpone tensions, not solve them.

Ralph Easley, who considered the anthracite operators "forty years behind the times in their attitude toward organized labor," recalled that it took "all the resources at the command of the (NCF) committee" to prevail upon them to attend the meeting with Mitchell.[11] Exactly why the operators chose to attend the meeting may never be known, but the hostility toward union demands led Mitchell to believe that their sole intent was to measure the strength of the union.[12] He nevertheless presented the union demands in clear and unemotional tones, earning himself the respect of employers on the NCF committee if not the operators. Committee member Marcus M. Marks congratulated Mitchell on his "magnificent effort," amazed that he did not for a moment lose his equanimity.[13] But the operators were unmoved and claimed they would rather go into bankruptcy than surrender to the union. The only agreement secured at this meeting was a commitment by Mitchell to postpone the threatened strike for thirty days.[14]

Mitchell emerged from this conference depressed, convinced more than ever that a strike was inevitable despite the thirty day respite. In a letter to his close friend, soft coal operator Harry Taylor, he spelled out his troubles and how they preyed on his personal life. "I oft' times wished that I were constituted differently," he wrote, "and could, after working hours, forget the troubles and cares of my office." But that was impossible for his "work is constantly in my mind; I think of it going to bed and even dream of it while asleep." Contemplating the grave possibility of a massive work stoppage, Mitchell, although not a religious man, wondered "what will be the Lord's position in our scrap" with the coal barons.[15] Moreover, his health once again failed him. Just prior to the Shamokin convention he complained of "heart pains" that forced him to cut short a speech he was making in Iowa, and in early April he confessed his condition had worsened. He complained of heart, lung, and back difficulties. "I fear that unless I can get a rest I am going to break down altogether," he wrote. He blamed "overwork and anxiety" for his troubles and wanted to visit a health resort where he could receive medical attention.[16]

Mitchell, Hanna, and Easley were tireless in their efforts throughout April to find a peaceful solution. Mitchell and Hanna even discussed the situation with President Roosevelt at Hanna's Washington, D. C. residence.[17] The only result of this diplomacy was an agreement by the operators to attend a second NCF conference with union officials on April 26. At this conference, the operators evinced less hostility. Some even expressed a growing fondness for Mitchell. According to Easley, two of the railroad presidents commented on "what a fair, square fellow he seems to be."[18] Nothing concrete resulted from this meeting, but a subcommittee composed of three railroad chiefs, the three district presidents and Mitchell was created to continue the talks on April 29. At this point Mitchell had all but abandoned the possibility of peace. On the day before the subcommittee met, he wrote that he had "little hopes of a settlement, as the operators persist in their statement that the industry will not justify any increase in the cost of production."[19]

The subcommittee met for two days and the only one to budge was Mitchell. The principal demands adopted at Shamokin conference had been a eight-hour day and a 20 percent increase for contract work. Mitchell now proposed a compromise of nine hours and a 10 percent increase. Even this the operators rejected as economically unfeasible.[20] The subcommittee disbanded without success. In a last ditch effort to avoid a strike, Mitchell then met with key NCF members including Easley. He agreed to back down once more, this time insisting on a mere 5 percent increase. Operators rejected this proposition as well.[21]

Was Mitchell willing to accept so small an advance? Was he willing to accept any settlement, even token concessions, to avert a confrontation? Most definitely. At least as early as the Shamokin convention, he knew that if a strike came, it would be a long, drawn out fight to the end. He realized then the strike could become "one of the most bitter struggles between employer and employee that this country has ever seen," that employers could last six months and afford to spend millions of dollars.[22] Such a struggle could easily deplete the union's treasury and destroy the UMWA in hard coal. No responsible union officer took these risks lightly. There were also personal considerations involved. Mitchell was not a well man, and he understood that "the work of the union official doubles and trebles as soon as a strike is declared."[23] Fatigue from the five-week strike of 1900 had nearly put him in the hospital.

Was he capable of that type of exertion for six months? The welfare of the anthracite mine workers and their families was another concern. Mitchell had personal knowledge from his own youth of the misery and deprivation that strikers and their families endured during long strikes. The labor leader "dreads the hardships, the suffering, the privation, the anguish of men whose wives and children are famished and freezing, the despair that comes at the end and destroys the slow patient work of long years."[24]

There were other factors that prompted Mitchell's 5 percent proposal. One was his desire to cultivate public opinion. Since the summer of 1901, he had been engaged in a media campaign to promote the trade agreement in hard coal. He wrote two articles for mass circulation magazines designed to rally public support behind efforts to combat the continuing misery of hard coal diggers through the trade agreement.[25] He concluded one of the articles with a direct emotional plea for public support of his efforts: "If the great sympathetic American public could see for itself, could know as I know the sorrows and the heartaches of those who spend their lives in the coal mines of our country, I am sure that they would give their unqualified support to every effort which is being made by the organizations of labor to ameliorate conditions under which these men work."[26] In order to maintain the public support he had worked so hard to create, especially for a second strike in less than two years, Mitchell understood that every effort must be made to appear reasonable and always ready to compromise.

Finally, and perhaps most importantly, Mitchell pursued the 5 percent proposal because of his perceived need to maintain his alliance with Hanna, Easley, and the NCF. He realized that displaying a willingness to compromise, every bit as much as demonstrating one's commitment to uphold the sanctity of contracts, was necessary to maintain the support of this "great and powerful organization." In Mitchell's eyes, if a suspension came, the services of the NCF would play a crucial role in its outcome. He thus had to make certain the union did not appear the aggressor in this conflict, that he had explored every possible avenue of peace, that he remained the labor leader they could trust.

For all these reasons Mitchell wanted peace, but he was playing a dangerous game. Unless he received concrete concessions from operators, he would have to call a strike or risk losing the support of the rank and file. The mine workers had allowed Mitchell to quell their desire to strike in the spring of 1901 with vague operator promises of future action that had proven meaningless. They would not be so easily deterred this year. Thus, Mitchell faced the ultimate crisis of a conservative labor leader. He was caught in the middle between a union membership hungry for economic justice and employers determined not to surrender absolute control. If he had promised employers he could discipline his men, he had also promised his men that he could secure redress of their grievances. These were the thoughts that caused his anxiety, these were the thoughts that invaded his dreams. On May 7 at Scranton, he convened a meeting of the anthracite districts' executive boards to decide whether a strike should be called.

When the board members met, Mitchell canvassed their attitudes and steered them toward one final, public appeal for peace. In a letter signed by himself and T. D. Nicholls of District 1, Mitchell offered to submit the demands of the Shamokin convention to arbitration "with the earnest desire and hope of averting the impending calamity." The arbitration proposal suggested the NCF Industrial Department appoint a committee of five to decide all questions in dispute, and that the committee's decision be made effective for one year. If that proposition proved unacceptable, Mitchell proposed that a committee of three, composed of Archbishop John Ireland of St. Paul, Minnesota, and Bishop Henry Potter of New York, and one other person these two selected, investigate and make binding recommendations.[27]

Willingness to arbitrate had been an effective propaganda technique in the strike of 1900, and the suggestion that two respected men of the cloth should be the arbiters was a nice touch. Who could be more fair? The coal barons, of course, dismissed arbitration out of hand, but Mitchell had attained his desired goal. Hanna wrote Mitchell on May 9: "I am glad to note that your committee are (*sic*) acting without haste and disposed to be conservative." Hanna believed Mitchell had once again taken advantage of "a *golden opportunity* to prove to the public that organized labor can command confidence and respect by their patience and prudence even under such conditions as surround the present situation."[28] Assured of Hanna's backing, and believing the public would now support him as well, Mitchell ordered a temporary suspension of work to begin May 12 and called a tri-district convention for May 14 at Hazleton to determine whether the suspension should be made permanent.[29]

Yet, Mitchell's anxieties concerning upcoming events still gnawed at him. On May 10, he described his fears in a letter to Mother Jones:

> You have, no doubt, learned from the daily papers of the situation in the anthracite field. . . . I have every reason to believe that the strike will be made general and permanent. I am of the opinion that this will be the fiercest struggle in which we have yet engaged. It will be a fight to the end, and our organization will either achieve a great triumph or it will be completely annihilated. Personally I am not quite satisfied with the outlook, as the movement for a strike is strongly antagonized by the officers of the lower District, and of course the success of the strike depends entirely upon all working in harmony and unison.[30]

Mitchell's dread of strike action was evident in his address to the Hazleton convention. A majority of the delegates had come under instructions to make the suspension permanent, and he did not ask them directly to violate their instructions and return to work under present conditions. He made abundantly clear, however, that he did not favor a strike at this time. Cherish as he did the confidence of the mine workers, he would not "do violence to my own conscience," he would not "advise that which is contrary to my own judgment." He then posed a question that went straight to the heart of the matter: "Is it better to go on improving conditions, little by little, or to risk everything in one great fight?" He believed the union had made strides since 1900. Operators had agreed to meet with representatives of employees and had at least talked to their union president. A strike loss might well set back the union's efforts for years to come. The sad history of every miners' union, he said, was that "once they met a Waterloo, once they met a crushing defeat, it took years and years for them to recover from that defeat and again organize and renew the struggle for better conditions of employment." This strike might not prove to be the UMWA's Waterloo, but one thing was certain, "the fight will be one to the finish." While Mitchell left no doubt of his personal opposition, nowhere in his speech did he explicitly oppose a strike call. He could not openly counsel against a strike without even a sop to placate the rank and file. As he acknowledged in his speech, "Many delegates have said that if this convention failed to order a strike, the United Mine Workers would vanish from this region." In the end, he asked delegates to vote according to their instructions, hoping they would follow his advice.[31]

On the afternoon of Thursday, May 15, soon after Mitchell's speech, delegates voted to strike by a sizeable majority.[32] As Mitchell put it, "the instructions of the delegates made it impossible for them to defer to my judgment."[33] When the decision was announced, delegates cheered wildly for Mitchell, despite his opposition to the strike. They roared until they went hoarse. According to one report, "Those who witnessed it say that no more dramatic scene has occurred in the history of the American labor movement."[34] Mitchell then walked to the entrance of the opera house, where the convention took place, and announced the decision to the small army of newspaper correspondents, who then rushed away to the telegraph wires and long distance telephones and spread the news to the world. At the conclusion of the convention, Mitchell admonished the delegates, and through them the mine workers, to remain law-abiding and peaceful, economical in their finances, and to have nothing to do with saloons. Delegates then joined in the singing of "My Country 'Tis of Thee," gave three cheers for Mitchell, three for the organization, and three for the American flag.[35] The strike was on.

As the Hazleton convention clearly demonstrated, Mitchell's interests were not identical to those of the mine workers. For the rank and file, the strike was perceived as an all-or-nothing fight to achieve some semblance of control over their work place. It was a full-scale confrontation in pursuit of economic justice, a rebellion against corporate hegemony. They had been fighting this hegemony in the small skirmishes of local strikes, but now they had united their forces and seized control of the union's apparatus to engage in a battle of titanic proportions. They revealed their true intent on the last day of the convention, after the decision had already been made to strike. Once again, they rejected Mitchell's sage counsel and passed a resolution requesting the districts of West Virginia, Maryland, and Michigan, where strikes were then in progress or contemplated, to join in petitioning for a special convention to consider a general strike of all miners.[36] For anthracite mine workers, this was to be Armageddon.

Mitchell, on the other hand, had been dragooned into the fray against his will. His health was questionable, the prospects of victory slim, the risks enormous. A few days after the convention, when the passions of the moment had subsided somewhat, he wrote his good friend Billy Ryan. In this letter, he described his plight as that of a man swept up in a great historical drama beyond his control and uncertain where he would land:

> Well, we are up against it, good and hard, and expect to be so for several months; however, permit me to say to you in confidence, that this strike and the attempt to inaugurate a National suspension is not of my choosing. In fact the movement is inaugurated over my most emphatic protest; but now that we are in it I am going to stay with the boys until they either succeed or fail; and if they fail I shall join the ancient order of has-beens and used-to-be's, and become one of its most revered members.[37]

Mine workers perceived Mitchell as a true labor leader. He was for them a champion of their cause, a spokesman and interpreter of their desires, and a fighter for their collective rights. The concerns that Mitchell expressed at the Hazleton convention and the start of the 1902 strike, however, revealed that he was less concerned with the mine workers' cause than he was with the preservation of the union and his own presidency. While mine workers were willing to risk the organization on a pitched battle, Mitchell most definitely was not. At the start of the 1900 strike, he could afford to be aggressive. Only a handful of hard coal mine workers belonged to the union, and he had not yet established a working alliance with Hanna or the NCF. Now, however, things were different. The union's membership had doubled, the funds in its treasury had multiplied, and there were important political alliances at stake. If operators were allowed to crush the union in anthracite, all the gains of the past two years would be wiped out. And Mitchell's own tenure was not so secure that he could withstand a strike loss of such magnitude and be certain of maintaining power. His fear of joining "the ancient order of has beens" was not an idle one.

Indeed, Mitchell had been so successful since assuming the presidency in creating a powerful union that his primary interest now had to be the consolidation of those gains and the protection of that union. He could no longer afford to take the risks he once had taken. By 1902, Mitchell revealed signs of the peculiar but natural metamorphosis common to all successful union heads from labor leader to labor bureaucrat, a man for whom the demands of the union as an institution, ultimately, shaped his behavior. Mitchell was slowly falling victim to the iron law of oligarchy: championship of the cause became secondary to the preservation of the institution. He remained a kind and caring man who felt deeply the sufferings and privations of mine workers. Moreover, he was a born risk-taker, a man who played high stakes poker, was deeply involved in various financial gambles, and on several occasions had faced serious personal harm on behalf of the union cause. But, as we shall see, he was unwilling to take the risks required to secure economic justice in anthracite—unwilling to risk depleting the union's treasury, unwilling to break existing contracts in the soft coal fields for the sake of a general mining strike, unwilling to threaten established relations with Hanna and Easley, unwilling to risk his own presidency—for such risks jeopardized the institution itself. In 1902, Mitchell was motivated not only by the cry for economic justice, but also by the bureaucratic imperatives of managing a modern union. For better or worse, he now had a strike to conduct with his future and that of the union in the balance.

As though the start of the hard coal strike were not enough to occupy his thoughts, Mitchell had to contend with another headache in the spring of 1902: West Virginia. If he opposed the strike in anthracite because it endangered the entire union, he faced the opposite problem in West Virginia. As we have seen, the failure to organize this state imperiled the interstate joint movement. At the January 1902 national convention, he reported that the West Virginia organizing campaign of the previous year had resulted in the creation of 80 locals with close to 5,000 members. Since operators routinely dismissed miners for union participation, however, he was forced to request that union funds be spent to maintain union members and their families. He also secured passage of a resolution that dealt with the problem of nonunion West Virginia operators who also controlled union mines in other states. If a strike took place, these operators would be in a position to continue their fight against the union in West Virginia while supplying their contracts through their union mines. The resolution stated that in the event of a strike the national executive board was empowered to suspend work in these operators' union mines.[38] It was apparent that Mitchell was already making preparations for a work suspension in the state.

In the spring of 1902, he received some positive news regarding West Virginia. Organizers in that state reported that the miners were exhibiting strong union sentiment. Mother Jones reported to "my dear comrade Mitchell" that she was holding "glorious meetings," and concluded that "the

Boys are responding" despite the threats of discharge.[39] If Mitchell was planning to call a strike at this time, the conflicting opinions expressed at an April meeting of the national executive board stayed his hand. While some believed a strike should be initiated at once, West Virginia district president Richards opposed taking any action that might provoke a strike until the field was better organized. He would not sanction any strike "until all the miners were organized who could be organized." A national organizer agreed. "I think a strike in West Virginia would be a failure at present," he said. Ultimately, Mitchell and the board agreed not to issue a strike call, but to continue the work of organizing "with as much vigor as possible."[40]

Events in the next few weeks, however, left Mitchell with little choice except to sanction a walk out. Operator discharge of union men became so rampant he was forced to admit "nothing can be done excepting to permit our men to be discharged without protest, or inaugurate a strike." Of the two courses, he was "inclined to favor the latter."[41] Operators then turned to physical violence against the organizers. On April 30, according to Tom L. Lewis, two "hirelings" of a major West Virginia coal company made a "deliberate attempt" to beat to death three national organizers, one of whom received serious internal injuries. After the assault, the two company "thugs" went before the mayor, confessed, and paid a fine. "They believe this ends it," wrote Lewis, his fighting spirit roused. But if the affair was indeed ended, if the union did not prosecute the assailants, "then it will be useless to attempt to do any more work in that region."[42]

Mitchell later recalled how the events of April 1902 changed attitudes regarding West Virginia. Even though he was "thoroughly consumed" by events in the anthracite region, "it became evident" to everyone at national headquarters "that we should be forced to inaugurate a strike or the organization which it had taken so many years to build would disintegrate."[43] Discharge and blacklisting of union miners would eventually decimate the union. He therefore issued a call for a meeting of organizers and officers to be held May 23 at Huntington. Because he was too busy to attend, he had no choice but to rely on Tom L. Lewis. He ordered Lewis to attend the Huntington conference, talk earnestly with the organizers, "and if it is the consensus of opinion that a strike movement could be made effective," to set a date "for the inauguration of a strike." Informing Lewis that the Fairmont region would prove the most difficult to move, he directed him to proceed there after the convention "and remain there until you are further advised."[44] He did not, however, place Lewis in charge of the conference. That job was given to Secretary-Treasurer Wilson, a man he trusted.

In his report on the Huntington meeting, Wilson noted that none of the twenty-four officers and organizers in attendance opposed strike action on the morning of the third day. He therefore appointed a committee to draft a circular announcing the strike and explaining the reasons this action was found necessary. That afternoon, when the conference was about to adjourn for the day, Tom L. Lewis arrived at the meeting place for the first time. Despite direct orders from Mitchell, Lewis had nearly missed the entire conference. But his insubordination had just begun. Wilson explained to Lewis the actions taken by the conference to that point. Lewis said nothing at the time. When the committee met to discuss the circular, however, Lewis immediately spoke out in opposition to the proposed walk out and gave two reasons for his opposition. First, he refused to take part in any strike call unless he was "first made conversant with the details of the general policy that was to be adopted in the strike." Second, a strike should not be called until the question was submitted to the rank and file. When the committee reported to the full conference, Lewis again spoke out. Due to Lewis's influence, seven of the twenty-four voted against the strike. Three of the seven who now opposed were district officials.[45] Whether Lewis had deliberately set out to sabotage the strike will never be known for certain, but he had surely jeopardized the success of the strike before it even started by breaking the unity of strike leaders. Nevertheless, the suspension began on June 7.

Even with the strike underway, Lewis continued to defy Mitchell. After the Huntington conference, contrary to Mitchell's instructions that he proceed to the Fairmont region of West Virginia, Lewis went home to Ohio. He penned Mitchell a note that revealed the depth of his contempt for Mitchell's authority. "I cannot believe that you without a well defined plan would advise a conference of organizers to declare a strike involving the entire state of West Virginia when there was so much at stake not only to the mine workers of that state but to those of the entire country." The strike had not been called by the national executive board and had not been approved by the rank and file in West Virginia. It was therefore because of his "obligation to the United Mine Workers of America" that he refused to participate. As far as going to the Fairmont field, Lewis refused to "grope around in the dark" without specific instructions.[46]

In one sense Lewis was correct. While several national executive board members had attended the Huntington conference, the board, as a body, had never sanctioned the strike call. Mitchell was so preoccupied with anthracite affairs that he was forced to break with precedent on this score. But Lewis's apparent commitment to principle was a sham masking his true intentions. Lewis banked on a failed strike, and he wanted to be on record as having opposed the strike from the beginning and having refused to participate. In his thirst for control of the union, Lewis contributed to a major strike loss that imperiled the future of the trade agreement in soft coal.

Mitchell chose to ignore Lewis, and Lewis chose to remain in Ohio. Twice during the next month Lewis sent telegrams to Mitchell asking for specific instructions. Mitchell curtly informed him that instructions had been given before the Huntington conference, and since Lewis chose not to comply, "I can see no necessity of advising or instructing you further until the question of my authority to do so has been fully and definitely determined."[47] Lewis did not arrive in West Virginia until July 20. Privately, Mitchell expressed his loathing for "the gentleman from Ohio who so vigorously antagonized the inauguration of a strike," who refused to take part in the struggle, and who remained at home "quibbling over technicalities."[48]

Mitchell's principal concern in the spring and summer of 1902, of course, was northeastern Pennsylvania and the anthracite strike, not Tom L. Lewis and West Virginia. He established strike headquarters in mid-May at the Hotel Hart in Wilkes-Barre to take personal charge of events. The first reports he received from organizers in the field were encouraging. From the first day of the strike, anthracite mine workers demonstrated their resolve by responding to the strike order with near unanimity. They shut down the mines and, in general, remained peaceful. Mitchell was elated. He claimed it was the "most wonderful strike" he had ever observed. Except for the fact there were more people on the street than usual, there was little evidence of a great industrial contest taking place. It may only be "the calm before the storm," but from all reports "the men are prepared to stand 'until the sun melts the pulley wheels on the tipple' before they will return to work." Indeed, the strikers were so calm that newspaper reporters were finding it difficult to find something to write about.[49] Elizabeth Morris noticed the same "quiet holiday" atmosphere, with mine workers fishing from the river banks and breaker boys enjoying the opportunity to play in the fresh air and sunshine.[50] Everything started so well that Mitchell left to spend the weekend in Chicago with his wife.[51]

Upon his return, he set about ending this strike as quickly as possible. At the very start of the strike, he had explained that while he hoped for victory, he planned to make "every possible effort to conciliate the coal operators and reach a settlement without a protracted contest."[52] The only way to obtain a quick settlement was to enlist the services of the NCF. Although this organization had failed to avert the strike, he knew of no other force powerful enough to end it. He found, however, that both Easley and Hanna were in a state of panic. The Hazleton convention's call for a special convention to initiate a general mining strike had created widespread sentiment among soft coal miners to break existing agreements and lay down their tools in a show of solidarity.

The NCF leaders had good reason for concern. The role of bituminous miners would prove one of the major points of departure in the two anthracite strikes. During the 1900 dispute, Hanna, in an effort to induce operators to compromise, had suggested that several soft coal districts were ready to walk out, although in actuality there was little likelihood of such a development.[53] In 1902, however, there was a great deal of sentiment among soft coal miners for a general mining suspension. This aspect of the strike merits close attention, for it reveals much about Mitchell's leadership imperatives.

In a dramatic letter to Mitchell, Hanna expressed his "alarm" about "the talk of a sympathetic strike." Such talk played into the hands of the railroad presidents who argued union agreements were useless because unions did not respect contract terms. Hanna claimed he always defended the UMWA because of its interstate joint agreement. To destroy the interstate movement now "would be the worst blow" possible for organized labor. A sympathy strike of bituminous miners would cost him public support and the assistance of the Civic Federation. He warned that Mitchell "cannot permit this strike to extend to soft coal interests where you control. I am not idle and will keep up the effort to have this strike settled but the suggestions in the newspapers of a National Convention to consider a general strike is already handicapping my efforts."[54]

Easley chimed in as well, informing Mitchell that Hanna was truly concerned. According to the NCF secretary, Hanna threatened to "throw up his hands and quit the whole work" of industrial conciliation if soft coal workers broke their contracts. "I never saw him so excited before." Easley also claimed other influential members of the NCF believed as did Hanna that the public would turn against the union should they conduct a sympathy strike.[55]

Among soft coal miners, however, the movement in favor of sympathetic action was growing. Perhaps more than any other occupation, coal mining created feelings of solidarity and brotherhood. When looking for a reason why miners bonded so tightly, one miner wrote that "we were all the same breed of cats; we shared the burdens of the mine."[56] A general strike appealed to this sense of solidarity which, after all, was the basis of all union organization. Moreover, a general strike might have paralyzed the national economy and forced a redress of grievances. The call for a general strike represented the type of labor action that marked the turbulent days of the 1870s and 1880s, when industrial relations resembled a state of anarchy. The call for a general strike also represented the type of labor action that Mitchell, as the champion of the trade agreement, would never initiate. He would not risk losing the support of Hanna and Easley and other men of importance who acted on behalf of the miners. He would never alienate the public opinion he had tried so hard to cultivate. Perhaps better than anyone else, he understood the politics of the trade agreement. Signed contracts must be kept inviolate without exception. The antipathy to breaking contracts he had expressed during the steel strike in 1901 was equally apparent in 1902.

In his reply to Hanna, Mitchell apologized that the strike had occurred and that the issue of a sympathy strike had arisen. He agreed with Hanna that the strike should have been postponed. He agreed as well that sympathetic action was a disastrous course. But he was forced to confess that the question of a sympathy strike posed a serious problem. The resolution to ask other districts to join in a call for a special convention had been "railroaded through" in the closing moments of the convention, and he had been powerless to stop it. According to the union constitution, he explained, the president was required to call a special convention after five districts had applied. And he had already received five applications! So far, he had "kept these requests from the public and even from my own colleagues, with the hope that something might occur which would bring about a peaceful settlement." If the NCF did not soon secure a resolution, however, "I shall be forced, even against my own judgment and desire, to call a National convention at an early date."[57]

Mitchell went on to explain that while he believed those soft coal miners currently under contract would strenuously oppose any violation of their agreements, they might be forced to do so. There were large numbers bituminous miners who were not working under joint agreements, and there were so many others presently on strike in Michigan, Kentucky, West Virginia, and other outlying districts that he feared the anthracite delegation, which would attend the special convention in full force, might be able to round up a majority of the votes. Moreover, as Hanna knew full well, "there are elements in our organization not in accord with the policy of conservatism that I have tried— in my own humble way—to establish." Mitchell assured Hanna he would do all he could to undermine efforts for sympathetic action, but the prospects for the upcoming special convention were not good. When a contract was signed, "I believe it should be observed under all circumstances," Mitchell concluded, "but there are things I cannot do, and it seems to me that the anthracite coal operators while proclaiming their confidence in me personally have, by their actions, done all it was possible for them to do to destroy my power for good; and have, unintentionally—no doubt—encouraged the less thoughtful element in our organization."[58]

The NCF had been busy in its mediational work since the start of the strike, and it needed no inducement to involve itself in this great industrial contest. Yet the very real threat of sympathetic action on the part of soft coal miners did intensify the efforts of both Easley and Hanna. On May 29, top NCF leaders George Perkins, Daniel Keefe, and Ralph Easley assembled in the Cleveland offices of Mark Hanna. Agreeing that the hard coal strike must be ended before Mitchell was forced to call the special convention, they contacted Mitchell by telephone to determine the absolute minimum demands he was willing to accept to call off the strike. Mitchell was willing to settle for very little indeed. He put forward several proposals he believed he could get the mine workers to accept. One proposal called for an advance of 10 percent and a union promise not to ask for wage increases for three years. A second proposal asked for a 5 percent increase with additional two and one half percent increases in each of the next two years. A third proposal, to be offered only if the others were rejected, called only for a 5 percent advance.[59] This last proposal once again revealed the divergence of interests between Mitchell and the mine workers. While mine workers were settling in for a long and resolute contest, he was willing to end hostilities for a modest pay increase that resolved none of the basic issues in the dispute.

Operators rejected all of these proposals. According to Easley, operators justified their intransigence by pointing to the union's apparent readiness to break existing contracts in the soft coal fields. They refused to deal with the union at all, calling it an "irresponsible outfit." Easley drew from his talk with the operators the lesson that violation of soft coal contracts "had to be prevented at all hazards."[60] Hanna then graciously offered to assist Mitchell in his effort to subvert sentiment for a sympathy strike. All Hanna needed was time and information. While he did not want Mitchell to act contrary to the union constitution, he did want him to hold off calling the special convention. "Time must be given," Hanna wrote, "to do missionary work among the bituminous coal men to prevent a sympathetic strike that . . . *must* be prevented at all hazards." The Captain then asked Mitchell for the names of people in the Central Competitive Field "who can work up a sentiment against a strike."[61]

With Mitchell's blessing, Hanna went about his "missionary" work. A Chicago newspaper reporter later confirmed that Hanna flooded the soft coal fields with agents in his employ spreading the gospel of the sanctity of contracts.[62] Easley and the labor representatives on the NCF executive committee were equally busy proselytizing in the anthracite fields, telling hard coal workers it would be better to lose their strike than break existing contracts in soft coal. He later boasted that the committee conducted "six weeks of hard, educational, missionary work," holding secret meetings at eight or ten different locations. "If the inside history of the work done to save those contracts could be written, it would be one of the proudest pages that organized labor could contribute to the industrial history of the United States."[63] These efforts graphically illustrated Mitchell's dependence on Easley and Hanna, and his willingness to grant them freedom of action in the internal affairs of his union. These efforts also demonstrated his utter abhorrence of the strong sentiment among the rank and file for acts of labor solidarity.

While the missionary campaign was underway, Mitchell continued to buy time for NCF negotiations by keeping secret the fact that he had received five requests for a special convention. Even with the extra time, however, NCF leaders found the railroad presidents so obstinate that they despaired of mediating the controversy without assistance. They thus tried to enlist the power and prestige of President Theodore Roosevelt to settle the strike. On June 8, Roosevelt ordered his Commissioner of Labor, Carroll D. Wright, to investigate the strike in full detail and submit a report of his findings. After interviewing Mitchell, the railroad presidents, and others involved, Wright turned in a voluminous report with specific recommendations to Roosevelt on June 20. Roosevelt read the report, commented favorably upon it, but after discussing the situation with his attorney general, decided he lacked constitutional authority to intervene in the strike at this time.[64]

Not only had the NCF failed once again, but Mitchell believed the NCF's appeal to the President had actually made matters worse. As Wright was conducting interviews, Mitchell and George Perkins met secretly in New York and Perkins suggested he might be able to arrange a conference with the railroad presidents. Mitchell was ecstatic. When the coal barons conferred, however, they decided against a conference. Mitchell was convinced that the threat of Roosevelt's intervention had made the operators even more determined to carry the fight to a finish. One reason they declined to attend a conference, Mitchell wrote, was their feeling "that if they were to make any settlement now it would be regarded as acknowledging fear of the President's action."[65] When the conference did not materialize, Mitchell expressed keen disappointment. The NCF had proven incapable of achieving a quick settlement, and he could no longer postpone the inevitable. "We shall now be forced to comply with our National constitution and call a National convention. What the outcome of that will be, no one can foretell, although I am apprehensive of the result."[66] On June 18, he sent out a circular call for a special convention to consider a general mining strike to commence July 17 at Indianapolis.[67]

Despite the missionary work of the NCF, the upcoming convention was a source of worry for Mitchell. He carefully monitored the situation, receiving reports from every mining section in the country. While he was convinced the "officers and conservatives" in the union would vigorously oppose any repudiation of "the spirit and letter" of signed contracts, "I know that the strike sentiment has been communicated to the less thoughtful and particularly the young men in the soft coal fields." The special convention represented a risk he did not want to take, and he made clear his hope that the strike would be settled before the convention opened.[68] On June 23, he admitted that he had not yet "mapped out" his strategy for the convention itself, but he believed that until the convention opened, "the best course to pursue would be one of silence." Perhaps the threat of a national strike might just bring to bear "powerful influences" against the coal barons and force them to settle.[69]

In this hope he was again to be disappointed. Through Daniel Keefe, he learned that Hanna was of the opinion that operators would like nothing better than to have soft coal miners call a sympathy strike. Such a step would prove to the nation that the union was untrustworthy. According to Hanna, "operators and business men generally are confident that the miners are whipped." Furthermore, the Captain contended that "if the Mine officials can't see that they are whipped, then they are not as practical as he gave them credit for." Hanna believed he could arrange a satisfactory settlement, but only if mine workers returned to work first. Mitchell replied tersely that Hanna's suggestions "won't do. The anthracite men will never go back to the mines, at least with my consent, unless they receive a substantial increase in wages."[70]

The strain of the strike, the obduracy of the operators, the inability of the NCF to find a solution, the backfiring of the appeal to Roosevelt, and the dread of the upcoming special convention were all taking their toll on Mitchell. At the end of June he resolved to go to Chicago to get away for a few days rest at his favorite hotel, McCoy's, and do nothing more exhausting than have Sunday dinner with his friend Harry Taylor.[71] Even this respite proved taxing, for as soon as he departed his secretary learned that reporters were sending stories to their editors that Mitchell had left for Chicago because his wife had begun divorce proceedings. Morris immediately sent out a coded message to warn Mitchell, but Mitchell could not decipher the code. Stories of Mitchell's impending divorce were printed in several papers the next morning, much to Mitchell's embarrassment. The divorce rumors were completely unfounded and the papers printed retractions, but Mitchell was so aggravated he declared his intention to find the source of the rumors "and seek redress through the courts."[72]

Back in Pennsylvania, Mitchell pursued one last desperate bid for peace before the special convention began. He consented to the offer of Father John J. Curran, pastor of a Catholic church in Wilkes-Barre, to confer with George Baer of the Reading Railroad and William Truesdale of the Lackawanna Railroad. The priest did gain an interview with the coal barons, but he found them as unyielding as ever. Both men seemed determined to destroy the union. Curran quoted Baer: "'Cripple industry, stagnate business or tie up the commerce of the world,' he says, 'and we will not surrender.'"[73] There would be no settlement before the special convention.

If Mitchell hoped to overcome the inherent appeal of sympathetic action, and thus save his reputation for conservative leadership, he needed an alternative plan that would allow soft coal miners to express solidarity with their brothers in anthracite and yet not involve violations of contract. Such a plan had been suggested to Mitchell by Thomas Kidd of the Woodworkers' Union in late June. Kidd advised Mitchell to assess every miner presently working one dollar per week and encourage district organizations to contribute as much as possible. This strategy might provide a two dollar per week strike benefit for anthracite men and allow them "to continue the fight for say two months longer." Mitchell thanked Kidd for the advice, although he made no comment on the suggestion at the time.[74] Apparently, however, Mitchell immediately began to act along these lines. By the eve of the convention, one paper reported that Mitchell had been active for weeks obtaining promises of financial aid for the strikers and was hinting that the special convention would vote for an assessment instead of a sympathy strike.[75] Just before embarking on the Grand Trunk train to Indianapolis, Mitchell for the first time was able to express confidence about the outlook for conservative action. "You may rest assured," he told a friend, "that if there is any trouble in the convention I shall not come out second best. If I do it will be the first time in my life."[76]

Between the day Mitchell received five petitions to call a special convention and the day the convention opened, two full months had elapsed. In that time, Mitchell, Hanna, Easley and all the forces at their disposal had been engaged in destroying sentiment for a sympathy strike. When the delegates finally gathered on July 17 at Tomlinson Hall in Indianapolis, the success of their efforts was readily apparent. And in a masterful display of control, Mitchell squelched the "less thoughtful" element that remained and directed the convention along conservative lines.

Mitchell's opening address was a brilliantly crafted denunciation of sympathy strikes, a superior blend of historical, rational, and emotional arguments. The anthracite struggle, he began, had great personal significance. He was so closely associated with the hard coal workers in the public mind, he felt so keenly their joys and sorrows "that it grieves me more than language can express" to disagree with those who wanted a sympathy strike. But he could not in good conscience advocate a policy that would "bring disaster and dishonor" upon the entire organization. He then lectured delegates on the "lessons" of the past. "As far as my knowledge goes I do not know of one solitary sympathetic strike of any magnitude which has been successful; on the contrary, the most conspicuous among the sympathetic labor struggles have resulted in ignominious and crushing defeat." Moreover, a sympathy strike would turn public opinion against the anthracite struggle:

> I have, during all my life in the labor movement, declared that contracts mutually made should during their life be kept inviolate; and while at times it may appear to the superficial observer or to those immediately concerned that advantage could be gained by setting agreements aside, such advantage, if gained, would, in the very nature of things, be temporary, and would ultimately result in disaster; because a disregard of the sacredness of contracts strikes at the very vitals of organized labor. The effect of such action would be to destroy confidence, to array in open hostility to our cause all forces of society, and to crystallize public sentiment in opposition to our movement.

He admonished delegates not to repeat past follies and not to lend credence to the "specious arguments" of the coal barons that the UMWA was irresponsible because it did not regard its contracts inviolate. If delegates voted against a sympathy strike, he promised them certain victory in the hard coal struggle. "Public sentiment would be so concentrated against the arrogant and unreasonable attitude of the anthracite coal operators" that they would be forced to yield. Delegates could demonstrate their solidarity in a more constructive way by supporting his recommendations for financial aid. Among other things, Mitchell called for an immediate appropriation of $50,000 from the national treasury to be placed at the disposal of the anthracite district officers; an assessment of not less than one dollar per week on all members of the union; an assessment of 25 percent of the incomes of all union officials and organizers; and an appeal to all trade unions and the public at large for financial assistance.[77]

After Mitchell's speech, the issue was opened to general discussion on the floor. Every bituminous delegate who spoke agreed with Mitchell that financial aid rather than strike action would be the most effective policy. One anthracite delegate, however, spoke forcefully in favor of a general strike. He appealed to the long standing tradition of solidarity among miners and the need to combine the forces of labor to battle the combined forces of capital. "In the name of humanity and civilization, and in the name of everything that is great and noble, I say stand together and make the strike general."[78] When others from anthracite questioned Mitchell's recommendations, the convention was forced to adjourn so that the anthracite delegation could confer.[79] What kind of pressure was brought to bear against the militants may never be known, but when the full convention reassembled, the anthracite delegates declared their support for Mitchell's plan.[80] On July 19, after the committee on resolutions made its report, Mitchell's recommendations were adopted unanimously.[81] The issue of a sympathy strike was never broached with any seriousness during the strike again.

With the assistance of the NCF, Mitchell had successfully sabotaged the general strike movement. According to one anthracite delegate, had the convention been held several weeks earlier, the majority of the delegates would have voted in favor of a sympathy strike.[82] The "missionary" work had indeed been the deciding factor. Whatever its impact on the outcome of the anthracite strike, Mitchell's maneuver was questionable for a number of reasons. First, by squelching the traditional expression of solidarity among miners, the special convention no doubt cut into the principal sources of union strength—militancy and unity. Mitchell was willing to pay this price, for he believed the strike would be settled by his corporate and political allies in the NCF, not through the militant might of workers united. Second, one must question Mitchell's tactics in achieving his goal. His stalling tactics and his use of Hanna's agents were devious and anti-democratic. Afraid that the popular will of the rank and file did not coincide with his interests, he showed no hesitation in employing underhanded means to overcome the prevailing sentiment among his own union brothers. Above all, the special convention showed the lengths Mitchell was willing to go to maintain his political alliances.

Certainly from Mitchell's perspective, stopping the general strike movement was a tremendous success. He had proven himself a truly reliable and trustworthy champion of the trade agreement, a thoroughly "practical" man of affairs. The national press rang out his praises. In a typical editorial, the *Baltimore News* extolled Mitchell's speech for its "soberness and discretion," in contrast with "the reckless and irresponsible utterances of men who in former years have misrepresented the laboring men and furnished ammunition to their enemies." The *Minneapolis Journal* predicted "organized labor will thrive when it commits the guidance of its affairs more generally to men of the Mitchell stamp."[83]

Hanna and Easley were quick to applaud their confederate. "I want to congratulate you and through you your associates," Hanna beamed, "in the successful outcome of your convention in upholding the honor and integrity of your organization."[84] Easley echoed these sentiments, claiming that by "insisting upon the sacredness of the contract and by inveighing against sympathetic strikes" Mitchell had accomplished "more for organized labor in that one speech than has been done by anyone else in my recollection." After he read the editorials praising Mitchell, Easley was even more enthusiastic. The speech "established a high water mark for organized labor and has helped the whole cause throughout the country."[85] Mitchell accepted their praise and expressed his confidence that he had in fact "demonstrated beyond all question the reliability of our organization."[86]

Despite all the accolades, the special convention had solved only one problem. Numerous others awaited immediate attention. Large strikes still raged in Michigan and West Virginia. Neither one was going particularly well for the miners. Upon his return to Wilkes-Barre, Mitchell found that "matters in the anthracite field are just as I left them went I went west." The railroad presidents had not been magically transformed by his efforts at Indianapolis. They remained as determined as ever to fight to the bitter end. Indeed, the only change in the anthracite situation was a cause for alarm rather than celebration. One week after the special convention, Mitchell complained that newspapers were printing such "extravagant stories of the fabulous sums" being collected by the union for the financial assistance of the strikers that the men were already "clamoring for their share of the wealth." Some of the mine workers who had left the region when the strike began had actually returned to the region, "expecting to be maintained in idleness."[87]

Within days, the special convention almost backfired in Mitchell's face by creating an unexpected crisis. Having undermined labor solidarity, Mitchell now confronted a high degree of jealousy and division over the distribution of strike funds. The secretary of District 9, George Hartlein, told Mitchell what was happening in the southern anthracite field. The men were "clamering (*sic*) like a lot of raging, tumbling, howling Hyenas, men who would not need one cents (*sic*) worth of aid for the next year to come, but because the actual needy cases get help, they swear they want the same, or else they would go to work." Hartlein claimed that while "the foreigners are the worst," he was "surprised and disgusted with the whole human family of wage earners."[88] Mitchell was not surprised but he was disgusted:

> Your letter portrays conditions as they exist here exactly. The companies have done effective work in persuading the miners to demand relief. I really believe that we should have been in better position if we had never held the Indianapolis convention. The newspaper stories that millions were pouring into the anthracite field have created a demand on the part of the miners that it is impossible to satisfy. Suspicions have been aroused and rumors are believed and it is going to tax the energies of every one of us to the utmost to get over this crisis.[89]

Mitchell later wrote that this situation in late July and early August was the most desperate period of the entire strike. Encouraged by antiunion newspapers, strikers developed wild expectations of relief payments. When these sums were not forthcoming, rumors of financial chicanery and mismanagement by union officials abounded. "I am fully convinced that the strike would have collapsed, had the operators at this time opened the mines and invited the strikers to return to work," Mitchell recalled. This was the only time in the five-month strike that there were "signs of wavering." Evidently the coal barons "did not realize the extent of the disaffection in the ranks of the strikers and failed to take advantage of the opportunity open to them."[90]

Luckily, Mitchell was able to avert the crisis through strong executive action. To counter misinformation spread by the newspapers, he issued a circular explaining what amount of aid strikers could expect and how it would be distributed. To ensure an equitable distribution of available funds, he advised locals to elect relief committees who would decide which strikers were truly needy.[91] Once this system was in place, passions soon subsided and few mine workers returned to work. Mitchell could take little comfort in the passing of this emergency, however, for he was no closer to a settlement in anthracite and the situation in West Virginia had grown bleak.

An estimated 16,000 of West Virginia's 33,000 miners had answered the strike call on June 7. In the first days of the strike, Mitchell received telegrams from organizers claiming 80 percent of the miners had quit work, and that the chances of a complete tie-up were encouraging.[92] Upon receiving the good news, he seemed both relieved and very enthusiastic. "I think that we are going to win that fight," he told Wilson. Less than a week into the strike he was "overjoyed" by the reports he received. The strike movement would prove "a severe rebuke" to Lewis.[93] Mitchell's glee would soon fade, however, due to trouble in the form of the court injunction.

Mitchell was well aware of the effectiveness with which West Virginia operators resorted to injunctions to stymie labor unions. Operators in that state had used injunctions in the 1897 strike and Mitchell himself had faced them during his organizing efforts in 1898. John Walker, future president of the Illinois district and at this time a UMWA organizer, had informed Mitchell in 1901 that in West Virginia "the court is practically controlled by the operators." And at the Huntington conference that issued the strike call, organizer Tom Haggerty predicted that the injunction was the only thing that could cause defeat.[94] Thus, Mitchell anticipated injunctions and had a strategy to cope with them. He was evidently not aware, however, of just how effective injunctions could be against the strike.

Less than two weeks after the start of the strike U.S. district court Judge Henry Jackson issued an injunction prohibiting the union from holding meetings at or near the mines or in any way interfering with the mining operations in the Fairmont region. A few days later, Mother Jones, four national board members, and six organizers were jailed for violating this injunction. Seven of these union representatives were sentenced to terms of between sixty and ninety days. Judge Jackson dubbed the men professional agitators, "vampires that live and fatten on the most honest labors of the coal miners of the country and who are busybodies creating dissatisfaction among a class of people who are quiet, well disposed and who do not want to be disturbed by the unceasing agitation of this class of people."[95]

Mitchell took this first assault by injunction in stride. Outside the Fairmont region, the strike was still "in good shape." Within the Fairmont field, Mitchell resolutely adopted a policy of nonviolent protest to overcome the crippling effect of the injunction. He would simply send other union men there to take the place of those who had been arrested. He therefore petitioned district officials to send as many reliable men as they could spare. If the districts could not afford to pay their expenses, the national would pick up the tab. Mitchell fully realized what he was asking these organizers to do. "Of course, men going there will, in all probability, (also) be arrested and sent to jail," he wrote, "but in this supreme crisis we must make any sacrifice to win."[96]

Even this militant stance could not withstand the legal onslaught of the next few weeks. Numerous injunctions were issued by federal and district courts prohibiting union action in most parts of the state. A warrant was issued for the arrest of William B. Wilson even before he entered the state.[97] Organizer Tom Haggerty, who had himself been arrested, believed it was the "evident intention of the courts to keep the organizers out of the field by calling them constantly into court." Although the strikers were still holding, "as long as the injunctions are in force our people will be defeated in the end."[98] By making it impossible for organizers to stay in contact with the strikers, keep up morale, and provide food and other types of relief, injunctions destroyed the strike movement. Because of the injunctions, Mitchell said, "the strikers became demoralized, and the strike, which at first held out such promises of success, rapidly disintegrated."[99]

Not content with mere legal action, operators resorted to other measures. They forcibly evicted miners from company homes, secured the services of the state militia, imported strikebreakers, and used their own private guards to intimidate and commit acts of violence. On the desperate state of affairs during the strike, Mother Jones recalled: "Men who joined the union were blacklisted throughout the entire section. Their families were thrown out on the highways. Men were shot. They were beaten. Numbers disappeared and no trace of them was found. Store keepers were ordered not to sell to union men or their families."[100]

By July 20, when Tom L. Lewis arrived in West Virginia, apparently having overcome his principled opposition to the strike, the strike had collapsed in the northern part of the state and the miners were forced to return to work on the company's terms. Elsewhere in the state the strike continued and in some areas did not officially end until the summer of 1903. Yet the union had little to show for its efforts. The only substantial success came in the Kanawha Valley in the south, where the union was able to secure favorable agreements with two large operators on October 4 covering approximately 7,000 miners.[101]

Mitchell had made a tremendous effort to organize West Virginia. It was a costly battle. Strike support, lawyers' fees, organizers' fees, all taxed the union treasury. Until the end of July 1902, the union spent more money on West Virginia than it did on the entire anthracite region. Even after that date, Mitchell maintained a high level of strike support for those regions still out.[102] The strike did not succumb through lack of effort. Nevertheless, other than the toehold achieved in the southern part of the state, Mitchell had failed once again to organize West Virginia. The reasons for this failure, the injunctions and the state militia, were beyond his control. But he would have to face the consequences. Tom L. Lewis would be able to use this strike loss in his ceaseless campaign to steal control of the union and, more importantly, union bituminous operators would once again have leverage at the upcoming joint conferences. If the West Virginia problem led to another year without wage advances for the UMWA's soft coal miners, Mitchell might have to prepare for a crisis in bituminous coal comparable to the one he was now grappling with in anthracite.

In his history of coal miners, Andrew Roy, a miners' union pioneer, wrote that the 1902 anthracite strike was "the best managed of any strike that ever occurred in the United States." He claimed "it was one of the most orderly strikes that ever occurred in any trade in any country of the world, and stamps John Mitchell as a peerless leader of men."[103] More recent historians have agreed that Mitchell's strike management in 1902 approached perfection.[104] And so it did. Taking into account the strike's duration, the number of strikers involved, the bitterness of feeling it engendered, Mitchell certainly deserved the homage he received at the time and since for his able control of 150,000 striking mine workers for more than five months.

Much of Mitchell's success stemmed from the results he had achieved in 1900. When the strike began, mine workers already regarded him a hero committed to their cause. For many in the isolated mine patches, he was the most famous man they had ever heard of. One story, perhaps apocryphal, revealed how important a figure Mitchell was. When news of President McKinley's assassination in 1901 spread through anthracite, many mine workers gathered, some actually shedding tears, asking "Who shot our President?" When informed that the deceased was McKinley and not Mitchell, the crowd quickly dispersed.[105] Thus from the very outset of the 1902 strike the men were ready to follow his instructions.

Moreover, Mitchell's leadership style was attractive to the rank and file. There were far greater orators who could better stir the passions of men, but Mitchell cultivated an image that proved equally effective in commanding a loyal following. The image he presented to the strikers was one of kindness, courage, and sincere concern for their grievances, big and small. The donning of the priestlike garb was a conscious attempt to command the same reverence as their clerics. He kept in constant contact with his men, touring the region often and encouraging them to voice their opinions. The Hotel Hart where he stayed was always open to mine workers who wanted to give or receive advice or simply meet their leader.[106] When talking to the men, he appealed not to their passion but to their reason. Breaker boys found him kind, and older mine workers who approached him found explanations rather than irrational oratory. "He is never dictatorial, only patient and reasonable," the famous muckraker Lincoln Steffens observed.[107] The success of this image in controlling the men was noted by Elizabeth Morris when she wrote that "never has there been a strike freer from grumbling and complaint; never has there been a strike where the men seemed so absolutely certain of their leadership and so willing to regard the wholesome advice given them."[108]

Mitchell's strongest rank-and-file support came from immigrant miners. These "cattle," as Mitchell called them in 1900, spoke of Mitchell as a god. According to one eyewitness, nearly every Slav in anthracite placed Mitchell's picture on the wall beside those of the saints.[109] Although Mitchell himself was perplexed by this devotion, he certainly was aware of it. He recalled one occasion when he arrived at a primarily immigrant town during the strike. Such a huge number had gathered to meet him at the train station, the local police were required to guide his carriage through the crowd toward his hotel. Mitchell noticed that many of the immigrants were more interested in the police than the parade. Eyeing the police with suspicion, many men pulled out revolvers and truncheons. Alarmed, Mitchell sought an explanation. He was told the immigrants "feared that the policemen might do me injury and they felt it incumbent on themselves to protect me." Later that day he noticed men stationed outside the hotel itself, and when he awoke the next morning, some of the men were still standing guard.[110]

One important reason for Mitchell's hold over the immigrants and rank and file in general was his careful recruitment of the Catholic clergy. In the largely Catholic immigrant community, according to one scholar, the priest was regarded "with profound respect and humility." He was not just a religious figure, he was "a teacher, adviser, and mediator as well."[111] Although not religious himself, Mitchell understood the important role played by priests and went to great pains to secure their support. He once remarked that his efforts in Pennsylvania had brought him "into close relationship with a large number of Catholic priests; and it has been rare indeed that I have found one of them out of sympathy with the work we are trying to do." He often received letters of support from priests and developed "an intimate acquaintance with several in this region."[112] His closest clerical friends were among the most important, Bishop Michael Hoban of Scranton and Father John J. Curran in Wilkes-Barre. Priests provided Mitchell with a valuable tool to keep the men in line.

The clergy supported Mitchell in part because of his determination to keep the strike peaceful. As he traveled from mining camp to mining camp, Mitchell continuously urged strikers to refrain from violence. He did not want to give Governor William Stone any excuse to call out the militia. In the early months of the strike, he was remarkably successful. There was some property damage. Several shafts were dynamited and a few company stores burned.[113] Mother Jones led the wives of strikers, armed with dish pans and mops, on a march to drive scabs out of the mines. Although no one was injured, even that kind of activity, she remembered, made Mitchell "nervous."[114] On July 30, the first major eruption of violence occurred when a shopkeeper in Shenandoah was beaten to death by a union mob for assisting a strikebreaker. Governor Stone then dispatched National Guard troops to restore order in the area. Mitchell immediately issued a public statement condemning the killing, regardless of where the fault lay, and insisting that "the person who violated the law was the worst enemy the strikers could have."[115]

After the Shenandoah "riot," other towns became scenes of violence. On October 6 the entire Pennsylvania Division of the National Guard was called out to keep the peace. Mitchell deftly protected his own image and that of the union, however, by claiming the level of violence was exaggerated by the operators. "There is no reign of terror," he told the press, "and the miners are conducting themselves peaceably as when the strike started."[116] He also argued that much of the violence that did occur resulted from efforts by the coal and iron police "to overawe peaceful strikers and provoke them to acts of violence."[117] Compared to other major strikes of the period, the anthracite struggle did remain a generally peaceful affair. The vast majority of mine workers followed Mitchell's counsel and maintained law and order. Curtailing violence was one of the key reasons Mitchell won the battle over public opinion against the operators.

He believed this victory was critical. Public opinion, along with a disciplined rank and file and political allies, represented the triumvirate of UMWA power from Mitchell's point of view. And of the three, rank and file strength was the least important. He was convinced that "the final judge of all social contests, whether wars or strikes, is the public."[118] Every press release, every conference, every public statement was designed to present himself and the union as reasonable, honorable, and peaceful. He never attacked the character of operators, he reiterated his willingness to arbitrate throughout the strike, and he often apologized for the shortage of coal the strike created.

Mitchell's brilliant handling of the press contrasted sharply with the unyielding, arrogant image the coal barons presented. Indeed, operators seemed intent on antagonizing the public with repeated statements that fanned the flames of antitrust sentiment. The most egregious example of operator callousness was the famous "divine right" letter of George Baer, president of the Reading Railroad. Writing on July 17 in response to a religiously inspired plea to end the strike, Baer lectured that "The rights and interests of the laboring man will be protected and cared for—not by the labor agitators, but by the Christian men to whom God in His infinite wisdom has given the control of the property interests of the country, and upon the successful Management of which so much depends."[119] The press ridiculed Baer for his crass and offensive assumption of divine sanction.[120] Statements such as this made it far easier for the public to side with the union.

Mitchell's ability to win over public sympathy contributed mightily to the ultimate outcome of the strike. According to Selig Perlman the anthracite strike of 1902 was the first time in American history a union had tied up a strategic industry for months "without being condemned as a revolutionary menace."[121] Yet, Mitchell paid a heavy price to maintain the support of the public. Because he perceived a need to appear reasonable and flexible, he abandoned all hope of securing union recognition. While a trade agreement was not one of the stated demands of the strikers, it was well known that Mitchell hoped to achieve in hard coal the same joint conference method that existed in soft coal. In late August, Abram Hewitt, ex-mayor of New York and member of the board of directors of the Erie Railroad, asserted that the real issue of the strike was not wages and hours but union recognition. At first Mitchell tried to avoid the issue, claiming Hewitt was "jesting."[122] But

Mitchell's rejoinder did not satisfy Easley, who pressed Mitchell to answer Hewitt "in detail."[123] Convinced the public would not endure a coal shortage for the sake of union recognition, Mitchell publicly declared that recognition of the UMWA "is not and never has been the paramount issue of the present strike." Mine workers were striking for living wages.[124] Mitchell's dedication to public sympathy was indeed an expensive proposition.

The "splendid action of the Indianapolis convention," Ralph Easley explained, went far toward restoring public confidence in organized labor, and thus the NCF was able to renew its efforts to secure a settlement in anthracite "with good grace." The NCF's new peace plan was first suggested by George Perkins, adopted by Easley, and eventually served as a general model for the coal commission appointed at the end of the strike. According to this plan, the mine workers would first return to work, then a committee of leading NCF members, assisted by a subcommittee of experts, would undertake an investigation mining conditions. Easley suggested the subcommittee might include "a mining engineer, a financial man, and some sociological expert." Once the evidence had been gathered, the committee would present its findings to J. P. Morgan. While neither the union nor the operators would be absolutely bound by the findings, the committee would have "the public so solidly behind its conclusions that it would be suicidal for either side to ignore it."[125]

When Easley suggested the plan to Mitchell, the union president sneered. "The men will not return to work and I shall not advise them to return to work until the strike is either won or lost or arbitrated." He then suggested Easley forget about the plan completely.[126] Mitchell had another solution in mind. He wanted to get Morgan directly involved. Morgan was the one man who could force the coal presidents into a settlement, and he had promised Mitchell in February he would do "what was right" if a strike was called. To secure Morgan, Mitchell needed Hanna's assistance. He wrote the senator twice in early August pleading for an interview with the great financier. The NCF had lost prestige by failing either to avert this strike or settle it, Mitchell informed Hanna, but if Morgan settled on a fair basis now, "I should be more than pleased . . . to have the Civic Federation receive credit for it." Hanna pledged his assistance in securing an interview but suggested it might take time for Morgan, who had been in Europe for some time, to become reacquainted with all the issues in the dispute.[127]

Evidently, the best Hanna could do was arrange for another interview between Mitchell and George Perkins. They met on August 31 in Philadelphia, and Perkins offered him a bargain. Morgan would employ experts to investigate mining conditions and use his influence to compel operator compliance with the findings, on the condition that the diggers returned to work before the investigation and agreed to be bound by the findings for three years.[128] This offer was quite similar to the one Easley had proposed earlier in August, and Mitchell condemned it on the same grounds. Perkins's proposal left "the entire matter in the hands of one more largely interested than anyone else."[129] While Mitchell wanted Morgan's involvement, he refused to put the men back to work without first receiving positive assurances that conditions would be substantially improved.

In an effort to prod Hanna to exert pressure on Morgan, Mitchell often made subtle political threats. Unlike 1900, there was no presidential election to prompt Hanna's intense concern, so Mitchell had to search for other ways to apply the political heat. In early August, he warned that the long strike was giving rise to third party political movements. He noted that "plans to place labor candidates in the field upon an independent ticket are gaining great head way here." In Wilkes-Barre and Scranton, the two largest towns in the region, the central labor unions were holding conventions to nominate labor candidates for all county, legislative, and congressional offices.[130] Several days later, he mentioned that business and professional leaders in the region were working to secure arbitration through the offices of Pennsylvania's senators, Boies Penrose and Matthew Quay.[131] When these senators did involve themselves, Mitchell warned Hanna through Daniel Keefe that "if they can do anything for the Miners, they want all the credit that is to be had. Of course, John has the utmost confidence in you, and wants you to have all the credit for settling the strike that is to be had."[132]

After the failed interview between himself and Perkins, Mitchell became more obvious in his attempts to goad Hanna by exploiting the political situation. In early September, he again referred to "the great and growing independent political sentiment in the coal fields," claiming many thousands of working men were arrayed against the Republican state administration of Governor William Stone. Democrats and Socialists were gaining strength. "If the sentiment prevailing at present continues up to the election, it is likely that there will be a number of Democratic Congressmen elected from districts now represented by Republicans." If Hanna were at all interested in the elections, he should send Daniel Keefe on a tour through the region. Keefe could then "advise you of the situation and of what steps should be taken to counteract the influence of the Socialist speakers, who are holding immense meetings in every mining community."[133]

If the threat of socialism could not move Hanna, nothing could. While Mitchell emphasized the economic aspects of trade agreements, Hanna worked for stable capital-labor relations primarily out of the fear that industrial strife radicalized working people. Hanna believed that by freely recognizing "responsible trade unionists," employers "would not only gain a peaceful labor situation but a ready and willing ally in the fight against Socialism."[134] Yet while Hanna did redouble his efforts to pressure Morgan, the stance of the coal barons remained unchanged. At the end of September, Hanna informed Mitchell that despite his best efforts, "nothing better can be accomplished" than to have Morgan renew the offer Perkins made on August 31. If Mitchell agreed and needed assistance to push this settlement through the UMWA convention, Hanna said he would "be glad to assist."[135] Once again, Mitchell refused to accept this settlement or any other that involved mine workers returning to work without any guarantee of improved working conditions.[136]

Mitchell's claims that the long strike was breeding radical politics was not an exaggeration. The ranks of socialists in Pennsylvania were growing dramatically. One socialist organizer believed the anthracite strike had accomplished "more for the cause of Socialism than all the events that ever happened in the United States before. There is nothing like an object lesson for instructing the people."[137] The "object lesson" was operator intransigence. The coal barons' refusal to arbitrate, their seeming disregard for the welfare of the mine workers, the arrogance of Baer's "divine right" letter, had all radicalized mine workers and their supporters. Moreover, the strike was encouraging anti-business sentiment across the entire nation. One popular magazine reflected the popular mood at the end of the summer: "The mine-owners, blind to the proofs of popular revolt against them, intoxicated with the power derived from profitable combination, have unwittingly done more in five months to promote in the United States that State socialism which they abhor than could without this help have been accomplished in a decade by all the avowed advocates and teachers of it."[138]

Morgan may not have been alarmed by the specter of political radicalism, but a lot of other people were, including President Roosevelt. Years later, when recalling the reason he intervened, Roosevelt wrote of his desire to "save the great coal operators and all of the class of big propertied men, of which they were members, from the dreadful punishment which their own folly would have brought on them if I had not acted."[139] Roosevelt was equally concerned about the rising cost of increasingly scarce anthracite coal in eastern cities. By mid-September the political fallout from a severe coal shortage in the East would cripple the Republican party in the upcoming congressional elections. On September 22, Roosevelt's close friend and political adviser, Senator Henry Cabot Lodge of Massachusetts, warned the President that "people" were saying they did not care whether the Republicans were responsible for the strike, the price of coal was rising "and the party in power must be punished."[140] Faced with the twin political threats of rising radicalism and rising coal prices, Roosevelt directly involved himself in the strike despite continuing doubts concerning his legal authority.

This was a joyous development for Mitchell. As early as September 8, he had suggested to Hanna that "the strike might be brought to a close if you could have the President invite the railroad presidents and our officers to meet him and you to try to adjust our differences."[141] Thus, when Roosevelt extended invitations on October 1 to Mitchell and the coal barons to confer with him in Washington on October 3, Mitchell quickly agreed, asking only that he be allowed to bring along the three anthracite district presidents. Roosevelt consented. The White House conference, however, was a failure. Mitchell offered to have Roosevelt name a tribunal to determine the issues involved in the strike. If the operators agreed to abide by the decisions of the tribunal, Mitchell told the President, "we will immediately call a convention and recommend a resumption of work." The coal barons rejected this plan. They described the strike field as being on the verge of anarchy and asked instead for Roosevelt to end the strike "by the strong arm of the military at your command." The conference ended without agreement.[142]

Mitchell could take heart, however, that his conduct at the meeting and his willingness to arbitrate had added immeasurably to his public image as both a gentleman and a trustworthy labor official. Roosevelt was very impressed with the young union president, who remained calm in the face of insults hurled by the operators. "There was only one man in that conference who behaved like a gentleman," Roosevelt said, "and that man was not I."[143] The *Des Moines Register and Leader* reflected the consensus of editorial opinion after the conference when it suggested that Mitchell had achieved "moral success" by winning over public sympathy. He was "cool, calm, self-controlled and polite, earnest and forceful in presenting the cause of the miners, yet never overstepping the bounds of gentlemanly courtesy." Despite his youth and lack of education, "he shows himself the mental equal, if not superior" of the operators.[144]

Roosevelt continued to press for a solution. Unable to move the operators, he tried to exploit Mitchell's reasonableness by offering to end the dispute along the lines put forth in the report of Commissioner of Labor Carroll D. Wright. Wright's report suggested an immediate return to work by the strikers, after which Roosevelt would set up a commission and move toward a settlement based on the findings. Hanna immediately urged Mitchell to accept this proposition, telling him it was the "best available solution of the miners' strike."[145] Mitchell, however, rejected Roosevelt's offer because there was no guarantee the operators would accept the commission's findings. Referring to the White House conference, Mitchell expressed his confidence that the President had been "impressed with the fairness of our proposition and the insincerity of those who maligned us." It was this insincerity that led Mitchell to question whether the coal barons would accept the commission's findings:

> Having in mind our experience with the coal operators in the past we have
> no reason to feel any degree of confidence in their willingness to do us jus-

tice in the future; and inasmuch as they have refused to accept the decision of a tribunal selected by you and inasmuch as there is no law through which you can enforce the findings of the commission you suggest, we respectfully decline to advise our people to return to work simply upon the hope that the coal operators might be induced or forced to comply with the recommendations of your commission.[146]

Rejecting a presidential proposal that had Hanna's backing was a strong display of courage and independence on Mitchell's part. But he did not want Hanna to consider his rejection a personal affront. Writing the senator on October 13, he expressed his sincere regret that he could not accept the proposal, but he could not call off the strike until either victory was achieved or "an impartial board of arbitration" established.[147] In a letter to his friend Harry Taylor, Mitchell gave some of the reasons why he was able to refuse President Roosevelt. Despite the failure of the White House conference, Mitchell was confident he had gained a "great deal of influence and prestige" while operators had "lost much of their support" as a result of that meeting. And even though the mine workers had been on strike for five months, they were "standing firm as the rocks of Gibraltar." Finally, Mitchell noted that "the pressure from the people in the east is becoming terrific, and it is entirely upon the operators." For all these reasons Mitchell was "hopeful of tangible results in the near future."[148]

Mitchell's letter to Taylor proved uncannily accurate. It was indeed public pressure that forced the operators to accept arbitration. But Mitchell could not have known how quickly the "near future" would be. On the very day he penned that missive, Secretary of War Elihu Root met with J. P. Morgan aboard the financial titan's yacht, the *Corsair*, to discuss a peace plan. Two days later, Morgan and Root brought President Roosevelt a statement signed by every major anthracite operator, including George Baer, calling for arbitration to end the strike. Root's plan called for the immediate resumption of work and the appointment of a presidential commission to consider the questions at issue. The difference between this and other proposals was that the contending parties in the arbitration hearings would be employers and employees, not employers and the United Mine Workers. This way operators could arbitrate their differences with their employees and still not have to deal with the union. One operator, Thomas P. Fowler of the New York, Ontario and Western, told reporters that acceptance of the Root plan "was chiefly due to the pressure of public opinion, or rather, you might say, public necessity."[149]

More accurately, acceptance by the operators meant succumbing to the pressure of Roosevelt. After efforts to pressure Mitchell failed, Roosevelt seriously contemplated sending in the army to take possession of the coal fields. At that point, Morgan realized the operators' position was untenable.

That Morgan was able to secure the coal barons' approval of this plan within twenty-four hours with only minor qualifications proved Mitchell had accurately assessed Morgan's control over the operators. The coal barons did insist on one alteration of Root's plan before signing, however. Because of their concern over membership of the arbitration board, they stipulated that the five-man board should include: an officer in the engineer corps of the army or navy; a mining engineer; a federal judge from eastern Pennsylvania; a man who had been active in mining and selling anthracite coal; and a "man of prominence, eminent as a sociologist."[150] The President's secretary, George Cortelyou, then informed Mitchell he was expected at the White House to discuss the proposal at his convenience. Mitchell wired back that he would be there the very next day.[151]

Before he left for Washington, Mitchell received a telephone call from Hanna. Hanna realized that Mitchell was upset by the failure to include a labor representative on the arbitration commission. The senator then assured Mitchell he just had a long conversation with the President, who assured him that in making up the commission he would appoint "one union man." The President also promised Hanna the commission would be fair and that "justice will be done the miners regardless of the railroad presidents."[152] Thus assured Mitchell met Roosevelt. As Roosevelt expected, the focus of their conversation was the composition of the commission. Mitchell requested not only a union representative, but also a "high Catholic ecclesiastic" because so many of the mine workers were Catholic. Roosevelt vowed to use his best efforts to meet the requests.[153]

George Perkins and Robert Bacon, representing J. P. Morgan, were summoned to the White House on October 15 to discuss the possibility of expanding the commission to seven men in order to accommodate Mitchell. They agreed to an expansion and to the prelate, but they adamantly refused to the naming of a labor representative and threatened to withdraw their offer to arbitrate. After two hours, an exasperated Roosevelt suggested he would name the labor representative as the "eminent sociologist." To his shock, Perkins and Bacon said they could convince the operators to agree to that plan. The absurdity of their position amazed Roosevelt. It appeared to him "that the mighty brains of these captains of industry would rather have anarchy than tweedle-dum, but that if I would use the word tweedle-dee they would hail it as meaning peace."[154]

On October 16, the White House made public the names of the commissions' members: Brigadier General John M. Wilson, retired army chief of engineers; Thomas W. Watkins, former mine owner; Edward Parker, editor of a mining industry journal; U.S. Circuit Court Judge George Gray; Bishop John L. Spalding of Illinois; and E. E. Clark, grand chief of the Order of Railway Conductors. Commissioner of Labor Carroll D. Wright was named recorder of the commission. Mitchell must have been quite pleased with the selection of Clark, for in early August the railroad brotherhood leader had written Mitchell expressing hope that "the men will win a signal victory."[155]

Roosevelt telegraphed Mitchell informing him that the operators had accepted these names and asked him to do likewise. Mitchell responded with a long letter informing Roosevelt that the executive boards of the anthracite districts had already met and unanimously agreed to call a delegate convention for October 20, at which they would recommend a return to work on the basis of the arbitration proposal. He reminded the President that he had always stood ready to arbitrate the strike. Had his offer been accepted "six months ago instead of now there need have been no strike." And he was anxious to thank the President for the "patriotic efforts" he made to end the strike honorably. As for the coal barons, Mitchell held no malice. He forgave their "arrogant refusal to deal with us," and he now "held out the right hand of friendship."[156]

In the few days before the start of the October 20 tri-district convention, Mitchell confessed that there would be "strong opposition" to ending the strike at this time and that "some of our officers are seeking to prevent a settlement." He admitted as well there was ground for opposition "because there was no guarantee that all our people will be reinstated."[157] Thus, when Mitchell addressed the delegates, he presented the settlement in the best possible light. Acknowledging there were "objectionable features" of the proposition and that it might not receive the "unanimous approval of our people," he then pressed hard for acceptance: "I am firm in my conviction that the prompt acceptance of this proposal will secure to the anthracite mine workers and those dependent upon them a greater measure of justice than they could attain by continuing the conflict. I believe that the prompt acceptance of this proposition will secure to the mine workers a greater degree of justice than they have enjoyed in the past."[158] The convention upheld the wishes of Mitchell, who then notified Roosevelt that on Thursday morning, October 23, the mine workers would return to work.[159] The strike was over.

Jubilant reaction from all quarters greeted the end of the strike. The majority of people in the labor movement or sympathetic to it hailed the settlement as a tremendous victory. Amidst the hurrahs, however, discordant voices could be heard. Within the UMWA, Mother Jones was the most vocal detractor. She believed the mine workers should have continued the strike until full recognition was achieved. "The strike was won," she wrote. "Absolutely no anthracite coal was being dug. The operators could have been made to deal with the union if Mr. Mitchell had stood firm." Jones considered Mitchell's "love of flattery" the real reason he backed down. With the President, press, priests, and politicians all singing his praises, Mitchell accepted a weak settlement. "Flattery and homage did its work with John Mitchell."[160] The head of the British miners' union, Benjamin Pickard, thought Mitchell had made a grave mistake.[161] Socialists also assailed Mitchell's acceptance of the settlement. John Spargo, a socialist who had worked for the union during the strike, castigated Mitchell for succumbing to his "friendship with T. R."[162] One socialist paper called it "one of the worst fiascoes ever presented by an impotently led labor movement."[163]

For those who believed the interests of capital and labor are irreconcilable and that the true power of the working class lies in its fighting strength, the settlement was indeed a fiasco Mitchell could have avoided. By his own admission, at the time the arbitration offer was made "the mine workers had practically won the strike." The assessments imposed by the special convention provided the union with more than funds it had ever possessed in its history. Nor did the presence of troops have a noticeable effect on strike sentiment. Mitchell was in fact confident the mine workers "were in a position to continue the contest indefinitely."[164] Had Mitchell placed his trust in the fighting spirit of the mine workers, he might well have spurned the offer to arbitrate and battled to achieve full recognition. Yet unlike Jones and the socialists, Mitchell did not place his faith in the rank and file. He depended on the friendship of elites and public approval to advance the union cause. His visit to the White House, in particular, had added immensely to his prestige. His constant willingness to arbitrate had earned him the sympathy of the public. Having worked so diligently to cultivate public opinion and political alliances, he could not contemplate jeopardizing these bases of support by reneging on his promise to arbitrate. As he put it, "as we had struggled for the principle of arbitration, we would not be justified in refusing to accept it because victory was in our hands."[165]

By keeping his word and ending the strike, he helped gain a measure of legitimacy for organized labor at a time when trade unions were considered part of the radical fringe. By his ability to control the rank and file and his ability to avert a sympathy strike, he ingratiated himself with some of the most powerful people in the nation. His gentile demeanor, in contrast with the arrogance of the operators, encouraged Roosevelt to bring the weight of presidential power to bear against the coal barons. The only thing he did not achieve was a clear cut victory for the anthracite mine workers.

Most mine workers and their families in the anthracite region were both relieved and happy now that the five-month ordeal was over and they could look forward to steady incomes. And once again Mitchell was worshipped like a deity. In premature celebration of a victory yet to be decided, a testimonial banquet was held in his honor on October 26 in the main function room at the Hotel Hart in Wilkes-Barre. This hotel had been Mitchell's residence for most of the strike. He was joined on stage by the three district presidents and Paul Pulaski, one of the leading Slavic organizers. Pulaski read a eulogy from a committee of immigrant mine workers:

Blessed be the moment when you, as salvator (*sic*) of our troubles and miseries arrived in our midst, and holding high the banner of human rights boldly and courageously stood like a hero against the tempest of mighty and seemingly unconquerable adverses. But nothing could withstand your ingenious leadership, a second Napoleon of labor, your every step was a conquest and a victory. Receive, dear leader, a thousand-fold blessing of all the poor, hard working and struggling people, who shall teach their children, that the embodiment of everything that is pure, just, right and sublime is our president, John Mitchell.[166]

Gifts were then offered to the hero. He received an expensive gold watch and an even more valuable ornate gold medallion with his initials set in diamonds across the top. Just three days after this celebration was Mitchell Day. A second round of festivities began, including parades and more gifts for the union official.[167]

The national spotlight shined brightly on Mitchell. At no other time in his career did Mitchell approach the "hero status" he attained in the months following the strike. One of the most popular magazines of the period carried his own account of the strike. The press dubbed him "the labor leader of to-day." He was hounded for interviews by reporters and begged to lecture by social organizations of every description. He was touted as the next AFL president and rumored to be running for the governorship of Illinois. Cheering crowds greeting him wherever he traveled. In mid-December Spring Valley threw a day long jubilee in honor of their most famous resident. On his train trip from Pennsylvania to Illinois large crowds gathered at every station just to see him. After the Spring Valley bash, he traveled to Springfield and dined with Governor Yate at the governor's mansion.[168]

Mitchell, of course, was eager to translate his fame into dollars and cents. His friend Harry Taylor advised him to go immediately on a lecture tour so he could "make a lot of money." The time to act was now, Taylor advised, and urged him to "strike while the iron is hot and the public is interested."[169] Mitchell replied that he fully appreciated "the importance of making some money" off his victory, but there were a number of reasons why he did not like the idea of a lecture tour. He could earn as much money for less effort simply by writing what he had to say for the magazines. His account of the strike in *McClure's*, for instance, was "a five hundred dollar article." Also the "terrible nervous strain" of the strike left him "physically and emotionally incapable" of undertaking more work. Finally, Mitchell was not comfortable in the role of national hero. The constant attention made him feel like a freak on display. Here was the lament of an intensely private man, still plagued by feelings of inferiority, who had achieved celebrity status. In a particularly revealing comment, Mitchell told Taylor how he longed for anonymity:

I have had the calcium light upon me so long that I wish to the Lord I could steal away to some place where people would not know me and where I could follow out my natural inclinations without attracting attention. As it is, wherever I go I am followed by the small boys and gazed after by the grown people. I am like some new beast that is brought into town with a circus; all of which is a source of much embarrassment to me.[170]

Although the public scrutiny and the strain of the strike had left him "fatigued, almost worn out," Mitchell had little time for rest. He had hoped to travel home to Spring Valley to be with his wife and children, whom he had not seen for some time. He also hoped once again to visit his sister and nieces in Fresno, where he truly felt at ease, but the need to prepare the union's case before the anthracite coal commission meant he would have to remain in the East and continue working. He estimated he would not get a moment's rest for the next four or five months. "It is a tremendous undertaking," he realized, "in fact the responsibility is greater than in the conduct of the strike."[171] The anthracite struggle was far from over; its venue had simply shifted from the strike field to the courtroom. And Mitchell would remain in the public eye until it was resolved.

Chapter 6

On the Witness Stand

Nothing better illustrated the emerging bureaucratic unionism of the Progressive Era years than John Mitchell's preparations for the Anthracite Coal Strike Commission. The terrain of capital-labor conflict in hard coal would no longer be the strike field, where there were too many risks involved for the union as an institution, but rather the conference room and the court room. Here, political alliances and public pressure took the place of rank-and-file militancy. Here, reasoned argument, backed by reams of facts and figures, took the place of pickets and rallies. The mine workers themselves were now important only for statistical purposes, and for the emotional impression their tales of woe might make on the public and the commissioners. Mitchell rented two floors of a house in Philadelphia and hired an army of labor's new mercenaries—investigators, economists, publicists, and secretaries. Above them stood Mitchell himself, the four-star general of bureaucratic unionism preparing for battle.

The artillery for this battle was information. Statistics on every conceivable aspect of the industry had to be gathered and processed. Not simply wages and and hours, but endless details on the costs of living, the costs of mining coal, production and distribution of coal, and profit levels were marshaled for the upcoming war of words. Mitchell was truly in his element. His success at the annual bituminous joint conferences testified to his expertise in the presentation of this type of confrontation. Because the anthracite industry was far more complex in its detail than soft coal, and because the commission would be far more exacting than a joint conference, Mitchell realized he needed more assistance than the union staff could supply. He therefore enlisted some of the best research talent available. One important figure was John R. Commons, assistant to NCF secretary Ralph Easley, and later one of the pioneers in the field of labor history. Isaac Hourwich, professor at Columbia University, and Peter Roberts, cleric and scholar, also contributed their skills. In charge of the research team, Mitchell placed Walter Weyl, an economist in the office of the Commissioner of Labor. Already an ardent admirer of the UMWA chief, Weyl would quickly establish a close working relationship with Mitchell. In the years to come Weyl would ably assist Mitchell in his literary efforts.[1]

Mitchell himself played a leading role in the gathering of information. He was adept at anticipating possible arguments operators might use to strengthen their case and directing researchers to counter those arguments. This ability reflected a thorough understanding of the complex social fabric of the anthracite region. For instance, he was certain operators would exploit the issue of drunkenness and the large number of saloons in the area to prove that mine workers squandered their money and that any wage increase would be spent recklessly as well. He instructed the research team to defend the argument that drunkenness was not the cause but the effect of low wages and that if "wages are increased drunkenness will decrease." To cite a second example, he directed researchers to gather evidence on the average age of bridegrooms in the area as well as averages for the various nationalities in Europe. If the union could prove mine workers tended to marry later than their European counterparts, this would help support their contention that they did not waste their earnings, but rather exhibited "a certain amount of forbearance and a certain period of saving."[2]

The justice of the mine workers' case, and the national attention the strike elicited, also earned for Mitchell the active support of one of the best known social critics of the day, Henry Demarest Lloyd. In addition to his famous anti-monopoly work, *Wealth Against Commonwealth*, Lloyd had also gained attention for his depiction of the 1889 Spring Valley miners' strike, *A Strike of Millionaires Against Miners*. Although Mitchell had never met the renowned reformer, he had applauded his relief efforts during the Spring Valley strike and welcomed his participation in the upcoming hearings. The two men had a mutual friend, Father John Power of Spring Valley. Lloyd had met Power before the 1889 strike and had kept in contact since, and, at the end of September 1902, Lloyd visited Power and obtained a letter of introduction to the union president. "He's one you may trust fully," Power wrote Mitchell.[3] Lloyd proved a worthy addition to the cause, adding not only research skills but prestige and oratorical abilities. It was Lloyd's suggestion that Mitchell hire Clarence Darrow to head up the UMWA's legal defense team. While the hearings would not be a legal trial, the commission would observe standard court procedure and thus courtroom skills were at a premium. Darrow had already achieved a measure of national acclaim for his defense of Eugene Debs during the Pullman strike in 1894. He knew little of mining, however, and therefore required the assistance of other lawyers with knowledge of anthracite.[4] These three men—Mitchell, Lloyd, and Darrow—were most responsible for representing the mine workers before the commission and the public. Among union supporters, they became known as the "miners' trinity."

On November 2 Mitchell formally submitted the miners' demands. The first two principal demands matched those adopted at the March tri-district convention in Shamokin—a 20 percent rate increase for contract miners and a 20 percent reduction in the hours of labor for all workers paid by the hour, day, or week. A third demand was now added—union recognition. Mitchell called for the "incorporation of an agreement between the United Mine Workers of America and the anthracite coal companies" to determine wages, conditions of employment, and "satisfactory methods for the adjustment of grievances."[5] Thus, Mitchell was trying to gain through arbitration what he so willingly gave up during the strike. Operators, of course, considered each of these demands arbitrary and unacceptable. They argued that present wages were generous enough to maintain a decent standard of living and were comparable to bituminous wages. The coal barons saved their real venom for the demand for union recognition. Not only did they believe this demand outside the scope of the commission, but in a loud and belligerent voice declared that under no circumstances would they recognize the UMWA.[6]

The Anthracite Coal Strike Commission opened hearings on November 14 at Scranton, and for the next four months it commanded national attention. The press was there in force, and the eyes of the nation watched to see if Roosevelt's commission would mete out justice as he had promised. The first noteworthy development was the appearance of lawyers on behalf of nonunion workers who asked for and received the right to present their case before the commission. Although they represented only a small percentage of the work force, these lawyers made a significant impression when they stridently opposed any agreement with the UMWA. Both Mitchell and Darrow argued that the nonunion lawyers were in the pay of the operators and that the nonunion men were being exploited and deceived, but the first blow had been struck against the demand for union recognition.[7]

On the second day of the hearings, the mine workers began the presentation of their case. Mitchell took the stand as Darrow's first witness. Denied the right to appear in his official capacity as president of the UMWA, he testified only as an interested spokesperson for the anthracite diggers. In clear and confident tones, he articulated the union's demands and the reasons for their acceptance. Among the justifications he cited for the wage increase: higher wages were paid to bituminous miners "for substantially similar work"; existing wages were insufficient compensation "in lieu of the dangerous character of the occupation"; wages were too low to "maintain the American standard of living"; and wages were so low that the children of mine workers "are prematurely forced into the breakers and mills instead of being supported and educated upon the earnings of their parents." In support of the 20 percent reduction of working hours, Mitchell put forth both ethical and economic arguments. The present ten-hour day, he said, was detrimental to the "life, health, safety and well-being" of mine workers, and therefore the reduction would greatly improve the "physical, mental and moral conditions" of their lives. This could be accomplished without loss of production. Experience in the soft coal fields showed "shorter hours increase the intensity and efficiency of labor" so that each worker produced the same in eight hours as he had earlier in ten.[8]

Mitchell then stated his case for the extension of the trade agreement to hard coal. First, trade agreements represented the wave of the future in all industries. They had been established in soft coal and other industries and thus were "in keeping with the spirit of the times." Second, union membership benefited the workers. In industries where unions were recognized by employers, they tended to improve workers' "physical, moral, and mental conditions." Third, trade agreements benefited employers. Only the union could establish labor peace. The UMWA imposed discipline on the work force, reduced work stoppages, and helped establish "friendly relations between employer and employee." Fourth, the trade agreement was the only effective means to establish employer-employee relations "on a just and permanent basis." It represented the only fair way to settle questions arising between workers and employers without resort to strikes and lockouts.[9]

Mitchell himself was pleased with his opening testimony. Writing in jest to a friend, he stated there had been a "magnificent address delivered by one John Mitchell."[10] He felt "quite well satisfied with the outlook so far," but he did not relish the coming cross-examination. The coal barons had hired "about thirty lawyers, the best they can get in the country." The thought of being dissected by this platoon made him anxious to retreat from the spotlight and join his friend Harry Taylor and their bowling chums, who planned to go on an ice skating excursion as soon as Mitchell could spare the time.[11]

He had good reason to fear cross-examination. It lasted four full days! Numerous attorneys for the operators challenged him, but it was Wayne MacVeagh, a former attorney general under President Garfield and now chief counsel for the Pennsylvania Coal Company, who took charge of the grilling. There were endless attempts to make Mitchell appear irresponsible and to force him to contradict himself. He withstood the test well, using his quick wit and debating skills to fend off his attackers and win over the reporters. For instance, when MacVeagh expressed concern that wage increases won by mine workers would lead to higher coal costs and thus fall on the "bowed backs of the poor," Mitchell suggested that operators need not raise coal prices. They might take the wage increase "out of their profits and so put it on the bowed backs of the rich." On another occasion MacVeagh argued the UMWA was not necessary to settle grievances between mine workers and the Pennsylvania Coal Company. In seventeen years, not a single worker had ever registered a complaint. Mitchell retorted he was not surprised because the source of the complaint—the mine worker himself—would surely have been removed.[12]

His skillful performance on the witness stand won praise from all sides. Henry Demarest Lloyd expressed admiration for the way Mitchell remained calm and forceful in the face of intense cross-examination. "He is admirably simple and straight-forward and as keen as anyone," Lloyd informed his wife.

Even Wayne MacVeagh was impressed, remarking at one point: "You are the best witness for yourself, Mr. Mitchell, that I have ever confronted." The press also applauded Mitchell's performance. One typical editorial claimed MacVeagh used all "the arts of his profession" to confuse, intimidate, and entrap Mitchell. And "if the labor leader did not really score the more points, he at least divided the honors."[13]

At one point during his cross-examination of Mitchell, MacVeagh asked to meet the union president and his counsel to settle the entire affair "out of court."[14] After a meeting between union representatives and the coal barons' attorneys, Darrow on November 22 asked for an adjournment of the commission until December 3 to explore the possibilities of an out of court settlement. The commission granted the request, with the chair of the commission, Judge Gray, declaring he would be pleased to see the dispute settled by any means.[15] Mitchell was ecstatic that operators had stepped forward in their first attempt to conciliate. The basis of the proposal was a 10 percent advance in wages (instead of the twenty the union demanded), a nine-hour day (instead of the eight the union demanded), and, as Mitchell put it, the union was to be "recognized in an indirect way, committees to be treated with in the settlement of grievances." Mitchell considered this proposal "satisfactory," and he hoped it would not be "bowled over in New York."[16]

Mitchell was optimistic about a successful resolution when J. P. Morgan wholeheartedly endorsed the plan, but his hopes were dashed when independent operators refused to go along and insisted the hearings continue. Mitchell was "sorely disappointed." Although he did not fear the outcome of the hearings, he did lament the loss of a golden opportunity for operators and the union to resolve their own dispute in a peaceful way and thus lay the basis for amicable negotiations in the future. With the resumption of the "court" battle, "personalities and disagreeable matters are bound to be injected into the fight now and as a result a bitter feeling will be left which it will take years to eradicate and replace by the confidence which should exist." Moreover, Mitchell desired to "get this thing off our hands so that I could take a little rest."[17]

When hearings resumed, the union paraded more than two hundred witnesses before the commission. These were mine workers of every description—immigrant and native born, adolescents and old men, skilled and unskilled, plus their wives, children, mothers, widows, and priests. They were brought forth to present firsthand evidence on a wide array of issues— dockage and size of the coal cars, safety and method of payment, irregular work and hours of labor, company housing and company stores. Their impact on the commission members and the press, however, was significant for its emotional impact. Their graphic descriptions of poverty, child labor, industrial accidents, drudgery, and exploitation went on for days, leading one scholar to refer to this testimony as "the moving spectacle of horrors."[18] Of the many heart wrenching personal stories, one that attracted a great deal of press commentary was that of twelve-year-old breaker boy Andrew Chippie, who was the sole means of support for his widowed mother and his three younger siblings.[19]

On December 17, the union concluded its case and the commission declared a holiday recess. When the hearings reopened on January 9 to begin testimony on behalf of the operators, the site had shifted from Scranton to Philadelphia. Mitchell and his secretary, E. C. Morris, took rooms at the posh Continental Hotel. According to one source, Mitchell's room had previously been occupied by General U.S. Grant and at another time by Dom Pedro, emperor of Brazil.[20] Mitchell flirted with high society in even more direct ways while in Philadelphia. Along with Darrow, Lloyd, and members of the commission, he attended a banquet at the Clover Club, the exclusive stomping ground of the city's elite. Labor's hero was wearing a tuxedo, smoking cigars, and drinking champagne while he crowed his now standard line: "If the laborers and capitalists might sit down to a banquet like this and look each other in the eye, strikes and lockouts would soon become things of the past."[21] Apparently Mitchell did not think the idea of Andrew Chippie and his widowed mother feasting with J. P. Morgan and George Baer at the Clover Club in any way absurd.

In his biography of Clarence Darrow, Irving Stone tells the story of a confrontation between Mitchell and Darrow that supposedly took place in early February when final summations were being prepared. Mitchell requested that Darrow tell him in broad outline what his principal arguments were to be. As Darrow talked, Mitchell became agitated, and at last he interrupted the lawyer, expressing shock that Darrow intended to make "a socialistic speech" before the commission. Darrow responded that he planned to use the "most effective" arguments he could. Then Mitchell, shouting: "And I tell you, Darrow, that this whole case must be argued upon the testimony that has been produced. I want an increase in wages and better living and working conditions as soon as I can get them. I'm not interested in the development of your private theories which may come into effect many years hereafter." After further shouts and threats, Darrow finally backed down.[22] Although probably apocryphal, the story is a beautiful illustration of Mitchell's conservative temperament. He had spent more than three months preparing and presenting this case, and he had been scrupulous in his avoidance of unnecessary acrimony. He did have a political agenda, but his agenda was class harmony rather than class conflict. He honestly believed, and he desperately had been trying to prove, that the union was a responsible institution capable of fostering close and friendly relations with the railroad chiefs through the trade agreement. Any discussion of the inherent friction between classes would subvert his purposes.

As it turned out, the final summations presented such radically contrasting social philosophies that Mitchell's belief in class harmony appeared naive. George Baer delivered the operators' summary. He spoke the language of social Darwinism, the unrestricted rights of capital, the evil of unionism, and the rights of individual workers to contract their labor. Darrow, on the other hand, argued for the social need of unions to organize so that the "downcast" might protect themselves against "cruel" capitalists. In his long and dramatic speech, Darrow captured the heart of the strike when he said that for the operators the whole debacle had been "a question of mastery—nothing else; because they felt and believed that upon this contest depended the question of whether they should be the masters or whether the men should be the masters."[23]

Much more memorable than the words of either man was the action of Mitchell. Upon the conclusion of Baer's speech, he walked across the room and shook his hand.[24] After five months of industrial warfare that required presidential intervention to quell, after more than two hundred witnesses had testified to the horrific exploitation resulting from absolute corporate dominance in the industry, and after the "divine right" coal baron had castigated him personally and disparaged his union as the root cause of the industry's problems, Mitchell professed no animosity. Mitchell never explained this action in print, but as were all his public actions and utterances, the handshake was quite obviously premeditated and calculated for its effect. It was pure theater intending to symbolize, for the benefit of commission members, operators, and the public, that he was the kind of reasonable, conservative labor leader who deserved recognition. It was also designed to soothe the hostilities that had arisen during the hearings and prepare for negotiations to come. Those who expected labor's hero to crucify the coal barons in this grand public forum did not know him. He had calculated that greater sympathy could be earned for the union, and greater prestige for himself, by a public turning of the cheek.

In all, the commission heard the testimony of 558 witnesses, of whom 240 had been called by the union, 153 by the attorneys for nonunion miners, 154 by the operators, and 11 by the commission itself. The testimony amounted to more than 10,000 legal cap pages, not including a vast array of statistics and other exhibits.[25] While the operators had frequently insisted that the question of union recognition did not fall within the parameters of the commission's authority, attorneys for both sides brought forth numerous witnesses to testify on just this issue. When the hearings finally closed in mid-February the commissioners traveled from Philadelphia to Washington and spent several weeks preparing their findings. Their final report was finally handed to the president on March 18 and made public on March 21.[26]

The findings of the commission consisted of a report and an award, the former being a theoretical discussion of general principles of capital-labor relations and the latter specific recommendations bearing on the anthracite industry. As to wages and hours, the commission's award resembled the attempted "out of court" settlement. The award provided for a 10 percent wage advance and a nine-hour day. As to union recognition, the UMWA was not formally recognized. There would be no trade agreement. Commissioners agreed with the coal barons that the issue of union recognition was not within their jurisdiction and that Mitchell had appeared before the commission solely "as the representative of the anthracite coal mine workers, and not in his official character as president of the United Mine Workers of America."[27] Instead, the commission created a permanent six-member Board of Conciliation to adjudicate disputes between miners and their employers. The board was to consist of one mine worker and one operator from each of the three anthracite districts. If the board could not resolve a dispute, the issue was referred to an umpire whose decision was to be final. No work suspensions were to be allowed during the grievance process.[28]

Even though the commissioners side stepped the issue of union recognition in their award, their report did expound views on unionization and the trade agreement. Considering the publicity surrounding their report, the pronouncements of the commissioners were of great significance for the future of the UMWA and the labor movement in general. The commissioners held that the right to join a union was a basic right of all workers. They also approved of collective bargaining, claiming that "the more full the recognition given to a trade union the more business-like and responsible it becomes." Because union recognition forced labor leaders to deal with "business men in business matters," over time the union's "more intelligent, conservative and responsible members come to the front" and gain control of the organization. In a warning to employers, the commissioners added that if employers' efforts were directed toward the "discouragement and repression" of unions, they "need not be surprised if the more radically inclined members are the ones most frequently heard."[29]

Yet the commissioners' report also explicitly condemned the closed shop and praised the open shop. There shall be, the report stated, "no discrimination against or interference with any employee who is not a member of any labor organization by members of such organization." The commissioners drove home this point by announcing that "the rights and privileges of nonunion men are as sacred to them as the rights and privileges of unionists. The contention that a majority in an industry, by voluntarily associating themselves in a union, acquire authority over those who do not so associate themselves is untenable." The board would fully protect the rights of those who chose not to strike or pay union dues because that was "part of the personal liberty of a citizen, that can never be surrendered."[30]

In short, both the report and the award represented compromises between the position of the coal barons and the union. And thus, both sides were able to claim victory. Because they had not been forced to recognize the UMWA, operators were quick to hail the award as a major triumph. Francis I. Gowan, an attorney for the coal barons, declared the decision a clear cut operator victory.[31] The emerging open shop movement of employers embraced the report as a vindication of its position. As one historian has written, the report was "tailored to specifications for the employers' drive against unions."[32] Socialists and radicals, of course, denounced both the award and the report on the same grounds. Debs simply called the entire settlement a "farce."[33]

Mitchell, however, was delighted. The day the decision was made public, he told reporters it represented "on the whole a decided victory for the miners, and I am pleased with it."[34] He had little to say regarding the report, with its contradictory endorsement of both the open shop and collective bargaining as the basis of industrial relations. While the commissioners were "fair-minded and intelligent men," the report showed "a lack of appreciation of some of the fundamental principles of unionism" and was "based upon premises which cannot be maintained."[35] But he applauded the wage gains and the hourly reduction contained in the award. And he chose to interpret the creation of the Board of Conciliation as a significant step toward a trade agreement for the industry. "While disclaiming the wish to compel the recognition of the United Mine Workers of America," he wrote, "the Commission in practice made that recognition inevitable."[36] As we shall see, the operators themselves did not agree with Mitchell's glowing assessment of the Board of Conciliation, and for many years they successfully blocked all union efforts to obtain more complete recognition.

Despite the failure to grant outright recognition to the UMWA, the press generally interpreted the award as a victory for the union.[37] And in no way did the award damage Mitchell's reputation as the foremost labor statesman of his day. Once again rumors surfaced that Mitchell was destined to leave the union to assume the AFL presidency or some political office. Some reports stated he would be the next governor of Illinois, some that he would become Roosevelt's vice president after the next election, and others that he would become the next secretary of the Department of Commerce.[38] Once again the offers of product endorsement came pouring into the union office. And once again the crowds swarmed to catch a glimpse of labor's celebrity. In mid-February when he attended a celebration at the Chicago Auditorium, the house was packed with 6,000 of his admirers while the band played "Hail, the Conquering Hero Comes."[39]

On February 26, a few weeks before the commission's award was made public, Mother Jones wrote Mitchell and warned him not to allow public acclaim to affect him. Many labor leaders before him, she wrote, had been carried away by praise and had lost sight of the interests of the rank and file. Mitchell assured her that no amount of praise would make him abandon the interests of union members:

I know, only too well, what has come in the past to those who have been applauded by the public. You may rest assured that the demonstrations which have been made have in no wise turned my head. They cannot shut out the picture of what I know to be the fate of those prominent in the labor movement, and they will not deter me from doing my level best for our people so long as I have opportunity.[40]

Mother Jones no doubt perceived that he already had allowed the applause to turn his head. She believed Mitchell had ended the strike in October against the best interests of the mine workers because he had been flattered by Roosevelt's compliments. And despite his protestations to the contrary, Mitchell was in many ways a far different person than he had been a year earlier. After five months of strike and four months of hearings, Mitchell looked different, his clothing style had changed, he belonged to new associations, and he had made new friends. The metamorphosis that had begun when Mitchell became union president and had intensified when he joined the NCF had once again taken hold of Mitchell's personality.

Mother Jones was not the only one who noticed the change. Clarence Darrow and Henry D. Lloyd both recognized it and disapproved. Just prior to the NCF's annual conference in December 1902, Lloyd wrote his wife that neither he nor Darrow liked the idea of Mitchell attending the affair. "The little fact that for this visit he bought a derby hat, discarding the black soft felt hat by which he is universally known, illustrates the tendency toward conformity resulting from such an association and likely to increase in the wrong direction."[41] Lloyd's analysis was remarkably perceptive. Mitchell was not simply donning a new hat. The derby symbolized the fact that he was adopting the outlook of those with whom he associated. And unfortunately, the UMWA president proved highly susceptible to this "tendency toward conformity."

One result of the strike was the significant expansion of Mitchell's social world. He was now familiar with some of the most powerful men in the nation—politicians, financiers, bishops, editors, and industrialists. Before the 1902 strike, he had his allies Hanna and Easley, but now there were numerous other associates, such as Senator Boies Penrose of Pennsylvania, George Perkins of U.S. Steel, and even President Roosevelt. Nor were his contacts with these men purely professional. Business and pleasure were often mixed. During the strike Easley asked Mitchell to "come and take dinner with me." He said Perkins would join them later to discuss business affairs, then perhaps the three of them could take in a Broadway show: "'When Knighthood was in Flower' with Julia Marlow is a lovely thing."[42] In the spring of 1903, Mitchell traveled to St. Louis to attend the dedication of the World's Fair. He informed Daniel Keefe that President Roosevelt, former President Grover Cleveland, Senator Hanna "and a lot of *us*" would be there. Keefe, who had close ties with Hanna himself, was nevertheless astounded by the company Mitchell was keeping. He joked about the "great presidents of the great country."[43] While certainly Mitchell and Roosevelt were not bosom buddies, they did establish a professional friendship and even had lunch together on occasion.[44] And as the number of such friendships with elites grew, so, too, did Mitchell's tendency to adopt their attitudes and aspirations.

One measure of Mitchell's emerging elite status was his desire to join exclusive clubs. His stay at the Continental Hotel and the banquet at the Clover Club must have whetted his appetite for the gathering places of the rich. In early March 1903, he applied for membership in the Chicago Athletic Club, a highbrow men's organization. He relied on his operator friend Harry Taylor's connections to gain admittance, and Taylor assured him he had friends on the membership committee. Mitchell was finally approved for membership in March 1904 and happily forked over the initiation fee of $100.[45] Soon after the coal commission hearings he expressed an interest in joining a costly "dining club" in Chicago, although again he was not certain if his application for membership would be approved.[46]

His new status also impacted his family life. At this point his connections to his wife and children were tenuous. When six-month-old John Jr. died from disease in the summer of 1901, he was distraught over the infant he "had learned to love so dearly."[47] But his love for his family was a distant one. Rarely home at the best of times, he had only a few brief encounters with his wife and children during the strike and hearings. From time to time, his eldest son, Richard, ten years old in 1903, would pen pathetic letters describing what was happening in his life and expressing his longing for his absent father: "I always think of you and ask the dear Lord to take care of my papa and bring and bring (*sic*) him safe home."[48] Even when Mitchell was able to slip away from union work for a few days, he would often not go home at all. He preferred to book a room at McCoy's Hotel in Chicago and spend his leisure time with Harry Taylor or his reporter friend E. R. Smith.

It is possible, although not certain, that Mitchell used these respites to drink heavily, adding a further strain on family ties. He and Taylor would often discuss going on "skating trips" and "fishing expeditions" together, and in the next breath would poke fun at prohibitionists. Both men were quite careful in their correspondence, however, not to discuss their drinking escapades candidly, perhaps because rumors abounded that Mitchell was often intoxicated in public during the strike.[49] After spending a weekend with his family at McCoy's at the beginning of the strike, Mitchell explained that he would never bring his family to the hotel again. His behavior had infuriated his wife. "A bunch of roses don't fix matters in Spring Valley," he admitted, and "I question very much if a new dress will do it."[50] When the hearings concluded, Mitchell had not seen his wife or children for over two months. He wrote his wife explaining his need for "a couple of week's rest," yet he was not coming home to reacquaint himself. He planned to join Taylor at Taylor's cabin in Wisconsin so the two men could enjoy some "fishing."[51]

Mitchell expressed his love for his family by providing for them, which also offered a means to symbolize his own rise in the world to Spring Valley neighbors. Throughout the strike and the hearings he actively searched for a new house in Spring Valley. By the time the coal commission's award was presented, he had arranged to purchase a $3,000 house in the wealthiest part of town. He wanted to install running water in all the bathrooms and electricity throughout the house, and he planned to build a cupola on one corner.[52] He also decided to take a hand, for the first time, in the upbringing of his three sons, Richard (age ten in 1903), Jim (age eight), and Robbie (age six).[53] The three boys attended a school run by Catholic nuns, and the eldest was an altar boy for Father Power at the Immaculate Conception church.[54] The day after the commission handed its findings to Roosevelt, Mitchell decided it was time "to pay considerable attention to their secular education as well as to their religious training." He did not object to the fact his children were being raised as "good Catholics." He appreciated the "moral influence of the Sisters' School." But he feared that his sons were not receiving the proper preparation for respectable careers. He insisted his boys learn how to "take care of themselves, and to know the business affairs of the world."[55] Perhaps Mitchell himself had learned during the strike and hearings that corporate values took precedence over all others, including morality and labor solidarity.

By the spring of 1903, the elitist Mitchell was also taking physical form. No longer did he look the way Lincoln Steffens described him during the strike: "a small, spare man, with black eyes steady in a white, smooth face, which, with his habitual clerical garb and sober mien, gives him the appearance of a priest."[56] The dark eyes and smooth complexion were still noticeable, but he was far from spare and hardly ministerial. He had begun to take on the appearance of a well-fed and well-paid corporate executive. Whether from alcohol or overeating, Mitchell at the age of thirty-three was starting to bloat. He admitted he was "stout" and heavier than he had ever been in his life. His five foot, seven inch frame was now carrying at least 180 pounds. He jested to his friend that he was "adding to my avoirdupois daily."[57] The added weight was noticeable not just on his now paunchy torso, but also on his face, which now looked puffy, his lips swollen and his eyes heavy. The weight gain also symbolized Mitchell's transformation from a lean and hungry fighter for the rank and file to the complacent and eminently comfortable labor bureaucrat.

The "clerical garb" mentioned by Steffens was also gone. Association with the wealthy called for a new executive wardrobe. In addition to the derby mentioned by Lloyd, Mitchell began to wear expensive tailor-made suits. By 1904, he had become dissatisfied with his present tailor. He told John B.

Lennon, president of the Journeymen Tailors' union, that he planned to spend between $150 and $200 on new suits, and he wanted Lennon to recommend a good union tailor.[58] He also sported a gold watch and diamond ring, and when enjoying tobacco, he preferred either expensive cigars or his meerschaum pipe.[59] There was nothing about his appearance to distinguish him from a successful businessman and nothing to remind one that just six years earlier he had been an unpaid union organizer tramping through the prairie of Illinois.

One of the most obvious advantages of Mitchell's elite status was the opportunity to make money, and after the strike he embarked on numerous financial ventures. If he wanted to look and act like the elite he so admired, he needed an income to suit his new life-style. But for Mitchell, making money was much more than a means to an end. It was a game, an adventure, and he loved it dearly. Although the January 1903 UMWA convention raised his salary to $3,000 per year,[60] Mitchell wanted more. Unfortunately, his aggressive pursuit of wealth and his readiness to exploit opportunities that came to him as union president often involved serious conflicts of interest. Despite his disclaimer that he was not "seeking to advance my personal welfare at the expense of those I am employed to serve,"[61] during the strike Mitchell surreptitiously began to invest in coal properties.

Soon after the special convention in July, when Mitchell derailed the general strike movement, he met Harry Taylor at McCoy's Hotel in Chicago. The two men discussed moves contemplated by Taylor's firm, the General Wilmington Coal Company. The company was anxious to purchase an operating coal mine, the Carbon Hill mine, from a rival firm, the Starr Coal Company. Taylor evidently offered Mitchell the chance to invest his money, for Mitchell wrote soon after that "the business matter is looking favorable, and I shall be glad when it is all fixed up."[62] The takeover of the Carbon Hill mine did not go through until October, when Taylor made an offer acceptable to the Starr Company. Mitchell then contacted Taylor and told him if it was "satisfactory to you to let me in there to the extent spoken of I shall be glad of the opportunity."[63] Since the Carbon Hill mine was a union mine, and Mitchell was ultimately in charge of bargaining for its miners, there can be no doubt that his purchase of this coal property represented a clear conflict of interest.

A second and equally clear case of conflict of interest originated during the hearings. Along with three of his closest friends—Harry Taylor, Frank S. Peabody, and Joseph B. Cavanaugh—all of them operators headquartered in Chicago, Mitchell not only invested in but also helped found a powder company. Since the price of powder sold to miners was determined by negotiations at joint conferences between operators and miners, his involvement in such a scheme was a serious breech of ethics. The original idea for the company probably came from Taylor, who wrote Mitchell in early December 1902 that he was "working on another line which . . . looks pretty good to me and you are in on it if I am." By the following March Mitchell had taken an active role. He told Taylor the "powder matter was getting along all right" and had discussed the plans with Peabody on the telephone.[64] Soon thereafter Taylor, Peabody, and Cavanaugh set up the Egyptian Powder Company. Mitchell's role was kept quiet, of course, but by September 1903 he had made three payments of $840 each to purchase stock. In all, he invested $8,400 in the company.[65]

Even his aboveboard money-making ventures involved the questionable use of his official authority. At the end of the strike, he became labor editor of a new labor paper published in Chicago called *Boyce's Weekly*. In addition to his editorial functions, he was to write one article per month for the first year and receive a total of $1,000. He then used his position to help this paper off to a good start. He agreed to bring a sales representative, R. N. Stevens, to the 1903 UMWA convention and show him around to the "right people," and when the convention concluded he sent the paper a list of all delegates who had attended to be used as a mailing list.[66] Even more aggressive was Mitchell's attempt to enlist breaker boys to work as newsboys in their spare time. He wrote a letter to Andrew Chippie, the hapless breaker boy whose testimony before the anthracite coal commission had attracted such national attention, and tried to get him to peddle the paper. Perhaps trying to capitalize on the boy's fame, Mitchell told him to "get as big a list of subscribers as you can," and enticed him with the Horatio Alger theme that "many a wealthy man got his start in life as a newsboy."[67] Despite his efforts, Mitchell did not supplement his income from *Boyce's Weekly* for long. The paper collapsed by September 1903.

During the commission's hearings, Mitchell also managed to squeeze some money out of the NCF. In an early 1903 meeting of the NCF's executive committee, Easley asked Mitchell if he and Daniel J. Keefe wanted to serve as advisors in the publication of the proposed National Civic Federation *Review*. Mitchell and Keefe quickly agreed.[68] Mitchell was anxious to learn when payment would begin, and he was disappointed to hear that "the compensation for our valuable services will begin on April 1st," the date the first issue was released. Mitchell then wrote Keefe: "I, of course, am indignant on accounts of it not starting earlier, particularly in view of the fact that we have rendered so much assistance in getting out this publication."[69] Keefe understood the humor in Mitchell's comment. As one scholar discovered, neither Mitchell nor Keefe seemed to have performed any work whatsoever for the publication. Yet, Mitchell did receive small sums for his "services" over the next few years.[70]

The quest for wealth was also the primary motivation behind his first book, *Organized Labor*. Toward the end of the anthracite hearings, he began to toy with the idea of presenting his ideas on the labor movement in book form. Walter Weyl, who had done research for the union during the hearings, encouraged Mitchell in this endeavor and agreed to help him write it. As it turned out, Weyl performed most of the actual work. By the end of April, Weyl had already arranged for a contract with the American Book and Bible House, a publisher located in Philadelphia, and had written 35,000 words.[71] Mitchell contributed in a meaningful way to the final product, however, and there is no reason to suggest that the ideas presented did not reflect his own. He told Weyl which topics he wanted addressed and what his specific views on those topics were, and he read over every phrase to make certain the ideas presented were consistent with his own. In August, the two men spent several weeks together in Philadelphia writing and revising the manuscript, and during the first weeks in September Mitchell worked on his own doing revisions.[72] By the time the book was in the hands of the publisher he could tell his wife that "I have never worked harder in my life."[73]

As the publication date drew near he became quite anxious. By early September, he admitted he was "on the ragged edge" waiting to find out whether his book would sell. "If everything turns out as I expect I shall be marching toward Easy Street," he informed a friend.[74] He actively recruited miners to serve as commissioned agents to sell the book, and he supplied a complete list of all UMWA local secretaries to the publisher. He expected nothing less than astronomical book sales. By mid-September he was "counting upon the sale of 500,000 books."[75]

Mitchell's dreams of "Easy Street" soon melted in the light of reality. By the end of 1903, Walter Weyl described the publisher, Charles Doe, as "rather discouraged." Doe claimed to have lost $10,000 "on the proposition," and he believed that sales would now "tend to decline."[76] In February 1904, Doe's prediction proved accurate. Sales were "growing smaller and smaller from month to month." Doe then requested that Mitchell agree to a reduction in royalties to help lower costs and thus boost sales. Mitchell replied emphatically in the negative and told the publisher that the royalties he had received thus far had been "a great disappointment."[77] "I would not have undertaken the work," Mitchell moaned to a friend, "if I had known the returns would be so small."[78] Judging solely by Mitchell's reaction, one would think the book earned him no money. Actually, royalties amounted to more than $2,600.[79] That such a tidy sum could prove so great a disappointment revealed how eager Mitchell had become for money, power, and prestige.

The "new" Mitchell, who dressed so well and associated so freely with the rich and powerful, received the scorn of radicals. Mother Jones, Henry D. Lloyd and other radicals were shocked and disgusted that Mitchell should contaminate himself by socializing with the bourgeoisie. Fraternization with the enemy class stripped labor leaders of their working-class values, poisoned them with riches, perverted them with praise. It led them to lose sight of the class struggle and become pawns of the elite. Radicals believed groups such as the NCF were conceived by powerful men to seduce labor leaders, fill their heads with false notions of class harmony, and thus "chloroform the labor movement into a more submissive mood."[80] Eugene Debs condemned Mitchell and other established labor leaders for having succumbed to "the blandishment of the plutocrats."[81] Joseph Buchanon put the radical view best when he wrote in 1903 that "when the daily press and the employing class begin to praise a labor 'leader,' it is time for workingmen to keep an eye on him."[82]

Mitchell undoubtedly resented the attacks of radicals, but he did not respond publicly. While he openly opposed the formation of a third party and the nationalization of the mines, he did not disparage socialists and consciously sought to maintain cordial relations as best he could. Indeed, he even praised socialists for their contributions during the 1902 hard coal strike at the 1903 AFL convention.[83] He was careful to avoid an open break with socialists because of the power they were beginning to wield in his own union, especially Illinois District 12.[84] By no means did radicals control the district administration in 1903, but their numbers were growing and he saw no sense in antagonizing them by an ugly public feud with Debs. Mitchell had also established close ties with several of the important socialist leaders in Illinois, especially John Walker, that he did not wish to jeopardize by lambasting radicals. Walker and Mitchell had known each other in Braidwood, had worked together in West Virginia in 1898, and despite their political differences, respected each other. Mitchell kept Walker employed as a union organizer. He did the same for another Illinois socialist, Duncan McDonald.[85]

Moreover, at this stage, Mitchell could afford to allow his accomplishments to speak for him. At the January 1903 UMWA convention, Secretary-Treasurer Wilson reported that the actual membership of the union was in excess of 300,000.[86] Nor had the failure of the West Virginia strike led an operator demand for a wage reduction at the 1903 joint conference. Mitchell had been spared the inevitable showdown with union operators over West Virginia competition by a year of "unparalleled prosperity" in bituminous coal. The loss of 22 million tons of anthracite coal in part accounted for high demand and high prices for soft coal.[87] At the interstate joint conferences in February 1903, soft coal miners won wage advances of 11 percent.[88] As long as Mitchell continued to build union strength and win wage increases, he had little to fear from the insults hurled by radicals.

But what of the merits of the radical argument that Mitchell had been seduced by the blandishment of capitalists? The argument presupposes a fatal character flaw that rendered him highly susceptible to seduction. A person of strong character dedicated to the advancement of the working class surely could withstand even champagne and caviar at NCF functions without selling out entirely. Did Mitchell have an Achilles' heel that plutocrats could lance with their poisoned darts? Did he have character flaws that could be exploited? Yes. And more than one. Mother Jones correctly identified one "weak point" as his "love of flattery." And of course she was not referring to the flattery of the rank and file. One pat on the head from Theodore Roosevelt was worth one thousand miners' parades in his honor.[89] Jones failed to mention his two other weaknesses, avarice and thirst for power. It had been greed that motivated his attempt to "mine the miners" for a house in Chicago and to entangle himself in dozens of get-rich-quick schemes. And it was love of power that kept him in the presidency despite the grinding work load and internal squabbling he so detested. When his name was bandied about for chief of the Bureau of Labor Statistics, Mitchell scoffed at the notion that he should abandon his present seat of power. "I recognize the fact that as President of the United Mine Workers," he informed James Duncan of the Granite Cutters, "I have more prominence, influence and prestige than I could have by holding any position with the Government unless it were one in the Cabinet or the Vice-Presidency."[90]

In this sense, Buchanon was right. By 1903, Mitchell was one labor leader earning the praise of both employers and the press who needed watching. He had adopted the life-style of the bourgeoisie, chose coal operators as his close friends, and had almost no contact with the rank and file outside conventions and parades. He had substantial investments in coal mines and powder that represented clear conflicts of interest, and he had proven his willingness to "mine the miners" for personal profit on several occasions. Moreover, his actions during the strike had been motivated as much by the bureaucratic imperatives of managing the union, political pressure, and public opinion as by commitment to the demands of the rank and file. If the radicals were correct, if capitalists had conspired to seduce labor leaders, then John Mitchell was a willing victim.

Yet, the radical's charge that Mitchell had abandoned the class struggle in return for wealth and privilege, while containing elements of truth, ultimately rings hollow. He had not "sold out" the class struggle. The truth was that Mitchell had never believed in class struggle. From the time he learned about capital-labor relations from Dan McLaughlin, he had been committed to accommodation and harmony between employer and employee in the form of the trade agreement. Nor was his commitment to class harmony a pipe dream completely divorced from economic reality. The joint conference established in soft coal demonstrated to his satisfaction that miners and operators, once organized, could cooperate to each other's mutual advantage. Miners received higher wages and shorter hours while operators could be assured of labor peace and more stable trade conditions. Through the principle of competitive equality, the joint conference had reduced ruinous competition among operators and spurred the growth of the industry. Mitchell sincerely believed that trade agreements could be adopted in all industries to the benefit of both workers and employers.

Mitchell's dedication to the trade agreement was also grounded in the historical reality of turn-of-the-century America. According to historian Philip Taft, the "five or six years around 1900" were the "honeymoon years of collective bargaining" when trade agreements flourished and were widely accepted by the American public.[91] Besides the coal industry, national trade agreements existed in newspaper publishing, iron molding, Great Lakes shipping, railroads, the building trades, and numerous other industries. Many leading representatives of labor, capital, and the public touted the trade agreement as the solution to the "labor question." "Though stoutly resisted in certain sectors," Taft continued, "collective bargaining was widely regarded and publicized as a method of industrial peace."[92]

Despite numerous contradictions and inconsistencies, the 1902 coal strike and the commission's report gave impetus to the trade agreement movement. While the commission's failure to grant recognition to the UMWA and its declared support of the open shop would also serve to inspire antilabor forces in the Progressive Era years, Roosevelt's condemnation of the railroad presidents, Mitchell's masterful strike leadership, and the justice of the union's cause helped win popular support for the trade agreement. If nothing else, the strike and the hearings highlighted the activities of the leading trade agreement crusaders of the period, Hanna, Easley, and especially Mitchell.[93]

Mitchell emerged from the 1902 strike as the principal spokesman for the entire labor movement. And while he exploited his fame to advance himself financially, he took his role as labor's ambassador seriously. He perceived himself a propagandist, a missionary among the public and employers. Labor's gains, Mitchell assumed, were dependent on the degree to which these groups accepted unionism and the trade agreement. Thus, in his public writings and utterances, he emphasized the "positive" aspects of unionism: its disdain of strikes and violence, its patriotism and anti-radicalism, and its readiness to cooperate with employers. In making these arguments, Mitchell was acting in a way similar to Gompers and other business unionists of the period. The difference, however, was the degree to which Mitchell was ideologically and emotionally committed to this conservative approach.

By 1903, Mitchell had become the recognized champion of the trade agreement. He perceived the growing number of agreements as a movement that would soon sweep the country and lift industrial relations out of the dark ages of conflict and violence. His book, *Organized Labor*, was in many respects an extended argument in favor of collective bargaining across industries. It was an effort to sell the idea to those who remained skeptical. "The hope of future peace in the industrial world lies in the trade agreement," he proposed. "There is nothing so promising to the establishment of friendly relations between capital and labor as the growing tendency of representatives of both sides to meet in friendly conference in order to settle conditions of employment." The joint conference was a magnificent affair, and he described it with a romantic flourish. It was "like a coming together of the representatives of two great nations, upon the basis of mutual respect and mutual toleration, for the formulation of a treaty of peace for the government of industry and the prosperity and welfare of the contracting parties."[94]

Before the "era of trade agreements," Mitchell argued, when industrial relations were anarchic, the disputes between capital and labor resulted not from irreconcilable class differences but from sheer ignorance. Workers routinely exaggerated the profits of employers and thus believed, "frequently without cause, that they were being exploited." Capitalists, on the other hand, often had no knowledge of their workers' true standard of living, obtained misinformation from foremen, and out of their ignorance developed "a feeling of superiority over the workmen and their representatives." But now industrial relations had entered a more enlightened stage, for the trade agreement imparted knowledge to both employer and worker. Through the joint conference, the veil of ignorance was "being obliterated."[95]

Formulation of a trade agreement acceptable to both employers and employees was a difficult and complicated process, Mitchell admitted. The rank and file, perhaps even their union leaders, might at first push for unreasonable goals, but the process of negotiations would soon force them "to appreciate the attitude and position of the employers." Through open and frank discussions with their bosses, workers would learn about costs of production, costs of transportation, and other factors that prevented employers from meeting all their expectations. They would learn, too, that even if they could insist upon all their demands, the result would be ruinous to the industry as a whole. In short, workers would soon "recognize the difference between what is desirable and what is attainable," and would begin to demonstrate "an unusual degree of self-restraint."[96]

The first trade agreement in an industry might be a simple affair dealing with wages and hours. But as both workers and employers came to appreciate its true significance, the agreement would cover an ever greater number of issues. It would set down, in precise terms, all the various provisions so there would be little possibility of misinterpretation by either party. If disagreements over interpretation did arise, the agreement provided a system of arbitration. By its exactitude, therefore, trade agreements "obviate hundreds of little misunderstandings which might otherwise lead to recrimination and to strikes and lockouts."[97]

The beauty of the trade agreement was so apparent that Mitchell could not help making a roseate prediction about the industrial future of the nation:

The recognition of the rights of organized labor by the making of trade agreements will with the coming years become more and more general in the United States. The American employer is too broad-minded not to realize the advantage of such a method of securing stable conditions and of ensuring a spirit of friendly cooperation among his men. The manufacturer of the future will no more forgo such an insurance of the goodwill of his workmen than he will permit his factory to remain uninsured against fire. The trade agreement makes for peace in the industrial world. . . . The frequent bickerings and constant irritation will vanish, and strikes themselves will be reduced to a minimum. To the present period of industrial war will succeed an era of peace, peace with honor to both sides.[98]

The trade agreement's promise of a peaceful future was founded on a number of conditions and assumptions. First and foremost was Mitchell's assumption that there was "no necessary hostility between labor and capital."[99] If the radicals were correct in their assertion that a fundamental antagonism existed between the two classes, if something more than ignorance created industrial strife, then not even the best laid trade agreement could prevent class warfare. Mitchell's assumption would be severely tested when the first economic downturn led employers to demand significant wage reductions. He would then be better able to ascertain the depth of the "friendly relations" between classes inspired by the trade agreement.

A second condition was the need to mobilize public opinion behind the movement. Unions needed to avoid breaches of contract, unjustifiable restrictions upon output, violence, radical politics, and all other actions that might alienate public sympathy. Organized workers could not and should not "hope for any permanent success unless their actions are in accord with the ideals of the American people." Only when the "great, humane public" was convinced of the justice and wisdom of trade agreements would the movement prosper.[100]

Third, the trade agreement movement necessitated the continuing growth of employer associations. Despite the fact that employer associations were better equipped to combat unions than individual competing employers, Mitchell encouraged the formation of employer associations in every industry. His "ideal of trade unionism" would be attained only when a strong union, embracing every worker in the trade, found itself face-to-face with an equally strong association of employers embracing every employer in the trade. The two would then meet on the basis of absolute equality. Only in this way could both parties be certain that "agreements arrived at will be kept inviolate; and thus strikes and lockouts, with their attendant sufferings and loss, will be reduced to a minimum, and peace and prosperity firmly established in American industry."[101]

Finally, the success of the trade agreement movement depended on the active involvement of enlightened elites in industrial affairs. And he was thankful that this condition had been met by the NCF. He described it as "one of the most potent influences in establishing amicable relations between organized labor and organized capital." He challenged the radical's assertion that the NCF was a conspiracy of the wealthy by pointing to the fact that every NCF committee contained members representing employers, the public, and organized labor. Policies were hashed out in such a way "so that the interests of all are conserved and the interests of none, sacrificed." Indeed, the NCF's policy of creating friendly relations between employer and employee, of averting strikes, and of promoting the trade agreement entitled it to the "hearty support of the community."[102]

While *Organized Labor* was not the commercial success that Mitchell wanted, it did receive critical acclaim from the commercial press. Mitchell, with the substantial assistance of Walter Weyl, had written what became the standard conservative interpretation of American labor for many years. The *Wall Street Journal* printed a positive review on the front page. While the reviewer did not agree with all that Mitchell had written, he did praise the book for its centrist views. He had even kinder words to say about the author. "Conservatism is the keynote throughout, and the work as a whole serves to strengthen the opinion formed by most fair minded people after the coal strike that Mr. Mitchell may be counted among the ablest, most responsible, and most farsighted of the labor leaders in power to-day."[103]

In many respects, Mitchell stood at the height of his prestige and power in 1903. Cheered by miners, the press, and the nation's elite, he seemed invincible. The attacks of the radicals could not dent his armor. The union was growing on a yearly basis, both soft coal and hard coal members had won significant wage increases, he had retained his alliance with the NCF and had even begun to cultivate powerful new ones. In his personal life, he had begun to taste some of the fruits of success. For the first time, his crass materialist desires were being fulfilled. And he could also imagine he was riding the wave of history as more and more people turned to the trade agreement, to which he was ideologically and emotionally wedded, as the solution to the labor problem.

Chapter 7

A Year of Reckoning, 1904

In 1903, Mitchell stood at the apex of his prestige and power. His national fame equaled that of AFL president Samuel Gompers, and within his own union he was almost beyond reproach. He was unique among labor leaders in that he enjoyed the respect of both employers and employees. Many business leaders and politicians regarded him as the living embodiment of conservative and cautious trade unionism, while miners and other wage earners considered him a hero, a fighter for the great cause of industrial justice. The adoration he received from the miners was somewhat remarkable, considering the large number of socialists in the union who wished to pursue more radical goals such as industrial unionism and political action, goals he rejected. Socialists also resented his participation in the National Civic Federation because its affairs were dominated by corporate capitalists. In 1903, however, socialists were careful not to attack Mitchell too aggressively, realizing that to do so meant alienating their own support among the rank and file.

Yet by early 1905, less than two years later, Mitchell's impervious armor was badly tarnished. Socialists had become emboldened and could denounce the UMWA president without fear of censure. A movement was underfoot to disallow Mitchell's participation in the NCF, a movement that would achieve its objective in 1911. Moreover, the rank and file was growing increasingly skeptical of their president. Policies that had once passed unnoticed became matters for acrimonious debate. Although Mitchell remained head of the union until 1908, the unquestioning support of the rank and file had vaporized.

A number of factors account for this dramatic reversal of fortune, but no one factor was more significant than the Colorado strike of 1903–1904. Colorado was not the site of Mitchell's first strike failure—he had met with defeat in West Virginia in 1902—but Colorado was the first major strike failure for which he was held personally responsible. Once miners began to question the strategy and tactics of their leader in this strike loss, it became much easier to scrutinize Mitchell's other actions and policies. The Colorado strike, therefore, was a major turning point for Mitchell, and as such it deserves a close investigation.

In order to determine whether Mitchell had in fact made any conspicuous errors in Colorado, it will be necessary to address the most important issues of the strike. There were three key questions: (1) Should Mitchell have called the strike? (2) Should he have allowed the strikers in northern Colorado to sign an agreement and return to work while the strike continued in southern Colorado? (3) And could a different strategy in southern Colorado have been more successful?

The first question, whether Mitchell should have called the strike, illuminates the pressures that impinged upon union decision making. Unions must continuously expand if they are to succeed. This was particularly true for the UMWA. If the union failed in its efforts to organize all coal fields, to force all coal operators to pay union wages, a very difficult proposition given the obduracy of capital, operators paying high union wages would be unable to compete for markets against non-union operators paying low wages. Such a situation would eventually force union operators to demand extensive wage cuts from the union. Mitchell recognized the threat of non-union fields all too well. His failure to organize West Virginia threatened to subvert the entire joint interstate movement. During the February 1903 joint conference, soft coal miners had secured a wage advance because of general economic prosperity and the removal of hard coal as an alternative fuel source. But Mitchell knew the ever increasing tonnage of non-union coal would lead union operators to insist on a significant wage reduction at their next annual joint conference with the union scheduled for January 1904. In order to avert a reduction, Mitchell required a demonstration of the union's resolve and ability to bring non-union operators into line.

If Mitchell needed a quick and substantial organizational victory to prove union strength to operators, Colorado was an unlikely place for action. When the national executive board met in October 1903 to discuss the request for strike aid from the Colorado district of the UMWA (District 15), board members and organizers explained the pitfalls of strike action at that time. First, very few Colorado miners were UMWA members. At best only 2,809 of the district's 16,000 miners belonged to the union. This concern was expressed most vocally by UMWA organizer and former District 15 President John Gehr, who stated that the strike could be won only if four-fifths of the miners joined but doubted that this many would in fact participate. "If they do," he said, "you can have my head. I have tried them and I know."[1] Second, mining in the southern part of the state was dominated by two powerful corporations, the Colorado Fuel and Iron Company and the Victor Fuel Company, which were unequivocal in their opposition to unionization. Together these two corporations employed more than half the miners in the state, and they had expressed in no uncertain terms they would fight the UMWA with all the resources at their disposal.[2]

A third problem was that if a strike was called, the UMWA could not expect the Colorado state government to remain neutral. Despite Governor William Stone's order to call in the national guard toward the end of the anthracite strike, the state government of Pennsylvania generally had maintained a "hands off" policy during that struggle, a policy that had been critical for the union's success. In Colorado, however, Governor James Peabody had demonstrated time and again his subservience to coal operators. He had done nothing when operators violated with impunity the state's mining laws, and he had on several previous occasions made liberal use of the state militia to quell mining strikes.[3] Fourth, the organization of Colorado miners was not vital to the success of the union. The tonnage of coal produced in Colorado was meager compared to that produced in West Virginia. Even if Mitchell was able to organize the district's miners through strike action, it was unlikely that victory would have sidetracked union operators from demanding a wage reduction at the upcoming interstate conference. If Mitchell really hoped to prove the union's viability to the nation's operators, West Virginia remained the obvious target, not Colorado.

If the possible gains of a strike in Colorado were slight and the prospects of victory slim, why did Mitchell sanction the strike? In large measure, the answer is fear. He was afraid that if he failed to throw the support of the national behind the strike, Colorado miners would abandon the UMWA and join a radical, rival union, the Western Federation of Miners (WFM). Were this to happen, he reasoned, the UMWA would not only lose the members of District 15, but the rival union would score an important propaganda victory which might lead to mass defections in other districts.

Founded in 1893, the WFM was, at this time, an avowedly revolutionary organization of metal miners in the Rocky Mountain states. Its leadership was confrontational and passionate. To radicals in the UMWA, the WFM represented the type of union they hoped to create in coal: a radical, industrial, and political organization. A number of socialists within the UMWA had established close ties with the leadership of the WFM.[4] By 1898, the WFM had spurned the AFL and had launched vitriolic attacks on Gompers, Mitchell, and other conservative union leaders as labor "fakirs." Mitchell was alarmed that coal miners in Colorado exhibited such solidarity with the WFM, gave the radical union financial and moral support in its repeated clashes with employers, and allowed this union to play a prominent role in the affairs of District 15. The extent to which the WFM involved itself in the affairs of Colorado coal miners could be seen at the August convention of District 15. The principal speakers calling for strike action were WFM President Charles Moyer and Secretary William D. "Big Bill" Haywood, who also took the occasion to blast Mitchell and his conservative policies.[5] Mitchell was aware of, and he agreed with, the findings of an AFL organizer in Colorado who wrote in September 1903 that the WFM was attempting to precipitate a coal strike in Colorado and that Mitchell would fail to support it with national strike funds and organizers. The certain failure of such a strike would create mass disaffection within the UMWA and allow the WFM to absorb the coal miners into their union.[6]

Thus, the question of whether Mitchell should have sanctioned the strike is intriguing. He believed he had been placed in a hopeless situation. If he refused to support the strike, the WFM would siphon off coal miners in the West and increase its influence with the radicals within the UMWA; if he did sanction the strike, he would engage himself in a desperate and expensive struggle against powerful corporations with little to gain even if victory could be secured. Faced with this insoluble dilemma, Mitchell chose to go ahead with the strike. He endorsed the strike call in October, and the strike began November 9.[7] His decision was based on fear of radical subversion, not on a rational assessment of the situation. Had he counteracted WFM propaganda with UMWA propaganda, perhaps he could have forestalled strike action until the district was better organized and thus increased the chances for success.

Much to the delight and surprise of Mitchell, on the morning of November 9, 95 percent of Colorado's miners answered the strike call and refrained from work.[8] It was the "biggest surprise party in the history of the West," the UMWA *Journal* declared. "Union and non-union, white and Mexican, all obeyed the strike order of President Mitchell and the tie up is complete."[9] If this early sign of success allowed Mitchell to entertain hopes of a quick victory, those hopes were soon dashed. Within a week, trouble appeared in the form of a proposed settlement plan put forth by the Northern Coal and Coke Company, the largest employer in the northern part of the state.

Northern Coal was a progressive firm that had negotiated with the UMWA in the weeks prior to the strike and continued negotiations after the strike began. Displaying attitudes that contrasted sharply with those maintained by the two large corporations in the south, Northern Coal agreed to many of the strikers' demands—the eight-hour day, an increase in wages, and adherence to state mining laws. Since the miners had not demanded union recognition, this was not an issue in the dispute.[10]

Once Northern Coal presented its offer, a sharp and public debate ensued among UMWA members. District 15 President William Howells and Mother Jones were among those who spurned the offer. They believed any lasting settlement in the north required victory in the south as well. Jones was especially adamant in her contention that the principal strength of the miners was solidarity and that operators would like nothing better than to have the miners make separate settlements. She argued the victory of miners in the north would disappear quickly if the miners of the south lost the struggle. "I would say we will all go to glory together or we will all die and go down together."[11] Mitchell and his supporters, however, argued for acceptance of Northern Coal's offer. He believed a settlement in the north would enable the UMWA to concentrate its financial resources in the south and thus increase the likelihood of victory. J. F. Ream, Mitchell's representative in Colorado, encouraged the northern miners to accept the settlement, telling them that this was the advice of their union president.[12]

The day before representatives of the northern miners were to vote on the proposed settlement, WFM President Moyer and Secretary Haywood attended the miners' conference and argued vociferously against the settlement.[13] Their interference, greatly resented by Mitchell, revealed the degree to which the WFM was involved in the affairs of District 15. Mother Jones was also there, urging miners to reject Mitchell's advice. The vote of the northern miners took place on November 22, with 165 representatives voting in favor of accepting the offer and 228 voting against it.[14] When the Denver press reported the speech Mother Jones had made, a copy was sent to Mitchell at Indianapolis. According to Jones, Mitchell was anguished by what he considered her treachery. "See what Mother Jones has done to me!," he cried.[15]

At Mitchell's insistence, a second vote was taken one week later. This time, he made better preparations. He flooded the north with organizers and instructed them to push for acceptance; he kept Mother Jones and District President Howells busy in the south so they could not argue against the settlement; and he prevented Moyer and Haywood from attending the union meeting. The tactics worked. This time, the northern miners voted 483 to 130 to accept Northern Coal's offer. On November 30, the 2,000 northern Colorado miners returned to work.[16]

The issue of the northern settlement was far from over. Indeed, Mother Jones, Howells, and other opponents of the settlement extended their critique into a full-blown condemnation of Mitchell's leadership. They castigated his overeagerness to compromise with operators, his participation in the National Civic Federation, his circle of friends that included operators and excluded miners, and his growing isolation from the problems and concerns of working people.[17] At the 1905 UMWA national convention, one delegate charged that Mitchell drove Mother Jones from the union after the northern settlement because she refused to "become a party to the betrayal of the southern miners."[18] Mother Jones considered herself Mitchell's implacable enemy from this point until his resignation in 1908. She held that Mitchell conspired to make covert attacks on her reputation. "From the day I opposed John Mitchell's authority, the guns were turned on me. Slander and persecution followed me like black shadows."[19]

Mitchell was quick to defend himself against the charge that he had forced the "miners' angel" to resign, although he did admit he admonished her for failing to support the northern settlement. As he told the 1905 convention:

> It is true that when Mother Jones went to Northern Colorado she disregarded the advice given her, and it is true I said she should not do it again, and that if

she expected to be employed by us she must carry out the orders of the National Board and the national convention. I will not allow any one to work for the organization, if I can help it, who does not carry out the policy of the National Executive Board and of the national convention. But Mother Jones was not discontinued.[20]

On this last point, at least, Mitchell was correct. At the April 30, 1904 meeting of the national executive board, Mitchell included Jones on his list of organizers submitted for the board's approval. The board confirmed her appointment by a vote of ten to seven on the condition that she be called to headquarters and informed of the policies of the union. "If she refuses to conform to those policies, her services will be dispensed with."[21] While Jones's services were retained, it was obvious that she was on probation. There was certainly a legacy of mutual suspicion between Mitchell and Jones resulting from the northern settlement.

Should the northern settlement have been made? From Mitchell's perspective, the decision was the bureaucratically correct one. It saved the union money by reducing strike funds, it offered strikers in the south a new safety valve where they could find work, and it reflected an established union policy that contracts would be signed with any company accepting strike demands. Nevertheless, Mitchell's push for the northern settlement was wrongheaded. In fact it crippled the strike in two ways. First, resumption of coal production in the north assisted the southern coal companies in their struggle against the union. The strike had forced these firms to purchase coal from midwestern states in order to keep their customers supplied, an expensive arrangement that could not be maintained for long. Now southern coal companies could purchase the coal mined in the north, which meant significant savings on transportation costs.[22] Second, and more importantly, the northern settlement created intense ill-will between UMWA officials and local union leaders in southern Colorado, a situation that made success there all but impossible. One national board member later recalled: "When I went to Trinidad (strike headquarters in the south) I was told by every national officer there that they never went into the district office that they were not insulted by the district officers."[23] Solidarity is the soul of the labor movement. Commitment to a common cause by all is the key to its success. Because it damaged the solidarity of the strikers and union officials, the northern settlement must be considered a grave mistake.

Mitchell himself did not travel to Colorado until December 2. Busy with an NCF meeting, an AFL Executive Council meeting, and the promotion of his book, he had failed to provide the personal leadership he had given anthracite mine workers in the weeks prior to the strike and during the strike itself. Indeed, his personal correspondence reveals he gave very little thought to the Colorado situation at all and that only when he grasped the serious divisions within southern Colorado did he make the trek to the West. He stayed less than one week. On his first day, he visited strike headquarters at Trinidad and spoke to district officers and national organizers. On the second day, he addressed a large public meeting, trying to drum up public support for the strike and warning the strikers to refrain from lawbreaking.[24] Several days later, he spoke to the assembled members of the Denver Chamber of Commerce, citing the reasons the strike was held and appealing to their sense of justice. He then met with Governor Peabody to discuss the situation.[25] And then he went home.

"My trip to Colorado did not result in any immediate benefit," Mitchell admitted, "although I had good meetings and gave the boys some encouragement."[26] The trip seemed perfunctory, and in contrast to anthracite, his presence inspired little enthusiasm. Many of the miners, feeling betrayed by the northern settlement, looked askance at their leader who paid so little attention to their struggle and instead went to dinners with the chamber of commerce and the governor. Many could agree with Mother Jones, who criticized Mitchell for coming to Colorado to be "wined and dined, flattered and cajoled" by the politicians and capitalists of the state rather than leading the strikers.[27]

While Mitchell politely discussed the labor question with the elites, the southern coal companies were busily crushing the strike in the south. They evicted miners from their homes, brought in scabs, and used private guards to beat and deport organizers and strike leaders. UMWA national board member Chris Evans, who was in charge of strike relief, was beaten bloody and unconscious with rifle butts while on a train from Trinidad to Pueblo. Stunned passengers sat paralyzed with fear until the masked attackers completed their job.[28]

Mitchell authorized $12,000 per week in strike support, set up tent colonies, and provided as much food, clothing, and medical attention as possible. At the January 4, 1904 national executive board meeting District President Howells expressed his conviction that $12,000 per week was simply not enough to support all the strikers. The board denied his petition for an increase, however. With the mines already filling with strikebreakers, Mitchell was looking for a resolution of the strike. He suggested that a meeting be arranged between the coal companies and a committee of employees, "using some prominent citizen, friendly to us, as a medium through which to arrange the meeting."[29] But no resolution was forthcoming. On January 19, Howells again went before the board to request more aid. "These men have answered your call nobly," he told board members, "and if you cannot furnish more aid than this, it would be wise to declare this strike off and not burn any more money there." Unless sufficient aid were given to provide transportation to strikers who wanted to leave and assistance to strikebreakers willing to join the strikers, the strike would be lost. Again Mitchell and the board refused to grant more aid.[30] Finally, after receiving numerous letters and telegrams from strikers themselves, Mitchell and the board on January 24 reluctantly agreed to increase support to $15,000 per week.[31]

The coal companies continued their program of intimidation, violence, and the use of strikebreakers, however, and by mid-March district and national officials were forced to concede that the futility of continuing the strike any longer. On March 18 district officials issued a call for a convention to be held March 24 at Trinidad to determine the best method to bring the strike to a close. But on the day before this convention, Governor Peabody dispatched 400 troops to Trinidad and declared the county under martial law. Incensed by what he considered the "unwarranted and uncalled for action of the governor," Mitchell immediately wired board member W. R. Fairley in Trinidad: "Delegates to convention can not afford to declare strike ended while troops are on the ground and civil law has been suspended." Delegates who had been prepared to call off the strike agreed with Mitchell that returning to work at this point would represent "a cowardly surrender to Peabody."[32]

Although Peabody had ordered out the national guard ostensibly to maintain law and order, strikers had in fact committed very little violence. Peabody's true intent could be seen on March 26, when the national guard began deporting strike leaders. Mother Jones was deported on that day. Defiant to the end, she penned a note to Peabody before she left: "I wish to notify you, governor, that you don't own the state."[33] In all, almost one hundred of the most active strike leaders were deported from the state and sixty-four others were incarcerated.[34]

Peabody's actions were so outrageous that even Mitchell, the stout defender of political nonpartisanship, felt compelled to instruct Colorado citizens on their duty to turn the governor out. While attending the April session of the AFL Executive Council in Denver, he addressed a mass meeting in which he openly called for Peabody's defeat in the fall elections that year. "I want to repudiate as far as I can the acts of the governor of this state," he told the audience. All trade unionists and all good citizens must actively work against Peabody to protect their rights. In conclusion, he announced his solidarity with all who desired justice:

> I am usually called a conservative labor leader—in fact in this Western Country I am said to be too conservative. Yet to the most radical of you, I announce myself as against any man who is against the people. I stand for a man who is a friend of the people, be he Republican, Democrat or Socialist.[35]

At the end of April, Mitchell and the national board again decided to end the strike as quickly as possible. This time District President Howells disagreed. He believed the actions of Peabody had shifted public opinion decisively in favor of the miners and that a continuation of the strike would result in a compromise victory for the union.[36] Obviously anxious to wrap up affairs in the state, Mitchell challenged Howells to "show the least ray of hope that the strike could be won." If Howells could demonstrate any possibility of success, Mitchell claimed he would recommend to the board that the strike be continued despite the fact the union had already spent over $400,000.[37] Thus, Howells was silenced, and Mitchell instructed the district to call a convention no later than June 20 to close up the strike.[38]

Could a different policy in southern Colorado have been more successful? Probably not. Once Mitchell's northern settlement had been made, and the rift between the national union and local leaders completed, defeat at the hands of the ruthless southern coal firms was a question of time. He could have demonstrated greater leadership by spending more time in Colorado, by attending local rallies, and by trying to maintain morale. That he would spend less time among Colorado's 16,000 strikers than he did among the 150,000 in anthracite was understandable, but his absence gave rise to a feeling among Colorado miners that he was insensitive to their plight. Moreover, he made the hopeless situation in southern Colorado even worse by committing key blunders as the strike wound down to its grisly conclusion.

Mitchell's most egregious blunder at the end of the strike was his ten-week jaunt to Europe from mid-June to the end of August. True, he had been selected by the UMWA's national convention in January 1904 to attend the International Mining Congress at Paris. But he considered the trip very much a working vacation, a chance to "get away from seven years of constant work and worry."[39] Before his departure, he and Daniel Keefe joked about his wearing a dress suit "morning, noon, and night" and walking around Paris in his "opera hat."[40] When District 5 Secretary William Dodds, who was to accompany Mitchell to Europe, wrote that he was making travel arrangements, Mitchell wrote back that he took "it for granted that our passage will be first-class, and that we will have comfortable accommodations." He then suggested each of them withdraw $1,000 from the national treasury for expenses.[41]

Mitchell sailed for England on June 11 aboard the St. Paul steamer. He spent several weeks touring London and the mining regions of Wales, the Midlands, the north of England, and Scotland. While in Scotland, he visited Skibo, Andrew Carnegie's castle, where he had dinner with the industrialist.[42] Carnegie and Mitchell had never met prior to this visit.[43] Mitchell then briefly toured Ireland for his own enjoyment before traveling to the Continent. He visited mining regions in Belgium, Germany, and France before attending the mining conference in Paris, which began on August 8. While in Europe, Mitchell apparently ate and slept well, for he charged $10 to his expense account for one night in a London hotel, excluding food, and $12 for one night at a Paris hotel. He returned to New York on August 27 feeling rejuvenated but unimpressed with the charm of the Old World. "My trip to Europe was very pleasant," he informed a friend, "although I do not care for the countries I visited and prefer to be back in the United States."[44]

Many Colorado miners would have preferred that Mitchell had never left the United States. In the eyes of many strikers, his "sin" was not that he had gone abroad, but rather the timing of the trip, the apparent luxury of his accommodations, and especially his get together with Andrew Carnegie. The image his trip created was one of grotesque contrast. As one strike leader put it, "Those strikers, having passed through a winter of suffering as pitiful as our forefathers passed through at Valley Forge, were in dire need of food, fuel and clothing, yet John Mitchell, the little tin labor God of the capitalistic class, spent the time in dining with . . . Andrew Carnegie . . . the man who has the blood of the Homestead men on his hands . . . Yet John Mitchell drank champagne and dined upon terrapin soup . . . while the women and children of the West were cold, hungry and naked."[45] Mitchell's display of crass insensitivity provided ammunition to his opponents. At the very least, he should have remained at union headquarters until the strike was officially concluded. Better yet, he should have traveled to Colorado if only to express his concern for the suffering miners.

On June 20, while Mitchell was sailing for England, District 15 held its convention to close up the strike. A letter from Mitchell was read to the delegates, explaining how much had been spent and why he believed the men should return to work. He also notified them that all strike aid would cease on July 1. Delegates, however, spent several days criticizing the national leadership before finally voting to continue the suspension even without strike funds. The strike lingered on until October 12, when the district officially conceded defeat and authorized the few remaining holdouts to return to work.[46]

The strike loss ended organizing efforts in Colorado for several years and left a legacy of suspicion of the union and hatred of Mitchell among the miners in the south. So intense was their feeling of betrayal that when the union again moved to organize the state in 1910, miners were still angry over the northern settlement. "So embittered are the mine workers in the southern field against the treatment they received six years ago," one organizer wrote, "that the very mention of the name John Mitchell precludes any possibility of securing any success."[47]

At the January 1905 UMWA national convention, several delegates from District 15 heaped abuse upon Mitchell's head for the failure of the strike. A few socialists quickly chimed in. This was a remarkable occurrence, for until this time, national conventions were usually joyous celebrations of Mitchell's leadership. But in 1905, Colorado miners, who had suffered through that terrible winter of 1903–1904, and socialists, who had always despised Mitchell's conservatism, vented their rage and reproached their president for the northern settlement, the break with Mother Jones, his participation in the NCF, and his trip to Europe while strikers were living in tent colonies. Mitchell was well aware that district officials and rank-and-file miners in Colorado blamed him for the strike loss, and he anticipated their criticism at the national convention. In his opening address, he tried to shift the blame to the district before anyone rose to attack him. The strike loss was "a source of sorrow and a keen disappointment," he said, but delegates to the district convention in June had made matters much worse for the strikers by failing to end a strike that had obviously failed. "Contrary to our expectations, and I unhesitatingly assert, contrary to the best interests of their constituents, the delegates attending this convention determined to disregard our advice at all hazards." When union officials became convinced beyond peradventure that a strike could not be won, he lectured, it became their "solemn duty, regardless of criticism or condemnation, to recognize the inevitable."[48]

Controversy at the convention began on the third day, when Adolph Germer, an Illinois socialist, introduced a resolution requesting "that our National President or anyone affiliated with the U. M. W. of A., sever all connection with the Civic Federation." Mitchell successfully tabled this resolution,[49] but he then faced a stronger challenge from a delegate named Robert Randall, a Colorado miner who had taken part in the strike. Randall launched into a history of the strike and bitterly denounced Mitchell for its failure. He castigated his president for forcing the northern settlement "against the wishes of the rank and file of miners in District 15." He condemned Mitchell for providing insufficient funds and for withdrawing those funds when they were most needed, "letting the miners starve, and starve, and starve until they were forced by hunger and suffering to return to the mines." He chastised Mitchell for drinking champagne with capitalists in Denver and lounging in fashionable hotels in Europe while the miners and their families were hungry and cold. And he dismissed Mitchell as one of the "little tin labor gods who are always fawning at the feet of the capitalistic class for a smile from their masters." Randall claimed he had more respect for Governor Peabody than Mitchell. At least Peabody "was true to his class and served his masters faithfully." But Randall could not "find words to express my contempt for a man who, having raised himself to power by the sufferings of the working class, falls a victim to the flattery of his capitalistic masters and proves himself false to the working men." In stunned silence, delegates heard Randall's parting shot. "In the name of the men in the West, whom you have proved a traitor to, I denounce you." To prove that many shared his contempt for Mitchell, Randall produced letters and signed statements by several miners and district officials.[50]

Mitchell rose to face his accuser. He claimed no malice toward Randall, only pity. He would not refer to him "in anything but a brotherly way" because he felt "sorry for him." Nor did he care that Randall referred to him as "a little tin god" because most men regarded him "simply as an ordinary man who has done his share in the struggle of our people." Randall, he said, was laboring under a false impression as to the powers of the union president. The UMWA was a democracy and the president's power was "extremely limited." He claimed he could not possibly have committed all the crimes of which he was accused because the board would have overruled him. Then he presented his version of events. As to the northern settlement, he stated it was "the proper course to pursue" and that "if I had to do it again I should advise the Northern Colorado miners to make the settlement they did." Nor was the settlement forced on the miners against their will. He had simply advised the men to accept the terms offered. As to drinking champagne with politicians and capitalists, he stated he was "glad at any time to address such a body as the Chamber of Commerce. I am glad to address employers whenever I get a chance, to tell them what we want and what our union stands for." If any man looked at the text of his speeches to employers, he would not find "one word that means surrender on our part." As to his European trip, he claimed he traveled as inexpensively as possible, and he challenged any delegate to go to Europe for ten weeks and spend less than he did.

In all, Mitchell spoke for nearly two hours in his own defense. At the end of his speech, he questioned Randall's motives for the attack, suggesting he was an agent for the Western Federation of Miners. "I know how much Mr. Randall cares for the United Mine Workers of America!" Mitchell shouted. "I know where his heart is! His heart is where the documents he has read here came from, and you do not need to tell us where you got them, Mr. Randall." And he concluded with what amounted to an ultimatum to the convention:

> Now, gentleman, if one of the charges this man makes is true, if there is a single one of those reflections upon me that can be sustained, I say that I am utterly unfit to represent you; I should be deposed and you should put in my place a man whom you believe to be trustworthy. On the other hand, if these statements are untrue, if they are not sustained, if you believe this man has made false statements concerning me, then I say I have a right to demand of you that you afford me protection. I cannot protect myself against the scandalmongers all over America. They hide behind closet doors; they get in out-of-the-way places and they seek to destroy my influence, my character, my standing. I cannot reach them all unless I get them here or unless I can get into their locals, I cannot answer them; but I have a right to demand of you that you afford me some degree of protection. Either this man or I should not be a member of this union.[51]

The confrontation between Randall and Mitchell represented much more than specific charges of failed leadership. It represented a clash between radical unionism, which sought to wage class war and overthrow capitalism, and conservative unionism, which sought class harmony within the existing system. Yet the battle of words did not neatly divide socialists and non-socialists. Several moderate socialists, who resented the dual unionism of the WFM more than the conservatism of Mitchell, sided with their president when the ultimatum was issued. Indeed, immediately after Mitchell sat down, John Walker, a moderate socialist from Illinois, rose to condemn Randall's speech as "a disgrace to the Socialist movement." Walker then served as Mitchell's henchman by introducing a resolution endorsing Mitchell's actions during the strike and calling for Randall's expulsion from the union unless he retracted his statements. William Wardjon, another moderate socialist, seconded the resolution, which was then carried by the convention. Randall refused to recant and left the convention hall.[52]

Mitchell had not emerged unscathed, however. The strike loss and the public altercation with Randall blemished his spotless reputation within the union. No longer was Mitchell immune to criticism. The editor of the UMWA *Journal* offered to help repair Mitchell's lost prestige by printing editorial comments from the commercial press praising Mitchell's handling of the strike and convention, but Mitchell declined. "I feel that if the work I have done for the miners is not sufficient evidence of my loyalty to them," he wrote an old friend, "I do not want to have the columns of our paper used in my behalf."[53] The Colorado coal strike by no means heralded the downfall of John Mitchell. He had a large enough reservoir of goodwill among the miners to ensure his reelection in 1905 and every year thereafter. Yet he had blundered in his handling of the strike, he had proven himself all too human, and as a consequence, he had undermined the unquestioning loyalty of the rank and file. He would never again reach the lofty height of prestige and power he held before the Colorado strike.

Equally important, the strike failure had underscored several weaknesses of Mitchell's approach to union advances in soft coal. He had pursued the old strategy of a peaceful walk out, the winning of public support, and the search for a quick settlement. And he had once again pinned his hopes on public opinion. Mitchell, of course, was a master of this approach and it had served him well in anthracite. The national press had been eager to cover the hard coal strike because it had involved 150,000 mine workers and had jeopardized the entire supply of a major energy source. His ability to secure public sympathy had resulted in Roosevelt's involvement and success for the union's cause. But way out West, with comparatively few miners and such a small portion of the coal supply involved, national attention was limited. He found public opinion was a weak weapon and that national politicians were not interested, even though the cause was equally just. But he did not fully realize the removal of public opinion as a factor offered opportunities as well as disadvantages. Because union actions were no longer under the public microscope, the strike offered a chance to be more aggressive.

One area of aggressive action Mitchell failed to exploit was politics. Coal companies in Colorado wielded tremendous political as well as economic power. Their control of the state's political machinery should have demonstrated to Mitchell that the union's economic muscle alone was insufficient. Successful strikes in states such as Colorado necessitated mobilizing working-class voting power to make certain state laws and the state militia did not work against trade unionism. His public denunciation of Governor Peabody in April revealed that he was aware of the political realities, but as one scholar has written, his speech was "a case of too little too late" and did not constitute a "sustained effort to appeal over the head of the controlling factions to the people of the state."[54]

Simultaneous with the disastrous defeat in Colorado came another setback for Mitchell. This one proved even more damaging to his reputation among the rank and file because it involved a majority of soft coal miners. An economic downturn beginning in 1903 led operators to demand a sizable wage reduction at the January 1904 interstate joint conference. This proved the first real test of the union's commitment to the trade agreement. Since 1898, when the trade agreement in soft coal was first established, the nation had experienced general economic prosperity. Profits and wages had both risen in the industry. Now that the economy had soured, would the union live up to its pledge that wages must be tied to market conditions? And could Mitchell force union members to accept a wage cut without resort to a strike?

In light of the ominous economic clouds hanging over the union, Mitchell's opening address to the January 1904 UMWA convention was remarkable for its belligerency. He posed as the general of a mighty union army, militant and defiant. With words that would later be thrown back at him, he portrayed the union as a force that would never retreat. While the union desired peaceful relations with operators, it would stand ever vigilant to maintain its integrity. It was "more honorable to strike than to accept employment upon conditions dictated solely by the operators." The union might not win all its strikes, "yet it is always better to resist injustice than meekly to submit to it. To paraphrase the words of Tennyson, it is better to have resisted and lost than not have resisted at all." He concluded with an emotional appeal. "Let the watchword be, Onward! Keeping everlastingly at it brings success!"[55]

It is probable that Mitchell's militant rhetoric was aimed more at restraining the coal operators' desire for a wage cut than inspiring the rank and file. But operators were apparently not listening. When the annual interstate joint conference of operators and miners met at the end of January in Indianapolis, operators demanded an incredible 15 percent reduction in wage scales. Francis L. Robbins, a powerful coal baron from the Pittsburgh district, presented the operators' case. He claimed 1904 to be the most important year in the history of the coal trade agreement. There were numerous critics of the joint agreement who predicted the agreement would break down as soon as it became necessary to make reductions, but Robbins did not believe this. He had no fear an agreement would be reached because the two sides could "reason together." The reduction was justified, he said, because of overproduction, low coal prices, and because cheap, non-union coal was taking over many of their markets. Requesting a reduction was unpleasant for "one who has in his heart a great friendship for his employees," but economic conditions necessitated wage cuts.[56]

Mitchell then spoke. He, too, believed the joint agreement would survive this pivotal year and that "the very cordial relationship" between the two sides would continue. He denied the existence of an economic depression, however, and he argued that if and when a depression did occur, a reduction in wages would worsen rather than help the situation. While the operators spoke of overproduction, Mitchell stressed underconsumption. "To my mind the only way to relieve over-production is by making it possible for people to consume; and the working man cannot consume unless he has his wages." If wages were cut in coal mining, ultimately every industry would be affected. "If you reduce one industry, it goes on and on and finally the wages of all workers are reduced, the purchasing power is cut off, and then you come back and start over and over again; it is an endless repetition."[57]

Several days of negotiations yielded no progress. On February 2, a subcommittee of two union and two operator representatives met to resolve the impasse. When the subcommittee reported the next day, operators had lowered their demand to a 12 percent reduction, but no agreement could be reached. Both sides then agreed to adjourn the joint conference until further notice. Mitchell agreed to an adjournment only with "keen regret," and he insisted that "we should leave no effort untried to perpetuate this movement."[58]

Mitchell was in trouble and he knew it. And as usual, he turned to Hanna to help get him resolve his difficulty. Unfortunately, Hanna was gravely ill at this time and Mitchell had to correspond with Hanna's personal secretary, Elmer Dover, in the hope that the Senator would be well enough in the next few days to come to his assistance. In his letter to Dover, Mitchell claimed he possessed information that some eastern railroads and U.S. Steel were "insisting that the operators give them cheaper coal, and this action is interfering with a settlement." The 12 percent reduction was unreasonable, he continued, and would never be accepted by the rank and file. He tried to impress upon the senator the urgency of the situation. "I do not feel that the miners should be required to accept a reduction this year and I know that the sentiment is universal among the members of our union against accepting a reduction."[59]

Dover responded that Hanna was a very sick man, suffering from "the natural and regular development of the typhoid fever," and that it would be weeks before he could look after any business matters.[60] Mitchell would have to solve this dilemma without Hanna's assistance. On February 15, Hanna died.

Mitchell was shaken with grief. "I cannot tell you how sorry I feel about him," he wrote Keefe on the day of Hanna's death. He was not only a "good friend of our organization," he was also "my good personal friend."[61] He attended the funeral on February 19 at Cleveland, and he issued glowing comments to the press about the man who "did all that lay in his power to fairly and honestly reconcile the interests of employers and employees" and who "did not desire either public notice or applause for his actions."[62] In a move that outraged radicals, Mitchell called on miners across the nation to refrain from work after noon on February 19 as a sign of mourning for the union's friend.[63]

Mitchell not only had to face this crisis without the "Captain," but also Ralph Easley and the NCF were exerting strong pressure on him to resolve the issue without resorting to a strike. Failure to effect a peaceful settlement would be a "great blow at the joint trade agreement movement," Easley wrote. The NCF had long held up the bituminous trade agreement as "the ideal" system of contracts, and the enemies of the NCF, the open shop employers, were "praying for a rupture." The fact that both Mitchell and Frank Robbins were on the NCF's executive committee gave Easley a "double interest in the matter." Moreover, Easley was busily setting up trade agreements in a number of industries, including New England textiles, "the music and theatrical worlds," and brewing. "So you can see we all have a vital interest in the successful working of the bituminous trade agreements."[64]

Despite NCF pressure, Mitchell was at first adamant that no reduction would be acceptable. To an operator friend, C. J. Devlin, he wrote that the situation was "far from encouraging." Operators were insisting upon a reduction, but "in my judgment industrial conditions are not such as to warrant the acceptance of less wages at this time." While he did not want to predict the outcome of negotiations, he confessed he feared strike action.[65] On March 1, the joint conference reconvened. Several days of talk again brought no breakthroughs. All previous arguments were simply reiterated by both sides. By March 4, just as newspapers began discussing the strong possibility of a bituminous strike when present contracts expired on April 1, the operators backed away from their demand for a 12 percent reduction. They now called for a $5^1/_2$ percent slash and a two-year contract, but they made clear this was their final offer. On March 5, the miners' representatives at the joint convention voted against the operators' final offer and the joint conference adjourned once again, this time without provision to meet again.[66]

The following day the miners' representatives met in special convention. For several hours arguments were made for and against acceptance of the $5^1/_2$ percent reduction. Mitchell himself, along with Vice President Lewis and Secretary-Treasurer Wilson, pressed for acceptance. While Mitchell realized that many miners "would never be convinced that their interests were properly protected by their officers" if the reduction were accepted, nevertheless he believed acceptance was the proper course to follow. He argued that a strike would not succeed. There were too many areas, such as West Virginia and central Pennsylvania, that were insufficiently organized. There were too many miners, even union miners, who would not respond to the strike call. The chances of success were too remote, and defeat in a national strike could well destroy the union. In any event, he concluded, a national soft coal strike would certainly destroy the joint conference that had brought such gains since 1898. "I believe that, rather than see this joint movement disrupted, rather than hazard all we have gained during six or seven years, by one great strike, it would pay us to accept this reduction."[67]

What prompted Mitchell, one of the greatest labor statesman of the day, to press vigorously for a two-year give-back he believed was not justified by market conditions? First, he was convinced the operators' offer was final and that there would indeed be a strike if the offer were rejected. As he informed his friend Keefe, miners had received the "best offer we could possibly obtain" and there was "no possibility of the operators receding from their position."[68] Second, he was again influenced by the bureaucratic imperative of protecting the institution under his control from possible destruction. As he had shown during the anthracite strike, championship of the cause was secondary to preservation of the union. It was far better to retreat than to risk everything in a strike gamble. Third and most importantly, having presented himself to the public as the champion of the trade agreement, Mitchell could not endanger the joint conference in coal without destroying his own credibility. His fame and fortune were intimately tied to the success of the trade agreement, of basing labor-capital relations on the high level of rational argument rather than the strike. By 1904, he was emotionally and ideologically committed to the principle that there were no irreconcilable differences between classes. To strike now, when capitalists believed the market justified wage cuts, would demonstrate that he was at best a fair weather friend of class harmony and at worst a hypocrite who failed to act on his own principles. In a sense, Mitchell had become a victim of his own rhetoric.

Other miners were not bound by public pledges to uphold labor peace, and Mitchell encountered a great deal of opposition at the special miners' convention. Many delegates exhibited the class consciousness their president abhorred. "We will strike, if necessary until hell freezes over and not concede anything to the millionaires," one Illinois delegate fumed. Indeed, the entire Illinois delegation, representing as they did the most solidly organized district, stood united against the reduction. Another delegate pleaded for rejection of the give-back to prove to the labor movement that the miners still retained their fighting spirit. "We have worked for years to build up this organization, and what will the world think of us if, in the midst of good times we accept a reduction without a contest."[69]

While no delegate directly challenged Mitchell's leadership, several class conscious delegates supported their opposition to the give-back with allusions to the elitist affectations of their president. Many resented Mitchell's tailored Prince Albert coat, his cane, and his derby. Mitchell had begun donning such garb several years before, but it was generally reserved for NCF meetings and other social occasions. Now he chose to wear such finery at union meetings, and it did not sit well with those who questioned his conservatism. One Illinois socialist took particular note of the cane, commenting that a cane was a sure sign of a social climber. Mitchell's attire was not the only thing delegates found disturbing. Several miners were surprised by his recently acquired accent. Mitchell pronounced "Nu Yok" and other words with an accent that sounded strangely affected to other Illinois miners. Some delegates began to question whether their president, who had adopted the dress and accent of operators, might have adopted their outlook as well.[70]

Before the vote was taken, Mitchell told the delegates to regard the issue as a vote of confidence in his presidency and asked them to remove him from office if they disregarded his advice and elected to strike. Despite this plea, the miners' representatives voted against acceptance of the reduction.[71] At this point, the strike order should have been issued. Yet Mitchell had not exhausted his efforts to sidetrack the will of the rank and file. He successfully maneuvered the convention to agree to a referendum vote of the entire soft coal union membership. In the guise of democracy, he was in fact trying to subvert the special miners' convention by going over the heads of the delegates to the rank and file. The referendum was a convenient tool to be used only when representative conventions took actions contrary to the will of the union head. As Mitchell put it, "a strike seems imminent. There is only one hope of averting it and that is a referendum vote."[72]

Ballots were to be distributed to the membership on March 15 and counted on March 17. The referendum afforded Mitchell the opportunity to apply all the coercive and persuasive power of the presidency against what appeared to be the majority sentiment of the miners. Indeed, the ballot itself revealed Mitchell's control. Attached to the ballot was a statement by Mitchell urging miners to accept the reduction. His reasoning in this statement was a direct contradiction of every argument he had used against the operators during the joint conference. First, at the joint conference he had denied the operators' charge that the country was heading toward a serious depression, but in his appeal to the miners he held that "we are slowly moving toward an industrial depression." Second, at the joint conference he had emphasized the need for high wages to maintain consumer purchasing power, but now he emphasized that "millions of people who have no voice in our negotiations would be compelled to suffer because of our quarrel with our employers." Third, at the joint conference he had played down the significance of non-union territories such as West Virginia, but now he stressed the "weak links in the chain of our organization." He then argued that because the reduction demanded by operators was "so small," miners could not expect the public sympathy in this struggle that anthracite mine workers received in 1902. On the other hand, if miners accepted the reduction, it would "strengthen us with the public because it will demonstrate that a Trade Union can, when the occasion arises, gracefully accept a reduction." Rather than demonstrate union weakness, acceptance of the reduction would leave the union "strengthened by conservatism."[73]

Unwilling to allow the weight of his arguments alone to sway the miners, he dispersed his flock of organizers throughout the coal fields to spread the nostrike gospel according to Mitchell. In his instructions to organizers, he was quite specific as to the arguments he believed would be the most effective. He counseled them to "call attention to importance of perpetuating joint movement" and that "public sentiment and metropolitan papers (were) unanimously opposed to a strike." He even encouraged his organizers to arouse sectional hostility among miners by suggesting that many miners in areas where employment was irregular saw strike action as a chance to "receive steady work."[74]

He also made use of the union *Journal* to effect the outcome of the referendum. The journal gave him a tremendous advantage over those who disagreed with his policies. By the time S. M. Sexton was named editor in 1903, the *Journal* could no longer be considered a democratic organ. It was simply a vehicle for pro-Mitchell propaganda. The *Journal* routinely extolled his leadership and provided little space for dissenting views. The few criticisms of the administration that were printed were ridiculed. Several days before the vote, the *Journal* printed an article praising the joint conference and pleading with miners not to abandon it. The article implied a vote against the reduction was tantamount to treason. The "man has never drawn a breath that can truthfully point to a single tactical blunder of John Mitchell."[75]

Despite all his precautions, Mitchell was very anxious about the outcome of the referendum. He kept in constant contact with his organizers and was forced to turn down a special NCF dinner arranged in part so that he could meet Andrew Carnegie.[76] The reports he received from organizers "indicate a very decided division of opinion." He predicted that miners in the east—Ohio, western Pennsylvania, and central Pennsylvania—would vote to accept the reduction while miners in the west—Iowa, Illinois, and Indiana—would vote in opposition to it.[77] On the day miners voted, Mitchell described his uneasiness to his lawyer friend William Hawthorne. He was "considerably worried" because sentiment among the western miners was so strongly opposed to the reduction. He then complained about the fickleness of the miners:

> I fear the miners will make the most serious mistake of their lives if they do
> not follow the advice given by their officers. In the last seven years they have

had an advance in wages of from seventy-five to one hundred per cent.; they are now asked to accept a reduction of five and one half per cent., with a two year contract.This would carry them over the election and to the time when the industrial affairs of the country would not be disturbed by either the prospect or the result of an election and I feel that at that time they can obtain an advance of from ten to fifteen per cent. The trouble with the miners, as with nearly every other laboring man, is that when times are good and wages on the increase, they think the union is all right, but when the tide turns the other way, they balk.[78]

Mitchell had underestimated the persuasive power of his personal appeal, his organizers, and the *Journal*. When the votes were tabulated, 102,026 miners voted to accept the reduction and 67,951 had voted to reject it. As he had predicted, the vote had split east and west. Ohio miners voted to accept the reduction, 26,888 to 6,885, while Illinois voted against the reduction, 34,168 to 14,411.[79] In Mitchell's home town, Spring Valley, miners rejected their president's advice and voted overwhelmingly to strike, 2,078 to 131.[80]

Mitchell had achieved his victory. He took great pride in having side-tracked majority sentiment for a strike, and he believed the miners would come to recognize the wisdom of their action. "I have no doubt that time will vindicate me in the course I have pursued," he wrote, "and that the miners will realize, eventually, that they were never more honestly nor more ably defended than they were in this emergency."[81] Above all, he was proud that he had preserved the interstate joint conference. He believed the referendum "has done more to strengthen and encourage this trade agreement than any other one thing that has happened in our industrial affairs."[82] Even though his own vigorous campaigning undoubtedly helped avert the strike, he chose to interpret the outcome as evidence of the conservative effect of trade unionism on the miners, and he chose to regard his own machinations as a form of practical education. In a letter to a friend, he wrote:

> It is a source of great pleasure to me to know that the miners have acted with such good judgment and so much discretion. It has demonstrated beyond all question of doubt that the effect of unionism and of conservative administration has made our people more thoughtful and has given them a much better understanding of the relations of capital to labor and of labor to capital. It is the first time, to my knowledge, either in our trade or in any other in this country, when a thoroughly organized body of men has, by referendum vote, decided to adopt a reduction in wages. It seems to me that the miners' action should for all time still the tongues of their calumniators.[83]

Operators were equally ecstatic that a strike had been averted, and they were quick to thank the man most responsible for undermining strike sentiment. In the days following the balloting, Mitchell received numerous congratulatory telegrams and letters from coal operators across the nation. "I cannot tell you what a great relief it was to me" that the miners took "a sensible view of the situation" and followed "the advice of their President," wrote a major St. Louis operator. "I realized what an undertaking it was to convince men that they should work for less money."[84] Another congratulated him on the "greatest victory of your career" and yet another applauded "the noble stand you took in the matter."[85] Frank L. Robbins, perhaps the most powerful soft coal operator, thanked Mitchell for his "friendship," and was happy to bear testimony that "with honest, conservative men at the head of labor organizations the liability of having trouble is decreased and it is a safer method of settling wage questions than by dealing with the rank and file of employees."[86] One cannot help but question a settlement that made operators so gleeful.

Others found reason to cheer Mitchell. Ralph Easley, of course, heaped praise upon the leading labor member of the NCF for preserving the joint conference in soft coal. "You certainly did a great thing for the joint trade agreement movement for the country at large," Easley beamed.[87] The commercial press joined in a chorus of praise for Mitchell's conservatism, his farsightedness, and his devotion to public welfare. In a typical editorial, the *Baltimore American* thanked the miners for following the wishes of their "worthy leader" rather than acting "like dumb, driven cattle."[88] The *Springfield Daily Morning Sun* complained that Mitchell was not receiving even greater recognition for his efforts. "John Mitchell has just prevented a coal strike that would have cost millions of money and many lives and much suffering, and yet nobody has stood John Mitchell up in line and kissed him, or decorated him with gold medals as a hero."[89]

Industrial relations scholars heralded the give-back as a red letter day in capital-labor relations. John R. Commons considered the miners' willingness to accept a wage cut in the face of poor market conditions "an unusual evidence of business sagacity" and claimed that such a happy result could only be secured under the trade agreement system. Frank J. Warne also believed Mitchell and the union had acted along sound business lines.[90]

Indeed, everyone seemed pleased by the action except the miners themselves. Those who had opposed acceptance of the reduction remained bitter long after the decision. And many long time supporters condemned Mitchell personally for his crusade to avoid strike action regardless of the consequences. In Spring Valley and elsewhere, miners turned Mitchell's picture to the wall. Others refused to speak to him. Even his friend and mentor, Billy Ryan, railed against him, causing a breach between the two men that never completely healed. One man with whom Mitchell had labored in the mines addressed his old comrade as "Mr. Mitchell." When the wounded Mitchell asked for an explanation of this formality, the miner explained he had come to doubt a labor leader who dined with the captains of industry.[91] The resentment against Mitchell among miners in Illinois was so high that he deemed it necessary to attend the annual district convention and justify his actions.[92]

Socialists also mercilessly attacked Mitchell's role in forcing the wage reduction. Indeed, the wage cut marked the decisive break between Mitchell and the socialists. Until 1904, he had maintained a cool but cordial relationship with socialists within the union and nationwide. Eugene Debs and Mitchell had until then expressed mutual admiration. Debs wrote in 1901 that "as far as Mitchell is concerned, I know he is honest and doing his best and I would not for the world say or do anything to weaken or discourage him, but do all in my power to strengthen his hands." Mitchell returned the compliment, calling Debs "an honest man" who had made great sacrifices for the labor movement. While he disagreed with Debs on numerous issues, he believed they were both in their own way "working toward the same end."[93] As mentioned previously, Mitchell also maintained good relations with the leaders of the UMWA socialists in Illinois, including John Walker and Duncan McDonald. The first serious socialist assault on Mitchell's leadership came at the conclusion of the 1902 anthracite strike, when the radicals berated Mitchell for agreeing to arbitration just when victory seemed within the union's grasp. But at that time Mitchell's popularity was so great that such criticism fell on deaf ears.

Socialists tried to advance their cause at national conventions by introducing resolutions calling on the union to endorse socialist political candidates or acknowledging the existence of the class struggle. While socialists realized they had little hope of securing passage of these resolutions, the principal motive for their introduction was to stir up debate and win converts. At almost every national convention during Mitchell's reign, socialists would argue with conservatives over the nature of capitalism and the merits of the two major political parties. Socialist resolutions would invariably be voted down, but not before the radicals had stated their case for a political solution to the plight of the working class. At the January 1903 convention, for instance, socialists put forth the following resolution: "We ask all workmen to unite for independent political action in a party having for its avowed object the overthrow of the capitalistic system of production and distribution." Although the resolution was not adopted, a lengthy discussion gave socialists the opportunity to proselytize.[94] Mitchell himself sometimes joined in the debate against the socialists, but until 1904 he did not fear the presence of socialists in the union. He considered the Socialist Party too doctrinaire to win over a majority of the miners. "I think the Socialist Party as at present organized in this country is on such narrow lines," he wrote Henry D. Lloyd in 1903, "that it does not command the support it would were it organized upon broader lines, and if the men who are its recognized leaders were more liberal in their views and expressions."[95]

Although Mitchell and the socialists disagreed on almost every major issue, socialists were careful to avoid making direct attacks against Mitchell's leadership before 1904. The wage gains secured between 1898 and 1903, the successful strikes and organizing drives, and Mitchell's own immense popularity made confrontational union politics a suicidal policy for the radicals. Attacks against Mitchell would have undermined their own standing among the rank and file. But the failure in Colorado and especially the wage reduction gave socialists their first major issues to exploit, and they were quick to turn their guns on the conservative presidency of John Mitchell.

Perhaps the socialists and the Illinois miners, those "dumb, driven cattle," understood the situation better than Mitchell or his admirers. While the giveback was a sign of levelheaded conservatism to the most sophisticated operators, it also represented a sign of weakness, and many operators outside the Central Competitive Field took advantage of this perceived union weakness by trying to force pay cuts larger than $5^1/_2$ percent. Operators in the outlying fields also brazenly refused to carry out the terms of the contracts they did sign with the union. Moreover, because Mitchell had sown dissension within the UMWA, during the battle over the referendum, the UMWA was less united and therefore less capable of defending its interests against such attacks. Thus, Mitchell was guilty of not anticipating the full impact of accepting a wage reduction, and he also was guilty of making the union more susceptible to attack by weakening the union from within.

Acceptance of the wage reduction was a severe blow to Mitchell's reputation in the UMWA. It gave radicals within the union ammunition with which to weaken his standing among the rank and file. He remained immensely popular among the miners, and there were no strong candidates on the left ready to challenge him, yet his near perfect image had been stained. He now appeared all too human. At the same time, Mitchell was becoming increasingly involved in the affairs of the National Civic Federation. At the end of 1904, he was named co-chair of the NCF's most important department. While Mitchell hailed his new role as an important step toward the popularization of the trade agreement and therefore the resolution of class conflict in America, socialists and other radicals spotlighted his coziness with NCF capitalists as further proof that he had sold out the interests of the working class.

Mark Hanna's death in February 1904 deeply wounded the NCF. While Ralph Easley remained the man behind the scenes, tackling the administrative chores and spurring members by reminding them of the NCF's vision, Hanna had provided the prestige and clout. As both industrialist and senator, Hanna was instrumental in securing the involvement of numerous influential figures. He was the marquis name who gave the NCF status and informal power. His commitment to NCF's vision of an industrial society in which reason, in the form of the trade agreement, prevailed over violence and chaos, made that vision respectable to the nation's power elite. Hanna's death meant not only the loss of an active president, but also the loss of the NCF's momentum.

Mitchell took an active role in the search for Hanna's replacement. For him the choice of a new president was surcharged with importance. He had viewed Hanna as a trusted ally of the union, a like-minded proponent of labor peace and justice, and a close personal friend. Indeed, Hanna's involvement in NCF affairs was, in the beginning, the principal reason he had cast his lot with the organization. He saw in Hanna the type of intellectual transformation he hoped would occur throughout the employing class. In a few short years, Mitchell declared, Hanna moved from an "enemy and opponent" of working people to "their friend and exponent." In an eloquent eulogy released to the press, Mitchell explained his feelings:

> I presume there is no representative of organized labor who enjoyed a more intimate acquaintance with Senator Hanna than myself, and no one can appreciate the many invaluable services he rendered organized labor without having as intimate contact with him. Senator Hanna did not seek credit for his work and I know of many sacrifices of time and energy made by him for which he received no public recognition. Indeed, he often told me that his highest ambition was to do all that lay in his power fairly and honestly to reconcile the interests of employers and employees, and that he did not desire either public notice or applause of his action. And from my own personal information I know this to be true.
>
> Senator Hanna's association with the National Civic Federation was an evidence of his sincere interest in the promotion of industrial peace. His connection with that body, his defense of the right of laboring men to organize and to act through their organization, did much to remove prejudice on the part of employers against labor organizations.[96]

At the semi-annual meeting of NCF leaders in May 1904, Mitchell opined that Hanna's death was "a well-nigh irreparable loss" to the labor movement.[97] Such a valuable comrade would be hard to replace.

Mitchell and other labor leaders above all were concerned that Hanna's successor be a nationally recognized industrialist who openly advocated trade agreements. Easley suggested Andrew Carnegie as the next president. A man of immense fame, Carnegie was now retired from steel making and could devote all his energies to the Federation. When Easley suggested Carnegie to Mitchell at Hanna's funeral in Cleveland, Mitchell responded warmly. "Since leaving Cleveland I have given the matter considerable thought and it appears to me that Carnegie would probably fill the bill about as acceptably as anyone we could get." He told Easley that "Mr. Carnegie is the person we should try to get."[98]

At first glance, Mitchell's support of Carnegie seemed outrageous. That a union leader would endorse a man renowned for his antiunion views and whose hands were "stained with the blood of the Homestead strikers" seemed incredible. According to Mitchell, however, Carnegie was just the man for the job. Like Hanna, he was known to be hostile to unions in the 1890s but had in recent years "seen the light" and now approved of both trade unions and trade agreements in principal. That so powerful an employer had undergone such a turnaround in outlook made him an ideal spokesperson for labor peace. As he explained to his friend Daniel J. Keefe, Carnegie was now "especially fond of trade unionists, particularly labor leaders."[99] Mitchell also would have agreed with Easley that Carnegie "could pull lots of wires" and that he could "land the organization on a permanent footing." Nor was Mitchell alone in his support of Carnegie. Samuel Gompers, T. J. Shaffer of the Iron, Steel and Tin Workers, James Duncan of the Granite Cutters, Daniel Tobin of the Teamsters, William D. Mahon of the Street Car Employees, and E. E. Clark of the Railway Clerks were among those supporting Carnegie.[100]

With the backing of Mitchell and the labor bloc of the NCF, Easley arranged a private dinner for Carnegie on March 15 at the New York home of Oscar Strauss. The dinner was to be a private affair, at which Carnegie would be offered the NCF presidency. Although Easley begged Mitchell to attend, Mitchell was too burdened with soft coal negotiations to make the trip.[101] Much to the chagrin of Easley and Mitchell, Carnegie, while flattered, was unable to accept the post. In his autobiography, Carnegie noted the support of the labor leaders and described it as "a balm to the hurt mind."[102] Health considerations, however, forced Carnegie to remain in Europe six months of every year, making it impossible to fulfill the required presidential functions. He did agree to accept membership on the NCF's national executive committee, and this, Easley explained to Mitchell, was better than nothing. The NCF would still "get all the benefit coming from his name and influence."[103] The search for a new president continued.

Some indication of Mitchell's attitude toward the NCF after the death of Hanna can be gleaned from a tongue in cheek missive to his friend Daniel J. Keefe. Four days had passed since the Strauss dinner, and Mitchell was miffed that Easley had yet to supply him with a complete report of the affair. "Unless one is received by the end of this week," Mitchell quipped, "I shall be compelled to remove him (Easley) and put a good man in his place."[104] Mitchell took the NCF seriously. His commitment to the organization and its promotion of trade agreements was not a sham for public consumption. Yet he was also aware that without his participation, the NCF carried little weight. He realized his charisma and public appeal were necessary to the success of the organization. Especially after the death of the "Captain," the NCF could not pretend to stand for peace between capital and labor without Mitchell's active involvement.

Mitchell's flippancy also underscored the fact that while the NCF was valuable for its promotion of the trade agreement, the ultimate worth of the NCF was what it could do for the UMWA during times of strike and negotiation. And from Mitchell's perspective, the NCF as an institution was less important in this regard than his personal friendship with Hanna. It is not surprising, therefore, that Mitchell searched for an equally valuable ally with the

"Captain's" passing. Perhaps he saw Carnegie as a possible replacement for Hanna. Although Carnegie lacked the political clout of the senator, his influence among industrialists remained strong. Mitchell's controversial visit to Carnegie's estate in Scotland in the summer of 1904 was perhaps an attempt to cultivate a lasting friendship that could work to the advantage of the union. If that was Mitchell's hope, he was quickly disappointed. Initially Mitchell's charisma won over the one-time steel giant. When Carnegie rearranged his busy schedule to attend the December 1904 annual meeting of the NCF, he did so primarily to see Mitchell again. Carnegie "has given up two or three meetings to attend our annual meeting," Easley informed Mitchell, "and expressly requested to meet with you as he wants to talk with you."[105] But while the two men developed warm personal feelings and admired each other, they never developed a close friendship, and Carnegie never intervened in industrial affairs to assist the UMWA.

Undaunted, Mitchell explored other possible replacements for Hanna. He ingratiated himself with Senator Boies Penrose of Pennsylvania, who was by 1904 the prime mover in that state's politics. In May 1904, Mitchell threw his support behind the effort to make Penrose Chairman of the Republican National Committee. He even went to the White House and spoke to Roosevelt about the matter. Although Penrose never obtained the post, he remained indebted to Mitchell and helped secure passage of several bills the UMWA favored at the state level.[106] Penrose, however, never proved to be the close and powerful ally Mitchell sought at the national level.

A more obvious choice than either Carnegie or Penrose was President Roosevelt. Roosevelt liked Mitchell—he admired his cautious and conservative conduct of the 1902 strike, and his quiet defiance of the obstinate railroad owners, and certainly no one was better situated to assist Mitchell than the President. It is interesting to note that while Mitchell remained in contact with Roosevelt throughout 1903 and early 1904, his level of communication increased dramatically after the death of Hanna. Before Hanna's demise, Roosevelt on several occasions had invited Mitchell to conferences and dinners at the White House. Yet, as one scholar has written, after Hanna's death Mitchell's relationship with Roosevelt became "a personal and direct one."[107] A genuine friendship was established. Mitchell began consulting with Roosevelt on labor matters, perhaps in an effort to ascertain just how useful Roosevelt's friendship could be. For instance, when Carroll Wright resigned as Commissioner of Labor in late 1904, Mitchell recommended Charles P. Neill, an academic who had served as recorder for the Anthracite Coal Commission. In part due to Mitchell's support, Neill obtained the post.[108]

That the public perceived Mitchell and Roosevelt as intimates could be seen in the widespread rumors that Mitchell would be Roosevelt's vice presidential running mate in the 1904 elections. Mitchell began hearing these rumors in late February. He was flattered, of course, but never believed Roosevelt contemplated selecting him. "About a year ago the chances seemed very favorable for the nomination of a labor man" as vice president, he explained to his AFL chum James Duncan, "but the sentiment has so changed that I do not believe it would be either possible or politic for the Republican party—or any other party—to nominate a trade unionist." As to the possibility of Roosevelt naming him to some other political office, Mitchell declared he would refuse any political appointment less powerful than a cabinet secretary.[109]

As Mitchell predicted, the vice presidential nomination was never offered. More importantly, Roosevelt never became the replacement for Hanna Mitchell sought. The two men remained close, however, and Mitchell continued to consult with Roosevelt on matters affecting the labor movement. Years later, Roosevelt fondly recalled his friendship for the union president, telling reporters: "John Mitchell! They didn't come any finer."[110] For all his charisma, his ability to charm the power elite, Mitchell never found a substitute for Hanna. The President did not serve Mitchell the way Hanna had. He did not apply the same kind of hands on pressure against anti-union coal operators during negotiations, nor did he work behind the scenes during strikes to secure quick settlements. Unlike Hanna, Roosevelt did not share Mitchell's vision of industrial capitalism transformed through the trade agreement. The only powerful men who did share this vision were active members of the NCF. This explains why Mitchell remained so active in the organization after Hanna's death and why he believed the search for a new president of the organization was so important.

At its December 1904 annual meeting, the NCF announced August Belmont, New York financier, its new president. Belmont had in fact been acting president since the summer of 1904, but the Federation decided to keep this secret until after the fall presidential elections to keep the organization free from partisan politics. Press reports declared that both labor leaders and employers were united behind the choice of Belmont.[111]

As a result of his future actions, Belmont is now recognized as an enemy of labor. In 1904, however, labor leaders considered Belmont an influential friend of the movement. As president of New York's Interborough Rapid Transit Company, he had negotiated an annual trade agreement with the Amalgamated Association of Street Railway Employees. William D. Mahon, president of this union, was an active member of the NCF, and he induced Belmont to join. Belmont quickly became an enthusiastic champion of labor peace and trade agreements, and Mahon convinced Mitchell and other labor members that Belmont would make a good successor to Hanna.[112] Having little personal knowledge of Belmont at this time, Mitchell apparently agreed to the choice because of his public record and the recommendation of Mahon.

In addition to electing a president, the NCF in 1904 revamped its organizational structure. Until that time, the only permanent department was the Industrial Department, the main purpose of which was to maintain labor peace by offering conciliation and arbitration services. Through its annual dinners, however, the NCF also emphasized the promotion of the trade agreement as the best means to ensure permanent labor peace. The NCF also developed an interest in gathering data on a whole range of capital-labor issues. To better serve these divergent ends, the NCF disbanded the Industrial Department in 1904 and created instead three new permanent departments: the Conciliation Department, the Trade Agreement Department, and the Industrial Economics Department.

The purpose of the Trade Agreement Department was simple. It was to promote collective bargaining in all industrial sectors. Because it was created at a time when trade agreements were held in high esteem by scholars, labor leaders, and many industrialists, the work of this department attracted a great deal of enthusiasm. At the May 1904 conference establishing the department, members were asked to come prepared with specific proposals on how best to "bring into concrete form the principles underlying collective bargaining."[113] The special committee, which established the department, consisted of fifty members, twenty-five employers and twenty-five labor leaders, including Mitchell. At the conference, Mitchell and others defined their goal: "to assist in educating employers and employees alike as to the basic elements common to all such agreements, and their adaptation to the requirements of specified industries."[114] In short, the department aimed to "sell" the idea of the trade agreement to all industries, then to assist in drawing up specific agreements tailor made to the specific needs of particular industries.

Who would head up this department? On this question there was little need for debate. Bituminous coal was the best example of an industry in which the trade agreement functioned smoothly to the benefit of both employer and worker. The recent acceptance of a wage reduction without recourse to strike action beautifully illustrated the proper functioning of collective bargaining. Moreover, both the union and employers in soft coal were ideologically committed to the trade agreement. In a move that surprised no one, therefore, John Mitchell was named co-chair of the Trade Agreement Department. The other co-chair was Francis Robbins, a Pittsburgh operator and the largest employer of coal workers.[115]

Mitchell embarked on his new task with enthusiasm. He quickly realized, however, that it was much easier to discuss trade agreements and labor peace in the abstract than it was to establish them in practice. Perhaps the most serious obstacle was the fact that trade agreements were possible only when both employers and workers were organized. Over three-fourths of the nation's work force in 1904 was unorganized and thus beyond the scope of the department. A second obstacle was the fact that conditions varied so greatly from one industry to the next that devising any type of universal trade agreement formula was impossible. Employers could not agree on the best features of the trade agreement. Nor could labor leaders.

Despite these and other barriers, Mitchell's enthusiasm grew as the months passed. By the end of 1904, he could look back with pride on the proliferation of trade agreements and the growing acceptance of the principle of collective bargaining. By that time more than fifty trade agreements existed in the nation's great industries. Among the most noteworthy were the agreements between the Newspaper Publishers Association and the Typographical Union, Erie Dock Managers and the Longshoremen, the Brewers' Association and the Brewers' Union, the New York Metal Trades Association and the Boilermakers, United States Steel and the Metalworkers, and the National Founders Association and the Iron Molders Union.[116] It must be noted that the vast majority of these had been established before the creation of the Trade Agreement Department, and many before the creation of the NCF itself. Yet, the NCF had successfully concluded a number of trade agreements and had played a leading role in maintaining existing ones.

As collective bargaining spread, Mitchell came to believe he was riding the wave of history. As he gathered information of existing trade agreements and spoke to industrialists and labor leaders on their beneficial results, he came more and more to believe that the trade agreement was the lasting and permanent solution to the "labor problem." Others agreed. The number of articles published by the NCF applauding collective bargaining rose dramatically after the creation of the Trade Agreement Department. One major NCF figure who sang the praises of collective bargaining was Louis Brandeis. Active in the New England Federation of Labor and a staunch supporter of organized labor, Brandeis wrote that trade agreements created a partnership between employers and employees. This partnership guaranteed not only industrial peace, but also industrial efficiency and economic progress.[117] Even Ralph Easley, who usually contented himself with remaining behind the scenes, declared that national trade agreements were the only vehicles that could "bring capital and labor into harmony."[118]

Employers and labor leaders often had divergent reasons for supporting trade agreements. Employers in the NCF believed such agreements made labor leaders more reasonable and conservative. Even radical trade unionists, once given the opportunity to bargain with employers in good faith, were forced to consider market conditions, operating costs, and all the other difficulties faced by employers, often became more temperate in their demands. Francis Robbins, co-chair of the department, was convinced that agreements had "an elevating effect upon the intelligence and character of the union leaders."[119]

Most labor leaders were equally pragmatic in their support of trade agreements. Samuel Gompers, for instance, participated in the NCF because it conferred on the AFL a measure of social recognition and respectability. He applauded the trade agreement because it rested on the organized strength of workers and did not depend on the apparatus of the state. Thus, trade agreements upheld his principle of voluntarism—his distrust of political solutions and his desire to rely exclusively on the economic power of trade unions.[120]

More than any other labor leader, Mitchell trumpeted the trade agreement as the dawn of a new day in labor relations. While Gompers and other labor leaders focused on the tangible rewards of collective bargaining, Mitchell was emotionally committed. He believed that agreements meant much more than improved wages and working conditions, or even increased union stability. He upheld the trade agreement as a mechanism capable of transcending the traditional hostility between labor and capital. In his address to the NCF's annual dinner in December 1904, Mitchell declared he was "glad to be part of this peace movement," by which he meant the NCF. As an upstanding American citizen concerned about "the progress and perpetuity of this republic," it was his duty to help resolve the greatest problem facing society—the relations between capital and labor. In recent years these relations had "become strained almost to the breaking point," and it was his duty to help "bring into closer and more harmonious relation these two apparently antagonistic forces." The trade agreement could do just that. It was "the great and ultimate factor in the solution of the industrial problem." In the "near future," the trade agreement would "establish an economic unity of interests between the two great contending forces, and the final relations will be that of business partnership."[121] It was a great speech and the crowd erupted in applause. Scholars and industrialists congratulated him enthusiastically. "The best speech of the evening was made by John Mitchell," commented the head of the New York Board of Education. "He was the only man of the lot who had anything to say."[122]

By 1904, Mitchell's support of the trade agreement was unconditional and wholehearted. The power of his union rested on the trade agreement; it had been the ideological connection between himself and Mark Hanna; he had tried to introduce it through two major strikes in the anthracite region; he had dedicated his book to it; he had accepted a significant wage cut for his soft coal miners in the face of strike sentiment in defense of it; and now he served as co-chair of the Trade Agreement Department of the NCF, a powerful voluntary agency devoted to it. Mitchell's career was now intimately tied to the fortunes of the trade agreement "movement." Failure of this movement would jeopardize Mitchell's status as a leading voice in industrial relations.

While the trade agreement had achieved clear successes by 1904, there were other forces at work in the economic sphere to which Mitchell seemed all but blind. By 1904, just when the trade agreement had reached its peak of influence, an employer anti-union offensive was already underway that would soon dominate industrial relations. Comprised of the open shop movement and welfarism, the anti-union offensive would soon cripple the trade agreement movement, redirect the affairs of the NCF, and undercut Mitchell's lofty perch atop the world of organized labor.

Anti-unionism increased at the same time the trade agreement movement flourished. Numerous factors account for this trend. After 1902, some employers abandoned their existing trade agreements, complaining that unions were irresponsible and could not uphold their contracts. Also, as the economic boom of 1898–1902 disappeared, turning to recession in 1904, many employers found resistance to unions a matter of competitive necessity. Other employers feared organized labor was becoming too powerful. Still other employers were determined to restructure work relations through the introduction of scientific management and found unions undesirable impediments.[123]

By 1903, anti-union employers were beginning to join forces in a determined campaign to prevent any further labor gains. Local groups known as industrial alliances emerged, and in 1903 met to create a national organization called the Citizens' Industrial Association (CIA). Under the presidency of C. W. Post, a cereal manufacturer from Michigan, the CIA used intensive lobbying and propaganda efforts to rouse public opinion against organized labor. Even more important at the national level was the National Association of Manufacturers (NAM). Originally organized in 1895 to promote foreign trade, by 1903, the NAM was dedicated to the principle of the open shop, a guarantee of the right to work regardless of union affiliation. Led by David M. Parry, president of the Overland Automobile Company, the NAM viewed all labor unions as socialistic and unpatriotic. In late 1904, just as Mitchell declared the trade agreement the solution of the industrial problem, Parry argued: "The labor question is a conflict between two antagonistic and opposing systems of political economics. In reality on the one side of this contest is the American system of government, while on the other side is a mixture of socialism and despotism."[124]

The tactics of anti-union employers associated with the NAM and the CIA were familiar ones. They utilized "yellow dog" contracts, in which workers agreed not to join unions as a condition of employment; they hired labor spies to identify pro-union workers in the shops and factories and, once these workers were fired, the employers used blacklists to make certain other firms would not hire them. Employers exploited ethnic and racial differences in their work force to forestall united action, and also made frequent appeals to courts in an effort to obtain injunctions against unions.[125]

Needless to say, NCF leaders perceived the NAM, the CIA, and their anti-union offensive as a direct threat to the NCF's existence. At the same time, the NCF was calling on employers to use its offices to solve their labor problems peacefully, the NAM and the CIA were urging those same employers to join with them in a great battle against the supposed evil of organized labor. Easley was especially venomous in his denunciation of the NAM and the CIA. He castigated them for their ignorance of labor history. Under the guiding influence of the NCF, labor unions were becoming less confrontational and more cooperative, he argued, and thus there was no need for employers to mount frontal attacks on unions. Along with socialists, the NAM and the CIA were "our enemies." "Diametrically opposed in their ultimate purpose," Easley wrote, socialists and anti-union employers "share a common opposition to the only organization that would bring capital and labor into harmony."[126]

While Mitchell in 1904 was not completely oblivious to the threat posed by these groups, he certainly underestimated their growing strength. Part of the reason for this was his own ignorance. Until he became co-chair of the Trade Agreement Department, Mitchell's knowledge of industrial relations stemmed almost entirely from relations between mine workers and operators. His NCF affiliation gave him insight into the attitudes of only the most progressive employers. It was therefore easy for him to believe that the success of the interstate agreement and the acceptance of conservative trade unionism among a relative handful of employers in the NCF were signs of things to come in industry as a whole. Even when faced with the growth of the anti-union offensive, Mitchell continued to believe this represented a temporary backlash among a small minority of reactionaries.

A second reason why Mitchell underestimated the threat of the anti-union insurgents was the fact that Easley often misled him on the relative strength of the organizations. By late 1903, Easley was already suggesting to Mitchell that the anti-union offensive was petering out. Parry and Post were failing to attract employers to their cause. "The same employers, and they outnumber the others at the rate of twenty-five to one, are with us," he assured Mitchell.[127] A year later, when Mitchell again expressed concern about the growth of the NAM, Easley scoffed that the NCF represented "more capital and men than the whole of the Parry outfit."[128]

Had Mitchell been more astute, however, he could have seen for himself the growing power of the NAM. He could have been more aware of the NAM's effective use of propaganda to attack unions in general and labor leaders in particular. After all, Mitchell himself had been the victim of David Parry's hostile insinuations. The story is instructive, for it not only highlights Parry's methods, but how sensitive Mitchell was to slanderous attack. The story began in November 1903, when Mitchell received a letter from Charles Stelzle, a major figure in the "Board of Home Missions" of the Presbyterian Church. Stelzle, who had been a New York machinist for eight years, now traveled from congregation to congregation encouraging employers in the flock to improve working conditions and accept conservative trade unionism.

Mitchell and Stelzle had met in December 1902 on a train between Scranton and Buffalo. Stelzle's letter described a recent meeting of the St. Paul Manufacturers' Association he had attended, at which Parry was the principal speaker.

According to Stelzle, Parry's speech focused on the evil of trade unionism and the general character of labor leaders. In the course of the speech, Parry illustrated his points by referring to Mitchell. Parry claimed Mitchell had recently purchased two pieces of property in Indianapolis valued at close to $80,000. Since Mitchell "could not have come by that money honestly," Parry stated the UMWA president had made the purchase "in the name of a relative." Then Parry told the audience about an encounter he had with Mitchell at a hotel in Indianapolis. Mitchell, Gompers, along with "a company of other Federation men," Parry recalled, were sitting around a table busily consuming alcohol from "steins." Parry passed by the table and remarked as he did that the labor men "had come down somewhat to drink beer." Mitchell then replied, according to Parry: "Oh, hell. This isn't beer, this is champagne. We're drinking it out of steins because some of those sons of bitches (referring to newspaper reporters) might see me." Stelzle related this story to Mitchell because he believed it "made an impression on these business men." And since he was to address the same audience in the near future, he wanted Mitchell to set the record straight so that he could preserve Mitchell's reputation.[129]

Mitchell was enraged. Although he ordinarily did not stoop to defend himself against attacks made on his character, he believed "Mr. Parry's position is such that I feel it my duty to enter an unqualified protest against his action." He emphatically denied the charges, claiming he owned no property in Indianapolis, he had never drank champagne or beer with Gompers in the hotel mentioned, and he had met Parry only one time at a public meeting in Scranton during the 1902 strike. He instructed Stelzle to refute the charges. Moreover, he wanted to make the charges and his refutation public by "meeting Mr. Parry face to face in the presence of those who were at the meeting in which he made these attacks."[130] Stelzle then wrote Parry, enclosing a copy of Mitchell's denial, asking Parry to either prove the charges or make a formal apology. Parry never responded. Instead, his secretary, John Maxwell, wrote Stelzle, telling the clergyman to drop the matter before it became a "campaign of personalities." "I cannot help but impress upon you the unpleasantness that confronts you and everyone else who presses this matter," Maxwell threatened.[131]

When informed of Maxwell's threat, Mitchell found it "very amusing." He was certain Parry had instructed Maxwell to write the letter and believed the threat was a sign of weakness. "Finding themselves against a stone wall," he concluded, "they are trying to escape by simply attempting to insult you and prevent a further investigation."[132] Stelzle agreed, promising to write

Maxwell and Parry once again, and if no satisfactory response was received, he would take the entire matter to the press.[133] Parry did not respond, and Stelzle took the story and all relating correspondence to a local paper. Although he was disappointed no major papers picked up the story, Stelzle hoped it would "make Mr. Parry more careful in the future as to the use of epithets and wholesale accusations."[134] While the matter ended there without any appreciable damage done to Mitchell's reputation, it should have been an indication of the effective techniques the anti-union insurgents used when appealing to employers.

Another indication of the growing strength of anti-unionism Mitchell failed to notice was the more than usual frenzy of activity surrounding the annual dinner of the NCF held in December 1904 in New York. Just one month earlier in that same city the CIA held its convention. In many ways the convention was a full-scale attack on the NCF, as several speakers ridiculed the NCF's approach to industrial relations. Easley tried to down play the CIA's convention, but recognized the NCF would have to redouble its efforts to maintain its support among employers. "I have been working night and day . . . to counteract the Parry influence throughout the country," he explained to Mitchell. He sent out special invitations to the most prominent New Yorkers, including John Jacob Astor and Cornelius Vanderbilt. Andrew Carnegie agreed to attend. Easley was determined to make this annual dinner a showcase of NCF prestige. Leaders from nearly every industry were invited, as were religious leaders from the major denominations. "We want to make this so big and so complete in every respect that it will make the Parryites look like 'thirty cents' in comparison."[135]

One can imagine Easley's dismay when Mitchell first told him he would be unable to attend the dinner in December. "You could have knocked me over with a feather," Easley wrote. First of all, the committee on arrangements, which included many prominent NCF members, insisted that Mitchell be the principal speaker from labor. Gompers was simply unacceptable. "Everybody wants to hear John Mitchell," Easley quoted the committee chair. Second, those industrialists who would be attending their first NCF convention were expecting to meet the hero of the miners. "These new people want to see you," Easley complained. "They want to hear you talk." And as if to stress that this dinner represented a showdown with the anti-unionists with dire ramifications for the labor movement, Easley stated: "You will do the greatest thing possible for the organized labor movement of this country to come here and let your voice be heard." Once he recognized the importance of the dinner, Mitchell did in fact agree to attend.[136]

The NCF dinner was a great success. The presence of Belmont, the new president, Carnegie, and Mitchell all guaranteed a wonderful evening for the organization. But it was in some respects the last great victory for the NCF. By the end of 1904, the anti-unionists were attracting more and more employers with their message of class warfare. By embracing the NCF, by agreeing to co-chair the Trade Agreement Department, by agreeing to serve as their principal labor spokesman, and by wholeheartedly endorsing the trade agreement, Mitchell was tying his future to a dying cause. Other trade unionists, as we will see, were prepared to take up the challenge of the anti-unionists and meet them on the economic battlefield, but Mitchell remained committed to the NCF and its doctrine of labor peace at all costs.

1904 had proven a difficult year for Mitchell. Within his union, the wage reduction soft coal miners were forced to swallow and the loss of the Colorado strike prompted some bitter attacks on his leadership. On the national level, the death of Mark Hanna and the emergence of a powerful open shop offensive served to undermine the NCF's effort to control the hearts and minds of employers. Mitchell's dream of a republic transformed by universal acceptance of the trade agreement, once shared by so many influential labor leaders and industrialists, seemed less and less plausible. The honeymoon years of the trade agreement were now nearing an end, and anti-unionism in the form of the NAM and the CIA increasingly dominated the industrial relations scene. How would the NCF respond? How would the labor movement respond? How would John Mitchell respond?

Chapter 8

Shattered Dreams of Cooperation, 1905–1906

In the years 1905 and 1906 both the National Civic Federation and the labor movement came to grips with the open shop movement. Easley and other NCF leaders, once they realized they could not compete with the "Parryites" by making vague appeals to labor peace and economic justice, took a decidedly conservative turn. While they did not espouse opposition to unions and did not completely abandon the promotion of trade agreements, they did begin emphasizing other aspects of labor relations that were of little benefit to organized labor. Within the labor movement, various responses to the anti-union offensive emerged. On the left appeared the Industrial Workers of the World, a syndicalist organization determined to organize all workers in "one big union" and square off against employers in direct class warfare. Even mainstream labor leaders were prepared to shift tactics in order to battle the anti-unionists. In 1906, Gompers and the AFL launched a full scale political attack on their enemies.

These developments provided Mitchell with the greatest challenges of his career. From the time of his youth, he had been inspired by the twin messages of conservative unionism and cooperation with employers through the trade agreement. The interstate agreement in coal had made the UMWA the largest union in America and offered proof of the rewards of cooperation with employers. Would he now abandon that approach when both unionists and employers seemed bent on conflict? Would he adopt a fighting stance and encourage workers to secure economic justice by battling those employers he so much admired and counted among his closest friends? Would he part with the NCF now that it no longer called for acceptance of conservative unionism in a loud and clear voice?

To all of these questions Mitchell responded with a resounding "No!" By the end of 1906, Mitchell was one of only a handful of labor leaders who continued to play an active role in the NCF and one who still considered it a vehicle for the advancement of the labor movement. As did all mainstream labor leaders, he assailed the Industrial Workers of the World and worked hard to diminish its influence within his own union. Yet, unlike most mainstream labor leaders, he refused to take part in the AFL's political action program of

1906. Rather than meet the challenge of the anti-unionists head on, Mitchell chose to cling to the increasingly irrelevant vision of a cooperative society based on trade agreements. In an effort to keep this vision alive, he once again in 1906 squelched widespread strike sentiment in the UMWA and refused to sanction a national walk out. Ironically, this action, rather than strengthening the interstate agreement, temporary destroyed it. As we shall see, Mitchell's inability to abandon his ideological commitment to the trade agreement after 1904 left him increasingly isolated in the labor movement, making him a force of reaction rather than progressive change.

One of the earliest indications that the tenor of the NCF had radically shifted in the face of the open shop offensive were the actions by its new president, August Belmont. Belmont's Interborough Rapid Transit Company of New York became embroiled in serious labor difficulties soon after his election. In late 1904, Belmont, despite his NCF post and the fact his company had contracts with three unions—the Brotherhood of Locomotive Firemen, Locomotive Engineers, and the Amalgamated Association of Street Railway Employees, made preparations to rid his company of unionism. Through his actions he seemed intent on provoking a strike. Workers complained of increased work loads, shortened rest periods, and other violations of their union contracts. By January 1905, union locals were preparing to walk out.[1]

Easley and the NCF immediately sprang to action. Needless to say, to have the new NCF president engaged in union-smashing would not be good for the organization's pro-union image. Rather than twist Belmont's arm, however, the NCF's New York conciliation committee went to work on Warren Stone of the Engineers and William D. Mahon of the Railway Employees. As Easley informed Mitchell, the committee worked throughout February, "trying to impress the labor end of the dispute with the importance of being fair and decent." While Stone and Mahon were prepared to forestall strike action, the question remained whether they could control the locals. As Mitchell learned, the unions were new and "not very amenable to discipline from national officers."[2]

When Belmont began importing strikebreakers and rejected demands that he abide by existing contracts, the besieged locals felt compelled to strike. The walk out began March 7. Under pressure from the NCF, national union officers refused to sanction the walk out. Easley immediately sent for Mitchell, who arrived in New York on March 9. Convinced the strike represented a violation of union law, Mitchell, along with Mahon and Stone, issued a public statement condemning the action and ordering employees back to work.[3] Mitchell also agreed to help protect Mahon from possible recriminations within his own union by writing a letter supporting Mahon's action in the Railway Workers' journal.[4] The strike was quickly broken by the combination of the repudiation of Mitchell, Mahon, and Stone, and the more than 1,000 strikebreakers Belmont had imported. Over two-thirds of the workers lost their jobs, the local unions were destroyed, and the Interborough became an open shop organization headed by August Belmont, NCF president.[5]

Belmont remained NCF president for the next three years. Mitchell certainly recognized the contradiction of having the open-shopper Belmont as head of the NCF. But it was not until 1907 that Mitchell tried to do something about the contradiction. He and Daniel J. Keefe, after consulting with Easley, met privately with Belmont in an effort to convince him to permit the unionization of his employees. The meeting accomplished nothing.[6] Despite Belmont's union busting efforts, Mitchell continued to like and respect the NCF president after the strike. When Belmont was hospitalized in October 1905, Mitchell, along with other NCF leaders, sent him flowers and a "get well" card.[7] And in late 1907 when Belmont was under criminal investigation by the public utilities commission of New York, Mitchell was forced to side with those who wanted to find a new NCF president, but he deeply regretted doing so: "You know I am very fond of him."[8]

Moreover, the fact that the Interborough had become an open shop company did not prevent Mitchell from purchasing stock in it. In response to his queries in the summer of 1907, Easley assured Mitchell that the Interborough's stock was completely safe. After some deliberation, he purchased an undetermined amount of stock at $64 per share. By November the stock price had dropped to 49 and he panicked. He wrote Easley to contact Belmont and ask if the stocks were "going any lower" and whether he should sell. Easley comforted Mitchell, explaining the declining stock price "means nothing."[9] Apparently Mitchell was not bothered by the fact that the Interborough was an open shop company and that he and the NCF had helped make it so.

An even more important indication the NCF was taking a conservative turn was the expansion of its welfare work. Originally established in 1904, the NCF's Welfare Department provided a framework in which employers could compare their experiences in implementing welfare or industrial betterment schemes, identify common problems, and refine their programs. Welfare work was not new in 1904. Numerous employers had already introduced programs designed to increase productivity by making workers more contented on the job. The NCF's Welfare Department, however, provided the first systematic approach to the process and helped make it a truly national movement. Headed by Gertrude Beeks, welfare manager at McCormick Harvester Company, the Welfare Department became one of the most successful NCF programs in 1905 and 1906.[10]

Although Beeks and other members of the Welfare Department insisted welfare schemes were designed to supplement rather than displace labor unions, in practice most employers saw the main goal of welfare work as the elimination of unions. By providing workers with a wide range of benefits, employers sought to undermine the need for labor organization.[11] The anti-union thrust of welfare work could be seen in the composition of the department. No labor leaders were invited to serve. By 1907, the department counted 250 members, all of them employers, plus a large permanent staff of experts. The Welfare Department was the only NCF department that excluded labor representatives.[12]

How did Mitchell respond to the creation and expansion of this department? Did he recognize the dangerous anti-union tendencies this movement signaled for the future of American industry? Did he object to the exclusion of labor leaders from the department? Mitchell was blind to the anti-union bias of the department and remained unwilling to criticize the NCF, which he believed was the only viable alternative to the NAM. Although he had little contact with the department in its early years, those few contacts he did have illustrate his tacit approval of its actions and his unconditional support of the NCF. In a 1906 article published in the *NCF Review*, Beeks reported on her first hand study of southern cotton mills and their employment of child labor. She concluded by calling for legislation to abolish the "evil of child labor," but she also applauded mill owners for "their remarkable, beneficent efforts" to educate these children and secure child labor laws.[13] The idea that mill owners should be praised for their beneficent views toward labor was so preposterous to unionists that S. M. Sexton, editor of the UMWA *Journal*, condemned both the article and Welfare Department in the pages of the journal.[14] Mitchell was aghast. He upbraided Sexton, telling him he considered the condemnation "an outrage." And in a personal apology to Beeks, he offered his "regret that an article of this kind . . . should appear in our own paper. I would be untrue to myself and remiss to my knowledge of the good work you have done," Mitchell concluded, "were I not to do whatever I can to correct this injury that has been done you."[15]

A second instance of Mitchell's cooperation with the Welfare Department involved a request Beeks made in late 1906. Much of her job comprised of travel and observation of working conditions. She was planning a trip to Illinois and asked Mitchell for letters of introduction to coal operators in that state to facilitate her investigation. Within days, Mitchell secured two letters from major Illinois operators and forwarded them to "dear Miss Beeks" with the observation that her tour of the mines was "an excellent idea."[16]

While the anti-union Welfare Department was growing by leaps and bounds in 1905 and 1906, Mitchell's Trade Agreement Department was already showing signs of decay. Even this development did not dilute Mitchell's enthusiasm for the NCF. Certainly by 1905, the NAM and the CIA were clearly winning the battle for the hearts and minds of employers. One sign of their success was a drop in total union membership for that year, the first decrease since 1897. Another sign was the loss of labor's weak foothold in mass-production industries. While labor remained strong in industries such as coal, where employers lacked sufficient unity or financial strength to remove it, employers nationwide were resisting Mitchell and the NCF's call to create trade agreements.

At the 1905 Trade Agreement conference, no employers representing major industries participated. Only small employers from printing, construction, and iron foundries bothered to attend. Nor did the participants focus on the major objective of the conference—the examination of means to extend trade agreements to other industries. Rather, they engaged themselves in heated squabbles with labor representatives for failure to prevent local strikes and unfair demands.[17] As one scholar has noted, by 1905 "the important manufacturers who were active in the NCF participated in the organization's safety and welfare work but not in its promotion of conciliation and trade agreements."[18]

As we have just seen, Mitchell fully participated in the rightward shift of the NCF. He abetted NCF president Belmont's crushing of unions at the Interborough, he endorsed and encouraged the expansion of the Welfare Department, and he stood by while the activities of his own Trade Agreement Department began to decline and the number of anti-union employers in the NCF multiplied. What had become of the man once touted as labor's hero and the champion of the working class? What possibly could have motivated Mitchell to sanction these blatantly anti-union thrusts?

While these are valid questions, perhaps a better question, one Mitchell must have asked himself, was "what are the alternatives?" Mitchell never believed the working class was capable of its own emancipation. He had always held that improvements in the lot of workers were primarily the result of policies pursued by enlightened employers. The role of workers was to stand united and remain peaceful and conservative, proving to those who controlled capital they were responsible citizens and therefore deserved economic justice. For Mitchell the NCF represented the most powerful and enlightened employers in America. He identified with them because he saw in them the only existing vehicle to advance worker interests. Now the sage policies of the NCF were under attack by the barbarian principles of the NAM, and to defend itself, the NCF had been forced to make certain compromises with the growing open shop tide in order to survive. In Mitchell's mind, however, the NCF still represented the most sagacious employers, those who held the future of the working class in their hands. Were he unwilling to support it now, were he unprepared to lend his unqualified support, the NCF would surely fail and industrial relations would be in the control of reactionaries bent on the destruction of all labor organization.

There are other factors to consider when analyzing Mitchell's continued commitment to an increasingly conservative NCF. One factor was certainly financial, an area of deep concern for the UMWA president. As we have seen, his involvement in the NCF was not without pecuniary rewards. Both he and Daniel Keefe continuously pressed Easley to keep the money coming. Another factor involved the respect and acceptance he was accorded by industrial magnates and political bigwigs associated with the NCF. To wine and dine with Andrew Carnegie, to form friendships with senators, to be accepted as an equal by some of the most powerful men in the nation meant a great deal to Mitchell. He respected these men above all others, and as we have seen, modified his dress, speech, and other habits to emulate them. The NCF provided the only forum in which Mitchell was treated as a bona fide member of the power elite. Yet another factor was the concrete economic experience of the UMWA. Mark Hanna had believed in the trade agreement, and through him the NCF had provided tangible assistance in Mitchell's efforts to extend the trade agreement to the anthracite fields. While not completely successful in this regard, the NCF had helped the UMWA grow dramatically between 1901 and 1903. In addition, the NCF had assisted him in squelching strike sentiment within the UMWA in 1902, when he believed a strike was not in the best interests of his union. The NCF had been useful in the past, and if it could weather the onslaught of the NAM, he had reason to believe it could be useful in the future. For all these reasons, Mitchell remained faithful to the NCF.

Although Mitchell's determination to stand by the NCF was perhaps understandable, it left him increasingly alienated from rank-and-file sentiment in his own union and in the nation as a whole. As he attempted to cling to the NCF lifeboat during the raging storm of anti-unionism, workers were developing their own solutions. One the most aggressive solutions emerged from the mining camps of the West and presented a clear cut challenge to the conservative union leadership of Mitchell himself. In June 1905 at Chicago radicals from across the nation attended the founding convention of the Industrial Workers of the World (IWW). The Western Federation of Miners provided the primary impetus behind the creation of the IWW, although Eugene Debs, Mother Jones and numerous leading socialists were also present. Denying any common interests between workers and employers, the "Wobblies," as they came to be known, called on workers to seize possession of the means of production. They scoffed at the class collaborationist AFL and declared their mission to be the overthrow of capitalism by means of economic action.[19]

Predictably, Mitchell was appalled by the rise of this radical outfit. His hostility was based on a fundamental difference in philosophy. Whereas Mitchell regarded the trade agreement as the basis of all positive union advances, the IWW rejected the concept of contracts, preferring to rely on the workers' ability to strike to enforce their demands. But Mitchell had another reason to fear the Wobblies. Because they had little respect for existing unions, they sought members from among organized as well as unorganized workers. The Wobblies made open attempts to attract support within the UMWA. Indeed, two UMWA locals—one from Red Lodge, Montana, and the other from Pittsburgh, Kansas—had affiliated with the IWW at its founding convention. It was the fate of the Illinois miners that concerned him most, however. Illinois was the largest district, and were the IWW to secure its support, the UMWA would be severely weakened and the IWW would have taken a major step toward success. At the February 1905 District 12 convention, delegates appointed a committee to observe the founding IWW convention. Although the complete membership of this committee is unknown, Adolph Germer, a leading Illinois socialist, was one member. A frightened Samuel Gompers wrote to Billy Ryan, secretary-treasurer of District 12, requesting he use his influence to prevent Illinois miners from attending. The Wobblies were already claiming "Illinois miners are with the movement," Gompers exclaimed, and if Illinois miners were present at the founding convention "still greater capital will be made of it, to the detriment of not only your State organization and the interests of the miners, but also the entire labor movement, and the interests of the working people of the country."[20]

Mitchell also wrote to Ryan soon after the Illinois miners' convention. Had he not been so busy, he would have been at the convention himself to block the action. He was disgusted by the decision and contended "nothing has happened since I have been officially connected with the organization that has caused me more sincere regret than this." While he realized there was little danger of the entire district "falling in line with the schemes" of the IWW, "the very fact that the Illinois convention has elected delegates, will give more encouragement to this movement than any one thing that could have occurred." The Wobblies could appeal to other workers "by pointing to the fact that the Illinois convention, representing over 50,000 miners, has elected delegates." The national press could then declare the IWW convention was successful and that a vast number of workers supported "industrial socialism." He feared any action which might sanction the IWW because he believed their "object is to disrupt the trade union movement as now organized." In conclusion, Mitchell told Ryan that if he had his way, the proposition to send delegates would be referred to local unions "with the information that a mistake has been made and the request that instructions to send delegates be revoked."[21]

Ryan responded that he felt "just as you do in regard to the whole business," but reminded Mitchell the Illinois delegates would have "neither voice nor vote." They were sent simply to observe the IWW convention and report back to the district. Ryan also had no doubt the report made would be an adverse one. Thus, he believed there was no need to refer the matter to the local unions and little harm in having Illinois delegates attend. As a safeguard, however, Ryan suggested Mitchell send to Chicago Tom Burke, a board member loyal to Mitchell, at the time of the IWW convention. Burke had a reputation as a skillful debater of socialists and other dissidents at conventions. Mitchell heeded Ryan's advice and Burke was sent to Chicago.[22]

Any fear that the Illinois miners might affiliate with the Wobblies failed to materialize, but Mitchell continued to regard to IWW with suspicion and hostility. In a passionate opening address to the 1906 UMWA convention, he condemned both the Wobblies and the NAM. Both were equally dangerous to the labor movement. "At the risk of giving offense and inviting controversy," he thundered, the UMWA needed to expose and attack its "open foes and professing friends." By open foes he meant the "Parry-Post aggregation of union wreckers," who threatened all labor organization. And by professing friends he meant the IWW and "its principal affiliated body, the Western Federation of Miners." While the leaders of these radical organizations "profess great solicitude for the welfare of the coal miners," they were every bit as threatening to organized labor as David Parry and his ilk. "These self-constituted advisers . . . justify their attacks on us by saying that we make trade agreements which so tie the hands of our members as to render us unable to strike at any time during the year when conditions would seem propitious." These radicals failed to recognize that if miners had no signed contracts and could strike at will, "the operators would have precisely the same right. They could lock us out whenever trade was dull and the ultimate consequence would be that we and our employers would be in continuous conflict." He reminded delegates the late nineteenth century had been a time of perpetual conflict between operators and miners and had resulted in poverty and misery for most miners. For half a century miners had struggled to create a trade agreement system to improve their lot. And now the IWW would have them abandon this system and return to the dark days of industrial warfare. "Surely, there is no honest, self-respecting man who would be so false to himself, so unfaithful to his craft as to commit one act which would bring back the conditions of life and labor that prevailed in former years."[23]

Mitchell's reasoning is instructive because it points out yet another reason he remained so committed to the NCF: opposition to working-class radicalism. The Wobblies and the Parryites, although fundamentally opposed in their ultimate aims, were both attempting to return to the years of chaos in industrial relations. In the 1880s and 1890s, before the heyday of trade agreements, employers and workers engaged in near constant warfare. From his own personal experience, Mitchell understood the working class had not fared well during these years. And he would not stand idly by while increasing numbers of employers and workers called for a resurgence of that warfare. Despite its recent conservative shift, the NCF stood as the only powerful agency opposing both the Parryites and the Wobblies. In Mitchell's eyes, the NCF remained the voice of reason.

The 1906 UMWA convention afforded Mitchell a chance to demonstrate his hostility to the WFM and the IWW. Radicals introduced a resolution urging that transfer cards issued by the WFM be accepted by the UMWA in lieu of initiation fees. Arguing on pragmatic grounds, the radicals contended that the frequency with which Western miners "change from camps within the jurisdiction of one organization to those within the jurisdiction of the other" made the acceptance of transfer cards necessary. But there were also ideological reasons for introducing the resolution. Radicals also argued that miners in both the UMWA and the WFM were like-minded and that only the conservative leadership of Mitchell forced the organizations down separate roads. Adolph Germer, the Illinois socialist, spoke eloquently in support of the resolution, declaring there was "no antagonism between the rank and file," only "between the officials" of the two organizations. He insisted the WFM leadership "expressed admiration for the membership" of the UMWA. The problem between the two unions, he implied, was Mitchell's kneejerk opposition to any form of radicalism.[24]

At this point, Mitchell rose angrily and interrupted the discussion. It was true, he began, that WFM leaders admired UMWA members. They admired them "so much that they are ready and trying to gobble them body and soul, boots and breeches." He then exploded into a tirade of denunciation for the dual unionist, radical WFM and, by implication, the IWW. He also expressed the anguish he felt in the face of jokes, insults, and personal attacks heaped upon him by the radicals, and the increasing difficulty of justifying his NCF membership:

> Let me say here publicly that I defy any miner, or any other person in this country, to cite one instance where I have made a personal attack upon the officers of the Western Federation of Miners. I assert that practically every issue of their journal contains malicious, malignant, untruthful and unmanly attacks on me. I ask delegate Germer if that is not true? Am I not maligned, are not my motives impugned? Is there one word more kind than "fakir" and "viper" and such terms applied to me? Am I not charged with associating with the enemies of labor and thereby being influenced through that association?[25]

As to the resolution at issue, Mitchell demanded its rejection. He stated that in 1904 he sent a UMWA committee to the WFM convention to arrange an agreement on transfer cards and respective jurisdictions. The WFM, however, refused to grant the UMWA jurisdiction over all coal miners. He also held the WFM guilty of scabbing during the recent Colorado strike. "Whenever the Western Federation of Miners is willing to meet us on a fair basis . . .

and when they stop sending their men to our striking mines to work," he barked, "it will be time enough to accept their cards."[26] His emotional plea carried the day, and the resolution was defeated overwhelmingly. Later during the same convention, however, Germer reopened the issue by reading aloud a letter from WFM secretary William D. Haywood, which described the charge of scabbing "a falsehood and a base calumny." And Eugene Debs praised Germer for his fortitude in battling Mitchell at the convention, calling his action a "fearless stand for the right."[27]

Mitchell certainly had no reason to believe soon after the UMWA convention he would have reason to support Haywood and the WFM. In February 1906, three major figures in the WFM—President Charles Moyer, Secretary Haywood, and former official George Pettibone—were arrested on charges of complicity in the murder of former Governor Frank Steunenberg of Idaho, resulting in one of the famous trials in American labor history. The WFM approached Clarence Darrow to defend the men. Darrow, in turn, contacted Mitchell and asked for advice. Although Darrow protested he would rather avoid the case "on account of the hard fight and serious odds," he believed the authorities were trying to "railroad these fellows" and saw no way to dodge his duty. He asked Mitchell in confidence to assess public sentiment in the case and also determine whether organized labor would contribute financially. As both he and Mitchell were well aware, public sympathy and lots of money were necessary components in any labor victory. Mitchell replied the WFM leaders would have a great deal of both. Although the WFM "has no standing in the American labor movement" and by its actions had alienated public sympathy, the prevailing public view was that the men were innocent. "My own judgment is that they are not guilty," he wrote, "and aside from any personal feeling that we have for them as labor leaders, we all feel that a good and sufficient defense should be secured for them." Mitchell was already collecting tens of thousands of dollars for their defense.[28] Thus, despite the ongoing war between Mitchell and the radicals within the house of labor, when the movement came under obvious attack from without, Mitchell at least in this instance was able to join forces with the IWW and other radicals. Although the accused men languished in jail for more than a year, they were eventually cleared of all charges.

While the IWW failed to attract a significant following among coal miners, it was in many ways an aggressive and positive response to the resurgence of anti-unionism after 1904. Within the AFL, the open shop offensive forced a response of a different kind: political action. Until this time official AFL policy was "voluntarism," and although the meaning of this word shifted over time, it meant the labor movement should rely almost exclusively on its economic rather than its political muscles. Among the manifestations of anti-unionism, however, were a growing number of adverse court decisions and a growing indifference to labor's demands by both major parties. In 1905 and 1906 pressure from the rank and file of union workers forced AFL leaders to reevaluate their political stance. The result was the famous document known as "labor's Bill of Grievances."

In early March 1906, Gompers held a meeting of the legislative committee of the AFL at which he addressed the problem of how to secure passage of labor's legislative demands from a hostile Republican Congress and Roosevelt Administration. He decided the best course of action was to hold a conference of all leading AFL officials, draw up a list of demands, and present those demands directly to Roosevelt and Congress. If the Republicans failed to adopt the suggested labor legislation, then the AFL "would hold the dominant party in Congress responsible."[29] Drafted by Gompers and Andrew Furuseth of the International Seamen's Union and adopted on March 21, 1906 by representatives of more than one hundred international unions and the AFL's Executive Council, the Bill of Grievances complained of government indifference toward the AFL's just and reasonable demands in the past. It enumerated most of the traditional legislative demands the labor movement had been voicing since the Civil War. It also called for the exemption of unions from the Sherman Act and relief from injunctions. That very day, AFL delegates presented the document to President Roosevelt, Senate President William Frye, and House Speaker Joseph G. Cannon.

March 21 was thus a banner day in the AFL's history. The Federation had certainly not abandoned either voluntarism or nonpartisanship, the belief that organized labor should not tie its fortunes to a particular party, but it had stepped up its political activity and had directly challenged the anti-union stance of the Republican party. Where was John Mitchell, second vice president of the AFL, on March 21? He was conveniently engaged in pressing UMWA business and was unable to attend the Washington conference of the AFL. He then instructed Gompers not to attach his name to the Bill of Grievances under the pretense that he had not seen the document.[30]

Why would Mitchell be reluctant to take this limited step toward political action? The answer lies in his conspicuously pro-administration and pro-Republican stance. His connection with the Republican party began during the 1900 anthracite strike when Republican leader Mark Hanna had used his influence on behalf of the UMWA. Upon Hanna's death, as we have seen, Mitchell cultivated the friendship of the Republican Roosevelt. Although his closeness to Roosevelt did not lead to a close working alliance, he dared not alienate that friendship by attaching his name to the Bill of Grievances, which represented an indictment of the Republican party. Indeed, he was at that very time attempting to secure Roosevelt's intervention in contract negotiations between the miners and operators.

When the Bill of Grievances received a cool hearing from Republican bigwigs, Gompers and the AFL prepared for an aggressive campaign in the fall of 1906 to defeat their enemies at the ballot box. The AFL established a Labor Representation Committee to coordinate its attack, and the committee identified Republican Congressman Charles E. Littlefield of Maine as their primary target. Not only was Littlefield "an implacable and conspicuous foe of labor legislation," according to Gompers, but since the Maine elections were being held on September 10, Littlefield's defeat would greatly increase the AFL's prestige among the existing parties prior to the general elections in November. Approximately fifteen AFL leaders traveled to Maine in mid-August to assist Gompers's anti-Littlefield campaign.[31]

The anti-Littlefield efforts did not proceed smoothly. Numerous Republican officials, including Speaker of the House Cannon, had also come to Maine and campaigned in support of Littlefield. Out of desperation, Gompers wrote Mitchell at the end of August begging his assistance. Littlefield "can and will be defeated," Gompers wrote. Cannon's presence, however, "will have considerable influence and everyone who has spoken to me upon the subject suggests that if you could and would come here and make two or three speeches, however brief, following Mr. Cannon, it would have the determining influence upon the campaign and Mr. Littlefield's defeat would be assured."[32] But Mitchell was not about to sabotage his relations with the Republican administration. He refused Gompers's request, again using the excuse that he was "overwhelmed with work."[33] Littlefield was reelected to Congress by the slim plurality of 1,362 votes, and as one historian has noted, "Mitchell's refusal to play an active part in the anti-Littlefield campaign certainly hurt the Federation's activities in Maine."[34]

Despite his unwillingness to participate in the AFL's 1906 political program, in many ways Mitchell was more progressive on the issue of labor and politics than Gompers and many other AFL leaders. To cite one example, he championed efforts to have union members elected to office. When a resolution at the 1906 UMWA convention called for a constitutional amendment that would force union officers to resign their posts after accepting nominations for political offices, he argued at length against the resolution. He believed union members should in fact be encouraged to run for political offices, for they could then use their positions to improve the welfare of workers. "If I were a member of Congress," he asked the delegates, "would I not have more influence there if I were president of your organization than I would if I were simply a private citizen?" In Britain, Mitchell continued, miners made certain their union leaders represented them in Parliament. The same should be true for miners and other workers in America.[35]

Mitchell also stood ready to spearhead legislative campaigns to improve working conditions. In 1906, for instance, he presented to the UMWA convention a model bill designed to improve safety in the mines. The bill called for the creation in each county of each state a miners' examining board. The board would grant "competency certificates" to any miner with two years' experience who could answer at least twelve questions in the English language. Once this bill was adopted by all the states, only those persons who obtained the competency certificate would be eligible for employment in the mines.[36] While operator resistance eventually crippled this legislative campaign, the campaign demonstrated Mitchell's determination to develop and push for positive legislation.

Throughout his presidency, UMWA lobbyists struggled in the state legislatures for passage of a wide variety of bills dealing with safety, child labor, hours of work, mediation services, and a host of other issues. And under his leadership UMWA officials actively sought political office, especially at the state level. 1906 was in fact one of the union's most active political years. Over thirty UMWA officials ran for political office in Ohio, Illinois, Kansas, Oklahoma, West Virginia, and Pennsylvania. The most impressive gains were made in Pennsylvania, where International Secretary-Treasurer William B. Wilson and District 1 President T. D. Nicholls were both elected to the U.S. Congress on the Democratic ticket.[37] In the fall of 1906, when Gertrude Beeks of the NCF wrote Mitchell requesting letters of introduction to district officials in the anthracite region, he informed her that most of the officials were so busy with their political campaigns they would probably have little time to talk with her.[38] As one scholar has observed, "In the United States, as in Europe, coal miners' unions were as strongly committed to political action and legislative reform as they were to collective bargaining."[39] And Mitchell himself was strongly committed to both. Unlike most AFL leaders and UMWA members, however, he believed political salvation lay in the hands of Roosevelt and the Republicans.

As he surveyed the national scene in 1906, Mitchell had reason for concern. With anti-unionism on the rise, with the growth of radical unionism, with AFL challenges to his beloved Republican party, he could not have been sanguine about the future. The one bright spot in this bleak picture was the state of the UMWA. In January 1906, the union topped the 300,000 mark of dues-paying members for the first time in its history. In the past year, nearly two hundred locals had been established, the treasury was strong, and the union had successfully checked unauthorized strikes. The price of both soft and hard coal had risen substantially since 1904, and he believed there was every reason to expect continued prosperity. And for the first time, all three major wage agreements—anthracite, the Central Competitive Field, and the southwestern field—expired on the same date. This gave Mitchell an incalculable edge. If negotiations stalled, he could threaten a general strike of all miners without having to break existing contracts. For all these reasons, Mitchell believed the union was in a powerful position to renegotiate its contracts. "I recognize the fact that there is little sentiment and no philanthropy in the determination of our general wage agreements," he told delegates to the 1906 convention. "However, it appears to me that inasmuch as we gave relief to our employers by accepting a lower wage rate at a time when there was little demand for coal and when prices were falling below a profitable margin, they should reciprocate now and voluntarily share with us their present and prospective prosperity."[40]

For every reason to be optimistic, however, there was a corresponding reason for Mitchell to dread the upcoming negotiations. First, there was his health to consider. Even if all went smoothly, the drawing up of three major contracts was a time-consuming, nerve wracking affair for any person at the best of times. And as negotiations began, Mitchell's health was already poor. In February, one journalist noted that he looked "haggard and worn" and that he had "great black rings under his eyes." He feared Mitchell might suffer a "recurrence of an attack of nervous prostration," which had put him in the hospital in 1900.[41] As early as January he complained of poor health and attributed it to the "pressure of work."[42] Second, he realized that rank-and-file expectations of a truly significant wage increase ran very high. If he failed to deliver, he would certainly feel the wrath of the miners. Third, he needed a union victory to silence his radical critics and overcome the reduction of 1904 and the Colorado strike fiasco. Fourth, at a time when trade agreements were in decline, he felt pressure to demonstrate the viability of collective bargaining, to prove that organized labor and capital could cooperate for mutual benefit. And fifth, he knew from his contacts among the operators they were prepared to contest union demands for a wage increase. Pressure mounted as negotiations began.

The joint conference with CCF operators began on January 25 in Indianapolis upon the conclusion of the UMWA convention. Convention delegates were instructed to remain in town until the joint conference had concluded. The wage scale committee had compiled a list of ten demands, including the admission of the southwestern states to the joint conference, a $12\frac{1}{2}$ percent increase in wages, and the eight-hour day where it did not already exist. The two leading spokespersons at the conference were Mitchell and Francis Robbins, the co-chairs of the NCF's Trade Agreement Department. Mitchell first made a plea for the inclusion of the southwestern districts, but the operators dismissed the suggestion out of hand. Mitchell then spoke on the prosperity of the industry and the prospect of high wages and increasing demand for the coming year. Such conditions, he argued, more than justified a $12\frac{1}{2}$ percent wage increase.[43]

Francis Robbins was not convinced. He pointed to the UMWA's inability to organize West Virginia, where only one in ten miners belonged to the union, and Kentucky and Tennessee, where at best 50 percent had joined. Non-union operators continued to capture markets by offering cheaper coal. In a familiar refrain, Robbins asked: "West Virginia shows an increase of five million tons of coal. What are you doing down there?" And before Mitchell could defend himself, Robbins supplied his own answer: "Practically nothing." He then declared his exasperation at "you people (who) come in here and talk about an advance of twelve and a half percent!"[44] One by one, each of the miners' demands were examined and rejected by the operators. Indeed, the operators believed the threat of non-union coal was grave enough to demand a reduction of wages rather than an increase.

By January 31, an impasse had been reached and operators requested a temporary adjournment in order to meet privately. Mitchell conceded to the request, but would not allow them to leave before introducing the threat of possible strike action. He declared that he would "not agree upon a settlement on any other basis except an advance in wages."[45] When negotiations resumed, operators offered to renew the present contract for another year. Enraged, Mitchell castigated operators for jeopardizing the joint conference by refusing to negotiate in good faith. He spoke of his own role in creating a viable trade agreement, but stressed that collective bargaining must be mutually advantageous in order to succeed. Unless operators were willing to make concessions when conditions justified them, the interstate movement was useless. Another year without a wage increase was not an acceptable concession. Again he played the trump card of strike action: "I want to emphasize this one point," he fumed, "if this is the end, if this is Utopia for the coal miners, then this movement means nothing for us." Robbins responded by asserting that operators were indeed concerned about keeping the interstate movement alive. Although present conditions justified a reduction, operators were willing to pay current wages in the interest of the movement. The impasse could not be broken, and both sides moved to adjourn once more. Before delegates left the hall, however, Mitchell mused on the significance of the failed conference. "We have been pictured by statesmen and philosophers as having the ideal arrangement for the adjustment of our trade relations." He, too, had considered it ideal, yet it "seems now that we have reached the limit and the parting of the way."[46]

Mitchell was no doubt dejected by the operators' stance, but he had certainly not abandoned the ideal of the trade agreement. His dramatics at the joint conference were part and parcel of the negotiating process. On February 1, the wage scale committee reported back to the convention delegates. After announcing the final proposal of the operators, Mitchell asked the men: "What is your pleasure?" Immediately, Billy Ryan, Mitchell's old friend and confidant, proposed a resolution. The "Ryan resolution," as it came to be called, stated that "no contract be signed in any district until we all get a settlement or go down in defeat together."[47] In all probability, Ryan had introduced the resolution at Mitchell's request, and it was adopted with near unanimity. The "Ryan resolution" symbolized the unity of UMWA members behind a possible strike. Only one delegate argued aggressively against the resolution. Patrick Dolan, Mitchell's old nemesis and still president of District 5, insisted the convention record he had voted against it.[48]

When the joint conference reconvened the next day, both sides voted on the operators' proposition to renew the contract for another year. One by one, the miners' delegates from Illinois, Indiana, and Ohio voted against the proposition. When the western Pennsylvania miners were asked to rise, Dolan voted in the affirmative and other delegates voted in the negative. Confusion ensued. Numerous miners denounced Dolan, and no one was certain how to record the vote. Mitchell then intervened and declared authoritatively that "the miners vote 'no.'" Francis Robbins retorted that the discussion was "entirely out of order. Mr. Mitchell had no right to cast his vote in that way unless he is the dictator of the mining interests of this country."[49] Amid this confusion the joint conference adjourned before resolving any of the major issues.

The conference had been a disaster. Unless Mitchell proved successful in last minute behind-the-scenes maneuvers, he faced a major strike in soft coal and the possible collapse of the interstate movement. Newspaper headlines were already screaming "Miners Declare for War."[50] Equally unnerving, the united front of the UMWA had been shattered by Dolan's machinations. Before he could salvage the bituminous agreement, Mitchell had to deal with Dolan once again. When delegates to the UMWA convention assembled the following day, Mitchell wondered aloud about Dolan's motivation for voting in favor of the operators' offer. Others were more interested in attacking Dolan. One delegate moved that Dolan be expelled from the union for "traitorous conduct," and another moved that the convention simply ask him to resign as president of District 5. Mitchell understood, however, that the national convention had no constitutional authority to remove a district officer. And while he was never a stickler on such niceties, he was not about to usurp district authority with a strike brewing and the national press watching. He first needed to determine why Dolan had sabotaged the unity of the miners. On his recommendation, the issue of Dolan's treason was referred to the District 5 convention.[51]

At the District 5 convention in Pittsburgh, Dolan proved a truly dangerous enemy. He cast numerous aspersions against Mitchell, all of them reprinted in the newspapers. Among other charges, Dolan stated that Mitchell had never conducted a successful bituminous strike. Nor should he be credited with the anthracite strike victory of 1900, which was won by Mark Hanna, or the anthracite strike victory of 1902. That was won by Theodore Roosevelt. According to Dolan, Mitchell was more concerned about his personal reputation than the welfare of the miners. He was conceited and out of touch with rank-and-file sentiment. Dolan completed the character assassination with the observation that it "takes something besides a Prince Albert coat and a carnation in the button hole to make a real labor leader."[52] Dolan then assailed Mitchell's actions at the recent joint conference with operators. When Mitchell argued for a wage increase based on rising coal prices, Dolan claimed, Robbins offered to open the companies' books if miners agreed to a contract based on the present coal price. Mitchell refused. From that point on operators controlled the negotiations. Mitchell's threats of a national strike were made out of desperation and had no impact on the operators' position.[53]

Dolan's motivation is an intriguing question, and the answer is not at all clear. While he had been a strident and resourceful opponent when Mitchell first became president, he had caused little trouble after 1901. Mitchell was not the only person puzzled. His friend James Duncan, president of the Granite Cutters and the AFL's first vice president, wrote Mitchell of his surprise. Duncan knew Dolan was "stubborn" and tended to "blurt out what comes first in his mind regardless of the after-effect," but he believed Dolan had rid himself of his anti-Mitchell views and had become "a strict administration man."[54] So, too, did Mitchell. Dolan's arguments in his own defense at the District 5 convention were unsatisfactory. He stated the scale offered by the operators was the best obtainable without a strike and that any strike would surely result in failure.[55]

Mitchell refused to get involved in a public debate with Dolan over his conduct at the recent conference or his own character. To the press he stated only that he "refused to be drawn into a newspaper controversy with Mr. Dolan or anyone else."[56] Privately, however, Mitchell had his own theory concerning Dolan's motivation, a theory he shared with his wife in a Valentine's Day letter. He presumed she had read in the newspapers of Dolan's "vicious attack" on his character. The attack, he believed, was the result of collusion between Dolan and certain western Pennsylvania operators to weaken the bargaining strength of the miners and undermine his leadership of the union. Exactly what consideration Dolan would receive Mitchell could not say, but he assumed it would be operator assistance in making him the next UMWA president. "It looks very much as though a conspiracy were formed between the operators of Pennsylvania and my enemies in the organization, for the purpose of destroying my usefulness and overthrowing my power." She could expect to read more hostile commentary in the press, but she should not believe anything she read, "as these men in their desperation may say anything calculated to do me injury." He assured his wife that she "need not be worried," that he could overcome this challenge. "I have no doubt of my ability to protect myself and to safeguard the interests of the miners in this emergency."[57]

Indeed, Mitchell already had taken steps to defend himself. No longer concerned about constitutional stipulations regarding district autonomy, he dispatched Vice President Tom L. Lewis to the district convention in Pittsburgh to make certain Dolan was ejected. By the time Lewis arrived, delegates had already moved, by a vote of ninety-six to six, to request the resignation of Dolan. Dolan, of course, refused to step down, claiming that only a district election could unseat him. Mitchell then ruled the district convention had "full power . . . to remove from office any official of the district."[58] Armed with this ruling, delegates voted to remove Dolan and all other district officers. On February 21 Mitchell himself arrived in Pittsburgh and placed three current national board members in charge of District 5 affairs until a district election was held. Dolan was finished. He refused to give up the union headquarters, forcing Mitchell's men to use a nearby hotel as their headquarters, but this maneuver only succeeded in making Dolan look foolish.[59]

Mitchell did not escape the Dolan affair unscathed, however. Much to his chagrin, the national press accepted many of Dolan's charges at face value. Numerous editorials in late February depicted Dolan as an admirable citizen. Believing that present conditions did not justify a wage increase, Dolan courageously attempted to sidetrack a strike movement that would cause a great deal of public hardship. Conversely, Mitchell was portrayed as an autocrat who squelched all criticism within his union through heavy handed tactics and a warlord who was pressing the union into combat against the operators whether or not coal prices merited an increase. Mitchell was blasted as a man who wanted industrial warfare, a man who felt his own prestige slipping and was willing to strike to save his own position, a man who would disrupt the nation's economy for selfish ends. More than one newspaper predicted he had so overreached himself that he would soon be dethroned as UMWA president.[60] At no other time in his career had he received a worse drubbing from the press.

These accusations placed Mitchell in an awkward position. On the one hand, he desperately needed to secure a significant wage increase to satisfy an expectant rank and file and recover whatever status he had lost after the 1904 retreat. On the other hand, if he was forced to threaten or actually lead a strike to obtain the wage increase, he would destroy his reputation as the conservative champion of labor peace, a reputation he cherished. He would also contribute ammunition to the forces on both the left and right who sought to undermine the trade agreement movement. Mitchell considered the situation serious but not desperate. He had more than a month before the existing contracts expired on April 1, he still had friends among the operators, the NCF, and even in the White House, and he was still adept at the game of behind-the-scenes negotiations.

Mitchell, in fact, already was deeply involved in secret talks with operators by the time the hostile editorials appeared. On February 18 in New York, he

met privately with Francis Robbins, chief spokesmen for the soft coal operators. Mitchell was certain Robbins had not been part of the Dolan conspiracy,
for Robbins was co-chair of the Trade Agreement Department, a strong supporter of the interstate movement, and a personal friend. The two men took a
drive in the country together to discuss the situation. The following day
Mitchell and Robbins met with two Illinois operators, also friends of
Mitchell's, Harry Taylor and Joseph Cavanaugh.[61] While these were secret
negotiations, on February 20, reporters spotted Robbins and Mitchell on a train
en route to Pittsburgh, and two days later they were seen returning to New York
together. When asked whether an effort was being made to prevent a strike,
Robbins replied that he had no authority to speak for the operators and Mitchell
could not settle for the miners. Only the joint conference could avert a strike,
and since the conference had adjourned without a commitment to meet again,
Robbins concluded that a strike would probably occur on April 1.[62]

Despite this public expression of pessimism, Mitchell and Robbins had in
fact come close to an agreement providing for an advances in wages. There
was only a stumbling block. The joint conference had ended sine die, meaning
without a day specified for a future meeting. Every previous conference had
ended with an official agreement to meet again on a specified date. While this
was a technicality, it was an important one because neither side could call for
a new conference without appearing weak. A way was needed to resume
negotiations without either side losing face. And Mitchell, ever resourceful,
again looked to his network of powerful friends to break this impasse. This
time he called upon the ultimate power broker, the president of the United
States. On the morning of February 22, he telephoned his friend President
Roosevelt. Writing Roosevelt that same day, Mitchell explained that a strike
would occur on April 1 unless the conference could be reconvened. He therefore asked Roosevelt's intervention. The "only way to relieve the situation
would be for you to write letters to each of us (Mr. Robbins, Mr. Taylor, and
myself) . . . advising us to have another meeting before a suspension of work
in the bituminous mines occurs." His postscript implored Roosevelt to keep
this request confidential because "we have so many interests involved which
we have to get into line" and "premature publicity might complicate matters.[63]

Mitchell's letter to Roosevelt reveals a great deal about his personal
power and his method of conducting union affairs. How many labor leaders
were in a position not only to telephone the President for favors, but to do so
more as an equal than a supplicant? The personal relationships with powerful
men he had developed over the years as the champion of conservative unionism gave him access to sources of authority denied most other labor leaders.
Indeed, Mitchell's labor philosophy stressed that the power elite and not the
rank and file would improve conditions for the working class. Thus, with a
strike looming, his first instinct was to contact Roosevelt and the operators to

achieve his ends rather than prepare the miners for industrial battle. And what better proof that he was adept at this approach than his ability to pick up the phone, dial the President, and ask him as a friend to intervene on his behalf?

Roosevelt was only too happy to comply. On February 24, the President forwarded two letters to Mitchell, one intended for public consumption at a future date, the other marked "confidential." In the first letter, Roosevelt stressed his "great concern" over the failure of the joint conference. Soft coal had "enjoyed a great industrial peace for many years, thanks to the joint trade agreement." A strike would be "a menace to the peace, the business interests, and the general welfare of the country," and he urged all parties concerned to "avert such a calamity." He also noted that since Mitchell and Robbins were co-chairs of the NCF's Trade Agreement Department, each had a special obligation to maintain peace, "an additional reason why each of you should join in making this further effort."[64] In his confidential letter, Roosevelt proved himself a willing participant in Mitchell's gambit. "Is the enclosed all right?," he asked of the first letter. Did it "fulfill the purposes you have in mind?" He gave Mitchell the chance to make any corrections he deemed necessary and asked only that he be advised of who would publish the letter and when.[65]

The scheme had been set in motion. Both Mitchell and Robbins understood that the key to success was secrecy. Open knowledge of this scheme would have robbed the UMWA of its sole leverage in negotiations, the threat of a strike. Operators would then feel no compulsion to grant a wage increase. In their public statements, therefore, Mitchell and Robbins continued to claim no progress had been made and that a major coal strike would in fact occur on April 1. On February 23, Robbins was quoted in the press declaring "I do not think there is any possibility of averting a strike." In the same article, Mitchell not only agreed with Robbins' prognosis but also kept alive rumors of a general mining strike of both hard and soft coal miners. When asked if the April 1 strike would involve the anthracite regions, Mitchell said: "You can draw your own conclusions."[66]

Mitchell and Robbins then called a meeting of leading UMWA officials and operators on February 26 in New York to discuss the situation. All was proceeding smoothly. Unfortunately, on the night prior to the meeting, Vice President Tom L. Lewis issued a press release assuring the nation there would be no soft coal strike on April 1. Robbins and Taylor, he explained, agreed to pay an advance in wages, and other operators would follow their lead.[67] Robbins desperately denied an agreement was near, but newspapers generally accepted Lewis's pronouncement. One journalist insightfully commented that Lewis may be "letting the cat out of the bag before the time agreed on," but he would not have issued his statement "if he were not intolerably sure of his facts."[68]

Why did Lewis break the secrecy before the miners and operators could be brought into line? It appeared as though Lewis was trying purposely to sabotage the deal being made, just as Dolan tried to subvert the joint conference. Mitchell was outraged. He believed that had secrecy been maintained for another ten days, "it would have been much better for all the parties concerned." But he did not believe that Lewis, like Dolan, was engaged in a conspiracy with operators opposed to the wage advance. Lewis, who had played no role in negotiations to this point, was simply trying to steal credit for successfully averting the strike. "Unfortunately Lewis got wind of what was being done and in order to give himself a little glory, he anticipated our movements by issuing a signed statement."[69] Nor did Mitchell believe Lewis's statement necessarily killed the scheme he had concocted with Robbins. He saw it as an inconvenience only that forced him to act earlier than he intended. On February 26, therefore, Mitchell released to the press Roosevelt's letter calling for the reestablishment of the joint conference.[70] On the same day, he ordered UMWA Secretary-Treasurer Wilson to issue a call for a special union convention to begin March 15.[71] Although the veil of secrecy had been lifted, Mitchell and Robbins continued to stress that unless the miners received an advance a soft coal strike would occur on April 1.

Events quickly proved Mitchell had grossly underestimated the impact of Lewis's statement. Now that miners understood Roosevelt's readiness to intervene and the operators' willingness to bargain, many of them raised their expectations and believed once again they could obtain their original demands. For example, district presidents in the southwest field, who had not been forced to accept a wage reduction in 1904, informed Mitchell that unless southwest miners received "the same relative advance" as miners in the Central Competitive Field, "there will be friction and possibly rebellion." Furthermore, these district heads believed the UMWA should now reassert its original demand that the southwest field be included in the CCF.[72] And now that operators understood Roosevelt's readiness to intervene and the miners' willingness to bargain, many of them, too, resolved to stand by their original demand that there be no wage increase. Concerned by numerous reports that operators in the Pittsburgh area were hostile to the proposed advance, Mitchell telegraphed Robbins on March 2, asking him to verify the stories. Robbins replied that not only were the reports true, but that numerous operators in Pennsylvania and Ohio "are doing a great deal of talking against settlement and would like to see a strike."[73]

These developments deeply troubled Mitchell. In a confidential letter to his friend Harry Taylor, he acknowledged his concern. Having received so many reports of operators hostile to any settlement "I became quite alarmed, fearing that after all our efforts, we might not succeed in getting all interests into line." He had hoped to give the impression that a wage advance "was being opposed by a large number of operators" so that when the settlement was reached, he could take credit for wresting the advance from unwilling operators. But he now found operator opposition so strong that he worried whether a satisfactory settlement could in fact be reached.[74]

Lewis's statement had certainly complicated negotiations, but there were other slips of the tongue that undermined Mitchell's scheme. On March 9, Francis Robbins detailed for journalists the manner in which Roosevelt became involved in negotiations. Robbins explained that Mitchell had approached Roosevelt and requested a letter calling for a resumption of the joint conference.[75] Whatever Robbins' intention, the effect of this statement was to further embolden recalcitrant operators. Since Mitchell had petitioned Roosevelt, operators opposed to any wage advance could now claim the union was too weak to strike and that Mitchell had been forced to seek outside support in an effort to maintain peace. "I see by this morning's papers that our friend Robbins has let the 'cat out of the bag,'" a disgusted Taylor wrote Mitchell. Even Illinois operators ready to accept a wage advance were now having second thoughts. Robbins' foolish comments "greatly complicates our situation."[76] Mitchell agreed. Yet, while disturbed, he still believed the scheme for peace had a chance: "I hope we may yet be able to overcome the many obstacles that have arisen."[77] Just as Mitchell had underestimated the ramifications of Lewis's statement, events would prove that he had misjudged the impact of Robbins' confession.

When the special UMWA convention opened on March 15, there were less than three weeks before contracts expired on April 1. In his opening address, Mitchell declared that despite recent complications he remained "hopeful, if not fully convinced" that operators would recognize the seriousness of the situation, grant an acceptable increase, and thereby "enable us to join them in the rehabilitation of our joint movement and the perpetuation of the practical business relationship under which we have worked with mutual advantage during the past eight years."[78] Rather than immediately prepare their strategy for the reconvening of the joint conference four days later, delegates spent most of their time debating whether Dolan should be allowed a seat.

Although Dolan had been removed from the District 5 presidency, he was still a member of the union in good standing. Numerous delegates rose to complain about his presence, challenging his credentials and demanding his expulsion from the union. On several occasions, however, Mitchell appealed to the convention not to remove Dolan, insisting such action would be a violation of the union's constitution. Only the district convention had the power to revoke Dolan's credentials as a delegate or expel him from the union. When John Walker, the Illinois socialist, queried whether it would be "a violation of the constitution for us to hang him," Mitchell cautioned him and other delegates to refrain from jokes that might be misinterpreted in the press.[79] In the end, Dolan was allowed to remain. A number of factors explain Mitchell's defense of Dolan. On the one hand, he hoped to placate rather than antagonize those miners who continued to support Dolan and Tom L. Lewis. Magnanimous treatment of Dolan was intended to dilute opposition from within. On the other hand, Mitchell no longer had reason to fear Dolan. On the opening day of the convention, the national executive board had met and rejected Dolan's appeal to overturn his removal from the district presidency.[80] Mitchell realized Dolan would never again be in a position to challenge his authority and thus he could afford to be generous.

While Roosevelt's intervention had succeeded in reopening the joint conference on March 19, the premature publicity given his letter made less likely the success of that conference. In his opening speech, Mitchell stated he had given the crisis considerable attention, and he remained convinced "beyond peradventure of doubt that the claims we made in this hall remained founded upon facts and justice, and that the industrial prosperity of our country justifies the coal miners in asking that they shall receive at least a fair share of the profits from great industrial activity."[81] He therefore reintroduced the demand for a $12\frac{1}{2}$ percent wage increase. He quickly found, however, that operators had not softened their opposition. Since the adjournment of the last joint conference, declared John H. Winder, a leading operator from Ohio, "nothing has developed in the trade to justify us in changing our position."[82] And so the joint conference dragged on for three days without result.

On the fourth day all seemed lost as miners and operators wasted their time debating secondary issues, prompting an infuriated Mitchell to ask for conferees to "stop quibbling."[83] That afternoon, a potential breakthrough occurred when Robbins openly declared he was willing to restore the 1904 wage cut, meaning he was offering a $5\frac{1}{2}$ percent increase, and willing to sign a new contract for two years. Mitchell quickly called for a vote on the proposal. Miners voted in favor of the offer, but operators from Ohio, Illinois, and Indiana voted against it.[84] On the ninth and last day, Robbins made an even more startling commitment. He stated that regardless of what other operators did, he was going to reopen his mines on April 1 and pay his miners a $5\frac{1}{2}$ percent increase. If operators elsewhere refused, they would surely face a long and costly strike. He trusted that miners would not strike his operations, however, since he was offering a wage scale to which they had agreed. When the conference adjourned, a few operators expressed their agreement with Robbins' position, but the majority of operators stated their determination to refuse any wage increase.[85]

The hostility of the majority of operators was demonstrated in an unusual way during the last day. For the first time in any joint conference, operators assailed Mitchell's character. In a discussion on coal company profits, miners pointed out that coal company profits were easily concealed because of their close relationship to railroads. As an illustration, Mitchell noted that one operator, Thomas Parker, was both president of the Madison Coal Company and purchasing agent for the Illinois Central Railroad. Inferring that some attack had been made on his character, Parker snorted: "Mr. Mitchell, you have seen the time, sir, when you were glad I was an officer in the railroad company." Now it was Mitchell's turn to take offense. He demanded an explanation. Parker charged that Mitchell had often received "free transportation" for himself and his family. Whether or not this specific charge was true cannot be determined, but as we have seen Mitchell often requested and received free train tickets from various railroads. Yet Mitchell rose and angrily defied Parker to offer proof. The chair then declared the matter trivial and irrelevant and asked to resume more important matters. Mitchell, however, would not let the issue drop. Parker's statement "reflects upon my personal integrity," Mitchell shouted. Even though on April 1 "we may be divided and engaged in a great industrial conflict, that does not justify you in leaving even one doubt in the minds of my people and the people of this country, that I ever did a dishonorable act." He contended he had watched the union grow from insignificance to its present position of power, he had established harmonious relations with the operators, and in all that time this was the first time "that any statement has been made that reflects upon my personal integrity." Billy Ryan then interrupted and accepted responsibility for the free tickets, claiming he had requested them without Mitchell's consent. After this admission, Mitchell forced Parker to apologize.[86] With Ryan's help, Mitchell had won this skirmish against the operators. He later expressed relief in a telegram to his wife that the personal attack had "done me no harm" and, in fact, his spirited self-defense had "increased my prestige."[87]

The larger issues, however, remained unresolved. Mitchell's scheme to establish peace through the involvement of President Roosevelt had failed. The joint conference was over without agreement on a new contract. All discussion with the operators was finished. When the special UMWA convention reassembled on March 30, delegates had only one question to consider: should the union accept Robbins' offer and endeavor to make separate settlements or should the "Ryan resolution" be enforced and a national strike initiated? Mitchell refused to answer reporters' queries on how the union would respond to Robbins' offer. Those same reporters, however, ascertained sentiment among UMWA convention delegates and found a strong desire to reject the offer and initiate a strike on April 1. Soft coal miners believed that contracts with individual operators or even entire districts should not be considered. Anything less than a contract covering all four districts would disrupt both the union and the interstate movement. In addition, the rank and file believed a strike might serve to organize the non-union miners of West Virginia.[88] If Mitchell still hoped to avoid a strike, he would have to work very hard to overcome this sentiment.

Meeting just two days before the April 1 deadline, the special UMWA convention buzzed with electric anticipation. All the chatter centered on the "Ryan resolution," union solidarity, and the need for a national suspension. From the first words of his opening address, however, Mitchell preached the wisdom of separate settlements with operators willing to grant the 1903 scale. He read aloud a telegram from operators claiming to represent 80 percent of all tonnage produced in the CCF to President Roosevelt dated March 29. These operators pleaded their inability to pay an increase and asked Roosevelt to establish a commission to study the industry and make binding recommendations.[89] In essence, Mitchell used this telegram to threaten miners that if they chose to strike, they might find themselves in the same situation as the anthracite miners, without clear recognition of the union.

Mitchell then demonstrated his ability to control the convention by giving the floor only to top level administration men certain to do his bidding. First, H. C. Perry, District 12 president, resolved that national and district officials be authorized "to make agreements with any and all parties" offering the 1903 scale.[90] Second, after several delegates complained that Perry's resolution could not be considered with the Ryan resolution still in effect, Billy Ryan himself rose to explain just what the Ryan resolution was all about. The resolution, he began, had already "done its work" by compelling many powerful operators to offer a wage increase. While at one time he had favored a national strike, he now believed separate settlements the proper course to pursue. He argued that a national strike would surely lead to disastrous arbitration proceedings: "I don't want your affairs to get into the hands of a commission that will not relieve any more of your complaints than our brothers in the anthracite field were relieved of." He then appealed to miner militancy by referring to districts settlements as "guerrilla warfare" and urging delegates to "go home and fight it out."[91]

Once his henchmen had prepared the way by raising the specter of arbitration, Mitchell was ready to address the delegates. Many of the men were still uncertain where their president stood on the issue of a strike, and he now hoped to set the record straight and make clear "what policy I believe would best conserve your interests." Stating his primary concern was the nation's coal miners and their organization, he had given the matter considerable thought and believed the best plan of action was "making settlements with the interests that are willing to comply with our demands." He knew "how popular it sometimes is to appeal to the sentiment and to the passion of men in favor of a general strike," but he also knew from experience "how different it is when their passions cool off and when their sentiment does not control their judgment."[92]

Mitchell offered only two reasons why delegates should side with him in support of separate settlements. First, a significant number of operators were willing to accept the miners' demands, including many who had voted against the miners in joint conference. Many operators had spoken to him personally and promised to sign contracts based on the 1903 scale, and he believed the intense competition in the coal industry would force many more to sign within a few days rather than face a protracted strike. In all, he believed that "one-half of the tonnage is ready to sign our scale."[93] Second, delegates should support their president simply because he deserved their respect. Indeed, he made the vote on the Perry resolution a vote of personal confidence. "Just as soon as I fail to have the confidence and the sincere respect of the miners, not only as to my personal integrity, but also as to my judgment as to what is best for them, then I ask you men to relieve me of my responsibility—let me go home, let me live as you live with your wives and your babies."[94]

Among the reasons against a national suspension Mitchell left unspoken was the financial condition of the union. On the surface, the union's finances looked good. There was some $400,000 in the national treasury and another $2.6 million in the various district and local treasuries. But there were hidden problems, most importantly the fact that money was not evenly distributed among the districts. Indeed, western Pennsylvania had just $14,000. If a strike lasted more than a month, the total resources at the union's command would not long provide benefits to more than 300,000 members. Another unspoken reason why Mitchell opposed a strike was his inability to count on widespread public sympathy. It would be difficult for him to claim operators had driven miners to initiate a national strike when by his own admission half the operators were willing to grant a wage increase. Once the strike began to impact the price of coal, he would have trouble explaining why separate settlements were not signed and why a strike was necessary to maintain labor solidarity.[95] A powerful argument Mitchell would later use against his detractors was his fear that the unorganized miners would not respond to the strike call. Their continued production would enable non-union operators to capture the markets of union operators, just as non-union operators in West Virginia had captured markets during the 1897 strike. As he stated at the 1907 UMWA national convention: "I do not believe that a national strike would have stopped any considerable number of men in any of the non-union fields of this country."[96]

There were other reasons, even more important than the paucity of funds, lack of public support, and non-union miners. One was Mitchell's desire to safeguard gains made by the union in years past. His statement to delegates that he hoped to "conserve" their interests revealed his bureaucratic mentality. As the head of a well established bureaucratic institution representing 300,000 members, his primary function was to preserve the institution entrusted to his care. Even though miners were prepared for battle, a national strike in the unfavorable climate of 1906 was an enormous gamble, one that might have led to the destruction of the union. Deathly afraid of making decisions that would damage the union, Mitchell chose to conserve through peace rather than expand through struggle. The militant spirit of the miners could be used as a threat during negotiations, but he no longer dared to unleash it.

The most salient reason for Mitchell's hostility to a national strike was his conviction that industrial strife in coal and the irreparable damage it would cause to the interstate movement would play into the hands of radicals on both the left and right who hoped to reintroduce open class warfare in America. Parryites and Wobblies both stood ready to applaud the failure of the joint conference in the CCF, the most celebrated trade agreement of the Progressive Era. Were it to fail, were the miners and operators unable to hash out their disagreements peacefully through reason rather than force, the agents of class warfare would stand triumphant. Mitchell's attempt to squelch rank-and-file strike sentiment in 1906, therefore, beautifully illustrated how his ideological commitment to the trade agreement served to undermine labor solidarity. The rank and file easily recognized the disruptive effects of separate settlements, but Mitchell remained more interested in keeping the interstate movement alive in the face of growing hostility to collective bargaining. By 1906, Mitchell's allegiance to the trade agreement left him increasingly divorced from the attitudes of union members.

Mitchell's appeal for separate settlements did not go unchallenged. Numerous delegates rose to point out the pitfalls of such an approach and contended that a national strike was the only viable option. No one spoke more eloquently on the subject of solidarity than Vice President Tom L. Lewis. The effect of signing separate agreements "means, to my mind, at least, demoralization," he began. "We have come together a united army, with solid phalanxes presented to the opposition, with arguments they could not meet, and now because some operators seek to pay the scale of 1903 we must disband this solidly organized, intelligent army and start out in a guerilla fashion to compel the operators of this country to give to us what we believe and what we have proven are our just rights as wage earners."[97]

An equally impassioned speech came from a young Ohio delegate, recently elected as president of District 6, William Green. Green was virtually unknown at this time, but by 1913 would become secretary-treasurer of the UMWA, and by 1924 he would succeed Gompers as AFL president. Green argued that far from destroying the interstate movement, a national strike might succeed in strengthening it by extending it to outlying districts. He also suggested that if 50 percent of the operators already favored a wage increase, a national strike would soon convince the other 50 percent to grant an increase. Nor did Green believe the public would be antagonistic to a national strike. The miners' cause was "just" and the public was "discriminating." Also, he reminded delegates that one reason for accepting a wage reduction in 1904 was to ensure the simultaneous expiration of all contracts in case a fight was necessary. A fight was now necessary, Green argued, and the only proper course was to stand united: "I think the old saying is applicable now, 'United we stand, divided we fall.'"[98]

When the debate on the Perry resolution ended, Mitchell called for order. He wanted to make certain all delegates had a chance to voice their opinions, declaring he had "violated every rule of proper parliamentary procedure to allow the delegates the fullest latitude" and that he was prepared to extend the discussion. No one rose to speak. Mitchell then ordered a vote be taken on separate settlements, and almost 90 percent of the 1,000 delegates voted in the affirmative.[99] Mitchell had snuffed the sentiment for a national strike. Only those miners employed by operators refusing to pay the 1903 scale were ordered to refrain from work beginning April 1. As they had in 1904, soft coal miners exhibited once again their faith in the conservative judgment of John Mitchell.

Mitchell of course was delighted by the outcome of the convention. To a friend, he expressed confidence that "within a short time the bituminous mines will be running under the scale demanded by the miners." Yet, he did not celebrate his victory. The long negotiating process and acrimonious debates had left him drained. "Physically and mentally, I am almost exhausted," he complained.[100] There was no time for recuperation, however, for Mitchell was still embroiled in equally tumultuous anthracite negotiations. 1906 was the year the anthracite coal commission's award expired.

Although Mitchell maintained the award of the anthracite coal strike commission in 1903 was a profound union victory, he quickly found the award was not nearly as satisfactory as a true trade agreement. Between 1903 and 1906, operators in no way had diluted their hostility to the UMWA. Discharging and blacklisting of union activists, unilateral changes in work rules, and a continued refusal to grant the check-off of union dues still characterized operator attitudes. When these and other charges were brought before the anthracite conciliation board, operators attempted to evade board decisions that went against them. Mitchell came to understand that while the award forced operators to sit with him at the conference table, he could not expect them to bargain in good faith.

Even worse, Mitchell soon discovered that unlike soft coal miners under the protection of the interstate movement, anthracite mine workers did not automatically remain in the union after the award was issued. The problem was the absence of the check-off. Without it, mine workers could come and go as they pleased, depending on what the union had done for them lately. By late 1904, union membership in anthracite had plummeted to 40,000.[101] Mitchell found this "apparent lack of interest" on the part of hard coal workers "a source of keen regret and disappointment." He was at a loss to explain this trend but was certain it was not due to "any failure on the part of the organization to protect and safeguard the welfare and the material advancement of the men employed there." While wages and conditions were still far from satisfactory, they had improved markedly since the union became active in the area.[102]

He began preparing for the expiration of the award very early. In the summer of 1905, he conducted an extensive tour of the anthracite region in order to bolster membership. "It is not reasonable to expect that the operators will recognize our union or enter into an agreement with it if the mine workers are only partially organized," he declared in a circular letter to the three hard coal districts. However, if all the men and boys were union members, "we would have a right to ask, to expect, and even to insist upon recognition." He hoped that prior to his tour, each union member would single out non-members or delinquent members, and personally call their attention to the importance of allying themselves with the UMWA.[103]

From early June until the end of September, with brief interruptions, he traveled from town to town, local to local in the anthracite districts. Into each town he rode with local priests and ministers, and his arrival was treated as a triumphal procession. As had happened during the 1902 strike, giant parades were held in his honor. While bystanders wore "Mitchell" buttons, participants carried placards reading "Mitchell Is Our Conquering Hero" and "Mitchell Is Our Hope." The parade invariably ended at the picnic grounds, where Mitchell and district officials delivered speeches. Huge crowds gathered and listened attentively while their champion spoke. When the speeches were over and the festivities concluding, Mitchell made a point of remaining a while longer so that anyone who wished to could shake the hand of their union president.[104]

In his addresses, Mitchell emphasized the need to overcome ethnic hatreds, pay union dues, and respect the authority of district officials. He sang the praises of those who had maintained their union status and chastised those who had left the flock. "I cannot understand the logic, I cannot understand the process of reasoning which impels men to leave the union and become non-unionists in times of victory," he bellowed. He held that he was not afraid of George Baer, nor was Baer afraid of him. "Do you know who I am afraid of: I am afraid of the men who don't belong to the union. If all men belonged to the union, Mr. Baer would be more afraid of me."[105]

By the end of June, he had delivered so many speeches his voice had become "exceedingly hoarse" and it was "painful for me to speak," but he kept going.[106] And the mine workers poured out to see him. At Plymouth on June 14, for instance, 10,000 people showed.[107] The highlight of the tour took place on August 10 in Wilkes-Barre, when Mitchell took center stage with President Roosevelt. Mitchell and Father J. J. Curran had worked hard to induce Roosevelt to attend.[108] While officially the event was a Catholic temperance meeting, Mitchell made sure the real focus was trade unionism. A throng estimated at 150,000 watched a parade featuring Mitchell and Roosevelt, and that evening the people were treated by speeches from both men. Mitchell gave a short history of the 1902 strike and flattered Roosevelt by crediting him with the strike's "happy termination." He then impressed upon the audience his belief that trade unionism was gaining acceptance among the public at large, and he quoted great historical figures who had upheld the principle of trade unionism, including Abraham Lincoln, Wendell Phillips, and William Gladstone. There was no need to continue quoting from the immortal dead, claimed Mitchell, for the honored guest was a man "whose name and deeds shall live as long as the Republic endures," a man "who has on innumerable occasions spoken in no uncertain terms in defense of the right of the workman to organize." And when he finally introduced Roosevelt, Mitchell bestowed upon him honorary membership in the UMWA.[109]

The anthracite tour was no doubt exhausting. Mitchell estimated that he talked to at least 225,000 people and shook hands with at least 25,000. He wanted time to recuperate.[110] But he also found the tour exhilarating. "At every place we visit the entire population of the town turns out," he informed his friend Billy Ryan, "and we are received more as a conquering hero than as an ordinary 'labor skate.'"[111] More importantly, he was pleased to see that, as intended, the tour was encouraging mine workers to return to the union. "The miners are joining the organization by the thousands," he gushed. By the beginning of November "we shall have practically a solid organization here."[112] Membership figures reveal that Mitchell was not exaggerating. By November anthracite membership stood at 80,000, a figure surpassing that on the eve of the 1902 strike.[113] As the membership of anthracite soared, so, too, did Mitchell's confidence. By the end of August, he was convinced that he could arrange a meeting with the railroad presidents and secure a signed contract by the spring of 1906.[114] Even when he learned operators had begun importing detectives as labor spies, he remained optimistic.[115]

In his efforts to secure formal recognition of the union in hard coal, Mitchell once again looked to the services of the NCF. By the fall of 1905, Ralph Easley was on the job, encouraging Frederick Underwood, president of the Erie Railroad, to come to terms with Mitchell. Easley reported that Underwood was impressed with the UMWA's record on upholding contracts, he already had signed contracts with the railroad brotherhoods, and he believed the UMWA also "belonged on that list." In addition, Underwood "thinks highly of Mr. Belmont," and since Belmont thought highly of Mitchell, Belmont might be able to play a useful role. As long as Mitchell could "keep your boys from putting out threats and 'ultimatums,'" Easley was certain he could arrange a conference between the railroad chiefs and the union that "will lead to a satisfactory settlement."[116]

Easley arranged a private dinner in New York on October 4 and invited Mitchell, Underwood, Francis Robbins, and President Mellen of the Ontario and Western Railroad. Mitchell jumped at the chance. He pleaded with Harry Taylor, whose opinions on anthracite he trusted, to meet him in New York the evening before the dinner in order to help him prepare.[117] While in New York, he stayed at the elegant Ashland House Hotel as usual, and along with the operators, went to see a Broadway play, George Bernard Shaw's "Man and Superman."[118] Although no specific agreements were made, this was the type of business dealing at which Mitchell excelled and he undoubtedly made a positive impression.

A special convention of the anthracite districts was slated for December 1905. Mitchell hoped that before this convention Easley and Belmont might be able to induce Underwood and the other railroad presidents to meet with him and arrange a settlement. Easley, however, was unable to comply. Belmont, who supposedly had such pull with the railroad presidents, "did not know that there was any trouble threatened or that any convention had been called." Even Easley realized how "strange this sounds." Easley had also talked with Underwood and learned that while there was "absolutely no bitterness in the minds of the operators" toward the UMWA, and while all of them "hoped a way would be found to avert any clash," they were not interested in "working out a plan" until after the tri-district convention. Easley counseled Mitchell to hold the convention, name a strong negotiating committee, then formally ask for a conference with the operators.[119]

Anticipating Easley's inability to arrange a conference, Mitchell had also enlisted Charles P. Neill, recently named U.S. Commissioner of Labor, to act on his behalf. Neill felt indebted to Mitchell because the UMWA president had helped secure his nomination. Dutifully, Neill met with the most powerful railroad president, George Baer. "There was an absence of bitterness in his attitude," Neill reported, "and I feel that the whole outlook is very encouraging." While Baer "will not consider the proposal of a contract," Neill believed he might be willing to meet formally with union representatives. Neill then offered Mitchell advice on the tri-district convention: all demands must be kept secret. If demands were made public, operators could contend they were unwilling to grant these demands and there would thus be no need for a joint conference. If demands were kept secret, however, operators could not take this stand.[120]

Mitchell acted on this advice and persuaded delegates to place all negotiations in the hands of a committee composed of himself and the executive boards of the three districts. He was now ready to open negotiations with the railroad presidents. "If they act at all diplomatically," he wrote Neill, "I feel quite sure that we can reach an agreement with them." But "if they hold aloof and refuse to do anything reasonable, there is danger that such action will lead to a rupture."[121] On December 20, Mitchell sent identical letters to all railroad presidents. He refrained from using the UMWA's letterhead so as not to antagonize them at the outset. And he asked them to join in a conference with anthracite representatives to determine conditions of employment effective after the expiration of the award.[122]

Within one week Mitchell received acknowledgements from all the railroad presidents. George Baer and William Truesdale, head of the Delaware, Lackawanna and Western Railroad, sent more informative responses. These two important operators declared their willingness to meet with representatives of the miners. They stressed, however, that they were speaking only for themselves and could not make commitments for other operators. Mitchell was nevertheless thrilled by this development. When Neill suggested that Easley and others in the NCF might apply pressure if other operators refused to meet with the UMWA, Mitchell suggested that in light of the positive responses from Baer and Truesdale, NCF leaders should not "take an active part in the affair at the present time. It is just possible that they may make some mistake that would throw everything overboard."[123]

After other operators consented to meet with the union, Baer and Mitchell agreed upon February 15 as the date for a conference. Mitchell had suggested that date, believing he could successfully conclude the CCF joint conference by then.[124] As we have seen, however, Mitchell remained mired in soft coal negotiations until the end of March. Thus, he was burdened with two sets of dangerous and wearisome contract talks simultaneously. Nevertheless, he entered anthracite negotiations with tremendous confidence. This confidence was bolstered by friendly sympathizers who assured him the railroad presidents were in no position to fight. Father Curran of Wilkes-Barre, a careful student of the industry, believed Mitchell was handling the situation deftly and suggested that "recognition of the union . . . will not be too hard to get." Operators were "just as haughty and hateful as ever," but they were "trembling" because of "upheavals in money circles." They would "concede a great deal rather than invite a public investigation of their business methods."[125] Clarence Darrow, who had kept abreast of anthracite since his participation in the Coal Strike Commission's hearings, also believed financial conditions favored the mine workers. The stock market was booming and therefore "the big fellows do not dare to have trouble." If Mitchell acted quickly in pressing his demands, the railroad presidents were in no position to refuse him.[126]

The long awaited joint conference with hard coal operators opened on February 15, 1906 in New York. Twenty-five operators squared off against thirty-four mine worker representatives. Mitchell's opening address expressed his hope that this first meeting "may mark the beginning of a better and more harmonious relationship." While relations in the past three years under the Coal Strike Commission had been "more satisfactory than any other period," there remained many sources of dissatisfaction. These problems could be removed if operators voluntarily entered into a trade agreement with the union. In no uncertain terms, he stated his desire to extend the joint conference to hard coal:

"We believe that it is possible to establish a condition of employment by agreement that will insure industrial peace in the anthracite coal fields." He then put forth the mine workers' specific demands, including recognition of the union, a wage increase, the eight-hour day, and reorganization of the Board of Conciliation to improve its efficiency in handling disputes.[127]

Once Mitchell had finished, Baer moved that each side create sub-committees of five or seven members to "formulate just what they desire and their reasons for it." He did not believe, nor did other operators, that a general discussion would be fruitful. Mitchell agreed. Sub-committees were standard procedure in the CCF joint conferences. In order to avoid controversy at a later date, Mitchell made clear to the operators that any agreement reached in joint conference would have to be ratified by the union membership. Baer seemed surprised that decisions reached at this level would represent only a "tentative arrangement" subject to convention approval. Mitchell then assured Baer that he had complete control of the rank and file. Convention approval "really amounts to nothing," adding "there will be no trouble." Once the two sub-committees were selected, the joint conference adjourned.[128]

This meeting with the railroad presidents marked a true milestone in anthracite. While Mitchell had sat down with hard coal operators at the bargaining table preceding the 1902 strike, operators had been forced to attend as a result of intense pressure applied through the NCF. This meeting represented the first voluntary bargaining session. Nothing concrete had been achieved, a clear statement of union recognition had by no means been made, and the two sides were far from establishing an annual joint conference to resolve grievances, but Mitchell was heartened by the operators' willingness to meet with the union. This bestowed upon the union a new level of legitimacy in hard coal. Until actual gains had been secured, however, mine workers themselves would not be satisfied.

Mitchell and his sub-committee forwarded their demands to Baer on February 27. When Baer complained they had not included reasons supporting their demands, Mitchell sent another letter on March 1.[129] On March 9 operators formally responded. They rejected every single demand. Concerning the central issue of union recognition and joint conferences, operators declared: "We stand unalterably for the open shop, and decline to make an agreement with the United Mine Workers of America." The UMWA, operators asserted, was "an organization controlled by a rival industry," meaning soft coal. Bituminous operators might offer wage increases to their miners and be able to "recoup themselves by an advance in price through a strike in the anthracite mines." The joint conference was dismissed as "an entirely new and untried arrangement." Not only the hard coal industry, but also the public welfare might be "seriously disturbed by these yearly contentions." Operators then made a counterproposal: renew the present award for three more years.[130]

Stunned by operator recalcitrance and saddled with pressing bituminous negotiations, Mitchell once again turned to the NCF for assistance. This time he called upon Seth Low rather than Easley. Low, recently mayor of New York, was fast becoming a prominent figure in the Federation, and Mitchell believed his powerful connections made him the only person capable of bringing sufficient force to bear on the railroad presidents. He informed Low that while bituminous talks were proceeding with great difficulty, the anthracite situation was "much more serious." He now had little hope that hard coal operators would make any concessions, "and it is almost certain that the anthracite miners will not renew the present wage agreement." If Low could somehow force operators to offer "any reasonable concessions, I believe I could induce our members to withdraw many of the demands." He then asked Low to arrange a personal meeting between himself and Baer. He had always found such informal talks much more productive than formal conferences, and if one could be arranged, "we might be able to 'iron out' some of the seemingly insurmountable obstacles." Low was happy to comply with this request but proved unable to set up the conference.[131] Baer's ability to repulse the NCF's efforts testified to the growing weakness of that organization.

On March 17, Mitchell penned a terse and strident reply to the operators. He informed Baer he was "keenly disappointed" the mine workers' demands were rejected and that arguments in favor of those demands "had received so little consideration." Since mine workers had upheld the letter and spirit of the award and had refrained from local strikes during the past three years, they deserved greater respect from operators. He then made a veiled threat: "We cannot, with any degree of contentment and satisfaction, continue to work under present conditions." Rather than break off negotiations, he suggested another meeting before April 1.[132] Baer replied that operators stood ready to meet mine worker representatives "at any time you may name," although he believed there was little to discuss. And as if to remind Mitchell that operators remained in control over their work force, Baer concluded with words reminiscent of those he had used during the 1902 strike: "The miners are contented. They have been fully employed. They have been paid large wages. They have saved money. All the conditions attending the workingman's prosperity are as favorable in the anthracite regions as it is possible to make them."[133]

Unfortunately, Mitchell was so involved with bituminous matters he was unable to arrange another conference with operators before the April 1 expiration of the award. In late March, he was presiding over the special UMWA convention and the question of a general soft coal strike. He did not write Baer until March 29, and then only to explain he could not attend a conference with the operators until April 3. Mitchell's delay was dangerous, for according to resolutions adopted at the December tri-district convention, unless an acceptable contract was in place, all work in anthracite would cease on April 1. He therefore had no choice but to order all mine workers, except the pump men necessary to preserve the mines, to "suspend work, on Monday morning, April 2nd, pending further instructions."[134] Newspapers reported the walk out was nearly complete the very first day.[135] Unless negotiations took a quick and dramatic turn, Mitchell was faced with his third major anthracite strike.

Mitchell and his sub-committee met with the railroad presidents on April 3 and April 5. Just as he had done at the outset of the 1902 strike, Mitchell proposed arbitration as a way to break the impasse. He suggested the present Board of Conciliation could serve as arbiters.[136] His proposal was an obvious ploy to win over public support in the struggle. And as the editor of the *Philadelphia North American* informed him, it was an effective gambit. Until now the public considered the operators' proposal of extending the existing agreement fair and reasonable, but with the proposal to arbitrate "the burden is plainly shifted and for the first time since the fight began your friends can defend your position without assuming to know anything of the real merits of the details of your demands."[137]

The railroad chiefs requested a recess to consider the arbitration proposal, but when the conference reassembled on April 10 they simply dismissed it as a "farce." They then issued their counterproposal: immediate resumption of work and the continuation of the present award, with only slight modification, for three years. Although Mitchell had asked for only a two-year agreement, operators believed maintaining the award until 1909 would "avoid introducing into purely business questions the political considerations of a presidential campaign." Mitchell told operators their "statement does not appeal to us favorably," but asked for an adjournment of two more days to give the counterproposal a full examination.[138]

When the conference reassembled on April 12, the mine worker representatives formally rejected the counterproposal. The conference had reached stalemate. Unless one side was willing to back down on important issues, the suspension would become another protracted strike. Mitchell was the first to back down. One by one he eliminated all of the mine workers' demands in a desperate effort to avoid another fight to the finish. The demand for union recognition was the first to go, then the demand for eight hours, then finally the reorganization of the Board of Conciliation. The only remaining demand was for a wage increase, and on April 26 he informed Baer that mine workers would agree to a renewal of the present award if wages were increased. He asked for an increase of 5 percent for the highest paid workers and 15 percent for the lowest paid workers. Operators rejected even this modest proposal, citing low profits.[139] What were Mitchell's options now? Involved in a strike he did not want, facing operators who, despite the claims of Darrow and Curran, seemed prepared to fight, Mitchell weighed the alternatives. He did not have long to ruminate, however, as he had arranged a special convention of the anthracite districts to begin on May 3 at Scranton.

Interestingly, in the days before the Scranton convention, Mitchell spent much of his spare time reading a novel. Upton Sinclair had sent him an auto-graphed copy of his new novel, *The Jungle*, a study of meat packers that con-tained a strong socialist message. Mitchell was "devoting my leisure moments to the perusal of the book,"[140] but if Sinclair hoped to convert Mitchell into a left-wing class warrior, he failed miserably. However angry he was at operator obstinacy, he never seriously entertained the possibility of an extended strike in hard coal. He had received information that operators desired a strike at this time and had stockpiles of coal that would last until the autumn. Railroad cor-porations were also gathering strikebreakers and bringing them to key mines in the region. His sources also told him many of the mine workers were opposed to a strike and were already hard pressed by the suspension. And finally, he learned that public sentiment would not tolerate a strike at this time.[141]

When the Scranton convention began, the seven hundred hard coal dele-gates were treated to a heavy dose of trade union conservatism. Although reporters described widespread strike sentiment among the delegates, most had come under instructions to vote in accordance with Mitchell's wishes.[142] Mitchell was therefore in a position to sit back, allow delegates to air their grievances, and thus give mine workers and the public the appearance of democratic action when in fact his decision would dictate the course followed. After several delegates rose to recommend turning the suspension into a strike, Mitchell called upon his staunch supporters to urge moderation and compromise. On the afternoon of the second day, Secretary-Treasurer William B. Wilson made a long speech. Although he claimed he was not necessarily opposed to a strike, he asked delegates "Can you win?" and answered in the negative.[143] Thereafter a motion was made to close the debate and refer the issue to the committee which had been negotiating with the railroad heads. The motion carried.[144] Mitchell now had complete control of the convention. When this committee met that afternoon in Scranton's Hotel Schadt, all mem-bers, reported the secretary, "stated that they were opposed to a strike at this time, each giving various reasons for opposing a strike."[145]

Armed with his negotiating committee's recommendation against strike action, Mitchell addressed the Scranton convention on May 5. He told them the best course was acceptance of the operators' offer to renew the award for three years. To strike now would mean defeat, he lamented, because the union did not have the same degree of public sympathy it had in 1902 and because the mine workers themselves were divided over the desirability of a strike: "If I were sure you could stand long enough to succeed, I would advise you to strike, to remain away from these mines until you secured greater consideration from your employers." He had received reports from every part of the region, however, that made him "fearful that our own people are not inclined to strike." And even though these men would probably respond to the strike call, "it would be a strike with which they would not be in sympathy." Any major strike under such conditions had little chance of success and would result in a severely weakened union. "We must retain what we have," he concluded, "rather than lose what we have gained in the last two strikes." When Mitchell sat down, delegates voted unanimously to accept a continuation of the present award.[146]

Mitchell and the negotiating team then traveled to New York, where he signed the agreement with the operators, and returned to Scranton to address delegates for the final time. He understood many were distraught because the negotiations, which had seemed so hopeful at the outset, had resulted in no gains whatsoever. He realized the readiness of so many to do battle with their employers for a third time in six years. To appease these men, he tried to convince them the union had achieved a victory of sorts in 1906. Had he not made his tour of the region in 1905 "there would have been a reduction in wages." The tour had also prevented railroad owners from increasing the hours of labor from nine to ten. He had not only prevented this action, he had secured a signed contract with the operators. True, the UMWA was not an official party to the contract, but it offered tacit recognition of the union because it was signed by union officers. "Your organization has done much for you," he concluded, and "it will do much for you in the future if you are true to yourselves and true to your union."[147]

Derailing strike sentiment in 1906 earned Mitchell the praise of journalists. The labor editor of the *Indianapolis News*, for instance, believed Mitchell had performed well under the circumstances. "The operators certainly had their guns cocked and primed and were waiting for that strike bird to put in its appearance," he wrote, and "I can't for the life of me see how Mr. Mitchell could have done other than he has done." If operators had been less prepared and had public sympathy been on the side of the mine workers, then more aggressive action would have been justified. Since those conditions did not exist, Mitchell deserved accolades for his "masterly retreat."[148] Nor did his opposition to a strike cost him the affection of the mine workers. At the close of the convention, delegates erupted in rounds of applause for their leader.[149]

Mitchell had emerged with his reputation intact and remained for many years something of a demigod in the hard coal region. "Mitchell Day" continued to be celebrated as a holiday, mine workers kept his picture on the wall along with those of their saints, songs about him could still be heard in the pubs, and for years men would tell their children tales about the day when John Mitchell came to town. Unlike John Siney, Mitchell never fell from grace in northeast Pennsylvania. Thus, it was a paradox that after May 1906 mine workers began leaving the union. Anthracite membership fell from approximately 80,000 to 30,000 between May and December.[150] Hard coal mine workers loved Mitchell because he was the first outsider to champion their cause, because he had fought alongside them in 1900 and 1902, and because he had taken the time to know them personally and understand their distress. There was an emotional bond between Mitchell and the men and boys of the region. There existed no such bond with the union, however. Without union recognition and the check-off, mine workers could view the UMWA pragmatically, joining when necessary and leaving when dues became an economic burden. The union had failed to increase their wages in 1906, and now there was no chance of an industry-wide strike at least until the expiration of the award in 1909. Thus, mine workers saw little point in remaining active in the union.

When Mitchell retired in 1908, anthracite membership had dwindled to 23,000. He continued to believe that apathy was the root cause. Operator hostility in the form of labor spies and the blacklist explained why miners refrained from joining the union in West Virginia and other soft coal regions where the UMWA was weak, Mitchell told delegates at the January 1908 convention. In hard coal, however, "the men are free to join or not to join the union without interference from the mine owners, and the actions of thousands of them in leaving it or in refusing to become members of it is due entirely to apathy and indifference, supplemented by a fallacious belief that it is necessary to establish a strong organization only on the eve of the expiration of their contract with the operators."[151]

Several years later, after Mitchell had severed all official connections with the union, the new UMWA president, John White, successfully negotiated a 5 percent wage increase in hard coal. Father Curran excitedly wrote Mitchell with the news that mine workers were once again joining the union in large numbers. Mitchell replied that hard coal had always been his greatest worry:

> During all the years I was president of the organization the principal source of pain to me was the failure of the anthracite men to protect themselves; I was constantly harassed by the thought that some failure on my part, some act of omission or of commission of which I was not conscious accounted in some measure for their lethargy. . . . I have often wondered if some man would not rise from their own ranks who would inspire them with hope and confidence, some man who had the wisdom to lead them wisely toward the goal of social and industrial justice.[152]

Mitchell had himself inspired hard coal men and had fought for his own version of industrial justice. But in 1906, when he could not even offer them a small wage increase, the ranks were quickly depleted.

On April 1, 1906, all soft coal miners without contracts guaranteeing a $5^{1}/_{2}$ percent increase struck. But the quick settlements Mitchell anticipated were not realized. Most operators in District 5 (western Pennsylvania) signed contracts within one week; most operators in District 11 (Indiana) and District 12 (Illinois) held out until the end of June; and in District 6 (Ohio), several powerful operators lasted until the end of August. Outside the CCF, the situation was even worse. While most Iowa operators signed by the end of April, operators in the southwest did not sign until July, and many operators in the central Pennsylvania district did not settle until October. Moreover, in Alabama, Tennessee, and the large Meyersdale district in central Pennsylvania, long strikes were lost and eventually called off by the union.[153]

Once the smoke cleared, the disaster of separate settlements became evident. Because each district had been allowed to bargain individually, the settlements were far from uniform. While most miners obtained the wage increase, a significant number either settled for less or were forced to agree to unfavorable contract provisions. In areas where strikes met with stiff operator resistance, Mitchell was quite willing to turn a blind eye to violations of the Perry resolution and allow miners to sign contracts which did not guarantee a $5^{1}/_{2}$ percent increase. In order to offset charges that he therefore sanctioned violations of instructions from a national convention, he had the union's executive board declare: "if miners decide by referendum not to accept the 1903 scale without any advance in the mining rate, they should be permitted to do so."[154] Most miners in the southwest fields returned to work before securing a $5^{1}/_{2}$ percent increase; in West Virginia union miners accepted an increase of less than 3 percent and were forced to give up the union shop; and while Illinois miners received the full increase, they reluctantly agreed to pay their own shot firers, a contract provision that cost them approximately half their wage increase.[155]

The true catastrophe of separate settlements was not the failure to gain wage increases for all miners but the damage done to the interstate movement. The future of the trade agreement in soft coal was now in jeopardy. When the 1906 contracts were about to expire in 1908, many CCF operators were unwilling to meet with UMWA officials in joint conference. Operators insisted on a continuation of the policy of separate settlements. In addition, district officials within the union also resisted a return to the interstate movement. Having assumed the role of negotiator, they were unwilling to transfer power back to the national. It was not until 1916 that the CCF was completely reestablished.[156] Ironically, while Mitchell had prevented class warfare in the coal fields in an effort to keep alive the most celebrated trade agreement in the nation, his policy of separate settlements might well have damaged the CCF more than a national strike could have.

A second catastrophic effect of separate settlements was the undermining of solidarity within the union. The solidarity of miners was the foundation of union strength. It had made the UMWA a powerful national movement. Separate settlements, however, drove a wedge between miners in the various districts. Miners in one district signed contracts and began working regardless of the impact such action had on strikes still in progress. Rather than maintaining a unified national movement, Mitchell had in fact placed miners in the various districts in competition with each other. He had abandoned the principle that miners were a national force and had to be dealt with on the national level. Quite understandably, miners themselves resented this policy and were quick to rebuke those responsible.

More than at any time during his presidency, Mitchell felt the wrath of a disgruntled rank and file. Ever since the wage cut of 1904, miners looked to 1906 with eager anticipation. With both hard and soft coal contracts expiring at the same time, miners fully expected to recoup their losses. They also understood that 1906 offered the perfect opportunity to extend the union into West Virginia and other unorganized and partially organized fields. Union miners recognized that non-union mines undersold union mines and thus served as daggers pointed at the heart of the union. Soft coal miners were prepared to initiate a national strike to secure their goals. Mitchell needed only to give the word. When he snuffed their militancy and failed to lead them in righteous conflict, miners openly criticized his leadership. He was certainly aware of the dissent and lamented that "so much unjust criticism has been made by those who disagree with the policies I have advocated."[157]

Dissent quickly gave rise to factionalism, as Vice President Tom L. Lewis tried to capitalize on the fiasco and mount yet another bid to unseat him. Mitchell knew full well that Lewis was traveling throughout the mining districts condemning the separate settlement policy.[158] Lewis also penned a letter for publication in the union *Journal* in an effort to reach a wider audience. Samuel Sexton, the *Journal* editor, immediately turned it over to Mitchell, who made certain the letter was not published.[159] But the letter does indicate the anti-Mitchell sentiment Lewis was spreading among the rank and file. Had miners remained united, Lewis wrote, they could have secured a significant wage increase. The policy of separate settlements had destroyed that unity: "I cannot and will not shut my eyes and silence my tongue in regard to the haphazard settlements that have been and are being made."[160] Obviously, Lewis was preparing for an open confrontation with Mitchell at the next national convention.

The demoralizing impact of both the hard and soft coal settlements could be seen at the January 1907 UMWA national convention. Rather than the usual 1,200 delegates, only 580 attended. Average paid-up membership in the union had dropped to 228,421. The bulk of Mitchell's opening address was thus an attempt to present the past year in the best light possible. "Taking a retrospective view of the whole struggle in the anthracite and bituminous fields from its inception to its close," he said, "I am constrained to the belief that, all things considered, the wisest policy was pursued and the best results obtained that could be secured under the circumstances." He recognized there were "many disappointments" and that many members were unhappy, but he believed the best interests of the institution had been "preserved and promoted." He concluded with a plea for unity and optimism: "We can well forget our vexations, congratulate ourselves upon our successes, join in a renewed effort to regain our comparatively small losses, and struggle on with untiring zeal for a larger and still larger share of the wealth that we produce."[161]

When Mitchell sat down, he braced himself for the report of the vice president and the attack he knew was coming. And Lewis did not disappoint him. His report was a vicious denunciation of Mitchell's policies. Although Lewis was inspired by personal motives, his report was not a character assassination, just a cold, hard examination of the facts from the perspective of a militant unionist committed to the expansion of the organization. Noting the "wide spread feeling of discontent" that now prevailed in the union and the "tremendous" membership loss of the past year, Lewis declared "the time has come when opinions should be expressed frankly." April 1, 1906, was to be a banner day in the history of the UMWA. Miners expected union recognition in hard coal, the complete organization of West Virginia and other problem areas, and significant wage advances. Nor did miners expect to achieve these goals without a fight. But "as a result of our policy last year," none of these goals were attained. Then Lewis took direct aim at the lunacy of separate settlements. "Sectional settlements cannot and will not permanently improve the condition of the mine workers," he fumed. "Sectional settlements would not maintain our wages or bring the unorganized up to our standard." Mitchell apparently had forgotten that the union was a national movement addressing national issues. "If States or districts are allowed and directed to legislate for themselves on questions of a National character, then there is no need for a National organization of miners."[162]

Lewis's report and that of Mitchell were then sent to the Committee on Officers' Reports. This was standard procedure. Usually the committee had an easy task of adjusting minor discrepancies in the reports. This time, however, the committee was faced with two contradictory views of the same set of events. Because the committee was packed with administration men, there was no fear that Mitchell would be repudiated. "We believe that the very best possible results have been attained under the circumstances," the committee ruled, and we "congratulate our organization upon the fact that it has emerged from the conflict with honor and that our organization has been preserved intact."[163]

The war of words was far from over. Until late the next day delegates battled each other over whether the proper policies had been pursued. The lengthy and often heated debate itself illustrated the lack of harmony within the union. Lewis and President William Green of the Ohio district led the assault against Mitchell. Green declared his disgust with separate settlements and his conviction that a national strike "would have prevented the dissolution of the interstate movement."[164] Secretary-Treasurer William B. Wilson and John Walker of Illinois led the pro-administration forces. The debate became so acrimonious, however, that Mitchell was forced to enter the fray in his own defense. In one of the most revealing convention speeches of his career, he discussed the tribulations of the union decision-making process. Departing from the roseate assessment of his opening address, Mitchell told delegates he was "not going to stand up here and make myself ridiculous by saying that we got all that was demanded by the Perry resolution. We did not get it. We were far from getting it."[165] He then reviewed all his reasons for opposing the strike during the spring, claiming that he had made the proper decision:

> I was not willing last year and if I had to do it again I would not be willing now to jeopardize all we have gained as a result of years of struggle and hardships and sacrifice for a matter of five and three cents a ton as long as I had a reasonable expectation that we could secure these same ends by the pursuit of a different policy.[166]

Even though he was unwilling to take the risks necessary to advance the union, maintain wage scales, and organize the unorganized, Mitchell insisted he was not a conservative labor leader. In his own way, he was fighting for the rights of the miners:

> They say that I am conservative. Some of my friends and some of those who are not my friends say that Mitchell is too conservative. I am not conservative, I am impatient and restless for advancement. There is not a man in this country who spends more sleepless nights, worrying and fretting because we do not go forward with more rapidity. I am not conservative in my expectations, or in what I want for our people. It is true I am temperate in my statements; it is true that I do not believe that the interests of the workingman are to be advanced are to be promoted by my standing up and calling every employer an exploiter and a robber and a thief. I am trying as best I can to promote a feeling of friendly business relations between the employers and ourselves; but my desire and my efforts to promote friendly reciprocal business relations does not detract one iota from my impatient desire to see the mine workers of this country among the best paid, the most humanely employed, of all the workers of this land.[167]

In the end Mitchell won the battle. His report was adopted. But ugly feelings continued to fester. He did not seem to recognize that it had been his policy of separate settlements, an effort to maintain "friendly business relations" with the operators, that had set miner against miner and broken the unity within the UMWA. Nor did he recognize that his unwillingness to "jeopardize all we have gained" had led to the collapse of the interstate movement.

1906 was a disastrous year for Mitchell and the union. The high expectations for recognition of the union in hard coal and wage increases in soft coal had been dashed. Membership losses in anthracite, the undermining of the CCF, a disgruntled rank and file, and a new surge by Lewis for control were the realities facing Mitchell by year's end. Yet, the story could have been different. Miners had been prepared for a national walk out to achieve their aims. They had expected Mitchell to fulfill his promise of 1904 to make this a year of victory. And they were sorely disappointed to find their leader once again instructing them to temper their militancy. By 1906, Mitchell the warrior was dead. Mitchell the bureaucrat, however, was alive and well. There was too little money in the treasury, too little public sympathy, too many gains to be risked, he told them. Conservation and patience and restraint were now his keys to victory. Unfortunately, this approach was slowly sapping the union of enthusiasm, solidarity, and membership. He was still the undisputed leader of the nation's miners, but he no longer shared their fighting spirit.

Mitchell understood the difficult tasks awaiting him in 1907. He needed to recreate unity within the UMWA. His growing number of detractors needed to be silenced. Faith had to be restored in his leadership abilities. The interstate movement needed to be revived. Each one of these jobs would tax his energies. Each one required a sophisticated exercise of both subtlety and power. Already weary from the lost campaigns of 1906, he approached the new year without enthusiasm.

Chapter 9
Years of Personal Crisis, 1907–1908

In 1907, all the strains inherent in Mitchell's public life began to cripple his private world. His commitment to labor peace at a time when class war was gaining momentum, his loyalty to the NCF when the influence of that body was in descent, his adherence to the trade agreement as the solution for industrial relations when national collective bargaining was on the wane—all made his public posture increasingly difficult. The perceived need to continuously squelch rank-and-file militancy and the endless attempts to establish friendly relations with hostile employers had proven over the years an emotionally as well as physically draining experience. The constant intrusion of the press, the day-to-day grind of speeches and conventions, the tension of behind-the-scenes negotiations, the ever-present fear that one wrong word uttered or one bad decision made might impact negatively hundreds of thousands of men and their dependents charged to his care—all took their toll on his psyche.

He sought escape through alcohol. He was plagued by insomnia and nagging physical ailments. In a desperate effort to find inner peace, he converted to Catholicism. He tried to forget his problems by focusing on stock market speculation, juggling his investments in a frenzy of compulsive activity. By the middle of the year, Mitchell had descended into a nightmarish world of alcoholism, illness, and loneliness. This assortment of woes would rattle the sanity of any person. Yet Mitchell was especially ill-equipped to face his personal challenges. A man without close family ties, without intimate friendships, a solitary man whose entire adult life had been the labor movement, Mitchell lacked the emotional resources to sustain him through his crises.

In the midst of his inner turmoil he made a fateful decision. If the root cause of his maladies was the pressure of the UMWA presidency, the first step on the road to recovery was resignation. Mitchell announced his intention to retire in October 1907 and finally stepped down on April 1, 1908. His health slowly returned and his shattered personal life was soon on the mend. Still a relatively young man with expensive tastes and a large family to support, he could not simply retire to Spring Valley. After weighing several job offers, he accepted a full-time position in New York with the National Civic Federation. The NCF position, so he believed, offered an opportunity to continue the fight for labor peace and industrial harmony based on the trade agreement. Although personal problems had forced his retirement from the UMWA, he had not abandoned his ideals. Unfortunately for Mitchell, he would quickly come to learn that few others in organized labor still shared those ideals.

Mitchell's personal woes certainly did not begin in 1907, nor did every difficulty spring from the tensions of his office. Two major setbacks occurred in 1905, for instance, and neither were related to union work. As he prepared to embark on his anthracite tour that spring, tragedy struck and delayed his departure. At 5:00 A.M. on May 17, his six-year-old daughter, Marie, died of pneumonia. Although he rarely had opportunities to visit Spring Valley during her short lifetime, he had grown especially fond of this girl and had nicknamed her "sweetheart." He was intensely saddened by what he described as the "very great loss" of a "sweet child." Harry Taylor, his operator friend, realizing Mitchell's attachment to the girl, sent "a pillow of flowers" reading "sweetheart" to the funeral. Mitchell spent ten days at home grieving.[1] Soon after this blow, he was struck with financial pain. In July, he lost $2,060 when the Spring Valley National Bank failed. The bank was run by another operator friend, Charles Devlin, whom he respected for his "personal honesty and business capacity." Thus, when he learned the bank was in financial straits, he did not remove his money and advised his friends not to remove theirs. The collapse came as something of a shock and eliminated "practically all my savings."[2] Although he was earning $3,000 per year in official salary and had numerous other investments at this time, the loss of such a large sum certainly wounded a man so money-oriented as Mitchell.

By the fall of 1905, with anthracite negotiations already underway and bituminous talks soon to begin, Mitchell began to complain on a regular basis of overwork, fatigue, and loneliness. The life of labor officials during the Progressive Era was taxing. As unions centralized and expanded, more and more work fell on the shoulders of union presidents. And as unions achieved greater social acceptance, their leaders gained a measure of prominence, a development that placed even more demands on their time. They were invited to lecture at educational institutions and a wide array of middle-class clubs; they were expected to take part in private and governmental committees; they were hounded by the press for their opinions.[3]

As the most prominent labor leader and head of the nation's largest union, Mitchell fully appreciated Gompers's observation that "the cause of labor is no easy mistress to serve."[4] Few men had more demands on their time than he. Most of his days were spent away from UMWA headquarters in Indianapolis. Traveling by train from town to town and staying in fine hotels was certainly far superior to his experience as an organizer in the 1890s, when he walked through the woods and often slept outside. He now ate well and slept well. And he knew his family was financially secure. But his relative ease and peace of mind did not compensate for the grueling pressure of public lectures, newspaper interviews, local union meetings, bargaining sessions, NCF functions, conferences with political leaders, and conventions. Even his days spent at headquarters were taxing. Each piece of correspondence had to be read and answered. Local developments had to be studied. A parade of visitors, from national officers and local delegations of miners to area businessmen and reporters, filed through the Stevenson Building each day. Mitchell tried to greet each one personally. Annual contracts required months of careful preparation. He usually ate lunch with other Indianapolis labor leaders at a nearby hotel restaurant. Even then he combined work with relaxation, discussing complex AFL affairs—jurisdictional disputes, boycotts, legislation—on which he was expected to vote. Often he did not retire until late at night.

His letters to his wife Kate revealed the physical and mental toll this life had taken after seven years. So harried was he that even these missives were dictated to his secretary. And so infrequently did he see his wife and family that these letters lacked much of the spontaneous intimacy one would expect between marriage partners. Perhaps sensing that time and distance was damaging their relationship, in mid-November 1905 Mitchell began to complain that he was "lonesome." He missed her and the children but was so "overwhelmed with work" he did not expect to be see them before Christmas.[5] By the beginning of December, however, an unforeseen development forced him home to Spring Valley. Returning to Indianapolis by train from Pittsburgh, where he had attended the annual AFL convention, he suffered a physical collapse. Under doctor's orders, he went home to recuperate. His friend Harry Taylor was not surprised by the collapse: "I knew the amount of work he has been doing and the strain he has been under would cause him to break down." But the nature of his job afforded him little chance to rest. As soon as he arrived home his secretary, Elizabeth Morris, wrote his wife to ask if he was able "to receive reports as to the work here." Mitchell returned to work after just two days. He was "still very weak" but decided to return to Indianapolis because he had "an immense amount of work to do."[6]

Between his return on December 4 and Christmas, Mitchell attended an NCF meeting in New York, made a speech in Dayton before the Structural Building Trades Alliance, presided over the tri-district anthracite convention in Shamokin, returned to New York for two days to discuss anthracite negotiations with NCF leaders, then returned to Indianapolis to clean up all outstanding union business so that he could travel home on December 23 to spend Christmas. On December 26, he returned to headquarters and began work the next day.[7] He then began the monumental chore of preparing for the January 16 opening of the UMWA national convention and the joint conferences with operators which followed. By January 6 he was again complaining of the impact of his workload on his health. "Owing to illness and the pressure of work," he told Gompers, "I have not even begun my annual report." He would be consumed with work until at least mid-February, he wrote, and much longer than that if the joint conferences were not successful.[8] The grueling workload and its effect on his health became a matter of public concern by the end of February. "John Mitchell Breaking Down," ran a headline in a Pittsburgh newspaper. "The miners' president is haggard and worn. Great black rings are under his eyes, and he is silent and seemingly more gloomy than ever."[9]

The first six months of 1906 was undoubtedly the most hectic and pressured period of his presidency. With all major union contracts expiring on April 1, he certainly had his hands full. It is significant that during these months correspondence between himself and his family increased and that the letters revealed a warmth and tenderness lacking for several years. Mitchell began to articulate a sense of loss and separation, a desire to reestablish close family ties. And his family reciprocated. Kate Mitchell was a good mother. Left alone to care for her brood, she nevertheless instilled in her children the solid moral values of the Catholic Church. She also instilled in them a sense of love and respect for their absent father. The Mitchell boys, Robert, James, and Richard, began writing him more often in 1906, expressing their love, asking for fatherly advice, and seeking his approval. For instance, when Richard wrote in January, he asked permission to join a local club for boys. "I think there will be no bad language used," he offered. He promised that "you will be better pleased this time" with his report card, and he concluded with his own view of the upcoming miners' convention: "We are longing to have you come home. We hope you do not get elected as you will be with us all the time." Mitchell's responses to such letters became increasingly affectionate. He expressed his love for "Mama, baby, Maggie, you, Jim and Rob."[10] He also expressed his love for his sons by taking the time to send gifts, something he had not been inclined to do before this. In November 1905, he had a kitten delivered, in February 1906 he surprised them with a subscription to *Scientific American*, and before the Fourth of July he posted a large box of fireworks.[11]

As the work intensified, so did Mitchell's longing for his family. At the end of February he was in New York conducting critical anthracite negotiations directly with the railroad presidents. When the talks started to sour, he telephoned his wife and invited her to join him. Never before had Kate stayed with her husband in New York. In a follow up letter, he suggested she should bring along their baby daughter, Catherine.[12] While Mitchell's days were consumed with work, Kate spent her time sightseeing and shopping, and the couple enjoyed several evenings together at the luxurious Ashland Hotel.[13] After Kate returned to Spring Valley, Mitchell once again felt the pangs of loneliness. He wrote to tell her he would soon be in Chicago and that she and the children could visit him there. "I cannot tell you how anxious I am to be home and to visit for a few days," he lamented, "so that I might enjoy the pleasure of seeing Catherine do her little stunts."[14] Pressing business forced the cancellation of the Chicago trip, and Mitchell again found himself "overwhelmed with work and worry."[15]

Job pressure, illness, and loneliness were not the only problems Mitchell faced in the first half of 1906. His consumption of alcohol also increased dramatically at this time. Mitchell had been a heavy drinker since at least the time of the 1902 strike, and probably all his adult life, but until 1906 there is no evidence that alcohol ever affected the performance of his duties as union chief. Along with so many of the other union officials in Indianapolis, he enjoyed smoking cigars, playing cards, and imbibing. He appreciated being considered "one of the boys." And as we have seen, he also liked to drink with his operator friends on little getaways to Chicago. None of his friends or associates ever chastised or lectured him about alcohol, however, before 1906. Perhaps the enormity of his tasks in early 1906 led to problematic consumption. Or perhaps he drank to escape from loneliness, or to overcome the insomnia with which he was often cursed, or to relieve his bouts of "nervous prostration." Another possible explanation is genetic. His full brother Robert was an alcoholic who had difficulty holding down jobs. When Robert asked Mitchell to secure work for him, Mitchell declined, saying he would be "embarrassed" if he got Robert a job and he could not continue "fighting booze."[16] Whatever the particular reason, his drinking in 1906 began to attract notice.

The only instance of intoxication affecting duty in 1906 occurred in late March during the special bituminous joint conference in Indianapolis. While Mitchell was drinking heavily and playing poker with operators, the spokesman for the operators secretly wired President Roosevelt and requested arbitration. A newspaper reporter, friendly to the union, had to rouse Mitchell from his stupor and apprise him of the situation. Once sober, he was able to block the operators' move, but the event revealed that operators were willing and able to exploit his drinking habits.[17] At the end of April, Mitchell was spotted in an Illinois bar drinking from late morning till evening for two straight days. His friend Billy Ryan suggested, half in jest, that if he wanted to continue such activity, he would have to "quit wearing Prince Albert coats and red carnations, and let your whiskers grow."[18] By the end of the year, his drinking was no longer a laughing matter. Friends now encouraged him to stop. One acquaintance told him the story of President Grant's successful struggle against alcoholism. Grant's "great, quiet nature responded in all its manhood and he won his greatest battle, he conquered himself." Mitchell, too, needed to abstain. He, too, was a leader of men. "Your future is wrapt up in the future of this cause so dear to you and millions of others, and we pray that you may respond to this faith of a people and win your greatest victory."[19] Despite this advice, Mitchell continued to drink.

By June 1906, the anthracite negotiations were completed and most of the bituminous strikes had been settled. But Mitchell still felt harried and sick and for the first time in many years seriously began considering the possibility of resigning. John McHenry planned to open a "chain" of banks in northeast Pennsylvania in early 1907, and he offered Mitchell the job of president. When Mitchell first spoke to McHenry about the post he was intrigued but wondered whether he was qualified. McHenry assured him: "understand that an experienced cashier is employed to take charge of the detail work of the bank. The real duties of the President are easily learned, and the detail intricacies in banking can be learned in a few months' time." Thus assured, Mitchell replied that he had "given very serious consideration" to the offer and was "disposed to look with favor upon the proposition." He was certain the chain would succeed if he were made president because "my official connection with it would secure the business of practically all the miners in that vicinity who make deposits, as well as that of many business firms." While he could not step down immediately as union head, he believed that "in the early part of next year the organization will be so situated and the conditions of employment among the miners so settled, that I could, at that time, sever my official connection with the union without doing injury to the men for whom I have worked so long." McHenry, however, was unwilling to meet Mitchell's salary demand of "about five thousand dollars annually," and the matter was dropped.[20]

Although the grind of duties offered few opportunities to enjoy the holidays, Mitchell insisted on a full five-day vacation on the Fourth of July in 1906. He spent two days with his family at Mount Olive, Illinois, at the home of a close friend of Kate's, Madge Dunn. The proud father took photographs of his family and mailed them to his brother-in-law, beaming that his baby daughter was "the sweetest 'kid' I ever saw."[21] Then Mitchell and his operator pals, including Joseph Cavanaugh, went on a fishing trip to Lake Winnebago, Wisconsin. Far from roughing it in the wilds, the men ate and slept on board a full-sized yacht.[22] These joyful days provided only a temporary respite, however. In less than three weeks, he once again found himself "overwhelmed with work." And by the end of August, the strain of his office had led to illness and fatigue.[23] Again in December 1906, he complained he had been "laid up by an attack of illness for the past week."[24] His life had become an endless cycle of overwork, exhaustion, and illness. Exactly in what way alcohol abuse contributed to this cycle is a matter of conjecture.

Just prior to the annual UMWA convention in January 1907, Mitchell became ill yet again, and when he appeared at the convention itself, he was noticeably haggard. A friend lectured him on the need to restore his "complete health. It is your duty," he counseled, "not only to yourself and your family, but to your country, that you shall abstain from work and worry until this desired end shall have been attained."[25] But the work did not cease. Nor did the desire to be at home with his family. When his son Rob failed to uphold his promise to write every week, Mitchell chided him with humor and exaggeration: "Unless you write me more letters in the future, you must not expect me to buy you punching bags, express wagons, rubber coats, rubber boots, foot balls, automobiles, horses, and dogs as I have been doing." He then concluded: "By the way, how do you like the bull dog I sent?"[26] But there was no time in his schedule to go home. In February, he was almost constantly on the road, making speeches and attending conferences in Pittsburgh, Chicago, West Virginia, Springfield, Illinois, and Columbus, Ohio.[27]

In late March 1907, Mitchell suffered his worst bout of illness. Too sick to travel to Spring Valley, he was confined to his bed in Indianapolis. Elizabeth Morris was alarmed. Obviously, he was incapable of performing union business. Indeed, he was so ill only one thing could rouse him—the scent of money. When Harry Taylor, who at this time was handling Mitchell's investments, wired that money was due immediately or he would miss out on a lucrative transaction, Morris wired back that she could not "get into communication with him" but would try later. That afternoon, from his sick bed, he gave the instruction that Taylor could "draw to full extent of account."[28] Although the nature of the illness was never determined, he was too sick to accept President Roosevelt's personal invitation to have lunch at the White House.[29] Within a week he was back on his feet, and his doctor had given him permission to return to work. Still he did not feel right. He turned down several speaking engagements and social functions, including dinner at Andrew Carnegie's home. As he told one person requesting his presence, "my regular work is so heavy and my health has suffered to such an extent of late that it is impossible for me to undertake any other than my regular duties."[30]

On April 23, he collapsed again, this time in Chicago at the home of his friend Frank Schnell. A doctor determined the cause of the illness to be complications from a hernia he had suffered while working in the mines, and he suggested surgery.[31] Gompers, apparently annoyed at Mitchell's physical weakness, wired that he must "show your grit for yourself this time."[32] By April 27, he was well enough to be taken to St. Margaret's Hospital in Spring Valley and was operated on that same day. At first doctors expected full recovery within ten days, but he remained weak. His secretary, who stayed with Mitchell's family throughout the ordeal, remarked on "his inability to sleep and his extreme nervousness." She read "harmless and non-irritating" romance novels to him in an attempt "to induce sleep with the dulcet tones of my voice."[33] For days on end, Mitchell was unable to sleep, however, and after a week he could not yet swallow solid food. After two weeks the doctor came to believe he may have made a mistake operating so quickly. Had he "realized the condition in which Mr. Mitchell's nervous system was, he would not have operated on him until he had a six week's rest," his secretary wrote. Mitchell's "general health is so impaired as a result of overwork that he has practically nothing to build upon in this emergency."[34]

His doctor concluded he had been "on the verge of a complete physical and mental breakdown" and that he required at least a full month's vacation after his release.[35] Certainly cognizant that his condition was serious, Mitchell asked for brochures of seaside resorts on the Atlantic coast. Almost a full month after the operation, he was capable of sitting in an "invalid's chair" for only a half hour every day. When asked by Easley whether he would be well enough to make a speech on the Fourth of July, he declined: "it will be a long while before I can make a public address."[36] Not until June 1 was he released from the hospital, and only then with the stipulation he not return to work before July. But the demands of his office once again summoned him. He never took his vacation. On June 19, he traveled to Chicago to attend a conference, and on June 21 he was once again behind his desk at UMWA headquarters.[37]

During his two month hospital stay, he performed minimal union work. Only the most urgent correspondence was brought before him, and only those with pressing union business were permitted to talk with him in his hospital room. In those periods when he was well enough to think clearly, Mitchell occupied his time shuffling his personal investments. Indeed, beginning in May, he bought and sold stock so often that friends and advisers cautioned him to slow down. Apparently, his compulsion to work, and perhaps his compulsion to drink, both of which were denied him in the hospital, now found an outlet in gambling on the stock market. Once started, his frantic financial maneuvers did not cease until October. By then he had gambled and lost more than $9,000.[38]

Before his hospital stay, Mitchell knew very little about the market. Most of his investments until that time were in the form of property. For advice on the market he looked to his two closest operator friends, Harry Taylor and Frank Peabody. Peabody served as his agent with the Chicago brokerage firm of Harris, Winthrop and Company, while Taylor served as his agent with another Chicago firm, Charles G. Gates and Company. The safety of his stock investments began to prey upon his mind just two days after his traumatic hernia operation, when his secretary, reading aloud from the newspaper, came across an article hinting that Charles G. Gates and Company was not financially sound. "Mr. Mitchell is considerably alarmed over this," she wrote to Taylor, because the company had $1,848 "of his money." He asked that his account be closed out, and Taylor dutifully sent him a check for the full amount.[39]

Immediately after receiving the check, Mitchell sent $2,000 to Peabody to purchase two convertible bonds.[40] And from his hospital room on May 16, he directed Peabody to purchase on margin 200 shares of Amalgamated Copper "if that stock goes down to 93." Although informed that he had been on the verge of a nervous breakdown, he now planned to buy over $18,000 worth of stock! Peabody placed the order without comment.[41] Mitchell then sold the two bonds, which left him with only $500 credit in his account to cover his 200 shares. The brokerage firm therefore asked Mitchell to send at least $1,000 "to apply as margin."[42] Peabody wrote him at the hospital with the unhappy news that the price of Amalgamated Copper was slipping and suggested that he send the $2,000 from the sale of the bonds. Mitchell complied. By May 28, the price of Amalgamated Copper had slipped to 83 7/8 and Harris, Winthrop and Company was asking for "additional margin." Mitchell was forced to send several secure investment bonds. Incredibly, on that same day, Mitchell directed Peabody to purchase 200 additional shares of Amalgamated Copper.[43]

At this point, Peabody advised extreme caution. "Don't you think it is wiser to go at it a little slow?" he asked. "My own opinion is that conservative work is better than overloading yourself." Mitchell at first accepted this advice, but then asked whether he should buy outright his 200 shares now on margin. Peabody thought the idea of buying these shares outright absurd because the market was "dull" and would continue to be so until the end of August. He urged Mitchell "not to make any further investments in the stock market."[44] Mitchell made no further moves until July. He confessed to Peabody he had shown "poor judgment" in buying Amalgamated Copper when he did, "but as I was lying in bed with nothing special to think about . . . I wanted some excitement, and . . . there is nothing that breaks the monotony of hospital life so effectively as the rise and fall of stock investments." Soon after, however, Mitchell disregarded Peabody's advice, bought the 200 shares outright, and began dealing directly with Harris, Winthrop and Company.[45] So began a flurry of compulsive buying and selling that ended with the loss of $9,000 by October.

Although Mitchell returned to work on June 21, 1907, his recent troubles had taken a heavy toll. No longer robust, consumed with nervous anxiety, he was a weak and lonely man plagued by alcohol dependency and absorbed in his compulsive financial speculations. Grappling once more with the work and worry was a prospect he did not relish. At just thirty-seven, he was burned out. While committed to the union and the cause of labor peace, he doubted his ability to continue the struggle. He had been in office eight years, as long as the combined tenures of all four previous UMWA presidents. He had had enough. Previous miners' leaders had abandoned their posts without mental anguish, securing employment with operators or the government as soon as a lucrative job was offered. Mitchell, too, had actively sought better paying opportunities until 1902. Since that time, however, he had brushed aside all job offers and had come to identify his own future with that of the miners. In the summer of 1907 things were different. His health was ruined and he was unwilling to maintain the pace necessary to perform at the level expected of him.

The first expression of his determination to resign came less than two weeks after his return to Indianapolis. To his sister he wrote he "was seriously thinking of giving up my official connection" with the UMWA, "although I cannot do so before the expiration of my present term."[46] Between July 1907 and April 1, 1908, the day his term officially expired, he evidently planned to make his life as easy as possible. He planned a trip to Washington state for the autumn. And although his presence was not essential, he traveled to Denver in mid-July to attend a joint conference of Wyoming miners and operators. He intended to spend several weeks after the conference relaxing in the Denver area. Staying with him at the "very comfortable" hotel was the physician who had performed his hernia operation, affording Mitchell the opportunity "to consult him regarding my condition."[47] When the conference ended, he and the doctor spent two weeks at a cabin in the mountains. And although his family did not accompany him, he kept in close contact. He sent home numerous gifts to his wife, including a piano, and even bribed his children with money to get them to write every week.[48] Union work seemed to be the farthest thing from his mind.

On August 14 he returned to union headquarters. The trip West had revived him, but he was more certain than ever retirement was the only permanent cure. By the end of August, his mind was made up, although he chose not to make the decision public. "I fear that I am going to be forced to give up my work," he wrote his brother in confidence, "in fact, I am looking around for some other position which should be less difficult to fill."[49] The "other position" he had in mind was membership on the U.S. Panama Canal Commission. He began putting out feelers in late August to see if a permanent post of Labor Commissioner for the Panama Canal would be created and what his chances were of getting that job.[50] But it is important to note that he had received no firm offers of employment before he made the decision to resign.

Mitchell spent the month of September traveling across the country meeting with soft coal operators in a desperate attempt to resuscitate the Central Competitive Field. Having heard reports that operators would resist reestablishment of the joint conference, he met personally with the major operators in each district in an effort to convince them of their interest in national collective bargaining. His plan to take things easy during his last months in office would have to be put on hold. To leave the union when the future of collective bargaining in coal was in doubt would hardly be a capstone to his career. For four days he was in Pittsburgh, for three days in Cleveland, for two days in eastern Ohio, for two days in Indiana, for three days in Chicago, and for one day in West Virginia.[51] Although the meetings were exhausting, he was quite pleased with the prospects. He set up a "preliminary joint conference" in October to pave the way for joint negotiations in the spring of 1908. "On the whole, everything looks satisfactory," he informed Francis Robbins, "and I have little doubt that we shall have a full and successful interstate meeting."[52]

To prepare for the preliminary joint conference, Mitchell arranged a September 24 meeting of union officials from the four districts. While presiding over this meeting he again became ill and had to be taken to a local Indianapolis hospital. The physician diagnosed the trouble as a recurrence of hernia problems coupled with appendicitis. He was rushed home to Illinois and placed in St. Mary's Hospital in nearby LaSalle.[53] On October 7, before he left Indianapolis, he issued a union circular announcing he would not be a candidate for UMWA president in the coming elections. He was forced "to arrive at this decision because I am no longer well enough to give your interests the consideration their importance demands."[54]

Mitchell's announcement touched off a whirlwind of activity. Reporters scrambled for details, a task made more difficult because of a telegraph strike; miners, politicians, and operators sent letters of condolence, many asking him to reconsider; and Vice President Tom L. Lewis began lining up votes for the upcoming union election. All the while Mitchell lay in agony. As with his earlier operation, recovery was slow. Only after three weeks did he begin to regain his strength. Then what doctors' described as "an intra abdominal abscess" formed. He had to undergo another operation to deal with this complication and his prognosis was questionable.[55] Not until December 6, two months after he was first admitted, was he able to leave the hospital.

While in the hospital he explained his decision to retire to inquiring friends and the rank and file of the union. In a letter to the union *Journal*, he countered rumors he was stepping down so that he might secure an appointment to "some high political office." No such office had been offered him, he wrote, "and if such a move is contemplated, I know absolutely nothing about it." There was nothing false in this denial, for the job with the Panama Canal Commission he was pursuing had not yet been offered, and he had no assurances that it ever would be. Moreover, he had decided to retire even before he asked about that post. His decision was "based solely upon impaired health." While he understood that it was natural to speculate on his future, he assured the miners that he had "made no arrangements and reached no conclusions as to what I shall do after April first."[56]

If health was not his only consideration, if he in fact wanted to retire to pursue a more lucrative career, he kept these motivations well hidden from his friends and family. When James Duncan, his friend on the AFL Executive Council, asked him to reconsider, he replied that while "the miners would elect me by practically a unanimous vote, my health is so seriously impaired that it is going to take a long time before I shall be fully strong again." He candidly admitted he had "no plans" for the future. Despite rumors to the contrary, he assured Duncan that "the prospect of easier or more lucrative work influenced in no manner my decision." In fact, "I should rather be president of the miners' organization than have any other position I know of in the country."[57] To another friend he argued he was acting in the best interests of the union:

> I am leaving at a time when the organization is safe. Its membership is greater now than ever before and we have a large sum in the treasury. . . . The interstate movement is sure of rehabilitation, and on the whole the future gives promise of peaceful relations between the operators and our members; under these circumstances I think it best both for my own self and for the organization, that I step aside and give someone more vigorous an opportunity to develop the organization to its full and ultimate fruition.[58]

As his health improved and he became restless in his hospital bed, he began wondering whether he had made the right decision. In his most revealing commentary, he discussed his qualms about his own future. Although he had often complained of the burdens of his charge, he found it strange that "instead of looking forward to the first of April as a release from care and worry, I look forward to it as the beginning of a new and painful restlessness." He felt as though he were "separating myself from an essential part of my being." More than likely this feeling would "wear off," and he would become "reconciled to a new life and get interested in new fields of work and activity."[59]

In the hospital, Mitchell began to devote serious consideration to his future. Notwithstanding his health problems, he possessed remarkable credentials. His youth, his unquestioned administrative talent, his peerless reputation as a champion of labor peace, all enabled him to attract intriguing job offers before April 1908. From the outset of his job search his greatest ambition was to land a permanent position with the National Civic Federation. The NCF appealed to him on a variety of levels. He assumed the work would be far less taxing than his present job, allowing him to spend considerably more time with his family and posing no threat to his health; he would be able to remain active in the labor movement, albeit as an interested outsider; he would be able to maintain his contacts among the nation's elite, engage in the elegant social life to which he had become accustomed, and continue to bask in the praise of men such as Andrew Carnegie; and he would not be forced to violate his principles because he could remain active in the great struggle for industrial peace. By any measure, the NCF suited perfectly his temperament, sensibilities, and convictions.

Mitchell did not wait for Ralph Easley to offer a job. In a letter to Easley written just ten days after his operation, he admitted that after his retirement he would "not in any way be a powerful factor in the industrial movement," but he believed "our own personal relations have been such that what I say will be given consideration by you." By no means was he shy in giving advice. He suggested the NCF "needed to undergo a process of reorganization." President

August Belmont, then under criminal investigation by the New York Public Utilities Commission, must be forced to step down. Seth Low would make an ideal replacement. In addition, the NCF had undertaken too many "side lines" and needed to conform more closely to its original purpose, namely, the promotion of industrial peace. He then begged Easley not to misconstrue his message, for he was "not looking for a position," but if the NCF "can be placed on a good, solid basis, and it should be deemed advisable for me to take charge of the Conciliation Department, I should be willing to do so." This not too subtle job request carried the "proviso" that satisfactory "conditions" be hammered out. Two days later he wrote Daniel Keefe, a friend active in the NCF, and asked him to "urge the idea" on Easley and other NCF leaders.[60]

Easley agreed with the need to reorganize, although he hoped Andrew Carnegie would assume the NCF presidency. He made no comment on Mitchell's job request. Never one to give up easily, Mitchell broached the subject again several weeks later. The choice of Carnegie, he wrote, was "entirely satisfactory to me." The only problem was that if Carnegie refused, Low might not consent "to fill the office as second choice." To demonstrate his commitment to the NCF, he announced that while he was still very weak, he would make every effort to attend the annual NCF dinner in mid-December. Although he was far too feeble to participate in all the meetings, "I shall to do everything in my power to be there and render whatever aid I can in carrying out the plans that will promote the interests of the Federation and help in maintaining industrial peace."[61]

Again Easley took no notice of the job request. He informed Mitchell that forces were hard at work trying to secure for him the post of Labor Commissioner of the Panama Canal. Mitchell feigned interest, but his reservations about the Panama job revealed he preferred to work with the NCF. First, President Roosevelt would probably expect to fill the position before April 1, but it would be impossible for him to assume the job before that date. If the joint conference was reestablished in soft coal, he would have to be present for negotiations. Second, he wondered how much real power would be vested in the position. Third, he would prefer to "remain in the States rather than locate to Panama." News that Carnegie had refused the NCF presidency allowed him to introduce once again his desire to work for the Federation. Seth Low would make a marvelous president because he appealed to working people and business elements. "I am sure that if it should be decided to associate me with him, as Chairman of the Conciliation Department, I could work in harmony with you and him and should feel an enthusiasm in the work that would make it congenial and effective."[62]

Mitchell was unable to attend the AFL convention held at the end of November in Norfolk, Virginia, but he was delighted to learn that, despite his resignation, delegates had unanimously elected him to remain second vice president.[63] Because this election allowed him to remain officially connected to the labor movement, it improved his chances of securing a post in the NCF. His dogged determination to work with the NCF was demonstrated in mid-December. The day after he was released from the hospital on December 6, Easley warned him not to let "anything keep you away" from the Federation's annual dinner beginning December 13. Despite lingering pain and fatigue, Mitchell attended. Held at the Hotel Astor in New York, the dinner was a lavish affair. Sumptuous food, expensive wine, and the nation's most powerful people—just the type of get together that made the NCF so attractive to Mitchell. A French journalist reporting on the dinner was amazed by the spectacle of Mitchell "sitting between Mr. Charles A. Moore, the manufacturer, and Mr. Percy A. Rockefeller, the capitalist." He later spotted Mitchell chatting with J. P. Morgan's daughter, Ann, and New York socialite Edith Harriman. "In France," the reporter concluded, "the workers would regard what happened at the Hotel Astor as proof that labor's leaders were playing into the hands of the capitalists."[64] Many American workers agreed. Unfortunately for Mitchell, his attendance did not lead to an immediate job offer. He heard nothing more from Easley until February 1908.

After the dinner, Mitchell returned to Indianapolis to preside over the preliminary joint conference of operators and miners in the Central Competitive Field, which had been delayed due to his illness. While addressing the conference, he was suddenly seized by intense pain in his abdomen. He was carried to his room by William B. Wilson, John Walker, and O. L. Garrison.[65] Although the pain stemmed from a rupture of his stitches, Mitchell at first believed he was dying. He asked for a priest, and Father Peter Killian was brought to his hotel room. With his friends Billy Ryan and O. L. Garrison as sponsors, he was formally baptized in the Catholic Church.[66]

While Mitchell's conversion to Catholicism may seem like the desperate act of a man convinced he was near death, few of his friends were surprised. Father John Power of Spring Valley, whom he had known since childhood, had "long expected" him "to take this step." Since the beginning of 1906 his constant health troubles and his inability to stop drinking to excess had led him to seek spiritual assistance. He had been in contact with Father J. J. Curran of Wilkes-Barre, and he had discussed the matter with his wife. Kate had been a Catholic all her life and she had raised her children in that faith. Thus, it was natural for him to look to the Catholic Church for succor. When this particular health crisis passed, Mitchell did not waver in his decision. "I propose taking the instructions as soon as I can do so," he informed his wife. "I know this will give you much happiness; it is, as you know, in line with an intention formed a long time ago." His conversion represented the act of a man in the throes of an ongoing physical and spiritual crisis. And once converted, he felt a deep sense of "relief and happiness."[67]

1907 marked the first Christmas Mitchell spent away from his wife since their marriage. He was well enough to leave Indianapolis on December 26. He then traveled directly to a health resort, Excelsior Springs, Missouri, known for its mineral waters and curative baths. Here he remained three weeks.[68] He spent his days leisurely, writing letters, meeting with friends who came to visit, slowly piecing together his report to the UMWA national convention which opened January 21, and keeping track of the moves to restore the Central Competitive Field. His conversion did not provide an immediate fix for his troubles, for his secretary noted that he suffered from insomnia his entire stay. And just before his departure, Mitchell wrote that he was still hampered by "brain fatigue."[69]

The January 1908 UMWA national convention was above all a magnificent display of affection for John Mitchell. Delegates from every district offered praise and gratitude for their leader. The committee on resolutions summed up the prevailing sentiment: "Resolved, that we appreciate, more than man can find words to express, the magnitude of his work and the brilliancy of his achievements in behalf of the downtrodden and oppressed wage workers in every sphere of toil." The resolution was carried unanimously.[70] Gratitude was expressed in gifts as well as words. An Illinois delegate presented him with a "loving cup." On behalf of the Wyoming District, one delegate announced "we came here with love in our hearts for President Mitchell and $2,700 in money, the check for which I now present to him." An embarrassed Mitchell claimed he did not want the money, but as a man always prepared to capitalize on generosity, he suggested that rather than offend the miners who made the gift, the check should be sent to his wife "and let her use it to educate our boys."[71]

Even more generous resolutions were introduced. A Texas delegate resolved that Mitchell offer his "able counsel" to the union on a part-time basis for the next two years at a salary of $5,000 per year. A Kentucky delegate resolved that a UMWA educational department be created and Mitchell be appointed its head. A local union in Kansas suggested each miner be levied ten cents and that the money raised be given to Mitchell upon his retirement. Mitchell demonstrated discretion by declining these offers. He did, however, accept a unanimously adopted resolution granting him a continuation of his present salary for six months to help him cover his medical expenses. In accepting this award, he pointed out how it demonstrated to the evolution of labor leadership in America:

It has been charged—and unfortunately it is true—that in the years of the past the champions of the workingmen have received their reward in kicks and blows. Scattered over our country in nearly every cemetery lie the bones of men, gone and forgotten, who rendered to our great cause as much service and made greater sacrifices than I have done. I wish it were possible for the spirit of the great John Siney to come back, as well as the spirits of Dan McLaughlin and those champions who fought and gave their lives without reward, who went to their graves—hungry in some cases, starved in others—not with the love of the people they unselfishly served. . . . And were it not that this stain may be removed from workingmen's organizations of our country I should ask you to defeat the resolution you have now under consideration.[72]

Mitchell was amazed at the opportunities for profit available to him at the 1908 convention. And despite the fact he walked away with $2,700 in cash, six months' salary and numerous momentos, he showed considerable restraint for a man so consumed by a love of money. He later claimed he could have obtained anything he wanted from the delegates, perhaps as much as $150,000, had he encouraged such sentiment.[73]

Other than celebrate Mitchell, the great task of the convention was to announce the new president. Balloting had taken place in November and December. The two principal candidates were Vice President Tom L. Lewis, the leading critic of Mitchell, and Secretary-Treasurer William B. Wilson, the top pro-administration man. Although too ill to take an active role in the campaign, from the very outset Mitchell pledged to support Wilson and promised to "line up my friends everywhere I can in your interest."[74] The election was bitter and close. Lewis was backed by many in the Ohio district as well as the socialists, who believed Lewis would abandon the conservative policies pursued by Mitchell and set the union on a more aggressive course. And while Wilson was a respected figure, he did not have mass appeal like Mitchell. Moreover, Wilson planned to keep his seat in the U.S. House of Representatives and therefore had to convince the miners he could perform two jobs at the same time.[75]

Throughout the campaign, Mitchell offered his invaluable advice on how to win union elections. He warned Wilson that Lewis was an unscrupulous competitor and urged him "to make a good, vigorous fight." Lewis had been waiting for this opportunity for years and had built "the machinery through which he can make a strong and effective campaign."[76] Mitchell suggested Wilson appeal to the national organizers and let them know they would not be routinely dismissed if he were elected. When he learned in mid-November that early returns put Lewis in the lead, he instructed Wilson to contact all locals through circulars which condemned Lewis and listed his own merits. Although this type of circular was illegal under the UMWA constitution and Mitchell did not want Wilson to violate his "standard of ethics," the situation warranted aggressive tactics. And to allay opposition to Wilson's drawing two salaries at the same time, he implored Wilson to declare that while in Washington he would not expect to receive payment from the UMWA.[77] Despite Mitchell's urging, Wilson ran a lackluster campaign. He refused to travel across the coal states, made few contacts among organizers, and refused to heed Mitchell's advice on circulars. He insisted the membership already knew where he stood on the issues.[78] In his sole campaign circular, Wilson pledged "to continue the policies of John Mitchell in the same conservative, yet constructive manner."[79]

Wilson's refusal to heed Mitchell's advice probably cost him the election. When the votes were tallied at the 1908 convention, Lewis had captured the presidency by a slim 2,000 vote majority out of 127,000 votes cast. Two of Mitchell's allies were elected to the other top posts. John P. White took the vice presidency and Billy Ryan became secretary-treasurer.[80] The election of Lewis was significant because it demonstrated that Mitchell had failed to build an effective political machine capable of surviving him. Over the years he had successfully dealt with internal opponents, controlled the union *Journal*, and built up a cadre of loyal organizers. Had he not been so ill he might well have been able to engineer a Wilson victory. Yet once he announced his retirement, his loyal followers began leaving the flock. They threw their support behind the next most powerful man in the union, Tom L. Lewis, in the hope that Lewis might favor them the way Mitchell had.

Although distraught by Lewis's election, Mitchell offered no criticisms of his successor. He proved gracious in defeat. Even when Lewis declared in his acceptance speech that he and Mitchell "never had one single personal difference during the time we worked together in the last seven years," he did not contradict him. Instead, he rose to congratulate his longtime foe. "If there is one man in this union who imagines that I would feel gratification at the failure of my successor," he said, "I hope that he will dispel from his mind that false and infamous idea." He then wished Lewis "more success than I have had."[81] Mitchell believed the best way to undermine an opponent was through behind-the-scenes maneuvers, and in the years to come he would coordinate the attack to remove Lewis from office.

If the Lewis victory alone was insufficient to spoil the celebration of Mitchell, William D. "Big Bill" Haywood came to the convention and assailed all that Mitchell stood for. Still secretary of the Western Federation of Miners and a major figure in the Industrial Workers of the World, he had recently been released from prison in connection with the murder of Governor Steunenberg of Idaho. The appearance of both men on the same platform provided a stark physical and ideological contrast. Haywood was tall and robust, and the loss of one eye made him look as tough and rebellious as the brand of unionism he represented. After months of illness, Mitchell looked small and pale. The puffiness around his eyes and facial swelling were telltale signs of his battle with alcoholism. His tailored suit made him look as conservative as his style of unionism. While Mitchell preached sound and cautious business unionism, albeit along industrial lines, in carefully crafted and logical speeches, Haywood thundered his revolutionary creed in loud and strident tones.

Haywood's speech was a bitter indictment of Mitchell's principles and a stirring plea for the UMWA to follow a new path. He recounted the WFM's history since its founding in 1893—the bloody strikes at Cripple Creek and Leadville, Colorado and Coeur D'Alene, Idaho. The lesson of these strikes, he suggested, was that all labor must join together in a meaningful way to subdue the combined power of capital and the state. The UMWA and the WFM must consolidate and undertake nationwide sympathy strikes for each other's benefit. If this meant abrogating signed contracts with employers, so be it. "Do not enter into agreements that are going to bind you for a period or make it impossible for you to do anything for yourselves or anybody else," he demanded. "Leave your hands free so that you can fight whenever a fight becomes necessary." When contracts are made, be sure to include a "saving clause" permitting miners to undertake sympathy strikes to help other workers in other industries. It was wrong for an international union such as the UMWA "to enter into an agreement unless that international takes into consideration the interest of the working class."[82]

Haywood's speech represented what Mitchell feared most—a call for workers to return to the days of class warfare. Left wing labor leaders such as Haywood and right wing employers such as David M. Parry both desired a fight to the finish. And in Mitchell's eyes, both were equally wrong. Neither realized that a middle ground had been established—the NCF—based on a harmony of interests between capital and labor. There was no irreconcilable conflict, no need for the overthrow of capitalism. There was a need, however, for responsible unionism. Haywood's disdain for the sanctity of contracts and his plea for sympathy strikes were dangerous ideas which had to be addressed. Mitchell rose when Haywood had finished.

Mitchell's response was short and to the point. He reminded delegates of the 1890s when class warfare raged in the coal fields, when miners had no signed contracts. "Every coal miner in America carries indelibly in his memory the history of the times when we had no contracts" he began. "Our contracts are not perfect; our system is not ideal; but there is not a man whose memory runs back ten short years who would go back to the system prevailing then." In those days miners worked longer hours for less pay. And when miners struck, their wives begged for food. While the present contracts were not ideal, miners should think long and hard before they "go back to the time when we could strike when we wanted to." As to the "saving clause," operators would never agree unless they were given the right to lock out miners when it served their interests. Nor did Mitchell want to hear talk of sympathy strikes involving miners and broken contracts. "I have the reputation of being opposed to sympathetic strikes," he said. The reputation was well deserved for "only in extreme cases" would he ever advocate one. In the history of the labor movement, he did not recall any of the great industrial struggles "in which the sympathetic strike proved of great advantage."[83]

He had refuted his radical opponent, accepted the accolades of his union brothers, and had congratulated his successor. The time had now come to say farewell. He thanked the miners for their "kindness and confidence," and spoke of the "sorrow" and "pain" of leaving office. He encouraged them to stay vigilant, to organize the unorganized fields, and remember his merits and not his deficiencies. If "I have in my life done aught to wound or injure any man, he will give me his forgiveness, just as now, as I pass from the limelight into the shadow, I forgive any man who may have done wrong to me." He asked also that he be allowed to face any man who charged him with misdeeds after he had left office. He asked this because "the man never lived whom I was afraid to face!" He then led the convention in the singing of the National Anthem.[84]

When the convention ended on February 2, Mitchell still had two months to serve as president. In that time, he hoped to repair the damage created by his separate settlement policy of 1906 and reestablish the joint conference in the Central Competitive Field. In previous years the joint conference took place immediately after the UMWA convention, but there were still many operators, especially in Illinois, who opposed the idea of recreating the interstate movement. Indeed, these Illinois operators agreed to attend an informal joint conference, beginning February 27 only if they were first allowed to meet with Illinois miners and iron out problems in that state. Mitchell reluctantly agreed.[85] The conference between Illinois operators and miners began in mid-February at Peoria. When difficulties arose, Mitchell was invited to attend. Union leaders in that state believed his presence might help to bring the operators into line. But he did not attend. A week after the UMWA convention, he had gone on an alcoholic binge and was now sick in his Indianapolis hotel room.[86]

The fact that Mitchell had tendered his resignation from the union did not automatically solve his personal and emotional difficulties. His loneliness might soon be cured, his physical health might well return, but he was still an alcoholic and recovery would be difficult. According to his secretary, an Indianapolis doctor had been treating Mitchell's alcoholism for some time, but this latest binge forced a temporary suspension of the treatment until Mitchell's "system is in condition to receive any benefit therefrom." The doctor assured Morris he could eventually "cure Mr. Mitchell of all desire for drink." Although the nature of the treatment involved was never specified, it was described by the doctor as "so changing the vibrations that it is impossible for him (meaning the man in the case) to get the liquor down."[87] To prepare for the February 27 informal joint conference Mitchell voluntarily placed himself in St. Vincent's Hospital in Indianapolis. Here he stayed for six days to recuperate. While there, he met with Father Peter Killian, the priest who had baptized him, and made a solemn pledge never to drink again.[88]

Just three days before the February 27 informal joint conference between operators and miners, Mitchell wrote that the situation was "not at all encouraging." In Illinois, Ohio, and western Pennsylvania, operators were stubbornly resisting the idea of reestablishing the CCF. "Some of the operators seem to want a suspension, others want a fight to the finish," he lamented, "and a good many inside movements are being made."[89] Whether or not a healthy and committed Mitchell could have brought about the resumption of the interstate movement is impossible to determine, but it is clear that his personal difficulties and his lack of attention to union business hindered the process. His drinking made him unfit in the critical days before February 27. His status as lame-duck president also weakened his authority among operators and allowed them to resist more easily. And while in the hospital, he devoted most of his attention to lining up a high paying job for himself.

From the time of the UMWA convention in January until April 1, Mitchell's primary concern was not the state of the union but rather his career prospects. During the convention, he dashed off a telegram to Ralph Easley asking whether there was any word on his bid to become head of the NCF's Conciliation Department. By February 1 Mitchell had happy news. Easley had discussed the matter with the other leaders of the NCF, including President Seth Low, and all were in agreement that Mitchell should be hired on a full time basis. He was not to become head of the Conciliation Department, however. He was to retain his position as chair of the Trade Agreement Department. Easley promised there would be sufficient funding and that "if the work of that department did not develop fast enough to interest you," Mitchell could assist "the other committees in their work." He also promised that NCF leaders were "unanimous in their determination to make this a great national organization."[90]

On February 21, Seth Low formally offered the post to Mitchell at a salary of $6,000 per year. As head of the Trade Agreement Department he would be responsible for "developing the idea of trade agreements" and thereby promoting industrial peace across the country. Without hesitation, Mitchell accepted. Writing from the hospital, he declared NCF work was "entirely in line with my highest and best conception of the industrial peace movement." He wanted to assist Low's efforts to make the NCF "the recognized tribunal of industrial peace in this country." The NCF was "a great organization, representative of all classes of society," and had "the sympathetic cooperation of all the people of our country." His only concern was his mental and physical health, and he asked for a few months' rest after his retirement to recuperate. He also asked that Low not make public his acceptance of the post until after April 1.[91] In brighter spirits, Mitchell left the hospital and at last prepared to address union matters.

CCF miners and operators finally got together on February 27, but their informal conference lasted just two days. On the first day, UMWA representatives moved that a call be issued for an interstate joint convention to begin March 10. Operators from Illinois, Ohio, and western Pennsylvania voted the motion down. On the second day, the miners moved that the question of calling an interstate convention be left in the hands of a committee of eight, one operator and one miner from each state. Operators voted down this motion as well and the conference adjourned.[92] With this failure, Mitchell issued a call for the UMWA national convention to reconvene on March 12 to determine what policies should be pursued. He fully understood that the situation was "very critical." Although he could not "forecast what will be done by our Convention," he recognized the very real possibility of a strike.[93]

Despite, or perhaps because of, the critical state of affairs, almost immediately after the informal conference Mitchell broke his pledge, went on another binge, and landed again in the hospital. "Cheer up, take heart, all are ready to lend a helping hand," Elizabeth Morris urged him. If he stayed in the hospital, followed his doctor's orders, and renewed his pledge, he could "win out."[94] But in a letter to Harry Taylor, Morris confessed she had "completely lost my courage and my hope" that her boss could win his battle against drink. She sent for his wife to come to Indianapolis. It was "the only thing to do."[95]

When the UMWA convention reopened on March 12, Mitchell was well enough to preside. He convinced delegates to allow the scale committee to draw up a report on the best course of action. Among others, the committee was composed of the present officers and those officers about to take office on April 1. During committee sessions, Mitchell and President-elect Lewis bickered over what should be done. As was the case in 1906, Mitchell believed that since the joint conference could not be reestablished, the only viable policy was the making of separate settlements. Lewis believed that a suspension of work in the Central Competitive Field on April 1 would force operators to renew the system of joint talks. In the end, the two men compromised on a policy of district settlements. District officers, rather than national officers, were directed to negotiate contracts for all miners under their charge. If district settlements were made prior to April 1 or if a district wage conference was in session on April 1, the men would continue to work. If no wage conference was in session on that date, the miners of that district would cease work.[96]

In his last official action as UMWA president, John Mitchell had squelched yet another movement for a national strike of soft coal miners. He pressed delegates to adopt the scale committee's report. "I know how attractive the proposition of a national strike is to men who work in the mines," he lectured. But not all miners wanted a strike and therefore a strike could not succeed. "I want you men who have accepted my advice year after year, in good times and in bad times . . . to give your support to this report." While he did not agree with all the details of the report, he believed it was "a policy that would protect and conserve the interests of the Union."[97] The report was duly adopted. Had the interests of the union been conserved? The union treasury doled out less money in strike assistance, and several districts made favorable contracts with operators. But the interstate movement, which represented the basis of union strength in the industry, had not been revived, and miners were once again placed in competition with each other and union solidarity therefore subverted.

After the convention adjourned, after the singing of the national anthem, delegates came forward to say their final farewell to Mitchell. Tears were shed by some of them. Mitchell was moved to make a final speech that revealed his newly developed religious faith. "I say to you now, gentlemen, may God bless our movement. May He look down on it with that favor, with that grace He has given it so far as I have been connected with it." He concluded: "My boys—and I will call you my boys even though some of you are nearly twice as old as I am, I regard you as my boys—be as good union men now, and in the time to come, as you have been while I was directing your affairs. God bless you again! I am leaving this movement, not because I want to, but because I have to leave you."[98]

Mitchell indeed had to leave the UMWA. By March, his problems with alcohol had reached a critical stage. He missed several sessions of the last convention, and stories circulated that he had been drinking at a local tavern. Whether or not these stories were true, the very day after the convention adjourned Mitchell collapsed at a meeting of the national executive board and a doctor was rushed to the scene.[99] He was immediately sent to a health spa at West Baden, Indiana and remained there a full week. By March 30, he was back in Indianapolis, but he did not spend his last two days as president at union headquarters. He admitted himself to St. Vincent's Hospital in Indianapolis to undergo treatment for alcoholism.[100]

On April 1 John Mitchell was no longer president of the miners. The troubles that befell him while he was in office, however, did not immediately melt away. He had told his wife he would take a few days to take care of his personal affairs and return to Spring Valley by April 9, but on that day he was in Chicago beginning a four-week intensive treatment program for alcohol addiction. In a letter to his wife written from his hospital bed, he tried to explain what had caused his illness:

For about twelve years I have lived away from home and necessarily away from those influences which home life brings to every man. . . . During that time I have worked as hard as any human being could work, and . . . many times I have felt so depressed and despondent that I foolishly believed that relief from worry and disappointment could be found in the use of intoxicants. I first drank in moderation, but as the habit grew and my appetite increased, I drank more and at more frequent intervals, until I finally became so weakened physically and mentally, as a result of overwork and too frequent indulgences, that I found myself, to use plain terms, a periodic inebriate.

He tried numerous methods to "escape the demon," but could not shake off his "appetite." His resignation from the union presidency, he admitted, was prompted by "the hope of regaining control of myself." He apologized for having so "offended" his wife, but held out hope that this new cure would be successful.[101]

This confession to his loving spouse was painful enough. Now he had to make a similar confession to his new employer and hope that Easley would still desire his services. "For some time I have not been either physically or mentally at my best," he wrote, but he was now taking treatment which promised to "restore permanently my physical and mental health." If for whatever reason the treatment failed, "I shall write you formally withdrawing my acceptance of the position tendered me by the National Civic Federation."[102] Easley proved sympathetic, telling Mitchell to take all summer if necessary to "get thoroughly well." Mitchell did not believe he needed that long. By the end of April, he reported that his "nervous system" was recovering rapidly, that within a few weeks he would be "in fine fettle," and that "all desire for consumption has ceased."[103] Relieved he was feeling better and that the NCF still wanted him, he wrote his wife with the exciting news that he would soon be working in New York and the family could settle down "somewhere in the suburbs."[104]

By May, however, Mitchell was becoming enthusiastic about an entirely different job prospect. Rumors began circulating as early as February that Mitchell would run for governor of Illinois on the Democratic ticket. At first he scoffed at the idea. But as more and more trade unionists and local politicians encouraged him to run, he became intrigued. "I have got a political bee in my bonnet," he wrote his friend John Walker in late May. In a confidential letter, he asked Walker to to ascertain "what fate will await me should I make so bold as to offer myself for the small office of Governor of Illinois."[105] The answer he received delighted him. The Chicago Federation of Labor would back him, the vast majority of trade unionists would support him, and a potential rupture in the state's Republican ranks heightened his chances of victory.[106]

However much the glamour and power of the governor's office tempted him, he remained committed to the NCF. He knew that in the Trade Agreement Department he would find "a field of activity that is more congenial than political life could possibly be."[107] Yet he also knew from years of negotiating experience he could use the call to politics as a bargaining tool with the NCF. In vintage Mitchell style, he wrote Seth Low in an effort to improve the NCF's $6,000 per year offer. While "political office held little attraction," he would find it difficult to "refuse the pressing claims, especially of the working people" respecting his candidacy "unless I am able to give some valid reasons." He wanted Low to guarantee a contract for "a number of years at least." Low replied by telegram he would guarantee at least three years' service.[108] Mitchell then travelled to New York and met with Easley. Apparently he wanted a salary increase as well. On June 16, Easley wired him that the salary offer was now $8,000 per year. Mitchell responded favorably. Once the contract was put in writing, he publicly announced he would not run for governor. And by the end of June, he formally accepted the NCF position.[109]

After two years riddled with personal traumas, Mitchell's fortunes began to revive in the summer of 1908. Once removed from the strains of office and and secure as to his future, his health began improving, his ongoing treatment for alcoholism began having a positive effect, and he was able to spend more time with his family in Spring Valley. He was slowing rousing from his nightmarish slumber. And as he regained his strength, he began to reflect upon the successes and failures of the UMWA in his last two years as president. The thoughts could not have been encouraging. Illness, booze, and concern over his future prospects, not union affairs, had consumed his time and energies. As a result, the interstate joint conference had not been reestablished, soft coal miners were engaged in another disaster round of separate settlements, and hard coal miners continued to leave the union in droves. Equally unsettling was the thought that his arch enemy, Tom L. Lewis, was now in command of the union's destiny. Although he consoled himself with the notion that "the organization, when I left it, was in better condition than ever before in its history,"[110] he understood that upon his retirement his successors were faced with enormous tasks.

Chapter 10
Decline and Death, 1908–1919

At the age of thirty-eight, Mitchell had abdicated his central role in the labor movement. And while he believed his new position in the National Civic Federation would allow him to exercise immense informal power on the industrial relations scene, he was soon disappointed with his own limited authority and the weakness of the NCF. His dream of championing a movement of workers, employers, and the public that would bring about industrial peace and economic justice died quickly. He stood by the NCF, however, and he continued to believe it was the only viable alternative to militant anti-unionism among employers and the rising tide of socialism among workers.

In 1911, Mitchell was aghast to find the NCF itself had become the target of radical unionists. Socialists in the UMWA joined hands with Tom L. Lewis to pass a resolution denouncing the NCF and forbidding any union member to associate with the organization. Thus, Mitchell was faced with the unpleasant choice of severing his ties with the NCF or facing expulsion from the UMWA. After days of soul searching, Mitchell resigned from his job. He continued to remain active in the NCF, however, and in 1911 he assisted Gompers in a dramatic battle against AFL socialists over the issue of the NCF.

After 1911, Mitchell sank into relative obscurity. He continued to intervene in the affairs of the UMWA, working behind the scenes to lead an insurgent movement that overthrew Tom L. Lewis; he played a role in a religious crusade within the AFL called the "Men and Religion Movement"; and he found employment first on the New York Workmen's Compensation Commission and later as Chair of the Industrial Commission of New York. This work, too, he found unsatisfying, and in his later years personal problems once again mounted. He began to drink heavily and in 1919 he died of pneumonia at age forty-nine, a sick and largely forgotten man.

Mitchell was so excited about his new job he started several days early. "I think I shall like the work I have undertaken," he wrote his brother-in-law.[1] Leaving his family in Spring Valley, he began acquainting himself with NCF headquarters at 281 Fourth Street in New York City even as painters, decorators, paper hangers, and carpet layers were still finishing his office.[2] Elizabeth Morris had quit her job at the UMWA when Mitchell did, and there was no question she would continue as his secretary at the NCF. She was his most dedicated and admiring friend. The position of Chair of the Trade Agreement Department excited him because it suited his most heartfelt convictions. He would be a salesperson who believed in his product. He would be an agent for progressive social change. In a letter to the UMWA journal written the day before his new career officially started, he gave an indication of the enthusiasm with which he took up his post. "While there are at this time some workingmen and many employers who question the advantage of these agreements," he wrote, "history and experience demonstrate beyond reasonable doubt that labor and capital alike profit by the adjustment of their relations through joint conference, and that industrial peace on an equitable basis has been and can be maintained through the collective bargain."[3]

Within weeks some of his initial enthusiasm began to subside as he got down to the daily routine of work. Rather than conventions, bargaining sessions, and strike headquarters, his new milieu was the stomping grounds of the wealthy. He met capitalists on their own turf, and he peddled the concept of the trade agreement at their banquets and social affairs. He quickly found his job an endless round of "pink teas, golf links, and yachting trips." And even for a man with such bourgeois tastes as Mitchell, the routine quickly lost its allure and he came to recognize the absurdity of some of these functions. On August 16, he was scheduled to attend a luncheon at Mount Kisco, the country home of Edith Harriman, a wealthy New York socialite who was active in the Women's Department of the NCF. "To-morrow I am going to have to take lunch with Mrs. Harriman, at her country home, and of course, incidentally, we shall solve the labor problem." He would rather visit Coney Island, but duty called.[4]

To his dismay, he also found that Seth Low and Ralph Easley expected him to perform many functions not associated with the Trade Agreement Department. One task he found particularly unpleasant was conciliation work in strikes that had already been lost. Unionists wrote requesting him "to straighten out disputes with employers—most of them strikes that have been lost beyond hope and in which the labor organizations have exhausted all their own resources."[5]

On the whole, however, Mitchell enjoyed his job in these early months and believed he he was well situated to act as a positive force for progressive change. There were many "attractive and pleasant" aspects to the work, he informed his brother David. "My work is not hard, I have no great responsibility, and my remuneration is entirely satisfactory." Of course, there were times when he longed for the excitement of the union presidency. And there were many old union associates who pleaded with him to retake charge of the UMWA. Yet he resisted this urge because he understood he could not stand the physical strain. There was no fear he would forget his trade union roots and sympathies, however. He kept active in AFL affairs, he was writing a second book on labor, and "I see daily enough misery in New York to keep me from falling unconsciously into the viewpoint of the rich." Moreover, his work offered the opportunity to influence important figures in the employing class:

> In this position here I am thrown into association with the great captains of industry and finance. On the whole they are an unsympathetic crowd, but my standing with them is peculiarly favorable; they know that I am honest in all that the word implies, and therefore they know that when I make a statement to them that I believe it to be true and this association gives me an opportunity of presenting labor's view to a class of people whose only knowledge of the working people is derived from the distorted portrayals appearing in an unfriendly press.[6]

Commitment to his work made him content. So, too, did the development of strong family ties. By the spring of 1909, he had purchased a fine suburban house at 3 Claremont Street in Mount Vernon, New York, and moved his family there. The entire family worked together for weeks on end to decorate the house and make it a real home. He was happy that "for the first time in years, my little ones are with me." He took great delight in the stability of his family life and especially his youngest daughter, Catherine, confiding that "every day I see something new and wonderful in her child nature."[7] For perhaps the first time ever he was enjoying a healthy and contented personal life.

As the months passed, however, Mitchell became increasingly frustrated and bored with his professional duties. He spent his days hobnobbing with the industrial elites, at formal and informal settings, pitching his message. But his work seemed to have no impact. No new trade agreements were established. In August 1909, he worked with Easley and Low to strengthen the Trade Agreement Department in an effort to stimulate greater interest among employers. They proposed a new executive committee for the department to consist of both employers and trade unionists. Thirty employers were invited to serve, but only nine accepted. All nine either represented industries such as building trades and printing, which already had established trade agreements, or were longtime officers of the NCF.[8] Equally unsettling was the negative response of many trade unionists when asked to serve on the executive committee. Abe Rosenburg of the International Ladies' Garment Workers refused to participate, and he made clear his reasons in a letter to Mitchell. "Our manufacturers do not believe in trade agreements," he stated bluntly. "I have not come across a single one that does, and I have had dealings with most of them. They only sign an agreement with us when they are pressed to the wall by the organization, and as soon as they sign one, they do all they possibly can do violate it."[9]

The failure of the NCF's Trade Agreement Department did not reflect Mitchell's weakness as a salesperson. The problem ran much deeper and involved national trends over which he had no control. As we have seen, aggressive anti-unionism had been on the rise since at least 1904. More and more employers shunned the NCF's call to accept responsible unionism. Without question, by 1908 the NAM was far ahead of the NCF in the struggle to control the hearts and minds of American employers. Thus, in large part, Mitchell had tied his fortunes to a dying cause. Other factors also account for the general lack of interest in trade agreements. A financial panic in 1907 resulted in several lean years for the American economy. During this period employers became fascinated by what one historian has dubbed "the efficiency craze."[10] Owners in major industries such as steel, textiles, and machine tools became obsessed with scientific management schemes to reduce operating costs and increase production. Employers intrigued with scientific management were generally hostile to the trade agreement because the success of their schemes hinged on complete control over the work process and labor force.

The open shop movement and scientific management dominated industrial relations in the years after 1907 just as collective bargaining and the trade agreement dominated the years 1898 to 1904. Not only was the trade agreement spurned in industries traditionally hostile to unions, but many employers who had signed trade agreements at the turn of the century were now refusing to renew them. Much to Mitchell's horror, in his first two years with the NCF dozens of employers dissolved existing collective bargaining agreements with their unions. According to one scholar's estimate, approximately half the trade agreements signed during the early years of the century were cancelled between 1907 and 1909.[11] Thus, while Mitchell continued to believe his association with employers provided them with "a broader and better view of the workingmen," he was in fact presiding over the wreckage of the trade agreement movement.[12]

Not only did Mitchell have to bear witness to the collapse of a movement he held so dear, he was called in on several occasions to participate in its unravelling. One such instance was the destruction of the trade agreement between the International Longshoremen's Association and Great Lakes Carriers' Association and the Dock Managers Association. This agreement had been set up years earlier by his two close friends and ideological allies, Daniel J. Keefe and Mark Hanna. Hanna was now dead and Keefe had retired, but the agreement continued to be touted as a model of capital-labor harmony. When the agreement was in danger of rupture in 1909, Mitchell and Seth Low intervened in an attempt to salvage it. H. G. Dalton, spokesperson for the dock managers, told Low the abrogation of the agreement came only after long and careful thought. The introduction of "very costly and complicated machinery" on the docks, however, required that labor policy be controlled entirely by management. Once this decision had been reached, Mitchell could do nothing.

When ILA officials demanded something be done, he feebly replied that "the indications are that we shall not be able to change the position taken by the Lake Carriers' Association or that of the dock managers."[13]

As the promotional work of the Trade Agreement Department foundered, Mitchell found himself increasingly unhappy. By August 1910, he candidly admitted much of his initial enthusiasm had waned over the past two years. "To be perfectly frank I am not entirely satisfied with the service I have been able to render," he explained to Sam Gompers. "In the well-organized trades the representatives of the union and the employers in interest have been able to work out their own problems." To this he had no objection. Where trade agreements were functioning smoothly, there was no need for NCF intervention. But he did expect to make headway in partially organized industries in which unions did not have a strong presence. In these industries, he found he was "handicapped" because of employer insistence on the open shop. It was impossible for him to exert influence because "it is well known among employers that I am in favor of the union shop."[14] The fact that so famous and respected a figure as John Mitchell, representing so notable an agency as the NCF, could not gain an audience with employers revealed how prevalent anti-union sentiment was by 1909.

Unable to make headway with employers, Mitchell was relegated to lesser tasks for the NCF. He toured the country with Easley in 1910 to establish state NCF councils, he assisted in the Federation's push for uniform legislation in the states, and, most interestingly, he worked closely with the Woman's Welfare Department, an auxiliary branch of Gertrude Beeks' Welfare Department. In 1908, Beeks had given a lecture at the most exclusive women's club in New York, the Colony Club. Several prominent club members, including Edith Harriman, Anne Morgan, the daughter of J. P. Morgan, and Ruth Hanna McCormick, the daughter of Mark Hanna, were so impressed with Beeks' discussion of industrial conditions they organized their own NCF department in May 1908.[15] From its inception this department was very active and its members were fascinated with Mitchell. Even before he began his NCF duty, members requested he come to their club and lecture on the meaning of trade unionism. "It goes without saying that the one labor man they care to hear is yourself," Beeks informed him.[16] This fascination with Mitchell continued and he found himself on numerous occasions preaching unionism to the well-intentioned wives and daughters of industrialists and financiers.

Often Mitchell was invited to speak at the country home of Harriman. She was the most visible member of the department and liked to surround herself with trade unionists. On one occasion in the summer of 1909 she invited Mitchell and Timothy Healy of the International Brotherhood of Locomotive Firemen to dinner. Healy brought along 150 members of his union, who were so impressed with her lavish praise and sumptuous food they made her an honorary member of the union.[17] According to the society columnist of the *Chicago Examiner*, the outdoor affair was a "fairyland" of beautifully decorated tables, waiters in "gorgeous livery," Japanese lanterns, and "pretty misses in costumes led by Miss Edith Harriman."[18] It was in such surroundings that Mitchell preached his vision of labor-capital harmony. Little wonder radical journalists denounced Mitchell and the NCF. As one labor reporter surveyed the scene, he suggested "every coal miner's shack should be ornamented with a copy of the photograph which was taken of the revellers."[19]

Although Mitchell came to recognize such activities were ineffectual and even absurd, and although he became discouraged with his inability to promote trade agreements, he never wavered in his conviction that the NCF and the trade agreement were the keys to perfecting industrial relations. With the open shop movement in full swing, with trade agreements dissolving by the dozens, with militancy on the rise among both employers and workers, he continued to emphasize the harmony of interests existing between capital and labor and the role of collective bargaining in bringing about industrial peace. "The trade agreement is the bridge between capital and labor," he sermonized. "It is an acknowledgment of the interdependence of labor and capital, a recognition of the reciprocity of interests of employer and employee."[20] In his eyes, the fact that few heeded this message did not make that message any less true.

The fact that few heeded this message, however, made his job very unsatisfying. And while he cheerfully fulfilled every duty out of a commitment to the cause, there was not enough work to keep such an active man occupied. As early as late 1908 he began to reassert his influence in the labor movement in a more direct way, taking a very active interest in the internal affairs of the UMWA. But most of his spare time in late 1908 was devoted to a labor issue he would have avoided if possible. He had to defend himself against criminal charges in the Buck's Stove and Range case, charges that almost landed him in prison.

One of the AFL's most effective weapons in the battle against the open shop was the union boycott. A labor movement united in its refusal to purchase goods which did not bear the union label restrained many hostile employers. Open shop employers, in turn, established the American Anti-Boycott Association to assist any employer who wished to challenge boycotts through the court system. And in the Progressive Era years, the courts proved valuable allies of the open shop movement. After two lengthy court battles spanning more than a decade, the AFL's right to boycott was severely undermined. The Danbury Hatters' case dragged on from 1902 until 1916 and resulted in a legal ban on secondary boycotts under the Sherman Act. Even more important was the Buck's Stove and Range case, in which Mitchell played a central role.

By 1906, James W. Van Cleave was the kingpin of the open shop movement. President of the St. Louis-based Buck's Stove and Range Company, he
was also a member of the American Anti-Boycott Association and had
replaced David M. Parry as president of the National Association of Manufacturers. Conspiring with other stove manufacturers, Van Cleave concocted a
detailed plan to establish the open shop in his own industry. The first step was
to drive the union from his company. By placing labor spies in his shop, refusing to negotiate with union representatives, and plotting to hire replacement
workers, he hoped to provoke a strike which would give him grounds to abro-
gate the existing trade agreement between the Stove Founders' Association
and the Iron Molders and Metal Polishers unions. When he cancelled the nine-
hour day in the polishing department, he got what he wanted. In late August,
the polishers went on strike.[21]

Following established custom, the union declared a boycott of the company, and the AFL Executive Council published the company's name on the
"We Don't Patronize List" of the *American Federationist*, the AFL's journal.
Mitchell, of course, agreed to the boycott, but it was hardly a major decision.
Dozens of firms were boycotted each year. This time things would be different. Van Cleave claimed the boycott was illegal and calculated to ruin his
company financially. He requested an injunction from Justice Ashley Gould
of the Superior Court of the District of Columbia to prohibit the AFL and its
officers from maintaining their "conspiracy" to boycott. In December 1907,
Justice Gould complied by issuing a sweeping injunction enjoining AFL officers from publishing the name of the company on the unfair list or in any way
calling attention to the existence of a boycott.[22]

Mitchell, Gompers, and the AFL Executive Council had been looking for a
test case on which to challenge the constitutionality of injunctions on labor
matters, and they resolved to fight this injunction to the end. Accordingly,
Gompers and AFL Secretary Frank Morrison continued to name the Buck's
Stove Company on the "We Don't Patronize" list. Mitchell did his part, too. For
years he had lambasted the use of injunctions. Eight years earlier, before the
U.S. Industrial Commission, he dubbed the injunction "the most dangerous
weapon that has ever been used against labor," and that its use in labor disputes
was destroying "the confidence of the working people in the judiciary."[23] At the
January 1908 UMWA convention, he endorsed a resolution calling for the continuation of the boycott against Buck's Stove, fining any UMWA member who
purchased a stove from this firm $5, and expelling any member who refused to
pay this fine. In February, he sent this resolution to Gompers and asked him to
print it in the AFL's journal with the request that Gompers "require other
Unions to take action along the lines indicated by this resolution."[24]

In July 1908, Van Cleave and his army of lawyers from the American
Anti-Boycott Association petitioned the Supreme Court of the District of

Columbia to find Mitchell, Gompers, and Morrison in contempt of court. Quite obviously, Van Cleave argued, these men had violated the injunction and continued their "conspiracy" to ruin the company. The court ordered this labor trio to appear in September and show cause why they should not be held in contempt. Until July Mitchell did not place much emphasis on the dispute. Consumed with illness, clouded by alcoholism, intent on winding up his affairs at the UMWA and securing new employment, he hardly gave Buck's Stove a passing thought. But when called to Washington on contempt charges, he was suddenly aware of the seriousness of the situation. "It looks to me now as though I may have to spend some time in jail," he wrote anxiously to John Walker.[25]

Mitchell would not face this possibility alone. Aside from the AFL, he had the support of the NCF. When he took up his post at NCF headquarters at the end of July, he learned his new employer had taken charge of the defense. Legal fees were privately financed by Andrew Carnegie, the NCF's biggest contributor, and the accused men were to be represented by Alton B. Parker, a Wall Street lawyer, presidential candidate, and future president of the NCF.[26] For the NCF the case was an opportunity to demonstrate their sympathy for conservative trade unionism against the truculence of the NAM. For Mitchell NCF support gave the case an entirely new meaning. In his eyes, the issue became not simply the use of injunctions and the right of boycott, but a titanic legal struggle between progressive and reactionary employers. This battle was not organized labor versus capital, but conservative labor and the NCF versus reactionary capital. The aim was not to raise class consciousness by winning a blow against injunctions; the aim was to demonstrate that an alliance of labor and progressive capitalists could win tangible benefits—such as a blow against injunctions. Here was a fight Mitchell relished. Thus, when Gompers made aggressively class conscious speeches blasting the judiciary and its subservience to the capitalist class, Mitchell pleaded with him to modify his language, telling him that "Dignity and proper restraint are at this time as essential as courage and candor."[27] This case afforded a golden opportunity to prove to the NCF that the AFL was conservative, that it did not condemn either capital or the state. In the days before the hearing, Mitchell publicly stated he did not "feel disposed to offer unjust criticism, or precipitately to condemn the judiciary. As a class I believe them to be men of high honor and integrity." The only problem was that a handful of judges, like open shop employers, clung to erroneous conceptions of property rights.[28]

Mitchell, Gompers, and Morrison testified in Washington on September 12 and 13, 1908. Over three months later, on December 23, the three men again appeared in court to hear Justice Daniel T. Wright's decision on the contempt charge. Gompers vividly described the scene. As they sat side by side facing Wright, Gompers wrote, "it was at once apparent to all in the court room, including the defendants ... that the flashing eyes, the twitching lips, and the contemptuous frown of Justice Wright but poorly concealed a volcano of surging, relentless hatred."[29] Wright upheld every one of Van Cleave's charges. After Wright read his lengthy finding, filled with such phrases as "the supremacy of law over the rabble" and "those who would unlaw the land are public enemies," he passed sentenced. Morrison was sentenced to six months in the U.S. jail in Washington, Gompers to twelve months, and Mitchell to nine months. All three men appealed and were released on bail.[30] Mitchell was shocked by the decision. So, too, was Seth Low. The NCF president believed that while the decision was deplorable, "it may ultimately lead to a more intelligent determination by the American people of the great principles involved." Mitchell agreed. He could bear this injustice without complaint if, through his suffering, freedom of speech and press were in the future better protected from injunctions.[31]

While the appeal process dragged on, the alliance of progressive employers and the labor movement held firm. The criminal convictions were eventually overturned by the U.S. Supreme Court in May 1911, but by then Buck's Stove had initiated civil proceedings. Again the three men were convicted and charged, and again they appealed. The civil suit eventually reached the Supreme Court in May 1914. To the dismay of all civil libertarians, when Justice Oliver Wendell Holmes read the court's opinion, he declined to comment on the basic issues of free speech, free press, and the legality of injunctions and boycotts. Rather, Holmes held that since all charges were more than three years old, the statute of limitations applied, and he dismissed the case. While Gompers railed that "the principles of justice have been lost in the maze of legalism," Mitchell found it "a great relief to have the contempt case finally disposed of." He also believed, unlike Gompers, that the years of litigation, the public awareness of the case, and the working relationship between the AFL and the NCF "shall be of benefit to the wage-earners of our country."[32]

Even though Mitchell had participated in the AFL's attempt to combat injunctions, he remained unwilling to join hands with Gompers in a forceful political campaign in the fall of 1908. The growing open shop movement and the legal challenges presented by the Buck's Stove and Danbury Hatters' cases convinced most members of the AFL Executive Council that the Federation must intensify its political efforts. From Gompers's perspective, the only hope for labor was a campaign to expel the Republicans and elect William Jennings Bryan and other Democratic candidates. While not officially endorsing the Democratic party, Gompers orchestrated a propaganda blitz of speeches, pamphlets, and cartoons blasting Republicans, especially their presidential candidate William Howard Taft, and praising the labor planks of the Democratic party.

Mitchell refused to cooperate for a variety of reasons. His lasting friendship with outgoing Republican President Theodore Roosevelt induced him to support privately his hand-picked successor, Taft.[33] His new position with the NCF, which sought to attract both Democrats and Republicans, required him to maintain a neutral stance. And he continued to believe the nonpartisan policy of the AFL was the only viable strategy in a movement composed of Democrats, Republicans, and Socialists. Were the AFL to establish close ties with the Democrats, others in the movement would be alienated and the movement ultimately weakened. For these reasons, he actively obstructed Gompers's plans. In late July, for instance, G. H. Hendren of the Indiana State Democratic Committee asked Gompers if Mitchell might speak to the coal miners of the state on behalf of the Democrats. Gompers relayed the request to Mitchell with the personal plea that "a few addresses by you in this campaign will have a tremendous influence." Mitchell declined, citing lingering illness as the excuse, and he would have to refrain from all speaking engagements for "at least two or three months."[34] The excuse of illness was mere subterfuge. In a letter written the same day to his friend Daniel Keefe, an outspoken Republican, he mentioned Gompers's request and stated he would never endorse publicly any candidate for office. To do so, he wrote, "would create division in the ranks of organized labor that might lead to irreparable injury."[35]

Early in August, Mitchell sent out a press release clarifying his position. "I favor the election of candidates, regardless of party affiliation, who are favorable to the political and legislative demands of the American workingmen." Because of time constraints imposed by his new job as chair of the NCF's Trade Agreements Department and because his physician advised him not to exert himself too strenuously, he would not "participate actively" in the AFL's campaign.[36] Yet in several instances, he applied pressure to terminate the pro-Democratic push of Gompers. For instance, when the AFL circulated a cartoon depicting Taft in the pocket of NAM President Van Cleave, Mitchell sent an official protest to the AFL's general organizer, Grant Hamilton. Such tactics were a mistake that "would embarrass the representatives of labor very seriously should perchance Mr. Taft be elected." If Taft were elected, the AFL would want to approach him "with perfect propriety and without embarrassment . . . and insist upon the consideration of labor's demands."[37]

Although Mitchell remained technically neutral during the campaign, he did nothing to dispel the widespread rumors that as an admirer of Roosevelt he supported the Republican party. As the election approached, Taft made political capital of these rumors. In a speech at Buffalo on October 30, Taft stated Gompers's support of Bryan did not represent the opinions of all labor leaders. He offered several names of AFL Executive Council members who did not share Gompers's views, and the name at the top of his list was Mitchell. When an excited Gompers pressed Mitchell for a response to Taft's speech, Mitchell stated publicly: "I am in full sympathy and in accord with the nonpolitical partisan policy of the American Federation of Labor."[38] Journalists were quick to notice that Mitchell failed to respond to the charge that he was opposed to Gompers's support of Democratic candidates. Many therefore assumed he supported Taft. On November 4 Elizabeth Morris informed him that "seventy-five news and editorial clippings have come in . . . either saying openly or intimating that you are against the Democratic campaign or against the policy of Mr. Gompers."[39] Whether or not Mitchell's comment was intended to sabotage Gompers's campaign, he did nothing to rectify the matter.

Taft's victory in the 1908 election was a severe blow to organized labor's legislative hopes. And Mitchell had without a doubt contributed to that victory. As he had in the 1906 congressional campaign, he worked to undermine the AFL's attempt to flex its political muscles and fight its open shop opponents on a new battle field. Even more than Gompers, Mitchell clung to the increasingly outdated view that the best the labor movement could do was to maintain relative silence during elections and try to establish harmonious relations with the winners of those elections. By 1912 so few labor leaders adhered to this policy the AFL was able to undertake a vigorous campaign to elect Woodrow Wilson. The slow turn to political action and the Democratic party came in spite of Mitchell, not because of him.

Resignation from the UMWA presidency did not cure Mitchell of his deep-seated concern for the interests of the union. In many ways, he considered the UMWA his child. He had nurtured it and watched it grow. He had suffered parental anxiety when the organization was troubled. Even as he settled into his NCF office in New York, he continued to follow every move within the union. And although he recognized his fragile health made it impossible for him ever to retake the reigns of power, he found it equally impossible to refrain from intervening in the affairs of the union. More than two years after his resignation, he wrote a friend regarding the miners: "There is not a day that passes during which their welfare is not a matter of deep concern to me."[40]

Union intrigue meant more to Mitchell than concern for the miners. It was also a source of genuine excitement in an increasingly dull routine of lunches, golf, tea parties, and dances. As his NCF post became less satisfying, his spent more of his time in clandestine efforts trying to direct the affairs of the union. In the summer of 1910, for instance, when Mitchell's UMWA machinations reached a peak, Elizabeth Morris admitted she was not earning her NCF salary. She had spent all week reading mining magazines, welcoming UMWA officials, who had come to speak with Mitchell, and writing letters to get up-to-date information on union matters. The only bit of NCF work her and Mitchell had accomplished was to select the winner of a first aid award given by the Red Cross.[41] Above all, Mitchell was obsessed with the ebb and flow of Tom L. Lewis's fortunes as UMWA president, and he followed Lewis's career even more closely than he followed his investments in the stock market.

President Lewis had trouble from the outset of his administration. Only with great difficulty was he able to settle the district negotiations bequeathed to him by Mitchell at the 1908 convention. On the heels of these settlements came disputes with district officials in Pennsylvania, Arkansas, and Kansas over the proper use of national organizers. An even more serious dispute arose in Indiana when Lewis revoked the charter of a local union engaged in what he labelled an illegal strike despite the fact that district officers had endorsed the strike. Lewis then moved to suspend the district officers, although district officers blocked this move by obtaining an injunction against Lewis.[42] These and other disputes convinced many miners Lewis would soon prove the ruination of the union. Many considered him a would-be dictator who ran roughshod over the interests of locals and districts. Although Lewis was no more militant than other UMWA leaders, he was a fighter by nature and his tendency to combat everyone around him, including his supporters, alienated him from the other top men in the union, such as John Walker of Illinois, Alex Howat of Kansas, John P. White of Iowa, and William Green of Ohio.

Mitchell, too, became convinced that Lewis had to go as early as September 1908. When John Walker, now president of the Illinois district, announced his intention to run against Lewis in the upcoming elections, Mitchell told him he was "glad you have decided to make the race." He promised to provide Walker with "every support that it is in my power to give," primarily because he believed that unless Lewis was defeated, "our organization is going to suffer even more than it is doing at this time."[43] Mitchell provided Walker with his expertise in how to run a campaign, how to select running mates with an eye to geography, and how to win the support of powerful allies.[44] Despite Mitchell's advice, Walker fared badly in early returns. Lewis's control of organizers and the UMWA *Journal* made him a fearsome opponent. Mitchell became so frustrated by mid-November he wrote a friend he was "seriously contemplating entering the field as a candidate" for union president, although he never did enter the race.[45] In the end, Lewis prevailed and Mitchell set his sights on defeating him the next year.

In the early summer of 1909, Mitchell pieced together a powerful opposition bloc. He gathered together in Chicago the most outspoken critics of Lewis: Green, Walker, White, Frank Farrington of Illinois, and Edwin Perry, recently elected UMWA secretary-treasurer. At this meeting, the leaders pledged to unite their forces and select a slate popular enough to unseat the incumbent. All present agreed that John P. White was the obvious choice. White, however, was unwilling to run for president so long as Edwin Perry, also from Iowa, retained his post as secretary-treasurer. White argued that two candidates for the top three slots in the union hailing from the same state would weaken his chances. When Perry refused to relinquish his post, the plotters had to make another selection. According to Mitchell, Green "seemed to be the logical choice." He represented the largest district, was popular himself, and his pleasant personality would contrast well with the bellicose Lewis. With all in agreement, Green was chosen to run for the presidency.[46]

Once again Mitchell served as the unofficial campaign director of the insurgent candidate. Even though he and Green had locked horns over the issue of separate settlements in 1906 and again in 1908, the two men shared similar union ideals. Both preferred the conference table to the strike field, both held high hopes for the cooperation of labor and capital, and both were anxious to rid the union of Lewis's dictatorial methods. Mitchell informed Green that it was "because of my anxiety to see preserved the integrity and helpfulness of our union that I feel it my duty to further your cause."[47] As he had done with Walker, Mitchell counseled Green on every aspect of his campaign, even devising the key campaign issue: "Green has heretofore been a consistent supporter of Lewis while at the same time retaining the confidence and esteem of those who disagreed with him. Consequently, he is the best man to restore the harmonious relationship that should exist between the various branches of the organization."[48]

During the campaign, Mitchell and the insurgents were treated to another demonstration of the power of Lewis's personal machine. Charges of corruption and dirty tricks abounded. Lewis refused to publish letters favorable to Green in the union journal, he fabricated membership increases in union rolls, and he hand-picked officials to administer the election itself. By mid-October most of the opposition leaders were resigned to the fact that Green had little or no chance of victory.[49] Green, however, refused to stoop to what he called the "immoral" tactics of Lewis and congratulated himself for having conducted a "clean and honorable campaign."[50] When the votes were tabulated at the January 1910 UMWA convention, the results revealed Lewis had administered a sound drubbing of Green and the other insurgents.

In 1910, Mitchell was finally able to engineer the overthrow of his old nemesis. Lewis assisted in his own downfall through his clumsy handling of the 1910 strike of Illinois miners. In settling this strike he demonstrated, more forcefully than ever, his determination to strip districts of their autonomy. The four-month strike of almost 100,000 Illinois miners centered on the issue of shot firers, those who set off explosives in the mines. Arguing that the national could not afford strike relief, Lewis overruled District 12 leaders and negotiated directly with Illinois operators. He negotiated a favorable settlement, but it included a provision stating that engineers and all other workers necessary to protect mine property during a strike were to be under the direction of the UMWA national executive board rather that district or local officials. When

District 12 leaders opposed the settlement, Lewis tried to go over their heads and appeal to the rank and file of Illinois in a referendum vote. The referendum, too, went against Lewis, who then called a special national convention on the issue. And again, despite his best efforts, the convention rejected Lewis's settlement. Two weeks later, District 12 officials themselves negotiated a settlement of the strike which did not include the obnoxious provision.[51]

Lewis was now in a very vulnerable situation, and Mitchell salivated at the thought of delivering the knockout blow. When Illinois miners rejected Lewis's settlement in the statewide referendum, an excited Mitchell wrote District 12 President Walker: "This is the opportunity of your life. Make the most of it." If only Walker could maintain the confidence of the miners for the rest of the year, "no power on earth can prevent your election to the international presidency." Ever the tactician, Mitchell calmed himself enough to remind Walker two days later not to declare his candidacy yet lest Lewis accuse him of opposing the settlement out of political ambitions. "Remember," he cautioned, "Lewis is adroit and will make use of anything that comes to him to rehabilitate himself and discredit you."[52]

When Lewis called the special national convention in August, Mitchell made certain he was sent as a delegate from his Spring Valley local. He was not about to miss this chance to drive a nail in Lewis's coffin. He learned, however, that he would have to miss the first days of this convention because of pressing NCF duties in New England. "I regret . . . that I cannot put every other thing aside and devote myself to the work of the convention," he wrote Green. But he also wrote Walker and instructed his ally how best to fight if Lewis challenged Mitchell's credentials. Walker followed his advice, secured a seat for Mitchell at the convention, and when Mitchell's name was read the "convention went wild."[53] Mitchell arrived soon after and became an active participant in the debate. While he was one of the few insurgents not to make a personal attack on Lewis's character, he did bolster the anti-Lewis forces when he charged Lewis with being the first president in UMWA history "to revise a scale of wages adopted in a district convention and submitted to a referendum vote."[54] After the convention rejected Lewis's settlement, Mitchell aided Walker in resolving the strike at the district level.[55]

Within days of the special convention, Mitchell met with his insurgent bloc in Chicago. Although Mitchell believed Walker was the logical choice, since he was the head of the Illinois miners who had humiliated Lewis, Walker declined in favor of a candidate more palatable to Lewis's supporters. Mitchell contended there were only two other men strong enough to defeat Lewis: one was William Green of Ohio and the other was John P. White of Iowa. The insurgents opted to run White for the presidency, the relatively unknown Frank Hayes of Illinois for vice president, and William Green for secretary-treasurer. Green was somewhat distraught at this slight and Mitchell had to convince him to accept the race for the lesser office.[56] The choice of White seemed to leave Mitchell out of the picture as campaign coordinator because the two men were not close friends. But when Mitchell offered his expertise, White quickly responded. Throughout October and November, White sought Mitchell's advice on a bewildering variety of campaign issues and strategies.[57] Perhaps because of the clear possibility of toppling the incumbent, Mitchell played an even stronger role in White's campaign than he had with Walker and Green in the two previous years.

Once again, cries of fraud and illegalities filled the air, but when the smoke cleared, both White and Hayes had won by substantial margins. Only William Green failed to win his race. Despite proof that Lewis forces intentionally failed to count the votes of forty-nine Illinois locals, Lewis had finally been unseated. In his farewell speech to the January 1911 UMWA convention, Lewis made an unsolicited promise that his knowledge and experience would never "be sold to the operators or employers of this country." Two years later, Lewis joined the ranks of one of the union's most formidable foes, the West Virginia Coal Operators' Association.[58] In accord with his reputation as a fighter, Lewis did not accept his fall from power without getting in his last licks. He did not need his spies to tell him the ringleader of the opposition was none other than his old nemesis, John Mitchell. Thus, before he left office, Lewis endeavored to exact his revenge.

As his defection to the operators indicated, Lewis was no socialist, but socialists in the UMWA had helped elect him, and he was anxious to exploit this alliance one last time at the January 1911 union convention to hurt Mitchell. The issue he chose was the National Civic Federation. Socialists had long derided Mitchell's participation in the NCF. Wining and dining with the corporate capitalists had "chloroformed" him, had led him to forget the class interests of the miners, had transformed him into "the little tin labor god of the capitalist class." Typical of such sentiment in Mitchell's early years was the comment by Mother Jones: "Poor John, he couldn't stand feasting with the rich. He is no good to his people any longer."[59] And as we have seen, his association with the elites of the NCF had in fact affected his dress and even his speech. When he retired from the UMWA to assume control of the NCF's Trade Agreement Department at the exorbitant salary of $8,000 per year, socialists often assailed him for "selling out" to the capitalists. They ridiculed his black tie and tail functions and his garden parties, and they were quick to contrast these affairs with the deplorable conditions of the working class.

Mitchell certainly made himself an easy target for socialists. He had a compulsion to look and act like a successful businessman. While his home in Mount Vernon was not opulent, it was located in an exclusive suburban neighborhood and was certainly beyond the means of ordinary workers. He dressed and ate very well, smoked expensive cigars, stayed at the most luxurious hotels, and worked in a plush high rise office in Manhattan. And when in public he was apt to display his wealth ostentatiously. To cite but one example, during the summer of 1910 Mitchell attended an AFL Executive Council session in Atlantic City. While playing a game of baseball on the beach with Gompers and the others, Mitchell lost his $1,000 diamond ring. When a lifeguard later found the ring, Mitchell, in full view of the press, took a $100 bill from a roll he carried in his pocket and presented it to the lifeguard as a reward. This exchange prompted one radical journalist to comment that labor leaders who wear such expensive rings and have such large rolls in their pocket "belong bodily to the capitalist class."[60]

In Mitchell's early years such socialist attacks were relatively easy to ignore, but by 1910 socialist influence in the UMWA, in the AFL, and in the nation at large was approaching an all-time high. In that year, Victor Berger became the first Socialist Party member elected to Congress and the party captured the mayoralty of Milwaukee. The next year, socialists were elected mayors in seventy-three cities across the country, and the mainstream press carried dozens of articles about the "rising tide of socialism." Within the AFL, socialist strength increased dramatically. In 1911, several socialists were elected to international office in Gompers's Cigar Makers' Union, and socialists were able to unseat the president of the Carpenters' union, William Huber, and capture the presidency of the Machinists' union.[61] Among the increasingly numerous socialist leaders of the UMWA were John H. Walker, Duncan McDonald, Frank Hayes, and Adolph Germer.[62] While socialists in the labor movement often disagreed over strategy and tactics, one issue on which most saw eye to eye was opposition to the National Civic Federation. And when Tom L. Lewis and socialists joined hands to condemn Mitchell's participation in that body, the struggle became, as one historian put it, "the most important public clash between the socialists and their opponents in the history of their relations throughout the labor movement at large."[63]

The occasion for the clash was the January 1911 UMWA convention, held in Columbus, Ohio. Mitchell did not attend the convention. He was ensconced at the Arlington Hotel in Washington, D. C. awaiting Supreme Court hearings in connection with the Buck's Stove and Range case. With Lewis presiding, several resolutions condemning the NCF were introduced. The most provocative was put forth by a young local union president from anthracite named Thomas Kennedy, later to become national secretary-treasurer, and eventually to succeed John L. Lewis as UMWA president in 1960. "The National Civic Federation, which is chiefly composed and wholly financed by the Belmonts, Carnegies, Morgans, and other bitter enemies of organized labor, is in existence only for the sole purpose of retarding the progress of the labor movement," Kennedy began. The NCF was guilty of attempting to "crush the ever growing militant spirit" of labor, guilty of "disseminating the infamous doctrine of 'identity of interests' and Brotherhood of Labor and Capital," and therefore guilty of implanting "economic falsehood . . . in the minds of the organized wage earner." He resolved that "each and every member" of the UMWA be "hereby prohibited, under penalty of expulsion, from affiliating with, or rendering aid to, financial or otherwise, the aforesaid labor-hating and designing National Civic Federation."[64]

All of the anti-NCF resolutions were referred to the Committee on Resolutions, which was composed of nine delegates hand picked by President Lewis. This committee, by majority vote, delivered to the convention a report denouncing the NCF and providing that any UMWA member be expelled who remained associated with the NCF. Three committee members refused to concur and presented a minority report advising that no action be taken that might be interpreted as an assault on Mitchell. During the debate over the majority and minority reports, Adolph Germer, a radical socialist, introduced a substitute denouncing the NCF but making no reference to Mitchell or his NCF affiliation. Out of fear that the majority report would be adopted, many of Mitchell's allies gave their support to the Germer substitute, which passed by a large majority. Lewis, however, was not satisfied. Revenge necessitated forcing Mitchell out of the NCF. Lewis therefore turned to the Committee on Constitution. Even though no resolutions had been referred to this committee, the committee reported to the convention an amendment to the union's constitution providing that members of the NCF could not also be members of the UMWA. When this proposed amendment was put forth, an acrimonious debate ensued.[65]

At first, Mitchell's allies were confident that they could squelch the amendment. John Walker, although a socialist himself, was a close friend of Mitchell's and generally conservative in his trade unionism. He informed Mitchell of the development but told him not to worry. "I think I have arrangements made which will spike that gun without any furor," he wrote. Mitchell, however, was alarmed. He dashed off a formal letter to Walker and asked him to read it before the convention. The letter read in part that his expulsion from the UMWA "would be the grossest ingratitude on the part of the Miners . . . at a time when I am standing in the shadow of a Federal prison." The ever supportive Elizabeth Morris was enraged that the convention would even contemplate such action. Declaring she was "as piping mad as Mother Jones," she threatened to "come over and personally go gunning for some of these fellows."[66]

The timing of the attack was filled with irony. While radical unionists were in effect placing Mitchell on trial for being too conservative, anti-union employers were trying him on charges of supporting the right to boycott and therefore being too radical. The irony was not lost on Mitchell, who commented at the 1912 UMWA convention that he was in court when a reporter informed him of the amendment denouncing him. At that very minute, NAM lawyer J. J. Darlington was informing the Court that Mitchell was a dangerous character. "As we sat there, tied hand and foot, that was the day and that was the time" the miners' considered the constitutional amendment.[67]

In the next few days, Mitchell received discouraging news from Columbus. He fully expected that President-elect White and Walker, president of the largest district, would use their combined influence to squelch the socialists and Lewis on this issue. Had he not after all been White's unofficial campaign director? And did not White and Walker easily control a majority of the delegates? But from one union friend he heard that White and Walker were uncertain as to the "most judicious method" of defeating the amendment and that "they both seem to have some fear that it will be carried." From Harriett Reid, a knowledgeable secretary with the Mining Investigative Committee of the State of Illinois, Mitchell learned that White and Walker were being "lazy and thoughtless." Rather than lining up votes to kill the amendment, they were staying up till 4:00 A.M. playing poker.[68]

John Walker, at least, proved not to be thoughtless. In the convention debates, Walker, along with many others, offered a vociferous defense of Mitchell. Although Walker conceded the aim of the NCF was "to chloroform the labor movement politically and economically," he believed "any man who tried to chloroform John Mitchell and have him use his services for the detriment of labor has . . . a job to accomplish." Duncan McDonald and Frank Hayes, two other moderate Illinois socialists, complained that Mitchell was not present to defend his connection with the NCF. McDonald also argued that since Mitchell was the only UMWA member in the NCF, and since many AFL leaders were members of that body, NCF membership was an issue on which the AFL should decide. Others charged the amendment represented a personal vendetta against Mitchell. And others wanted concrete examples of the "chloroforming" effect of the NCF.[69]

The fact that moderate socialists supported Mitchell was important. All of these men—Walker, Hayes, McDonald—were highly critical of the NCF and believed in the class struggle, but they broke with their more extreme brethren on this issue. These men hoped to advance socialism by proving to workers that radicals were capable of improving their daily lives in terms of wages, hours, and working conditions. And they believed collective bargaining was the best way to address these bread and butter issues. Thus, despite their politics, they supported John Mitchell, the interstate movement, and the sanctity of contracts. Although they recognized this process of "boring from within" would be slow, they were convinced it was a much more practical approach than the more militant tactics of the IWW's William Haywood, who held that constant class warfare would radicalize the working class.[70]

There were other, more radical socialists in the UMWA, however. Led by Adolph Germer of Illinois and Charles Gildea of the anthracite region, this group hoped their assault on the NCF and Mitchell's conservatism would educate the rank and file on socialist principles and the exploitative nature of capitalism. Germer therefore openly attacked Mitchell and labor leaders of his ilk as "nothing more or less than sheep in wolves' clothing." Reminding delegates of Mitchell's role in the Colorado strike of 1903–1904, he asked delegates what Mitchell and the NCF had "done for the men in the Colorado jail?"[71] To get his points across, Germer was more than willing to join hands with outgoing President Lewis and his supporters who were out for revenge.

In the end, the combination of radicals and pro-Lewis forces proved too powerful. Lewis closed debate. On a standing vote, the amendment was adopted by a majority of about 100. A roll call vote was then taken, and the amendment was adopted by a vote of 1,213 to 967.[72] When he learned of the vote, Mitchell sent the following telegram to the convention: "I am advised that by an amendment of constitution I am deprived of my membership in the United Mine Workers of America unless I relinquish my membership in the National Civic Federation. While I regard this action as a cruel injustice . . . I recognize the legal right of the convention to enact this legislation . . . although I shall live in the consciousness that the men and women at home, for whom I worked for so many years, will not concur in your conclusions."[73]

In two long letters written immediately after this vote, Walker tried to explain to Mitchell why he had been unable to prevent adoption of the amendment. The letters are a remarkable study in contrast. In the first letter, he consoled Mitchell with the thought that while Mitchell now had a difficult choice, he should be warmed by the knowledge that "a large number of the men who spoke in favor" of the amendment "took occasion first to make clear their high regard for you." He claimed the constitutional amendment lacked much of "the sting and thunder" of the original resolutions because it did not mention Mitchell by name. In the second letter, Walker was more callous, and he revealed an inkling of his disgust for the NCF and Mitchell's bourgeois lifestyle. "I do not see how you can complain much," he wrote. "You have been settling all of your disputes by the 'pink tea method' for so long that a little bump like this will be good for you."[74]

Mitchell did not believe this "bump" was in any way beneficial. To Harriett Reid, his trusted confidante, Mitchell poured out his feelings of hurt and anger. "I feel more keenly than will ever be known the rebuke and condemnation so poorly disguised in the action of the convention," he moaned. And referring to his indictment in the Bucks' Stove and Range case, he wailed that "ten years in prison for defending labor would not sting as much as even one implication of unfaithfulness to labor." He did not believe the convention, packed as it was with Lewis supporters, represented the true wishes of the rank and file. The true sentiment of the miners was revealed in the union election, in which he was elected UMWA delegate to the AFL convention by the largest majority he had ever received. But he worried that passage of the resolution would eventually destroy the miners' faith in him. "Naturally and properly they, or at least large numbers of them, will accept the conclusions of the convention." He did not blame Walker, Frank Hayes, William Green or any of his other friends. They had done their best to protect him. He did, however, rebuke John P. White, the man he had helped capture the presidency. "I cannot help observing that the one man in that convention who had the greatest power, namely the president-elect, did not, so far as the minutes show, raise his voice in my defense."[75]

Why had White failed to defend Mitchell? Elizabeth Morris was convinced he was too busy playing poker and celebrating his election to remain vigilant. She thought it was "disgusting" that White, a man who was "so really good at heart," did not possess "the earnestness of purpose to sacrifice a little fun for the sake of being alert and watchful." But poker alone does not explain White's inaction. A more plausible explanation was White's unwillingness to confront directly the large number of radicals over an issue that had no bearing on important union matters. If he hoped to secure radical support for his administration, he dared not cross them on a matter about which they were so adamant. In essence, Mitchell was sacrificed by the insurgent movement he helped create. Mitchell himself came to this conclusion after the convention ended. "I presume John (White) reasoned it would make his administration less tempestuous if he refrained from participation in the factional strife," he noted. But he added caustically that if White "defends policies with as little zeal as he defends his friends, his administration will not pass into history as a brilliant achievement."[76]

Hurt and angry though he was, Mitchell still had a difficult decision to make. He had to decide quickly, before April 1, the day the amendment took effect. The choice proved one of the most difficult in his life. While he was not officially connected with the UMWA, the union had for many years been his lifeblood. He said later he had come to regard the union "largely as the child of my own creation."[77] And he remained emotionally tied to the union. He had kept up his membership with his Spring Valley local, he served as its representative on the AFL's Executive Council, and he spent many hours every week keeping current with union affairs. "From a material standpoint the miners' organization is nothing to me," he confided to a friend, but "sentimentally it is everything."[78] Indeed, one of his greatest concerns after passage of the amendment was the impact it would have on the UMWA. Victory at the convention would encourage "the forces of disruption" within the union, he worried, and in the future they would undertake "further assaults" against conservative leadership.[79]

The NCF, on the other hand, remained in many ways attractive. The $8,000 salary was no minor consideration for a man with bourgeois tastes and a family to support. His oldest son, Richard, was now a senior at the private Fordham University High School and was looking forward to college that autumn. His two other sons were now sixteen and fourteen, and they too hoped to attend college. His house in Mount Vernon was still mortgaged. Thus, Mitchell worried whether he could afford to resign from the NCF. But he did not believe money was the "determining consideration." The NCF represented much more than a high-paying job. It was also a calling. Although his day-to-day duties in the NCF had been unfulfilling, he still considered the NCF the leading proponent of "righteous industrial peace." He described his chairmanship of the Trade Agreement Department "a position honorable in every respect, a position in which I have done and can do good service for the labor movement."[80]

At first, Mitchell tried to find a way out of the convention's verdict. He pleaded with President-elect White to submit the amendment to a referendum vote. The referendum was justified, he argued, because the convention had contravened the wishes of the rank and file, who had expressed their support of Mitchell by electing him AFL delegate. If such a move were not possible, he asked White to grant him a one-year "stay" of the decision to give him sufficient time to think the matter through. "The interests of the United Mine Workers of America cannot suffer by permitting me to remain a member of the union for another year," he wailed.[81] White, however, had a better offer. On February 1, Walker, Green, and White had met to discuss Mitchell's future. They decided to offer him the job of editor of the UMWA's *Journal.* "We all agreed that nobody but yourself could take hold of that paper with such prospects of making it the real, live sheet it should be," Walker excitedly informed Mitchell. In addition, Mitchell could be in charge of a yet to be created "publicity bureau." By delivering lectures, writing articles, and editing the journal, he could once again become a leading force in the union.[82]

Mitchell rejected this offer out of hand. For him it was a question of pride. "Could I retain my self-respect if I accepted an office in the miners' union following the repudiation of the Columbus convention?," he asked Walker. In a letter to James Duncan, first vice president of the AFL, he explained his reasoning. He had built the union to a position of strength, had won wage increases and hourly reductions. He had worked long and hard as their president, to the point where his physical and mental health had become so impaired he was forced to step down. Three years later, while facing prison because of an action taken by the miners' convention, he learned the miners' had "denounced" him. And he was not even given the opportunity to defend himself. "Do you know, Jim, of another case in the history of the labor movement wherein so gross an injustice was done?" He resolved that "there were no circumstances imaginable that would induce me to accept an official position in the miners' union."[83]

To help him decide, Mitchell sought advice from just three people—John Walker, James Duncan, and Frank Peabody. Duncan was not only a friend in the labor movement, he was also a leader in the NCF. Peabody was an operator whose opinion he had valued for years. All three men encouraged him to resign his NCF post. Peabody advised that the miners needed him now more than ever. Under the Lewis administration the miners had been "inspired with insubordination . . . and will not heed the commands or demands of their officers, and are paying absolutely no attention to the contracts with the operators." If this situation was not rectified by the spring of 1912, the miners would be in no position to restore collective bargaining, and the result would be "chaos." "If this is all true, do not the men again need a leader, one who has shown by his own actions that his heart is wrapped up in their interests?" He urged Mitchell to resign from the NCF "and take part as a member of your local union in the deliberation of the miners."[84] Duncan was even more forceful in his advice. "Stay with your union," he implored. The greatness of the UMWA was built upon "your personality and your ability." Quitting the union would play right into the hands of the Lewis forces, "who since the first day your name was mentioned as a successor to M. Ratchford have been planning your downfall and belittling your work." Moreover, resignation from the union would force him from the AFL Executive Council and out of the labor movement altogether. If Mitchell were ever to make "such a change it must be of your own free will and accord, and in your own way."[85]

That Mitchell sought advice from the socialist Walker reveals he was probably leaning toward a decision to resign from the NCF. After all, Walker had condemned the NCF at the miners' convention. If Mitchell was simply looking for encouragement to carry out a decision he had already made, Walker did not disappoint him. If Mitchell remained in the NCF, those miners who condemned him "will go forward with the slogan that you hold the Civic Federation in higher esteem than you do the Miners' Organization." Unless he quit the NCF the miners would believe that he "would rather have the dollars of the labor crushers than to work for the men that you were raised and associated with all your life." They would believe "that you would rather feast, drink and orgy with the plutocracy than to work for the cause of human uplift." And the extremists such as Adolph Germer would rejoice that they had "compelled you at least to stand out in your true colors."[86]

In the end it was not fear that workers would consider him a capitalist lackey that determined his course of action. Rather, it was fear he would be cut adrift from the child of his creation. On February 15, Mitchell officially tendered his resignation to Seth Low, NCF president. On April 1, he would sever all connection with that organization. He regretted the action of the UMWA convention, not so much because it forced him to choose between the two organizations, but "because of the unjust and gratuitous attack" upon the NCF. He apologized for breaking his contract. And he thanked Low and the NCF officers for having confidence in his abilities and allowing him to be "of assistance in promoting industrial peace through the medium of the trade agreement."[87]

In accepting Mitchell's resignation, Low condemned the action of the miners that had made it necessary. Under the circumstances, however, he believed Mitchell's decision was "both natural and proper." He commended Mitchell for his past work in the cause of industrial peace. Only NCF colleagues, he wrote, "fully understand how helpful you have been in bringing about a better understanding between employers and employees in all sorts of directions." Low asserted that because of Mitchell's presence he personally had a more profound appreciation of "the workingmen's point of view on many questions of vital interest."[88]

Samuel Gompers and Ralph Easley recoiled in horror to the radical attack on Mitchell. From their perspective, the humiliation of Mitchell marked the opening salvo in a war for control of the labor movement. Socialist gains in the various affiliates of the AFL had emboldened the radical leaders, who were now determined to displace the "old guard" of conservative business unionists who had controlled AFL policy since the 1880s. Mitchell was the first trophy to be "bagged," and it was only a question of time before others fell, perhaps even Gompers himself. Gompers, ever the fighter, was not about to wait for the socialists' next move. He wanted to strike now and crush his opponents before they gained greater strength. And he pressed Mitchell to join him in a full scale propaganda war against the radicals. Easley, too, wanted Mitchell to return the fire against those who would sever the alliance between conservative trade unionists and progressive employers, which represented the basis of NCF influence. Gompers and Easley quickly prepared for all out war over control of the labor movement.

In mid-February, Gompers wrote Mitchell, praising him for making the proper decision. "If the same situation were presented to me I would not hesitate for one moment, I would resign from the Civic Federation and I would remain in the Miners' Union," he declared, "and then within the ranks I would fight for the cause of right, for the cause of labor." He asked Mitchell to write, "fully and completely," his account of the convention and the socialists' attack. This account could then be published in the AFL's magazine, the *American Federationist*, and would prove to the nation's rank and file the treachery and evil nature of socialists. He pleaded with Mitchell to "do a service to the cause of labor and justice—the cause of trade unionism—for which no like opportunity might present itself in a decade." Gompers had already written an article on the subject for the March issue of the journal, but he wanted an account written by the victim, who would not be afraid to name names and expose the intrigue. He wanted Mitchell to act quickly, while the issue was still fresh in the public's mind. Easley excitedly wrote that he had talked with Gompers and the AFL president was prepared to press this matter until vengeance was secured. "He has no idea of letting down for a minute," Easley gushed.[89]

Mitchell balked. He questioned the wisdom of writing or saying anything on the subject before he had a chance to do so through the miners' journal. And that opportunity would not arise until April 1, when White assumed the UMWA presidency. Tom L. Lewis still held the reigns and would undoubtedly refuse to publish anything he wrote prior to that date. While he agreed the radicals who censured him deserved to be "pilloried," he felt duty bound to challenge his opponents within the union first before involving the entire labor movement. If Gompers wanted him to join in his holy war against socialism, he would have to wait.[90] Privately, Mitchell agreed with Gompers that the action taken against him was of national importance. He wanted his case to "awaken the trade unionists" of America, to prompt them to take greater interest in their unions and watch "more carefully the maneuvers of the element that is trying so hard to secure control of all our organizations."[91] But he also had selfish reasons to maintain silence. At their February district convention, the miners of Illinois had condemned, by nearly unanimous vote, the amendment adopted at the national convention. Other districts were contemplating similar action. Mitchell was overjoyed by this news and believed he could yet be vindicated by the miners.[92] The last thing he wanted to do was raise the ire of the rank and file by airing the union's dirty linen in the pages of the public press. The "manly" thing was to confront his enemies directly.

Gompers refused to wait. His article for the AFL's magazine combined a scathing, vituperative smear of socialists in the labor movement with a *rational*, detached defense of the NCF. Socialists knew nothing of the Civic Federation, he charged. Their charge that AFL leaders were duped by corporate capitalists revealed a "perverted intellect," an "abandonment of sincerity and truthfulness," and was "designed to stir up the meanest of passions." In truth, the NCF performed valuable work in regulating corporations, settling labor disputes, and pressing for positive legislation such as workers' compensation. If socialists were less ignorant of the NCF, they would not be so quick to attack it.[93] The article marked only the beginning of Gompers's campaign. In a widely publicized letter to Mitchell on March 3, Gompers declared the action of the UMWA convention was not only a mistake and an injustice, but also a blow to all "constructive trade union work, the work for the common and general uplift of the toilers." The humiliation of Mitchell was the work of socialists, those "false pretenders who mask behind a pretended interest in and friendship for labor." Their destructive philosophy was "wholly at variance" with constructive trade unionists and surprisingly similar to "the Posts and the Kirbys of the National Association of Manufacturers."[94]

Throughout the month of March numerous other conservative unionists took up the cause. One by one, they defended Mitchell, denounced socialism, vented their condemnation of the miners' action, and voiced their support for the NCF. Daniel Tobin of the Teamsters, recently elected member of the NCF's executive committee, J. L. Rodier, a leading unionist from Washington state, and several others made their voices heard. In May and June, Easley inserted himself into the propaganda war, carrying on a well publicized debate with Morris Hillquit, New York labor lawyer and moderate socialist.[95] But it was Mitchell that Gompers wanted to enlist in the anti-socialist crusade. And after April 1, when it became clear the new UMWA president would do nothing to exonerate Mitchell for fear of alienating the radicals, Mitchell finally stepped forward to tell his story. He wrote a series of articles for publication in the coal miners' journal, and he had secured President White's promise that they would in fact be published. He informed Gompers the account was "not so strong as I should like to make it, but there are some things I cannot find the heart to say." Nevertheless, he believed that when the mine workers read these articles, "the revulsion of feeling . . . will be crystallized."[96]

In his first article, he recounted the "injustice" perpetrated by the UMWA convention, the "misrepresentation" of the real character of the NCF, and the "impertinence" of not allowing him to defend himself in person. He stressed, however, that while "a great wrong has been done me," he in no way "held the rank and file of our membership in any degree responsible for this injustice." The fault lay with those officials and radicals who acted "for purposes best known to themselves." The second article was a vigorous defense of the NCF against the "silly charge" of socialists that the NCF was "chloroforming the labor movement." The labor men in the NCF were "champions." The "strongest and most progressive" unions in the nation were officered by men connected with the NCF. Under his leadership the UMWA had become "the most powerful, and among the most feared and respected of all the organizations of labor on this continent." And yet during this same period, if the socialists were correct, "we were lulled to sleep by the soothing effects of chloroform administered by the National Civic Federation!" The third and fourth letters were attempts to educate the miners on the true principles and purposes of the NCF. He discussed its history, its open membership, its finances, the functions of the various departments, and its administrative structure. He then focused on its valuable contributions to the labor movement. The NCF actively promoted trade agreements by providing a clearinghouse of information on these increasingly complicated collective bargaining contracts, and the NCF assisted in the amicable resolution of strikes, which often benefited the trade unions involved.[97]

Gompers's propaganda war set the whole labor movement afire by the early summer of 1911. In union conventions across the country, delegates grappled with the larger issues arising from Mitchell's resignation from the NCF. Socialist insurgents battled business unionists aligned with the NCF in several pitched battles for control. In the Brotherhood of Locomotive Firemen, incumbent President Timothy Healy crushed a socialist attempt to oust him. President Denis Hayes of the Glass Bottle Blowers' union repelled socialists at his convention. But the socialists had their victories as well. The socialist William H. Johnston defeated the conservative incumbent James O'Connell in the Machinists' union presidential race. And socialists removed from office John B. Lennon, secretary of the journeymen tailors' union and AFL treasurer.[98]

Mitchell, Gompers, and Easley prepared for an ultimate showdown between the two forces at the November 1911 AFL convention in Atlanta. In Mitchell's eyes, the coming confrontation assumed the dimensions of an Armageddon, the conclusive battle between the forces of good and evil. Reflecting on the labor movement as a whole, he wrote his friend Lennon "I wonder sometimes, whither we are drifting?" Had conservative unionists "built up a structure that is to be torn upon our heads?" Interestingly, he viewed the battle with socialists in religious terms, viewing their philosophy as heretical. The AFL was "passing through a great crisis," he wrote, "and that we may emerge from the clouds of discord and heresy is my earnest hope and constant prayer."[99] He was ready to plot as well as pray.

In May he met with Gompers and Easley to plan their strategy for the convention. They carefully prepared a defense for every possible socialist attack against the NCF. One of the strongest socialist arguments was control of the NCF by savagely anti-union employers such as Andrew Carnegie, who had "the blood of the Homestead strikers on his hands," and August Belmont, the ex-NCF president who had provoked the Interborough strike to establish the open shop. Easley was assigned the task of gathering evidence. He asked Carnegie to provide any information he could concerning his actions before the Homestead strike. "Both Gompers, Mitchell and I want this material," Easley explained, "because we are going to make those lying Socialists eat their words." Mitchell and Gompers would find it easy to defend Carnegie because "they admire and love you." According to Easley, Mitchell was to take personal charge of the defense of Carnegie at the AFL convention, and he was eager to do so.[100]

At the Atlanta convention of the AFL, the long awaited battle began. As Mitchell and Gompers anticipated, radicals introduced several resolutions condemning the NCF and calling on all AFL members to sever their connection with that body. Gompers, of course, had packed the Resolutions Committee, which was ready to burst forth with a defense of the NCF against all charges, a defense that sounded as if it were written by Easley himself. When the Resolutions Committee recommended non-concurrence with the anti-

NCF resolutions, a general debate ensued that Gompers characterized as "one of the most fundamental and most spirited in convention records."[101] Leading the radical faction were Adolph Germer of the UMWA and Max Hayes, perhaps the most popular trade union socialist and a member of the Typographers' union. When they were finished, conservative union presidents and AFL vice presidents, one by one, arose to defend the Civic Federation. Gompers himself made the longest speech, but Mitchell unquestionably made the most effective one.

By order of the January 1911 miners' convention, all UMWA delegates to the AFL convention were instructed to vote against the NCF. Thus, it was ironic that Mitchell was duty bound to censure the NCF even as he rose to praise it. His argument was familiar, although perhaps more emotional. He once again recounted the treachery of Lewis and his allies in the union that forced him to retire from the NCF. That action had caused "a sting in my heart, (and) as long as God gives me life, I shall remember the circumstances surrounding me at the time this action was taken." He again praised the beneficial work of the Civic Federation. And then he fulfilled his promise to Easley and Gompers by defending Andrew Carnegie's role during the Homestead strike of 1892. Carnegie had been in Europe at the time of the strike, he said, and had he been in Pennsylvania no violence would have occurred. He concluded by appealing to delegates to vote on the resolution without regard to personality or prejudice, but with an unbiased assessment of what was best for the labor movement. When he concluded delegates voted 11,851 to 4,924 to uphold the report of the Resolutions Committee. Mitchell and Gompers had dealt the socialists a stunning defeat.[102]

Mitchell was quite satisfied with the results of the convention. He relished the abuse heaped upon Tom L. Lewis for packing the UMWA convention and forcing his retirement from the NCF out of selfish reasons. What impressed Mitchell most was the way Lewis "sat there like a whipped dog through it all." As for socialism, the convention had intensified his contempt for its practitioners and principles. He had always "studied socialism with an open mind," but as a result of his recent experience, he came to the conclusion that "the practices of many socialists repel me." The only real solution for the labor problem was conservative collective action through the trade union movement. "Progress is being made," he declared, "the workers are better off than they have been in the past, and . . . measured by decades great progress has been achieved."[103]

Unfortunately, the agency which Mitchell perceived as one of the great contributors to that progress had suffered as much as he had in 1911. While the NCF had been saved from denunciation at the 1911 AFL convention, Mitchell's resignation on April 1 marked the end, in a very real sense, of its active promotion of trade agreements. The loss of Mitchell, by far the nation's most popular and committed champion of the trade agreement, forced Easley to abandon his grandiose dream of reconciling capital and labor through national collective bargaining. Easley did attempt to revive the Trade Agreement Department by contemplating the hiring of co-chairs, one employer and one labor leader, who exemplified the viability of trade agreements. But Samuel Gompers objected to the appointment of another trade unionist to the department on the ground it would most likely prompt another anti-NCF campaign by socialists in the AFL. Thus, Mitchell's departure forced a major shift in the focus of the NCF. While the Trade Agreement Department continued to decline, the Welfare Department received greater attention. And as we have seen, the Welfare Department was undeniably anti-union in its makeup and objectives. By 1913, the NCF's new direction attracted so many open shop employers that James Duncan, Mitchell's friend on the AFL Executive Council, quit the NCF in disgust.[104] While Mitchell continued to attend NCF functions as an observer and adviser, he no longer looked to the organization as the vehicle to establish capital-labor harmony.

Ironically, the defeat of socialists at the "Armageddon" of 1911 did nothing to weaken their strength in the UMWA and the labor movement as a whole. Much to Mitchell's chagrin, socialists at the 1912 UMWA convention secured resolutions calling for a restructuring of the AFL along industrial union lines and favoring "government ownership of all industries," and they came close to winning a resolution that would have endorsed the Socialist Party as the political party of the working class. Both Adolph Germer and Duncan McDonald recalled the Mitchell era when socialists were an isolated minority faced with constant hostility and contrasted those dark years with their present strength. Socialists at the 1912 AFL convention gained thirty-five percent of the vote on their demand for industrial union organization.[105]

Mitchell remained adamantly opposed to what he perceived as the twin evils of open shop employers and radical workers, but he was no longer in a position to combat them. As of April 1, 1911, Mitchell was out of a job and out of the limelight. The action of the UMWA in 1911 shattered his pride, and he no longer took an active part in union affairs. His resignation from the NCF left him without a platform to publicize his views and without an official connection to unions and employers. His one remaining tie to the labor movement was his seat on the AFL Executive Council. And in November 1913, he voluntarily gave up this position to make room for someone more active in the movement. Thus, while Mitchell was still a very popular figure, his role as a major player in the industrial relations scene ended in 1911.

By no means did he slip quietly into retirement. He was still young, only forty-one, and he was possibly healthier than he had been at any time since 1906. And he still needed to earn a living to support his family. Even before he vacated his office at NCF headquarters, Mitchell received numerous job offers, including the editorship of three newspapers. But the avenue he found most appealing was the lecture circuit. Ever since the 1902 anthracite strike, he had toyed with the idea of capitalizing on his fame by delivering lectures across the country. And when the opportunity presented itself in the spring of 1911, he jumped at the chance. He signed contracts with the Lyceum and Chautauqua circuits, agencies that made all travel and hotel accommodations and paid him handsome salaries. In addition, he sold his services to individual groups and clubs, usually charging $50 a lecture plus expenses. Thus, for the next two years Mitchell spent much of his time on the road.[106]

The content of his speeches were usually taken from his book, *Organized Labor*, on the principles and practices of trade unionism. His mission, such as it was, was to allay fears among the general public that trade unions were radical, corrupt, or un-American. This proved to be a far more difficult task than he at first envisioned. Especially in rural areas and small towns in the Midwest and South, he found his audiences largely composed of farmers and small businessmen. These people had "peculiar notions" about unions, he discovered, and many audiences were "obviously hostile." In all he found his lecture tour the "hardest work I have ever undertaken."[107]

Mitchell also remained active on a wide array of committees and commissions, not all of which dealt with labor questions. Always a joiner, he found himself lecturing before and serving on the executive committees of such groups as the Travelers' Aid Society, the American Academy of Political and Social Science, the American Association for Labor Legislation, the National Committee on Prison Labor, and the National Child Labor Committee. He also lectured before the National Woman's Trade Union League. For the first time in his life, he spoke out publicly for the need to organize women workers. Indeed, he became so interested in women workers that he made a special plea on their behalf in the middle of his retirement speech to the November 1913 AFL convention: "I belong to a craft that has no women workers, but, my friends, I am more interested in the organization of women than I am of men, and I hope . . . that you and those you represent will do even more than you have in the past in furnishing protection to that weaker part of the great industrial army."[108] While he had not become an outspoken supporter of feminism, he did join the New York branch of the Men's League for Women's Suffrage in 1912.[109] It is interesting to wonder what actions he might have taken on behalf of women workers had he remained active in the movement.

One question that intrigued Mitchell more than almost any other after 1911 was the role of religion in the labor movement. With the rapid growth of socialist influence in the AFL, and with the NCF apparently in the hands of open shop employers, Mitchell, along with other notable Catholic labor leaders, joined hands with Father Peter Dietz in the Militia of Christ for Social

Service. Father Dietz was an arch anti-socialist active in the labor movement who organized the Militia of Christ at the November 1910 AFL convention. According to the Militia's constitution, it was "a religious, patriotic and unionist fraternity" of Catholic labor leaders who hoped to "cultivate the aspirations of the workers to better their conditions through organization in conservative trade unions, through collective bargaining and trade agreements, (and) conciliation and arbitration of industrial disputes." Other than Dietz and Mitchell, the leaders of the Militia included P. J. McArdle of the Amalgamated Association of Iron, Steel, and Tin Workers, and Thomas J. Duffy of the Brotherhood of Operative Potters.[110]

The Militia of Christ perfectly matched Mitchell's agenda. Like the NCF, the Militia worked to advance the cause of trade unionism by promoting trade agreements and industrial peace. Also like the NCF, the Militia was just as concerned with stemming the socialist tide within the movement as it was with challenging the anti-union employers who attacked from outside the movement. As a Catholic organization, the Militia serviced Mitchell's recently developed religious predilections. And finally, it was an agency that promoted pro-labor legislation, an area in which Mitchell was developing great interest. Mitchell defined the Militia as "a movement for progressive social reform." Whether or not the charge was true, "there is a widespread impression that our Church is just a little over-conservative in matters of this kind." It seemed to him, therefore, that "our people should adopt and pursue a systematic program for social betterment . . . for the protection of that great part of the people in our country who are least able to protect themselves."[111]

In 1911, Mitchell delivered several lectures at Catholic churches on the East coast on behalf of the Militia, and he actively tried to enlist other Catholic trade unionists in the cause. He met with members of the Militia several times during the year in an effort to get the movement off the ground. But at the end of 1911, the Militia was simply surviving, not prospering in the way Dietz had hoped. Dietz complained that Catholic labor leaders "have done little beyond lending their names." The contributions of Mitchell and a handful of others were generous, but they "did not fan the spark to the point of ignition." Mitchell regretted he could not be more active, but he was constantly on the road giving lectures trying to make ends meet. Whenever time allowed, however, he promoted the cause. In fact, he had just returned from Scranton where he lectured at a benefit for Slavish workers hoping to erect a church. And he did suggest methods by which Dietz could raise more money "to carry on the work."[112]

Despite Dietz's fears, the Militia grew by leaps and bounds in 1912 and became a major fixture on the industrial relations scene for the remainder of the Progressive Era. With the assistance of Mitchell and Gompers, the Militia printed weekly newsletters and distributed them to over three hundred labor papers. It sponsored hundreds of trade union meetings and conferences to spread its ideas and combat socialism.[113] Indeed, Mitchell and Gompers so ably assisted the Militia that one of its most able lecturers, David Goldstein, offered them his highest praise. In answer to the question of whether socialists would capture the AFL, Goldstein wrote: "Fear not!" Men such as "Samuel Gompers and John Mitchell stand as good security against so dreadful a fate. They are too well versed in the principles of socialism not to heed the danger—they are too well acquainted with socialist tactics not to understand their modes of attack."[114]

Just as Gompers, a Jew, was ready to support a Catholic trade union movement because he deemed it an ally in his fight against radicalism, so, too, did Mitchell support conservative union activists in the Protestant churches. In 1912, Mitchell became active in the Protestant-based "Men and Religion Movement." This movement was the brainchild of Charles Stelzle, a former machinist and Presbyterian minister who remained active in the AFL. Stelzle combined the techniques of evangelical religion with the philosophy of conservative trade unionism to increase union strength and weaken the influence of socialists. In hundreds of cities across the nation, teams of organizers held parades, mass meetings, and lectures lasting for several days. Even though he was in the midst of a hectic lecture schedule, Mitchell contributed by delivering lectures in Washington, D. C. and New York City.[115]

Mitchell's interest in religion as the key to advance the cause of labor waned as quickly as it developed. While he remained a committed Catholic and continued to believe that organized religion, whether Catholic or Protestant, could play a positive role in thwarting radicalism among workers and anti-unionism among employers, by mid-1912 he despaired that churches would never assume that role in practice. Only when the church "could see its way clear to declare in an emphatic manner its endorsement of the principles of trade unionism," he informed a priest, would the church be valuable to the labor movement and the nation as a whole. Many of the ideals of conservative trade unionism "have been endorsed by individual clergymen or by associations of clergymen," he continued, "but it would seem to me that it would be advantageous . . . if clergymen everywhere could see their way clear to assert positively that these principles . . . are essential to the welfare of the people and the prosperity of the nation."[116]

If religion would not serve as the vehicle to advance the interests of the working class, and if the NCF could no longer fulfill this role, what agency could possibly promote progressive social change? Mitchell became increasingly convinced, after his departure from the NCF, that only the state could fulfill this role. In the remaining years of his life, he devoted most of his energy to the passage of positive social legislation benefiting both organized and unorganized workers. Among the laws he came to favor were those endorsing a minimum wage, shorter hours, safety and sanitation in factories and mines, prohibition of child labor, and workers' compensation. As we have seen, while president of the UMWA, he had been somewhat less doctrinaire than Gompers on the positive role of state intervention in economic affairs. He had, for instance, voted for AFL support of a maximum hour law despite Gompers's opposition. Yet by and large he had agreed with the AFL president that trade union economic power was the best method to advance working-class interests, and he therefore upheld the voluntarism of the AFL. Mitchell by no means abandoned voluntarism in his declining years, but he did begin to speak out more forcefully for positive government intervention.

Exactly why Mitchell turned to the state is difficult to determine. Perhaps he realized the trade agreement movement, which he considered for so many years to be the solution for labor relations, was all but dead by 1911. Perhaps he understood that far too few workers belonged to unions for the labor movement to be the only instrument to promote the welfare of the entire working class. Perhaps he was simply reflecting the influence of Theodore Roosevelt's thinking. Or perhaps he recognized socialist advances could be stymied only by securing concrete gains for all workers. Whatever the reason, Mitchell became a vocal critic of the AFL's knee jerk opposition to political action. At the 1914 AFL convention, for instance, he made an eloquent, if unsuccessful, plea on behalf of AFL support for minimum wage and maximum hour laws. He had traveled throughout much of the country and had heard the cries of workers for such laws. "Have you a right, then, to deny all the men and women in these various states the right to legislate themselves into a legal eight-hour day?"[117] Gompers argued against support for this legislation and hinted that it was sponsored by socialist influences.

One area of pro-labor legislation in which Mitchell and Gompers were in agreement was workers' compensation, and here Mitchell played an important role in shaping legislation. His interest in compensation dated from the autumn of 1909, when he served on a commission created by authority of the New York state legislature. This commission studied workers' compensation questions in detail and made the first legislative report in the country on the subject. Mitchell also helped the commission draft a bill which the state legislature enacted. The act was compulsory, but it applied only to "extra-hazardous and non-competitive industries." While he admitted the act was "limited in scope," he believed that since this was the "first measure of this kind enacted by any state, it was thought best to make the 'trial trip' on lines of least resistance."[118] Despite this caution, in March 1911, the New York Court of Appeals ruled that an employer without fault could not be compelled to pay workers injured on the job, and further, that compulsory compensation was a violation of the state's constitution.[119] This decision notwithstanding, the New York law spurred other states to pass similar legislation. During 1911 alone, twelve states passed compensation or accident insurance laws.[120]

The NCF was also vitally interested in workers' compensation. It was in many ways an ideal issue for Easley and Low. Supported by progressive businessmen, labor leaders, and the general public, workers' compensation was an issue that might help the NCF reassert itself. In 1913, the NCF appointed a commission of six members to study the operation of the various state laws. The intent was to frame a model bill to aid states which had not yet passed such legislation, to point out the relative merits and defects of existing laws, and in general to inspire cooperation between employer and employee on this vital question. Mitchell agreed to serve on this NCF commission, and he spent part of 1913 visiting California, Washington, Illinois, Michigan, Ohio, New Jersey, and other states. He assisted in the collation and analysis of data culled from questionnaires sent to workers in the twelve states where laws were already in operation. And he helped prepare a model bill for the NCF which was circulated throughout forty-one state legislatures during the winter of 1913–1914.[121]

In December 1913 the New York legislature passed its second workers' compensation act. The new act borrowed many features from the NCF's model bill Mitchell had helped frame. When Governor Martin H. Glynn looked around for commissioners to help administer the act, Seth Low quickly recommended Mitchell. Mitchell was interested in securing a regular job, for as early as April 1912 he had been unhappy with his lecture tour. "There are many features connected with the work that are distasteful," he wrote. He found especially bothersome the fact he was "kept away from home more than I want to be." Thus, when Glynn considered him for the New York Board of Compensation, Mitchell was interested but by no means ecstatic. And he was certainly not thrilled about the salary. The best he could say about the $7,000 per year salary was that it was "better than nothing." The next day Glynn appointed Mitchell to a term of four years.[122]

Mitchell's obvious lack of enthusiasm can be attributed to his failure to obtain the more powerful and prestigious post of New York Commissioner of Labor in 1913. Governor William Sulzer appointed him to that post in April of that year, but leading state senators, the Tammany organization, and even state labor officials opposed his confirmation. Mitchell was very excited about the job, and he was pleased when Sulzer decided to fight for Mitchell's confirmation to the bitter end. Unfortunately, the end came for Sulzer as well as Mitchell. Sulzer was impeached, and the appointment cancelled.[123] This turn of events proved to be a major disappointment for Mitchell, who now had to settle for the position of Board of Compensation Commissioner.

His prospects brightened somewhat in the spring of 1915, when the state legislature consolidated the work of the Board of Compensation and the State Labor Department, and placed them under a new, five member State Industrial Commission. In late May Mitchell was appointed to a one year term as chair of this new commission, but he would ultimately hold this position until his death in 1919.[124] The Commission was responsible for a wide variety of activities, from factory inspection and enforcement of factory laws to compensation claims and payments, from mediation and arbitration services to labor statistics and information, from immigration records to fire safety inspection in factories.

His new position kept him extremely busy. He was constantly on the go between the Commission's New York City offices and Albany, and he also worked out of his home at Claremont Street in Mount Vernon. In addition, he was expected to speak at local business clubs and labor organizations throughout the state, and he personally handled many of the most complicated compensation claims. To assist him, he retained the administrative services of Elizabeth Morris, his faithful servant since 1899. Far from a cushy political appointment, he found the job almost too demanding. He complained the work "keeps me busy from early morning until late at night" and gave him little time for family and friends. "I have always worked hard," he confided to a friend in early 1916, "but I have never worked harder than during the past seven months."[125] Despite the onus of overwork, he found his new job reasonably satisfying, and he believed it to be important work. Nor did he have to hide his pro-union attitudes. Never once did a politician ask him to mute his trade union bias. "Indeed, I do not believe politicians would have the least respect for me," he bragged to old chum John Walker, "if I were to permit my position . . . to change my opinions in the slightest degree."[126]

Perhaps Mitchell could have lived to a ripe old age as an important state official. He might have grown fat and content in his comfortable Manhattan office, now that he was far removed from the turmoil of union politics. His two oldest boys, Richard and James, were both working, and the younger son and daughter, Robert and Catherine, would soon be old enough to leave the nest. While his wife was sickly, periodically stricken by one minor disease after another, no doubt John and Kate looked forward to many happy years together as a bourgeois suburban couple. Unfortunately, such was not to be. In late 1915 trouble struck. Mitchell and the entire Commission came under attack by a state legislative investigating committee. The charges were negligence, incompetence, and misuse of funds, and as head of the Commission Mitchell felt the political heat.

The cause for the investigation was the November 6, 1915 Diamond Candy Corporation factory fire in Brooklyn, which left twelve workers dead. Since inspection of fire hazards in factories five stories or higher fell under the jurisdiction of Mitchell's Commission, the state legislature undertook a routine investigation to determine whether the Commission had been aware of potential problems. The investigating team was appalled by what they found. The interior stairway of the Brooklyn factory where the fire started was not enclosed with fireproof material. And while the Industrial Commission had inspected the building and ordered the stairway to be fireproofed, the Commission had failed to pursue the matter and force company compliance. As the investigators dug deeper, they uncovered a pattern of negligence on the part of the Commission, citing repeated examples of "lax enforcement" and charging the Commission was "incompetently administered." Moreover, investigators charged that the five person Commission and its staff had used state-owned automobiles for private purposes and made "improper charges for meals and hotel bills," amounting to nearly $24,000 in less than a year! In view of these findings, the investigators called for the removal of all present members of the Commission.[127]

Investigators withheld one name from their list of Commission members to be removed—John Mitchell. They found that he was not responsible for factory inspections. The Commission had early on decided to divide up their tasks and Mitchell was to take charge of workers' compensation claims, agreements, awards, and payments. He therefore could not be charged with negligence in the Diamond factory fire. Nor could investigators link him to false meal and hotel billing or misuse of state vehicles. The investigators concluded that while the chair should have kept a closer eye on his underlings, his own actions were without fault: "On account of his experience in the administration of the workmen's compensation law, his grasp of the subject, the great respect and esteem in which he is held by the citizenship of this State generally, and his standing among and almost life-long interest in the welfare of the great mass of organized workers, we feel that he should remain upon the Commission."[128]

While relieved there was "little criticism of me personally" by the legislature or in the press, Mitchell was profoundly shaken by the "unfortunate fire" and the charges against the Commission and its members. He was also frightened when the District Attorney of Kings County interviewed him and contemplated criminal charges for his "alleged failure to enforce labor laws."[129] Although no charges were filed, he was upset enough to consider retirement. He realized Governor Charles Whitman planned to renominate him, but in confidence he wrote that "frankly, I should be as well satisfied if I were not appointed." As the weeks passed, the press and others continued to assail the Commission, and while few ever made attacks against Mitchell's leadership, he complained that "my reputation is nevertheless affected by these charges."[130]

Ultimately, Governor Whitman renominated him for a five-year term and the state senate duly confirmed him. He was grateful for the governor's expression of confidence and he promised never to fail again.[131] Perhaps because he recognized for the first time the seriousness of his duties, the fact that human lives depended on his abilities as an enforcer of the law, or perhaps because he understood that another mistake of the same magnitude would deprive him of his livelihood, Mitchell absorbed himself in his work with even greater zeal. His life became an endless cycle of meetings, hearings, and speaking engagements. While he continued to believe the work itself was worthwhile, he quickly began to feel the strain of overwork. In his private letters, he continuously complained of the "exacting demands" of his office. The "pressure is so heavy," he sighed, that he no longer had time for a personal life. Elizabeth Morris, noting the furious pace at which he worked, commented in early 1917 that he was "pressed up to the limit of his strength by a multitude of official matters requiring attention."[132]

As had happened a decade earlier when he was an overburdened UMWA president, the frenzied Mitchell began to display compulsive behavior in regard to investments and alcohol. Once again he sought escape through reckless financial speculation and alcoholic binges. And this time there would be no exit from the self-destructive behavior. Signs of trouble began in mid-1916 when his investment activity increased dramatically. In June he purchased $10,000 worth of stock in a strip mining operation in the Hocking Valley of Ohio. Although the company was not to begin operations until November, Mitchell purchased another $5,000 worth of stock in August. In November, he invested over $2,500 in a grocery chain and less that two weeks later purchased $10,000 worth of stock in the Baltimore and Ohio Railroad.[133] While he bought almost all of this stock on the margin, in less than six months he became responsible for investments totalling $27,500!

By January 1917, he began exhibiting the second stage of the pattern. He fell ill and found himself in the hospital. Morris described his illness as "la grippe," or influenza. When he tried to return to work after being released from the hospital, he became sick again and spent the next ten days recovering at a health spa in Lakewood, New Jersey.[134] Once back at the office, he found the routine even more taxing. "My work here as chairman . . . requires every moment of my time," he wrote in disgust, "and much of the work is of such a character that makes imperative my moving from place to place in the State without advance notice." Although he had been absent only two short weeks, he found that his "work accumulates to such an extent that I am obliged to devote the evenings to its disposition."[135] And within weeks he was again gambling on a reckless scale. In February, he purchased $5,200 worth of Allis-Chalmers stock, in June he invested another $1,500 in the Ohio strip mine, and in July he bought over $10,000 worth of stock in the International Petroleum Company.[136]

The only respite in his spiraling decline was America's entry into World War I. The chance to demonstrate his love of country seemed to rejuvenate him. As the debate over whether America should join the Allies reached a peak in the spring of 1917, he became more and more active in various patriotic organizations. His fighting spirit was roused, and he even dreamed of engaging in active duty himself. At the end of March, he wrote Secretary of War Newton D. Baker that if the federal government issued the call for "a volunteer army, I would like to be permitted to undertake the formation of a regiment composed of coal miners."[137] As did President Wilson, he viewed the war in Europe in idealistic terms, a struggle between democracy and autocracy. He called upon all Americans to contribute in any way they could. In May, he made a stirring and unsolicited appeal to young men, asking for a "generous and enthusiastic response" to the Marine Corps' call for volunteers. And he beamed with pride when all three of his sons enlisted in the Navy and began their training at Pelham Bay Park, New York.[138]

As American entry in the war drew near, both the state of New York and the federal government called upon Mitchell to play his part. And he enthusiastically embraced every opportunity to demonstrate his patriotism. By the end of 1917, in addition to his duties as chair of the State Industrial Commission, Mitchell was president of the State Food Commission, chair of the State Farms and Markets Council, member of the Federal Milk Commission, and head of the Federal Food Board for New York state. In all of these posts his principal duty was to make certain food production continued without interruption. As the number of commissions began to mount, he joked that his secretary was starting a card index to keep track of them all.[139] He was the proud bureaucrat giving his all to defeat autocracy.

Soon, however, his ignorance of the economics of food, combined with the sheer volume of work he had taken on, began to impact his personal life. The patriotism he had exuded faded into exhaustion and nervous strain. When he began his work on the State Food Commission, he likened his post to being in the "wilderness." He was "totally without experience" and was "not over well equipped," but he hoped through sheer effort to "familiarize myself with the subject" as quickly as possible. His other jobs required similar preparation. And since he believed the presidency of the State Food Commission was "the most conspicuous position in the State government," he felt the pressure of being in the public spotlight once again. Moreover, the constant travel between Washington, Albany, and New York City was wearing him down. By early December 1917 he looked back to the time "when I was working until eight o'clock at night at the Industrial Commission offices" and wished he were "back at that 'easy job.'" In January 1918, the weary Mitchell complained he was "working beyond my strength" and his health was "suffering as a result."[140]

Excessive work was not his only source of tension. In late March 1918, his two youngest sons, James and Robert, were shipped to France in the Naval Aviation Service. His eldest son Richard remained at Pelham Bay Park until the summer, when he was assigned to convoy duty. Richard eventually made three trips across the Atlantic. Fear for the safety of his two youngest sons prompted Mitchell to write long, rambling letters full of fatherly advice. "To serve your country well it is not necessary to be reckless," he counseled. "On the contrary, along with being brave, as I know you both will be, it is important that you be prudent and careful."[141] Yet he remained convinced his sons' lives were being risked in a noble cause, and he was prepared to lose them in the fight if necessary. To a trade union friend, he confessed it would be "a thousand times better for the future of civilization and the liberty of all the people that our boys should never come back than that the Prussian monarch and his military caste should be permitted to impose their will upon the liberty-loving, free, and democratic people of the world."[142]

Already harried by overwork, Mitchell could not stand the added strain of a father's fear for his children in the midst of a bloody total war. At the end of May 1918, Mitchell collapsed. His health, which had been "considerably impaired" for several months, now became a serious problem. At the direction of his physician he was compelled to spend three weeks at home recuperating.[143] And from the confines of his bedroom on Claremont Street, he tried to forget about the commissions and his sons. Instead, he engaged in his favorite pastime, gambling on the stock market. Buy and sell orders were sent out as quickly as Morris could take dictation.[144] In early August, stress forced him to take another rest. He spent ten days on a friend's house boat on the St. Lawrence River.[145]

This pattern of overwork and stress leading to doctor-ordered periods of recuperation continued until armistice in November 1918. With the end of the war came the relief that all three sons were safe and would be home for Christmas. But the volume of work did not diminish. At the end of November, he wrote in despair that his State Food Commission work would drag on for the foreseeable future. He longed for an end to his wartime burdens, noting that "life has been much too strenuous for comfort and well being during the past year."[146]

He had been so constantly occupied with bureaucratic work since 1915 that he had little spare time to keep abreast of developments within the UMWA. His letters to union officials grew less frequent and his ties to the union weakened. His new circle of friends included fellow bureaucrats and New York State Federation of Labor officials, but on rare occasions an old chum from his union days would visit him in New York to reminisce about days long since past. Referring to his life in New York, he once wrote that while he had made a few close friends, "we have so little in common. They know nothing of mining. You can't know what it means to fall in with some old mining friends and talk over the old days."[147] With America's entry into World War I, opportunity for such chats all but vanished, and he was simply too harried to comprehend the enormous significance of the war for miners and their union.

By the end of the summer of 1917, the Committee on Coal Production, of which Mitchell was nominally a part but played no active role in, had been displaced by a new agency, the Federal Fuel Board. UMWA President John P. White resigned in October to accept a full-time position on the Fuel Board as labor adviser to administrator Harry A. Garfield. White's resignation had profound implications for the future of the UMWA. Frank Hayes became president, and together with William Green, who had become secretary-treasurer in 1913, they chose to make John L. Lewis, at that time union statistician, the new vice president. Although a popular figure among the rank and file, Hayes quickly succumbed to the illness that had been the cause of Mitchell's downfall—alcoholism. Long before his illness forced him to resign on January 1, 1920, Hayes was physically incapable of running the union. By the end of the war, therefore, John L. Lewis had risen from obscurity to control over the affairs of the union.[148]

If Mitchell was too overworked to take much notice of John L. Lewis's rise, he was also blind to the growing militancy of the miners and the entire labor movement. In the nine months following American entry in April 1917 more strikes occurred than in any previous full year in American history, and 1918 witnessed an equally impressive strike wave. The UMWA conducted aggressive and partially successful organizing drives in several outlying districts, and by the end of the war union membership stood at 400,000. It was by far the nation's largest trade union.

The coming of peace promised a new era in labor relations. With the removal of wartime restraints and government controls over wages and prices, unions and employers readied for a resumption of their historic contests. Unions were prepared to fight to keep the gains they had won during the war and extend their influence, while employers were equally determined to reassert their power. The result was an industrial upheaval in 1919 the likes of which the nation had never experienced. Tense and often violent strikes rocked industry after industry. For many Americans, the fact that these strikes followed on the heels of the Bolshevik Revolution and Russian Civil War made them appear even more ominous. And employers were quick to exploit the growing anti-socialist hysteria by charging that the industrial war was the first step toward the spread of Bolshevism in America.

Although the wartime wage agreement signed by the miners did not expire until April 1, 1920, John L. Lewis was militant in his determination to redress the miners' grievances before that date. As acting president he called a national convention in September 1919 and formulated a list of demands, including a 60 percent wage increase and a thirty-hour week to combat unemployment resulting from the decline of the wartime fuel needs. Unless these demands were met, Lewis was ready to initiate a national coal strike on November 1.[149]

Buried in paperwork and chained to various committees, Mitchell was hardly aware let alone involved in the mounting labor strife of 1919. Indeed, he was so far removed from the fray that in March his secretary wrote John Walker asking him to send Mitchell some union news. As a result of his workload "Mr. Mitchell is almost completely out of touch with his old-time friends," she explained. She understood that "this is a source of great regret to him and that he would be very happy to hear from you." By the end of that month, he fell ill and spent the next week in bed. He returned to his chores without enthusiasm. Confiding to his son that he "very badly" needed an extended vacation, he resolved to "go to the country, perhaps to some sanatorium where I can receive the right sort of exercise and rest." In early May, he resigned from the presidency of the State Council of Farms and Markets, citing poor health. "I now find that as the result of my attempt to discharge the duties of these numerous positions," he told Council members, "my health has been so impaired as not only to justify but to demand relief from some of these responsibilities."[150]

By the summer of 1919, the wartime committees had disbanded, but Mitchell never recovered his health. Although he was only forty-nine, his paunchiness, his recently developed baldness, and especially the heavy, dark bags under his eyes made him appear much older. Even though his workload had lessened, his physician again ordered him to take a vacation. He agreed. "I have lost a good deal of weight and am nervous and sleepless," he moaned.[151] But he continued to take expensive risks on the stock market. And rumors that he had started drinking again flourished. Exactly when Mitchell resumed his old drinking habits cannot be determined, but that he had broken his pledge by 1919 is certain. When he learned that UMWA District 1 President John Dempsey was an alcoholic, Mitchell wrote Dempsey a moving letter in which he admitted his continuing and not always successful fight with drink. He offered advice as much for himself as for Dempsey: "I understand perfectly how you are constituted, because I am constituted the same way myself; in other words, you must either leave the stuff alone absolutely or be its victim."[152]

In mid-August, Mitchell left the offices of the State Industrial Commission intending to take a ten day vacation. On the drive up to the St. Lawrence River, however, he suffered an acute attack of gall stones and spent over a week in an upstate New York hospital. When he was well enough to return to Mount Vernon, doctors told him he would need an operation to remove the gall stones. He wanted to wait until he felt stronger, but the pain forced him to act quickly. On August 30, he entered Post Graduate Hospital in New York City and doctors successfully removed the stones. Before the operation, Mitchell informed his secretary that if all went smoothly, and there was no pressing business at the Industrial Commission, he planned to attend the September 1919 UMWA convention. Acting President John L. Lewis had invited him to address the convention, and he was looking forward to rekindling friendships and helping the miners grapple with the great issues confronting them in postwar America. "I do not need to tell you how happy Mr. Mitchell would be if he could attend the convention," Morris informed William Green on September 5.[153]

But Mitchell never recovered. Pneumonia set in soon after the operation and his health rapidly deteriorated. On September 7 doctors suggested a blood transfusion to help restore his strength. All three sons volunteered to give their blood to keep their father alive. Doctors chose Robert, the youngest at age twenty-two. The infusion had no effect, however. By noon on September 9 all hopes that Mitchell would recover were abandoned. With his wife and children at his bedside, he died at 5:00 P.M.[154]

Mitchell's death hardly created a ripple in the labor movement. Caught up in the great battles of that year—the Boston Police strike which began the day he died, the steel strike which began two weeks later—as well as the hundreds of lesser strikes, the labor movement barely noticed the demise of one of their greatest leaders. The miners placed an oversized photograph of their former president in the convention hall, paid tribute, and then resumed business. He had been so long removed from their day-to-day activities his death was like the fading of a memory. Only in the anthracite region, where Mitchell remained a hero, did crowds assemble to mourn his passing. According to his own wishes, his body was laid to rest in Scranton, Pennsylvania, the site of his greatest victory.[155]

Outside the labor movement, even fewer noted his passing. His tiny obituary in the *New York Times*, for instance, was tucked away on page eight alongside those of a Kansas judge and a Brooklyn politician. The only issue surrounding his death to grab headlines was the size of his fortune. When probate records revealed he had accumulated a personal fortune of nearly $350,000, surprised reporters questioned how a man who never earned more than $10,000 per year could amass such wealth, and a few intimated he made money through collusion with operators while UMWA president. His friends resented such editorial attacks and came to his defense. Ralph Easley spoke for many when he wrote that anyone who knew the man also knew he never "took a dishonest dollar or was capable of doing a dishonest thing." Easley was convinced that Mitchell accumulated his wealth after he retired from the union and had succeeded due to "keen business sense" and "almost uncanny shrewdness."[156] But as we have seen, Mitchell began building his fortune while in the union. While there is no evidence of collusion with operators, he certainly had engaged in questionable business dealings. He had also exploited his ties to corporate capitalists in the NCF for inside information on stocks. By the time he stepped down in 1908, he was already a wealthy man.

One scholar who has analyzed Mitchell's finances in detail estimated that his investments totalled at least $55,000 as of June 1907.[157]

In the eleven years after his resignation, Mitchell was able to parlay that healthy sum into a not-so-small fortune. Indeed, his greatest success after leaving the union was in the stock market. Successful investment strategies would not have drawn criticism from other conservative trade unionists. Samuel Gompers himself acquired a tidy sum of $40,000 by investing in stocks, bonds, and real estate.[158] But criticism would have been made had it been known that Mitchell had invested heavily in three notoriously anti-union corporations—the Baltimore and Ohio Railroad, the New York Central Railroad, and the meat packing firm of Armour and Company.[159] Quite obviously, in his declining years Mitchell placed his desire to make money before his commitment to the labor movement.

That Mitchell died a largely forgotten man testified to his relative insignificance in national affairs after he resigned the UMWA presidency in 1908. His unimportance came as a rude awakening, for he had embarked on his NCF career with the zeal of a crusader, and he believed he could single-handedly resuscitate a languishing trade agreement movement. But the forces of reactionary anti-unionism among employers proved too powerful, and he soon found that his message of peaceful coexistence fell on deaf ears. Within the labor movement, the growth of socialist sentiment revealed that many workers had also spurned his vision of capital-labor harmony. When radicals in his beloved UMWA engineered his ouster from the NCF, he was cut adrift, a leader without followers. By the time of his death, he was hopelessly dated, the champion of a cause long forgotten.

Afterword

In the spring and early summer of 1908, after he resigned his union post and before he took up his duties at NCF headquarters, Mitchell had time to battle his alcoholism and reacquaint himself with his family. He also found time to reflect upon the successes and failures of his UMWA presidency. How effectively had he dealt with the problems plaguing miners? How skillfully had he managed the union? What problems did he bequeath to his successors? Were there opportunities and avenues for the advancement of labor he failed to explore? These and other questions ran through his mind as he looked back over his ten year reign. And on the whole, Mitchell was quite pleased with his accomplishments. "The organization, when I left it, was in better condition than ever before in its history," he wrote a friend.[1]

Mitchell's legacy is indeed an impressive one. He took command of a small union of 30,000 members which was in many ways weak. In 1898, the union lacked financial resources, a stable and effective bureaucratic structure, and a strong central authority. By 1908, the UMWA was the largest trade union in America. Its 300,000 members were welded together under a highly centralized and still largely democratic administrative authority. Considering the political, economic, and social conditions of the Progressive Era that made the very existence of trade unions precarious, the expansion and consolidation of the UMWA under Mitchell's leadership was truly remarkable. In the face of a hostile court system ready to issue injunctions on the whims of employers, pro-business politicians at all levels who challenged the legal right of unions to exist, and a public that often equated unionism with extremism and violence—in the face of all such opposition, Mitchell had erected a powerful and unified working-class organization.

In terms of concrete and immediate gains for miners, no one can deny Mitchell's accomplishments. In 1898, the coal industry was infamous for its low pay, long hours, and dangerous conditions. Under Mitchell's tenure, dramatic improvements were made in all three areas. Wages doubled for the soft coal miners and rose significantly for hard coal miners. Working hours had dropped from ten to eight in soft coal and ten to nine in hard coal. Mitchell was equally proud of his record on safety. At his retirement, the fatality rate in fully organized districts was 2.47 per thousand workers compared with 5.07 in partially organized districts and 9.49 where the UMWA was not present.[2] These were the figures Mitchell considered most important. He had helped improve the daily lives of miners. He had helped them achieve greater material comfort, more leisure, and increased peace of mind. For him the labor movement could serve no higher purpose. In language that epitomized "pure and simple" unionism, Mitchell declared in the fall of 1908: "For ten years I was president but I did not revolutionize the industrial world. I did not solve the labor problem. It will never be solved. We only hope to gain little by little more and more of our proper share of what we produce."[3]

His one regret was his inability to complete the organization of the anthracite fields. The two great strikes he conducted had made him a hero to hard coal miners, but had not established collective bargaining. He confessed he was "much disappointed at the result of my efforts to maintain a strong organization in the anthracite fields." Yet he did not attribute this "failure to either the wisdom or the unwisdom of the policies pursued there." The crux of the problem was "the criminal indifference of a large majority of the men themselves." He was perplexed by the paradox of anthracite mine workers who worshipped him but did not remain loyal to the union he headed. "It was neither my fault nor my suggestion that the anthracite miners worshipped me," he wrote. As far as he knew the parades and celebrations were "spontaneous" and "reflected their true feelings." Thus, he could not understand why they had abandoned the UMWA.[4]

Mitchell beamed with pride when he reflected on his ability to create a strong central authority and at the same time maintain a semblance of democracy within the union. In large measure, centralization was the result of the interstate movement he had inherited. When bargaining took place at the local level, national officers played a limited role. But when bargaining involved more than one district, the union president had to step in, arm himself with statistics and arguments that were national in scope, balance conflicting demands among local and district leaders, and produce a contract in the best interests of the union as a whole. Centralization also involved national control over strike funds and a weakening of district authority.

Mitchell's authority and popularity would have made it easy for him to squelch union democracy altogether and assume dictatorial control. Yet unlike his successors Tom L. Lewis and John L. Lewis, he was in some ways careful to uphold free speech and rank-and-file input. Socialists and other radicals were allowed to openly criticize his policies during conventions. Examples of this came at the 1905 convention when socialists mounted a lengthy attack on his handling of the Colorado strike and at the 1908 convention when he gave "Big Bill" Haywood free reign to plea for syndicalism. Another action demonstrating concern for democracy was his expansion of the national executive board to include one delegate from each district to be chosen by that district. He also sought rank-and-file approval for his policies through the use of referendums.

In other ways, however, Mitchell foreshadowed the dictatorial methods of John L. Lewis. When union democracy stood in the way of a desired policy,

Mitchell often cast it aside. His handling of internal enemies in his early years, notably Tom L. Lewis and Patrick Dolan, involved questionable covert schemes and, in the case of Dolan, a messy cover-up. He also could be quite devious when expecting opposition at national conventions. In 1902, for instance, he illegally delayed calling the special convention to consider a sympathy strike of soft coal miners. And when he believed miners would press for a national strike at the 1906 convention, he instructed his allies in Illinois to purchase several thousand fake membership cards to increase their voting strength.[5] There were other, more subtle techniques of one-man control. He routinely sent organizers to already organized fields to campaign for his policies during referendums and his allies in district elections; he controlled the union *Journal*, often denying access to his opponents, and used its pages to propagandize his own policies; and he jealously guarded his authority to make appointments to convention committees, thus guaranteeing that his policies would receive a favorable hearing. Mitchell was by no means dictatorial, but neither was he a staunch defender of democratic principles.

At the same time Mitchell shifted authority from the local and district levels to the national office, he often used district autonomy as an excuse for failure to act on important issues, especially the issue of racism. The UMWA had from its inception one of the best records on the organization of African-Americans and immigrants. And while Mitchell often expressed racist and anti-foreign views in private, as union president he upheld the liberal policies on the union. In anthracite, his speeches were peppered with calls for unity between native and foreign born mine workers. At national conventions, he also spoke on the need for camaraderie between the races. At the 1904 convention, for instance, he secured a unanimous vote on the resolution that all AFL affiliates end discrimination. But his speeches had little impact on white coal miners in the South who insisted on segregated locals. In his tours of Southern states, he never challenged this practice for fear of sowing dissent among white miners. He never attempted to use his authority to outlaw segregation, and when he stepped down, the practice continued.[6]

Mitchell's legacy is marred by an even more notable failure. As the president of the largest industrial union in America, many expected him to play a leading role in shifting the AFL away from its narrow craft union base. If the AFL ever hoped to organize the growing number of unskilled and semi-skilled workers in mass-production industries such as steel, rubber, automobiles, and meat packing, it would have to become more flexible in its organizational structure. At Mitchell's insistence, the AFL had in 1901 proved itself capable of making exceptions to craft jurisdictions. The so-called Scranton Declaration of that year awarded the UMWA an industrial charter. But Mitchell proved unwilling to fight for the principle of industrial unionism outside the coal industry. One reason for this failure was his general lack of attention to AFL activities. His primary focus during his tenure was the UMWA, and although he succeeded to the second vice presidency of the Federation, he had no appetite for the time-consuming and often unrewarding challenge of AFL policy-making. A second reason was the absence of an industrial union movement of any significance before 1912 outside the ranks of socialists. Mitchell was not about to ally himself with the left wing element on this or any other issue.

Mitchell's ultimate contribution to the labor movement, however, went beyond concrete gains for miners or missed opportunities to crusade for industrial justice outside the coal fields. His lasting legacy was to provide a new model for union leadership. At a time when labor leaders were denounced as demagogues, radicals, and men of violence, he was able to cultivate a new image, one which has held sway in mainstream labor circles ever since. Through his words and actions, he carefully crafted an image of himself as a responsible, respectable, trustworthy, cautious, conservative, and peaceful trade union leader. He became all things to all people. To the miners, he was a leader who could be trusted to care for their interests, a fighter when necessary and a skillful negotiator capable of securing the most favorable contract; to employers, he was a man who squelched unauthorized strikes, upheld the sanctity of contracts, and opposed radicalism; and to the general public, he was the prince of moderation, a progressive who called for a measure of justice and not revolution, a man who stood ready to arbitrate any dispute. He had risen to fame as a result of class warfare in anthracite, but his image was that of a man of peace.

This pacifist image was often untenable and the chief victims were union solidarity and militancy. In 1906 and again in 1908, his commitment to labor peace led him to undermine widespread strike sentiment and adopt the disastrous policy of separate settlements, which pitted miner against miner. The fighting spirit and solidarity of the miners, the twin bases of union strength, were sacrificed time and again so that Mitchell could present himself and the union to employers and the public as acceptable and responsible. In hard coal this stance had led to mass desertion from the union's rolls, and in soft coal it placed the future of the interstate movement in doubt. Mitchell had accomplished a great deal for the miners, but upon his retirement in 1908 his successors were faced with enormous tasks.

Above all, Mitchell's career symbolized the promises and pitfalls for organized labor in the Progressive Era. With the return of prosperity at the turn of the century, progressive businessmen and politicians were prepared to accept conservative labor leaders as junior partners in the production process. As long as these labor leaders assisted capitalists by crushing unauthorized strikes, preventing sympathy strikes, and upholding collective bargaining agreements, they could expect a measure of legitimacy and acceptance

unthinkable in earlier years. As long as these leaders helped rationalize industry by guaranteeing continued production and steady profits, capitalists would
refrain from their perennial war against the organization of their workers.
More clearly than any other labor leader, Mitchell recognized the opportunities for trade union advance in the Progressive Era, as well as the obligations
such opportunities demanded. In a remarkably short time, he constructed the
type of union Progressives desired, and he was rewarded with praise, influence, and acceptance. Quite naturally, he convinced himself that the strategy
of peaceful coexistence heralded a new day in labor relations and would eventually establish industrial justice for all workers.

Unfortunately, the progressive vision of cooperation between capital and
organized labor died quickly. Employers soon found more expedient methods
to rationalize industry, methods such as welfarism and scientific management,
methods which could be implemented without the assistance of labor. The
new anti-union offensive necessitated new and more aggressive strategies and
tactics on the part of unions and their leaders. But Mitchell balked. He clung
to the increasingly irrelevant dream of labor peace and capital-labor partnership as embodied in the declining National Civic Federation. Insisting that
cooperation was still viable, he refused to unleash the force he had worked so
hard to crush—worker militancy. By the time of his retirement from the NCF,
he had become an increasingly estranged and isolated voice for capital-labor
harmony based on the trade agreement.

John Mitchell was in many ways likeable and admirable. His leadership
talent and negotiating skills helped establish coal unionism on a sound and
permanent basis and helped lift hundreds of thousands of wage earners and
their dependents out of poverty and oppression. And despite his conflicts of
interest, selfishness, and lust for personal gain, he remained earnestly devoted
to the welfare of the rank and file. His shortcomings and failures stemmed not
from a lack of sympathy for the plight of working people, but from an unwillingness to place his faith in the militancy of the miners themselves. As do so
many labor leaders, Mitchell placed his faith in political and economic elites,
hoping that they would voluntarily embrace unionism. He failed to recognize
the irreconcilable conflict between labor and capital, and he never understood
that the labor movement can become a powerful instrument for economic justice only through the fighting spirit and solidarity of working people themselves.

Notes

Preface

1. Leo Wolman, *The Growth of American Trade Unions, 1880–1923* (New York: National Bureau of Economic Research, 1924), p. 33.

2. Philip Taft, "Collective Bargaining Before the New Deal," in *How Collective Bargaining Works*, ed. Twentieth Century Fund (New York: The Twentieth Century Fund, 1942), p. 881.

3. Robert Michels, *Political Parties*, trans. Eden and Ceder Paul (New York: Dover Publications, 1959), pp. 310–311.

Chapter 1: The Emergence of a Labor Leader

1. George Woodruff, et al., *The History of Will County, Illinois* (Chicago: William LeBaron, Jr. and Company, 1878; reprint edition, Joliet: Peterson Printing Craftsmen, 1973), pp. 466–467.

2. *Workingmen's Advocate*, 10 May 1873.

3. Information on Braidwood's early development can be found in John H. M. Laslett, *Nature's Noblemen: The Fortunes of the Independent Collier in Scotland and the American Midwest, 1855–1899* (Los Angeles: Institute of Industrial Relations, UCLA, 1983), pp. 40–43; Herbert G. Gutman, "The Braidwood Lockout of 1874," *Journal of the Illinois State Historical Society* 53 (Spring 1960): 5–8; Michael Ray McCormick, "A Comparative Study of Coal Mining Communities in Northern Illinois and Southeastern Ohio in the Late Nineteenth Century," (Ph. D. diss., Ohio State University, 1978), pp. 9–15; Richard P. Joyce, "Miners of the Prairie: Life and Labor in the Wilmington, Illinois, Coal Field, 1866–1897," (M. A. thesis, Illinois State University, 1980), pp. 6–15; Amy Zahl Gottlieb, "British Coal Miners: A Demographic Study of Braidwood and Streator, Illinois," *Journal of the Illinois State Historical Society* 72 (August 1979): 183.

4. Quoted in Gottlieb, "British Coal Miners," p. 179.

5. Ibid., pp. 183–185; Laslett, *Nature's Noblemen*, p. 35; Joyce, "Miners of the Prairie," p. 28.

6. McCormick, "Comparative Study," p. 28.

7. *Chicago Tribune*, 22 June 1874.

8. *Workingman's Advocate*, 25 July 1874.

9. JM to S. Lewis, November 27, 1899; JM to Jane Mitchell, January 30,

February 4, 1905, John Mitchell Papers, Microfilm Edition. (Hereafter cited as JMP.) On the service of immigrant miners in the Civil War, see Edward A. Wieck, *The American Miners Association, A Record of the Origin of Coal Miners' Unions in the United States* (New York: Russell Sage Foundation, 1940), pp. 112–114.

10. Elsie Gluck, *John Mitchell, Miner: Labor's Bargain with the Gilded Age* (New York: John Day, 1929), p. 4.

11. JM to M. M. Patterson, undated letter, circa 1899; JM to Jane Mitchell, January 30, February 4, 1905; JM to B. E. Guthrie, September 21, 1904, JMP.

12. While in Braidwood in 1867, Alexander MacDonald and local union leader John James called upon miners to support laws guaranteeing "Compensation to the widow and orphan." See Clifton K. Yearly, *Britons in American Labor: A History of the Influence of the United Kingdom Immigrants on American Labor, 1820–1914* (Baltimore: The Johns Hopkins Press, 1957), p. 127.

13. *Wilmington Advocate*, 26 March 1875.

14. George McNeill, ed., *The Labor Movement: The Problem of Today* (New York: M. W. Hazen Company, 1897), p. 248.

15. Priscilla Long, *Where the Sun Never Shines: A History of America's Bloody Coal Industry* (New York: Paragon House, 1989), p. 42.

16. On the care of boarders, bathing, and water in coal communities, see Dorothy Schwieder, *Black Diamonds: Life and Work in Iowa's Coal Mining Communities* (Ames: Iowa State University Press, 1983), pp. 90, 95–98.

17. Ibid., pp. 92–94; Gluck, *John Mitchell*, p. 5.

18. JM to Margaret Mitchell, undated letter, circa 1900, JMP.

19. John Mitchell, "The Boyhood of a Miner's Son," *The Circle* (June 1909): 331–332; Elizabeth Catherine Morris, "John Mitchell, the Leader and the Man," *The Independent* (December 25, 1902): 3073. Morris was Mitchell's secretary and confidante from 1899 until his death. She probably knew him better than anyone, including his wife.

20. Quoted in Gluck, *John Mitchell*, p. 5.

21. JM to Robert Mitchell, January 13, 1899, JMP.

22. John Mitchell, "Boyhood of a Miner's Son," pp. 331–332.

23. JM to Margaret Mitchell, undated letter, circa 1900, JMP.

24. Ibid.

25. Elizabeth Catherine Morris, "John Mitchell, the Leader and the Man," p. 3074; John Mitchell, "Boyhood," pp. 331–332; Gluck, *John Mitchell*, pp. 6–7.

26. For a good description of mines in the area, see James McFarlane, *The Coal Regions of America: Their Topography, Geology, and Development* (New York: D. Appleton and Company, 1873), pp. 407–436.

27. Unless otherwise noted, the following description of a typical soft

coal mine is based on Priscilla Long, *Where the Sun Never Shines*, pp. 24–36.

28. On the problems of "black damp" and drainage in Braidwood mines, see Illinois Bureau of Labor Statistics, *Second Biennial Report* (Springfield: H. W. Rokker, 1883), p. 22.

29. John Brophy, *A Miner's Life* (Madison: University of Wisconsin Press, 1964), pp. 41–42.

30. JM to M. M. Patterson, undated letter, circa 1899, JMP.

31. Upton Sinclair, *King Coal* (Published by author, 1921), p. 22.

32. Joseph E. Finley, *The Corrupt Kingdom: The Rise and Fall of the United Mine Workers* (New York: Simon and Schuster, 1972), p. 206.

33. Illinois Bureau of Labor Statistics, *Second Biennial Report*, 1883, p. 112.

34. JM to Robert Mitchell, January 13, 1899, JMP.

35. Andrew Roy, *A History of the Coal Miners of the United States, from the Development of the Mines to the Close of the Anthracite Strike of 1902* (Columbus, Ohio: J. L. Traeger Printing Company, 1905), pp. 202–207; Illinois Department of Mines and Minerals, *A Compilation of Reports of the Mining Industry of Illinois from the Earliest Records to the Close of the Year 1930* (Springfield: n. p., 1931), pp. 68–78.

36. Gluck, *John Mitchell*, pp. 8–9.

37. Carter Goodrich, *The Miners' Freedom* (New York: Workers Education Bureau of America, 1926), pp. 110–121; Michael Nash, *Conflict and Accommodation: Coal Miners, Steel Workers, and Socialism, 1890–1920* (Westport, Ct.: Greenwood Press, 1982), pp. 28–29.

38. JM to J. L. Gilpin, August 7, 1917, JMP.

39. Brophy, *A Miner's Life*, pp. 49–50; Gluck, *John Mitchell*, pp. 10–11.

40. JM to J. L. Gilpin, August 7, 1917, JMP.

41. Woodruff, et al., *The History of Will County, Illinois*, p. 468.

42. Alex Gottfried, *Boss Cermak of Chicago* (Seattle: University of Washington Press, 1962), p. 5.

43. Mitchell's testimony in the *Report of the Industrial Commission on the Relations of Capital and Labor Employed in the Mining Industry*, vol. 12 (Washington, D. C.: Government Printing Office, 1901), pp. 44–45.

44. Joyce, "Miners of the Prairie," p. 44.

45. Ibid., pp. 41–42.

46. *Wilmington Advocate*, 24 October, 31 October 1879.

47. Ibid., 4 June 1880; *Chicago Tribune* first edition, 31 July 1877.

48. *Wilmington Advocate*, 2 April, 16 April 1875.

49. Ibid., 7 July 1882.

50. *Chicago Tribune* first edition, 31 July 1877.

51. Gottfried, *Boss Cermak of Chicago*, p. 10.

52. *Wilmington Advocate*, 4 June 1880.

53. Ibid., 224 August 1883.

54. Ronald Lewis, *Black Coal Miners in America: Race, Class, and Community Conflict, 1780–1980* (Lexington: University of Kentucky Press, 1987), pp. 82–85.

55. George McKay to JM, April 19, 1899, JMP.

56. Gutman, "Braidwood Lockout," pp. 8–9.

57. Yearly, *Britons in American Labor*, p. 133.

58. On MacDonaldism and James's attitude toward strikes, see Laslett, *Nature's Noblemen*, pp. 24–25, 53.

59. On the 1874 strike, see Gutman, "Braidwood Lockout," pp. 5–28; Laslett, *Nature's Noblemen*, pp. 53–56; Joyce, "Miners of the Prairie," pp. 67–86.

60. On the 1877 strike, see Laslett, *Nature's Noblemen*, pp. 73–80; Joyce, "Miners of the Prairie," pp. 87–111.

61. Illinois Bureau of Labor Statistics, *Second Biennial Report*, p. 100.

62. Ibid., *Third Biennial Report* 1884 (Springfield: H. W. Rokker), p. 401.

63. Ibid., *Fourth Biennial Report* 1886 (Springfield: H. W. Rokker), p. 318.

64. Quoted in Norman Ware, *The Labor Movement in the United States, 1860–1895: A Study in Democracy* (New York: D. Appleton and Company, 1929), p. 117.

65. Arthur E. Suffern, *The Coal Miner's Struggle for Industrial Status* (New York: Macmillian, 1926), p. 35; see also Chris Evans, *The History of the United Mine Workers of America*, vol 1 (Indianapolis: United Mine Workers of America, 1914, 1918), pp. 137–145.

66. Both the lettter and the call for a joint convention are located in Andrew Roy, *A History of the Coal Miners*, pp. 248–249.

67. Ibid., pp. 250–254; Evans, *United Mine Workers*, vol. 1, p. 146.

68. *Wilmington Advocate*, 6 November 1885.

69. Roy, *A History of the Coal Miners*, pp. 256–257.

70. David Montgomery, *Beyond Equality: Labor and the Radical Republicans, 1862–1872* (New York: Random House, 1967), p. 219.

71. Roy, *A History of the Coal Miners*, p. 257.

72. *Wilmington Advocate*, 23 July 1886.

73. McCormick, "Comparative Study," p. 16; Joyce, "Miners of the Prairie," p. 21.

74. McCormick, "Comparative Study," pp. 28–29.

75. Gottfried, *Boss Cermak*, p. 5.

76. Brophy, *A Miner's Life*, p. 51.

77. *Wilmington Advocate*, 27 July 1883; *Joliet Daily News*, 9 July 1897.

78. George McNeill, *The Labor Movement*, pp. 241–242.

79. Mitchell, "Boyhood of a Miner's Son," p. 332.

80. Laslett, *Nature's Noblemen*, p. 72 f. 133.

81. *The Biographical Record of Bureau, Marshall, and Putnam Counties* (Chicago: S. J. Clarke, 1896), pp. 11–12. Spring Valley is located in Bureau County.

82. *Wilmington Advocate*, 13 November 1885; McCormick, "Comparative Study," p. 26; Grace Abbott, "The Immigrant and Coal Mining Communities of Illinois," *Bulletin of the Immigrants' Commission* 1 (1920): 10–11; Ronald Lewis, *Black Coal Miners*, pp. 84–85.

83. JM to Irving Munson, June 12, 1918, JMP.

84. JM to Charles Duncan, January 8, 1900; JM to J. L. Gilpin, August 7, 1917, JMP.

85. Quoted in Evans, *United Mine Workers,* vol. 1, p. 446. On the collapse of the interstate movement, see Suffern, *The Coal Miner's Struggle*, pp. 47–52; Roy, *A History of the Coal Miners*, pp. 248–261; Frank Julian Warne, *The Coal Mine Workers* (New York: Longmans, Green, and Company, 1905), pp. 201–205.

86. Lloyd presents a dramatic analysis of this lockout. Henry D. Lloyd, *A Strike of Millionaires Against Miners, or The Story of Spring Valley* (Chicago: Belford Clarke Company, 1890).

87. *Chicago Tribune*, 7 May, 20 June, 25 June, 5 July, 31 July, 1889.

88. *Black Diamond*, 15 June 1889.

89. *Chicago Tribune* first edition, 23 June 1889.

90. *New York World*, 25 August 1889, quoted in Nash, *Conflict and Accommodation*, p. 32.

91. Lloyd, *Millionaires Against Miners*, pp. 92–93, 136.

92. McCormick, "Comparative Study," pp. 133–134, 168–169.

93. JM, press release, "Henry D. Lloyd," dated 30 November 1904, JMP. This was issued at Lloyd's death.

94. Quoted in McCormick, "Comparative Study," p. 151.

95. *New York Times*, 15 December 1889.

96. On the founding of the UMWA, see Long, *Where the Sun Never Shines*, pp. 151–165; Maier B. Fox, *United We Stand: The United Mine Workers of America, 1890–1990* (Washington, D. C.: United Mine Workers of America, 1990), pp. 17–19, 22–29. The quote is from John B. Rae, the UMWA's first president, and is cited in Long, p. 152.

97. Lloyd, *Millionaires Against Miners*, pp. 240–241.

98. Ibid., pp. 235–236.

99. Evans, *United Mine Workers,* vol. 2, pp. 184–185.

100. Roy, *A History of the Coal Miners*, pp. 260–261.

101. *Danville* (Illinois) *Daily News*, 5 December 1898, cited in Gowaskie, "A Study in Leadership," p. 4.

102. G. Tilse Tilton to JM, December 21, 1903; JM to Tilton, January 2, 1903, JMP. A photograph as well as an unidentified newspaper clipping was included in Tilson's letter.

103. Evidence of their affectionate marriage can be found in the numerous letters he wrote his wife while union president. Two of the six children did not survive childhood. John, Jr. lived only six months and died in 1900, and Marie died at the age of six in 1905.

104. Gluck, *John Mitchell*, p. 20.

105. *United Mine Workers' Journal*, 23 April 1891 (Cited hereafter as *UMWJ*); Lloyd, *Millionaires Against Miners*, pp. 238–239.

106. John Hawthorne to JM, August 20, 1903; JM to Charles Duncan, January 8, 1900, JMP.

107. JM to Irving Munson, June 12, 1918, JMP.

108. Evans, *United Mine Workers,* vol. 2, pp. 150–154.

109. Ibid., vol. 2, pp. 181, 249, 269–270.

110. *UMWJ*, 20 July 1893.

111. Richard Jensen, *The Winning of the Midwest: Social and Political Conflict, 1888–1896* (Chicago: University of Chicago Press, 1971), pp. 244–249.

112. *UMWJ*, 8 October 1893; for a discussion of Populist sentiment in the UMWA see John H. M. Laslett, *Labor and the Left: A Study of Socialist and Radical Influences in the American Labor Movement, 1881–1924* (New York: Basic Books, 1970), pp. 199–202.

113. *UMWJ*, 14 September 1893.

114. Fox, *United We Stand*, pp. 44–45.

115. *Chicago Tribune*, 30 May, 2 June 1894.

116. *UMWJ*, 16 August 1894.

117. *Chicago Tribune*, 24 May 1894.

118. Ibid., 26 May, 27 May 1894. Interestingly, Governor Altgeld in August would eloquently protest President Cleveland's decision to send troops to break the Pullman strike.

119. Ibid., 27 May, 2 June, 4 June 1894.

120. *UMWJ*, 17 June 1894; *Chicago Tribune* first edition, 17 June 1894.

121. *Chicago Tribune*, 10 August, 11 August 1894.

122. Gluck, *John Mitchell*, p. 24; Joyce, "Miners of the Prairie," pp. 172–173.

123. On Ryan's background, see Roy, *A History of the Coal Miners*, pp. 420–422.

124. Modesto Donna, *The Braidwood Story* (Braidwood, Ill.: by the author, 1957), p. 27.

125. Gluck, *John Mitchell*, pp. 24–25; Gowaskie, "A Study in Leadership," p. 7.

126. JM to James Lord, April 12, 1914, JMP.

127. JM to Will Craig, June 22, 1909, JMP.

128. *Joliet Daily News*, 19 July 1895.

129. Ibid., 10 September 1897; *Report of the Industrial Commission on the Relations of Capital and Labor Employed in the Mining Industry*, vol. 15 (Washington, D. C.: Government Printing Office, 1901), p. 408.

130. Quoted in Long, *Where the Sun Never Shines*, p. 154.

131. Fox, *United We Stand*, pp. 47–49.

132. *Chicago Tribune*, 5 August 1895.

133. "Notebook of Elizabeth Catherine Morris," no date, JMP. Morris was Mitchell's secretary during his tenure as UMWA president.

134. *Joliet Daily News*, 10 July, 13 July, 18 July, 19 July 1895.

135. Gluck, *John Mitchell*, p. 25; Gowaskie, "A Study in Leadership," p. 8.

136. On Mitchell's legislative accomplishments, see *UMWJ*, 17 February 1898; Joyce, "Miners of the Prairie," p. 180.

137. Fox, *United We Stand*, pp. 50–51.

138. Quoted in Jensen, *The Winning of the Midwest*, p. 245.

139. *Joliet Daily News*, 7 July, 16 July 1897.

140. On Mitchell's activities in southern Illinois, see Marion Kinneman, "John Mitchell in Illinois," *Illinois State University Journal* 32 (September 1969): 29; Roy, *A History of the Coal Miners*, pp. 353; John H. Keiser, "John H. Walker: Labor Leader from Illinois," in *Essays in Illinois History*, edited by Donald Tingley (Carbondale: Southern Illinois University Press, 1968), p. 78; Gluck, *John Mitchell*, pp. 29–30; McAlister Coleman, *Men and Coal* (New York: Farrar and Rinehart, 1943), p. 60.

141. *Chicago Tribune*, 15 August 1897.

142. Illinois Bureau of Labor Statistics, *Coal in Illinois, 1897* (Springfield: Phillips Brothers, 1898), p. 164.

143. James P. Johnson, *The Politics of Soft Coal* (Urbana: University of Illinois Press, 1979), pp. 49–50; K. Austin Kerr, "Labor-Management Cooperation: An 1897 Case," *Pennsylvania Magazine of History and Biography* 49 (January 1975): 60–62.

144. Joyce, "Miners of the Prairie," p. 186; Kerr, "Labor-Management Cooperation," 159; Fox, *United We Stand*, pp. 51–52; Roy, *A History of the Coal Miners*, pp. 355–356; J. E. George, "The Coal Miners' Strike of 1897," *Quarterly Journal of Economics* 12 (1898): 200–203.

145. Gluck, *John Mitchell*, pp. 31–32; William E. Forbath, *Law and the Shaping of the American Labor Movement* (Cambridge, Mass.: Harvard University Press, 1991), p. 139.

146. JM, "Labor Day Address," 1899, delivered in Hocking Valley, Ohio, JMP.

147. George, "The Coal Miners' Strike of 1897," pp. 204–207; Roy, *A History of the Coal Miners*, pp. 356–358; Fox, *United We Stand*, p. 52; Kerr, "Labor-Management Cooperation," pp. 66–68.

148. John R. Commons, "A New Way of Settling Labor Disputes," *The American Monthly Review of Reviews* 23 (March 1901): 328–333.

149. *Joliet Daily News*, 16, 17, 18, 19 November 1897; *Chicago Tribune*, 17 November 1897.

150. *UMWJ*, 28 October 1897; Gowaskie, "A Study in Leadership," p. 11. In early 1898, the Illinois miners commended Smith for giving "valuable assistance to us through his paper during our strike." *UMWJ*, 3 March 1898.

151. *Joliet Daily News*, 4, 8, 9, 11 November 1897; *Chicago Tribune*, November 9, 10, 11, 1897.

152. *Joliet Daily News*, 23, 24 November 1897; *Chicago Tribune*, 24 November 1897.

153. UMWA, *Proceedings of the Ninth Annual Convention* in Columbus, Ohio, 1898, pp. 3–10.

154. Gowaskie, "A Study in Leadership," pp. 12–13; Gluck, *John Mitchell*, p. 40; UMWA, *Proceedings*, 1898, p. 22.

155. For a discussion of Patrick Dolan, see Roy, *A History of the Coal Miners*, pp. 343–345; and Gluck, *John Mitchell*, pp. 40–41.

156. "Notebook of Elizabeth Catherine Morris," no date, JMP; Gluck, *John Mitchell*, p. 41.

157. UMWA, *Proceedings*, 1898, pp. 22–23; *UMWJ*, 20 January 1898.

158. The following discussion of the 1898 interstate joint conference in based on Fox, *United We Stand*, pp. 53–54; John E. George, "The Settlement in the Coal Mining Industry," *Quarterly Journal of Economics* 12 (July 1898): 447–457; Arthur E. Suffern, *Conciliation and Arbitration in the Coal Industry of America* (New York: Houghton Mifflin, 1915), pp. 154–155.

159. The object of the conference was not to establish equal pay for miners, but rather to equalize the costs of production for all operators. Because of differences in the distance from markets, seam thickness, coal quality, and numerous other factors, some operators had natural advantages. Rates were adjusted at the district level so that all operators in the CCF could compete on an equal footing. See the testimony of John Mitchell in the *Report of the Industrial Commission*, vol. 12, p. 698.

160. *UMWJ*, 20 January 1898.

161. For the impact of the joint conference on social and economic thought, see Kerr, "Labor-Management Cooperation," pp. 70–71.

162. JM, "Labor Day Address," 1899, delivered in Hocking Valley, Ohio, JMP.

163. The second child, James, was born in 1895.

164. *UMWJ*, 10 March 1898.

165. "Copy of the Agreement Between the Miners and Operators of Illinois, Indiana, Ohio, and Western Pennsylvania, 1898," in JMP.

166. See Mitchell's letter in the *UMWJ*, 17 March 1898.

167. JM to M. D. Ratchford, March 6, 1898, JMP.

168. Ibid., March 9, 1898, JMP.

169. Ibid., March 21, 1898, JMP.

170. Ibid., March 6, March 9, 1898, JMP.

171. Ibid., March 9, March 21, March 29, 1898, JMP.

172. Ibid., March 21, March 29, April 5, 1898, JMP.

173. Ibid., April 5, 1898, JMP.

174. Fox, *United We Stand,* p. 60; a copy of the circular, dated 16 May 1898, is located in the JMP.

175. JM to M. D. Ratchford, April 27, May 1, May 7, May 11, 1898, JMP.

176. Ibid., May 7, May 11, May 14, May 14, May 22, May 30, 1898, JMP.

177. Ibid., May 31, 1898, JMP; Paul M. Angle, *Bloody Williamson: A Chapter in American Lawlessness* (New York: Alfred A. Knopf, 1952), pp. 98–100; Daniel Jensen Prosser, "Coal Towns in Egypt: Portrait of an Illinois Mining Region, 1890–1930," (Ph. D. diss. , Northwestern University, 1973), pp. 53–54.

178. JM to M. D. Ratchford, June 5, June 7, 1898, JMP.

179. Ibid., June 7, June 9, June 13, 1898; Ratchford to JM, June 8, June 10, June 20, 1898, JMP.

180. Victor Hicken, "The Virden and Pana Mine Wars of 1898," *Journal of the Illinois State Historical Society* 52 (Summer 1959): 263–266; see also the report of the State of Illinois Board of Arbitration, dated May 29, 1899, located in the JMP.

181. Hicken, "The Virden and Pana Mine Wars," p. 266; JM to M. D. Ratchford, August 24, August 25, August 28, 1898, JMP.

182. JM to M. D. Ratchford, September 3, 1898, JMP.

183. Ibid.

184. *UMWJ*, 22 September 1898; JM to W. R. Russell, 24 September 1898, JMP. The case never came to trial.

185. Fox, *United We Stand,* pp. 25–26, 54; Warren Van Tine, *The Making of the Labor Bureaucrat: Union Leadership in the United States, 1870–1920* (Amherst: University of Massachusetts Press, 1973), p. 16.

186. JM to W. R. Russell, September 24, 1898, JMP.

187. See Roy, *A History of the Coal Miners*, pp. 343–345, 381–383.

188. On the new skills required by the interstate agreement, see Bruno Ramirez, *When Workers Fight: The Politics of Industrial Relations in the Progressive Era, 1898–1916* (Westport, CT: Greenwood Press, 1978), p. 53.

189. In her discussion of Mitchell's assumption of the acting presidency, Gluck, *John Mitchell,* pp. 48–49, implies that the subversion of the constitution was simply a practical consideration to avoid "political wrangles." It should also be mentioned that once in office, Mitchell would demonstrate the same cavalier attitude toward constitutional questions.

190. Van Tine, *The Making of the Labor Bureaucrat,* pp. 170–171.

191. On Mitchell's salary as acting president, see James O. Morris, "The Acquisitive Spirit of John Mitchell, UMWA President (1898–1908)," *Labor History* 20 (Winter 1979): 29–30.

192. Lewis, *Black Coal Miners,* p. 83; JM to M. D. Ratchford, October 10, 1898, JMP; *UMWJ,* 20 October 1898.

193. Quoted in George Korson, *Coal Dust on the Fiddle* (Hatboro, PA: Folklore Associates, 1965), p. 378. Many of the African-American strikebreakers were often ex-convicts. Both Alabama and Tennessee used convict labor in the mines, and most of these convict apprentices were African-American. See Fox, *United We Stand,* p. 108. On the Virden Massacre, see Victor Hicken, "The Virden and Pana Mine Wars," pp. 273–275; Nash, *Conflict and Accommodation,* pp. 60–61.

194. Fox, *United We Stand,* pp. 61–62; Lewis, *Black Coal Miners,* p. 83; Hicken, "The Virden and Pana Mine Wars," pp. 276–278.

195. John H. Keiser, "The Union Miners Cemetery at Mt. Olive, Illinois: A Spirit-Thread of Labor History," *Journal of the Illinois State Historical Society* 62 (Autumn 1969): 248–249.

196. Mitchell's testimony in the *Report of the Industrial Commission on the Relations of Capital and Labor,* vol. 12, pp. 51–52.

197. *UMWJ,* 8 December 1898.

198. JM to M. D. Ratchford, September 21, 1898; *UMWJ,* 8 December 1898.

199. UMWA, *Proceedings of the Tenth Annual Convention,* 1899, pp. 3–6.

200. Gowaskie, "A Study in Leadership," p. 31.

201. Ibid., pp. 31–32; Gluck, *John Mitchell,* p. 52.

202. JM to James O'Rourke, January 13, 1899, JMP; UMWA, *Proceedings,* 1899, p. 37.

CHAPTER 2: THE BOY PRESIDENT

1. JM to M. M. Patterson, undated letter, circa 1899, JMP.

2. See, for instance, Lincoln Steffens, "A Labor Leader of Today: John Mitchell and What He Stands For," *McClure's Magazine* (August 1902): 355; Gluck, *John Mitchell,* p. 79; Gowaskie, "A Study in Leadership," p. 165; Donald L. Miller and Richard E. Sharpless, *The Kingdom of Coal: Work, Enter-*

prise, and Ethnic Communities in the Mine Fields (Philadelphia: University of Pennsylvania Press, 1985), p. 249.

3. Thomas I. Kidd to JM, May 3, 1900, JMP.

4. JM to Sybil Wilbur, October 8, 1899, JMP.

5. JM to "My dear Wife," January 31, 1900, JMP.

6. Van Tine, *The Making of the Labor Bureaucrat*, pp. 23–24 states that after 1895 union leaders took an average of five years to attain their highest office, whereas earlier leaders reached their highest union post one year after joining the national administration.

7. The average age of a male labor leader in 1900 was 41.6 years. Gary M. Fink, ed., *Biographical Dictionary of American Labor* (Westport, CT: Greenwood Press, 1984), p. 8.

8. JM to Adam Russell, March 29, 1899, JMP.

9. Untitled speech given at Spring Valley, February 2, 1899, JMP.

10. JM to Adam Russell, March 29, 1899, JMP.

11. JM to Ed McKay, September 15, 1899, JMP.

12. JM to John P. Reese, September 16, 1899, JMP. See also JM to J. J. McGovern, October 4, 1899, JMP.

13. JM to Adam Russell, March 29, 1899, JMP.

14. Morris, "The Acquisitive Spirit of John Mitchell," pp. 5–43. This is an excellent examination of one important, albeit narrow, aspect of Mitchell's personality. I am indebted to Morris's essay for much of my analysis of Mitchell's finances.

15. JM to William Hawthorne, April 20, May 2, 1899; Hawthorne to Mitchell, April 21, June 14, 1899, JMP. The question of how Mitchell raised $1,000 to invest by June 1899 is intriguing. Unfortunately, the Mitchell Papers are silent on his financial activities before 1899. It is reasonable to believe, however, that Mitchell's investments began before he was elected to the union presidency.

16. JM to William Ryan, September 14, 1899, JMP.

17. JM to T. R. Jones, May 11, 1900, JMP.

18. JM to Robert Mitchell, February 23, 1899, JMP.

19. See JM to Robert Mitchell, January 31, 1911; JM to "My dear Wife," January 31, 1900, JMP.

20. JM to "My dear Wife," January 31, 1900, JMP.

21. JM to "My dear Wife," January 31, March 9, 1900, JMP.

22. JM to Robert Mitchell, January 13, February 23, 1899; Robert Mitchell to JM, March 2, 1899; Ed Mitchell to JM, July 3, 1899; David Mitchell to JM, August 13, 1899; JM to David Mitchell, August 22, 1899; JM to E. R. Smith, July 13, 1899, JMP.

23. JM to Robert Mitchell, February 23, 1899; JM to E. R. Smith, June 7, 1899; JM to Charles J. Devlin, June 28, 1899; E. R. Smith to JM, June 29,

1899, JMP. It is interesting to note that at the May 1900 session of the UMW executive board, Fred Dilcher, probably at Mitchell's request, introduced a motion giving the union president a three-week vacation every year "to be taken at whatever time, in his judgment, the work of the organization can best spare him." The motion was carried unanimously. See UMWA, Minutes of the National Executive Board, May 18, 1900, in JMP.

24. E. C. Morris to JM, July 1, 1899; JM to Ralph Mason, July 10, 1899; JM to T. W. Davis, July 12, 1899; JM to E. R. Smith, July 13, 1899; JM to David Mitchell, August 22, 1899; Mae Ludon to JM, October 6, November 20, 1899; Agnes MacDonald to JM, December 29, 1899, JMP.

25. JM to W. H. Wright, July 12, 1899; W. R. Russell to JM, June 15, 1899; JM to "My dear Wife," January 31, March 9, 1900; JM to Mae Leedom, February 9, 1900; JM to Irene Andrews, February 9, 1900, JM to James O'Rourke, March 9, 1900, JMP.

26. JM to E. R. Smith, August 10, 1900, JMP.

27. JM to James O'Rourke, January 13, 1899; JM to Ralph Mason, December 27, 1899; JM to N. O. Gray, January 8, 1900; H. S. Baisenhers to JM, January 20, 1900; JM to Baisenhers, January 20, 1900; JM to "My dear Wife," January 31, 1900, JMP.

28. Van Tine, *The Making of the Labor Bureaucrat*, p. 28.

29. JM to Robert Mitchell, February 23, 1899; Robert Mitchell to JM, March 2, 1899, JMP.

30. JM to Thomas Davis, Jr., June 3, 1899, JMP.

31. On Morris, see Gluck, *John Mitchell*, pp. 58–60; May Wright Sewall to E. C. Morris, July 11, 1896; E. C. Morris to Edward O'Rourke, February 16, 1900, JMP.

32. Ralph Easley to JM, n. d., JMP.

33. UMWA, *Proceedings of the Eleventh Annual Convention*, 1900, p. 17.

34. *UMWJ*, 16 March 1899.

35. For details of this federal law and its effect, see the circular written by Mitchell, "Appeal for Financial Aid," April 11, 1899, JMP. An 1894 strike in Indian Territory had resulted in similar federal action. See the letter from Dan McLaughlin to Phil Penna, June 2, 1894, JMP.

36. Mitchell, "Appeal for Financial Aid," April 11, 1899, JMP.

37. *Indianapolis News*, 27 November 1899, quoted in Gowaskie, "A Study in Leadership," p. 62 n. 88.

38. Roy, *A History of Coal Miners*, p. 374.

39. JM to William Hawthorne, May 2, 1899, JMP; *UMWJ*, 4 May 1899.

40. JM to William Hawthorne, May 2, 1899, JMP; *UMWJ*, 11 May 1899.

41. *UMWJ*, 11 May 1899; John P. Reese to JM, April 14, 1899; JM to E. R. Smith, June 7, 1899, JMP.

42. *UMWJ*, 30 November 1899; JM to E. R. Smith, November 22, 1899, JMP.

43. On this last point, see Gowaskie, "A Study in Leadership," p. 62.

44. Charles Devlin to JM, December 14, 1899; JM to Devlin, December 22, 1899, JMP.

45. *UMWJ*, 11 January 1900.

46. John Brophy, *A Miner's Life*, p. 71.

47. These and other complaints were brought forth at the Tyrone conference. The proceedings of this conference can be found in Evans, *United Mine Workers*, vol. 2, pp. 705–708.

48. Ibid.

49. John Brophy, Columbia University Oral History Project, p. 195, cited in Gowaskie, "A Study in Leadership," p. 66.

50. William Warner to JM, May 3, 1899, JMP.

51. William Warner to JM, June 21, 1899; Warner to T. W. Davis, June 29, 1899, JMP.

52. JM to E.R. Smith, July 13, 1899, JMP.

53. JM to Ed McKay, December 6, 1899, JMP.

54. Thomas Cairns to JM, March 8 and July 15, 1899; Ralph Mason to JM, May 7, 1899, JMP.

55. Ralph Mason to JM, May 7 and June 4, 1899, JMP.

56. Ralph Mason to JM, August 28, 1899, JMP.

57. JM to Ralph Mason, September 12, 1899, JMP.

58. Ralph Mason to JM, October 5, 1899; JM to Ralph Mason, October 6, 1899, JMP.

59. JM to Richard Neason, October 5, 1899; JM to Ralph Mason, October 6, October 7, and October 11, 1899, JMP.

60. JM to Ralph Mason, October 6, 1899, JMP.

61. JM to Ralph Mason, October 23, 1899, JMP.

62. Ibid.

63. JM to George Schachert, November 10, 1899, JMP.

64. JM to Ralph Mason, November 11, 1899, JMP.

65. Ralph Mason to JM, September 14, 1899; JM to Mason, September 15 and November 11, 1899, JMP

66. JM to Ralph Mason, November 20, 1899, JMP.

67. Ralph Mason to JM, December 21, 1899; JM to Mason, December 22, 1899, JMP.

68. William Warner to JM, January 26 and January 27, 1899, JMP.

69. William Warner to JM, November 9, 1898, JMP.

70. JM to Patrick Dolan, January 28 and January 30, 1899; William Warner to JM, January 30, 1899, JMP.

71. Patrick Dolan to JM, telegram and letter, both dated January 31, 1899, JMP.

72. This was partially true. District 5 was notoriously disorganized. Operators often violated the terms of the national contract with impunity. Thus, Mitchell sent organizers into the district at least in part to better organize this vital portion of the CCF.

73. JM to Patrick Dolan, telegram, January 31, 1899; JM to Dolan, February 1, 1899, JMP.

74. JM to William Warner, February 1 and February 2, 1899, JMP.

75. Dolan to Mitchell, February 4, 1899, JMP.

76. Circular "To the Members of District 5, United Mine Workers of America," 21 February 1899, JMP.

77. JM to Patrick Dolan, February 21 and February 27, 1899; Dolan to JM, February 23, 1899; JM to William Dodds, April 8, 1899; Dodds to JM, April 7 and April 10, 1899, JMP.

78. John Mitchell, *Organized Labor, Its Problems, Purposes, and Ideals* (Philadelphia: American Book and Bible House, 1903), p. 75. In his *The Making of the Labor Bureaucrat*, p. 115, Warren Van Tine argues that most proponents of centralization generally displayed a "rather weak adherence to constitutionalism."

79. JM to Edward Soppitt, April 4, 1899, JMP.

80. JM to Edward Soppitt, April 19, 1899, JMP.

81. William Warner to JM, May 9, 1899; JM to E.R. Smith, November 22, 1899, JMP.

82. JM to Ed McKay, July 15, 1899, JMP.

83. JM to William Warner, September 22, 1899; Warner to JM, September 27, 1899, JMP.

84. JM to James Buchan, October 10, 1899; JM to Edward Soppitt, October 13, 1899, JMP.

85. See, for example, JM to John Trew, October 25, 1899, JMP. Trew was secretary of a local in District 5.

86. JM to William Warner, October 25, 1899, JMP.

87. JM to William Warner, November 27, 1899, JMP.

88. JM to Edward Soppitt, November 18, 1899; Soppitt to JM, November 17 and November 28, 1899; on the use of organizers in District 5, see also Soppitt to JM, October 2, October 11, October 23, and November 14, 1899, JMP.

89. Edward Soppitt to JM, November 28, 1899; Patrick Dolan to JM, December 6, 1899, JMP.

90. Van Tine, *The Making of the Labor Bureaucrat*, pp. 154–155; Robert Christie, *Empire in Wood: A History of the Carpenters' Union* (Ithaca: Cornell University Press, 1956), p. 139.

91. JM to Ed McKay, September 15, 1899; see also JM to T. W. Davis, September, 15, 1899; JM to Ralph Mason, September 15, 1899; JM to John P. Reese, September 16, 1899; JM to Edward Soppitt, October 4, 1899, JMP.

92. JM to Edward Soppitt, October 4, 1899, JMP.

93. JM to E. R. Smith, July 13, 1899, JMP.

94. JM to Edward Soppitt, November 11, 1899, JMP.

95. M. F. Tighe to JM, September 27, 1899; JM to Ralph Mason, September 22, 1899; JM to Tighe, September 26, 1899; JM to E. R. Smith, September 26, 1899; JM to W. D. Ryan, September 26, 1899; JM to W. D. Russell, September 26, 1899; JM to Mason, September 27, 1899; Mason to JM, October 19, 1899, JMP.

96. These are the terms Gowaskie uses to criticize Mitchell's handling of the affair. See "A Study in Leadership," pp 74–75.

97. M. F. Tighe to JM, December 8, 1899; JM to Tighe, December 23, 1899, JMP.

98. JM to Ed McKay, November 1, 1899, JMP.

99. JM to John P. Reese, September 16, 1899; JM to William Fairley, October 10, 1899, JMP.

100. JM to E. R. Smith, October 14, 1899, JMP.

101. JM to John McGarity, November 15, 1899, JMP.

102. John P. Reese to JM, November 19, 1899; JM to Reese, November 21, 1899, JMP.

103. JM to John P. Reese, February 7, 1900, JMP.

104. JM to T. I. Roberts, November 20, 1899; JM to E. R. Smith, November 22, 1899; JM to Ralph Mason, December 22, 1899, JMP.

105. UMWA, *Proceedings of the Eleventh Annual Convention*, 1900, pp. 49, 63, 64.

106. JM to Tom W. Davis, February 10, 1900, JMP.

107. UMWA, *Proceedings*, 1900, pp. 17, 27–28. Gompers's address can be found on pp. 2–7.

108. JM to E. R. Smith, June 7, 1899, JMP.

109. UMWA, *Proceedings*, 1900, p. 57.

110. JM to Irene Andrews, February 9, 1900, JMP.

111. UMWA, *Proceedings*, 1900, p. 57.

112. E. C. Morris, "John Mitchell, the Leader and the Man," *Independent* (December 25, 1902): 3073–3078.

113. UMWA, *Proceedings*, 1900, p.15.

114. Ibid., p. 23.

115. Ibid., pp. 50–51.

116. Ibid., pp. 20–21.

117. Ibid., pp. 56, 65–67.

118. Ibid., p. 24.

119. *Third Annual Joint Conference of Coal Miners and Operators of Illinois, Indiana, Ohio, and Pennsylvania* (Indianapolis: n. p., 1900), p. 74.

120. Ibid., pp. 65, 99.

121. Ibid., pp. 141–142.

122. Ibid., p. 141; JM to Tom W. Davis, February 10, 1900, JMP.

123. JM to Neal Hughes, October 4, 1899, JMP.

124. *Chicago Inter-Ocean*, September 20, 1901, quoted in Marion Kinneman, "John Mitchell in Illinois," *Illinois State University Journal* 32 (September 1969): 21.

125. JM to Ed O'Rourke, February 21, 1899, JMP.

126. JM to Neal Hughes, October 4, 1899, JMP.

127. JM to W. D. Ryan, December 26, 1899, JMP.

128. JM to Neal Hughes, February 15, 1900, JMP.

129. JM to W. D. Ryan, March 29, 1900, JMP.

130. "To the Twelfth Annual Convention of the United Mine Workers of America," December 1900, JMP.

131. Paul W. Pritchard, "William B. Wilson: The Evolution of a Central Pennsylvania Mine Union Leader," (Ph.D. diss., University of Pennsylvania, 1942), p. 214; W. D. Ryan to JM, April 5, 1899, JMP.

132. William B. Wilson, "Annals of an Immigrant," p. 36. This is an autobiographical effort by Wilson and is located in the William B. Wilson Papers (Historical Society of Pennsylvania, Philadelphia) According to Pritchard (pp. 3–4), there was an interesting connection between Mitchell and Wilson. Dan McLaughlin used to stay at the home of Wilson's parents during his trips to Scotland.

133. UMWA, Minutes of the Executive Board, May 17, 1900.

134. This sketch of Wilson is taken from Gary M. Fink, ed., *Biographical Dictionary of American Labor*, pp. 588–589; and Clarke L. Wilhelm, "William B. Wilson: The First Secretary of Labor" (Ph.D. diss., Johns Hopkins University, 1967), pp. 1–11.

135. William B. Wilson, *Memories* (Washington: by the author, 1916). Contains some of his own poems.

136. *UMWJ*, 18 June 1903.

CHAPTER 3: THE ANTHRACITE STRIKE OF 1900

1. UMWA, *Proceedings of the Eleventh Annual Convention*, 1900, p. 24.

2. On the process of monopolization in anthracite, see Eliot Jones, *The Anthracite Coal Combination in the United States* (Cambridge, Mass.: Harvard University Press, 1914), chapters 2 and 3; Robert J. Cornell, *The Anthracite Coal Strike of 1902* (Washington, D. C.: Catholic University of America Press, 1957), pp. 33–37.

3. Arthur E. Suffern, *Conciliation and Arbitration in the Coal Industry of America* (New York: Houghton Mifflin, 1915), p. 232; George O. Virtue, "The Anthracite Mine Laborers," *Bulletin of the Department of Labor* 13 (Washington, D.C.: Government Printing Office, November 1897), p. 750.

4. Gluck, *John Mitchell*, pp. 68–70; Bruno Ramirez, *When Workers Fight: The Politics of Industrial Relations in the Progressive Era, 1898–1916* (Westport, CT: Greenwood Press, 1978), pp. 34–35.

5. Frank Julian Warne, "Organized Labor in the Anthracite Coal Fields," *Outlook* (May 24, 1902): 274.

6. JM to John Fahy, February, 1899; Fahy to JM, March 4, 1899, JMP. A brief account of Fahy's activities is given in the *UMWJ*, 17 March 1898.

7. JM to Ed McKay, July 15, 1899, JMP.

8. Charles Thain to JM, July 23, 1899; George Hartlein to W. C. Pearce, July 24, 1899; James Dorsett to JM, July 29, 1899, JMP.

9. John Fahy to JM, July 31, August 2, and August 18, 1899; JM to Fahy August 8, 1899, JMP.

10. Mitchell first noted his intent to call this convention in his letter to Fahy of August 8, 1899.

11. JM to Tom W. Davis, August 14, 1899, JMP.

12. JM to Tom W. Davis, August 31, 1899, JMP.

13. JM to Ed McKay, October 24, 1899, JMP.

14. JM to John Fahy, November 20, 1899, JMP.

15. Philip S. Foner, *History of the Labor Movement in the United States* Vol. 3 (New York: International Publishers, 1964), p. 87.

16. Gluck, *John Mitchell*, pp. 67–74, claims that Mitchell spent the last five months of 1899 in anthracite, assisting the organizers, establishing relationships with the local clergy and business community, and becoming well known to the miners. She claims that by August 1900 he had been in the area almost a year. This was not the case at all. Mitchell returned to national headquarters after the Wilkes-Barre convention, where he returned to business as usual. He made numerous trips in late 1899, but none to northeast Pennsylvania.

17. John Mitchell, "The Miner's Life and Aims," *Cosmopolitan* (October 1901): 624.

18. JM to Tom W. Davis, August 31, September 14, 1899; John Fahy to JM, September 22, 1899, JMP.

19. *UMWJ*, March 10, August 24, December 21, 1899; JM to Tom W. Davis, August 31, 1899, JMP.

20. *UMWJ*, 11 January 1900; JM to Charles J. Thain, January 4, 1900, JMP; UMWA, Minutes of the National Executive Board, February 3–4, 1900.

21. UMWA, *Proceedings*, 1900, pp. 17–18.

22. Ibid., p. 28.

23. Ibid., pp. 48–49.

24. UMWA, Minutes of the National Executive Board, February 3–4, 1900.

25. Ibid.

26. T. D. Nicholls to JM, June 9, 1900, JMP.

27. John Fahy to JM, July 1, 1900, JMP.

28. So Mitchell referred to West Virginia miners in JM to Michael Ratchford, March 21, 1898, and anthracite mine workers in JM to Ryan, September 24, 1900, JMP.

29. JM to Ed McKay, July 10, 1900, JMP.

30. JM to W. D. Ryan, March 29, 1900, JMP.

31. "Address of President John Mitchell," stating his position on what course the convention should follow regarding the calling of a strike. Delivered to the delegates of the joint convention of Districts 1, 7, and 9, UMWA, Grand Opera House, Hazleton, Pa., May 15, 1902, JMP.

32. "Circular Call for Convention of Districts One, Seven and Nine," July 17, 1900, located in JMP.

33. JM to William Hawthorne, August 10, 1900, JMP.

34. J. P. Gallagher, John T. Dempsey, and George Hartlein to the Operators of the Anthracite Coal Fields of Pennsylvania, August 16, 1900, located in JMP.

35. UMWA, Minutes of the National Executive Board, September 8, 1900, JMP.

36. "Address of President John Mitchell," May 15, 1902, JMP. The vice president of the Erie Mitchell met was G. M Cummings.

37. Copy of telegram in JMP.

38. Copy of appeal in JMP.

39. John Fahy to JM, September 18, 1900, JMP.

40. "Bulletin No. 1," September 17, 1900, JMP; John Mitchell, *Organized Labor*, p. 366.

41. JM to Daniel Keefe, September 14, 1900; JM to Sybil Wilbur, October 8, 1900; E. C. Morris to W. C. Scott, September 18 and September 21, 1900, JMP. It is probable that the hotel heated its rooms with anthracite coal and the manager wished to conserve fuel.

42. JM to Tom W. Davis, September 22, 1900, JMP.

43. JM to W. D. Ryan, September 29, 1900, JMP.

44. JM to W. D. Ryan, September 24, 1900, JMP.

45. E. C. Morris to W. C. Scott, September 23, 1900, JMP.

46. For a comparison of union attitudes toward immigrants, see Robert Asher, "Union Nativism and the Immigrant Response," *Labor History* 23 (Summer 1982): 325–348.

47. Victor R. Greene, *The Slavic Community on Strike: Immigrant Labor*

in Pennsylvania (Notre Dame, Ind.: University of Notre Dame Press, 1968), pp. 160–164.

48. JM to Tom W. Davis, September 22, 1900, JMP.

49. JM to W. D. Ryan, September 24, 1900; Mitchell made the same complaint to his brother-in-law. See JM to James O'Rourke, September 28, 1900, JMP.

50. JM to W. D. Ryan, September 24 and September 29, 1900, JMP.

51. On Mitchell's popularity in anthracite, see the contemporary observations in E. C. Morris, "John Mitchell, the Leader and the Man," *Independent* (December 25, 1902): 3073–3078; Lincoln Steffens, "A Labor Leader of To-Day," *McClure's* (August 1902): 355–357; Frank Julian Warne, "John Mitchell, the Labor Leader and the Man," *Review of Reviews* (November 1902): 1044–1049; Walter Weyl, "The Man the Miners Trust," *The Outlook* (March 24, 1906): 657–662. See also the assessment of historians in Gluck, *John Mitchell,* pp. 70–74; Greene, *The Slavic Community on Strike,* pp.199–203. There is no evidence in the Mitchell Papers or in any other source to indicate that Mitchell ever uttered these exact words.

52. JM to Tom W. Davis, October 11, 1900, JMP.

53. JM to David Mitchell, October 16, 1900; JM to M. M. Patterson, October 20, 1900, JMP.

54. JM to Tom W. Davis, October 11, 1900, JMP.

55. JM to David Mitchell, October 16, 1900, JMP.

56. An excellent summary of the daily routine of breaker boys is found in Miller and Sharpless, *The Kingdom of Coal*, pp. 121–125.

57. JM to Tom W. Davis, October 11, 1900, JMP.

58. A survey of the press's reaction on the eve of and during the strike is provided by *Literary Digest* (September 29, 1900): 361–362.

59. This discussion of press relations is taken from Gowaskie, "A Study in Leadership," pp. 93–94.

60. Charles J. Devlin to W. H. Truesdale, August 31, 1900; Devlin to JM, October 3, 1900, JMP.

61. JM to John F. Power, September 17 and September 22, 1900; Power to JM, September 20, 1900, JMP.

62. UMWA, *Proceedings of the Twelfth Annual Convention,* 1901, p. 28.

63. John Mitchell, "The Great Coal Strike," *Independent* (November 1, 1900): 2615.

64. Cornell, *The Anthracite Coal Strike of 1902*, pp. 47–48.

65. Nash, *Conflict and Accommodation,* p. 64; Greene, *Slavic Community on Strike*, pp. 166–170.

66. Press statement, September 22, 1900, JMP.

67. Ibid.

68. JM to W. D. Ryan, September 24, 1900, JMP.

69. "Open Letter to the Public," September 21, 1900, JMP.

70. One popular journal declared the reasons operators gave for refusing to arbitrate were "anything but convincing to the impartial mind." *Review of Reviews* (November 1900): 533, cited in Cornell, *The Anthracite Coal Strike*, p. 50.

71. Cornell, *The Anthracite Coal Strike*, pp. 51–52; Mitchell's argument is taken from his "Open Letter to the Public," September 21, 1900, JMP.

72. Edward S. Phillips, "Letter to the Editor," *The Scrantonian*, 9 April 1901, copy JMP.

73. Phillips was so taken by Mitchell that the two became fast friends. Phillips even defended Mitchell when Irish Catholics in the area challenged Mitchell's Irish Protestant background, stating that Mitchell's wife and children were Catholic and that many Irish patriots, including Robert Emmett, Wolfe Tone, and Charles Stuart Parnell had been Protestant. See Ibid.

74. Cited in Greene, *The slavic Community on Strike*, p.164.

75. JM to W. D. Ryan, September 24, 1900, JMP.

76. *New York Sun*, quoted in *Literary Digest* (September 22, 1900): 335.

77. Press release, 5 October 1900, JMP; for his private disavowal, see JM to Tom W. Davis, September 22, 1900, JMP.

78. "Proceedings of the Anthracite Coal Strike Commission, 1902–1903," vol. 4, (Mimeographed copy in the Library of Congress), vol. 4, pp. 354–355.

79. Daniel J. Keefe to JM, September 19, 1900, JMP.

80. JM to Daniel J. Keefe, September 24, 1900, JMP.

81. *New York Times* final edition, 27 September 1900.

82. "Report of Interview of Commissioner of Labor with Messrs. George F. Baer, R. M. Olyphant, E. B. Thomas, and David Wilcox," in Carroll D. Wright, "Report to the President on the Anthracite Coal Strike," *Bulletin of the Department of Labor* 43 (Washington: Government Printing Office, 1902), Appendix E, p. 1204.

83. JM to W. D. Ryan, September 29, 1900, JMP.

84. Copies of these notices are found in the JMP.

85. Copy of speech in JMP; see also E. C. Morris to W. H. Scott, October 1, 1900, JMP.

86. JM to Daniel J. Keefe, October 4, 1900, JMP.

87. JM to Daniel J. Keefe, October 8, 1900, JMP.

88. Minutes of the convention at Scranton, Pa., October 12–13, 1900, are found in JMP.

89. "Minutes of a meeting," October 24, 1900, located in JMP.

90. End of strike order, October 25, 1900, located in JMP.

91. E. C. Morris to Tom W. Davis, November 6, 1900; E. R. Smith to JM, November 12, 1900; JM to Mae Leedom, October 26, 1900, JMP.

92. UMWA, *Proceedings*, 1901, pp. 28, 36, 61.

93. JM to Ralph M. Mason, July 25, 1900, JMP.

94. W. D. Ryan to JM, November 17, 1900; JM to Ryan, November 19, 1900, JMP.

95. JM to Daniel J. Keefe, October 4, 1900, JMP. Emphasis added.

96. JM to Daniel J. Keefe, November 26, 1900; Marcus A. Hanna to JM, November 27, December 5, and December 13, 1900; JM to Hanna, December 11, 1900, JMP.

97. JM to Daniel J. Keefe, December 22, 1900, JMP.

98. JM to Daniel J. Keefe, February 16, 1901, JMP.

99. JM to Daniel J. Keefe, February 27, 1901, JMP.

100. John Mitchell, "The Great Coal Strike," *Independent* (November 1, 1900): 2613–2616.

101. JM to W. B. Wilson, December 8, 1900, JMP. Mitchell publicly denied these reports. Privately, he believed those behind the campaign were Tom L. Lewis and Patrick Dolan, who hoped to kick him upstairs to the AFL post and thus out of the UMWA. "It is simply amazing how solicitous they (Dolan and Lewis) are for my future welfare," he wrote Billy Ryan, "but I see the point; and have concluded that the Presidency of the United Mine Workers of America is a bigger job than the Presidency of the A. F. of L." JM to W. D. Ryan, November 16, 1900, JMP; see also JM to Edward Soppitt, November 1, 1900; Ryan to Mitchell, November 17, 1900, JMP.

102. JM to Mae Leedom, October 26, 1900, JMP.

103. Quoted in Robert L. Reynolds, "The Coal Kings Come to Judgment," *American Heritage* 11 (April 1960): 61.

104. JM to W. D. Ryan, November 19, 1900, JMP.

105. JM to E. R. Smith, October 30, 1900, JMP.

106. JM to Mattie Patterson, November 12, 1900, JMP.

107. JM to Ralph Mason, November 12, 1900, JMP.

108. Morris, "The Acquisitive Spirit of John Mitchell," pp. 20–21, also discusses the house scheme.

109. Fred Dilcher to JM, December 17 and December 26, 1900, JMP.

110. George Harris to JM, January 10, 1901, JMP.

111. JM to M. M. Paterson, January 11, 1901, JMP.

112. Fred Dilcher to JM, December 1, 1901; JM to Dilcher, December 3, 1901, JMP.

113. JM to George Harris, December 31, 1901, JMP.

114. Mary Harris Jones, *Autobiography of Mother Jones*, ed. Mary Field Parton (Chicago: Charles H. Kerr, 1925), pp. 87–88.

115. JM to William Hawthorne, November 10, 1900, JMP.

116. A. P. O'Donnell to JM November 1, November 15, and November 30, 1900; JM to O'Donnell, November 12, 1900, JMP.

117. Daniel J. Keefe to JM, November 24, 1900; JM to John C. Dernell, January 6, 1902. See also Morris, "The Acquisitive Spirit of John Mitchell," p. 17.

118. Reinhold R. Koch to JM, November 3, November 15, November 17, November 21, 1900, and April 12, 1901, JMP.

119. JM to Mattie Paterson, January 23, 1901, JMP.

120. JM to William Hawthorne, October 25, 1901, JMP.

121. JM to James O'Rourke, October 22, 1901, JMP.

122. JM to Ralph Mason, July 1, 1901, JMP.

123. JM to James O'Rourke, November 26, 1901, JMP.

124. JM to Daniel J. Keefe, November 26, 1900, JMP.

125. H. N. Taylor to JM, November 23, 1900, JMP.

CHAPTER 4: MITCHELL ENTERS THE NATIONAL SCENE, 1901

1. Wolman, *The Growth of American Trade Unions*, p. 33.

2. Ralph Easley to JM, April 6, 1900, JMP.

3. Samuel Gompers to JM, April 9, 1900, JMP.

4. Ralph Easley to JM, October 11, 1900, JMP.

5. Mitchell's NCF speech is located in the JMP under title "Chicago Civic Federation Conference, 1900." According to Gowaskie, "A Study in Leadership," p. 100 n. 43, Mitchell's speech was reprinted in the Hearst newspaper chain.

6. Cited in Marguerite Green, *The National Civic Federation and the American Labor Movement, 1900–1925* (Washington, D. C.: Catholic University of America Press, 1956), p. 11.

7. *New York Tribune*, 21 December 1901, cited in Foner, *History of the Labor Movement,* vol. 3, p. 62.

8. JM to M. A. Hanna, March 20, 1901, JMP.

9. Herman Justi to JM, March 20, 1901; JM to Justi, March 22, 1901, JMP.

10. JM to Daniel J. Keefe, March 25, 1901, JMP.

11. John Mitchell, *Organized Labor*, p. 369.

12. JM to W. B. Wilson, February 16, 1901, JMP. The two respondents were Robert M. Olyphant of the Delaware and Hudson Company and Alexander J. Cassatt of the Pennsylvania Railroad. A copy of the February 18 call for the March Hazleton convention can be found in the JMP.

13. Mitchell mentioned these notices in a letter to W. B. Wilson, March 9, 1900, JMP.

14. JM to H. N. Taylor, March 9, 1901, JMP.

15. JM to W. R. Fairley, March 13, 1901, JMP. Part of the problem stemmed from a controversy surrounding Benjamin James, ex-president of

District 7, who was accused by some of sabotaging efforts to secure changes in Pennsylvania's mining laws. See T. D. Nicholls to JM, March 3, 1901; JM to Nicholls, March 7, 1901, JMP.

16. Cornell, *The Anthracite Coal Strike*, pp. 63–64.

17. JM to W. D. Ryan, March 19, 1901, JMP.

18. Chris Evans to JM, March 12, 1901; H. J. Gray to JM, March 13, 1901, JMP.

19. Ralph Easley to JM, no date (probably March 1901), JMP. Easley wrote five undated letters to Mitchell describing his efforts to arrange a conference.

20. Ralph Easley, "Report of the Executive Committee of the National Civic Federation on the Anthracite Coal Strike," circa 1902, copy in JMP.

21. Ralph Easley to JM, undated letter (probably March 1901), JMP.

22. JM to H. N. Taylor, March 20, 1901, JMP.

23. JM to Daniel J. Keefe, March 25, 1901, JMP.

24. JM to M. A. Hanna, March 20, 1901, JMP.

25. M. A. Hanna to JM, March 21, 1901, JMP.

26. JM to W. B. Wilson, March 25, 1901, JMP.

27. JM to W. D. Ryan, March 21, 1901, JMP.

28. JM to Mattie Paterson, March 21, 1901; W. B. Wilson to JM, March 22, 1901; JM to Wilson, March 25, 1901, JMP. Mitchell did in fact bring a libel suit against the newspaper. The case was settled out of court and the newspaper paid Mitchell's legal fees and printed a retraction. See JM to Joseph O'Brien, May 11, 1901; Richard Little "To the Public," June 12, 1901; JM to W. B. Wilson, June 13, 1901; JM to H. N. Taylor, June 15, 1901; Fred Dilcher to JM, August 4, 1901, JMP.

29. JM to Daniel J.Keefe, March 25, 1901, JMP.

30. JM to W. B. Wilson, March 26, 1901, JMP.

31. Ibid.

32. M. A. Hanna to JM, undated letter (probably March 1901), JMP.

33. E. C. Morris to W. B. Wilson, March 30, 1901, JMP.

34. "To Miners and Mine Workers of the Anthracite Region," March 29, 1901, JMP.

35. JM to W. B. Wilson, March 26, 1901, JMP.

36. JM to Ralph Easley, April 1, 1901, JMP.

37. Green, *National Civic Federation*, p. 19 n. 53.

38. Ralph Easley to JM, April 26, 1901, JMP.

39. Green, *National Civic Federation*, pp. 19–20; Ramirez, *When Workers Fight*, pp. 66–69.

40. JM to Ralph Easley, May 13, 1901, JMP.

41. Ralph Easley to JM, undated letter (probably May or June 1901), JMP.

42. JM to E. R. Smith, April 25, 1901; JM to M. M. Paterson, April 26, 1901; JM to Mae Leedom, June 16, 1901, JMP.

43. Ralph Easley to JM, June 11, 1901; JM to Easley, June 12, 1901, JMP; on the Murray Hill agreement and its collapse, see David Montgomery, *The Fall of the House of Labor: The Workplace, the State, and American Labor Activism, 1865–1925* (New York: Cambridge University Press, 1987), pp. 261–269.

44. Ralph Easley to JM, June 14, 1901; JM to Easley, June 19, 1901, JMP.

45. The following information is taken from Foner, *History of the Labor Movement*, vol. 3, pp. 78–80; David Brody, *Steelworkers in America: The Nonunion Era* (Cambridge, MA: Harvard University Press, 1960), pp. 62–66; John A. Garraty, "The United States Steel Corporation Versus Labor—The Early Years," *Labor History* I (Winter 1960): pp. 6–13.

46. M. A. Hanna to JM, July 16, 1901, JMP.

47. JM to M. A. Hanna, July 19, 1901; Hanna to JM, July 22, 1901, JMP.

48. Foner, *History of the Labor Movement*, vol. 3, pp. 79–81.

49. Ralph Easley to Louis Brandeis, November 4, 1912, cited in Green, *National Civic Federation*, p. 27.

50. UMWA, Minutes of the National Executive Board, August 10, 1901, JMP.

51. Tom L. Lewis to Samuel Gompers, September 8, 1901, cited in Foner, *History of the Labor Movement*, vol. 3, p. 82.

52. Mitchell, "Statements Regarding Efforts to Settle the Steel Strike," 1901, JMP.

53. T. J. Shaffer to JM, August 29, 1901, JMP.

54. JM to M. A. Hanna, August 29, 1901, JMP.

55. JM to Ralph Easley, August 31, 1901, JMP.

56. JM to W. B. Wilson, September 6, 1901, JMP.

57. Several telegrams were passed between Mitchell and Shaffer, September 4 and 5, 1901, JMP. On Shaffer's failure to comply, see JM to John P. Reese, September 14, 1901, JMP.

58. President's Report, *Proceedings of the Amalgamated Association of Iron, Steel and Tin Workers*, 1901, pp. 6317–6318, copy in JMP.

59. JM and Samuel Gompers to T. J. Shaffer, September 25, 1901, JMP.

60. Henry White to JM, October 11, 1901; J. M. Jenks to JM, October 27, 1901, JMP.

61. Ralph Easley to JM, October 9, 1901, JMP.

62. JM to Ralph Easley, October 18, 1901, JMP.

63. JM to T. J. Shaffer, October 18, 1901, JMP.

64. JM to Samuel Gompers, June 13, 1903, JMP.

65. Ralph Easley to JM, no date (probably August 1901), JMP.

66. JM to W. B. Wilson, September 6, 1901, JMP.

67. Frank Sargent to JM, September 23, 1901, JMP.

68. Green, *National Civic Federation*, p. 39.

69. E. C. Morris to JM, May 23, 1901, JMP. Whenever Mitchell went on vacation, Morris laboriously summarized all his official correspondence for him.

70. T. D. Nicholls, T. P. Duffy, and John Fahy to JM, August 11, JMP.

71. JM to M. A. Hanna, August 29, 1901, JMP.

72. M. A. Hanna to JM, September 3, 1901, JMP.

73. JM to M. A. Hanna, September 6, 1901, JMP.

74. Ralph Easley to JM, October 11, 1901, JMP.

75. JM to Ralph Easley, October 18, 1901, JMP.

76. Ralph Easley to JM, November 13, 1901; JM to Easley, November 15, 1901, JMP.

77. Ralph Easley to JM, October 23, 1901, JMP.

78. Herbert Croly, *Marcus Alonzo Hanna: His Life and Work* (New York: Macmillan, 1912), p. 391.

79. Cited in Green, *National Civic Federation,* p. 41.

80. A copy of Mitchell's speech, December 17, 1901, located in JMP.

81. Cited in Ramirez, *When Workers Fight,* pp. 71–72.

82. Green, *National Civic Federation,* p. 43

83. JM to Ralph Easley, December 28, 1901, JMP.

84. *Report of the Industrial Commission on the Relations of Capital and Labor Employed in the Mining Industry,* vol. 12 (Washington, D.C., Government Printing Office, 1901), pp. 45–52.

85. Ibid.

86. UMWA, *Proceedings of the Twelfth Annual Convention,* 1901, pp. 13, 90.

87. Philip Taft, *The A. F. of L. in the Time of Gompers* (New York: Harper, 1957), pp. 194–198.

88. JM to John P. Reese, November 14, 1901; see also JM to James O'Rourke, November 26, 1901, JMP.

89. W. D. Ryan to JM, January 8, 1901; JM to Ryan, January 9, 1901, JMP.

90. John Mitchell, *Organized Labor,* pp. 211–213.

91. Ibid., p. 206.

92. JM to John P. Reese, November 24, 1901, JMP.

93. UMWA, Minutes of the National Executive Board, August 9, 1901, JMP.

94. JM to W. B. Wilson, August 31, 1901, JMP.

95. JM to T. L. Lewis, September 21, 1901, JMP.

96. T. L. Lewis to JM, October 3, 1901, JMP.

97. JM to T. L. Lewis, October 10, 1901, JMP.

98. T. L. Lewis to JM, October 15 and October 20, 1901; JM to Lewis, October 17 and October 22, 1901, JMP.

99. See JM to W. B. Wilson, September 14, 1901, JMP.

100. JM to James O'Rourke, October 22, 1901, JMP.

101. Copy of circular, November 19, 1901, JMP.

102. JM to T. L. Lewis, November 7, 1901, JMP.

103. T. L. Lewis to JM, November 14, 1901; JM to Lewis, November 22, 1901, JMP.

104. See J. A. Springer to JM, November 15, 1901; JM to Louis Goaziou, November 23, 1901, JMP.

105. UMWA, *Proceedings of the Thirteenth Annual Convention*, 1902, pp. 40–41.

106. Cited in Gowaskie, "A Study in Leadership," p. 130 n. 31.

107. See JM to Ralph Easley, March 13, 1902; JM to Ed McKay, March 13, 1902, JMP.

108. JM to H. N. Taylor, April 2, 1902, JMP.

Chapter 5: The Great Strike of 1902

1. UMWA, *Proceedings of the Thirteenth Annual Convention*, 1902, pp. 42–43.

2. Ibid., p. 129.

3. JM, T. D. Nicholls, Thomas Duffy, and John Fahy to E. B. Thomas, February 13, 1902, JMP.

4. A copy of this letter, dated February 14, 1902, is located in the JMP.

5. E. B. Thomas to JM, February 20, 1902; W. H. Truesdale to JM, February 18, 1902, JMP.

6. Ralph Easley to JM, February 11 and March 5, 1902; JM to M. A. Hanna, August 25, 1902, JMP.

7. Copy of convention call, dated February 26, 1902, and company notices, dated March 14, 1902, found in JMP.

8. JM to Ralph Easley, March 13, 1902, JMP.

9. "President Mitchell, to the Convention of the Three Anthracite Districts," March 22, 1902, JMP; notes on Shamokin convention, March 18–24, 1902, JMP.

10. See telegrams, JM to Ralph Easley, March 22, 1902; JM to M. A. Hanna, March 22, 1902; Hanna to JM, March 22, 1902; Easley to JM, March 24, 1902, JMP.

11. Ralph Easley to Frank Sargent, August 4, 1902, JMP.

12. UMWA, *Proceedings of the Fourteenth Annual Convention*, 1903, p. 28.

13. Marcus M. Marks to JM, April 2, 1902, JMP.

14. Ralph Easley, "Report of the Executive Committee of the National Civic Federation on the Anthracite Coal Strike," circa 1902, JMP.

15. JM to H. N. Taylor, April 2, 1902, JMP.

16. JM to H. N. Taylor, March 18, April 21, 1902; JM to David Mitchell, April 21, 1902, JMP.

17. JM to Ralph Easley, April 2, 1902, JMP.

18. Ralph Easley to Frank Sargent, August 4, 1902, JMP.

19. JM to H. N. Taylor, April 28, 1902, JMP.

20. "Report of President John Mitchell to the Delegates of the Joint Convention of Districts 1, 7, and 9, United Mine Workers of America, Hazleton, Pa.," May 15, 1902, p. 4, JMP.

21. Cornell, *The Anthracite Coal Strike*, pp. 87–88.

22. See his speech at this convention. "President Mitchell, to the Convention of the Three Anthracite Districts," March 22, 1902, JMP

23. John Mitchell, *Organized Labor*, p. 305.

24. Ibid., p. 306

25. "Recognition of Trade Unions," *Independent* (15 August 1901), 1895–1898; Mitchell, "The Mine Worker's Life and Aims," *Cosmopolitan* (October 1901): 622–630. For a solid examination of these two articles, see Gowaskie, "A Study in Leadership," pp. 151–156.

26. Mitchell, "The Mine Worker's Life and Aims," p. 630.

27. "Minutes of Meetings of the Joint Executive Boards of the Three Anthracite Districts, held in Carpenters' Hall, Scranton, Pa., May 7th to 10th, 1902," located in the JMP. Both Archbishop Ireland and Bishop Potter were members of the NCF's executive committee.

28. M. A. Hanna to JM, March 9, 1902, JMP.

29. JM, T. D. Nicholls, John Dempsey, Thomas Duffy, J.P. Gallagher, John Fahy, and George Hartlein to the Anthracite Mine Workers, May 9, 1902, JMP.

30. JM to Mother Jones, May 10, 1902, JMP.

31. "Address of President John Mitchell, Stating His Position on What Course the Convention Should Follow Regarding the Calling of a Strike. Delivered to the Joint Convention of Districts One, Seven and Nine, U. M. W. A., Hazleton, Pa., May 15, 1902," JMP.

32. "Minutes of the Joint Meeting of Districts 1, 7 and 9, U. M. W. A., Hazleton, Pa., May 14–16, 1902," partial copy, JMP. The exact vote was 461 1/3 to 349 2/3.

33. JM to Ralph Mason, May 17, 1902, JMP.

34. William Mailly, "The Anthracite Coal Strike," *The International Socialist Review* (August 1, 1902), 81, cited in Cornell, *The Anthracite Coal Strike*, p. 93 n. 109.

35. E. C. Morris to S. M. Sexton, May 16, 1902, JMP. Morris was in attendance at the convention and wrote a description of it for Sexton, the new editor of the union's journal.

36. "Minutes of the Joint Meeting of Districts 1, 7 and 9, U. M. W. A., Hazleton, Pa., May 14–16, 1902," partial copy, JMP.

37. JM to W. D. Ryan, May 19, 1902, JMP.

38. UMWA, *Proceedings*, 1902, pp. 40–41, 144.

39. Mother Jones to JM, March 14, 1902, JMP.

40. UMWA, Minutes of the Executive Board, April 8, 1902, JMP.

41. JM to B. F. Berry, April 28, 1902, JMP.

42. T. L. Lewis to W. R. Fairley, May 5, 1902; Lewis to JM, May 3, 1902, JMP.

43. UMWA, *Proceedings*, 1903, p. 37.

44. JM to T. L. Lewis, May 21, 1902, JMP.

45. W. B. Wilson to JM, May 24, 1902, JMP.

46. Tom L. Lewis to JM, June 1, 1902, JMP.

47. Tom L. Lewis to JM, June 9 and June 30, 1902; JM to Lewis, July 5, 1902, JMP.

48. JM to Mother Jones, June 13, 1902, JMP.

49. JM to T. W. Davis, May 23, 1902, JMP.

50. E. C. Morris to S. M. Sexton, May 24, 1902, JMP.

51. See telegrams, Mrs. Mitchell to JM, May 23, 1902; JM to Mrs. Mitchell, May 23 and May 24, 1902, JMP

52. JM to Bishop Michael Hoban, May 16, 1902, JMP.

53. Carroll D. Wright, "Report to the President on the Anthracite Coal Strike," *Bulletin of the Department of Labor* 43 (Washington, D.C.: Government Printing Office, 1902), Appendix E, p. 1024.

54. M. A. Hanna to JM, May 20, 1902, JMP.

55. Ralph Easley to Hanna, no date (probably May 1902), JMP.

56. John Brophy, *A Miner's Life*, p. 34.

57. JM to M. A. Hanna, May 22, 1902, JMP.

58. Ibid.

59. JM to Hanna, May 29, 1902; Ralph Easley, "Report of the Executive Committee of the National Civic Federation on the Anthracite Coal Strike," circa 1902, JMP.

60. Ralph Easley, "Report of the Executive Committee of the National Civic Federation," JMP.

61. M. A. Hanna to JM, May 29, 1902, JMP.

62. *Chicago Record-Herald*, 21 July 1902.

63. Ralph Easley, "Report of the Executive Committee of the National Civic Federation," JMP.

64. Cornell, *The Anthracite Coal Strike*, pp. 103–110.

65. JM to W. B. Wilson, June 11, 1902, JMP.

66. JM to Frank Sargent, June 11, 1902, JMP.

67. Copy of circular, June 18, 1902, in JMP.

68. JM to H. N. Taylor, June 20, 1902, JMP.

69. JM to John P. Reese, June 23, 1902, JMP.

70. Daniel J. Keefe to JM, June 26, July 7, 1902; JM to Keefe, July 9, 1902, JMP.

71. JM to H. N.Taylor, June 23, 1902; Taylor to JM, June 26, 1902, JMP.

72. E. C. Morris to JM, June 28, 29, and 30, 1902; JM to J. J. Sweeney, July 3, 1902, JMP.

73. John J. Curran to JM, July 12 and July 16, 1902, JMP.

74. Thomas I. Kidd to JM, June 23, 1902; JM to Kidd, June 26, 1902, JMP.

75. *Minneapolis Journal*, 16 July 1902, cited in Cornell, *The Anthracite Coal Strike*, p. 116.

76. JM to Ralph Mason, July 11, 1902, JMP.

77. UMWA, *Minutes of Special Convention Called to Consider the Anthracite Strike*, July 17–19, 1902, pp. 1–4.

78. ibid, pp. 15–16.

79. Ibid., pp. 22–23.

80. Ibid., pp. 33–34.

81. Ibid., p. 95.

82. Ibid., p. 11.

83. *Baltimore News*, 18 July 1902; *Minneapolis Journal*, July 18, 1902, both quoted in Cornell, *The Anthracite Coal Strike*, p. 118.

84. M. A. Hanna to JM, July 18, 1902, JMP.

85. Ralph Easley to JM, July 29, 1902, JMP.

86. JM to M. A. Hanna, July 21, 1902, JMP.

87. JM to John P. Reese, July 26, 1902, JMP.

88. George Hartlein to JM, July 27, 1902, JMP.

89. JM to George Hartlein, July 28, 1902, JMP.

90. John Mitchell, *Organized Labor*, pp. 380–381.

91. Copy of circular, August 4, 1902, in JMP.

92. Selig Perlman and Philip Taft, *History of Labor in the United States*, vol. 4 (New York: Macmillan, 1935), p. 328; UMWA, *Proceedings*, 1903, p. 38.

93. JM to W. B. Wilson, June 11, 1902; JM to Mother Jones, June 13, 1902, JMP.

94. John H. Walker to JM, July 9, 1901; Huntington conference minutes, May 23–25, 1902, JMP.

95. Cited in Gowaskie, "A Study in Leadership," pp. 140–141.

96. JM to John P. Reese, June 23, 1902, JMP.

97. Mother Jones to JM, July 25, 1902, JMP.

98. Haggerty's comments are contained in a letter from E. C. Morris to JM, June 30, 1902, JMP.

99. UMWA, *Proceedings*, 1903, p. 38.

100. Jones, *Autobiography*, p. 63.

101. UMWA, *Proceedings*, 1903, pp. 52–54; Chris Evans to JM, October 6, 1902, JMP; Perlman and Taft, *History of Labor*, p. 329.

102. Gowaskie, "A Study in Leadership," p. 145.

103. Roy, *A History of Coal Miners* , p. 440.

104. See, for example, Selig Perlman, *A History of Trade Unionism in the United States* (New York: 1923), p. 177; Gluck, *John Mitchell*, chapter 6; Cornell, *The Anthracite Coal Strike*, pp. 258–259; Gowaskie, "A Study in Leadership," pp. 165–169, 189; Ramirez, *When Workers Fight*, pp. 40–41; Robert Wiebe, "The Anthracite Strike of 1902: A Record of Confusion," *Mississippi Valley Historical Review* 48 (September 1961): 240.

105. Steffens, "A Labor Leader of To-day, p. 355.

106. Morris, "John Mitchell, the Leader, pp. 3073–3078.

107. Steffens, "A Labor Leader of To-Day," p. 355.

108. E. C. Morris to S. M. Sexton, August 27, 1902, JMP.

109. Cited in Greene, *The Slavic Community on Strike*, p. 200.

110. John Mitchell, "An Exposition and Interpretation of the Trade Union Movement," in Charles S. McFarland, ed., *The Christian Ministry and the Social Order* (New Haven, CT: Yale University Press, 1913), pp. 95–96.

111. Greene, *The Slavic Community of Strike*, p. 47.

112. JM to Father John Power, August 9, 1902, JMP.

113. Nash, *Conflict and Accommodation*, p. 69

114. Jones, *Autobiography*, pp. 91–92.

115. Quoted in Cornell, *The Anthracite Coal Strike*, p. 152.

116. Ibid., p. 155.

117. John Mitchell, "The Voice of Labor," *Collier's Weekly* (September 6, 1902): 5.

118. Mitchell, "The Coal Strike," *McClure's Magazine* (December 1902): 219.

119. A copy of this letter, George Baer to William F. Clark, July 17, 1902, is located in the JMP.

120. For the reaction of the press to this letter, see Cornell, *The Anthracite Coal Strike*, pp. 170–172.

121. Perlman, *A History of Trade Unionism*, p. 177.

122. Press statement, August 27, 1902, JMP.

123. Ralph Easley to JM, August 27, 1902, JMP.

124. John Mitchell, "Dictation by the Unions," *Independent* (18 September 1902), 2228.

125. Ralph Easley to Frank Sargent, August 4, 1902, JMP.

126. Ralph Easley to JM, August 4, 1902; JM to Easley, August 6, 1902, JMP.

127. JM to M. A. Hanna, August 9 and August 15, 1902: Hanna to JM, August 20, 1902, JMP.

128. Easley, "Report of the Executive Committee of the National Civic Federation," JMP.

129. JM to M. A. Hanna, September 8, 1902, JMP.

130. JM to M. A. Hanna, August 6, 1902, JMP.

131. JM to M. A. Hanna, August 9, 1902, JMP.

132. Daniel Keefe to M. A. Hanna, September 6, 1902, JMP.

133. JM to M. A. Hanna, September 8, 1902, JMP.

134. Marcus Alonzo Hanna, "Industrial Conciliation and Arbitration," *Annals of the American Academy of Political and Social Science* 40 (December 1902): 28–29.

135. M. A. Hanna to JM, September 30, 1902, JMP.

136. JM to M. A. Hanna, October 2, 1902, JMP.

137. Quoted in Foner, *History of the Labor Movement*, p. 96.

138. *Independent* (16 October 1902), 2483.

139. Quoted in Richard Hofstadter, *The American Political Tradition and the Men Who Made It* (New York: Alfred A. Knopf, 1948), p. 223.

140. Quoted in Cornell, *The Anthracite Coal Strike*, p. 174.

141. JM to M.A. Hanna, September 8, 1902, JMP.

142. The quotes are from Cornell's account of the conference, pp.181–188.

143. Quoted in Gluck, *John Mitchell,* p. 126.

144. *Des Moines* (Iowa) *Register and Leader*, 5 October 1902, clipping in JMP.

145. M. A. Hanna to JM, October 7, 1902, JMP.

146. JM to Theodore Roosevelt, October 8, 1902, JMP.

147. JM to M. A. Hanna, October 13, 1902, JMP.

148. JM to H. N. Taylor, October 11, 1902, JMP.

149. This account of the plan and its acceptance by the operators, including Fowler's quote, is taken from Cornell, *The Anthracite Coal Strike*, pp. 215–223.

150. Ibid., pp. 224–225.

151. George Cortelyou to JM, October 14, 1902; JM to Cortelyou, October 14, 1902, JMP.

152. Telephone memorandum, Senator Mark Hanna and John Mitchell, October 14, 1902, JMP.

153. Theodore Roosevelt, *Theodore Roosevelt: An Autobiography* (New York: Macmillan, 1919), p. 467.

154. Ibid., pp.468–469.

155. E. E. Clark to JM, August 1, 1902, JMP.

156. JM to Theodore Roosevelt, October 16, 1902, JMP.

157. JM to M. J. Hoban, October 18, 1902, JMP.

158. "Opening Address of President John Mitchell to Delegates of the Joint Convention of Districts 1, 7 and 9, U. M. W. A., at Wilkes-Barre, Pa., October 20, 1902," JMP.

159. JM and W. B. Wilson to Theodore Roosevelt, October 21, 1902, JMP.

160. Jones, *Autobiography*, pp. 59–61.

161. Gluck, *John Mitchell*, p. 132.

162. Quoted in Laslett, *Labor and the Left*, p. 205.

163. *Social Democratic Herald*, 31 January 1903, quoted in Gowaskie, "A Study in Leadership," p. 195.

164. John Mitchell, *Organized Labor*, p. 390.

165. Ibid.

166. Copy of eulogy, October 26, 1902, JMP.

167. Greene, *The Slavic Community on Strike*, pp. 202–203.

168. Mitchell, "The Coal Strike," pp. 219–224; Steffens, "A Labor Leader of To-day," pp. 355–357; JM to George T. Lennon, October 30, 1902; JM to William Hawthorne, December 6, 1902; Hawthorne to JM, December 4 and December 22, 1902; *Chicago Inter Ocean*, 14 December 1902; *UMWJ*, December 18, 1902.

169. H. N. Taylor to JM, October 23, 1902, JMP.

170. JM to H. N. Taylor, November 7, 1902, JMP.

171. JM to Mae Leedom, November 1, 1902, JMP.

CHAPTER 6: ON THE WITNESS STAND

1. Information on the research team and its investigations gathered from numerous letters and documents found in the JMP. See also Gowaskie, "A Study in Leadership," pp. 184–185.

2. JM to John R. Commons, October 29, 1902, JMP.

3. John Power to JM, September 20, 1902, JMP.

4. Irving Stone, *Clarence Darrow for the Defense* (New York: Doubleday and Co., 1941), p. 141.

5. Copy of demands in JMP.

6. Operator responses can be found in Anthracite Coal Strike Commission, *Report to the President on the Anthracite Coal Strike of May–October 1902* (Washington, D.C.: Government Printing Office, 1903), Appendix A, pp. 96–171. (Hereafter cited as *Report to the President*.)

7. Cornell, *The Anthracite Coal Strike*, pp. 240–241.

8. *Report to the President*, pp. 39–41.

9. Ibid.

10. JM to W. R. Russell, November 16, 1902, JMP.

11. H. N. Taylor to JM, November 10, 1902; JM to Taylor, November 15, 1902, JMP.

12. Caro Lloyd, *Henry Demarest Lloyd* (New York: G. P. Putnam's Sons, 1912), p. 210; see also Gowaskie, "A Study in Leadership," p. 186.

13. Lloyd, *Lloyd*, p. 210; "Proceedings of the Anthracite Coal Strike Commission, 1902–1903," (mimeographed copy in the Library of Congress), vol. 4, p. 430 (hereafter cited as "Proceedings"); *Buffalo Courier*, 18 November 1902, cited in Cornell, *The Anthracite Coal Strike*, p. 242 n. 24.

14. *Scranton Truth*, November 24, 1902.

15. Cornell, *The Anthracite Coal Strike*, p. 243.

16. JM to H. N. Taylor, November 22, 1902, JMP.

17. JM to W. B. Wilson, November 27, 1902, JMP.

18. Gluck, *John Mitchell,*, p. 147.

19. "Proceedings," vol. 13, pp. 1619–1628.

20. Estella Lightner to E. C. Morris, January 4, 1903, JMP.

21. *Philadelphia North American*, 16 January 1903, clipping in JMP.

22. Stone, *Clarence Darrow for the Defense*, pp. 151–152.

23. Clarence Darrow, *The Story of My Life* (New York: Charles Scribners' Sons, 1932), pp. 354–363.

24. Gluck, *John Mitchell*, p.148.

25. Mitchell, *Organized Labor*, p. 392.

26. Cornell, *The Anthracite Coal Strike*, p. 252.

27. *Report to the President*, pp. 60–61.

28. Ibid., pp. 67–68.

29. Ibid., pp. 62–63.

30. Ibid., pp. 64–65, 76–78.

31. *New York Times*, 22 March 1903.

32. Robert Wiebe, "The Response of American Business Men to the National Progressive Movement, 1901–1916," (Ph. D. diss., University of Rochester), 1957, pp. 177–178, quoted in Foner, *History of the Labor Movement*, p. 100.

33. Quoted in Laslett, *Labor and the Left*, p. 204.

34. *New York Times*, 22 March 1903.

35. Mitchell, *Organized Labor*, p. 392.

36. Ibid., p. 394.

37. Cornell, *The Anthracite Coal Strike*, p. 257.

38. JM to Mrs. Mitchell, March 18, 1903; *Frostburg* (Maryland) *Herald*, 13 November 1903, clipping in JMP.

39. Gluck, *John Mitchell,* pp. 152–153.

40. Mother Jones to JM, February 26, 1903; JM to Jones, March 3, 1903, JMP.

41. Quoted in Gluck, *John Mitchell,* p.150.

42. Ralph Easley to JM, no date, probably 1902, JMP.

43. JM to Daniel J. Keefe, April 27, 1903; Keefe to JM, May 1, 1903, JMP. Emphasis added.

44. See E. C. Morris to Harriet Reid, September 23, 1903, JMP. The letter reads in part, "Just under your hat, the boss lunches with the President next Tuesday at one."

45. JM to H. N. Taylor, March 11, 1903; Taylor to JM, March 13, 1902; T. G. Moran, Jr. to JM, March 14, 1904, JMP.

46. JM to H. N. Taylor, April 28, 1903, JMP.

47. Mrs. Mitchell to JM, August 3, 1901; JM to Mrs. Mitchell, August 3, 1901; E. C. Morris to JM, August 5, 1901; JM to Joe Vasey, August 12, 1901, JMP.

48. Richard Mitchell to JM, October 7, 1902, JMP. There are two other undated letters from Richard to his father written approximately the same time in the JMP.

49. JM to H. N. Taylor, April 2, August 10, and November 15, 1902, JMP; for a discussion of the rumors, see Gluck, *John Mitchell,* p. 141.

50. JM to H. N. Taylor, June 11, 1902, JMP.

51. JM to Mrs. Mitchell, March 2, 1903, JMP.

52. JM to William Hawthorne, April 25, 1903; see also Hawthorne to JM, January 19, 1903; JM to Mrs. Mitchell, March 2 and March 19, 1903; and JM to Hawthorne, March 17, 1903, JMP.

53. He also had a daughter at this time, Marie, who was not yet in school.

54. Richard mentioned his being an altar boy in the letter to his father dated October 7, 1902.

55. JM to Mrs. Mitchell, March 19, 1903, JMP.

56. Steffens, "A Labor Leader of To-Day, p. 355.

57. JM to Mrs. Mitchell, March 2, 1903; JM to H. N.Taylor, April 2, 1903, JMP.

58. JM to John B. Lennon, December 10, 1904, JMP.

59. JM to John B. Wilson, May 5, 1903, JMP.

60. UMWA, *Proceedings of the Fourteenth Annual Convention,* 1903, pp. 495, 497–98.

61. JM to H. N. Taylor, April 12, 1902, JMP.

62. H. N. Taylor to JM, August 8, 1902; JM to Taylor, August 10, 1902, JMP.

63. H. N. Taylor to JM, October 8, 1902; JM to Taylor, October 11, 1902, JMP.

64. H. N. Taylor to JM, December 4, 1902; JM to Taylor, March 11, 1903, JMP.

65. H. N. Taylor to JM, September 9 and November 3, 1904, January 4, 1904; JM to Taylor, November 6, 1903, January 22, 1904, JMP.

66. William D. Boyce to JM, January 18 and February 10, 1903; Judson Grennell to JM, December 29, 1902; JM to Grennell, February 7, 1903, JMP.

67. JM to Andrew Chippie, January 6, 1903, JMP.

68. JM to Ralph Easley, February 11, 1903, JMP.

69. JM to Daniel J. Keefe, March 8, 1903, JMP.

70. Morris, "The Acquisitive Spirit of John Mitchell, pp. 24–26.

71. Charles A. Doe to Walter E. Weyl, March 16, 1903; Weyl to JM, April 24, April 26, and April 28, 1903; JM to Weyl, April 25, 1903, JMP.

72. JM to Walter E. Weyl, April 29, May 7, September 17 and September 21, 1903; Weyl to JM, May 2 and May 20, 1903; JM to Charles A. Doe, August 5, 1903, JMP.

73. JM to Mrs. Mitchell, September 15, 1903, JMP.

74. JM to William Hawthorne, September 6, 1903, JMP.

75. JM to Charles A. Doe, August 17 and September 17, 1903, JMP.

76. Walter E. Weyl to JM, December 29, 1903, JMP.

77. Charles A. Doe to JM, February 5 and February 27, 1904; JM to Doe, March 7, 1904, JMP.

78. JM to William Hawthorne, March 15, 1903, JMP.

79. Morris, "The Acquisitive Spirit of John Mitchell," p. 23.

80. This was how Duncan McDonald, UMW official and socialist, described the NCF at the 1911 AFL convention. Quoted in James Weinstein, *The Corporate Ideal in the Liberal State* (Boston: Beacon Press, 1968), p. 22.

81. Quoted in Marc Karson, *American Labor Unions and Politics, 1900–1918* (Carbondale, Ill.: Southern Illinois University Press, 1958), pp. 160–161.

82. Quoted in Van Tine, *The Making of the Labor Bureaucrat*, p.177.

83. American Federation of Labor, *Proceedings*, 1903, pp. 188–199.

84. Laslett, *Labor and the Left*, p. 205.

85. On Walker, see the biographical sketch in the John H. Walker Collection, Illinois State Historical Survey, University of Illinois; on McDonald, see "Autobiography," in Duncan McDonald Collection, Illinois State Historical Society.

86. UMWA, *Proceedings*, 1903, p. 61.

87. Ibid., pp. 45–46.

88. Copy of agreements signed at 1903 interstate convention in JMP.

89. Jones, *Autobiography*, pp. 56–57, 59.

90. JM to James Duncan, March 11, 1904, JMP.

91. Philip Taft, "Collective Bargaining Before the New Deal," in *How Collective Bargaining Works*, ed. Twentieth Century Fund (New York: The Twentieth Century Fund, 1942), p. 881.

92. Ibid.

93. An excellent discussion of the contradictions of the report is in Ramirez, *When Workers Fight*, pp. 41–45.

94. Mitchell, *Organized Labor*, p. 347.

95. Ibid., p. 352.

96. Ibid., p. 348.

97. Ibid., p. 353.

98. Ibid., p. xi.

99. Ibid., p. ix.

100. Ibid., p. 423.

101. Ibid., p. 194.

102. Ibid., pp. 192–193.

103. *Wall Street Journal*, 28 October 1903.

CHAPTER 7: A YEAR OF RECKONING, 1904

1. UMWA, Minutes of the National Executive Board, October 6, 1903.

2. On the power and labor practices of these corporations, see George McGovern,"The Colorado Coal Strike, 1913–1914," (Ph.D. diss., Northwestern University, 1953), chapter 1; and J. Warner Mills, "The Economic Struggle in Colorado," *Arena* 34 (July–December 1905): 1–10, 248–265, 379–399.

3. On Governor Peabody's labor policies, see George G. Suggs, Jr., "Colorado Conservatives Versus Organized Labor: A Study of the George Hamilton Peabody Administration, 1903–1905," (Ph.D. diss., University of Colorado, 1964).

4. For instance, a prominent Illinois UMWA socialist, Adolph Germer, corresponded frequently with John M. O'Neill, editor of the WFM's official journal.

5. Typed copy of a confidential, unsigned report from an organizer of the AFL to Samuel Gompers, September 1903, JMP.

6. Ibid.

7. UMWA, Minutes of the National Executive Board, October 9, 1903.

8. U. S. Commissioner of Labor, "A Report on Labor Disturbances in the State of Colorado from 1880 to 1904, Inclusive," Senate Document 122, 58th Congress, Second Session, p. 335. (Hereafter cited as U. S. Commissioner of Labor, "A Report on Labor Disturbances.")

9. *UMWJ*, 19 November 1903.

10. U. S. Commissioner of Labor, "A Report on Labor Disturbances," p. 335.

11. Quoted in Philip S. Foner, editor, *Mother Jones Speaks: Collected Speeches and Writings* (New York: Monad Press, 1983), p. 104.

12. U. S. Commissioner of Labor, "A Report on Labor Disturbances," p. 336.

13. Long, *Where the Sun Never Shines*, pp. 229–230.

14. U. S. Commissioner of Labor, "A Report on Labor Disturbances," p. 336.

15. Jones, *Autobiography*, p. 100.

16. U. S. Commissioner of Labor, "A Report on Labor Disturbances," p. 336; Colorado Bureau of Statistics, *Ninth Biennial Report, 1903–1904*, p. 190.

17. Long, *Where the Sun Never Shines*, p. 231.

18. UMWA, *Proceedings of the Sixteenth Annual Convention*, 1905, p. 179.

19. Jones, *Autobiography*, p. 101.

20. UMWA, *Proceedings*, 1905, p. 228.

21. UMWA, Minutes of the National Executive Board, April 30, 1904.

22. See the speech by Robert Randall in UMWA, *Proceedings*, 1905, p. 179.

23. Speech by W. R. Fairley, *Proceedings*, 1905, p. 179. On the problems created by the northern settlement, see Long, *Where the Sun Never Shines*, pp. 228–232.

24. *UMWJ*, 10 December 1903.

25. U. S. Commissioner of Labor, "A Report on Labor Disturbances," p. 339.

26. JM to John P. Reese, December 15, 1903, JMP.

27. Jones, *Autobiography*, p. 101.

28. *UMWJ*, 17 March 1904; see also Emma Longdon, *The Cripple Creek Strike: A History of Industrial Wars in Colorado, 1903–1905* (Denver: Great Western Publishing, 1905), pp. 265–269.

29. UMWA, Minutes of the National Executive Board, January 4, 1904.

30. Ibid., January 19, 1904.

31. Ibid., January 24, 1904.

32. JM to W. R. Fairley, March 23, 1904, JMP; UMWA, *Proceedings*, 1905, pp. 11–12.

33. Jones, *Autobiography*, p. 103; U. S. Commissioner of Labor, "A Report on Labor Disturbances," p. 351.

34. *UMWJ*, 24 March 1904.

35. *UMWJ*, 21 April 1904; U. S. Commissioner of Labor, "A Report on Labor Disturbances," pp. 353–354.

36. UMWA, Minutes of the National Executive Board, April 27, 1904.

37. UMWA, *Proceedings*, 1905, p. 211.

38. UMWA, Minutes of the National Executive Board, April 30, 1904.

39. JM to H. N. Taylor, June 10, 1904, JMP.

40. Daniel J. Keefe to JM, April 18, 1904; JM to Keefe, April 20, 1904, JMP.

41. William Dodds to JM, May 16, 1904; JM to Dodds, May 17 and May 18, 1904, JMP.

42. The information on Mitchell's trip is taken from his expense account, dated September 21, 1904, JMP.

43. So stated Carnegie in his invitation. See Carnegie to JM, June 14, 1904, JMP.

44. JM to Neal Hughes, September 13, 1904, JMP.

45. UMWA, *Proceedings*, 1905, p. 184.

46. U. S. Commissioner of Labor, "A Report on Labor Disturbances," pp. 357, 359.

47. Quoted in Long, *Where the Sun Never Shines*, p. 257.

48. UMWA, *Proceedings*, 1905, p. 14.

49. Ibid., pp. 168–169.

50. Ibid., pp. 176–185.

51. Ibid., pp. 189–196, 227–230.

52. Ibid., pp. 230–232.

53. JM to T. W. Davis, February 13, 1905, JMP.

54. Gowaskie, "A Study in Leadership," p. 277.

55. UMWA, *Proceedings of the Fifteenth Annual Convention*, 1904, pp. 31, 38.

56. *Seventh Annual Joint Conference of Coal Miners and Operators of Western Pennsylvania, Ohio, Indiana, and Illinois* (Indianapolis, 1904), pp. 7–8. (Hereafter cited as *1904 Joint Conference*.)

57. *1904 Joint Conference*, pp. 8–10.

58. Ibid., pp. 53–54.

59. JM to Elmer Dover, February 9, 1904, JMP.

60. Elmer Dover to JM, February 11, 1904, JMP.

61. JM to Daniel J. Keefe, February 15, 1904, JMP.

62. JM to H. N. Taylor, February 17, 1904; "Prepared for the Cleveland Press," February 18, 1904, JMP.

63. *UMWJ*, 18 February 1904.

64. Ralph Easley to JM, February 8, 1904, JMP.

65. JM to C. J. Devlin, March 1, 1904, JMP.

66. *1904 Joint Conference*, pp. 57–114.

67. UMWA, *Proceedings of the Special National Convention*, March 5–7, 1904, pp. 28–29.

68. JM to Daniel J. Keefe, March 7, 1904, JMP.

69. UMWA, *Proceedings of the Special National Convention*, March 5–7, 1904, pp. 2, 10.

70. Duncan McDonald, unpublished "Autobiography," p. 37, located in the Duncan McDonald Collection, Illinois State Historical Society. See also Gowaskie, "A Study in Leadership," p. 240 n. 14.

71. UMWA, *Proceedings of the Special National Convention*, March 5–7, 1904, pp. 28, 33.

72. JM to Walter Weyl, March 7, 1904, JMP.

73. "Recommendations of the National Officers Issued in Accordance with Instructions of the Special National Convention," March 9, 1904, JMP.

74. JM to John H. Walker, March 12, 1904, JMP.

75. *UMWJ*, 10 March 1904.

76. Ralph Easley to JM, March 8, 1904; JM to Easley, March 10, 1904, JMP.

77. JM to E. R. Smith, March 10, 1904, JMP.

78. JM to William Hawthorne, March 15, 1904, JMP.

79. The tellers' report, dated March 25, 1904, located in the JMP.

80. Gowaskie, "A Study in Leadership," p. 244.

81. JM to John P. Reese, March 17, 1904, JMP.

82. *NCF Monthly Review* (July 1904): 12.

83. JM to George Harrison, March 18, 1904, JMP.

84. O. L. Garrison to JM, March 16, 1904, JMP.

85. W. S. Bogle to JM, March 18, 1904; C. J. Devlin to JM, March 18, 1904, JMP.

86. Frank L. Robbins to JM, March 26, 1904, JMP.

87. Ralph Easley to JM, March 18, 1904, JMP.

88. *Baltimore American*, 18 March 1904, clipping in JMP.

89. *Springfield Daily Morning Sun*, 23 March 1904, clipping in JMP.

90. Ramirez, *When Workers Fight*, p. 80.

91. Gluck, *John Mitchell*, pp. 164–165.

92. Gowaskie, "A Study in Leadership," pp. 246–247.

93. Eugene Debs to Mother Jones, May 15, 1901; JM to Jones, August 3, 1901, JMP.

94. UMWA, *Proceedings*, 1904, p. 90.

95. JM to Henry D. Lloyd, May 27, 1903, JMP.

96. Copy of press release, dated February 13, 1904, in JMP. Mitchell wrote this eulogy while Hanna was still alive, then released it to the press on the day of his funeral.

97. Minutes of the Semi-Annual Meeting of the NCF, May 6, 1904, Easley Papers, New York Public Library.

98. JM to Ralph Easley, February 24, 1904, JMP.

99. JM to Daniel J. Keefe, March 9, 1904, JMP.

100. Ralph Easley to JM, March 8, 1904, JMP.

101. JM to Ralph Easley, March 10, 1904, JMP.

102. Andrew Carnegie, *Autobiography* (New York: Houghton Mifflin, 1928), p. 228.

103. Easley to JM, March 18, 1904, JMP.

104. JM to Keefe, March 19, 1904, JMP.

105. Ralph Easley to JM, December 8, 1904, JMP.

106. Frank Robbins to JM, May 8, 1904; JM to Robbins, May 13, 1904; Louis Hammerling to JM, March 18, 1905; see also Gowaskie, "A Study in Leadership," pp. 217–218.

107. Ramirez, *When Workers Fight*, p. 61.

108. JM to Neill, December 10, 1904; Neill to JM, December 10, 1904, JMP.

109. JM to James Duncan, March 15, 1904, JMP; see also JM to Father John Power, February 27, 1904; JM to James Duncan, February 27, 1904; Duncan to JM, March 11, 1904, JMP.

110. Quoted in Coleman, *Men and Coal*, p. 71. When this comment was made, Coleman was a reporter and heard the comment first hand.

111. *New York Times*, 17 December 1904.

112. On Belmont's election, see "Labor Wrests Victory from Defeat," *NCF Review* (March 1905): 1–4; Green, *The National Civic Federation*, pp. 61–62.

113. Ralph Easley to JM, April 20, 1904, JMP. This letter was also sent to all members of the special committee establishing the Trade Agreement Department.

114. Ralph Easley to JM, May 25, 1904, JMP.

115. "A National Conference on Trade Agreements," *NCF Monthly Review* (July 1904): 11–16; Green, *National Civic Federation*, pp. 85–86.

116. For a more complete list, see Gordon Jensen, "The National Civic Federation: American Business in an Age of Social Change and Social Reform, 1900–1910" (Ph.D. diss., Princeton University, 1956), pp. 125–126.

117. Louis D. Brandeis,"The Employer and Trade Unionism," *NCF Monthly Review* (August 1904): 11.

118. Ralph Easley, "Our Enemies," *NCF Monthly Review* (October 15, 1904): 8.

119. Quoted in the *NCF Review* (April 1913): 13.

120. On Gompers' attitudes toward trade agreements, see Ramirez, *When Workers Fight*, pp. 76–78; and William M. Dick, *Labor and Socialism in America: The Gompers Era* (Port Washington, New York: Kennikat Press, 1972), p. 113.

121. "John Mitchell to the Annual Dinner of the NCF, December 15, 1904," *NCF Review* (January 1, 1905): 6.

122. The comment was made by Henry Leipziger and is quoted by Kellogg Dunland in a letter to Mitchell, dated December 16, 1904, JMP.

123. On the origins of the antiunion movement, see Montgomery, *The Fall of the House of Labor*, pp. 272–275; Van Tine, *The Making of the Labor Bureaucrat*, pp. 81–82; Clarence E. Bonnett, *History of Employers' Associations in the United States* (New York: Vantage Press, 1956), pp. 443–447; Taft, "Collective Bargaining Before the New Deal," *How Collective Bargaining*, pp. 898–900.

124. Quoted in Green, *National Civic Federation*, p. 105.

125. A good discussion of the tactics and strategies of the anti-union movement can be found in Foner, *History of the Labor Movement*, vol. 3, pp. 32–60.

126. Ralph Easley, "Our Enemies," *NCF Review* (October 15, 1904): 8.

127. Ralph Easley to JM, October 3, 1903, JMP.

128. Ralph Easley to JM, December 8, 1904, JMP.

129. Charles Stelzle to JM, November 19, 1903, JMP.

130. JM to Charles Stelzle, November 27, 1903, JMP.

131. John Maxwell to Charles Stelzle, January 25, 1904; JM to Stelzle, January 15, 19, 21, 1904; Stelzle to JM, November 30, 1903, January 16, 19, 20, 1904, JMP.

132. JM to Charles Stelzle, February 12, 1904, JMP.

133. Charles Stelzle to JM, February 13, 1904, JMP.

134. Charles Stelzle to JM, February 18, 1904, JMP.

135. Ralph Easley to JM, December 8, 1904, JMP.

136. Ralph Easley to JM, December 8, 1904; JM to Easley, December 10, 1904, JMP.

CHAPTER 8: SHATTERED DREAMS OF COOPERATION, 1905–1906

1. A good description of the background of the conflict and the strike itself can be found in Philip S. Foner, *History of the Labor Movement*, vol. 3, pp. 102–106.

2. Ralph Easley to JM, February 24, 1905, JMP.

3. "Labor Wrests Victory from Defeat," *NCF Review* (March 1905): 1–4.

4. William D. Mahon to JM, March 13, 1905; JM to Mahon, March 17, 1905, JMP. The letter stated that the men had "no right' to strike without Mahon's consent and that Mahon "took the only logical position he could assume" by refusing to sanction the strike.

5. Foner, *History of the Labor Movement*, vol. 3, pp.104–105.

6. Ralph Easley to JM, March 30, 1907, JMP.

7. Foner, *History of the Labor Movement*, vol.3, p. 105.

8. JM to Ralph Easley, October 21, 1907, JMP.

9. JM to Ralph Easley, September 1, November 16, 1907; Easley to JM, September 6, November 20, 1907, JMP.

10. "How the Welfare Department was Organized," *NCF Review* (June 1904): 13–14; Ramirez, *When Workers Fight*, pp. 148–150.

11. On the anti-union tendency of welfare work, see Daniel Nelson and Stuart Campbell, "Taylorism Versus Welfare Work in American Industry," *Business History Review* 46 (Spring 1972): 1–4.

12. *NCF Review* (March–April 1907): 11; Green, *The National Civic Federation*, p. 268.

13. Gertrude Beeks, "Welfare Work and Child Labor in Southern Cotton Mills," *NCF Review* (July–August 1906): 14 ff.

14. *UMWJ*, 8 November 1906.

15. JM to Gertrude Beeks, December 6, 1906, JMP.

16. Gertrude Beeks to JM, December 28, 1906; JM to Beeks, January 2, 1907, JMP.

17. This conference is discussed in Green, *National Civic Federation*, pp. 108–111.

18. Montgomery, *The Fall of the House of Labor*, p. 274.

19. The best single study of the IWW is Melvyn Dubofsky, *We Shall Be All: A History of the Industrial Workers of the World* (Chicago: Quadrangle Press, 1969); see also Joseph R. Conlin, *Bread and Roses Too: Studies of the Wobblies* (Westport, CT: Greenwood Press, 1969); and Patrick Renshaw, *The Wobblies: The Story of Syndicalism in the United States* (Garden City, NY: Anchor Books, 1968).

20. Samuel Gompers to W. D. Ryan, May 13, 1905, cited in Laslett, *Labor and the Left*, p. 210.

21. JM to W. D. Ryan, March 3, 1905, JMP.

22. W.D. Ryan to JM, March 6, 1905; JM to Ryan, March 10, 1905, JMP.

23. UMWA, *Minutes of the Proceedings of the Seventeenth Annual Convention*, January 1906, pp. 53–54.

24. UMWA, *Proceedings*, 1906, pp. 158–159.

25. Ibid., p. 159.

26. Ibid., pp. 159–160.

27. Both quotes are cited in Gowaskie, "A Study in Leadership," p. 290 n. 25.

28. Clarence Darrow to JM, March 13, 1906; JM to Darrow, March 14, 1906, JMP.

29. Cited in Foner, *History of the Labor Movement*, vol. 3, p. 315.

30. JM to Samuel Gompers, March 21, 1906, JMP.

31. Foner, *History of the Labor Movement*, vol. 3, p. 322.

32. Samuel Gompers to JM, August 26, 1906, JMP.

33. JM to Samuel Gompers, August 30, 1906, JMP.

34. Foner, *History of the Labor Movement*, vol. 3, p. 328.

35. UMWA, *Proceedings*, 1906, pp. 201–203.

36. Ibid., pp. 45–48.

37. Laslett, *Labor and the Left*, p. 213.

38. JM to Gertrude Beeks, October 1, 1906, JMP.

39. Montgomery, *Fall of the House of Labor*, p. 339.

40. UMWA, *Proceedings*, 1906, pp. 36, 52–53.

41. *Pittsburgh Leader*, 24 February 1906, clipping in JMP.

42. JM to Samuel Gompers, January 6, 1906, JMP.

43. *Proceedings of the Joint Conference of Coal Miners and Operators*, January 25–February 2, March 20–March 29, 1906, pp. 9, 14.

44. Ibid., p. 17.

45. Ibid., p. 90.

46. Ibid., p. 93, 113.

47. UMWA, *Proceedings*, 1906, p. 246.

48. Ibid., pp. 247–248.

49. UMWA, *Proceedings of the Joint Conference of Coal Miners and Operators*, January 25–February 2, March 20–March 29, 1906, pp. 122–123.

50. Quoted in Gluck, *John Mitchell*, p. 185.

51. UMWA, *Proceedings*, 1906, pp. 249–251.

52. *Pittsburgh Gazette*, 19 February 1906, cited in Gowaskie, "A Study in Leadership," p. 300.

53. Ibid.

54. James Duncan to JM, February 24, 1906, JMP.

55. Cited in Gowaskie, "A Study in Leadership," p. 299.

56. Press release, issued February 12, 1906, in JMP.

57. JM to "My Dear Wife," February 14, 1906, JMP.

58. JM to T. L. Lewis, February 7, 1906, JMP.

59. *Pittsburgh Post*, 25 February 1906, clipping in JMP. The three national board members were Joseph Sharp, Thomas Haggerty, and William Little.

60. *New York Times*, 24 February 1906; see also *Pittsburgh Leader*, 25 February 1906, cited in Gowaskie, "A Study in Leadership," pp. 303–304.

61. Manuscript, "Dates of Interest in Connection with Negotiations for Bituminous Settlement," 1906, JMP.

62. *Pittsburgh Chronicle-Telegraph*, 23 February 1906, clipping in JMP.

63. JM to Theodore Roosevelt, February 22, 1906, JMP.

64. Theodore Roosevelt to JM, February 24, 1906, JMP.

65. Theodore Roosevelt to JM, "Confidential," February 24, 1906, JMP.

66. *Pittsburgh Chronicle-Telegraph*, 23 February 1906, clipping in JMP.

67. *Pittsburgh Dispatch*, 26 February 1906, cited in Gowaskie, "A Study in Leadership," p. 307.

68. *Pittsburgh Press*, 26 February 1906, clipping in JMP.

69. JM to H. N. Taylor, March 3, 1906, JMP.

70. JM to Theodore Roosevelt, February 26, 1906, JMP.

71. JM to William B. Wilson, February 26, 1906, JMP.

72. George Colville, George Richardson, and Peter Hanraty to JM, March 6, 1906, JMP.

73. JM to Francis Robbins, March 2, 1906; Robbins to JM, March 3, 1906, JMP.

74. JM to H. N. Taylor, March 3, 1906, JMP.

75. *Pittsburgh Dispatch*, 10 March 1906, cited in Gowaskie, "A Study in Leadership," p. 312.

76. H. N. Taylor to JM, March 10, 1906, JMP.

77. JM to H. N. Taylor, March 12, 1906, JMP.

78. UMWA, *Minutes of the Special Convention*, March 15–30, 1906, p. 5.

79. Ibid., pp. 9–10.

80. UMWA, Minutes of the National Executive Board, March 15, 1906.

81. UMWA, *Proceedings of the Joint Conference of Coal Miners and Operators*, January 25–February 2, March 20–March 29, 1906, p. 144.

82. Ibid., p. 145.

83. Ibid., p. 177.

84. Ibid., p. 178.

85. Ibid., pp. 260–261, 264–272.

86. Ibid., pp. 261–264.

87. JM to Mrs. John Mitchell, March 31, 1906, JMP.

88. *Pittsburgh Dispatch*, 25 March 1906; *Indianapolis News*, March 26, 1906, cited in Gowaskie, "A Study in Leadership," p. 317 n. 81.

89. UMWA, *Minutes of the Special Convention*, March 15–30, 1906, p. 57.

90. Ibid., p. 58.

91. Ibid., pp. 64–65.

92. Ibid., pp. 72–73.

93. Ibid., p. 73.

94. Ibid., pp. 73–74.

95. Gowaskie, "A Study in Leadership," pp. 321–322.

96. UMWA, *Proceedings of the Eighteenth Annual Convention*, 1907, p. 275.

97. UMWA, *Minutes of the Special Convention*, March 15–30, 1906, p. 87.

98. Ibid., pp. 78–80.

99. Ibid., p. 92, JM to Mrs. John Mitchell, March 31, 1906, JMP.

100. JM to Denis A. Hayes, April 3, 1906, JMP.

101. UMWA, *Minutes of the Proceedings of the Sixteenth Annual Convention*, January 1905, p. 8.

102. Ibid., p. 9.

103. JM to the "Officers and Members of Local Unions of Districts Nos. 1, 7, and 9," April 24, 1905, JMP.

104. *UMWJ*, 8 June, and 27 July 1905.

105. "Address Delivered at Old Forge, Pa., June 20, 1905," JMP

106. Ibid.

107. "Mr. Mitchell's Meetings in the Anthracite, June, 1905," JMP.

108. On preparations for the event, see JM to Father J. J. Curran, July 19, 31, August 4, 5, 1905; Curran to JM, July 23, August 4, 8, 1905, JMP.

109. The speech, marked "Wilkes-Barre, August 10, 1905," in JMP; see also *UMWJ*, 17 August 1905.

110. JM to W. D. Ryan, September 29, 1905, JMP.

111. JM to W. D. Ryan, August 26, 1905, JMP.

112. JM to Ralph Easley, September 11, 1905, JMP.

113. See membership figures at the end of December, 1905, in JMP.

114. JM to H. N. Taylor, August 28, September 4, 1905, JMP.

115. JM to Samuel Gompers, September 4, 1904, JMP.

116. Ralph Easley to JM, September 8, 1905, JMP.

117. Ralph Easley to JM, September 8, September 11, September 14; JM to H. N. Taylor, September 20, October 2, 1905; JM to Easley, September 22, 1905; Taylor to JM, September 23, 1905, JMP.

118. E. C. Morris to Harriett Reid, October 4, 1905, JMP.

119. Ralph Easley to JM, December 12, 1905, JMP.

120. Charles P. Neill to JM, December 13, 1905, JMP.

121. JM to Charles P. Neill, December 15, 1905; JM to Easley, December 15, 1905, JMP.

122. See, for example, JM to George Baer, December 20, 1905, JMP.

123. JM to Charles P. Neill, December 27, 1905; Neill to JM, December 23, 1905, JMP.

124. JM to George Baer, January 8, 16, 1906, JMP.

125. Father J. J. Curran to JM, January 6, 1906, JMP.

126. Clarence Darrow to JM, January 4, 1906, JMP.

127. *Minutes of a Joint Conference of Mine Operators and Mine Workers and Correspondence Connected Therewith*, February, April and May, 1906, pp. 2–5. Hereafter cited as *Anthracite Joint Conference*.

128. Ibid., pp. 8–12.

129. JM to George Baer, February 27, March 1, 1906; Baer to JM, February 28, 1906, reprinted in Ibid., pp. 13–33.

130. George Baer, et al, to JM, March 9, 1906, reprinted in Ibid., pp. 34–52.

131. JM to Seth Low, March 16, 1906; Low to JM, March 19, 1906, JMP.

132. JM to George Baer, March 17, 1906, reprinted in *Anthracite Joint Conference*, pp. 52–54.

133. George Baer to JM, March 20, 1906, reprinted in Ibid., pp. 55–57.

134. The strike order, dated March 29, is located in the JMP.

135. *New York Times*, 3 April 1906.

136. *Anthracite Joint Conference*, pp. 107–108.

137. E. A. Van Valkenburg to JM, April 6, 1906, JMP.

138. *Anthracite Joint Conference*, pp. 123, 127, 129

139. JM to George Baer, April 26, 1906, reprinted in Ibid., pp. 141–142; Baer to JM, April 27, 1906, reprinted in Ibid., pp. 145–151.

140. Upton Sinclair to JM, April 23, 1906; JM to Sinclair, April 28, 1906, JMP.

141. Mitchell's key source for information was Father Peter O'Donnell of Carbondale, Pennsylvania. See O'Donnell to J. J. Curran, May 2, 1906, located in JMP.

142. *New York Herald*, 3 May 1906; *Philadelphia Inquirer*, May 3, 1906.

143. UMWA, *Proceedings of the Special Convention of Districts 1, 7, and 9*, May 3–8, 1906, pp. 74–79.

144. Joseph Gowaskie, John Mitchell and the Anthracite Mine Workers: Leadership Conservatism and Rank-and-File Militancy," *Labor History* 27 (Winter 1985–1986): pp. 78–79.

145. Notes on this committee meeting are found in UMWA, Minutes of the National Executive Board, 1906, following p. 175.

146. UMWA, *Proceedings of the Special Convention of Districts 1, 7, and 9*, May 3–8, 1906, pp. 82–85.

147. Ibid., pp. 107–108.

148. E. I. Lewis to E. C. Morris, May 6, 1906, JMP.

149. *Philadelphia Press*, 9 May 1906.

150. Membership figures are located in JMP.

151. UMWA, *Proceedings of the Nineteenth Annual Convention*, 1908, pp. 26–29.

152. JM to Father J. J. Curran, January 6, 1906; Curran to JM, January 3, 1913, JMP.

153. *UMWJ*, 14 J, 1906; UMWA, Minutes of the National Executive Board, June 4, August 1, 1906; UMWA, *Proceedings of the Eighteenth Annual Convention*, 1907, pp. 37–38.

154. UMWA, Minutes of the National Executive Board, June 4, 1906.

155. Fox, *United We Stand*, p. 80.

156. Ibid., pp. 127–128; David J. McDonald and Edward A. Lynch, *Coal and Unionism: A History of the American Coal Miners' Unions* (Silver Spring, Md.: Lynald Books, 1939), pp. 78–79.

157. JM to J. H. Turner, July 11, 1906, JMP.

158. JM to John Walker, August 27, 1906, JMP.

159. UMWA, Minutes of the National Executive Board, June 6, 1906.

160. A copy of this letter is located in the JMP.

161. UMWA, *Proceedings of the Eighteenth Annual Convention*, 1907, pp. 34–38.

162. Ibid., pp. 51–61.

163. Ibid., p. 273.

164. Ibid., p. 285.

165. Ibid., p. 277.

166. Ibid., p. 313.

167. Ibid., p. 280.

CHAPTER 9: YEARS OF PERSONAL CRISIS, 1907–1908

1. James O'Rourke to JM, May 17, 1906; H. N. Taylor to JM, May 18, 1906; JM to David Mitchell, June 17, 1906, JMP; *New York Evening Mail*, 18 May 1906, clipping in JMP.

2. JM to Samuel Gompers, July 19, 1905; JM to W. Barton, August 12, 1905; JM to W. W. Stetson, August 12, 1905, JMP.

3. Van Tine, *The Making of the Labor Bureaucrat*, pp. 161–163.

4. Samuel Gompers, *Seventy Years of Life and Labor,* vol. 1 (New York: E. P. Dutton, 1925), p. 273.

5. JM to "My dear Wife," November 15, 20, 1905, JMP.

6. JM to Bennett Brown, December 5, 1905; JM to James B. Morrow, December 5, 1905; E. C. Morris to H. N. Taylor, December 4, 1905; Morris to Mrs. Mitchell, December 2, 1905; Taylor to Morris, December 2, 1905; Morris to Ralph Easley, December 2, 1905, JMP.

7. Pieced together from his correspondence of December 1905, JMP.

8. JM to Samuel Gompers, January 6, 1906, JMP.

9. *Pittsburgh Leader*, 24 February 1906, clipping in JMP.

10. Richard Mitchell to JM, January 11, 1906; JM to Richard Mitchell, January 15, 1906; see also Richard Mitchell to JM, February 2, 1906; JM to Richard Mitchell, February 5, 1906, JMP. "Maggie" referred to Madge Dunn, a close friend of Kate who stayed with the family in Spring Valley for several years. "Baby" referred to Catherine, the last of the Mitchell children, born in 1905.

11. JM to "My dear Wife," November 15, 1905; JM to Richard Mitchell, February 9, 1906; JM to Neil Hughes, July 2, 1906, JMP.

12. JM to "My dear Wife," February 24, 1906; see also E. C. Morris to Harriett Reid, February 28, 1906, JMP.

13. JM to James Mitchell, March 1, 1906, JMP.

14. JM to "My dear Wife," April 9, 1906, JMP.

15. JM to David Mitchell, April 9, 1906, JMP.

16. JM to Robert Mitchell, February 6, 1908, JMP.

17. Gluck, *John Mitchell,* p. 198.

18. W. D. Ryan to JM, April 27, 1906, JMP.

19. M. E. McDowell to JM, November 22, 1906, JMP.

20. John G. McHenry to JM, June 11, July 12, 1906; JM to McHenry, June 18, July 9, July 16, 1906, JMP.

21. JM to James O'Rourke, July 19, 1906, JMP

22. JM to William Gilbert, July 23, 1906; JM to J. B. Cavanaugh, July 23, 1906, JMP.

23. JM to Daniel J. Keefe, July 24, 1906; JM to David Mitchell, August 28, 1906, JMP.

24. JM to H. N. Taylor, December 8, 1906, JMP.

25. Richard Beamish to JM, January 20, 1907; H. N. Taylor to JM, January 9, 1907, JMP.

26. JM to Robert Mitchell, February 1, 1907, JMP.

27. See JM to "My dear Wife," February 14, 1907; E. C. Morris to H. N. Taylor, February 9, 1907; D. H. Sullivan to JM, February 25, 1907, JMP.

28. H. N. Taylor to JM, March 27, 1907; E. C. Morris to Taylor, March 28, 1907 (two telegrams), JMP.

29. E. C. Morris to Theodore Roosevelt, March 26, 1907, JMP.

30. JM to Felix Addler, April 2, 1907; JM to Ralph Easley, April 3, 1907, JMP.

31. E. C. Morris to "My dear Mrs. Mitchell," April 24, 1907; Daniel J. Keefe to Frank Schnell, April 24, 1907; JM to Morris, April 24, 1907; Morris to Harriett Reid, April 26, 1907, JMP.

32. Samuel Gompers to JM, April 24, 1907, JMP.

33. E. C. Morris to Harriett Reid, April 30, 1907, JMP.

34. E. C. Morris to Thomas Burke, May 8, 1907; Morris to W. D. Ryan, May 6, 1907; Morris to Harriett Reid, May 1, 1907, JMP.

35. E. C. Morris to Samuel Gompers, May 11, 1907, JMP.

36. JM to Ralph Easley, May 25, 1907; JM to H. N. Taylor, May 23, 1907; E. C. Morris to Harriett Reid, May 11, 1907, JMP.

37. JM to John D. Fallon, June 1, 1907; JM to Louis Hammerling, June 21, 1907, JMP.

38. Morris, "The Acquisitive Spirit of John Mitchell," *Labor History* 20 (Winter 1979): 13.

39. E. C. Morris to H. N. Taylor, April 30, May 5, 1907; Taylor to Morris, May 4, 1907, JMP.

40. Harris, Winthrop and Company to F. S. Peabody, May 5, 1907; Peabody to E. C. Morris, May 9, 1907; Harris, Winthrop and Company to JM, May 17, JMP.

41. E. C. Morris to F. S. Peabody, May 16, 1907; Peabody to Morris, May 17, 1907, JMP.

42. Harris, Winthrop and Company to F. S. Peabody, May 20, 1907, JMP.

43. E. C. Morris to F. S. Peabody, May 28, May 29, 1907; Harris, Winthrop and Company to JM, May 23, May 28, 1907; JM to Harris, Winthrop and Company, May 29, 1907; Peabody to JM, May 21, 1907, JMP.

44. F. S. Peabody to JM, May 30, June 11, 1907; JM to Peabody, June 4, 1907, JMP.

45. JM to F. S. Peabody, July 10, July 20, 1907, JMP.

46. JM to Mrs. M. M. Patterson, July 2, 1907, JMP.

47. JM to J. H. Crawford, July 2, 1907; JM to W. D. Ryan, July 15, 1907; JM to William Hawthorne, July 17, 1907, JMP.

48. JM to "My dear Wife," August 16, 1907; JM to James Mitchell, August 13, 1907; JM to Robert Mitchell, August 7, 13, 1907; Richard Mitchell to JM, August 10, 1907; JM to Richard, James and Robert Mitchell, July 26, 1907, JMP.

49. JM to David Mitchell, August 27, 1907, JMP.

50. JM to Gertrude Beeks, August 27, September 10, 1907; Beeks to JM, August 30, September 18, 1907; Ralph Easley to JM, September 6, 1907, JMP.

51. Details of his trip can be gleaned from JM to H. N. Taylor, August 29, 31, September 21, 24, 1907; JM to Francis L. Robbins, September 1, 11, 1907; JM to O. L. Garrison, September 11, 1907; and a memo dated September 1, 1907, JMP.

52. JM to Francis L. Robbins, September 11, 1907, JMP.

53. JM to William D. Ryan, October 11, 1907; JM to George Hartlein, October 11, 1907; E. C. Morris to H. N. Taylor, October 8, 1907; Morris to Samuel Gompers, October 8, 1907, JMP.

54. "To the Officers and Members of the U. M. W. of A.," October 7, 1907, JMP.

55. E. C. Morris to Harriett Reid, October 30, 1907; Morris to P. F. Sweeney, October 31, 1907, JMP.

56. JM "To the Editor of the United Mine Workers' Journal," November 11, 1907, JMP.

57. JM to James Duncan, November 5, 1907, JMP.

58. JM to Richard Beamish, October 26, 1907, JMP.

59. JM to J. B. Cavanaugh, November 7, 1907, JMP.

60. JM to Ralph Easley, October 21, 1907; JM to Daniel J. Keefe, October 23, 1907, JMP.

61. Ralph Easley to JM, November 1, 1907,; JM to Easley, November 20, 1907, JMP.

62. Ralph Easley to JM, November 20, 1907; JM to Easley, November 20, 22, 1907, JMP.

63. JM to Samuel Gompers, November 26, 1907, JMP.

64. *New York Evening Mail*, December 17, 1907, cited in Foner, *History*

of the Labor Movement, vol. 3, pp. 148–149; Ralph Easley to JM, December 7, 1907, JMP.

65. E. C. Morris to John G. Taylor, December 20, 1907; O. L. Garrison to Morris, December 21, 1907, JMP.

66. JM to "My dear Wife," December 24, 1907, JMP.

67. JM to Reverend F. B. Dickman, December 31, 1907; JM to "My dear Wife," December 24, 1907; Father John Power to JM, December 23, 1907, JMP.

68. JM to Richard Beamish, December 24, 1907; JM to Samuel Gompers, December 31, 1907, JMP.

69. JM to Father Peter Killian, January 16, 1908; E. C. Morris to H. N. Taylor, January 17, 1907; JM to David Mitchell, January 13, 1907, JMP.

70. UMWA, *Proceedings of the Nineteenth Annual Convention,* 1908, pp. 291–292.

71. Ibid., p. 24.

72. Ibid., pp. 295–296.

73. JM to Thomas Burke, February 24, 1908, JMP.

74. JM to William B. Wilson, October 25, 1907, JMP.

75. On socialist support for Lewis, see Gowaskie, "A Study in Leadership," p. 354 n. 146. On Wilson's decision to retain his House seat, see Clarke L. Wilhelm, "William B. Wilson: The First Secretary of Labor," (Ph.D. diss., Johns Hopkins University, 1967), p. 29.

76. JM to William B. Wilson, October 25, 1907, JMP.

77. JM to William B. Wilson, October 28, November 14, November 26, 1907, JMP.

78. William B. Wilson to JM, November 27, 1907, JMP.

79. William B. Wilson "To the Officers and Members of the United Mine Workers of America," November 25, 1907, JMP.

80. UMWA, *Proceedings,* 1908, p. 366.

81. Ibid., pp. 373–374.

82. Ibid., pp. 273–283.

83. Ibid., pp. 284–285.

84. Ibid., pp. 374–375.

85. JM to H. N. Taylor, February 6, 1908, JMP.

86. E. C. Morris to "My dear Mrs. Mitchell," February 18, February 20, 1908, JMP.

87. E. C. Morris to "My dear Mrs. Mitchell," February 20, 1908, JMP.

88. E. C. Morris to "My dear Mrs. Mitchell," February 24, 1908; JM to "My dear Wife," February 24, 1908, JMP.

89. JM to Thomas Burke, February 24, 1908, JMP.

90. Ralph Easley to JM, February 1, January 26, 1908, JMP.

91. JM to Seth Low, February 24, 1908; Low to JM, February 21, 1908, JMP.

92. "Minutes of Informal Joint Conference," February 27 and 28, 1908, located in JMP.

93. JM to Robert Erskine Ely, March 3, 1908; "To the Delegates of the Nineteenth Annual Convention of the United Mine Workers of America," February 29, 1908, JMP.

94. E. C. Morris to JM, March 2, 1908, JMP.

95. E. C. Morris to H. N. Taylor, March 7, 1908, JMP.

96. UMWA, *Proceedings of the Reconvened Nineteenth Annual Convention*, March 12–March 20, 1908, pp. 67–68.

97. Ibid., pp. 70–73.

98. Ibid., pp. 111–112; on the emotional response of delegates, see Randolph Smith to JM, March 21, 1908, JMP.

99. UMWA, Minutes of the National Executive Board, March 21, 1908. On the rumors of drinking during the convention, see Gluck, *John Mitchell*, pp. 219–220.

100. JM to "My dear Wife," March 30, March 31, 1908; JM to Randolph Smith, March 27, 1908, JMP.

101. JM to "My dear Wife," April 9, 1908, JMP.

102. JM to Ralph Easley, April 9, 1908, JMP.

103. JM to Ralph Easley, April 24, 1908; Easley to JM, April 21, 1908, JMP.

104. JM to "My dear Wife," April 29, 1908, JMP.

105. JM to John H. Walker, May 25, 1908, JMP.

106. JM to Denis A. Hayes, May 25, 1908, JMP.

107. Ibid.

108. Seth Low to JM, undated, 1908; JM to Low, May 27, 1908, JMP.

109. JM to Seth Low, July 2, June 25, 1908; JM to Easley, June 17, June 21, June 22, 1908; Easley to JM, June 16, 1908, JMP.

110. JM to F. E. Waite, July 2, 1908, JMP.

CHAPTER 10: DECLINE AND DEATH, 1908–1919

1. JM to James O'Rourke, July 31, 1908, JMP.

2. JM to Daniel J. Keefe, July 31, 1908, JMP.

3. JM "To the Editor of the United Mine Workers' Journal," July 31, 1908, JMP.

4. JM to John H. Walker, August 15, 1908, JMP.

5. Ibid.

6. JM to David Mitchell, September 16, 1908, JMP.

7. JM to H. N. Taylor, June 21, 1908, JMP.

8. Ramirez, *When Workers Fight*, p. 139.

9. Cited in Ibid., p. 140.

10. Samuel Haber, *Efficiency and Uplift: Scientific Management in the Progressive Era* (Chicago: University of Chicago, 1964), p. 52.

11. George Barnett, "National and District Systems of Collective Bargaining in the United States," *Quarterly Journal of Economics* 26 (1912): 427–428.

12. JM to H. N. Taylor, June 21, 1909, JMP.

13. H. G. Dalton to Seth Low, June 19, 1909: JM to T. V. O'Connor, June 28, 1909, cited in Ramirez, *When Workers Fight,* pp. 137–138.

14. JM to Samuel Gompers, August 9, 1910, cited in Gluck, *John Mitchell,* pp. 227–228.

15. On the Woman's Welfare Department, see Green, *The National Civic Federation,* pp. 279–281.

16. Gertrude Beeks to JM, June 20, 1908, JMP.

17. Edith Harriman, *From Pinafores to Politics* (New York: Henry Holt and Company, 1923), pp. 89–92.

18. Chicago *Examiner*, 25 August 1909, cited in Foner, *History of the Labor Movement,* vol. 3, pp. 147–148.

19. Cited in Foner, *History of the Labor Movement,* vol. 3, p. 148.

20. NCF *Review* (15 November 1909), 15.

21. Bernard Mandel, *Samuel Gompers: A Biography* (Yellow Springs, Ohio: Antioch Press, 1963), pp. 262–265; Leo Wolman, *The Boycott in American Trade Unions* (Baltimore: Johns Hopkins University Press, 1916), pp. 80–82.

22. J. C. Kennedy, "Important Labor Injunction in the Buck's Stove and Range Company Suit," *Journal of Political Economy* 16 (1908): 98.

23. *Report of the Industrial Commission on the Relations and Conditions of Capital and Labor Employed in the Mining Industry,* vol. 12 (Washington: Government Printing Office, 1901), pp. 38–40.

24. UMWA, *Proceedings of the Nineteenth Annual Convention,* 1908, pp. 203–204, 346–349; JM to Samuel Gompers, February 17, 1908, JMP.

25. JM to John H. Walker, August 21, 1908, JMP.

26. Weinstein, *The Corporate Ideal,* p. 16.

27. Cited in Gluck, *John Mitchell,* p. 247.

28. JM "To the Editor of the United Mine Workers' Journal," August 24, 1908, JMP.

29. *American Federationist* (February 1909), 129, 151.

30. Mandel, *Samuel Gompers,* pp. 272–275; Foner, *History of the Labor Movement,* vol. 3, pp. 361–364.

31. Seth Low to JM, December 27, 1908; JM to Low, December 29, 1908, JMP.

32. *American Federationist* (June 1914), 483–486; Mandel, *Samuel Gompers,* pp. 275–283; JM to Hugh Frayne, May 13, 1908, JMP.

33. JM to Theodore Roosevelt, February 12, 1908, JMP.

34. Samuel Gompers to JM, July 31, 1908; JM to Gompers, August 3, 1908, JMP.

35. JM to Daniel J. Keefe, August 3, 1908, JMP.

36. "Press release," dated 3 August 1908, in JMP.

37. JM to M. Grant Hamilton, October 6, 1908, JMP.

38. "Press release," dated 29 October 1908, in JMP.

39. E. C. Morris to JM, November 4, 1908, JMP.

40. JM to John Hawthorne, August 8, 1910, JMP.

41. E. C. Morris to Harriett Reid, August 13, 1910, JMP.

42. On Lewis's trouble in 1908, see Fox, *United We Stand*, pp. 126–129.

43. JM to John H. Walker, September 21, 1908, JMP.

44. JM to John H. Walker, October 1, October 8, October 19, October 24, 1908; Walker to JM, October 10, October 17, October 24, October 28, 1908, JMP.

45. JM to H. N. Taylor, November 13, 1908, JMP.

46. JM to William B. Wilson, July 20, 1909, JMP.

47. JM to William Green, July 17, 1909, JMP.

48. JM to William Green, July 16, July 17, 1909; Green to JM, July 20, 1909; William B. Wilson to JM, July 28, 1909; JM to John H. Walker, July 27, 1909, JMP.

49. JM to John H. Walker, September 22, 1909; Walker to JM, September 25, 1909; JM to William Green, September 29, 1909; Edwin Perry to JM, October 13, 1909, JMP.

50. William Green to JM, December 13, 1909, JMP.

51. On the 1910 Illinois strike, see A. C. Everling, "Tactics Over Strategy in the United Mine Workers of America: Internal Politics and the Question of the Nationalization of the Mines, 1908–1923," (Ph.D. diss., Pennsylvania State University, 1976), pp. 38–41; Fox, *United We Stand*, pp. 132–134.

52. JM to John H. Walker, July 30, August 1, 1910, JMP.

53. JM to William Green, August 8, 1910; JM to John H. Walker, August 8, 1910; Walker to JM, August 12, 1910, JMP.

54. Mitchell's speech at the 1910 special convention located in the JMP.

55. JM to John H. Walker, August 29, September 2, 1910; Walker to JM, August 27, 1910, JMP.

56. JM to John H. Walker, August 24, 1910; JM to Francis Feehan, August 26, 1910: Walker to JM, August 27, 1910; William Green to JM, August 30, 1910; JM to Green, September 1, September 10, 1910, JMP.

57. John P. White to JM, October 2, October 10, October 15, October 19, October 24, November 4, 1910; JM to White, September 30, October 5, October 7, October 13, October 17, October 22, October 27, November 1, November 9, 1910, JMP.

58. JM to John P. White, December 23, 1910, JMP; Everling, "Tactics over Strategy," p. 41; UMWA, *Proceedings of the Twenty-Second Annual Convention*, 1911, p. 68; Long, *Where the Sun Never Shines*, pp. 259–260. Long concluded that since at least early 1910 Lewis had been "surreptitiously working in the interests of the operators."

59. Quoted in Harriman, *From Pinafores to Politics*, p. 173.

60. *Appeal to Reason*, July 16, 1910, cited in Foner, *History of the Labor Movement*, vol. 3, pp. 146–147; the story was also picked up by the mainstream press. See the *New York World*, 12 July 1910.

61. Weinstein, *The Corporate Ideal*, pp. 120–122.

62. For a discussion of socialist strength in the UMWA, see Laslett, *Labor and the Left*, chapter 6.

63. Ibid., p. 214.

64. UMWA, *Proceedings*, 1911, p. 521.

65. Ibid., pp. 521–575.

66. John Walker to JM, January 19, 1911; JM to Walker, January 21, 1911; E. C. Morris to Walker, January 23, 1911; JMP.

67. UMWA, *Proceedings of the Twenty-Third Annual Convention*, 1912, vol. 1, p. 464.

68. W. R. Fairley to JM, January 24, 1911: Harriett Reid to E. C. Morris, January 27, 1911, JMP.

69. UMWA, *Proceedings*, 1911, pp. 519–575.

70. Nash, *Conflict and Accommodation*, pp. 89–90. Unfortunately, Nash incorrectly places Adolph Germer in the camp of moderate socialists.

71. UMWA, *Proceedings*, 1911, p. 542.

72. Ibid., pp. 573–575.

73. JM to UMWA convention, January 31, 1911, JMP.

74. John H. Walker to JM, January 29, January 30, 1911, JMP.

75. JM to Harriett Reid, January 30, 1911, JMP.

76. E. C. Morris to Harriett Reid, January 30, 1911; JM to Reid, February 3, 1911, JMP.

77. JM's address before the AFL convention. AFL, *Proceedings*, 1912, p. 228.

78. JM to Frank Peabody, February 2, 1911, JMP.

79. JM to Samuel Gompers, February 2, 1911, JMP.

80. JM to Robert Mitchell, January 31, 1911; JM to John P. Reese, February 6, 1911; JM to Seth Low, February 16, 1911; JM to James Duncan, February 7, 1911, JMP.

81. JM to John P. White, February 3, 1911, JMP.

82. John H. Walker to JM, February 2, 1911, JMP.

83. JM to James Duncan, February 7, 1911, JMP.

84. Frank Peabody to JM, February 11, 1911, JMP.

85. James Duncan to JM, February 13, 1911, JMP.

86. John H. Walker to JM, February 14, 1911, JMP.

87. JM to Seth Low, February 15, 1911, JMP.

88. Seth Low to JM, February 28, 198911, JMP.

89. Samuel Gompers to JM, February 16, 1911; Ralph Easley to JM, February 16, 1911, JMP.

90. JM to Samuel Gompers, February 23, 1911, JMP.

91. JM to Thomas Tracy, February 23, 1911, JMP.

92. Edward Dagget to JM, February 26, 1911; John H. Walker to JM, February 23, 1911; JM to Walker, February 27, 1911, JMP.

93. Samuel Gompers, "Organized Labor and the National Civic Federation," *American Federationist* (March 1911), 181 ff.

94. Samuel Gompers to JM, March 3, 1911, JMP.

95. Cited in Green, *National Civic Federation,* pp. 162–163, 165–167.

96. JM to Samuel Gompers, March 29, 1911, JMP.

97. JM "To the Editor of the United Mine Workers' Journal," March 29, April 26, May 6, and May 9, 1911, JMP.

98. "Socialists in the Trade Unions," *America* (September 16, 1911), 542; Montgomery, *The Fall of the House of Labor*, pp. 289–290; Green, *National Civic Federation,* pp. 167–169.

99. JM to John B. Lennon, June 22, 1911, JMP.

100. Quoted in Green, *National Civic Federation,* pp. 171–172.

101. Samuel Gompers, *Seventy Years*, vol. 1, p. 400; AFL, *Proceedings*, 1911, pp. 218–257.

102. AFL, *Proceedings*, 1911, pp. 235–241, 257.

103. JM to W. D. Ryan, December 6, 1911; JM to David Mitchell, December 6, 1911, JMP.

104. Weinstein, *The Corporate Ideal,* p. 122; Ramirez, *When Workers Fight,* pp. 140–141.

105. UMWA, *Proceedings*, 1912, vol. 1, pp. 194–213, 218–233, 258–271, 432–434; AFL, *Proceedings*, 1912, pp. 265, 309–312; On the UMWA convention and politics, see Everling, "Tactics over Strategy," pp. 56–57. On industrial unionism in 1912, see Laslett, *Labor and the Left,* pp. 216–217; and Dick, *Labor and Socialism*, pp. 83–84; and James O. Morris, *Conflict Within the AFL: A Study of Craft Versus Industrial Unionism, 1901–1938* (Ithaca: Cornell University Press, 1958), p. 45.

106. JM to John H. Walker, March 6, 1911; JM to Richard Beamish, March 10, 1911; JM to William Greisler, March 10, 1911; JM to W. R. Fairley, March 10, 1911; JM to Frank Peabody, May 1, 1911, JMP.

107. JM to Harriett Reid, September 13, 1914, JMP.

108. "Speech of Mr. Mitchell at Convention of the American Federation of Labor," November 22, 1913, JMP.

109. See James L. Laidlaw to JM, February 1, 1912.

110. Foner, *History of the Labor Movement,* vol. 3, pp. 119–121.

111. Quoted in Mary Harrita Fox, *Peter E. Dietz, Labor Priest* (Notre Dame, Ind.: Notre Dame Press, 1953), pp. 51–52.

112. JM to Peter Dietz, June 8, 1911; January 3, 1912; Dietz to JM, May 29, June 6, December 30, 1911, JMP.

113. Weinstein, *The Corporate Ideal,* p. 123; Marc Karson, *American Labor Unions,* chapter 9.

114. David Goldstein, *Socialism: The Nation of Fatherless Children* (Boston: Astor Station, 1912), pp. 368–369.

115. Charles Stelzle to JM, January 15, 1912; Fred B. Smith to JM, January 25, 1912; Peter J. Brady to JM, April 2, April 6, 1912, JMP. For an excellent discussion of this movement, see Elizabeth and Kenneth Fones-Wolf, "Trade Union Evangelism: Religion and the AFL in the Labor Forward Movement, 1912–1916," in Michael H. Frisch and Daniel Walkowitz, eds., *Working-Class America: Essays on Labor, Community, and American Society* (Urbana: University of Illinois Press, 1983), pp. 153–184.

116. JM to Reverend Walter Spooner, April 18, 1912, JMP.

117. AFL, *Proceedings,* 1914, p. 434.

118. JM to J. F. Callbreath, March 9, 1911, JMP.

119. "Appeal to the Voters of the State of New York," no date, JMP.

120. Weinstein, *The Corporate Ideal,* p. 55.

121. Green, *National Civic Federation,* pp. 253–261; Gordon M. Jensen, "The National Civic Federation: American Business in an Age of Social Change and Social Reform, 1900–1910," (Ph.D. diss., Princeton University, 1956), pp. 201–208.

122. JM to Reverend J. J. Curran, April 5, 1912; JM to Daniel Keefe, March 14, 1914; JM to William Green, March 16, 1914, JMP.

123. William Sulzer to JM, March 15, March 26, March 29, April 9, April 22, April 23, April 27, May 5, 1913; JM to Sulzer, March 19, March 25, April 22, April 24, April 25, 1913, JMP.

124. JM to W. D. Ryan, May 20, 1915; Meyer Wolff to JM, May 24, 1915; Edwin Storms to JM, May 25, 1915; JM to William Green, May 26, 1915, JMP.

125. JM to John Hays Hammond, January 5, 1916; JM to T. J. Comerford, January 5, 1916, JMP.

126. JM to John H. Walker, June 16, 1916, JMP.

127. The report of the legislative investigating committee, its recommendations, and the testimony of Commission members is located in the JMP.

128. Ibid.

129. JM to W. D. Ryan, January 5, 1916; JM to John J. Irving, January 5, 1916, JMP.

130. JM to John H. Walker, January 5, 1916; JM to John Hays Hammond, January 17, 1916, JMP.

131. JM to Charles Whitman, March 21, 1916, JMP.

132. JM to John Ferguson, March 13, 1917; E. C. Morris to Warren J. Haig, January 11, 1917, JMP.

133. JM to W. W. Keefer, June 3, August 15, 1916; JM to Frank Peabody, November 26, 1916; George Havernan to JM, December 8, 1916, JMP.

134. E. C. Morris to Ernst Bohm, January 11, 1917; Morris to W. R. Fairley, January 12, 1917; Morris to JM, January 16, 1917; Morris to W. D. Ryan, January 16, 1917, JMP.

135. JM to Frederick Almy, January 22, 1917, JMP.

136. JM to F. W. Shepard, February 9, 1917; JM to W. W. Keefer, June 18, 1917; JM to Harris Hammond, July 19, 1917, JMP.

137. JM to Newton D. Baker, March 28, 1917, JMP.

138. JM to United State Marine Corps, May 31, 1917; E. C. Morris to W. R. Fairley, October 15, 1917; JM to Ralph Easley, November 30, 1917, JMP.

139. JM to John B. Lennon, November 12, 1917; E. C. Morris to John B. Lennon, November 23, 1917; JM to W. R. Fairley, December 3, 1917, JMP; *New Rochelle Daily Star*, 3 October 1917, clipping in JMP.

140. JM to James Duncan, October 6, 1917; JM to Elon R. Brown, October 6, 1917; JM to John B. Lennon, November 12, 1917; JM to W. R. Fairley, December 3, 1917, January 16, 1918, JMP.

141. JM to John H. Walker, January 3, 1919; E. C. Morris to Frank Farrington, March 19, 1918; JM to Robert and James Mitchell, May 22, June 11, July 13, August 17, 1918; JMP.

142. JM to Marsden G. Scott, July 2, 1918, JMP.

143. JM to W. K. Field, May 18, 1918; JM to William Johnson, May 25, 1918, JMP.

144. The transactions are detailed in correspondence in the JMP from late May to mid-June 1918.

145. JM to Frank Farrington, July 6, 1918; JM to Charles Betts, August 2, 1918; JM to W. R. Fairley, August 14, 1918, JMP.

146. JM to W. D. Ryan, November 26, 1918, JMP.

147. Quoted in Gluck, *John Mitchell,* pp. 252–253.

148. Melvyn Dubofsky and Warren Van Tine, *John L. Lewis: A Biography* (New York: Quadrangle Books, 1977), pp. 37–41.

149. Ibid., pp. 47–50; Fox, *United We Stand*, pp. 187–188.

150. E. C. Morris to John H. Walker, March 19, 1919; JM to Richard Mitchell, April 6, 1919; JM "To the Members of the Council of Farms and Markets," April 7, 1919, JMP.

151. E. C. Morris to John H. Walker, April 24, 1919; JM to W. D.Ryan, April 24, 1919, JMP.

152. JM to John T. Dempsey, August 2, 1919, JMP.

153. JM to John H. Walker, August 20, 1919, E. C. Morris to Fred W. Upham, September 4, 1919; Morris to William Green, September 5, 1919; JMP.

154. *New York Times*, 10 September 1919.

155. *Scranton Times*, 14 September 1919.

156. Ralph Easley "To the editor of the Evening Sun," December 31, 1919, JMP. Elsie Gluck largely accepts this interpretation. See Gluck, *John Mitchell*, pp. 257–260.

157. Morris, "The Acquisitive Spirit, p. 29.

158. Mandel, *Samuel Gompers,* p. 431.

159. William Z. Foster, *Misleaders of Labor* (Chicago: Trade Union Educational League, 1927), pp. 128–129.

AFTERWORD

1. JM to F. E. Waite, July 2, 1908, JMP.

2. Fox, *United We Stand*, pp. 205–206.

3. Gluck, *John Mitchell*, pp. 228–229.

4. JM to George Hartlein, July 2, 1908, JMP.

5. See JM to W. D. Ryan, September 29, 1908, JMP.

6. On segregated locals, see Lewis, *Black Coal Miners*, p. 46.

Bibliography

PRIMARY SOURCES

Manuscript Materials

Adolph Germer Papers. State Historical Society of Wisconsin, Madison.

Duncan McDonald Papers. Illinois State Historical Society, Springfield.

John Mitchell Papers. Microfilm edition.

National Civic Federation Papers. New York Public Library.

William B. Wilson Papers. Historical Society of Pennsylvania, Philadelphia.

Convention Proceedings and Journals

American Federation of Labor. *Report of the Proceedings of the Annual Conventions*, 1898–1914.

American Federationist

Black Diamond

National Civic Federation Review

United Mine Workers of America, *Proceedings of the Conventions*, 1891–1919.

United Mine Workers of America, *Minutes of the National Executive Board*, 1900–1908.

United Mine Workers' Journal

Government Documents

Abbott, Grace. "The Immigrant and Coal Communities of Illinois." *Bulletin of the Immigrants' Commission* 1 (1920): 10–14.

Anthracite Coal Strike Commission. *Report to the President on the Anthracite Coal Strike of May–October, 1902, by the Anthracite Coal Strike Commission*. Washington, D.C.: Government Printing Office, 1903.

Illinois Bureau of Labor Statistics. *Biennial Report*, 1883, 1884, 1886.

———. *Coal in Illinois, 1897*. (Springfield: Phillips Brothers, 1897).

Illinois Department of Mines and Minerals. *A Compilation of Reports of the Mining Industry of Illinois from the Earliest Records to the Close of the Year 1930.* Springfield: n. p., 1931.

U. S. Commissioner of Labor. "A Report on Labor Disturbances in the State of Colorado from 1880 to 1904, Inclusive." Senate Document 122, 58th Congress, Second Session.

U. S. Industrial Commission, *Report of the Industrial Commission on the Relations and Conditions of Capital and Labor Employed in the Mining Industry.* vol 12. Washington, D.C.: Government Printing Office, 1901.

Wright, Carroll D. "Report to the President on the Anthracite Coal Strike." *Bulletin of the Department of Labor* 43 (Washington, D.C.: Government Printing Office, 1902): 1147–1228.

Reminiscences and Autobiographies

Brophy, John. *A Miner's Life.* Edited and supplemented by John O. P. Hall. Madison: University of Wisconsin Press, 1964.

Carnegie, Andrew. *Autobiography.* New York: Houghton Mifflin, 1928.

Darrow, Clarence. *The Story of My Life.* New York: Charles Scribner's Sons, 1932.

Gompers, Samuel. *Seventy Years of Life and Labor.* 2 vols. New York: Dutton, 1925.

Harriman, Edith. *From Pinafores to Politics.* New York: Henry Holt and Company, 1923.

Jones, Mary Harris. *Autobiography of Mother Jones.* Edited by Mary Field Parton. Chicago: Kerr, 1925.

Lloyd, Caro. *Henry Demarest Lloyd.* New York: G. P. Putnam's Sons, 1912.

Roosevelt, Theodore. *Theodore Roosevelt: An Autobiography.* New York: Macmillan, 1919.

Books and Articles by Contemporaries

Barnett, George. "National and District Systems of Collective Bargaining in the United States." *Quarterly Journal of Economics* 26 (1912): 425–443.

The Biographical Record of Bureau, Marshall, and Putnam Counties. Chicago: S.J. Clarke, 1896.

Commons, John R. "A New Way of Settling Labor Disputes." *The American Monthly Review of Reviews* 23 (March 1901): 328–333.

Cummings, John. "The Passing of the Coal Strike." *The Journal of Political Economy* 11 (December 1902): 55–74.

"Dissensions Among Operators and Mine Workers." *The Outlook* (March 17, 1906), 577–578.

Durand, E. Dana. "The Anthracite Coal Strike and Its Settlement." *Political Science Quarterly* 18 (September 1903): 385–414.

Easley, Ralph. "Senator Hanna and Labor Problem." *Independent* (March 3, 1904), 483–487.

"The End of the Coal Miners' Suspension." *The Outlook* (July 21, 1906), 634.

Evans, Chris. *The History of the United Mine Workers of America.* 2 vols. Indianapolis: United Mine Workers of America, 1914, 1918.

George, John E. "The Coal Miners' Strike of 1897." *The Quarterly Journal of Economics* 12 (January 1898): 186–208.

———. "The Settlement in the Coal-Mining Industry." *The Quarterly Journal of Economics* 12 (July 1898): 447–460.

Hanna, Marcus Alonzo. "Industrial Conciliation and Arbitration." *Annals of the American Academy of Political and Social Science* 40 (December 1902): 28–29.

"John Mitchell, The Man Who Kept His Head." *Current Literature* 52 (April 1912): 401–404.

Jones, Eliot. *The Anthracite Coal Combination in the United States.* Cambridge, MA: Harvard University Press, 1914.

Lloyd, Henry D. *A Strike of Millionaires Against Miners, or The Story of Spring Valley.* Chicago: Belford Clarke Company, 1890.

MacFarlane, James. *The Coal Regions of America: Their Topography, Geology, and Development.* New York: D. Appleton and Company, 1897.

McNeill, George, ed. *The Labor Movement: The Problem of Today.* New York: M. W. Hazen Company, 1897.

Mitchell, John. *Organized Labor; Its Problems, Purposes and Ideals.* Philadelphia: American Book and Bible House, 1903.

———. *The Wage Earner and His Problems.* Washington: P. S. Risdale, 1913.

———. "The Ascent of Labor." *Collier's Weekly* (April 11, 1903): 12.

———. "The Boyhood of a Miner's Son," *The Circle* (June 1909): 330–332.

———. "The Coal Strike." *McClure's Magazine* (December 1902): 219–224.

———. "Dictation by the Unions." *Independent* (September 18, 1902): 2228–2230.

———. "An Exposition and Interpretation of the Trade Union Movement." In *The Christian Ministry and the Social Order*, ed. by Charles S. McFarland. New Haven, CT: Yale University Press, 1913.

———. "The Great Coal Strike." *Independent* (November 1, 1900): 2613–2616.

———. "The Mine Worker's Life and Aims." *Cosmopolitan* (October 1901): 622–630.

———. "Recognition of Trade Unions." *Independent* (August 15, 1901): 1895–1898.

———. "The Voice of Labor." *Collier's Weekly*, (September 6, 1902): 4–5.

Morris, Elizabeth Catherine. "John Mitchell, The Leader and the Man." *Independent* (December 25, 1902), 3073–3078.

Nichols, Francis H. "Children of the Coal Shadow." *McClure's Magazine* (February 1903): 435–44.

Parker, U. S. "Collective Bargaining in the Soft Coal Industry." *Journal of Political Economy* 12 (September 1904): 546–554.

Raymond, R. W. "The 'Matchless' Mitchell." *Engineering and Mining Journal* (August 30, 1902): 270–271.

Roberts, Peter. "The Anthracite Coal Situation." *Yale Review* 11 (May 1902): 29–37.

———. *The Anthracite Coal Industry*. New York: Macmillan, 1901.

———. *Anthracite Coal Communities*. New York: Macmillan, 1904.

Roy, Andrew. *A History of the Coal Miners of the United States, from the Development of the Mines to the Close of the Anthracite Strike of 1902.* Columbus, Ohio: J. L. Traeger, 1905.

Steffens, Lincoln. "A Labor Leader of To-Day: John Mitchell and What He Stands For." *McClure's Magazine* (August 1902): 355–357.

Virtue, George O. "The Anthracite Combinations." *Journal of Political Economy* 9 (December 1900): 1–23.

———. "The Anthracite Mine Laborers." *Bulletin of the Department of Labor* 13 (November 1897): 728–774.

Warne, Frank Julian. *The Coal Mine Workers*. New York: Longman, Green, and Company, 1905.

———. *The Slav Invasion and the Mine Workers*. Philadelphia: J. B. Lippincott Company, 1905.

———. "The Anthracite Coal Strike." *Annals of the American Academy of Political and Social Science* 17 (January 1901): 15–52.

———. "The Effect of Unionism Upon the Mine Worker." *Annals of the American Academy of Political and Social Science* 21 (January 1903): 20–35.

———. "The Miner's Union: Its Business Management." *Annals of the American Academy of Political and Social Science* 25 (January 1905): 67–86.

———. "Organized Labor in the Anthracite Coal Fields." *Outlook* (May 24, 1902): 273–276.

Wellman, Walter. "The Inside History of the Great Coal Strike." *Collier's Weekly* (October 18, 1902): 6–7.

Weyl, Walter. "John Mitchell, The Man the Miners Trust." *Outlook* (March 24, 1906): 657–662.

Woodruff, George, et al. *The History of Will County, Illinois, Containing a History of the County, Etc.* Chicago: William LeBaron, 1878.

SECONDARY SOURCES

Books

Angle, Paul M. *Bloody Williamson: A Chapter in American Lawlessness.* New York: Alfred A. Knopf, 1952.

Aurand, Harold W. *From the Molly Maguires to the United Mine Workers.* Philadelphia: Temple University Press, 1971.

Berthoff, Roland Tappan. *British Immigrants in Industrial America, 1790–1950.* Cambridge, Mass.: Harvard University Press, 1953.

Bodnar, John. *Anthracite People: Families, Unions and Work, 1900–1940.* Harrisburg, Pa.: Pennsylvania Historical and Museum Commission, 1983.

Bonnett, Clarence E. *History of Employers' Associations in the United States.* New York: Vantage Press, 1956.

Brody, David. *Steelworkers in America: The Nonunion Era.* Cambridge, MA: Harvard University Press, 1960.

Christie, Robert. *Empire in Wood: A History of the Carpenters' Union.* Ithaca: Cornell University Press, 1956.

Coleman, McAlister. *Men and Coal.* New York: Farrar and Rinehart, 1943.

Corbin, David Alan. *Life, Work and Rebellion in the Coal Fields: The Southern West Virginia Miners, 1880–1922.* Urbana: University of Illinois Press, 1981.

Cornell, Robert J. *The Anthracite Coal Strike of 1902*. Washington, D.C.: The Catholic University of America Press, 1957.

Croly, Herbert. *Marcus Alonzo Hanna: His Life and Work*. New York: Macmillan, 1912.

Dick, William. *Labor and Socialism in America: The Gompers Era*. Port Washington, N.Y.: Kennikat Press, 1972.

Dix, Keith. *What's a Coal Miner to Do? The Mechanization of Coal Mining*. Pittsburgh: University of Pittsburgh Press, 1988.

——. *Work Relations in the Coal Industry: The Hand-Loading Era, 1880–1930*. Morgantown: West Virginia Institute for Labor Studies, 1977.

Donna, Modesto. *The Braidwood Story*. Braidwood, Ill.: by the author, 1957.

Dubofsky, Melvyn. *We Shall Be All: A History of the Industrial Workers of the World*. Chicago: Quadrangle Books, 1969.

——. *"Big Bill" Haywood*. New York: St. Martin's Press, 1987.

Duboksky, Melvyn, and Warren Van Tine. *John L. Lewis: A Biography*. New York: Quadrangle/The New York Times Book Co., 1977.

Eavenson, Howard Nicholas. *The First Century and a Quarter of the American Coal Industry*. Baltimore, Md.: Waverly Press, 1942.

Erickson, Charlotte. *American Industry and the European Immigrant, 1860–1885*. Cambridge, Mass.: Harvard University Press, 1957.

Featherling, Dale. *Mother Jones, the Miners' Angel*. Carbondale, ill.: Southern Illinois University Press, 1974.

Fink, Gary M., ed. *Biographical Dictionary of American Labor Leaders*. Westport, CT: Greenwood Press, 1974.

Finley, Joseph F. *The Corrupt Kingdom: The Rise and Fall of the United Mine Workers*. New York: Simon and Schuster, 1972.

Foner, Philip S. *The History of the Labor Movement in the United States*. Vol. 3: *The Policies and Practices of the AFL 1900–1909*, and Vol. 5: *The AFL in the Progressive Era 1910–1915*. New York: International Publishers, 1964 and 1980.

——. *Organized Labor and the Black Worker, 1619–1973*. New York: International Publishers, 1974.

——, ed. *Mother Jones Speaks: Collected Speeches and Writings*. New York: Monad Press, 1983.

Forbath, William E. *Law and the Shaping of the American Labor Movement*. Cambridge, Mass: Harvard University Press, 1991.

Forcey, Charles. *The Crossroads of Liberalism*. New York: Oxford University Press, 1961.

Foster, William Z. *Misleaders of Labor*. Chicago: Trade Union Educational League, 1927.

Fox, Maier B. *United We Stand: The United Mine Workers of America, 1890–1990*. Washington, D.C.: United Mine Workers of America, 1990.

Fox, Mary Harrita. *Peter E. Dietz, Labor Priest*. Notre Dame, Ind.: Notre Dame University Press, 1953.

Gluck, Elsie. *John Mitchell, Miner: Labor's Bargain with the Gilded Age*. New York: The John Day Company, 1929.

Goodrich, Carter L. *The Miners's Freedom*. Boston: Marshall Jones, 1925.

Gottfried, Alex. *Boss Cermak of Chicago*. Seattle: University of Washington Press, 1962.

Graebner, William. *Coal-Mining Safety in the Progressive Period: The Political Economy of Reform*. Lexington: University Press of Kentucky, 1976.

Green, Archie. *Only a Miner: Studies in Recorded Coal Mining Songs*. Urbana, Ill.: University of Illinois Press, 1972.

Green, James R. *Grass-Roots Socialism: Radical Movements in the Southwest, 1895–1943*. Baton Rouge, La.: Louisiana State University Press, 1978.

Green, Marguerite. *The National Civic Federation and the American Labor Movement, 1900–1925*. Washington: The Catholic University of America Press, 1956.

Greene, Victor R. *The Slavic Community on Strike: Immigrant Labor in Pennsylvania Anthracite*. Notre Dame, Ind.: University of Notre Dame Press, 1968.

Grob, Gerald N. *Workers and Utopia: A Study of Ideological Conflict in the American Labor Movement, 1865–1900*. Evanston, Ill.: Northwestern University Press, 1961.

Haber, Samuel. *Efficiency and Uplift: Scientific Management in the Progressive Era*. Chicago: University of Chicago Press, 1964.

Harvey, Katherine A. *The Best Dressed Miners: Life and Labor in the Maryland Coal Regions, 1835–1910*. Ithaca, N.Y.: Cornell University Press, 1969.

Jensen, Richard. *The Winning of the Midwest: Social and Political Conflict, 1888–1896*. Chicago: University of Chicago Press, 1971.

Johnson, James P. *The Politics of Soft Coal*. Urbana: University of Illinois Press, 1979.

Karson, Marc. *American Labor Unions and Politics, 1900–1918*. Carbondale, Ill.: Southern Illinois University Press, 1958.

Korson, George. *Coal Dust on the Fiddle*. Hatboro, Pa.: Folklore Associates, 1965.

Laslett, John H. M. *Labor and the Left: A Study of Socialist and Radical Influences in the American Labor Movement, 1881–1924*. New York: Basic Books, 1970.

———. *Nature's Noblemen: The Fortunes of the Independent Collier in Scotland and the American Midwest, 1855–1899*. Los Angeles: Institute of Industrial Relations, UCLA, 1983.

Laurie, Bruce. *Artisans into Workers: Labor in Nineteenth-Century America*. New York: The Noonday Press, 1989.

Lewis, Ronald L. *Black Coal Miners in America: Race, Class, and Community Conflict, 1780–1980*. Lexington, Ky.: University of Kentucky Press, 1987.

Long, Priscilla. *Where the Sun Never Shines: A History of America's Bloody Coal Industry*. New York: Paragon House, 1989.

Lorwin, Lewis. *The American Federation of Labor: History, Policies, and Prospects*. Washington, D.C.: The Brookings Institute, 1933.

Madison, Charles A. *American Labor Leaders: Personalities and Forces in the Labor Movement*. New York: Ungar Publishing, 1950.

Mandel, Bernard. *Samuel Gompers: A Biography*. Yellow Springs, Ohio: Antioch Press, 1963.

Marks, Gary. *Unions in Politics: Britain, Germany, and the United States in the Nineteenth and Early Twentieth Centuries*. Princeton: Princeton University Press, 1989.

McDonald, David J., and Edward A Lynch. *Coal and Unionism*. Silver Spring, Md: Cornelius Printing, 1939.

McGovern, George S., and Leonard F. Guttridge. *The Great Coalfield War*. Boston: Houghton Mifflin, 1972.

Miller, Donald L. and Richard E. Sharpless. *The Kingdom of Coal: Work, Enterprise, and Ethic Communities in the Mine Fields*. Philadelphia: University of Pennsylvania Press, 1985.

Mink, Gwendolyn. *Old Labor and New Immigrants in American Political Development: Union, Party, and State, 1875–1920*. Ithaca, N.Y.: Cornell University, 1986.

Minton, Bruce, and John Stuart. *Men Who Lead Labor*. New York: Modern Age, 1937.

Montgomery, David. *The Fall of the House of Labor: The Workplace, the State, and American Labor Activism, 1865–1925*. New York: Cambridge University Press, 1987.

———. *Beyond Equality: Labor and the Radical Republicans, 1862–1872*. New York: Random House, 1967.

Morris, James O. *Conflict Within the AFL: A Study of Craft Versus Industrial Unionism, 1901–1938*. Ithaca: Cornell University Press, 1958.

Nash, Michael. *Conflict and Accommodation: Coal Miners, Steel Workers, and Socialism, 1890–1920*. Westport, CT: Greenwood Press, 1982.

Nyden, Paul. *Black Coal Miners in the United States*. New York: American Institute for Marxist Studies, 1974.

Perlman, Selig, and Philip Taft. *History of Labor in the United States, 1896–1932*. New York: Macmillan, 1935.

Ramirez, Bruno. *When Workers Fight: The Politics of Industrial Relations in the Progressive Era, 1898–1916*. Westport, CT: Greenwood Press, 1978.

Robb, John M. *The Black Coal Miner of Southeast Kansas*. Topeka: State of Kansas Commission on Civil Rights, 1969.

Schwieder, Dorothy. *Black Diamonds: Life and Work in Iowa's Coal Mining Communities, 1895–1925*. Ames, Iowa: Iowa State University Press, 1983.

Seltzer, Curtis. *Fire in the Hole: Miners and Managers in the American Coal Industry*. Lexington, Ky.: University of Kentucky Press, 1985.

Sinclair, Upton. *King Coal* (a novel). n. p., 1921.

Steel, Edward M., ed. *The Correspondence of Mother Jones*. Pittsburgh: University of Pittsburgh Press, 1985.

Stone, Irving. *Clarence Darrow for the Defense*. New York: Doubleday, 1941.

Suffern, Arthur E. *The Coal Miners' Struggle for Industrial Status*. New York: Macmillan, 1926.

———. *Conciliation and Arbitration in the Coal Industry of America*. New York: Houghton Mifflin, 1915.

Taft, Philip. *The A. F. of L. in the Time of Gompers*. New York: Harper, 1957.

———. *Organized Labor in American History*. New York: Harper, 1957.

Van Tine, Warren. *The Making of the Labor Bureaucrat: Union Leadership in the United States, 1870–1920*. Amherst: University of Massachusetts Press, 1973.

Ware, Norman J. *The Labor Movement in the United States, 1860–1895*. New York: D. Appleton and Company, 1929.

Weinstein, James. *The Corporate Ideal in the Liberal State, 1900–1918.* Boston: Beacon Pres, 1968.

Wiebe, Robert. *Businessmen and Reform.* Chicago: Quadrangle Books, 1968.

Wieck, Edward A. *The American Miners Association, A Record of the Origin of Coal Miners' Unions in the United States.* New York: Russell Sage Foundation, 1940.

Wolman, Leo. *The Growth of American Trade Unions, 1880–1923.* New York: National Bureau of Economic Research, 1924.

Yearly, Clifton K. *Britons in American Labor: A History of the Influence of the United Kingdom Immigrants on American Labor, 1820–1914.* Baltimore: The Johns Hopkins University Press, 1957.

Yellowitz, Irwin. *Labor and the Progressive Movement in New York State, 1897–1916.* Ithaca: Cornell University Press, 1965.

Articles

Amsden, Jon, and Stephen Brier. "Coal Miners on Strike." *Journal of Interdisciplinary History* 7 (Spring 1977): 583–616.

Asher, Robert. "Union Nativism and the Immigrant Response." *Labor History* 23 (Summer 1982): 325–348.

Aurand, Harold W. "Diversifying the Economy of the Anthracite Regions, 1880–1900." *Pennsylvania Magazine of History and Biography* 94 (January 1970): 54–64.

————. "'Do Your Duty!': Editorial Responses to the Anthracite Strike of 1902." In *Hard Coal, Hard Times: Ethnicity and Labor in the Anthracite Region*, ed. by David L. Salay. Scranton, Pa.: The Anthracite Museum Press, 1984.

Bailey, Kenneth R. "A Judicious Mixture: Negroes and Immigrants in the West Virginia Mines, 1880–1917." *West Virginia History* 34 (January 1973): 141–161.

Berthoff, Roland Tappan. "The Social Order of the Anthracite Region, 1825–1902." *Pennsylvania Magazine of History and Biography* 89 (July 1965): 261–291.

Brier, Stephen. "Interracial Organizing in the West Virginia Coal Industry." In *Essays in Southern Labor History*, ed. by Gary M. Fink and Merl E. Reed. Westport, CT: Greenwood Press, 1977.

Cline, Catherine Ann. "Priest in the Coal Fields: The Story of Father Curran." *Records of the American Catholic Historical Society of Pennsylvania* 68 (June 1952): 67–84.

Corn, Jacqueline. "Protective Legislation for Coal Miners, 1870–1900: Response to Safety and Health Hazards," pp. 67–82. In *Dying for Work: Workers' Safety and Health in Twentieth-Century America*, ed. by David Rosner and Gerald Markowitz. Bloomington: Indiana University Press, 1989.

Destler, Chester. "On the Eve of the Anthracite Coal Strike Arbitration: Henry Demarest Lloyd at the United Mine Worker Headquarters." *Labor History* 13 (Spring 1972): 286–293.

Fones-Wolf, Elizabeth and Kenneth. "Trade-Union Evangelism: Religion and the AFL in the Labor Forward Movement, 1912–16," pp. 153–184. In *Working-Class America: Essays on Labor, Community, and American Society*, ed. by Michael H. Frisch and Daniel J. Walkowitz. Urbana: University of Illinois Press, 1983.

Garraty, John A. "The United States Steel Corporation Versus Labor—The Early Years." *Labor History* 1 (Winter 1960): 6–13.

Ginger, Ray. "Managerial Employees in Anthracite, 1902." *Journal of Economic History* 14 (1954): 146–157.

Gottlieb, Amy Zahl. "British Coal Miners: A Demographic Study of Braidwood and Streator, Illinois." *Journal of the Illinois State Historical Society* 72 (August 1979): 179–192.

Gowaskie, Joseph M. "John Mitchell and the Anthracite Mine Workers: Leadership Conservatism and Rank-and-File Militancy." *Labor History* 27 (Winter 1985–86): 54–83.

———. "From Conflict to Cooperation: John Mitchell and Bituminous Coal Operators, 1898–1908." *Historian* 38 (August 1976): 669–688.

Graebner, William. "Great Expectations: The Search for Order in Bituminous Coal, 1890–1917." *Business History Review* 48 (Spring 1974): 49–72.

Greene, Victor R. "A Study in Slavs, Strikes, and Unions: The Anthracite Strike of 1897." *Pennsylvania History* 31 (April 1964): 199–215.

Gutman, Herbert G. "The Negro and the United Mine Workers of America; the Career and the Letters of Richard L. Davis." In *Workers in the Industrial Revolution*, ed, by Peter N. Stearns and Daniel Walkowitz, 194–231. New Brunswick, N.J.: Transaction, 1974.

———. Gutman, Herbert. "Five Letters of Immigrant Workers from Scotland to the United States." *Labor History* 9 (1968): 384–99.

———. "The Braidwood Lockout of 1874." *Journal of the Illinois State Historical Society* 53 (Spring 1960): 11–12.

Harris, Sheldon H. "Letters from West Virginia: Management's Version of the 1902 Coal Strike." *Labor History* 10 (Spring 1969): 228–240.

Hicken, Victor. "The Virden and Pana Mine Wars of 1898." *Journal of the Illinois State Historical Society* 52 (Spring 1959): 262–278.

Keiser, John H. "Black Strikebreakers and Racism in Illinois, 1865–1900." *Journal of the Illinois State Historical Society* 65 (Autumn 1972): 314–322.

———. "John H. Walker: Labor Leader from Illinois." In *Essays in Illinois History*, ed. by Donald Tingley. Carbondale: Southern Illinois University Press, 1968.

———. "The Union Miners Cemetery at Mt.Olive, Illinois: A Spirit-Thread of Labor History." *Journal of the Illinois State Historical Society* 62 (Autumn 1969): 248–249.

Kerr, K. Austin. "Labor-Management Cooperation: An 1897 Case." *Pennsylvania Magazine of History and Biography* 49 (January 1975): 45–71.

Kinneman, Marion. "John Mitchell in Illinois." *Illinois State University Journal* 32 (Sept 1969): 21–35.

Morris, James O. "The Acquisitive Spirit of John Mitchell, UMW President (1899–1908)." *Labor History* 20 (Winter 1979): 5–43.

Rogin, Michael. "Voluntarism: The Political Functions of an Antipolitical Doctrine." *Industrial and Labor Relations Review* 15 (1962): 521–35.

Scheinberg, Stephen. "Theodore Roosevelt and the AFL's Entry into Politics, 1906–1908," *Labor History* 3 (Spring 1962): 131–148.

Steel, Edward M. "Mother Jones in the Fairmont Field, 1902." *Journal of American History* 57 (September 1970): 290–307.

Suggs, George G., Jr. "The Colorado Coal Miners's Strike of 1903–1904: A Prelude to Ludlow?" *Journal of the West* 12 (January 1973): 36–52.

Taft, Philip. "Collective Bargaining Before the New Deal." In *How Collective Bargaining Works*, ed. by Twentieth Century Fund. New York: Twentieth Century Fund, 1942.

Turner, George A. "Ethnic Responses to the Lattimer Massacre." In *Hard Coal, Hard Times: Ethnicity and Labor in the Anthracite Region*, ed. by David L. Salay. Scranton: The Anthracite Museum Press, 1984.

Weitz, Eric. "Class Formation and Labor Protest in the Mining Communities of Southern Illinois and the Ruhr, 1890–1925." *Labor History* 27 (Winter 1985–86): 85–105.

Wiebe, Robert. "The Anthracite Coal Strike of 1902: A Record of Confusion." *Mississippi Valley Historical Review* 48 (September 1961): 229–251.

Unpublished Material

Blatz, Perry K. "Ever-Shifting Ground: Work and Labor Relations in the Anthracite Coal Industry, 1868–1903." Ph.D. diss., Princeton University, 1987.

Cary, Lorin L. "Adolph Germer: From Labor Agitator to Labor Professional." Ph.D diss., University of Wisconsin, 1968.

Everling, Arthur C. "Tactics over Strategy in the United Mine Workers of America: Internal Politics and the Question of the Nationalization of the Mines, 1908–1923." Ph.D. diss., Penn State University, 1978.

Gowaskie, Joseph Michael. "John Mitchell: A Study in Leadership." Ph.D. diss., The Catholic University of America. 1968.

Greene, Julia Marie. "The Strike at the Ballot Box: Politics and Partisanship in the American Federation of Labor, 1881–1916." Ph.D. diss., Yale University, 1990.

Jensen, Gordon M. "The National Civic Federation: American Business in an Age of Social Change and Social Reform, 1900–1910." Ph.D. diss., Princeton University, 1956."

Joyce, Richard P. "Miners of the Prairie: Life and Labor in the Wilmington, Illinois, Coalfield, 1866–1897." M.A. Thesis, Illinois State University, Normal, 1980.

McCormick, Michael Ray. "A Comparative Study of Coal Mining Communities in Northern Illinois and Southeastern Ohio in the Late Nineteenth Century." Ph.D. diss., Ohio State University, 1978.

McGovern, George S. "The Colorado Coal Strike, 1913–14." Ph.D. diss., Northwestern University, 1953.

Pritchard, Paul. "William B. Wilson: The Evolution of a Central Pennsylvania Mine Union Leader." Ph.D. diss., University of Pennsylvania, 1941.

"Proceedings of the Anthracite Coal Strike Commission, 1902–1903." 56 vols. Mimeographed Copy in the Library of Congress.

Stroh, Paul. "The Catholic Clergy and American Labor Disputes, 1900–1937." Ph.D. diss., Catholic University of America, 1939.

Suggs, George G., Jr. "Colorado Conservatives Versus Organized Labor: A Study of the George Hamilton Peabody Administration, 1903–1905." Ph.D. diss., University of Colorado, 1964.

Wilhelm, Clarke L. "William B. Wilson: The First Secretary of Labor." Ph.D. diss., Johns Hopkins University, 1967.

Index